SCOTT, FORESMAN AND COMPANY
EXPLORING
MATHEMATICS ®

AUTHORS

L. Carey Bolster
Coordinator of Mathematics
Baltimore County Public Schools
Towson, Maryland

Clem Boyer
Coordinator of Mathematics, K-12
District School Board of Seminole
County
Sanford, Florida

Thomas Butts
Associate Professor, Mathematics
Education
University of Texas at Dallas
Richardson, Texas

Mary Cavanagh
Math/Science Coordinator
Solana Beach School District
Solana Beach, California

Marea W. Channel
Mathematics Resource Teacher
Los Angeles Unified School District
Los Angeles, California

Warren D. Crown
Associate Professor of Mathematics
Education
Rutgers, The State University of
New Jersey
New Brunswick, New Jersey

Jan Fair
Mathematics Department
Allan Hancock College
Santa Maria, California

Robert Y. Hamada
District Elementary Mathematics
Specialist
Los Angeles Unified School District
Los Angeles, California

Margaret G. (Peggy) Kelly
Associate Professor
California State University, Fresno
Fresno, California

Miriam Leiva
Professor of Mathematics
University of North Carolina at
Charlotte
Charlotte, North Carolina

Mary Montgomery Lindquist
Callaway Professor of Mathematics
Education
Columbus College
Columbus, Georgia

William B. Nibbelink
Professor, Division of Early
Childhood and Elementary
Education
University of Iowa
Iowa City, Iowa

Linda Proudfit
University Professor of Mathematics
and Computer Education
Governors State University
University Park, Illinois

Cathy Rahlfs
Mathematics Coordinator
Humble Independent School District
Humble, Texas

Rosie Ramirez
Assistant Principal
Charles Rice Elementary School
Dallas, Texas

Jeanne F. Ramos
Mathematics Adviser
Los Angeles Unified School District
Los Angeles, California

Gail Robinette
Elementary Mathematics
Coordinator
Fresno Unified School District
Fresno, California

David Robitaille
Head, Department of Mathematics
and Science Education
University of British Columbia
Vancouver, British Columbia,
Canada

James E. Schultz
Associate Professor of Mathematics
The Ohio State University
Columbus, Ohio

Richard Shepardson
Professor, Division of Early
Childhood and Elementary
Education
University of Iowa
Iowa City, Iowa

Jane Swafford
Professor of Mathematics
Illinois State University
Normal, Illinois

Benny Tucker
Professor of Education; Chairman,
Education Department
Union University
Jackson, Tennessee

John Van de Walle
Associate Professor of Education
Virginia Commonwealth University
Richmond, Virginia

David E. Williams
Former Director of Mathematics
Education
School District of Philadelphia
Philadelphia, Pennsylvania

Robert J. Wisner
Professor of Mathematics
New Mexico State University
Las Cruces, New Mexico

Editorial Offices: Glenview, Illinois
Regional Offices: Sunnyvale, California • Tucker, Georgia
Glenview, Illinois • Oakland, New Jersey • Dallas, Texas

CONTRIBUTING AUTHOR
Janet K. Scheer
Director of Field Services
    for Mathematics
Scott, Foresman and Co.
Glenview, Illinois

CONSULTANTS

Reading
Robert A. Pavlik
Professor and Chairperson,
Reading/Language Arts
    Department
Cardinal Stritch College
Milwaukee, Wisconsin

At-Risk Students
Edgar G. Epps
Marshall Field
Professor of Urban Education
Department of Education
University of Chicago
Chicago, Illinois

**Limited-English-Proficient
Students**
Walter Secada
Department of Curriculum
    and Instruction
University of Wisconsin
Madison, Wisconsin

Mainstreaming
Roxie Smith
Associate Provost
Northwestern University
Evanston, Illinois

Gifted Students
Christine Kuehn Ebert
Assistant Professor of Education
University of South Carolina
Columbia, South Carolina

Critic Readers
Mary P. Brown
Old Town Elementary School
Winston-Salem, North Carolina
Joyce Buratti
Hoover School
Oklahoma City, Oklahoma
Bruce C. Burt
East Bradford Elementary
    School
West Chester, Pennsylvania
Desdra J. Butler
Los Angeles Unified School
    District
Los Angeles, California
Howard Cohn
Lone Star Elementary School
Jacksonville, Florida
Rachel Carter Cole
District Six Office, Philadelphia
    Public Schools
Philadelphia, Pennsylvania

Laura Dunn
St. Brendan School
San Francisco, California
Ruth Elliott
Pembroke Elementary School
Pembroke, Kentucky
Herlinda Garza
Zavala Elementary School
Corpus Christi, Texas
Ruth Harbin
Olathe District Schools
Olathe, Kansas
Barbara J. Kane
Bridgewater-Raritan Schools
Bridgewater, New Jersey
Norma P. Lowe
Daniel E. Morgan School
Cleveland, Ohio
Carol Newman
Broward County Schools
Fort Lauderdale, Florida
Clara Parker
Fayette County Public Schools
Lexington, Kentucky
Henry W. Richard
Governor Wolf School
Bethlehem, Pennsylvania
Barbara F. Wallace
The John B. Russwurm School
New York, New York

ACKNOWLEDGMENTS
Design
Cover and Special Features:
SHELDON COTLER + ASSOCIATES

Art Direction and Production/
    Core Lessons: Taurins Design
    Associates, Inc./NYC

Scott, Foresman Staff and Rosa +
    Wesley Design Associates

Editorial Development
Scott, Foresman Staff and
    Falletta Associates

Photographs
Cover: Richard Chesnut, Fred
Schenk. xi (tl): Richard
Hutchings, InfoEdit xi (bl):
Stephen Frisch, Stock Boston xi
(l): Brent Jones xi (br) Lawrence
Migdale xv (t): Courtesy Compaq
Computer Corporation xvi (t):
Lawrence Migdale xx-1: Charles
Gupton, Click/Chicago/Tony
Stone Scott, Foresman
photographs by: Richard
Chesnut 61, 129, 160, 180–181,
193, 222, 223, 244, 245, 262,
306–307, 318, 373, 395, 507,
528–529; Arie deZanger 44–45,
120–121, 161, 262, 299,
340–341, 384–385, 506; Fred
Schenk 80–81, 327, 319,
450–451; unless otherwise
acknowledged, all photographs
are the property of Scott
Foresman and Company. Clara
Aich: 24, 52, 86, 105, 134, 154,
155, 163, 165, 168, 195, 196,
210, 224, 225, 250, 252, 268,
284, 309, 320, 338, 464, 465,
474, 475, 478, 502, 503, 512,
513 Animals Animals: Breck P.
Kent 150 Peter Arnold, Inc.:
Stephen J. Kraseman 414–415
Craig Aurness: 150 The
Bettmann Archive: 494–495
Click/Chicago/Tony Stone: Chris
Baker 244 Duomo: Paul J.
Sutton 44–45; Steve E. Sutton
244, 245 Ellis Wildlife Collection:
Ken Deitcher 414–415; Gerry
Ellis 44–45, 116, 117, 414–415
FPG: Joel Elkins 44–45; Gerald
L. French 280–281; Richard
Laird 280–281; John Turner
44–45 Judy Gurovitz: 30, 132,
133 Richard Hutchings: 14, 16,
26, 28, 126, 184, 194, 254, 256,
260, 282, 288, 289, 296, 308,
316, 390, 424, 425, 472

(Continued on page 572)

Contents

Chapter 1   Place Value, Addition, and Subtraction

Chapter 2   Multiplication

Chapter 3 Measurement and Geometric Figures

Chapter 4 Division with One-Digit Divisors

Chapter 5   Division with Two-Digit Divisors

Chapter 6   Geometric Solids and Measurements

Chapter 7 Addition and Subtraction of Decimals

Chapter 8 Multiplication of Decimals

Chapter 9   Patterns and Coordinate Graphing

Chapter 10   Fraction Concepts

Chapter 11 Exploring Addition and Subtraction of Fractions

Chapter 12 Exploring Multiplication of Fractions

Chapter **13** Statistics, Graphing, and Probability

Chapter **14** Geometry

Chapter **15** Ratio, Proportion, and Percent

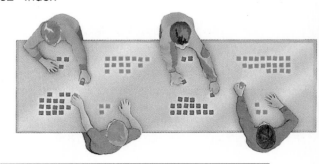

WELCOME TO
EXPLORING
MATHEMATICS

Mathematics is valuable and
interesting. The next ten pages
describe some of the ways your book
will help you explore and discover
more of the wonders of mathematics.

Your book will help you build your

Math Power

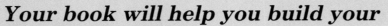

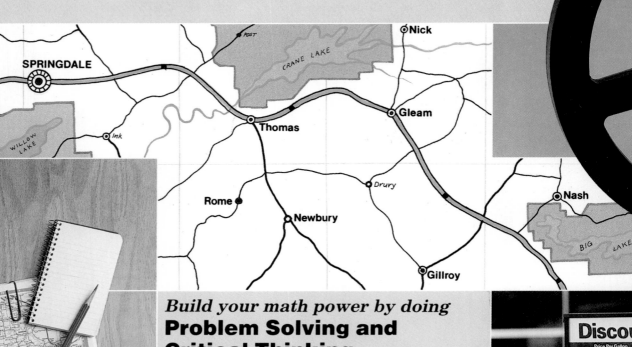

Build your math power by doing

Problem Solving and Critical Thinking

You'll need to use your math to solve problems all your life. So, as you solve problems in your book, you will do more than find answers. You will also learn how to think mathematically.

In Chapter 1, tell the page numbers where you first find these.

1 "Problem-Solving Guide"
   • Understand
   • Plan and Solve
   • Look Back

2 "Tips for Problem Solvers"

3 An exercise called "Critical Thinking"

Build your math power by looking for **Connections**

Your book will help you explore connections between math and the real world, between math and other school subjects, and between different topics within mathematics.

4 On what page does "Social Studies Connection" first appear at the top of the page?

5 On page 31, find a problem that involves a consumer decision?

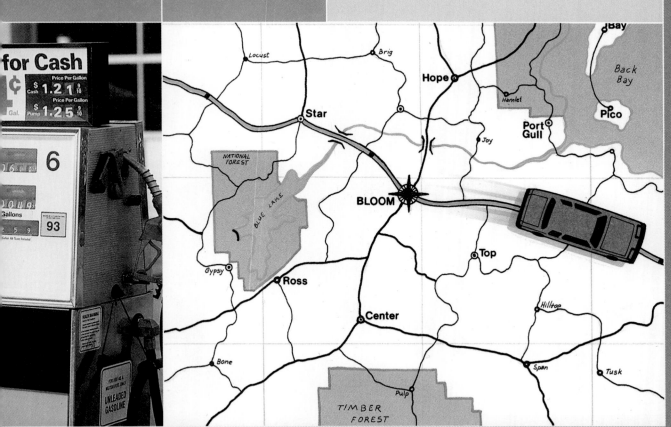

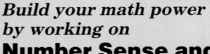

Build your math power by working on
Number Sense and Using Data

1 Find a chapter that begins with a Number-Sense Project about kites of different shapes. Then find where this project is continued. (Hint: Find the Problem-Solving Workshop within the chapter.) On what page is the project continued?

2 On page 12, Example A estimates the sum by using what kind of digits?

3 On what page is the Data File that you'll use with Exercise 7 on page 72?

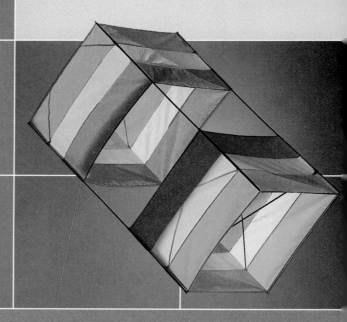

Scott, Foresman
GRAPHING and
PROBABILITY
WORKSHOP

Press Return.

Build your math power by using
Calculators and Computers

4 On page 250, what math topic does a calculator help you learn?

5 On page 319, what math topic does a computer help you learn?

6 In Chapter 3, which full page lesson asks you to "Explore with a Calculator" to find a missing length of a side?

7 Which exercises on page 59 ask you to tell whether or not you would use a calculator?

Use your book to help you
Do Your Best

To do your best,
Expect to Succeed

When you want to learn something, it helps to believe in yourself. Whether you are learning a sport, a musical instrument, or mathematics, a positive attitude can make a big difference.

To do your best,
Build Your Understanding

When you understand what you're doing, you do it better and remember it longer. So it pays to study the "Build Understanding" part of the lessons.

1 On page 24, why is it easy to see what new math word is being taught?

To do your best, learn ways to do
Independent Study

One of the most important things you can learn from a math book is how to learn math even when a teacher is not there to help.

2 On page 7, look to the right of the words "Check Understanding." On what page can you find another example for that lesson?

3 On page 7, look to the right of the word "Practice." On what page can you find more practice for that lesson?

4 There is an Independent Study Handbook in the back of your book. On what page does the "Math Study Skills" section begin?

5 Name the first and last words defined in the glossary on page 559.

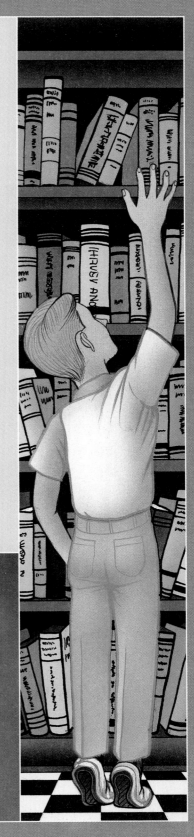

Your book will help you experience
Active Learning

You'll learn math by doing
Math Activities

Activities help you understand math. Some activities use materials that help you show numbers, measure objects, do experiments, explore shapes, or solve problems.

1 What materials are used in the activity on page 46?

2 Use your "Math Sketcher" or a ruler to draw pictures that show $\frac{1}{2}$ of three shapes.

Doing math includes
Reading, Writing, Talking, Listening

Reading, writing, talking, and listening in math class will help you think mathematically.

3 In Chapter 1, tell the page number where these first occur.

"Talk About Math"

"Write About Math"

"Reading Math"

A good way to learn is by
Working in Groups

In real life and in math class, people can often solve problems better by working together.

4 How many students should work together in a group to do the "Subtracting Whole Numbers" activity on page 26?

5 In the "Explore As a Team" on page 20, what is the "Tip for Working Together"?

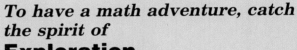

To have a math adventure, catch the spirit of
Exploration

Be a Math Explorer and discover new things. Look for patterns, check out your hunches, and try different approaches to problems.

6 What lesson in Chapter 9 explores number patterns by folding paper and drawing steps?

7 In the "Explore Math" on page 23, what are you asked to do in Problems 20–24?

A key ingredient to learning math is
Enjoying Math

Your book will help you
Enjoy Math at School

The explorations in your book will help you discover and enjoy the wonders of mathematics.

1 In Chapter 3, what page asks you to explore the area of squares and rectangles by counting squares?

2 Use a sheet of grid paper. See how many different figures you can cut out having exactly 5 squares.

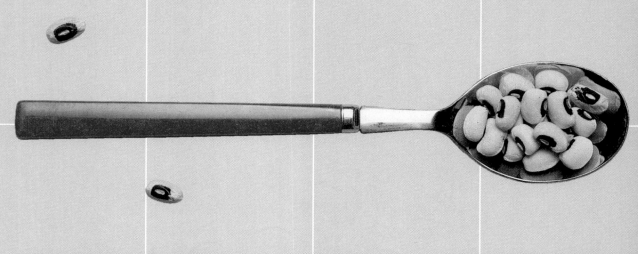

To make math a part of your life

Enjoy Math at Home

Outside of school, share math ideas with others and continue to explore math your whole life.

3 In the Math-at-Home activity on page 61, what type of activity is suggested?

4 What is the name of the family game suggested in the Problem-Solving Workshop in Chapter 9?

5 Play this Estimation game with someone at home. Use a bag full of items such as peanuts, beans, bottlecaps, or pennies. Each player guesses how many items will fit in a spoon. The player with the closest estimate scores 1 point. Repeat this estimation activity with other containers, such as a jar lid, a cup, a saucer, a handful. The player with the most points wins.

Place Value, Addition, and Subtraction

1

Did You Know: Today, the average life expectancy for a person living in the United States is about 75 years. In 1950, the average life expectancy in the United States was about 68 years. Today, the average life expectancy for the world is about 65 years. In 1950, the average life expectancy for the world was about 47 years.

Number-Sense Project

Estimate
If you ask 5 older people to estimate the population of your state, what do you think will be the greatest estimate?

Gather Data
Ask 5 older people to estimate the population of your state. Record their estimates.

Analyze and Report
List the estimates in order from greatest to least. Write a sentence comparing your prediction to the greatest estimate you recorded.

Place Value

Build Understanding

A. In 1986, the Internal Revenue Service collected $782,251,812,000 in taxes. The commas separate this number into ***periods***.

Taxes Collected by IRS

Year	Amount
1984	$680,475,229,000
1985	$742,871,541,000
1986	$782,251,812,000
1987	$886,290,590,000

April 15, 19 9

PAY TO: *I.R.S.*

SUM OF: *OO Dollars and* 0⁄100 *cents*

⑈123456789⑈

billions period			millions period			thousands period			ones period		
hundred-billions	ten-billions	billions	hundred-millions	ten-millions	millions	hundred-thousands	ten-thousands	thousands	hundreds	tens	ones
7	8	2	2	5	1	8	1	2	0	0	0

782,251,812,000

782 billion, 251 million, 812 thousand

seven hundred eighty-two billion, two hundred fifty-one million, eight hundred twelve thousand

B. *Standard form*   *Expanded form*
108,507   **100,000 + 8,000 + 500 + 7**

■ **Talk About Math**   Read aloud each of the numbers in the table. Why is it necessary to include the zeros when you write these numbers?

Check Understanding

For another example, see Set A, pages 38–39.

1. Tell which digits are in the thousands period in 2,940,335.

2. Tell what the 6 means in 168,475,043.

3. Write 5,403,008,925 in words.

4. Write 92 million, 48 thousand, 28 in standard form.

5. Write 300,000,000 + 40,000 + 800 + 5 in standard form.

6. Write 50,036,504 in expanded form.

Practice

For More Practice, see Set A, pages 40–41.

Tell which digits are in the millions period in each number.

7. 843,909,002   **8.** 52,555,821,905   **9.** 80,752,224   **10.** 4,254,896

Tell what the 8 in each number means.

11. 5,790,823   **12.** 45,678,421   **13.** 3,845,241   **14** 8,000,657,221

Write each number in words.

15. 3,051,003   **16.** 452,005,020   **17.** 100,000,000,001

Write in standard form. **Remember** to use commas where needed.

18. 5 thousand, 243

19. 52 million, 523 thousand, 342

20. 800,000 + 30,000 + 50 + 9

21. 3,000,000 + 8,000 + 400 + 9

Write each number in expanded form.

22. 840,005   **23.** 30,907,030   **24.** 48,009,700,820   **25.** 5,002,050,600

Problem Solving

26. Use the table at the beginning of the lesson. If $100 billion more was collected in 1988 than 1987, what was the total for 1988?

27. Critical Thinking My thousands digit is twice my hundreds digit. The sum of my tens and one digits is my thousands digit. My hundreds digit is 2 more than my tens digit. My tens digit is greater than 1 and less than 3. What 4-digit number am I?

Comparing and Ordering Whole Numbers

Build Understanding

A. Which park is larger, Katmai or Glacier Bay?

Compare 3,716,000 and 3,225,284.

What do you notice about the digits in the millions place? What do you notice about the digits in the hundred-thousands place?

same

3,716,000 ⠿ **3,225,284**

7 hundred-thousands is more than 2 hundred-thousands.

3,716,000 > 3,225,284   > means "is greater than."
< means "is less than."

Katmai National Park is larger than Glacier Bay National Park.

Alaska is the largest state in the United States.

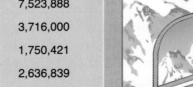

National Parks in Alaska	
Park	Number of Acres
Denali	4,716,726
Gates of the Arctic	7,523,888
Katmai	3,716,000
Kobuk Valley	1,750,421
Lake Clark	2,636,839
Glacier Bay	3,225,284

B. List the numbers 52,384, 52,525, and 50,981 in order from least to greatest.

50,981   52,384   52,525

50,981 < 52,384
52,384 < 52,525

■ **Talk About Math** Discuss ways to help you remember which symbol means "is greater than" and which symbol means "is less than."

6

Check Understanding

For another example, see Set B, pages 38–39.

Compare these numbers. Use >, <, or =.

1. 582 ⬚ 589   **2.** 3,765 ⬚ 3,981   **3.** 61,002 ⬚ 61,020

List the numbers in order from least to greatest.

4. 207   270   200   **5.** 8,457   8,472   7,484   **6.** 53,002   5,302   53,302

Practice

For More Practice, see Set B, pages 40–41.

Compare these numbers. Use >, <, or =.

7. 754 ⬚ 745   **8.** 5,891 ⬚ 6,857   **9.** 7,942 ⬚ 7,942

10. 38,924 ⬚ 38,752   **11.** 59,387 ⬚ 59,984   **12.** 380,521 ⬚ 392,521

List the numbers in order from least to greatest.

13. 785   724   758

14. 983   872   827

15. 3,045   3,542   3,425

16. 8,542   8,540   85,420

17. 35,426   35,624   35,246

18. 72,584   72,589   72,857

Problem Solving

Use the table at the beginning of the lesson.

19. Which park is the largest? How can you tell?

20. Which park is the smallest? Explain how you know.

21. List the parks in order from the largest to the smallest.

22. 🖩 **Calculator** Find the total number of acres in the parks in Alaska.

Use the table of national parks at the right.

23. Which park is larger, Haleakala or Wind Cave?

24. Which park is the largest?

25. Arrange the national parks in order, largest first.

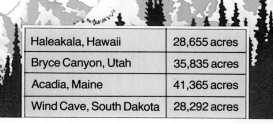

Haleakala, Hawaii	28,655 acres
Bryce Canyon, Utah	35,835 acres
Acadia, Maine	41,365 acres
Wind Cave, South Dakota	28,292 acres

Rounding Whole Numbers

Build Understanding

A. In 1987, the population of the Cherokee Reservation was 58,232. To the nearest thousand, what was the population?

58,232 is between 58,000 and 59,000, but it is closer to 58,000.

To the nearest thousand, the population of the Cherokee Reservation was 58,000.

B. Round each number to the nearest thousand.

18,458   18,925   18,512

Between which thousands do these numbers fall? Each number is between 18,000 and 19,000.

What digit can help you round to the nearest thousand?

18,458	18,925	18,512
The hundreds digit is less than 5. The thousands digit stays the same.	The hundreds digit is greater than 5. Add 1 to the thousands digit.	The hundreds digit is 5. Add 1 to the thousands digit.
18,000	**19,000**	**19,000**

■ **Talk About Math** What number is in the middle between 2,000 and 3,000? If you follow the directions in Example B, what is this number when rounded to the nearest thousand? Discuss other similar situations.

The Cherokee have many art forms but are best known for their beautiful baskets.

Check Understanding

For another example, see Set C, pages 38–39.

1. The digit in the ___?___ place helps to round to the nearest hundred.

2. In thousands, 24,354 is between ___?___ and ___?___.

3. To the nearest ___?___, 48,215 rounds to 50,000.

Round 83,852 to the nearest

4. ten-thousand.   5. thousand.   6. hundred.   7. ten.

Practice

For More Practice, see Set C, pages 40–41.

Round to the nearest ten.

8. 56   **9.** 73   **10.** 185   **11.** 398   **12.** 5,142   **13.** 3,778

Round to the nearest hundred.

14. 136   **15.** 350   **16.** 483   **17.** 1,291   **18.** 4,549   **19.** 4,550

Round to the nearest thousand.

20. 1,343   **21.** 5,789   **22.** 7,062   **23.** 786   **24.** 12,382   **25.** 71,500

Round to the nearest ten-thousand.

26. 13,875   **27.** 37,951   **28.** 78,928   **29.** 45,000   **30.** 9,842

Problem Solving

31. Name some situations where it would be helpful to use rounded numbers.

32. Describe what happens when **996** is rounded to the nearest hundred; the nearest thousand.

33. When rounding to the nearest thousand, what is the greatest number that rounds to **5,000**?

34. When rounding to the nearest thousand, what is the least number that rounds to **5,000**?

35. Write a number with a **5** in the tens place that rounds to **8,000** when rounded to the nearest hundred.

Reading ———— **Math**

Vocabulary   Use the telephone buttons to decode these math terms. You can find these terms in this chapter.

1. 786   **2.** 78287228   **3.** 3433373623

4. 233363   **5.** 6468363   **6.** 7828724363

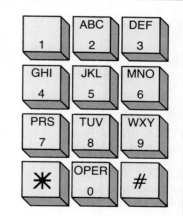

Using a Problem-Solving Guide

Understand
QUESTION
FACTS
KEY IDEA

Plan and Solve
STRATEGY
ANSWER

Look Back
SENSIBLE ANSWER
ALTERNATE APPROACH

Build Understanding

Solving a problem is like taking a journey. There may be more than one road that leads to an answer. Some roads turn out to be dead ends. Sometimes you need to turn back and start over. The Problem-Solving Guide is like a map that can help you find your way.

The Silver Boot Award is given to campers who hike 250 miles in a month. Jim has hiked 140 miles so far this month. How many more miles does he need to hike to earn a Silver Boot?

Understand

QUESTION
What are you asked to find?

FACTS
What facts are given?

KEY IDEA
How are the facts and question related?

Plan and Solve

STRATEGY
What can you do to solve the problem?

ANSWER
Give the answer in a sentence.

Look Back

SENSIBLE ANSWER
Did you check your work?

ALTERNATE APPROACH
Is there another way to get the same answer?

Understand

QUESTION   How many more miles does Jim have to hike?

FACTS   Jim has hiked 140 miles. He has to hike a total of 250 miles.

KEY IDEA   One part of the 250 miles is 140 miles. Find the other part.

Plan and Solve

STRATEGY   Subtract to find the number of miles Jim has to hike.

$$\begin{array}{r} 250 \\ -140 \\ \hline 110 \end{array}$$

ANSWER   Jim needs to hike 110 miles more.

Look Back

SENSIBLE ANSWER   Add 110 to the number of miles Jim has already hiked. $140 + 110 = 250$. The answer checks.

■ **Talk About Math**   Can you think of a different way to solve the problem?

Check Understanding

1. What are the three steps of the Problem-Solving Guide?

Answer each exercise about the problem at the right.

2. What are you asked to find?

3. What label will you use for the answer to show what the number represents?

> On a hiking trip, Jim and his two friends hiked 15 miles the first day, 10 miles the second day, and 4 miles the third day. How much farther did they hike on the first day than on the second day?

Practice

Answer each exercise about the problem at the right.

4. What facts are given?

5. What facts are not needed to solve the problem?

> A canteen costs $15. A backpack costs $23. Hiking boots cost $65. How much will it cost for Leon to buy a canteen and a backpack?

6. Rewrite the problem in your own words.

7. The answer is 38. Give this answer in a sentence.

8. Complete this sentence. "I know that the answer to Exercise 7 makes sense for this problem because . . . ."

Solve each problem. Use the Problem-Solving Guide to help you.

9. Chuck bought lunches for a one-day hike along the Delaware River. Each lunch cost $4. What is the total cost of lunch for 21 hikers?

10. The total distance of a three-day hike in the Pocono Mountains is 75 miles. What would be the average number of miles hiked per day?

Estimating Sums

Build Understanding

Here are some estimation strategies to use when estimating sums.

A. Estimate 3,168 + 2,594 *using front-end digits.*

3,168 + 2,594
↓   ↓
3,000 + 2,000 = 5,000

The actual sum will be more than the estimate of 5,000.

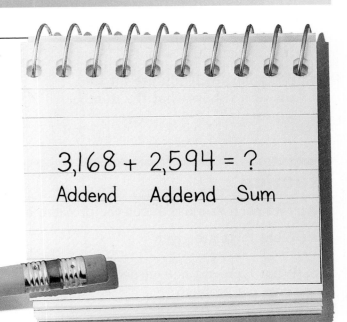

3,168 + 2,594 = ?
Addend   Addend   Sum

B. Estimate 568 + 429 by *finding a range.*

Round down.	Round up.
568 + 429	568 + 429
↓ ↓	↓ ↓
500 + 400 = 900	600 + 500 = 1,100

The actual sum will be between 900 and 1,100.

C. Estimate 189 + 228 by *rounding* both addends to the same place.

189 + 228
↓   ↓
200 + 200 = 400

The actual sum should be close to 400.

D. Estimate 48 + 47 by *comparing to a reference point.*

Each addend is less than 50. The sum must be less than 50 + 50 or 100.

E. Estimate 22 + 28 + 24 + 29 *using clustering.*

All the addends are close to 25. The sum should be close to 25 + 25 + 25 + 25 or 100.

■ **Talk About Math** Suppose you have estimated the sum of two numbers. What can you say about the actual sum if both numbers were rounded down? If both numbers were rounded up?

Check Understanding

For another example, see Set D, pages 38–39.

1. Estimate 342 + 584 using front-end digits.

2. Estimate 2,859 + 6,051 by finding a range.

3. Estimate 7,654 + 1,821 by rounding to the same place.

4. Estimate 21 + 24 by comparing to a reference point.

5. Estimate 47 + 52 + 53 using clustering.

6. For Exercise 3, will the actual sum be less than or more than the estimate?

Practice

For More Practice, see Set D, pages 40-41.

Estimate each sum. Tell which strategy you used.

7. 59 + 58

8. 328 + 219

9. 5,852 + 6,071

10. 3,825 + 3,157

11. 29 + 32 + 31

12. 298 + 342 + 687

13. 513 + 225 + 401

14. Choose two of the exercises above. Explain why you chose the strategy that you used.

Choose the best estimate for each sum.

15. 46 + 54 + 47 + 59

   2,000   20   200

16. 379 + 423

   8,000   800   700

17. 189 + 176

   200   400   500

18. 3,759 + 3,549

   6,000   8,000   600

19. 203 + 192 + 219 + 197

   200   2,000   800

20. 578 + 192

   800   600   700

Problem Solving

21. Jack said that the actual sum for 577 + 483 is more than 900 but less than 1,100. Do you agree? Which estimation strategy did he use?

22. Sally agreed with Jack but said that the actual sum is closer to 1,100. What estimation strategy did she use?

23. Benita said that the sum of 893 and 768 is less than 1,500. Do you agree? Explain why or why not.

24. Andy said that the answer to 29 + 34 + 27 + 32 is close to 150. Is that a reasonable estimate?

Adding Whole Numbers

Build Understanding

The two sentences at the right are alike in some way. How are they alike?

The letters in each sentence read the same, forward or backward. These are called *palindromes*. Here are some numbers that are palindromes:

323   1,331   265,562

Was it a cat I saw?

Step on no pets!

323

265,562

1,331

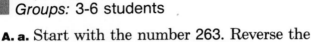

Exploring Palindromes
Groups: 3-6 students

A. a. Start with the number 263. Reverse the digits to create another number. Then add.

b. If the sum is not a palindrome, reverse the digits and add again. Continue reversing the digits and adding until the result is a palindrome.

c. How many additions did it take to make a palindrome?

B. a. Make several palindromes. Start with 2- or 3-digit numbers. Keep track of how many additions it took to make each palindrome.

b. Share your results with the others in your group. Who found the palindrome that took the most additions to make?

■ **Write About Math** Explain how you would use place value to help do the renamings for the addition in Example A.

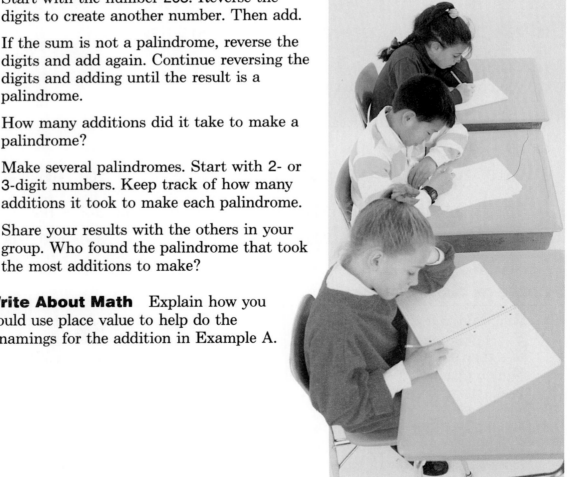

14

Check Understanding

For another example, see Set E, pages 38–39.

For each exercise, which statement at the right is needed
to find the answer? Then give the sum.

1. 387
  + 531

2. 7,326
  +   813

3.   58
     14
   + 23

4. 9,526
  + 3,471

> a. 10 hundreds = 1 thousand
> b. 10 tens = 1 hundred
> c. 10 thousands = 1 ten-thousand
> d. 10 ones = 1 ten

5. **Estimation** Len said that the
    actual sum for 4,942 + 2,816 was
    8,758. Is this answer reasonable?
    Explain your reasoning.

6. How is finding $25.36 + $51.91
    like adding two 4-digit numbers?

Practice

For More Practice, see Set E, pages 40–41.

For each exercise, estimate the sum. Then find the actual sum.

7.   76
   + 23

8.   35
   + 54

9.   236
   + 62

10. 174
   + 413

11. 689
   + 110

12. 53
   + 28

13. 94
   + 25

14. 173
   + 142

15. 628
   + 207

16. 273
   + 84

17. 1,234
   +   354

18. 6,743
   +   239

19. 8,230
   +   294

20. 7,483
   +   508

21. 5,118
   + 3,225

22. 7,356
   + 1,229

23. 6,692
   + 2,213

24. $12.50
   + 31.25

25. $54.25
   + 12.18

26. $20.53
   +   8.91

27. 29 + 32 + 24

28. 52 + 31 + 46

29. 253 + 121 + 316

30. 1,320 + 545 + 324

31. 1,523 + 4,005 + 258

32. 1,009 + 2,110 + 3,237

Problem Solving

33. **Estimation** The sum of which
    two of these palindromes is closest
    to 7,000?

    5,665   2,772   1,441

34. **Number Sense** Use each of the
    digits 1 through 7 once to write a
    4-digit number plus a 3-digit
    number that gives the greatest
    possible sum.

Mental Math for Addition

Build Understanding

Here are some mental math strategies to use when adding mentally.

A. Look for **special numbers** that are easy to add, such as numbers that end in one or more zeros.

45 + 30 = 75   **295 + 400 = 695**

B. Look for numbers that you can **break apart** into numbers that are easy to add.

$$\overset{20 + 3}{\downarrow}$$
54 + 23 = 77   **235 + 144 = 379**
$$\overset{100 + 40 + 4}{\downarrow}$$

C. Look for **combinations** that give numbers that are easy to add, such as numbers that add up to 10 or 100.

$$\overset{\lceil\text{—}10\text{—}\rceil}{}$$
7 + 18 + 3 = 28   **(42 + 75) + 25 = 142**
$$\overset{\lceil\text{—}100\text{—}\rceil}{}$$

You can change the order of addends and get the same sum. This is the **commutative property of addition.**

7 + 18 + 3 = 7 + 3 + 18

You can change the grouping of addends and get the same sum. This is the **associative property of addition.**

(42 + 75) + 25 = 42 + (75 + 25)

D. Change one number to make it easy to add. Then **compensate** by changing the answer.

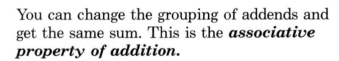

■ **Write About Math**   List ten pairs of numbers where each pair has a sum of 100. None of the numbers can end in 5 or 0. For which mental math strategy will these pairs of numbers be useful?

16

Check Understanding

For another example, see Set F, pages 38–39.

1. Find 8 + 5 + 2 + 6 + 4 using combinations of numbers.

2. Find 30 + 468 using a special number.

3. Find 154 + 322 by breaking apart one addend.

4. Find 38 + 47 using compensation. Explain your thinking.

5. Look ahead to Exercises 6–13. Which answers do you think can be found using combinations that give numbers that are easy to add?

Practice

For More Practice, see Set F, pages 40-41.

Use mental math to find each sum. Tell which strategy you used.

6. 76 + 47 + 24
7. 103 + 465
8. 589 + 300
9. 102 + 99

10. 68 + 32
11. 45 + 33
12. 85 + 98
13. 84 + 58 + 16

14. Choose two of the exercises above. Explain why you chose the strategy you used.

Use mental math to choose the correct sum.

15. 9 + 8 + 1 + 12

   20   30   40

16. 37 + 198

   137   237   235

17. 642 + 205

   842   847   805

18. 299 + 76

   376   276   375

19. 64 + 13 + 36

   103   93   113

20. 104 + 97

   191   101   201

Problem Solving

21. Luis said he would use mental math to find 135 + 248 by breaking apart both addends. Explain how this could be done.

22. What mental math strategy would you use to find 317 + 483? Explain your thinking, and give the sum.

Take risks. Try your hunches. They often work.

Give Sensible Answers

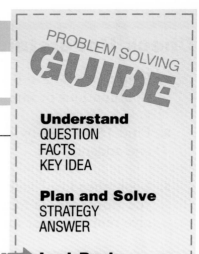

PROBLEM SOLVING
GUIDE

Understand
QUESTION
FACTS
KEY IDEA

Plan and Solve
STRATEGY
ANSWER

Look Back
SENSIBLE ANSWER
ALTERNATE APPROACH

Build Understanding

Sean and his friends went skating at the Central Roller-Rama on Friday. Which choice is the most sensible for the time they skated?

$\frac{1}{4}$ hour $2\frac{1}{2}$ hours   5 hours

Understand How long did Sean and his friends skate? The group skated on Friday night. The rink is open from 7:30 to 11:00 P.M. Determine which of the choices is the most sensible.

Plan and Solve The rink is open for only $3\frac{1}{2}$ hours on Friday nights. One fourth hour is only 15 minutes.

Consider the three choices. The only reasonable choice that is less than $3\frac{1}{2}$ hours is $2\frac{1}{2}$ hours.

Sean and his friends skated for $2\frac{1}{2}$ hours.

Look Back SENSIBLE ANSWER   The other choices are not sensible.

Sean and his friends could not have skated for longer than the rink was open. So 5 hours is not a sensible answer.

Unless there were some kind of emergency that would force the group to leave early, they probably would not skate for only $\frac{1}{4}$ hour. So $\frac{1}{4}$ hour is not a sensible answer.

■ **Talk About Math**   How did the context of this problem affect the answer? What could Sean and his friends have done instead of skating so $\frac{1}{4}$ hour would have been the sensible answer?

Check Understanding

1. Choose the most sensible answer. How many people were skating at the rink on Friday night?

   3 people   50 people   700 people

2. Explain why the other two choices are not sensible.

Practice

Choose the most sensible answer. Explain why the other choices are not sensible.

3. Sean rented a pair of skates. How much was the skate rental fee?

   $2 $20 $200

4. What was the temperature in the roller rink?

   20°F   72°F   105°F

5. A Roller-Rama T-shirt costs $5 more than skate pompons. How much do pompons cost?

   $3 $20 $35

6. Sean's brother drove Sean and his friends home from the rink. How many people were in the car?

   1 person   2 people   5 people

7. A chartered bus was used to bring a youth group home from the rink. How many people were on the bus?

   4 people   40 people   400 people

Midchapter _____ Checkup

1. What does the 6 mean in 265,291?

2. Use >, <, or =.
   18,429 ⬚ 18,249

3. Round 24,581 to the nearest thousand.

4. Use mental math to find 39 + 58.

5. Estimate 8,295 + 357. Then find the actual sum.

6. Liz bought a movie ticket. How much change could she have received from $5? Choose the most sensible answer.
   $8 $4.95 $3

7. If the three choices were not given for Exercise 6, what other fact would you need to know to solve the problem?

Problem-Solving Workshop

Explore as a Team

1. Discuss how you might estimate the number of squares or parts of squares in Drawing A.

> **a.** You may count only up to 10 squares before you estimate.

> **b.** Ask yourselves questions like: Does the drawing include more than 10 squares? 20 squares? 30 squares? 100 squares?

2. **Estimate** the number of squares in Drawing A.

3. **Estimate** the number of squares or parts of squares in Drawing B. (You may count up to 25 squares only before you estimate.)

4. What questions did you ask yourselves before making your estimate?

5. Use 1-centimeter-square paper to make a drawing.

6. **Estimate** the number of squares you will include in your drawing. After you have made the drawing, count the actual number of squares. Secretly record the total.

7. **Estimate** the number of squares or parts of squares in your teammates' drawings. After estimating, compare the actual number of squares with your estimates.

Drawing A

Drawing B

TIPS FOR **WORKING TOGETHER**

Involve your whole group. Help everyone to participate.

Real-Life Decision Making

Consider crowds such as these:

a. in a park

b. in the auditorium

c. at recess

d. in a football stadium

1. Discuss situations in which you would estimate the number of people in a crowd. When would you need to know the exact number of people in a crowd?

2. Evaluate how far off your estimate could be if you were writing a newspaper article about a crowd.
10? 25? 200? 1,000? 5,000? 20,000?

Explore with a Computer

Use the *Graphing and Probability Workshop Project* for this activity.

1. Find the differences between the height and reach of the students in your class. As a team, use a tape measure to measure each person's height and reach in inches.

2. At the computer, enter the data into a table.

3. Display the information using the **Bar Graph** option.

4. Compare the results for each student.

Number-Sense Project

Look back at pages 2-3.

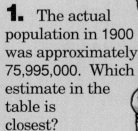

1. The actual population in 1900 was approximately 75,995,000. Which estimate in the table is closest?

2. What do you think the actual population of the United States is today?

3. How could you find the current estimated population of the United States?

Estimates of U.S. population in 1900	
1.	1,300,000
2.	500,000,000
3.	10,000,000
4.	2,000,000
5.	25,000,000

Adding Larger Numbers

Build Understanding

A. The observation level of Toronto's CN Tower is 1,136 feet above the ground. The tower with its antenna continues upward for another 679 feet. What is the height of the CN Tower?

Find 1,136 + 679.
Estimate: 1,100 + 700 = 1,800

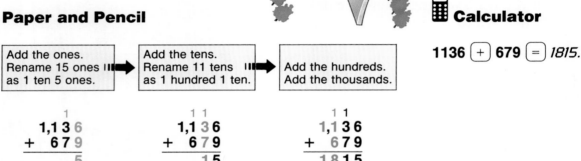

Paper and Pencil

Add the ones. Rename 15 ones as 1 ten 5 ones.	➡	Add the tens. Rename 11 tens as 1 hundred 1 ten.	➡	Add the hundreds. Add the thousands.

$$
\begin{array}{r}
\overset{1}{} \\
1,1\,3\,6 \\
+\ \ 6\,7\,9 \\
\hline
5
\end{array}
\qquad
\begin{array}{r}
\overset{1\ 1}{} \\
1,1\,3\,6 \\
+\ \ 6\,7\,9 \\
\hline
1\,5
\end{array}
\qquad
\begin{array}{r}
\overset{1\ 1}{} \\
1,1\,3\,6 \\
+\ \ 6\,7\,9 \\
\hline
1,8\,1\,5
\end{array}
$$

Calculator

1136 ⊞ **679** ⊟ *1815.*

The height of the CN Tower is 1,815 feet. The estimate shows that the answer is reasonable.

B. Estimation Use *front-end digits with adjusting.*

Use front-end digits.

273 + **4**12 + **1**48
  ↓   ↓
200 + **4**00 + **1**00 = 700

Then adjust the estimate.

73 + 12 + 48 > 100

The sum is more than 800.

C. Mental Math Use *compensation.*

Change one number to make it easy to add. Then change the other number.

29 + 1 = 30		45 − 1 = 44		30 + 44
29	+	45	=	74

Change both numbers to make them easy to add. Then change the answer.

98 + 2 = 100		97 + 3 = 100		200 − 5
98	+	97	=	195

Talk About Math Explain how you would use mental math to find $3.25 + $2.60 + $4.75 + $1.45.

Check Understanding

For each exercise, estimate the sum. Then give the sum.
Which statements at the right are needed to find the answer?

1. 2,868
   + 2,043

2. 8,237
   + 8,369

3. 824
    341
  + 516

4. 31,328
  + 19,925

a. 10 hundreds = 1 thousand
b. 10 tens = 1 hundred
c. 10 thousands = 1 ten-thousand
d. 10 ones = 1 ten

5. **Mental Math** Use mental math to find 298 + 327.

Practice

For each exercise, estimate the sum. Then find the actual sum.

6. 4,009
  + 3,171

7. 21,467
  + 6,425

8. 87,027
  + 23,058

9. 41,666
  + 22,335

10. 51,008
   + 27,165

11. 27,463
   + 10,008

12. 14,298
   + 3,506

13. $307.96
   + 408.73

14. $642.54
   +   88.79

15. $142.67
   + 238.54

Mental Math Find each sum using mental math.

16. 124 + 59

17. 197 + 196

18. $8.65 + $1.35

19. $32.05 + $3.95

Problem Solving

Explore ——— Math

Write 4-digit numbers beneath one another as described here.

20. Write two numbers. Write a third so, for each place, the sum of the digits in the second and third numbers is 9.

21. Write a fourth number. Write a fifth so, for each place, the sum of the digits in the fourth and fifth numbers is 9.

22. **Calculator** Find the sum. Compare the sum to the first number. What do you notice?

23. Try this again with other sets of numbers. Try to predict the answer before you add.

24. Explain why you were able to make the prediction.

Estimating Differences

Build Understanding

Here are some estimation strategies to use when
estimating differences.

A. Estimate 3,217 − 1,229 *using
front-end digits.*

3,217 − 1,229
   ↓   ↓
3,000 − 1,000 = 2,000

The actual difference should be about
2,000.

B. Estimate 693 − 219 by *rounding*
both the minuend and subtrahend to
the same place.

693 − 219   Round to the
   ↓   ↓   nearest hundred.
700 − 200 = 500

The actual difference should be
about 500.

■ **Talk About Math**   Why would using front-end digits not have been a
good strategy to use with the numbers in Example B?

Check Understanding

For another example, see Set G, pages 38–39.

1. Estimate 9,581 − 4,623 using
front-end digits.

2. Estimate 5,841 − 2,104 by rounding
to the same place.

For each exercise, if you were to estimate the difference by
rounding, to what place would you round the numbers?

3. 98 − 57   **4.** 592 − 45   **5.** 4,730 − 285

Practice

For More Practice, see Set G, pages 40–41.

Estimate each difference. Tell which strategy you used.

6. 82 − 23 **7.** 78 − 49 **8.** 585 − 329 **9.** 717 − 521

10. 6,642 − 2,591 **11.** 8,472 − 5,924 **12.** 5,217 − 1,388 **13.** 7,246 − 984

14. Choose two of the exercises above. Explain why you chose the strategy you used.

Choose the best estimate for each difference.

15. 91 − 32

30 50 60

16. 87 − 39

30 50 60

17. 623 − 384

100 200 300

18. 894 − 321

400 500 600

19. 7,157 − 4,852

1,000 2,000 3,000

20. 5,827 − 952

4,000 5,000 6,000

Problem Solving

21. Kazuko said the actual difference between 472 and 295 is close to her estimate of 300. Does this seem reasonable? Explain.

22. Brenda said the actual difference between 4,376 and 2,977 was close to her estimate of 1,000. Do you agree? Explain why or why not.

23. Tomas used rounding to the same place. The rounded minuend was 800. The estimated difference was 300. Give the least possible number and the greatest possible number that the actual subtrahend could have been.

24. Critical Thinking Suppose you estimate a difference where the minuend rounds up and the subtrahend rounds down. Will the actual difference be less than or greater than the estimate? Explain your reasoning.

Use Data Use the information in the table on page 7.

25. Round the number of acres for Haleakala to the nearest thousand.

26. Which is larger, Bryce Canyon or Wind Cave?

27. Estimate the difference in the number of acres between Acadia and Wind Cave.

Subtracting Whole Numbers

Build Understanding

The sums below are alike in some way. How are they alike?

4 + 5 = 9
28 + 71 = 99
342 + 657 = 999

Each sum contains only digits of 9. Two numbers with a sum that has only digits of 9 are called **complements.** Here are some more complements:

6 and 3   51 and 48   1,111 and 8,888

A. Adding to Subtract
Groups: 3-6 students

a. Start with a subtraction problem involving two 3-digit numbers. Find the complement of the lesser number.

b. Add the complement to the greater number. Subtract 1 from the first digit of the sum. Add 1 to the digit in the ones place.

c. Compare this answer with the difference you get by actually subtracting. Are the results the same?

d. Make up more subtraction problems with 3- or 4-digit numbers. Take turns with the others in your group to find the differences by adding and by subtracting.

e. Does the addition method always work? Share your results with others in your group.

B. You can check subtraction by using addition.

```
 7 14
 8̸ 4̸ 5        Check
- 3 8 2       4 6 3
-------      + 3 8 2
 4 6 3       -------
              8 4 5
```

■ **Talk About Math**   For Example B, explain the renaming that was done in order to subtract.

Check Understanding

For each exercise, which statement at the right is needed to find the answer? Then give the difference.

1.	2.	3.	4.
84 − 37	529 − 74	7,062 − 5,431	8,463 − 5,431

a. 1 hundred = 10 tens
b. 1 ten = 10 ones
c. 1 thousand = 10 hundreds

5. Estimation Is 2,036 a reasonable difference for 5,827 − 3,791? Explain your reasoning.

6. Find $125.39 − $18.25.

Practice

For each exercise, estimate the difference. Then find the actual difference. **Remember** to check your work.

7.	8.	9.	10.	11.
87 − 29	98 − 32	584 − 91	607 − 293	5,735 − 824

12.	13.	14.	15.	16.
9,704 − 5,362	5,468 − 3,124	$27.08 − 14.24	$32.58 − 11.24	$154.38 − 42.75

17. 792 − 438   **18.** 7,596 − 342   **19.** 6,270 − 4,155

Mixed Practice **Remember** to watch the signs.

20.	21.	22.	23.	24.
852 + 183	527 − 313	2,539 − 627	7,624 − 3,483	5,437 + 5,622

25. $32.59 + $19.62   **26.** $62.59 − $31.24   **27.** $31.60 − $20.47

Problem Solving

28. Number Sense Use each of the digits 1 through 7 once to write a 4-digit number minus a 3-digit number that gives the greatest possible difference.

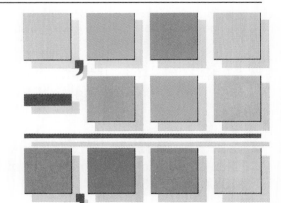

Mental Math for Subtraction

Build Understanding

Ellen Logan is the manager of a store that sells party supplies. She often uses mental math when taking inventory.

Here are some mental math strategies to use when subtracting mentally.

A. Look for *special numbers* that are easy to subtract, such as numbers that end in one or more zeros.

80 − 20 = 60   **78 − 30 = 48**

500 − 300 = 200   **642 − 200 = 442**

B. Look for numbers that you can *break apart* into numbers that are easy to subtract. This works best when there is no renaming.

$$\overset{\overset{20 + 4}{\downarrow}}{67 - 24} = 43$$

C. Look for numbers where you can use *compensation*.

Change one number to make it easy to subtract. Then change the other number.

$$\overset{177 + 2 = 179}{177} \quad \overset{98 + 2 = 100}{-98} \quad = \quad \overset{179 - 100}{79}$$

Change one number to make it easy to subtract. Then change the answer.

$$165 \quad \overset{97 + 3 = 100}{-97} \quad = \quad \overset{65 + 3}{68}$$

■ **Talk About Math**   Explain how Ellen could use mental math to find $10.00 − $5.75.

Check Understanding

For another example, see Set H, pages 38–39.

1. Find $359 - 40$ using a special number.

2. Find $254 - 32$ by breaking apart one number.

3. Find $94 - 68$ using compensation. Explain your thinking.

4. Explain how to use mental math to find $20.00 - $15.99.

Practice

For More Practice, see Set H, pages 40–41.

Use mental math to find each difference.
Tell which strategy you used.

5. $84 - 40$ 6. $275 - 99$ 7. $872 - 521$ 8. $729 - 300$

9. Choose one of the exercises above. Explain why you chose the strategy you used.

Problem Solving

Remember to use mental math when it is helpful.

10. Ellen counted 185 bags of balloons. Some contained red balloons and others contained blue balloons. If there were 100 bags of red balloons, how many bags of blue balloons were there?

11. Ellen found 98 packs of paper plates in the storeroom. There were 14 packs on the shelves in the store. How many packs were there all together?

12. Ellen knows that $82 + 18 = 100$. How will this help her use mental math to give change to a customer who paid for items costing $5.82 with a $10 bill?

Skills Review
pages 4–5

1. Tell what the 8 means in 359,802,443.

2. Tell what digit is in the ten-thousands place in 24,805,271.

3. Write 20,503,064 in expanded form.

4. Write $8,000,000 + 50,000 + 300 + 40$ in standard form.

Subtracting Larger Numbers

Build Understanding

A. Giants Stadium seats 76,891 people. In Chicago, Soldier Field can seat 65,793 people. How many more fans can watch a football game in Giants Stadium than in Soldier Field?

Find 76,891 − 65,793.
Estimate: 77,000 − 66,000 = 11,000

Paper and Pencil

| Rename 9 tens 1 one as 8 tens 11 ones. Subtract the ones. | → | Rename 8 hundreds 8 tens as 7 hundreds 18 tens. Subtract the tens. | → | Subtract the hundreds. Subtract the thousands. Subtract the ten-thousands. |

$$
\begin{array}{r}
^{8\,11} \\
76,89\cancel{1} \\
-\,65,793 \\
\hline
8
\end{array}
$$

$$
\begin{array}{r}
^{18}\\
^{7\,\cancel{8}11} \\
76,\cancel{8}\cancel{9}\cancel{1} \\
-\,65,793 \\
\hline
98
\end{array}
$$

$$
\begin{array}{r}
^{18}\\
^{7\,\cancel{8}11} \\
76,\cancel{8}\cancel{9}\cancel{1} \\
-\,65,793 \\
\hline
11,098
\end{array}
$$

Calculator

76891 $\boxed{-}$

65793 $\boxed{=}$

11098.

Giants Stadium can seat 11,098 more people than Soldier Field. The estimate shows that the answer is reasonable.

Check
$$
\begin{array}{r}
11,098 \\
+\,65,793 \\
\hline
76,891
\end{array}
$$

B. Find 2,700 − 1,487.

$$
\begin{array}{r}
^{9}\\
^{6\,10\,10} \\
2,\cancel{7}\cancel{0}\cancel{0} \\
-\,1,487 \\
\hline
1,213
\end{array}
$$

Estimate:
2,700 − 1,500 = 1,200

■ **Talk About Math** Explain the renaming that is shown in Example B.

Check Understanding

For another example, see Set I, pages 38–39.

For each exercise, estimate the difference. Then give the difference.
Which statements at the right are needed to find the answer?

1.	2.	3.	4.
5,192 − 1,223	4,037 − 3,419	70,258 − 34,619	33,000 − 19,004

a. 1 hundred = 10 tens
b. 1 ten = 10 ones
c. 1 thousand = 10 hundreds
d. 1 ten-thousand = 10 thousands

Practice

For More Practice, see Set I, pages 40–41.

For each exercise, estimate the difference. Then find the
actual difference. **Remember** to check your work.

5.	6.	7.	8.	9.
9,711 − 3,645	38,704 − 9,295	81,008 − 64,029	32,436 − 21,647	54,782 − 26,295

Mixed Practice **Remember** to watch the signs.

10.	11.	12.	13.	14.
92,516 + 38,745	37,005 − 15,129	12,000 − 7,859	74,612 + 99,953	95,817 − 87,908

Problem Solving

15. The Ruiz family planned to spend $100 to see the
Giants play football. They spent $54.75 on tickets,
$18.29 on food, and $17.50 on transportation. Did they
have any money left over? If so, how much?

Explore ———— **Math**

16. Write a 4-digit number with the
first digit greater than the fourth
and the second digit less than the
third.

17. Reverse the digits to create
another number. Then subtract.

18. Reverse the digits of the
difference. Then add.

19. Try this several times with other
4-digit numbers.

20. Describe the pattern you see in
your answers.

21. For Ex. 16, why can't the first
digit be less than the fourth?

Write an Equation

Build Understanding

The two-day Highland School Health Fair was a big success. On Thursday, 312 people attended the fair. Another 259 people attended on Friday. What was the total attendance at the fair?

Understand   The fair lasted two days. There were 312 people on the first day and 259 people on the second day. The total attendance is the sum of the attendance for both days.

 **Plan and Solve**   STRATEGY   To find the total attendance, add the attendance for each of the two days. An *equation* is a number sentence that can be used to show how the parts of the problem are related. *Write an equation* using n for the total attendance. Then solve.

Thursday's attendance	Friday's attendance	Total attendance
312 +	**259** =	n

Estimate: 300 + 300 = 600

Paper and Pencil    **Calculator**

```
  312
+ 259
─────
  571   n = 571
```

312 (+) **259** (=) *571.*

$n = 571$

ANSWER   There were 571 people at the fair.

Look Back   The answer is reasonable because the answer is close to the estimate. Check your addition by subtracting either addend from the sum.

■ **Talk About Math**   Could you solve the problem using this equation: 259 + 312 = n? Explain why or why not.

PROBLEM SOLVING
GUIDE

Understand
QUESTION
FACTS
KEY IDEA

Plan and Solve
STRATEGY
ANSWER

Look Back
SENSIBLE ANSWER
ALTERNATE APPROACH

Check Understanding

The planning committee expected 500 people to attend the fair. How many more people attended than were expected?

1. Which equation can you use to solve this problem?

   a. $500 + 571 = n$ **b.** $571 - 500 = n$

2. Solve the equation and give the answer in a sentence.

Practice

Write an equation. Then find the answer.

3. Eye tests were given to 208 people on Thursday. On Friday, 185 people had their eyes tested. How many fewer people had their eyes tested on Friday?

4. The dental display booth had 575 toothbrushes to give as prizes. At the end of the fair, there were 98 toothbrushes left. How many were given away?

5. The heart rate of one fifth grader was 72 beats per minute. After she rode an exercise bike, her rate was 128 beats per minute. How much did her rate increase?

6. The snack booth sold 485 bran muffins. Of these, 248 were sold individually and the rest were sold with fruit salad. How many were sold with fruit salad?

7. During the two days, the snack booth sold 247 glasses of orange juice, 245 glasses of milk, and 108 glasses of grapefruit juice. How many glasses were sold in all?

8. Hearing tests were given to 179 people on Thursday. On Friday, 74 more people were tested than on Thursday. How many people were tested on Friday?

Choose a _____ Strategy

Rainbow Math   The numbers in the red and blue parts of the rainbow count double.

9. What 3 numbers give a total sum of 120?

10. What 5 numbers give a total sum of 122?

11. What 5 numbers give a total sum of 158?

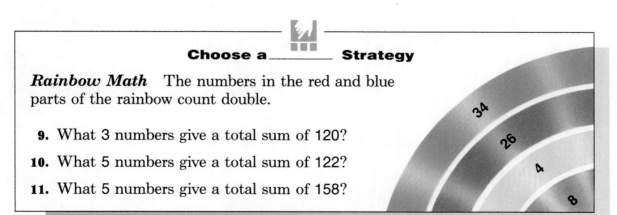

Missing Addends

Build Understanding

The fourth and fifth graders at Meyer Elementary School went to Orchestra Hall to see a concert. There were 98 fifth graders. All together there were 173 students on the trip. How many fourth graders were there?

	Number of fifth graders		Number of fourth graders		Total number of students	
Use this equation. How can it be solved?	98	+	n	=	173	
Subtract to find the missing addend.			n	=	173 − 98	
			n	=	75	

$$\begin{array}{r} 173 \\ -\ 98 \\ \hline 75 \end{array}$$

There were 75 fourth graders.

■ **Write About Math**   To find a missing addend, it is helpful to think of a family of facts such as the family shown at the right. Which fact would help you find n in $7 + n = 16$?

$$7 + n = 16 \qquad 16 - 7 = n$$
$$n + 7 = 16 \qquad 16 - n = 7$$

Write a family of facts for the equation in the example above.

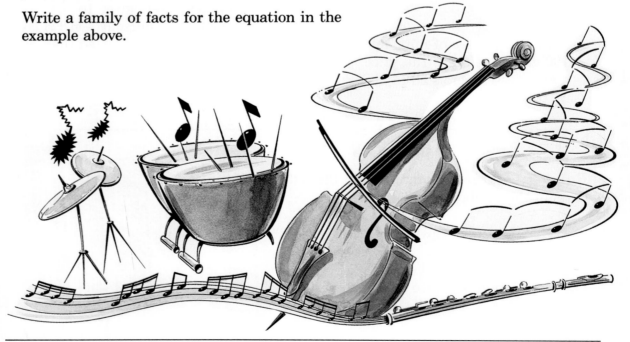

Check Understanding

For another example, see Set J, pages 38–39.

Find the missing addend. Use families of facts to help.

1. $45 + n = 82$ **2.** $n + 53 = 101$ **3.** $134 = 78 + n$

Practice

For More Practice, see Set J, pages 40–41.

Find the missing addend.

4. $57 + n = 93$ **5.** $n + 17 = 45$ **6.** $67 = 41 + n$

7. $138 = n + 94$ **8.** $87 + n = 129$ **9.** $n + 59 = 148$

10. $n + 363 = 787$ **11.** $784 = n + 137$ **12.** $517 + n = 638$

13. $2,496 = 712 + n$ **14.** $317 + n = 1,548$ **15.** $918 = 421 + n$

16. $4,002 = n + 1,642$ **17.** $n + 3,165 = 3,916$ **18.** $2,043 + n = 6,571$

Calculator   Find the missing addend.

19. $n + 38,176 = 67,145$ **20.** $98,176 + n = 142,631$ **21.** $380,162 = n + 145,002$

Problem Solving

22. Orchestra Hall seats 2,560 people. It was sold out for this performance. In addition to the 173 students, how many other people were in the audience?

23. The concert tickets and transportation cost $1,384. It was paid out of the $2,000 school activity account. How much was left after this expense?

24. There were 105 orchestra members performing on stage. Later, the chorus performed with the orchestra. Then there were 223 performers on stage. How many people were in the chorus?

25. In the orchestra, the violin players and the 21 players of other stringed instruments make up the 67 members of the string section. How many violin players are there?

26. A student pass to attend 3 concerts costs $15. The ticket cost for one concert is $6.50. Is it cheaper to buy the pass than to buy 3 separate tickets? If so, how much money would a student save? What reasons are there why someone would not want to buy the pass?

Problem Solving REVIEW

Solve each problem.

1. In 1790 the population of the United States was 3,929,213. Round the number to the nearest million.

2. How many songs an hour can a radio station play? Which choice is a reasonable answer? Why?

5 15 35

3. Use the digits, 0, 3, 4 and 7 to write the least number.

4. The attendance at the first game of a baseball double-header was 56,221. Before the second game, 1,927 people left. How many fans stayed for the second game?

5. Use mental math to find the least number of bills and coins this customer got in change. He paid for his purchases of $18.36 with two $10 bills, 2 quarters, and a penny.

6. The continental shelf of the Northeast Atlantic Ocean covers 1,162,250 square miles. For the Northwest Atlantic, the area is 486,360 square miles. How much larger is the area for the Northeast Atlantic?

7. Data File
Use the map on pages 116–117. Find the difference in height between Longs Peak, the highest point in Rocky Mountain National Park, and Mt. Julian, which is also in the park.

8. Make a Data File Use a map of North and South America. Make a list of places that are about 1,000 miles, 2,000 miles, 3,000 miles and so on, up to 10,000 miles away from your town.

Explore with a Calculator

"Numbers Around Us"

Numbers are found in many places and used in many ways in our world.

52,123 people see the Eagles win

$17,184 raised in fund drive

4,350 students are enrolled at Central High School

The population of Cedar Creek has risen to 673,801

2,196 acres for sale

My dad's new car cost $8,912

3,007 miles of coastline

Johnson wins the election by 28,355 votes

The 7,016 yard golf course

Only 2,399 tickets left

1. Go on a number hunt to check out your knowledge of place value. Use your calculator and the numbers above to do each problem.

a. Find the sum of all the four-digit numbers.

b. Find the sum of all the numbers with an 8 in the thousands place.

c. Find the sum of all the numbers with a 1 in the hundreds place.

d. Find the difference between the greatest and the least numbers.

e. Find the sum of the numbers greater than 25,000.

f. Find the difference between the two numbers that are the least.

g. Find the sum of the three numbers that are the least.

h. Find the sum of all the numbers with a 0 in the hundreds place.

2. Find the sum of your answers for Problems 1. a.–h.

a. Add 3,799,547 to your answer for Problem 2.

b. Turn your display upside down. Read the "word" in your display. If it is something swimmers wear, your knowledge of place value is okay.

Reteaching

Set A pages 4–5

Billions period			Millions period			Thousands period			Ones period		
hundred-billions	ten-billions	billions	hundred-millions	ten-millions	millions	hundred-thousands	ten-thousands	thousands	hundreds	tens	ones
	1	0	6	0	2	5	4	0	0	0	0

The number 10,602,540,000 is read ten billion, six hundred two million, five hundred forty thousand. **Remember** that the comma separates each group of three digits, or period.

Give the standard form. **Remember** to use zeros as placeholders.

1. 285 million, 806 thousand

2. 9 billion, 3 million, 80 thousand, 912

Set B pages 6–7

Compare 46,469 and 46,584. The ten-thousands digits and the thousands digits are the same in both numbers. So compare the hundreds.

Since 4 < 5, then 46,469 < 46,584.

Remember that > means greater than and < means less than.
Compare these numbers. Use >, <, or =.

1. 647 ▦ 649   2. 48,030 ▦ 48,303

Set C pages 8–9

Round 14,287 to the nearest thousand. To round to the nearest thousand, look at the hundreds digit. Since 2 is less than 5, the thousands digit stays the same.

So 14,287 rounds to 14,000.

Remember to add 1 to the digit in the place to be rounded if the digit to its right is 5 or more. Round to the nearest thousand.

1. 3,429   2. 14,192   3. 804

Set D pages 12–13

Estimate the sum by rounding to the nearest thousand.

$$\begin{array}{r} 4,913 \rightarrow 5,000 \\ +7,086 \rightarrow +7,000 \\ \hline 12,000 \end{array}$$

Remember that the digit in the place to be rounded stays the same if the digit to its right is less than 5. Estimate each sum.

1. 6,215 + 5,831   2. 7,902 + 7,092

Set E pages 14–15

Estimate the sum. Find the actual sum.

$$\begin{array}{r} & & 1 \\ 7,296 \rightarrow & 7,000 & 7,296 \\ +2,642 \rightarrow & +3,000 & +2,642 \\ \hline & 10,000 & 9,938 \end{array}$$

Remember that the actual sum will be less than the estimate if both addends are rounded up.
Estimate the sum. Find the actual sum.

1. 283 + 174   2. 5,309 + 3,102

Set F   pages 16–17

Using combinations can help you to find a sum using mental math. Look for numbers whose sum is 10 or 100.

$$68 + 75 + 32 = 100 + 75$$
$$= 175$$

Remember you can add numbers in any order. Use mental math to find each sum.

1. 39 + 84 + 61   **2.** 44 + 97 + 56

3. 81 + 19 + 48   **4.** 76 + 27 + 73

Set G   pages 24–25

Estimate 6,413 − 3,806 by rounding both the minuend and the subtrahend to the nearest thousand.

$$\begin{array}{r} 6{,}413 \rightarrow \quad 6{,}000 \\ -\ 3{,}806 \rightarrow -\ 4{,}000 \\ \hline 2{,}000 \end{array}$$

Remember when estimating by rounding to round the numbers to the same place. Estimate each difference.

1. 86 − 57   **2.** 431 − 276

3. 629 − 318   **4.** 6,809 − 4,570

Set H   pages 28–29

Use mental math to find 364 − 97. Change 97 to 100 in order to make it easier to subtract.

$$364 − 100 = 264$$

Since you added 3 to 97, add 3 to this answer, 264. So

$$364 − 97 = 267$$

Remember that if you add a number to the subtrahend, you must add the same amount to the difference. Use mental math to find each difference.

1. 179 − 98   **2.** 86 − 48

3. 147 − 38   **4.** 238 − 27

Set I   pages 30–31

Find 18,546 − 9,752.

Estimate: 19,000 − 10,000 = 9,000

Rename to show 10 more tens.

$$\begin{array}{r} {}^{4}{}^{14} \\ 1\,8{,}\cancel{5}\cancel{4}\,6 \\ -\ 9{,}7\,5\,2 \end{array}$$

Rename to show 10 more hundreds.

$$\begin{array}{r} {}^{14} \\ {}^{7}\,\cancel{4}\,{}^{14} \\ 1\,\cancel{8}{,}\cancel{5}\cancel{4}\,6 \\ -\ 9{,}7\,5\,2 \\ \hline 8{,}7\,9\,4 \end{array}$$

Remember to estimate the difference to be sure your answer makes sense. Estimate the difference. Then find the actual difference.

1. 8,924   **2.** 46,275   **3.** 14,000
    − 4,675   − 32,489   − 6,532

Set J   pages 34–35

Use subtraction to find the missing addend in this addition equation.

$$\begin{aligned} 83 + n &= 276 \\ n &= 276 − 83 \\ n &= 193 \end{aligned}$$

Remember that it is helpful to think of a family of facts to find a missing addend. Find the missing addend.

1. 46 + n = 90   **2.** n + 68 = 135

3. 374 = n + 298   **4.** 733 + n = 1,038

More Practice

Set A   pages 4–5

Tell which digits are in the millions period in each number.

1. 108,627,831   **2.** 31,846,225,006   **3.** 14,396,025   **4.** 4,027,834

Tell what the 6 in each number means.

5. 4,630,147   **6.** 3,486,091   **7.** 6,107,052   **8.** 719,060,005

Write in standard form.

9. 14 thousand, 38   **10.** 3 million, 80 thousand, 452

Write each number in words and in expanded form.

11. 407,003   **12.** 2,400,070   **13.** 320,000,900   **14.** 5,060,008,000

Set B   pages 6–7

Compare these numbers. Use >, <, or =.

1. 649 ▦ 647   **2.** 4,286 ▦ 4,301   **3.** 53,102 ▦ 53,012

List the numbers in order from least to greatest.

4. 436   463   419   **5.** 2,305   2,053   2,530

Set C   pages 8–9

Round to the nearest ten and to the nearest hundred.

1. 83   **2.** 145   **3.** 551   **4.** 249   **5.** 4,036   **6.** 3,091

Round to the nearest thousand and to the nearest ten-thousand.

7. 8,483   **8.** 16,544   **9.** 52,426   **10.** 12,420   **11.** 68,035

Set D   pages 12–13

Estimate each sum. Tell which strategy you used.

1. 64 + 86   **2.** 419 + 624 + 733   **3.** 3,821 + 7,125

Choose the best estimate for each sum.

4. 279 + 486
600   700   800

5. 107 + 92 + 101 + 96
300   3,000   400

6. 4,820 + 6,021
10,000   11,000   1,100

Set E   pages 14–15

For each exercise, estimate the sum. Then find the actual sum.

1.   68
+ 19

2.   147
+ 39

3.   374
+ 138

4.   5,528
+   391

5.   7,629
+ 3,392

Set F pages 16–17

Use mental math to find each sum. Tell which strategy you used.

1. 76 + 96   **2.** 68 + 40   **3.** 32 + 47 + 68   **4.** 86 + 59

Use mental math to choose the correct sum.

5. 12 + 13 + 14
     29   39   49

6. 426 + 563
     983   986   989

7. 153 + 95
     148   184   248

Set G pages 24–25

Estimate each difference. Tell which strategy you used.

1. 93 − 54   **2.** 679 − 442   **3.** 523 − 325   **4.** 7,394 − 4,833

Choose the best estimate for each difference.

5. 74 − 45
     20   30   400

6. 438 − 296
     100   200   300

7. 6,246 − 3,908
     2,000   3,000   4,000

Set H pages 28–29

Use mental math to find each difference. Tell which strategy you used.

1. 657 − 432   **2.** 387 − 96   **3.** 97 − 50   **4.** 59 − 36

5. Choose one of the exercises above. Explain why you chose the strategy you used.

Set I pages 30–31

For each exercise, estimate the difference. Then find the actual difference.

1.   8,617
    − 4,705

2.   26,842
    − 8,356

3.   74,064
    − 35,206

4.   43,562
    − 32,683

5.   85,626
    − 76,337

Mixed Practice Remember to watch the signs.

6.   73,468
    + 37,654

7.   49,006
    − 31,238

8.   14,000
    − 6,483

9.   48,391
    + 86,829

10.   78,625
    − 69,816

Set J pages 34–35

Find the missing addend.

1. $29 + n = 43$ **2.** $317 + n = 508$ **3.** $3,006 = n + 2,086$

Calculator Find the missing addend.

4. $n + 49,268 = 62,497$ **5.** $86,695 + n = 103,708$

Enrichment

Roman Numerals

The Roman numeral system was used many years ago to name numbers.
The basic symbols are:

I V X L C D M

I (1)	V (5)	X (10)	L (50)	C (100)	D (500)	M (1,000)

Study these samples.

1	I	19	XIX	39	XXXIX	200	CC
2	II	20	XX	40	XL	300	CCC
3	III	21	XXI	41	XLI	400	CD
4	IV	24	XXIV	44	XLIV	500	D
5	V					600	DC
6	VI	29	XXIX	50	L		
7	VII	30	XXX	60	LX	900	CM
8	VIII	31	XXXI	70	LXX	1,000	M
9	IX	34	XXXIV	80	LXXX		
10	X			90	XC		
11	XI			100	C		

Write each Roman numeral in standard form. Follow these examples.

LXVIII	XCII	CDXLII	MMCMXCIX
60 + 8	90 + 2	400 + 40 + 2	2,000 + 900 + 90 + 9
68	**92**	**442**	**2,999**

1. XV   **2.** XXXVII   **3.** XLIX   **4.** LXVIII   **5.** LXXIV

6. LXXXIX   **7.** XCV   **8.** XCIX   **9.** CXVI   **10.** CXL

11. CDIX   **12.** MCXV   **13.** MDCLXI   **14.** MDCCL   **15.** MCMXL

16. Section XII   **17.** King Louis XIV   **18.** Chapter XXIX

19. Date on a building:
MDCCCXXIV

20. Book copyright date:
MCMXLIX

21. Movie copyright date:
MCMXCI

Chapter 1 Review/Test

1. What does the 7 in 7,000,826,354 mean?

2. List the following numbers in order from least to greatest:

   47,189   47,028   40,008

3. Round 89,127 to the nearest ten-thousand.

Choose the best estimate.

4. 689 + 788

   150   1,300   1,500

5. 5,168 − 2,850
   1,000   2,000   3,000

For each exercise, estimate the sum or difference. Then find the actual sum or difference.

6.   6,224
   $+ 2,198$

7.   28,168
   $+ 39,667$

8.   7,821
   $- 1,587$

9.   40,007
   $- 22,188$

Use mental math to chose the correct sum or difference.

10. 72 + 65 + 35

    162   172   272

11. 683 − 199

    482   384   484

Find the missing addend.

12. $38 + n = 89$

13. $n + 3,078 = 5,924$

14. Name the three steps of the Problem-Solving Guide.

15. Mr. Donovan bought 4 baseball tickets costing $12 each. What was the total cost?

16. Pablo said that the sum of 687 and 792 is more than 1,300. Do you agree? Why or why not?

17. Choose the most sensible answer.

    Amy bought a sandwich. How much change could she have received from $10?

    $9.95 $6.95 $12.25

Read the problem below. Then answer the question.

On Monday, Sarah sold 78 papers. On Tuesday, she sold 92 papers, and on Wednesday, she sold 50 papers. How many more did she sell on Tuesday than on Monday?

18. Which equation can you use to solve the problem?

    a. $78 + 92 = n$
    b. $78 + 92 + 50 = n$
    c. $92 - 78 = n$
    d. $92 - 50 = n$

19. **Write About Math** Explain the mental-math strategy you used in Exercise 11.

Multiplication

Did You Know: The average American watches 968 hours of television a year. That is just over 40 days.

Number-Sense Project

Estimate
Predict how many hours of television you watch in a week. Is it more than 24 hours?

Gather Data
Keep a record of how many hours you watch television during a week.

Analyze and Report
Summarize your results. Make a chart or graph to display your data. Compare your results with another student.

Multiples

Build Understanding

The *Lightning Bolt* roller coaster leaves the station every 6 minutes. The *Thunder Wave* leaves every 4 minutes. If they start at the same time, how long before they both leave the station again at the same time?

A. Exploring Multiples
Materials: Grid paper, scissors
Groups: Small groups of 2-4

a. Cut strips of paper that are each 1 unit wide. Make some 6 units long to represent the time for *Lightning Bolt.* Make some 4 units long for *Thunder Wave.*

b. Put the 6-unit strips end to end. Put the 4-unit strips end to end next to the row of 6-unit strips. Line up the beginnings of both rows.

c. For each row, how many units are in 1 strip? in 2 strips? in 3 strips? What do these numbers represent for each roller coaster?

d. Find the first place where ends of strips from both rows line up. How many units from the start is this? What does this tell you about the two roller coasters?

e. Find other places where ends of strips line up. How many units from the start are they? If you add more strips, can you continue to find more places where the strips line up?

B. If *Lightning Bolt* runs 3 times, how long will it take before it leaves again?

3 × 6 = 18   Since each run takes the same
                  amount of time, you multiply.
Factor Factor Product

It will take 18 minutes. The number 18 is a ***multiple*** of 6. Here are some multiples of 6.

6	12	18	24	30	36
1 × 6	2 × 6	3 × 6	4 × 6	5 × 6	6 × 6

46

c. Multiples of 6 and 4 tell when each roller coaster leaves its station. The *common multiples* of 6 and 4 tell when the roller coasters leave their stations at the same time.

Lightning Bolt
Multiples of 6:   6   12   18   24   30   36   42   48   54 . . .

Thunder Wave
Multiples of 4:   4   8   12   16   20   24   28   32   36 . . .

The *least common multiple* of 6 and 4, which is 12, tells that it takes 12 minutes from the start before roller coasters are leaving their stations at the same time again.

■ **Write About Math**   Describe how you can tell if a number is even or odd.

Check Understanding

For another example, see Set A, pages 74–75.

1. List six multiples of 9.

2. What is the greatest multiple of 9?

3. List three common multiples of 9 and 6.

4. Find the least common multiple of 9 and 6.

Practice

For More Practice, see Set A, pages 76–77.

List five multiples of the following numbers.

5. 2   **6.** 3   **7.** 5   **8.** 7   **9.** 8

List three common multiples of the following.

10. 2 and 4   **11.** 3 and 9   **12.** 6 and 8

13. Find the least common multiple for the numbers in Exercises 10-12.

Problem Solving

14. For *Lightning Bolt* and *Thunder Wave,* how many runs did each make in 12 minutes?

15. Critical Thinking   Does every pair of whole numbers have a common multiple?

16. Is there a greatest common multiple of 6 and 8? Explain why or why not.

Mental Math for Multiples of 10, 100, and 1,000

Build Understanding

On December 17, 1903, near Kitty Hawk, N.C., Wilbur and Orville Wright were the first to fly a power-driven airplane. The plane was a single engine biplane named *Flyer*. The longest flight made that day reached a speed of about 30 miles per hour (mi per h). How does this compare with the speed of other planes?

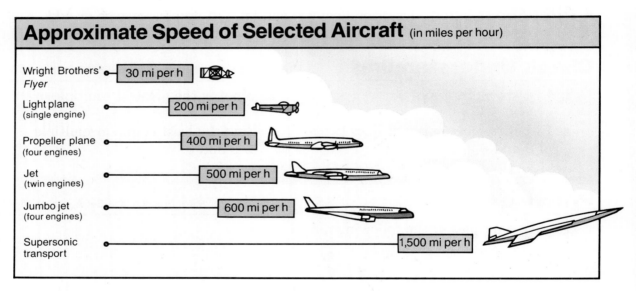

Approximate Speed of Selected Aircraft (in miles per hour)

Wright Brothers' *Flyer*	30 mi per h
Light plane (single engine)	200 mi per h
Propeller plane (four engines)	400 mi per h
Jet (twin engines)	500 mi per h
Jumbo jet (four engines)	600 mi per h
Supersonic transport	1,500 mi per h

How far can a jumbo jet travel in 3 hours?

Think of 3 lengths of 600 miles each. Add to find the answer.

600 + 600 + 600 = 1,800

Or, since you know the rate for one hour, you can multiply the number of hours and the rate to get the total distance. Use mental math.

3 × 600 = 1,800   3 × 6 hundreds = 18 hundreds

■ **Talk About Math**   How far can a supersonic transport travel in 1 hour? in 0 hours? What does this tell you about multiplying by 1 and multiplying by 0?

Check Understanding

For another example, see Set B, pages 74-75.

Complete each with *tens*, *hundreds*, *thousands*, or *ten-thousands*.

1. 30 × 600 = 18 __?__   **2.** 30 × 60 = 18 __?__   **3.** 6,000 × 30 = 18 __?__

Copy and complete.

4. 4 × 3,000 = ▦,000   **5.** 80 × 50 = 4,▦0   **6.** 500 × 20 = ▦,000

Multiply using mental math.

7. 1,000 × 80   **8.** 400 × 1   **9.** 100 × 100   **10.** 0 × 800

Practice

For More Practice, see Set B, pages 76–77.

Multiply. **Remember** to use mental math.

11. 50 × 7   **12.** 9 × 20   **13.** 30 × 1   **14.** 10 × 1,000

15. 90 × 40   **16.** 600 × 7   **17.** 0 × 300   **18.** 60 × 70

19. 1 × 4,000   **20.** 800 × 600   **21.** 5 × 800   **22.** 100 × 1,000

23. 50 × 6,000   **24.** 9,000 × 0   **25.** 52 × 1,000 **26.** 9 × 3,000

27. 200 × 800   **28.** 500 × 200   **29.** 7 × 1,000   **30.** 60 × 9,000

Problem Solving

Use the data at the beginning of the lesson.

31. How far does a propeller plane travel in 3 hours?

32. How far does a jumbo jet travel in 5 hours?

33. Which plane can travel 3 times as fast as a jet?

34. Which plane can travel 20 times as fast as the Wrights' *Flyer*?

35. Write a problem that can be answered by using some of the data about airplane speeds.

36. Find four pairs of factors with a product of 400. The factors should each have only one nonzero digit.

49

Multiplying by a One-Digit Number

Build Understanding

A. The Freewheeler Bike Shop sold 6 times as many ten-speed bikes as three-speed bikes last year. If the shop sold 127 three-speed bikes, how many ten-speed bikes did it sell?

The number of ten-speed bikes sold is a multiple of the number of three-speed bikes sold. Multiply to find the number of ten-speed bikes. Find 6 × 127.

Estimate: Since 127 is between 100 and 200, the product must be between 6 × 100 = 600 and 6 × 200 = 1,200. Since 127 is closer to 100, the product will be closer to 600.

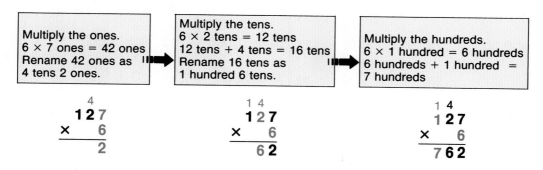

Multiply the ones. 6 × 7 ones = 42 ones Rename 42 ones as 4 tens 2 ones.	Multiply the tens. 6 × 2 tens = 12 tens 12 tens + 4 tens = 16 tens Rename 16 tens as 1 hundred 6 tens.	Multiply the hundreds. 6 × 1 hundred = 6 hundreds 6 hundreds + 1 hundred = 7 hundreds

$$\begin{array}{r} \overset{4}{12}7 \\ \times\ \ \ 6 \\ \hline 2 \end{array} \qquad \begin{array}{r} \overset{1\ 4}{12}7 \\ \times\ \ \ 6 \\ \hline 62 \end{array} \qquad \begin{array}{r} \overset{1\ 4}{12}7 \\ \times\ \ \ 6 \\ \hline 762 \end{array}$$

The shop sold 762 ten-speed bikes last year. The answer is reasonable because 762 is between 600 and 1,200.

B. Find 8 × 3 × 5.

Multiply two factors.

Then multiply by the third factor.

$$8 \times 3 = 24 \qquad \begin{array}{r} 24 \\ \times\ \ 5 \\ \hline 120 \end{array}$$

C. Find 3 × $2.98.

Think of $2.98 as 298 cents. Write the answer in dollars and cents.

$$\begin{array}{r} 298 \\ \times\ \ \ 3 \\ \hline 894 \end{array} \qquad \begin{array}{r} \$2.98 \\ \times\ \ \ \ 3 \\ \hline \$8.94 \end{array}$$

■ **Talk About Math** In Example B, would the product be different if you changed the order of the factors? How would this help you find the product mentally?

50

Check Understanding

For another example, see Set C, pages 74–75.

Copy and complete.

1. 27 tens = ▦ hundreds ▦ tens   **2.** 35 hundreds = ▦ thousands ▦ hundreds

Multiply.

3. 5 × 2,056   **4.** 4 × $5.26   **5.** 8 × 7 × 3

6. Mental Math For Example C, how will thinking of $2.98 as 2 cents less than $3 help you find the product mentally?

7. Estimation Choose three exercises from Exercises 8-19. Explain how you would estimate each product.

Practice

For More Practice, see Set C, pages 76–77.

Multiply. **Remember** to estimate to tell if the answer is reasonable.

8.   17
   × 8

9.   87
   × 3

10.   40
   × 6

11.   75
   × 7

12.   861
   × 5

13.   579
   × 7

14.   403
   × 8

15.   640
   × 3

16.   2,413
   × 2

17.   3,592
   × 9

18.   7,053
   × 4

19.   4,006
   × 6

20. $0.45
   × 4

21. $8.20
   × 9

22. $4.97
   × 3

23. 4 × 3 × 9   **24.** 7 × 1 × 5   **25.** 5 × 7 × 6   **26.** 8 × 8 × 8   **27.** 3 × 0 × 7

Problem Solving

28. Critical Thinking Today is Sue's birthday. Her father gave her a new bike. He is 4 times as old as Sue is now. In 4 years, his age then will be 3 times her age then. How old is Sue now?

 Calculator What does Sue do when she gets a birthday gift that she likes? Use a calculator to do Exercises 29-31. Turn your calculator upside down to read the words. Fill in the blanks in Exercise 32.

29. 3 × 23 × 5   **30.** 768,088 × 7   **31.** 8 × 422

32. __29.__ __30.__ with __31.__ .

51

Draw a Diagram

PROBLEM SOLVING
GUIDE

Understand
QUESTION
FACTS
KEY IDEA

IIII▶ **Plan and Solve**
STRATEGY
ANSWER

Look Back
SENSIBLE ANSWER
ALTERNATE APPROACH

Build Understanding

Kenji is shopping for a new bike. He can choose between three models: the Falcon, the Eagle, and the Hawk. Each model comes in two colors: red and silver. How many choices for a new bike does Kenji have?

Understand You need to find the number of different choices. There are three different models and two different colors for each model. You need to count each model matched with each color.

 **Plan and Solve** STRATEGY   To consider the choice of colors for each model of bike, one by one, you can *draw a diagram*. A ***tree diagram*** will show each model matched with each color.

Models	Colors	Choices
Falcon	red	red Falcon
	silver	silver Falcon
Eagle	red	red Eagle
	silver	silver Eagle
Hawk	red	red Hawk
	silver	silver Hawk

ANSWER   Kenji has six possible choices for a new bike.

Look Back Be sure that all the colors were listed with each model and that all models were listed.

■ **Talk About Math** Would the answer be different if you started your diagram by first listing the colors and then listing the type of models for each color?

Check Understanding

Tires come in two types: gumwall or blackwall. Each tire comes in four colors: white, black, blue, or red.

1. List the types of tires.

2. For each type, list the colors.

3. Make a tree diagram to show all the different tire combinations.

4. How many different choices for tires are there?

Practice

5. Handlebars are made from two different materials and come in three different styles. How many choices are there for handlebars?

Materials	Styles
steel	standard
chrome	high-rise
	racing

6. The pedal assembly comes in two styles of crank and two styles of pedal. How many choices are there for pedal assemblies?

Cranks	Pedals
1-piece	rubber platform
3-piece	metal trap

7. Bike saddles come in standard, racing, or touring styles. Each style comes in red or black. How many choices is this?

8. The combination for a bike lock has two digits. Each digit can be 1, 2, 3, or 4. How many combinations are there?

Explore ———— Math

Look back at the information in this lesson and your answers.

9. How many bike choices were there? How many models? colors?

10. How many tire choices were there? How many types? colors?

11. How many handlebar choices were there? How many materials? styles?

12. Describe how you might find the number of possible choices without drawing a tree diagram.

13. How many bike choices would there be if each model came in three colors?

14. How many tire choices would there be if each tire type came in five colors?

Multiplying by a Multiple of 10 or 100

Build Understanding

A. An Airedale needs about 20 pounds of dog food a week. At this rate, how many pounds of dog food will an Airedale need in a year?

Since the rate is the same each week, multiply the rate and the number of weeks (52) in a year to find the total amount. Find 20 × 52.

Estimate: Using front-end digits, the product will be about 20 × 50 = 1,000.

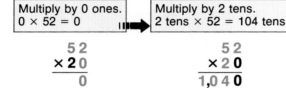

Multiply by 0 ones. $0 \times 52 = 0$	Multiply by 2 tens. 2 tens × 52 = 104 tens

$$\begin{array}{r} 52 \\ \times 20 \\ \hline 0 \end{array} \qquad \begin{array}{r} 52 \\ \times 20 \\ \hline 1,040 \end{array}$$

An Airedale will need about 1,040 pounds of dog food. The answer is reasonable because it is close to the estimate.

B. Find 200 × 368.

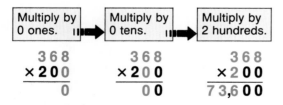

Multiply by 0 ones.	Multiply by 0 tens.	Multiply by 2 hundreds.

$$\begin{array}{r} 368 \\ \times 200 \\ \hline 0 \end{array} \quad \begin{array}{r} 368 \\ \times 200 \\ \hline 00 \end{array} \quad \begin{array}{r} 368 \\ \times 200 \\ \hline 73,600 \end{array}$$

■ **Write About Math** Write a rule for multiplying by a multiple of 10 or 100. Then try your rule on the product 300 × 320.

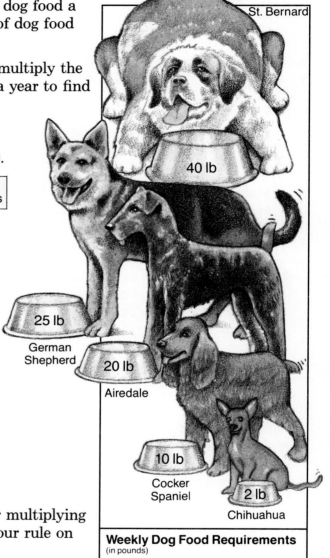

St. Bernard — 40 lb

German Shepherd — 25 lb

Airedale — 20 lb

Cocker Spaniel — 10 lb

Chihuahua — 2 lb

Weekly Dog Food Requirements
(in pounds)

Check Understanding

For another example, see Set D, pages 74–75.

Multiply.

1. 4 × 614   **2.** 40 × 614   **3.** 400 × 614

Practice

For More Practice, see Set D, pages 76–77.

Multiply. **Remember** to estimate to tell if the answer is reasonable.

4.	47 × 30	**5.**	31 × 70	**6.**	65 × 90	**7.**	38 × 50	**8.**	24 × 40
9.	940 × 50	**10.**	728 × 80	**11.**	502 × 30	**12.**	622 × 80	**13.**	708 × 40
14.	416 × 200	**15.**	325 × 500	**16.**	907 × 400	**17.**	989 × 200	**18.**	605 × 700

Problem Solving

Use the information about dog food at the beginning of the lesson.

19. Dog food costs $0.79 per pound. How much will it cost to feed a cocker spaniel for one week?

20. How much more will it cost to feed a St. Bernard for one week than a cocker spaniel?

21. ▦ **Calculator** Find how much food a German shepherd would eat in one year. Use only the number keys and ⊕ and ⊜ keys.

22. A kennel charges $1.26 per pound of dog food. How much will the kennel charge to feed 8 German shepherds for one week?

Reading_____ Math

Numbers and Symbols Match each situation on the left with the most likely expression on the right.

1. A St. Bernard eats more than a German shepherd.

a. $8 \times \$0.79 = \$6.32$

2. Billy bought a can of dog food and a box of dog biscuits.

b. $\$1.00 - \$0.79 = \$0.21$

3. After buying a can of dog food, Anna received some change.

c. $40 > 25$

4. Juanita bought several cans of dog food.

d. $\$0.79 + \$1.24 = \$2.03$

Mental Math for Multiplication

Build Understanding

Here are some mental math strategies to use when multiplying mentally.

A. Look for **combinations** that give numbers that are easy to multiply, such as numbers that give multiples of 10 or 100.

$$\overset{\lceil\ 20\ \rceil}{4 \times 9 \times 5} = 180$$

You can change the order of the factors and get the same product. This is the **commutative property of multiplication.**

4 × 9 × 5 = 4 × 5 × 9

$$\overset{\lceil\ 100\ \rceil}{(29 \times 4) \times 25} = 2{,}900$$

You can change the grouping of the factors and get the same product. This is the **associative property of multiplication.**

(29 × 4) × 25 = 29 × (4 × 25)

B. Look for numbers that you can **break apart** into numbers that are easy to multiply.

Multiply each part, and then add the products back together.

$$\begin{array}{ccccc} & \overset{20+3}{\downarrow} & & \overset{8\times 20}{\downarrow} & \overset{8\times 3}{\downarrow} \\ 8 \times & 23 & = & 160 & + & 24 \\ & & = & 184 \end{array}$$

This is the **distributive property**.

8 × 23 = (8 × 20) + (8 × 3)

C. Look for numbers where you can use **compensation**.

Change a difficult factor into the difference of two easy factors. Multiply each part, and then subtract to compensate.

$$\begin{array}{ccccc} & \overset{30-1}{\downarrow} & & \overset{5\times 30}{\downarrow} & \overset{5\times 1}{\downarrow} \\ 5 \times & 29 & = & 150 & - & 5 \\ & & = & 145 \end{array}$$

■ **Talk About Math**   Explain how you can use the mental math strategy in Example C to find 4 × $4.99.

56

Check Understanding

For another example, see Set E, pages 74–75.

1. Find 4 × 6 × 25 using combinations of numbers.

2. Find 8 × (50 × 3) using combinations of numbers.

3. Find 3 × 53 by breaking apart one factor. Explain your thinking.

4. Find 8 × 19 using compensation. Explain your thinking.

Look ahead to Exercises 7-22.

5. Which answers can be found using combinations that give numbers that are easy to multiply?

6. Which answers can be found using compensation by changing a difficult factor into the difference of two easy factors?

Practice

For More Practice, see Set E, pages 76–77.

Use mental math to find each product. Tell which strategy you used.

7. 12 × 3

8. 29 × 2

9. 9 × 5 × 4

10. 6 × 21

11. 4 × 39

12. 5 × 7 × 6

13. 5 × 66

14. 98 × 4

15. 8 × 199

16. 205 × 4

17. 2 × 17 × 5

18. 2 × 9 × 50

19. 4 × 8 × 25

20. 4 × 26

21. 8 × $4.03

22. 8 × $2.97

23. Choose four of the exercises above. Explain why you chose the strategy you used.

Problem Solving

Remember to use mental math when it is helpful.

24. The pet shop sells rawhide bones for $3.98 each. How much will it cost to buy four of them?

25. A leash costs $4.25. How much will it cost to buy two leashes?

4.25

TIPS FOR PROBLEM SOLVERS

Be flexible. If you get stuck, try another idea.

Choosing a Computation Method

Greenbriar
Theater Ticket Prices
Adults $6.00
Under 12 . . . . $3.50
Seniors $4.75

Build Understanding

Three friends went to the Greenbriar Mall. After shopping for a while, they wanted to see a movie. Their tickets for the movie would cost $3.50 each. Between them they had $10. The three girls decided to see if they could afford a movie.

Patient Penelope reached for a notebook and wrote:

$$\begin{array}{r} \overset{1}{\$\,3.5\,0} \\ \times \quad 3 \\ \hline \$10.50 \end{array}$$

Merry Martha scratched her head and thought:

$3 \times \$3 = \$9$ $3 \times \$0.50 = \$1.50$

$\$9 + \$1.50 = \$10.50$

Careful Carolyn took out her calculator and entered:

$3 \;\boxed{\times}\; 3 \;\boxed{\cdot}\; 5 \;\boxed{=}\; 10.5$

"We don't have enough money!" they all agreed. But they could not agree on whose computation method was most appropriate. What do you think?

Here are some general guidelines to help you choose a computation method.

When an exact answer is needed,
• use *mental math* if you can find the exact answer in your head.
• use *paper and pencil* if you cannot do it in your head easily.
• use a *calculator* if there are many numbers or the numbers are complicated.

■ **Talk About Math** Do you think Carolyn got her answer faster than Penelope did? Discuss when you might find it easier or faster to use paper and pencil rather than a calculator.

Check Understanding

For another example, see Set F, pages 74–75.

1. What method would you choose to total the ticket sales for the day if you were the theater manager? Explain your thinking.

2. What method would you choose to figure the change from $20 for seven tickets that cost $2 each? Explain your thinking.

Tell which computation method you would use.

3. 20 × 40   **4.** 1,939 + 5,386   **5.** 7 × $1.10   **6.** 854 − 399

Practice

For More Practice, see Set F, pages 76–77.

Tell which computation method you would use. Then find each answer.

7. 5 × 348   **8.** 5,000 − 924   **9.** 30 × 90   **10.** 224 + 105

11. $96.83 + $64.57   **12.** 4 × $10.25   **13.** 25 × 478 × 4   **14.** 184 − 79

Problem Solving

Tell which computation method you would use. Then find each answer. Use the information about ticket prices given at the beginning of the lesson.

15. The theater lobby has 4 walls of movie posters with 10 posters on each wall. How many posters are there?

16. Can a family of two adults and two children under 12 see a movie for under $20? Explain your answer.

17. Attendance at six showings of a new movie was 186, 179, 191, 182, 187, and 189. How many people attended?

18. There were 213 boxes of popcorn sold at the first show and 426 sold at the second. How many more were sold at the second show?

19. The theater has 408 seats. What is the greatest amount that could be collected from a sold-out movie?

Midchapter **Checkup**

Multiply using mental math.
1. 4 × 30   **2.** 5 × 7 × 4

Multiply.
3. 8 × 74   **4.** 924 × 300

5. List three common multiples of 2 and 3.

6. Would you use paper and pencil, mental math, or a calculator to find 8 × 947?

7. Tents come in cabin or dome models. Each model comes in canvas or nylon. How many choices is this? Draw a tree diagram.

Problem-Solving Workshop

Explore as a Team

The numbers 1, 4, and 9 are *square numbers*. We can show them as squares.

$1 \times 1 = 1$

$2 \times 2 = 4$

$3 \times 3 = 9$

1. Discuss the dot arrangements. How are they the same? How are they different?

2. Use counters to find the next two square numbers.

3. Invent ways to "mark off" and record square numbers. Here are some examples for 9.

$9 = 3 \times 3$ $\qquad$ $9 = 4 + 2 + 2 + 1$ $\qquad$ $9 = 1 + 3 + 5$ $\qquad$ $9 = 1 + 2 + 3 + 2 + 1$

$9 = 4 + (2 \times 2) + 1$

4. Try to "mark off" and record the next two square numbers. Discuss the patterns you find in the recording of square numbers.

What tools do we use in arithmetic?

ANSWER: Multipliers

Number-Sense Project

Look back at pages 44-45.
The chart at the right shows the number of hours that Jeffrey watched television during a week.

1. About how many hours of television does Jeffrey watch per month?

2. About how many hours of television does Jeffrey watch in a year?

3. Write a sentence telling how Jeffrey's yearly total compares to yours.

Day	Television Viewing
Monday	1 hour
Tuesday	1 hour
Wednesday	2 hours
Thursday	1 hour
Friday	3 hours
Saturday	5 hours
Sunday	2 hours

Math-at-Home Activity

Gather Data Take a survey of 12 people who live with or near you. Ask them to guess a, b, or c for the following census question.

At the time of the first census, in 1790, about how many people were living in the United States?

a. *500,000*   **b.** *4 million*

c. *100 million*

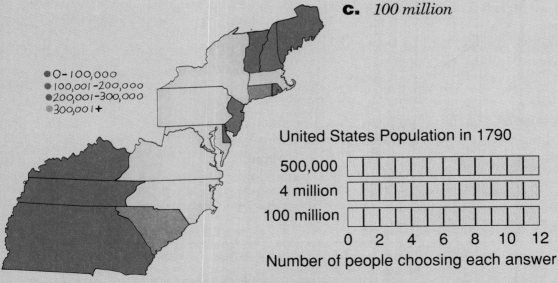

●0–100,000
●100,001–200,000
●200,001–300,000
●300,001+

United States Population in 1790

500,000
4 million
100 million

0 2 4 6 8 10 12
Number of people choosing each answer

Estimating Products

Build Understanding

Here are some estimation strategies to use when estimating products.

A. Estimate 17 × 305 by *rounding* both factors so each has only one nonzero digit.

17 × 305
↓   ↓
20 × 300 = 6,000

The actual product is about 6,000.

B. Estimate 58 × 24 by *finding a range*.

Round down.   Round up.

58 × 24   58 × 24
↓   ↓   ↓   ↓
50 × 20 = 1,000   60 × 30 = 1,800

The actual product will be between 1,000 and 1,800.

c. Estimate 26 × 4 using *compatible numbers*.

Substitute a number that is close to an original number and can be multiplied easily.

26 × 4   25 × 4 = 100

The actual product should be close to 100.

■ **Talk About Math** If you estimate a product by rounding, what can you say about the actual product if both factors round down? if both factors round up? if one factor rounds down and one rounds up?

Check Understanding

For another example, see Set G, pages 74–75.

1. Estimate 591 × 784 using rounding.

2. Estimate 625 × 297 by finding a range.

3. Estimate 98 × 7 using compatible numbers.

4. For Exercise 1, will the actual product be less than or more than the estimate?

5. How can you tell that 27,824 is a more reasonable answer for 752 × 37 than 21,824?

Practice

For More Practice, see Set G, pages 76–77.

Estimate each product. Tell which strategy you used.

6. 29 × 31

7. 8 × 59

8. 98 × 17

9. 6 × 197

10. 205 × 42

11. 59 × 687

12. 2 × 49 × 8

13. 4 × 6 × 26

14. Choose two of the exercises above. Explain why you chose the strategy you used.

Choose the better estimate for each product.

15. 32 × 485

   12,000   15,000

16. 89 × 72

   5,600   6,300

17. 307 × 81

   24,000   32,000

Problem Solving

18. Kazuko said that 346 × 28 is between 6,000 and 12,000. Give a better estimate.

19. Do you think 20 × 100 or 18 × 100 will give a better estimate for 18 × 99? Explain why.

20. **Use Data** Use the information about ticket prices on page 58. Would $50 be enough to pay for the nine members of the Senior Citizen Club to see a movie? Explain.

Skills _____ **Review** pages 6-7

Compare these numbers. Use >, <, or =.
1. 538 ▦ 583
2. 947 ▦ 938
3. 5,049 ▦ 5,409

List the numbers in order from greatest to least.
4. 849 857 728
5. 957 1,089 846
6. 648 693 629

Deciding When an Estimate Is Enough

PROBLEM SOLVING GUIDE

 **Understand**
QUESTION
FACTS
KEY IDEA

Plan and Solve
STRATEGY
ANSWER

Look Back
SENSIBLE ANSWER
ALTERNATE APPROACH

Build Understanding

The Olivers are planning a raft trip down the Colorado River through the Grand Canyon. It will cost them $1,102.50 each for the seven-day trip. Will $5,000 cover the cost for the four of them to make this trip?

Understand QUESTION Is $5,000 enough for four people?

FACTS The rate for one person is $1,102.50. There are 4 people.

KEY IDEA Since the problem is not asking for the exact cost for four people, an estimate may be enough.

An estimate is enough if:
• you cannot get exact amounts, or
• an exact answer does not make sense, or
• you do not need an exact answer and you are certain that an estimate will answer the question.

Plan and Solve Since the rate is the same for everyone, you would multiply the rate by 4 to find the exact answer. To estimate the product, think:

$1,102.50 is less than $1,200, so 4 × $1,102.50 is less than 4 × $1,200.   4 × 1,200 = 4,800

The raft trip for the Olivers will cost less than $4,800, so $5,000 will cover the cost of the trip.

Look Back An estimate was enough to solve this problem because the exact cost will be less than the estimate, and the estimate is less than $5,000.

The Grand Canyon extends 277 miles in northwest Arizona.

64

■ **Talk About Math**   If you were sending a check as payment for your family to take a raft trip, would an estimate of the total cost be enough? Explain.

Check Understanding

Suppose the Olivers decide that they can spend no more than $4,500 on the trip.

1. **Estimation**   Will the exact cost of the Olivers' raft trip be more or less than $4,400?

2. **Estimation**   Will the exact cost of the Olivers' raft trip be more or less than $4,800?

3. Is the estimate of the range given in Problems 1 and 2 enough to tell if the Olivers can make the trip?

4. What must you do to see if the exact cost of the trip is no more than $4,500?

Practice

5. A two-day trip down the river costs $435.75. Round-trip fare to the canyon costs $372. Will $1,000 cover the entire cost? Tell whether an estimate is enough.

6. Is an estimate enough to tell if $800 will cover the entire cost for the situation in Problem 5? Explain.

7. Raft tours are offered for 18 weeks of the year. If all the rafts are full, 39 people can take the tours each week. Can 900 people take the tours during the year? Tell whether an estimate is enough.

8. For the situation in Problem 7, is an estimate enough to tell how many people can take the raft tours during the year? Explain.

Explain each answer. Would an estimate be enough to decide

9. how far you hiked on a hiking trip?

10. whether you have enough money to pay for your lunch?

11. how much allowance you will earn during the summer?

12. how much you plan to spend on souvenirs during your vacation?

Multiplying by a Two-Digit Number

Build Understanding

A. How long would a train of 37 covered hopper cars be, not counting the engine and caboose?

Since all the cars are the same length, multiply. Find 37 × 54.

Estimate: 40 × 50 = 2,000

```
    5 4
  × 3 7      30 + 7
  ─────
    3 7 8    7 × 54
  1 6 2 0    30 × 54
  ─────
  1,9 9 8
```

The train would be 1,998 feet long. The answer is reasonable because it is close to the estimate.

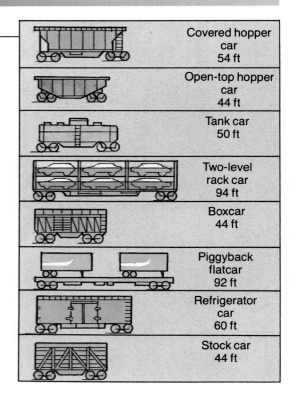

	Covered hopper car 54 ft
	Open-top hopper car 44 ft
	Tank car 50 ft
	Two-level rack car 94 ft
	Boxcar 44 ft
	Piggyback flatcar 92 ft
	Refrigerator car 60 ft
	Stock car 44 ft

B. Find 84 × 673.

Paper and Pencil

```
    6 7 3
  ×   8 4      80 + 4
  ─────
  2 6 9 2      4 × 673
  5 3 8 4 0    80 × 673
  ─────
  5 6,5 3 2
```

 Calculator

84 ⊗ 673 ⊜ *56532.*

■ Talk About Math

Discuss how this diagram relates to the multiplication in Example A.

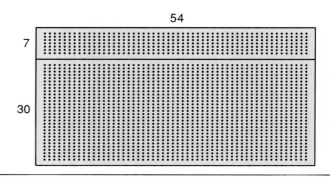

Check Understanding

For another example, see Set H, pages 74–75.

The rectangle represents the product
23 × 35. Which part represents each of
the following?

1. 3 × 35   **2.** 20 × 35   **3.** 23 × 35

Multiply.

4. 40 × 97   **5.** 27 × 582

6. 39 × $0.47   **7.** 82 × $5.35

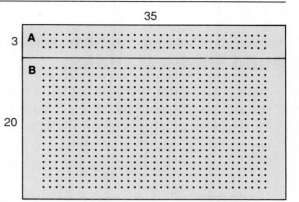

Practice

For More Practice, see Set H, pages 76–77.

Tell whether you would use paper and pencil, mental
math, or a calculator. Then find each product.

8. 48 × 63	**9.** 52 × 20	**10.** 30 × 51	**11.** 75 × 44	**12.** 80 × 49	**13.** 86 × 60
14. 284 × 53	**15.** 408 × 20	**16.** 830 × 65	**17.** 907 × 19	**18.** 211 × 80	**19.** 238 × 85

20. 31 × $0.82   **21.** 23 × $7.10   **22.** 30 × $4.99   **23.** 75 × $2.00

Mixed Practice   **Remember** to watch the signs.

24. 381 − 274	**25.** 738 + 81	**26.** 203 × 6	**27.** 937 − 61	**28.** 731 × 12	**29.** 826 + 957

Problem Solving

Use the information at the beginning of the lesson.

30. What is the length of 42 piggyback
flatcars?

31. What is the length of 24 open-top
hopper cars?

32. Estimation   Which is closer to
the length of 28 two-level rack cars,
1,800 feet or 2,700 feet?

33. Number Sense   Is the product
even or odd if you multiply two odd
numbers? two even numbers? one
even and one odd?

34. What is the length of 52 refrigerator
and 52 tank cars?

35. What is the length of 21 stock cars
and 30 boxcars?

Choose an Operation

Build Understanding

Jesse owns a dairy store that sells milk, cheese, yogurt, and frozen yogurt. Last month, the store sold 12 times as much low fat milk as whole milk. There were 156 gallons of whole milk sold. How many gallons of low fat milk did the store sell last month?

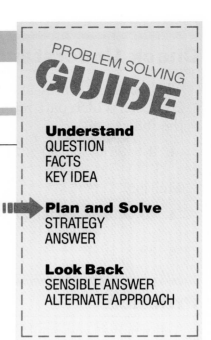

PROBLEM SOLVING GUIDE

Understand
QUESTION
FACTS
KEY IDEA

➡️ **Plan and Solve**
STRATEGY
ANSWER

Look Back
SENSIBLE ANSWER
ALTERNATE APPROACH

Understand How many gallons of low fat milk were sold? Jesse sold 156 gallons of whole milk and 12 times as much low fat milk. One amount is a multiple of the other.

➡️ **Plan and Solve** STRATEGY Since the amount of low fat milk sold is a multiple of the amount of whole milk sold, you multiply. Find 12×156.

Paper and Pencil

$$\begin{array}{r} 156 \\ \times\ 12 \\ \hline 312 \\ 1560 \\ \hline 1,872 \end{array}$$

🖩 **Calculator**

12 $\boxed{\times}$ 156

$\boxed{=}$ *1872.*

ANSWER The store sold 1,872 gallons of low fat milk last month.

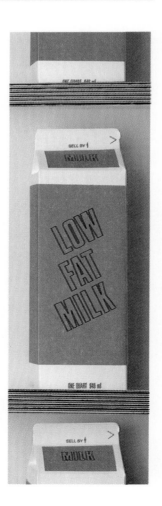

Look Back The answer is sensible since:
12×156 is about 12×150.
12×150 is 12×100 plus half of 12×100.
So, $12 \times 150 = 1,200 + 600 = 1,800$.

■ **Talk About Math** Decide which method you would have used for the computation in the example—paper and pencil, calculator, or mental math. Explain why you chose the method you would use.

Check Understanding

How much milk, whole and low fat, did Jesse's store sell all together?

1. Will you add, subtract, or multiply?   **2.** Find the answer.

3. Explain why you chose the operation you used.

Practice

Tell whether to add, subtract, or multiply. Then solve the problem.

4. The store sold 501 quarts of vanilla frozen yogurt and 437 quarts of chocolate. How much more vanilla than chocolate was sold?

5. Each shelf in the dairy case holds 15 rows of milk cartons. Each row has 5 cartons. There are 25 shelves. How many cartons of milk can the dairy case hold?

6. A gallon of frozen yogurt is enough to make 32 cones. How many cones can Jesse make if he has a gallon each of 8 different flavors?

7. Whole milk sells for $1.78 a gallon. A gallon of skim milk sells for $0.27 more. What is the cost of a gallon of skim milk?

8. Each person in the U.S. drinks about 25 gallons of milk per year. At this rate, how many gallons would a fifth-grade class of 26 drink in a year?

9. If milk costs $1.78 a gallon and each person in the U.S. drinks 25 gallons per year, how much does the average person spend on milk in a year?

Choose a _____ Strategy

Pretty Petunias

10. Kim is planting 4 petunias of different colors in a long pot. The white petunia is closer to the purple petunia than to the red petunia. The purple petunia is just to the left of the pink petunia. The red petunia is on the right. From left to right, what is the order of the colors?

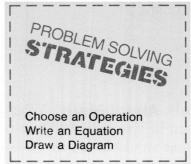

PROBLEM SOLVING
STRATEGIES

Choose an Operation
Write an Equation
Draw a Diagram

Multiplying by a Three-Digit Number

Build Understanding

Most people of the world rely on milk as a food source. Milk is produced by dairy cows, goats, camels, llamas, sheep, and water buffalo. In the U.S., there are about 11 million cows which produce about 17 billion gallons of milk each year.

A. A herd of Holstein cows needs 720 pounds of hay and 645 pounds of grain each day. How many pounds of grain does the herd need in one year?

The herd needs the grain at the same rate each day, so multiply. There are 365 days in one year. Find 365 × 645.

Estimate: 400 × 600 = 240,000

```
    645
  × 365      300 + 60 + 5
  ─────
   3225      5 × 645
  38700      60 × 645
 193500      300 × 645
 ──────
 235,425
```

The herd needs 235,425 pounds of grain each year. The answer is reasonable because it is close to the estimate.

There are more Holsteins in the U.S. than any other breed of dairy cattle.

B. Find 109 × 247.

```
    247
  × 109        Estimate using
  ─────        compatible numbers.
   2223        100 × 250 = 25,000
  24700        The product is about
  ─────        25,000.
  26,923
```

■ **Talk About Math** What estimation strategy was used in Example A? Do you think that finding a range would have given a better estimate?

Check Understanding

For another example, see Set I, pages 74–75.

How much hay does the herd need in one year?

1. Estimate by finding the range.
2. Estimate by rounding.
3. Find the answer.
4. Which strategy gave the best estimate?

Multiply.

5. 420 × 347
6. 800 × 614
7. 237 × 806

Practice

For More Practice, see Set I, pages 76–77.

Use paper and pencil or a calculator to multiply.
Remember to estimate to tell if the answer is reasonable.

8.	291	9.	202	10.	563	11.	433	12.	604
	× 400		× 125		× 325		× 102		× 500

13.	909	14.	722	15.	413	16.	499	17.	862
	× 230		× 502		× 210		× 300		× 593

Estimation Estimate to choose the most reasonable answer.

18. 806 × 257   a. 127,142   b. 167,142   c. 207,142   d. 277,142

19. 489 × 312   a. 122,568   b. 152,568   c. 202,568   d. 232,568

20. 673 × 585   a. 293,705   b. 313,705   c. 393,705   d. 423,705

Problem Solving

21. A Holstein cow gives an average of 1,714 gallons of milk each year. A Jersey cow gives 616 gallons less. How much does a Jersey cow give?

22. Wisconsin is the leading dairy state. It has twice as many dairy cows as California. If California has 1,336,000 dairy cows, how many does Wisconsin have?

Choose which way you would write each problem if you were using paper and pencil to find the product. Then explain why you chose as you did.

23. 305 × 346   a. 346   b. 305
                   × 305   × 346

24. 800 × 492   a. 800   b. 492
                   × 492   × 800

Problem-Solving Review

Solve each problem.

1. How much did Janice pay for 3 birthday cards that cost $1.25 each?

2. You can see the rock opera *Frankie* on Thursday, Friday, or Saturday. You can buy a ticket for $8, $12, or $20. How many choices are there for seeing the show?

3. Vince bought a $7.60 gift and a $0.90 card. How much change did he get back from $10.00?

4. The first ocean-going diesel ships were launched in 1912. *Nautilus*, the first nuclear-powered submarine, was launched 42 years later. In what year was *Nautilus* launched?

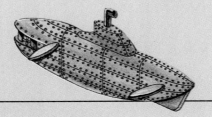

5. At an air show, plane rides cost $37.50 per person. Is $200 enough to buy tickets for the 5 members of the Sheldon family?

6. Find the cost of 26 weeks of *Magic Magazine*, a weekly magazine. Find the cost of 52 weeks.

Magic Magazine	
26 weeks	$0.54 per issue
52 weeks	$0.47 per issue

7. **Data File** Use the chart of animal champions on pages 116–117 to find the slowest reptile in the world. How many feet can it travel in 8 minutes? What is the fastest land animal? How fast can it travel?

8. **Make a Data File** Find the meaning of each of the numbers on the face of a dollar bill. Show your findings by making a drawing of the bill and labeling it.

Explore with a Calculator

"Multiplication Daze"

Anthony had multiplication exercises to do for homework. He arranged the exercises and their products in a grid. While he was helping his mom with the dishes, his younger brother colored some of the numbers.

1. Use your calculator to help Anthony find the colored numbers.

X	24			27
		391		
	1,344		1,736	
18		306		
41				1,107

2. The next day at school, Anthony's teacher played *Guess My Number* with the class. He wrote 12 numbers on the chalkboard and read the questions below. Use the numbers to answer the questions. Once you use a number, it cannot be used again. All 12 numbers will be used to answer the questions.

46	24	8
27	35	123
489	17	37
64	9	26

a. Find two numbers with a product of 1,107.

b. Find two numbers with a product of 459.

c. Find two numbers with a product of 3,912.

d. Find three numbers with a product of 82,880.

e. Find three numbers with a product of 28,704.

Reteaching

Set A   pages 46–47

Find the least common multiple of 6 and 10.

List the first few multiples of 6 and of 10.

Multiples of 6: 6, 12, 18, 24, ⃝30, 36

Multiples of 10: 10, 20, ⃝30, 40, 50

The least common multiple is 30.

Remember that the least common multiple of two numbers is the least number that is a multiple of both numbers.

Find the least common multiple of

1. 3 and 4.   **2.** 2 and 8.

3. 6 and 9.   **4.** 8 and 10.

Set B   pages 48–49

A twin-engine jet can fly about 500 miles per hour. How far can it go in 4 hours?

Add: $500 + 500 + 500 + 500 = 2,000$

Multiply: $4 \times 500 = 2,000$

4×5 hundreds $= 20$ hundreds

Remember that multiplication is repeated addition.
Multiply using mental math.

1. 40×6 **2.** 40×60

3. 500×5 **4.** $60 \times 8,000$

Set C   pages 50–51

Find 148×6.

Rename 48 ones as 4 tens 8 ones.

```
    4
  1 4 8
× 	  6
-------
      8
```

Rename 28 tens as 2 hundreds 8 tens.

```
  2 4
  1 4 8
× 	  6
-------
    8 8
```

```
  2 4
  1 4 8
× 	  6
-------
  8 8 8
```

Remember to estimate the product to see if the answer is reasonable.
Multiply.

1. $\begin{array}{r} 19 \\ \times\ 8 \\ \hline \end{array}$ **2.** $\begin{array}{r} 77 \\ \times\ 6 \\ \hline \end{array}$ **3.** $\begin{array}{r} 328 \\ \times\ 5 \\ \hline \end{array}$

4. 304×4 **5.** $5,607 \times 3$

Set D   pages 54–55

Find 300×137.

Multiply by 0 ones.

```
  1 3 7
× 3 0 0
-------
      0
```

Multiply by 0 tens.

```
  1 3 7
× 3 0 0
-------
    0 0
```

Multiply by 3 hundreds.

```
    1 3 7
  × 3 0 0
---------
4 1, 1 0 0
```

Remember to put as many ending zeros in the product as there are in the two factors.

Multiply.

1. 346×200 **2.** 891×400

Set E   pages 56–57

Find 4×27.

Break apart 27 into $20 + 7$.
Multiply each part by 4.
$4 \times 20 = 80 \qquad 4 \times 7 = 28$

Now add the two products.
$80 + 28 = 108$

Remember that some numbers are easy to multiply after you break them apart. Use the break-apart strategy to find each product mentally.

1. 41×6 **2.** 33×4

3. 62×8 **4.** 306×9

Set F pages 58–59

When an exact answer is needed,

- use mental math if you can find the exact answer in your head.
- use paper and pencil if you cannot do it in your head easily.
- use a calculator if there are many numbers or the numbers are complicated.

Remember that paper and pencil can sometimes be as fast as a calculator.

Tell which computation method you would use. Then find each answer.

1. 8×687 **2.** $297 + 148$

3. 40×90 **4.** $382 - 167$

Set G pages 62–63

Estimate 47×489.

Round each factor so each has only one nonzero digit.

$$47 \times 489$$
$$\downarrow \qquad \downarrow$$
$$50 \times 500 = 25,000$$

Remember to add 1 to the digit in the place to be rounded if the digit to its right is 5 or more.

Estimate each product by rounding.

1. 7×48 **2.** 5×95

3. 64×483 **4.** 56×271

Set H pages 66–67

Find 578×62.

Estimate: $600 \times 60 = 36,000$

```
    5 7 8
  ×   6 2      62 = 60 + 2
  -------
  1 1 5 6      2 × 578
3 4 6 8 0      60 × 578
  -------
3 5,8 3 6
```

Remember that the actual answer will be less than the estimate if both factors are rounded up.

Tell whether you would use paper and pencil, mental math, or a calculator. Then find each product.

1. $\begin{array}{r} 36 \\ \times 28 \end{array}$ **2.** $\begin{array}{r} 62 \\ \times 30 \end{array}$ **3.** $\begin{array}{r} 58 \\ \times 22 \end{array}$

4. 307×50 **5.** 670×54

Set I pages 70–71

Find 423×528.

Estimate: $400 \times 500 = 200,000$

```
      4 2 3
    × 5 2 8      528 = 500 + 20 + 8
    -------
    3 3 8 4      8 × 423
    8 4 6 0      20 × 423
2 1 1 5 0 0      500 × 423
    -------
2 2 3,3 4 4
```

Remember to estimate the product to tell if the answer is reasonable.

Use paper and pencil or a calculator to multiply.

1. $\begin{array}{r} 692 \\ \times 300 \end{array}$ **2.** $\begin{array}{r} 837 \\ \times 255 \end{array}$ **3.** $\begin{array}{r} 808 \\ \times 504 \end{array}$

4. $\begin{array}{r} 506 \\ \times 483 \end{array}$ **5.** $\begin{array}{r} 715 \\ \times 320 \end{array}$ **6.** $\begin{array}{r} 962 \\ \times 243 \end{array}$

Independent Study RETEACHING

More Practice

Set A pages 46–47

List five multiples of the following numbers.

1. 4　　　　**2.** 6　　　　**3.** 9　　　　**4.** 7　　　　**5.** 8

List three common multiples of the following.

6. 2 and 7　　**7.** 3 and 6　　**8.** 6 and 10　　**9.** 8 and 12

10. Find the least common multiple for the numbers in Exercises 6–9.

Set B pages 48–49

Multiply. **Remember** to use mental math.

1. 40 × 8　　**2.** 30 × 10　　**3.** 500 × 9　　**4.** 50 × 60

5. 700 × 900　　**6.** 40 × 300　　**7.** 64 × 1,000　　**8.** 30 × 7,000

Set C pages 50–51

Multiply. **Remember** to estimate to tell if the answer is reasonable.

1. 18 × 9　　**2.** 46 × 5　　**3.** 80 × 7　　**4.** 782 × 4　　**5.** 609 × 3

6. 6,580 × 6　　**7.** 5,004 × 8　　**8.** 3,648 × 4　　**9.** $0.62 × 9　　**10.** $5.10 × 8

Set D pages 54–55

Multiply. **Remember** to estimate to tell if the answer is reasonable.

1. 53 × 20　　**2.** 49 × 40　　**3.** 87 × 50　　**4.** 26 × 60　　**5.** 660 × 40

6. 821 × 70　　**7.** 504 × 30　　**8.** 685 × 600　　**9.** 307 × 300　　**10.** 451 × 500

Set E pages 56–57

Use mental math to find each product. Tell which strategy you used.

1. 9 × 41　　**2.** 306 × 7　　**3.** 8 × 9 × 5　　**4.** 2 × 14 × 5

5. 6 × 195　　**6.** 4 × 6 × 25　　**7.** 4 × $8.07　　**8.** 7 × 199

9. Choose three of the exercises above. Explain why you chose the strategy you used.

Independent Study MORE PRACTICE

Set F   pages 58–59

Tell which computation method you would use.
Then find each answer.

1. 6 × 438

2. 346 − 208

3. 8,000 − 648

4. 80 × 70

5. $103.46 + $73.84

6. 5 × $20.20

7. 263 − 49

8. 20 × 392 × 5

Set G   pages 62–63

Estimate each product. Tell which strategy you used.

1. 48 × 52

2. 9 × 37

3. 19 × 104

4. 8 × 205

5. 38 × 492

6. 408 × 64

7. 4 × 82 × 24

8. 9 × 28 × 11

9. Choose two of the exercises above. Explain why you
chose the strategy you used.

Choose the better estimate for each product.

10. 41 × 312
    12,000   16,000

11. 32 × 98
    2,700   3,000

12. 408 × 68
    28,000   30,000

Set H   pages 66–67

Tell whether you would use paper and pencil, mental
math, or a calculator. Then find each product.

1.   39
    × 53

2.   40
    × 82

3.   238
    × 45

4.   306
    × 18

5. $6.20
    ×   24

Mixed Practice   **Remember** to watch the signs.

6.   408
    ×   7

7.   683
    − 367

8.   846
    × 14

9.   783
    − 92

10.   539
    + 768

Set I   pages 70–71

Use paper and pencil or a calculator to multiply.
Remember to estimate to tell if the answer is reasonable.

1.   438
    × 300

2.   647
    × 135

3.   303
    × 352

4.   566
    × 106

5.   318
    × 410

Estimation   Estimate to choose the most reasonable answer.

6. 509 × 386   **a.** 156,474   **b.** 196,474   **c.** 176,474   **d.** 206,474

7. 376 × 418   **a.** 127,168   **b.** 137,168   **c.** 147,168   **d.** 157,168

8. 627 × 892   **a.** 639,284   **b.** 589,284   **c.** 559,284   **d.** 489,284

Enrichment

Lattice Multiplication

Lattice multiplication is a way of multiplying that is based on an ancient calculating instrument.

To find 482 × 63, make a lattice as shown here.

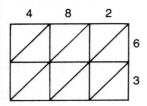

Lattice multiplication is based on "Napier's Rods" which were used in the 16th century.

Next, multiply the digits of the two factors. Record the products in the lattice.

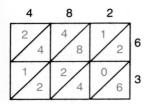

Finally, add along the diagonals within the lattice.

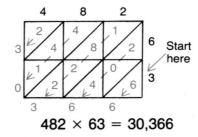

482 × 63 = 30,366

Lattices can be any size. Try these. Copy each lattice, and find the product.

1. 47 × 58

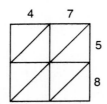

2. 258 × 367

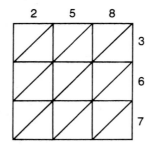

Find each answer using lattice multiplication.

3. 53 × 64   **4.** 27 × 16   **5.** 38 × 246   **6.** 293 × 824   **7.** 814 × 452

Chapter 2 Review/Test

1. List three common multiples of 3 and 4.

Multiply.

2. 9×87

3. $2,386 \times 5$

4. 18×60

5. 705×700

6. $\begin{array}{r} 295 \\ \times\ 57 \\ \hline \end{array}$

7. $\begin{array}{r} 863 \\ \times\ 82 \\ \hline \end{array}$

8. $\begin{array}{r} 524 \\ \times\ 18 \\ \hline \end{array}$

9. $\begin{array}{r} 706 \\ \times\ 795 \\ \hline \end{array}$

10. Complete with *tens, hundreds, thousands,* or *ten-thousands.*

    $70 \times 40 = 28 \underline{\quad?\quad}$

11. Copy and complete.

    48 tens = ▦ hundreds ▦ tens

Multiply using mental math.

12. 700×6

13. 800×700

14. 12×4

15. $2 \times 18 \times 5$

Choose the best estimate for each product.

16. 79×42

    2,800   3,200

17. 609×23

    12,000   18,000

Tell which computation method you would use. Then find each answer.

18. 80×60

19. 7×123

20. A car travels at an average rate of 60 miles per hour for 4 hours. How far does the car travel?

21. One car comes with black, brown, or blue upholstery. The material can be vinyl or leather. How many choices are there? Make a tree diagram to show your answer.

22. Connie can earn $38 a week at her part-time job. She is saving to go to a computer camp that costs $600. If she works for 22 weeks, will she save enough to go to camp? Tell whether an estimate is enough.

Read this problem. Then answer the questions below.

The Gonzalez family spent $532 on home heating last year. This year they spent $670. How much did heating costs increase this year?

23. Which do you need to find for this problem?

    a. The family's total heating costs for the two years
    b. How much greater this year's costs were than last year's
    c. The cost per month for heating

24. Solve the problem.

25. **Write About Math** In Exercises 16 and 17, explain the method of estimation you used.

Measurement and Geometric Figures

3

Did You Know: The first ribbon factory in the United States was started in Philadelphia in 1815. Around 1865, most ribbon in the United States was produced in the Paterson, New Jersey, area.

Number-Sense Project

Estimate
Estimate how many inches of ribbon it took to wrap this present and make the bow.

Gather Data
Wrap a piece of ribbon around an object such as a book, a basketball, or a stuffed animal.Remember the actual length you use. Ask ten people to estimate the length of the ribbon.

Analyze and Report
Record the estimates you collect. Record whether the estimates were greater or less than the actual length and by how much. Compare your results with those of other students.

Customary Units of Length

Build Understanding

Macie paints signs on trucks and vans. Some letters may be only a few inches tall while other letters could be a foot or more tall.

A. Inches, feet, yards, and miles are *customary units of length*.

One *inch* (in.) is about the length of a paper clip.

One *foot* (ft) is about the length of a notebook.

One *yard* (yd) is about the distance from a doorknob to the floor.

One *mile* (mi) is about the length of 5,280 notebooks placed end to end.

B. Macie used a ruler to measure the heights of the two letters shown below. She said each letter measured $2\frac{1}{4}$ inches. Did she measure correctly?

You can tell by looking at the two letters that their heights are not the same. Macie did measure correctly, however. Both letters are $2\frac{1}{4}$ inches to the nearest $\frac{1}{4}$ inch.

You can also measure to the nearest $\frac{1}{8}$ inch. The letter A is $2\frac{3}{8}$ inches to the nearest $\frac{1}{8}$ inch. The letter R is $2\frac{2}{8}$ inches to the nearest $\frac{1}{8}$ inch.

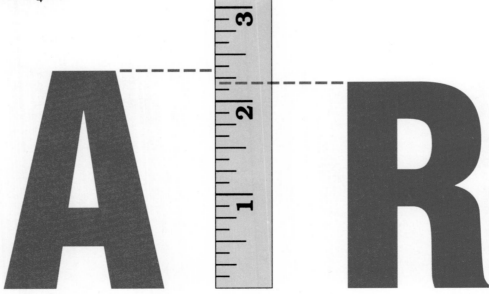

■ **Talk About Math** Explain how you could estimate the length of your classroom.

Check Understanding

Estimation Choose the most sensible measure.

1. Height of a ladder
   a. 8 in.   b. 8 ft   c. 8 mi

2. Width of a paint brush
   a. $2\frac{1}{2}$ in.   b. $2\frac{1}{2}$ yd   c. $2\frac{1}{2}$ ft

3. Height of a woman
   a. $5\frac{1}{2}$ ft   b. $5\frac{1}{2}$ yd   c. $5\frac{1}{2}$ in.

4. Distance from home to work
   a. 5 in.   b. 5 ft   c. 5 mi

Practice

Estimation Tell whether you would use inches, feet, yards, or miles to measure each of the following.

5. Length of a spoon

6. Distance from the earth to the moon

7. Width of a backyard

8. Length of a kitchen table

Use a ruler. Measure to the nearest $\frac{1}{4}$ inch and to the nearest $\frac{1}{8}$ inch.

9. _____

10. _____

11. _____

12. _____

Use a ruler to draw a line of each length.

13. $2\frac{3}{8}$ inches

14. $3\frac{1}{4}$ inches

15. $1\frac{7}{8}$ inches

Problem Solving

16. The letters on the door of a truck are 2 inches tall. How tall will the letters on the side of the truck be if they are 10 times as tall?

17. **Visual Thinking** Macie needed to paint three large letters on the side of a truck. Each of the three letters could be 2 feet wide and still leave the following amounts of blank space: 1 foot before the first letter, 1 foot after the last letter, and 6 inches between letters. How long was the side of the truck?

Equal Customary Measures of Length

Build Understanding

What do you notice about these pairs of words?

little—small   far—distant   strong—powerful

The two words that make up each pair are synonyms, or words that mean almost the same thing. With synonyms, you have different ways to describe the same thing.

A. "Five feet" and "60 inches" are two different ways to describe the same length.

> 1 foot = 12 inches
> 1 yard = 3 feet
> 1 mile = 5,280 feet
> 1 mile = 1,760 yards

One foot is 12 inches, or the length of some rulers. Something that is 5 feet long is like 5 rulers, or $5 \times 12 = 60$ inches.

B. Is 500 yards the same as 1,500 feet?

1 yard = 3 feet

You can think of 500 yards as 500 groups of 3 feet.

500 × 3 = 1,500

500 yards is the same as 1,500 feet.

C. Which is longer, 6 feet 10 inches or 77 inches?

1 foot = 12 inches

You can think of 6 feet as 6 groups of 12 inches.

6 × 12 = 72

6 feet 10 inches is 10 inches longer.

72 + 10 = 82

6 feet 10 inches, or 82 inches, is longer than 77 inches.

■ **Talk About Math**   Why do you multiply when you change a larger unit, like feet, to a smaller unit, like inches?

Check Understanding

For another example, see Set A, pages 110–111.

Read this story. Then match each measure in Exercises 1-4 with an equal measure from the story.

Tamara and her grandfather were driving to the river to go fishing. Tamara's grandfather parked the truck and said, "The river is not far from here—only about *900 feet*. You know, when I was a boy, I used to walk *5,280 yards* to school every day." After they had walked a while, Tamara asked her grandfather how big the biggest fish he ever caught was. He said, "It was *1 foot 9 inches* long." Walking in the tall weeds behind him, Tamara wondered what it would be like to be *76 inches* tall, just like her grandfather.

1. 3 miles   **2.** 6 feet 4 inches

3. 21 inches   **4.** 300 yards

Practice

For More Practice, see Set A, pages 112–113.

Change each of the measures in Exercises 5-9 to inches.

5. 7 ft   **6.** 7 ft 5 in.   **7.** 2 yd   **8.** 12 ft   **9.** 128 ft

Change each measure to feet.

10. 8 yd   **11.** 2 mi   **12.** 8 yd 2 ft   **13.** 2 yd

Number Sense Choose the larger measure.

14. 32 in. or 2 ft   **15.** 15 yd or 15 ft   **16.** 56 in. or 4 ft 7 in.

17. 2 yd or 7 ft   **18.** 5 yd or 20 ft   **19.** 3 mi or 15,000 ft

Problem Solving

20. A newspaper article stated that the new mall would be "3 football fields long." A football field is 100 yards long. How many feet long will the new mall be?

21. Brian saw an advertisement for 66-inch-long extension cords. Would one of these extension cords be long enough to reach an outlet that is 5 feet away?

Metric Units of Length

Build Understanding

Michael couldn't understand why none of the wrenches in his dad's toolbox would fit the bolt on his bike.

Later, his father explained it. The wrenches were designed for bolts with measures involving customary units, like $\frac{1}{2}$ inch, $\frac{3}{4}$ inch, and $\frac{5}{16}$ inch. The measure of the head of the bolt on Michael's bike involved metric units.

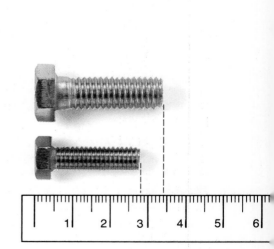

A. Here are some common *metric units of length*.

One *millimeter* (mm) is about the thickness of a dime.

One *centimeter* (cm) is about the length of the fingernail on your little finger.

A soup can is about 1 *decimeter* (dm) tall.

A baseball bat is about 1 *meter* (m) long.

One thousand baseball bats placed end to end would be about 1 *kilometer* (km) long.

B. Michael measured these two bolts and told his dad that they were both 3 centimeters long. Did Michael measure correctly?

You can see that the top bolt is longer than the bottom bolt. Michael measured correctly, however. The length of both bolts is 3 centimeters to the nearest centimeter.

You can also measure to the nearest millimeter. The top bolt is 34 millimeters. The bottom bolt is 28 millimeters.

■ **Talk About Math**   How many millimeters long is the longest line that you could draw that would measure 5 centimeters if measured to the nearest centimeter?

Check Understanding

Estimation Choose the most sensible measure.

1. Length of a nail
   a. 8 cm   b. 8 km   c. 8 dm

2. Width of a button
   a. 12 m   b. 12 km   c. 12 mm

3. Length of a board
   a. 2 m   b. 2 cm   c. 2 mm

4. Distance from home to school
   a. 1 dm   b. 1 cm   c. 1 km

Practice

Estimation Tell whether you would use centimeters, meters, or kilometers to measure each of the following.

5. Length of a backyard

6. Length of a river

7. Width of a dollar bill

8. Width of a car

Use a ruler. Measure each line to the nearest centimeter and to the nearest millimeter.

9. _____

10. _____

11. _____

12. _____

Use a ruler. Draw a line of each length.

13. 42 mm   14. 8 cm   15. 2 dm   16. Between 5 and 8 cm

Problem Solving

17. How many millimeters long is the shortest line that you could draw that would measure 5 centimeters if measured to the nearest centimeter?

Reading ———— **Math**

Looking for Main Ideas Look at the Build Understanding section on page 82. Write three main ideas you can find in this section.

Equal Metric Measures of Length

Build Understanding

A purple martin birdhouse is divided into separate sections so the birds can nest in groups called *colonies*.

A. Roger's aunt owns Rosie's Posies, a garden shop. She asked Roger to help her display a new purple martin birdhouse she has for sale. The instructions said that the birdhouse should be 450 centimeters above the ground. The pole Roger wants to use is 4 meters long. Is it long enough?

1 meter = 10 decimeters
1 meter = 100 centimeters
1 meter = 1,000 millimeters
1,000 meters = 1 kilometer

Since 1 meter is 100 centimeters, 4 meters is 4 × 100 centimeters, or 400 centimeters.

The birdhouse needs to be 450 centimeters above the ground, and the pole is only 400 centimeters long. The pole is not long enough.

B. The height of the birdhouse is 6 decimeters. What is the height in centimeters?

Since 1 decimeter is 10 centimeters, 6 decimeters is 6 × 10 centimeters, or 60 centimeters.

The height of the birdhouse is 60 centimeters.

C. The openings to the birdhouse are 7 centimeters apart. How many millimeters is that?

One centimeter is 10 millimeters, so 7 centimeters is 7 × 10 millimeters, or 70 millimeters.

The openings are 70 millimeters apart.

■ **Talk About Math** For Example A, if Roger had found a pole that was 4,200 millimeters long, would it have been long enough? Explain.

Check Understanding

For another example, see Set B, pages 110–111.

Use the information on page 88 to fill in the blanks.

1. 1 m = ▦ mm   **2.** 1 m = ▦ cm   **3.** 1 cm = ▦ mm

4. 1 dm = ▦ cm   **5.** 1 dm = ▦ mm   **6.** 1 ▦ = 100 cm = ▦ mm

If 1,000 millimeters is 1 meter, how many millimeters is

7. 5 meters?   **8.** 17 meters?   **9.** 9 meters?

If 100 centimeters is 1 meter, how many centimeters is

10. 2 meters?   **11.** 6 meters?   **12.** 22 meters?

Practice

For More Practice, see Set B, pages 112–113.

Write each measure in millimeters.

13. 35 cm   **14.** 7 m   **15.** 4 dm   **16.** 4 m   **17.** 10 dm   **18.** 8 cm

Write each measure in centimeters.

19. 15 dm   **20.** 39 m   **21.** 2 km   **22.** 6 m   **23.** 5 km   **24.** 4 dm

Number Sense Tell which of these is the larger measure.

25. 67 m or 720 km   **26.** 67 m or 720 cm   **27.** 239 mm or 239 cm

28. 239 mm or 23 cm   **29.** 42 dm or 3 m   **30.** 42 m or 3 dm

Problem Solving

Read for the facts to solve the problems.

31. A wren birdhouse is 22 centimeters tall. How many millimeters is that?

32. Rosie's delivery van goes about 2,000 km each month. How many kilometers is that every year?

33. Rosie's store has two bird baths. One is 5 centimeters deep and the other is 45 millimeters deep. Which is deeper? By how much?

34. If Roger filled the 45 millimeter deep bird bath with 3 centimeters of water, how many millimeters from the top would the water be?

Perimeter

Build Understanding

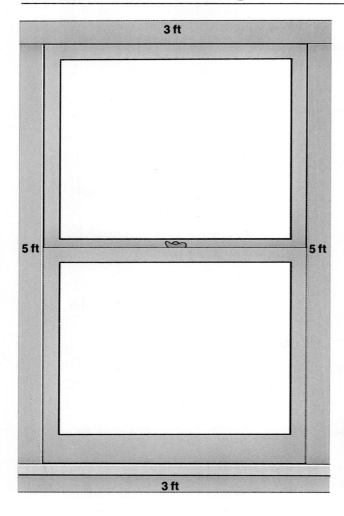

The **perimeter** of the window, or the distance around, is the sum of the lengths of all four sides of the window.

Irene used a tape measure to measure the length of each side of the window. Then Irene added the measures of the sides to find the perimeter.

The perimeter of the window is 3 ft + 5 ft + 3 ft + 5 ft, or 16 feet.

■ **Talk About Math** How would you have found the perimeter of this window if some of the measurements had been in inches?

Check Understanding

For another example, see Set C, pages 110–111.

1. If the window above were 10 feet tall instead of 5 feet, what would the perimeter be?

2. Draw a sketch of a square window. Find its perimeter if a side is 3 decimeters long.

3. Why do you need to label the unit of measure when giving the perimeter?

4. How would you find the perimeter of a figure with 5 sides?

Practice

For More Practice, see Set C, pages 112–113.

Measure the length of each side in centimeters. Then find the perimeter of each figure.

5.

6.

Find the perimeter of each figure. **Remember** to label the unit of measure.

7.
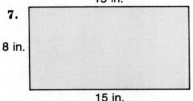
15 in.

8 in.

8 in.

15 in.

8.
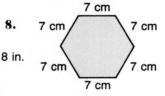
7 cm

7 cm

7 cm

7 cm

7 cm

7 cm

9.
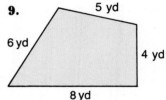
5 yd

6 yd

4 yd

8 yd

Problem Solving

10. A rectangular window is 3 feet long and 2 feet wide. What is its perimeter?

11. Another window is 32 inches long and 26 inches wide. What is its perimeter?

12. 🖩 **Calculator** Sealer is used around the perimeter of a window. A tube of sealer will seal 125 feet. Will one tube be enough to seal 8 windows that are each 5 feet long and 2 feet wide?

Midchapter ✓ Checkup

Choose the most sensible measure for each of the following.
1. Width of a door
   a. 1 km   **b.** 1 mm   **c.** 1 m

2. Length of a car
   a. 12 ft   **b.** 12 in.   **c.** 12 mi

Choose the larger measure.
3. 3 ft 2 in. or 40 in.   **4.** 3 km or 300 m   **5.** 4 yd or 13 ft

6. Find the perimeter.
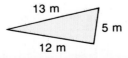
13 m

5 m

12 m

Problem Solving **WORKSHOP**

Real-Life Decision Making

You are at the zoo with 1 adult and another child. The three of you want to take each ride once. You have $12 and some coupons that allow two people to ride for the price of one.

1. What is the least the Elephant Ride will cost if you use the pay adult price coupon?

2. What is the least the Bus Tour will cost if you use the pay child price coupon?

3. Decide which coupon you will use on which ride.

PAY ADULT PRICE
CHILD RIDES FREE
2 for 1
Good on any zoo ride

PAY CHILD PRICE
ANOTHER CHILD RIDES FREE
2 for 1
Good on any zoo ride

ZOO RIDES

	Sky Ride	Elephant Ride	Bus Tour
ADULT	$2.25	$1.50	$3.00
CHILD	$1.75	$0.75	$2.00

Explore with a Computer

Use the *Geometry Workshop* Project for this activity.

1. Suppose you want to make a rectangle that has a perimeter of 24 units. How many different size rectangles can you make?

2. Use the **Draw** option to make the rectangles. Record the length, width, and perimeter of each one.

3. Use the **Measure** option to check your answers.

File Edit Draw Measure Extras Help

MEASURES
pABCD 24.00

Perimeter of:
Type a label. Then press Return.

Number-Sense Project

Look back at pages 80-81.

1. This table shows the estimates Ben collected for the length of a cord he tied around a box.

Estimate	Under by	Over by
20 ft	12 ft	
18 ft	14 ft	
60 ft		28 ft
33 ft		1 ft
50 ft		18 ft
30 ft	2 ft	
50 ft		18 ft
24 ft	8 ft	
30 ft	2 ft	
26 ft	6 ft	

a. How long was Ben's cord?

b. Write a summary telling how accurate the 10 estimates that Ben collected were.

c. Were the people who estimated too high more accurate than those who estimated too low?

Visual-Thinking Activity

You have built a fence in the shape of a square. There are 4 fence posts on each side. How many posts did you use altogether?

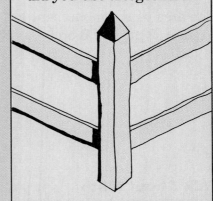

Finding Area by Counting Squares

Build Understanding

Lenny's mother is designing a new park for the city. She drew a plan showing the park's buildings, monuments, and playgrounds on grid paper.

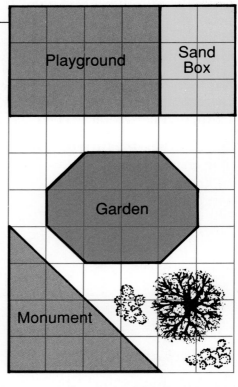

A. Lenny counted 12 shaded squares labeled "playground."

 The length of each side of this square is 1 centimeter. The **area** of the square is 1 **square centimeter** (1 cm²).

Each square shown on the grid paper is 1 square centimeter.

On the plan, the playground covers three rows of 4 square centimeters.

The area of the playground on the plan is 12 square centimeters.

B. What is the area of the monument on the plan? There are 6 whole squares and 4 half squares.

 4 half squares equal 2 whole squares.

The area of the monument is 6 cm² + 2 cm², or 8 cm².

C. Find the area of the figure. Each square represents 1 **square inch** (1 sq in.). There are 4 whole squares and 8 half squares.

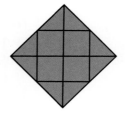 2 half squares equal 1 whole square, so 8 half squares equal 4 whole squares.

The area of the figure is 4 sq in. + 4 sq in., or 8 square inches.

Talk About Math Is it possible for two figures with different shapes to have the same area? Explain.

Check Understanding

For another example, see Set D, pages 110–111.

Find the area of each shaded figure on the plan on page 94. Each square is 1 square centimeter. **Remember** to label the unit of measure.

1. Sandbox

2. Garden

Find the area of each figure. Each square represents 1 square inch. **Remember** to label the unit of measure.

3.

4.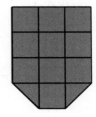

Practice

For More Practice, see Set D, pages 112–113.

Find the area of each figure. Each square is 1 cm².

5.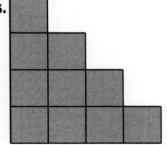

6.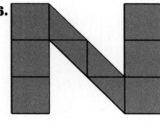

7.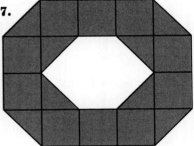

Problem Solving

Critical Thinking Use grid paper for Exercises 8-9.

8. Put four square inches together so the perimeter is 10 inches. How many different ways can you do this?

9. Put four square inches together so the perimeter is 8 inches. How many different ways can you do this?

TIPS FOR PROBLEM SOLVERS

Don't give up. Some problems take longer than others.

Area of Squares and Rectangles

Build Understanding

A. A Square Deal
Materials: Pieces of paper 1 inch square
Groups: Groups of 3-6 students

a. Arrange your squares into the figures shown.

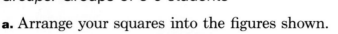

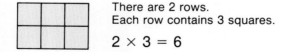

b. All of the figures are ***rectangles***. The two rectangles with four equal sides are ***squares***.

c. Find the area of each square or rectangle by counting.

d. Think about the figures as rows of squares. For example, the first figure has 1 row containing 1 square. The second figure has 1 row containing 2 squares. Write the number of rows each of the other figures has and the number of squares in each row.

e. For each figure, multiply the number of rows by the number of squares in each row.

f. Compare your answers in step e with your answers in step c. What do you notice?

B. Each square in this figure represents 1 square foot. What area is represented by this figure?

There are 2 rows.
Each row contains 3 squares.

$2 \times 3 = 6$

The area represented by the figure is 6 square feet.

Check You can count 6 squares. Each square represents 1 square foot, so the answer checks.

■ **Talk About Math** Tell how you can find the area of a square or a rectangle if the length and width are given.

Check Understanding

For another example, see Set E, pages 110–111.

1. How many rows of 1-foot squares would fit in the rectangle?

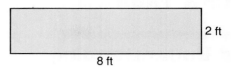

2 ft

8 ft

2. How many squares would be in each row?

3. What is the area of the rectangle?

Practice

For More Practice, see Set E, pages 112–113.

Measure the length and width of each figure in inches. Then find the area of the figure.

4.

5.

Measure the length and width of each figure in centimeters. Then find the area of the figure.

6.

7.

Problem Solving

8. Estimation Do you think a figure twice as long and twice as wide will have an area twice as large? Explain.

1 ft

3 ft

Make a Table

PROBLEM SOLVING
GUIDE

Build Understanding

Harvey has 24 yards of chicken wire. He will use 1-yard sections of the wire to fence in a rectangular garden. Harvey wants to have the largest possible area. How should he arrange the fence?

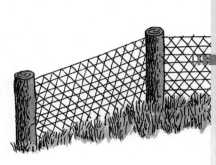

Understand
QUESTION
FACTS
KEY IDEA

Plan and Solve
STRATEGY
ANSWER

Look Back
SENSIBLE ANSWER
ALTERNATE APPROACH

Understand   QUESTION   What is the largest rectangular area that can be made from 24 yards of chicken wire?

FACTS   Each side must be a whole number of yards since the fence is to be built in 1-yard sections.

KEY IDEA   The perimeter of the garden must be 24 yards.

**Plan and Solve**   STRATEGY   Use a table to make an organized list.

ANSWER   The garden measuring 6 yards long and 6 yards wide has the largest area for a 24-yard perimeter.

Width (yd)	Length (yd)	Perimeter (yd)	Area (sq yd)
1	11	1 + 11 + 1 + 11 = 24	1 × 11 = 11
2	10	2 + 10 + 2 + 10 = 24	2 × 10 = 20
3	9	3 + 9 + 3 + 9 = 24	3 × 9 = 27
4	8	4 + 8 + 4 + 8 = 24	4 × 8 = 32
5	7	5 + 7 + 5 + 7 = 24	5 × 7 = 35
6	6	6 + 6 + 6 + 6 = 24	6 × 6 = 36
7	5	7 + 5 + 7 + 5 = 24	7 × 5 = 35

Look Back   SENSIBLE ANSWER   The largest rectangular area for Harvey's garden uses all 24 yards of fence and is 6 yards wide and 6 yards long.

■ **Talk About Math** Does the table include all possibilities? Why does it stop with the width at 7 yards? Explain.

Check Understanding

1. Suppose Harvey has only 20 yards of fencing. Make a table to show the possible gardens.

2. What is the area of the largest rectangular garden Harvey could put 20 yards of fencing around?

3. What do you notice about the shapes of the largest gardens for both 24 yards of fencing and 20 yards of fencing?

Practice

Lupe has 12 meters of chicken wire. She will use 1-meter sections of the wire to fence in her garden.

4. What is the area of the largest rectangular garden Lupe could build a fence around?

5. What is the area of the largest rectangular garden Lupe could enclose with 12 meters of fencing in 1-meter sections if she used the wall of a barn for one side of the fence?

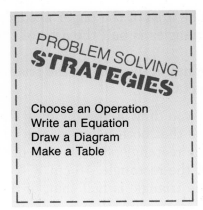

Choose a ⬛ Strategy

Neighborly Fences One piece of chicken wire is 28 meters long. Another piece of chicken wire is 36 meters long. Each piece of chicken wire is to be made into a fence with 1-meter sections.

6. Could these two lengths of chicken wire fence two gardens with the same area? Explain.

PROBLEM SOLVING STRATEGIES

Choose an Operation
Write an Equation
Draw a Diagram
Make a Table

Area of Triangles

Build Understanding

Tammy and Consuela are building a kite for science class. The color on each of the four sections of the kite they have designed is different. How much paper will they need for each color?

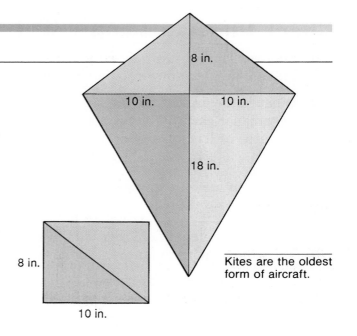

A. Each section of the kite is a *triangle*. The two top triangles are the same size. If you put them together, the triangles form a rectangle.

The area of the rectangle is 8 in. × 10 in., or 80 sq in. You can see that the area of each triangle is half the area of the rectangle.

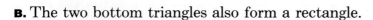

The area of the paper needed for each of the top triangles is half of 80 sq in., or **40 sq in.**

Kites are the oldest form of aircraft.

B. The two bottom triangles also form a rectangle.

The area of the rectangle they form is 10 in. × 18 in., or 180 sq in.

The area of the paper needed for each of the bottom triangles is half the area of the rectangle, or **90 sq in.**

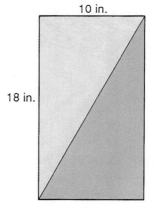

C. What is the area of the triangle inside this rectangle?

If you draw a line dividing the triangle in half, you can see that both halves of the triangle would fit inside half the rectangle. So the area of the triangle is half the area of the rectangle. 18 cm × 4 cm = 72 cm², so the area of the triangle is half that, or **36 cm²**.

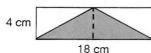

■ **Talk About Math** What must be true about two triangles if they form a rectangle when put together?

100

Check Understanding

For another example, see Set F, pages 110–111.

For Exercises 1-2, draw a sketch that will help you find the area of each triangle.

1.

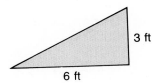

3 ft

6 ft

2.

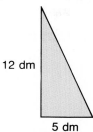

12 dm

5 dm

Practice

For More Practice, see Set F, pages 112–113.

Find the area of each triangle. **Remember** to label each unit of measure.

3. The triangle in Exercise 1

4. The triangle in Exercise 2

5.

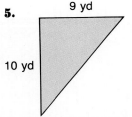

9 yd

10 yd

6.

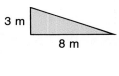

3 m

8 m

7.

2 ft

3 ft

8.

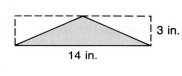

3 in.

14 in.

Problem Solving

Tammy made another kite. The rectangle formed by the 2 top triangles was 12 inches wide and 14 inches long. The rectangle formed by the bottom triangles was 20 inches wide and 14 inches long.

9. Draw a diagram of the kite.

10. Find the areas of the four triangles.

11. Find the area of the whole kite.

Explore ———— Math

This kite has two crossbars that are 60 cm long. The crossbars intersect in the middle.

12. Find the area of each triangle formed by the crossbars.

13. What is the total area of the kite?

14. What do you notice about this kite?

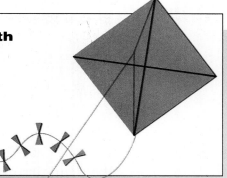

Use Data from a Picture

Build Understanding

Matt Allison is a roofing contractor. What is the area of this roof?

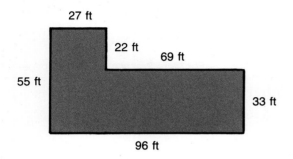

27 ft

22 ft

69 ft

55 ft

33 ft

96 ft

Understand
QUESTION
FACTS
KEY IDEA

Plan and Solve
STRATEGY
ANSWER

Look Back
SENSIBLE ANSWER
ALTERNATE APPROACH

Understand QUESTION   What is the area of the roof?

FACTS   The measurements of the roof are shown.

KEY IDEA   Think of the roof as two rectangles.

Plan and Solve   STRATEGY   Find the area of each rectangle. Then add to find the total area.

Area of large rectangle
96 ft × 33 ft = 3,168 sq ft

Area of small rectangle
27 ft × 22 ft =   594 sq ft

Total area   **3,762 sq ft**

ANSWER   The area of the roof is 3,762 sq ft.

Look Back   ALTERNATE APPROACH   You could divide the figure into two different rectangles. Then find the area of each.

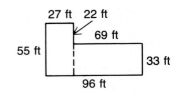

27 ft 22 ft

69 ft

55 ft

33 ft

96 ft

■ **Write About Math**   Explain how to find the area of the roof in the example if you think of the roof as a rectangle with a small rectangle missing from it.

Check Understanding

1. Divide the figure at the right into shapes whose areas you know how to find.

2. Find the areas of the shapes you drew.

3. Find the total area.

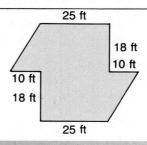

Practice

Find the area of each figure.

4.

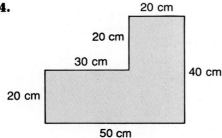

5.

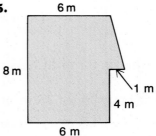

6.

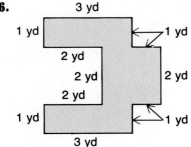

7.

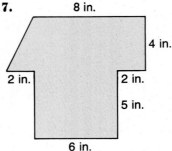

Skills ⟲ Review   pages 8–9

Round each number to the nearest hundred.
1. 8,456   **2.** 29,491   **3.** 3,924   **4.** 984   **5.** 49,999

Time

Build Understanding

A. Soo Kim schedules flights for passengers at the airport. One flight started at 7:45 A.M. and ended at 12:15 P.M. How long was the flight?

Count the hours from 7:45 A.M. to 11:45 A.M.

Count the minutes from 11:45 A.M. to 12:15 P.M.

7:45 A.M.

11:45 A.M.
4 hours

12:15 P.M.
30 minutes

The flight was **4 hours 30 minutes** long.

B. What time will it be 9 hours 35 minutes after 8:20 P.M.?

Count 9 hours past 8:20 P.M.

Count 35 minutes past 5:20 A.M.

8:20 P.M.

5:20 A.M.

5:55 A.M.

The time will be **5:55** A.M.

C. Write 5 hours 25 minutes in minutes.

```
    60
  ×  5
  ─────
   300
 +  25
 ─────
   325
```

Multiply the number of hours and the number of minutes in each hour.

Add the rest of the minutes.

1 minute (min) = 60 seconds (sec)
1 hour (h) = 60 minutes
1 day (da) = 24 hours

5 h 25 min = 325 min

■ **Talk About Math** Does A.M. mean from midnight to noon? What does P.M. mean?

Check Understanding

For another example, see Set G, pages 110–111.

1. What is the length of time from 4:25 A.M. to 6:10 A.M.?

2. What time will it be 3 hours 25 minutes after 10:15 P.M.?

3. Write 3 minutes 45 seconds in seconds.

Practice

For More Practice, see Set G, pages 112–113.

What is the length of time from

4. 8:25 A.M. to 10:30 A.M.?

5. 3:35 P.M. to 6:15 P.M.?

6. 10:40 A.M. to 2:00 P.M.?

7. 9:45 P.M. to 6:15 A.M.?

Remember to label A.M. or P.M. What time will it be

8. 2 h 5 min after 3:50 P.M.?

9. 5 h 35 min after 6:35 A.M.?

10. 7 h 45 min after 4:10 P.M.?

11. 3 h 20 min before 5:45 A.M.?

Remember to label the unit of time.

12. Write 3 hours in minutes.

13. Write 15 minutes in seconds.

14. Write 7 hours 19 minutes in minutes.

15. Write 8 days 14 hours in hours.

Problem Solving

On the first Sunday in April, most areas in the U.S. change from standard time to *daylight savings time*. The clocks are set *ahead* one hour. In the fall, when standard time resumes, the clocks are set *back* one hour.

16. On the first Sunday in April, an airline passenger was surprised to find that he had missed his flight by almost 1 hour. What do you think happened?

105

Temperature: Celsius and Fahrenheit

Build Understanding

A. The temperature is 30 degrees Celsius (30°C). Rachel is wearing shorts and a T-shirt. Should she put on heavier clothing before going outside?

In most places of the world, *degree Celsius* is the unit of measure used for temperature. In the United States, *degree Fahrenheit* is the unit of measure used for temperature.

On the Celsius thermometer, 30 degrees is the same as 86 degrees on the Fahrenheit thermometer (86°F). Rachel does not need to change her clothes.

B. Give the temperature.

The temperature is −5°F.

■ **Talk About Math** Not all thermometers are marked for every degree. Suppose a thermometer was marked for every 2 degrees. Explain how you would read this thermometer.

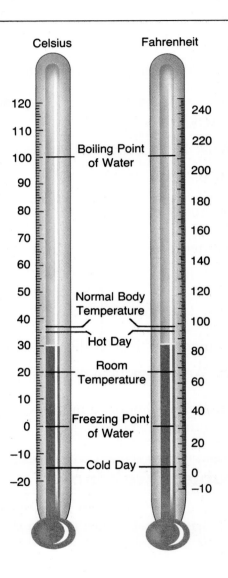

Check Understanding

For another example, see Set H, pages 110–111.

Estimation Choose the more sensible temperature.

1. The temperature for swimming
35°C   60°C

2. The temperature for ice skating
29°F   65°F

Practice

For More Practice, see Set H, pages 112–113.

Estimation Choose the more sensible temperature.

3. Cold day
 20°C   − 20°C

4. Hot cocoa
 20°C   80°C

5. Classroom
 23°C   70°C

6. Freezing water
 32°F   50°F

7. Melting butter
 30°F   100°F

8. Boiling water
 100°F   212°F

Give the temperature shown on each thermometer.

9.   **10.**   **11.**   **12.**   **13.**   **14.**

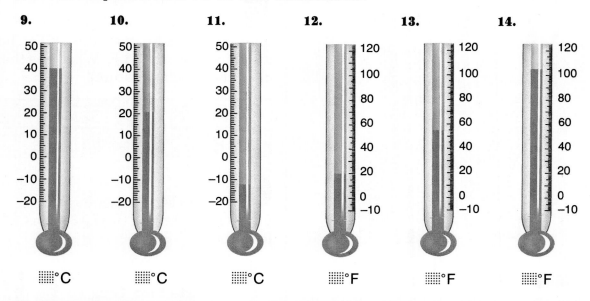

Problem Solving

15. The radio said it was − 20°C in Duluth, Minnesota, and − 10°C in Winnipeg, Canada. Which city had the colder temperature?

16. Estimation Ham should be cooked to an internal temperature of 50°. Would this be degrees Celsius or degrees Fahrenheit?

17. Estimation The printing in a cookbook is smudged. Should soup be heated to 60°F or 160°F in a microwave oven?

18. Use Data If you were going to put gutters around the roof on page 102, how many feet of gutter would you need?

19. A microwave oven has been programmed to defrost and cook a 5-pound beef roast. It takes 8 minutes per pound to defrost and 7 minutes per pound to cook. How many minutes will defrosting and cooking take?

Solve each problem.

1. Jumbo the elephant is 10 feet tall. How many inches tall is Jumbo?

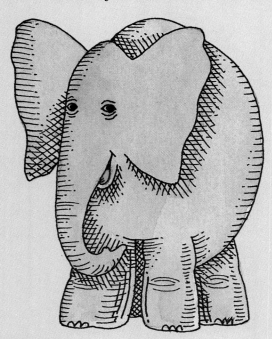

2. Mrs. Reiner's house is on a lot shown by the diagram below. She plans to put a fence inside the edge. What is the perimeter of the lot shown below?

180 ft

120 ft

3. If Mrs. Reiner put the fence around her lot 3 feet inside the edge, how many feet of fence does she need? Use the diagram above.

4. The Harris family left home for the beach at 7:00 A.M. They returned home at 4:40 P.M. How long were they away from home?

5. The daytime high temperature in Fremont was 76°F. The nighttime low was 53°F. What was the difference in temperature?

6. Can Mrs. Visser buy two $1.79 notebooks and two $0.89 pens for $5.00?

7. **Data File** Greg is 5 ft 2 in. tall and weighs 109 lb. Jane is 4 ft 6 in. tall and weighs 80 lbs. Find the right size baseball bat each person should buy using the chart on pages 116–117.

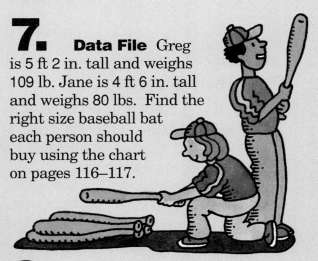

8. **Make a Data File** Look up the regulation length and width of fields or courts for some sports. Make a table showing length, width, perimeter, and area.

Explore with a Calculator

"Choosing Up Sides"

Mrs. Court held a contest among the teams in her class. She distributed the problem cards shown below. The team that could find all the missing lengths of sides of the figures would win.

Use the facts and your calculator to solve the problems. Remember to label your answers.

1. Facts: Rectangle
   length = 13 ft
   perimeter = 42 ft
   width = ?

2. Facts: Square
   perimeter = 68 yd
   length of a side =?

3. Facts: Triangle
   sides of 23 cm, 34 cm
   perimeter = 86 cm
   length of other
   side = ?

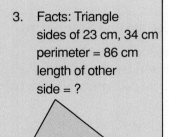

4. Facts: Rectangle
   width = 9 m
   area = 162 m²
   length = ?

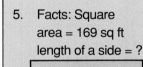

5. Facts: Square
   area = 169 sq ft
   length of a side = ?

6. Facts: Triangle
   perimeter = 42 in.
   2 sides same length,
   each 12 in.

   other
   side = ?

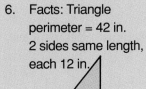

7. Facts: Hexagon
   all sides same length
   perimeter = 102 yd
   length of a side = ?

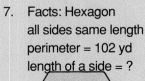

8. Facts: Square
   area = 961 cm²
   length of a side = ?

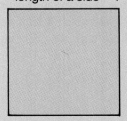

Reteaching

Set A pages 84–85

Change 3 miles to feet.

The chart on page 84 shows that
1 mile = 5,280 feet.

So 3 miles = 3 × 5,280 or 15,840 feet.

Remember to multiply when changing a larger unit to a smaller unit.

Change each of the measures as described. Use the equal measures given in the chart on page 84.

1. 9 feet to inches

2. 6 yards to feet

3. 2 miles to yards

Set B pages 88–89

Write 5 centimeters in millimeters.

Since 1 centimeter = 10 millimeters,
5 centimeters is 5 × 10 or 50 millimeters.

Remember that since 1 centimeter equals 10 millimeters and 10 centimeters equals 1 decimeter, 1 decimeter equals 100 millimeters.

Use the chart of equal metric measures on page 88 if necessary.

Write each measure in millimeters.

1. 45 cm   **2.** 6 dm   **3.** 3 m

Write each measure in centimeters.

4. 12 dm   **5.** 6 m   **6.** 3 km

Set C pages 90–91

Find the perimeter of this figure.
Add the lengths of the sides:

15 cm + 9 cm + 9 cm + 9 cm + 9 cm
or 51 cm

Remember to label the unit of measure.

For Exercise 1, measure each side in centimeters. Then find the perimeter. For Exercise 2, use the measurements given to find the perimeter.

1.    **2.**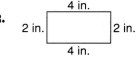

Set D pages 94–95

Find the area.
Each square represents 1 square inch.

Think: There are 5 whole squares and 4 half squares. 4 half squares equals 2 whole squares. So the area is

5 + 2 = 7 sq in.

Remember that area is measured in square units.

Find the area of each figure. Each square represents 1 sq in.

1.    **2.**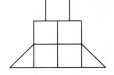

Set E   pages 96–97

This rectangle is 2 cm long and 1 cm wide.

The area is 2 × 1 or 2 cm².

Remember that the area of a figure is the number of square units needed to cover the figure.

Measure the length and width of each figure in centimeters. Then find the area of the figure.

1.    **2.**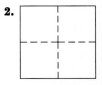

Set F   pages 100–101

Find the area of this triangle.

Think of the triangle as one half of a rectangle.

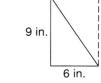

9 in.

6 in.

Rectangle: 9 × 6 = 54 sq in.
Triangle: one half of 54 sq in., or 27 sq in.

Remember that you can sketch a rectangle to help you find the areas of these triangles.

Find the area of each triangle.

1. 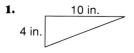   **2.**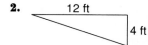

10 in.   12 ft

4 in.   4 ft

Set G   pages 104–105

The drive to the mountains began at 9:15 A.M. We arrived 4 hours 10 minutes later. What time did we arrive?

Count 4 hours past 9:15 A.M.

Count 10 minutes past 1:15 P.M.

We arrived at 1:25 P.M.

Remember that A.M. means from midnight to noon. P.M. means from noon to midnight.

What time will it be

1. 3 hours 15 minutes before 1:30 P.M.?

2. 6 hours 35 minutes after 7:15 A.M.?

3. 3 hours 25 minutes after 10:10 P.M.?

Set H   pages 106–107

On this thermometer, every two degrees is marked. What temperature is shown?

The color in the thermometer is 4 marks above 20°C.

Since every 2 degrees is marked, the temperature is 4 × 2 or 8 degrees above 20°C, or 28°C.

30°C
20°C
10°C
0°C

Remember that not all thermometers are marked for every degree. Give the temperature shown on each thermometer.

1.   **2.**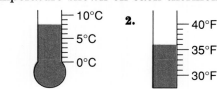

10°C
5°C
0°C

40°F
35°F
30°F

More Practice

Set A pages 84–85

Change each of the measures in Exercises 1–4 to inches.

1. 8 ft   **2.** 4 ft 9 in.   **3.** 4 yd   **4.** 146 ft

Change each measure to feet.

5. 7 yd   **6.** 3 mi   **7.** 10 yd 2 ft   **8.** 6 yd

Number Sense Choose the larger measure.

9. 14 in. or 3 ft   **10.** 6 yd or 16 ft   **11.** 52 in. or 4 ft 6 in.

Set B pages 88–89

Write each measure in millimeters.

1. 45 cm   **2.** 6 m   **3.** 5 dm   **4.** 10 m   **5.** 9 dm   **6.** 30 cm

Write each measure in centimeters.

7. 12 dm   **8.** 44 m   **9.** 4 km   **10.** 60 m   **11.** 7 km   **12.** 10 dm

Number Sense Tell which of these is the larger measure.

13. 94 m or 500 km   **14.** 188 mm or 18 cm   **15.** 9 dm or 96 cm

Set C pages 90–91

Find the perimeter of each figure. For Exercises 1 and 2 you need to measure the length of each side in centimeters.

1.   **2.**    **3.** 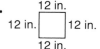   **4.**

Set D pages 94–95

Find the area of each figure. Each square represents 1 cm².

1.   **2.**   **3.**   **4.**

Set E   pages 96–97

Measure the length and width of each figure in inches.
Then find the area of the figure.

1.

2.

Measure the length and width of each figure in
centimeters. Then find the area of the figure.

3.

4.

Set F   pages 100–101

Find the area of each triangle. **Remember** to label each
unit of measure.

1.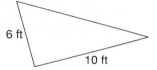

6 ft

10 ft

2.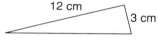

12 cm

3 cm

3.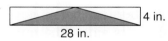

4 in.

28 in.

Set G   pages 104–105

What is the length of time from

1. 6:20 P.M. to 10:10 P.M.?

2. 11:50 A.M. to 4:55 P.M.?

3. Write 5 hours in minutes.

4. Write 3 minutes 18 seconds in seconds.

What time will it be

5. 4 hours 20 minutes after 1:10 P.M.?

6. 6 hours 45 minutes after 7:15 P.M.?

Set H   pages 106–107

Estimation   Choose the more sensible temperature.

1. Bath water
    10°C   35°C

2. Snow skiing
    25°F   65°F

3. Hot soup
    30°C   80°C

Give the temperature shown on each thermometer.
Remember to determine the number of degrees each mark represents.

4.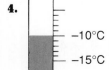

−10°C

−15°C

5.

30°C

20°C

6.

0°F

−5°F

−10°F

7.

50°F

40°F

30°F

Enrichment

Numbers Greater Than and Less Than Zero

Most thermometers show temperatures both above and below 0°. Numbers above zero are greater than 0°. Numbers below zero are less than 0° and are written with a negative sign. A temperature of 5 degrees below zero is written as −5°.

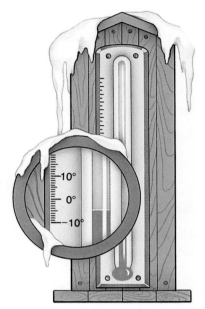

By counting degrees on the thermometer, you can find the new temperature after it rises or falls.

Temperature at 7:00 A.M. was −5°. It rose 11° during the day. Count up 11 degrees from −5°. The new temperature is 6°.

Temperature at 7:00 P.M. was 3°. It fell 7° during the night. Count down 7 degrees from 3°. What is the new temperature?

The number line below is like a thermometer turned on its side. The numbers less than 0 are at the left of 0. You can use the number line to add and subtract. Think of a rise or fall in temperature.

Find −7 + 3.

Add 3 to −7.
Move 3 units to
the right from −7.
−7 + 3 = −4

Find 6 − 9.

Subtract 9 from 6.
Move 9 units to
the left from 6.
6 − 9 = −3

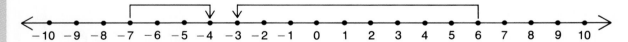

The temperature at 6:00 A.M. was −2°.
Find the new temperature if it

1. rises 1°.   **2.** falls 3°.   **3.** rises 6°.   **4.** falls 8°.

Use the number line to add or subtract.

5. −6 + 2   **6.** −3 + 4   **7.** −4 + 4   **8.** −8 + 0   **9.** −1 + 7

10. 4 − 7   **11.** 1 − 5   **12.** 0 − 2   **13.** −1 − 5   **14.** −6 − 4

Chapter 3 Review/Test

Choose the most sensible measure.

1. Length of a hammer

    a. 13 in.   **b.** 13 ft   **c.** 13 mi

2. Width of a nail

    a. 2 m   **b.** 2 km   **c.** 2 mm

Change each measure to feet.

3. 5 yd   **4.** 3 mi

Write each measure in centimeters.

5. 17 m   **6.** 12 dm

Use a ruler.

7. Measure the line to the nearest $\frac{1}{4}$ inch.

———————————

8. Draw a line that is 36 mm long.

Which is larger?

9. 38 in. or 3 feet

10. 57 m or 600 cm

11. Find the perimeter.

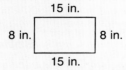

12. Find the area. Each square represents 1 sq in.

13. Measure the length and width in centimeters. Then find the area.

14. Find the area of the triangle.

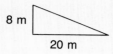

15. Write 6 hours 12 minutes in minutes.

16. Which is the more sensible temperature for a hot day, 32°C or 32°F?

17. An eraser is 5 centimeters long. How many millimeters is this?

18. One room is 20 feet long and 12 feet wide. Another room is 18 feet long and 16 feet wide. Which has the greater perimeter?

19. Collette is making a rectangular pen for her puppy. She has 24 feet of fencing. What is the area of the largest pen she can make?

20. Which is an appropriate method to use in finding the area of the lot shown below?

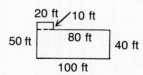

    a. Add 100 × 40 and 20 × 10.
    b. Add 100 × 50 and 20 × 10.
    c. Add 100 × 50 and 80 × 10.
    d. Add the lengths of all the sides.

21. Write About Math What other method could be used to find the area in Problem 20?

Data File

1. Animal Champions

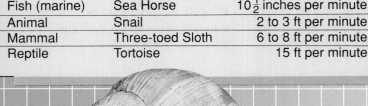

Fastest		
Bird	Indian Swift	200 miles per hour
Land animal	Cheetah	70 miles per hour
Ocean swimmer	Sailfish	68 miles per hour
Slowest		
Fish (marine)	Sea Horse	$10\frac{1}{2}$ inches per minute
Animal	Snail	2 to 3 ft per minute
Mammal	Three-toed Sloth	6 to 8 ft per minute
Reptile	Tortoise	15 ft per minute

1. List
The fastest and slowest speed of some kinds of animals are listed here.

2. Tables
Batter's height is given in feet (') and inches (").

3. Map
The elevation of peaks in Rocky Mountain National Park are on this map.

4. Graph
The graph shows the growth in world population from 1450 to 1980.

5. Chart
The chart shows the size of bat used by some major league baseball players.

2. Baseball Bat Sizes

Boys

Batter's weight in lb	Batter's height							
	3'5"-3'8"	3'9"-4'	4'1"-4'4"	4'5"-4'8"	4'9"-5'	5'1"-5'4"	5'5"-5'8"	5'9"-6
under 60	27"	28"	29"	29"				
61-70	27"	28"	29"	29"	30"			
71-80	28"	28"	29"	30"	30"	31"		
81-90	28"	29"	29"	30"	30"	31"	32"	
91-100	28"	29"	30"	30"	31"	31"	32"	
101-110	29"	29"	30"	30"	31"	31"	32"	
111-120	29"	29"	30"	30"	31"	31"	32"	
121-130	29"	30"	30"	30"	31"	32"	33"	33"
131-140	29"	30"	30"	31"	31"	32"	33"	34"
141-150		30"	30"	31"	31"	32"	33"	34"
151-160		30"	31"	31"	32"	32"	33"	34"
Over 160			31"	31"	32"	32"	33"	34"

116

4. World Population Growth

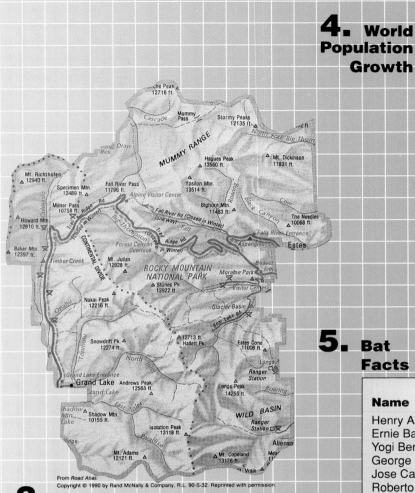

Millions

5,000	
4,500	**1980:** 4,469,934,000
4,000	
3,500	**1970:** 3,677,837,000
3,000	
2,500	**1950:** 2,501,000,000
2,000	
1,500	
1,000	**1850:** 1,091,000,000
500	

AD   1450   1650   1850
                              1980

3. Rocky Mountain National Park

From *Road Atlas.*
Copyright © 1990 by Rand McNally & Company. R.L. 90-S-32. Reprinted with permission.

5. Bat Facts

Name	Length (inches)	Weight (ounces)
Henry Aaron	35–36	32–34
Ernie Banks	Varied	32
Yogi Berra	35	33
George Brett	$34\frac{1}{2}$	32
Jose Canseco	35	35
Roberto Clemente	Varied	40–42
Alvin Dark	Varied	28
Joe DiMaggio	36	34–35
Lou Gehrig	34	38 +
Tony Gwynn	32	30
Rogers Hornsby	34–35	37–39
Reggie Jackson	$34\frac{1}{2}$	33
Ted Kluzewski	35	35–39
Mickey Mantle	35	32–34
Willie Mays	35	33–34
Dale Murphy	$34\frac{1}{2}$	32
Stan Musial	$34\frac{1}{2}$	32–33
Dave Parker	$35\frac{1}{2}$	$34\frac{1}{2}$
Frank Robinson	36	35
Pete Rose	34–36	31–35
Al Rosen	36	36
Babe Ruth	35–36	37–54
Mike Schmidt	35	$32\frac{1}{2}$
Willie Stargell	$36\frac{1}{2}$	38
Darryl Strawberry	35	33
Ted Williams	33–35	32–34
Carl Yastrzemski	35	33

Girls

Batter's weight in lb	Batter's height					
	3'10"-4'	4'1"-4'4"	4'5"-4'8"	4'9"-5'	5'1"-5'4"	5'5"-5'9"
under 40	26"	27"	28"			
40-45	27"	28"	29"	30"		
46-50	27"	28"	29"	30"		
51-60	27"	28"	29"	30"	31"	
61-70	28"	29"	30"	31"	32"	
71-80	28"	29"	30"	31"	32"	33"
81-90	29"	30"	31"	32"	33"	33"
91-100	29"	30"	31"	32"	33"	34"
101-110		30"	31"	32"	33"	34"
111-120		31"	32"	33"	34"	34"
121-130		31"	32"	33"	34"	34"
Over 130			32"	33"	34"	34"

Cumulative Review/Test Chapters 1-3

1. What does the 6 in 6,000,124,008 mean?
   - **a.** 6 billions
   - **b.** 6 millions
   - **c.** 6 ten-millions
   - **d.** 6 ten-billions

2. Round 76,524 to the nearest ten-thousand.
   - **a.** 70,000
   - **b.** 76,000
   - **c.** 77,000
   - **d.** 80,000

3. Choose the best estimate.

   489 + 308
   - **a.** 800
   - **b.** 700
   - **c.** 8,000
   - **d.** 1,000

4. Subtract.

   15,000
   − 9,724
   - **a.** 6,724
   - **b.** 5,276
   - **c.** 6,276
   - **d.** 5,724

5. Find the missing addend.

   $n + 92 = 150$
   - **a.** 58
   - **b.** 48
   - **c.** 242
   - **d.** 68

6. Which number is a common multiple of 5 and 6?
   - **a.** 15
   - **b.** 30
   - **c.** 24
   - **d.** 25

7. Multiply.

   800 × 700
   - **a.** 560
   - **b.** 5,600
   - **c.** 56,000
   - **d.** 560,000

8. Multiply.

   137
   × 85
   - **a.** 11,545
   - **b.** 11,645
   - **c.** 10,545
   - **d.** 10,645

9. Multiply.

   536
   × 324
   - **a.** 173,564
   - **b.** 174,664
   - **c.** 173,664
   - **d.** 162,624

10. Choose the best estimate.

    28 × 495
    - **a.** 1,500
    - **b.** 15,000
    - **c.** 8,000
    - **d.** 10,000

11. Choose the most sensible measure.

    Height of a table
    - **a.** 3 in.
    - **b.** 6 ft
    - **c.** 3 yd
    - **d.** 30 in.

12. Change 30 yd to feet.
    - **a.** 90 ft
    - **b.** 360 ft
    - **c.** 10 ft
    - **d.** 300 ft

13. Write 90 meters in centimeters.

   a. 9 cm   **c.** 9,000 cm
   b. 900 cm   **d.** 90,000 cm

14. Find the perimeter.

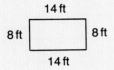

   a. 22 ft   **c.** 112 ft
   b. 44 ft   **d.** 224 ft

15. Find the area of the rectangle.

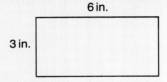

   a. 16 sq in.   **c.** 9 in.
   b. 18 sq in.   **d.** 17 in.

16. Write 2 hours 20 minutes in minutes.

   a. 220 minutes   **c.** 120 minutes
   b. 140 minutes   **d.** 80 minutes

17. Find the area of the triangle.

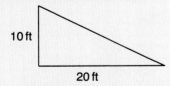

   a. 100 sq ft   **c.** 50 sq ft
   b. 200 sq ft   **d.** 60 sq ft

18. Choose the operation that could be used to solve this problem. Then solve the problem.

In a field there are 27 rows of corn. Each row has 36 corn plants. How many corn plants are in the field?

   a. Addition; 63 corn plants
   b. Multiplication; 972 corn plants
   c. Subtraction; 9 corn plants
   d. Division; 862 corn plants

19. Find the area of the figure.

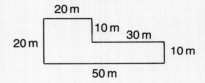

   a. 1,000 m^2 **c.** 140 m^2
   b. 700 m^2 **d.** 1,300 m^2

Read the problem below. Then answer the question.

In the fifth grade there are 112 students, and 60 of the students are girls. How many boys are in the fifth grade?

20. Which equation can you use to solve the problem?

   a. $112 + 60 = n$
   b. $n + 112 = 60$
   c. $112 \times 60 = n$
   d. $n + 60 = 112$

Division with One-Digit Divisors

Did You Know: In international parachuting contests the jumpers try to hit a 10-centimeter disk in the drop zone. Parachutes are used to deliver cargo. Airplanes and helicopters drop food and medicine by parachute.

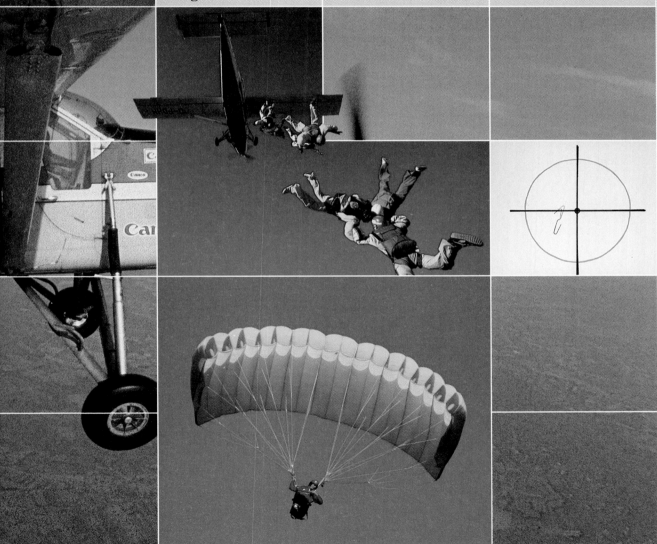

Number-Sense Project

Estimate
In a "drop the paper clip" contest, how accurate do you think you will be? Estimate in centimeters how close a paper clip will land to an X on a piece of paper. Drop the paper clip from a height of 1 meter.

Gather Data
Bend the paper clip into different shapes and experiment to find the shape that is easiest to drop near the target. Then drop the paper clip 5 times. Record the distance from the X for each drop.

Analyze and Report
Add the distances from the target for your 5 trials. The sum is your total error. Compare your results with those of other students.

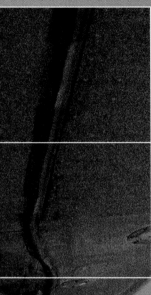

Dividing Whole Numbers

Build Understanding

A. There were 114 students in the Choral Club. The students were divided equally into 4 groups for rehearsals. How many students were in each group? How many students were left? Find 114 ÷ 4.

| You cannot divide 1 hundred among 4 groups. | Rename 1 hundred. How many tens all together? Divide the tens among 4 groups. How many tens in each group? How many tens left? | You cannot divide 3 tens among 4 groups. Rename the tens. How many ones all together? Divide the ones among 4 groups. How many ones in each group? How many ones left? |

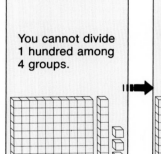
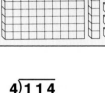

$$4\overline{)114}$$

$$\begin{array}{r} 2 \\ 4\overline{)114} \\ \underline{8} \\ 3 \end{array}$$

Divide.
Multiply.
Subtract and compare.
Is 3 less than 4?

$$\begin{array}{r} 28 \text{ R2} \\ 4\overline{)114} \\ \underline{8}\downarrow \\ 34 \\ \underline{32} \\ 2 \end{array}$$

Bring down.
Divide.
Multiply.
Subtract and compare.
Is 2 less than 4?
Are there any more digits to bring down?

There were 28 students in each group with 2 students left.

B. You can check division using multiplication.

Quotient → **3 R4** ← Remainder
Divisor → 8)28 ← Dividend

Check

$$\begin{array}{r} 3 \leftarrow \text{Quotient} \\ \times 8 \leftarrow \text{Divisor} \\ \hline 24 \\ +4 \leftarrow \text{Remainder} \\ \hline 28 \leftarrow \text{Dividend} \end{array}$$

■ **Talk About Math** If the divisor is 6, what can you say about the remainder? Explain your thinking.

122

Check Understanding

For another example, see Set A, pages 142-143.

Divide.

1. $2\overline{)9}$ **2.** $7\overline{)31}$ **3.** $6\overline{)96}$ **4.** $8\overline{)286}$ **5.** $9\overline{)\$8.28}$

6. If the divisor is 7, will the remainder be less than or more than 7?

7. If the remainder is 8, could the divisor have been 6? Why or why not?

8. Explain how you would check your work for Exercise 4.

Practice

For More Practice, see Set A, pages 144-145.

Divide. **Remember** to check your work.

9. $2\overline{)19}$ **10.** $9\overline{)65}$ **11.** $5\overline{)37}$ **12.** $4\overline{)39}$ **13.** $5\overline{)48}$

14. $4\overline{)75}$ **15.** $5\overline{)94}$ **16.** $6\overline{)96}$ **17.** $8\overline{)94}$ **18.** $7\overline{)84}$

19. $6\overline{)215}$ **20.** $4\overline{)358}$ **21.** $7\overline{)616}$ **22.** $3\overline{)230}$ **23.** $5\overline{)418}$

24. $75 \div 8$ **25.** $87 \div 5$ **26.** $615 \div 8$ **27.** $839 \div 9$

Problem Solving

28. There were 8 chairs in each row in the practice room. If 97 students filled as many rows as possible, how many rows were filled? How many students were in the incomplete row?

29. The audience for the Choral Concert filled 24 rows of the auditorium. There were 20 seats in each row. How many people attended the concert?

30. Ron said he divided by 7 and got an answer of 15 R7. Is this correct? Why or why not?

31. What are the possible remainders if you divide by 5?

Critical Thinking Will there always be a remainder if you

32. divide an even number by an odd number?

33. divide an odd number by an even number?

Try and Check

Build Understanding

PROBLEM SOLVING
GUIDE

Understand
QUESTION
FACTS
KEY IDEA

▐▐▐▶ **Plan and Solve**
STRATEGY
ANSWER

Look Back
SENSIBLE ANSWER
ALTERNATE APPROACH

You are applying for a job at the Who-Done-It Detective Agency. Before you can be hired, you have to take a test to show your mystery-solving abilities. Can you solve this mystery?

The product of two numbers is 48. The sum of the numbers is 19. What are the numbers?

Understand   Two numbers multiplied together give 48. The same two numbers added together give 19. You need to find the two numbers.

▐▐▐▶ **Plan and Solve**   STRATEGY   You can *try and check* pairs of numbers until you find the pair that works. Find two numbers whose product is 48. Check to see what their sum is. Continue trying and checking until you find the correct numbers.

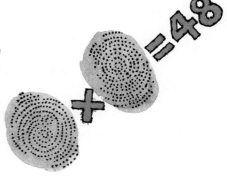

1 × 48 = 48	Does 1 + 48 = 19?
2 × 24 = 48	Does 2 + 24 = 19?
3 × 16 = 48	Does 3 + 16 = 19?

ANSWER   The numbers are 3 and 16.

Look Back   Could you solve this problem by trying numbers whose sum is 19 and checking to find a product of 48?

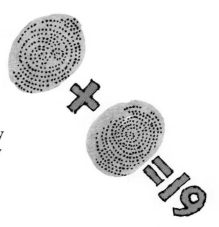

■ **Talk About Math**   Could you solve this problem by randomly picking numbers? Why was it helpful to try and check in an organized manner?

Fingerprinting became a method of identification in the 1880s.

Check Understanding

The product of two numbers is 40. The sum of the numbers is less than 15. What are the numbers?

1. List all the pairs of numbers that have a product of 40.

2. Check the sum of the numbers in each pair. Give each sum.

3. What pairs of numbers have a sum less than 15?

Practice

Solve each problem using try and check.

4. The product of two numbers is 20. The sum of the numbers is 12. What are the numbers?

5. The sum of two numbers is 10. The product is 24. What are the numbers?

6. What two numbers have a product of 12 and a sum of 7?

7. What two single-digit numbers have a product of 36 and a sum of 13?

8. What two numbers have a sum that is a multiple of 5 and a product of 36?

9. What two pairs of numbers have a product of 72 and a sum that is less than 20?

10. What two numbers have a product of 144 and a sum of 25?

Choose a Strategy

11. *Time Ticks Away*   The test for the detective job took 3 hours 45 minutes. What time did the test start, and what time did it end? Use each of the digits 0, 1, 2, 3, 5, and 6 once to write the starting and ending times.

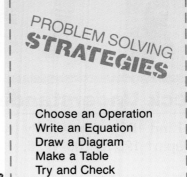

PROBLEM SOLVING
STRATEGIES

Choose an Operation
Write an Equation
Draw a Diagram
Make a Table
Try and Check

Mental Math and Estimating Quotients

Build Understanding

A. Here is a mental math strategy to use when dividing mentally. Look for numbers that you can ***break apart*** into numbers that are easy to divide.

Divide each part, and then add the quotients back together.

$$\overset{210 + 6}{\underset{\downarrow}{216}} \div 3 = \overset{210 \div 3}{\underset{\downarrow}{70}} + \overset{6 \div 3}{\underset{\downarrow}{2}}$$
$$= 72$$

B. Here is another mental math strategy for division. Look for numbers where you can use ***compensation***.

Think of a division fact that will be helpful, and then use multiples.

Think: $40 \div 8 = 5$

$$\overset{40 \times 3}{\underset{\downarrow}{120}} \div 8 = \overset{5 \times 3}{\underset{\downarrow}{15}}$$

C. Here is an estimation strategy to use when estimating quotients. Estimate $468 \div 9$ using ***compatible numbers***.

Substitute numbers that are close to the original numbers for the divisor, the dividend, or both. Choose numbers that can be divided easily.

$468 \div 9$

$450 \div 9 = 50$	$470 \div 10 = 47$
$500 \div 10 = 50$	$480 \div 8 = 60$

Since there can be more than one way to choose compatible numbers, all these estimates are reasonable.

■ **Talk About Math** In Example A, explain how $21 \div 3 = 7$ helps you find $210 \div 3$. How can you use this idea to find $2,100 \div 3$?

Check Understanding

For another example, see Set B, pages 142-143.

1. Find $125 \div 5$ mentally by breaking apart 125 as $100 + 25$.

2. Find $70 \div 5$ mentally using compensation.

3. Estimate $295 \div 6$ using compatible numbers. Explain your thinking.

Practice

For More Practice, see Set B, pages 144-145.

Use mental math to find each quotient. Tell what strategy you used.

4. 328 ÷ 4   **5.** 80 ÷ 5   **6.** 160 ÷ 5   **7.** 248 ÷ 8

8. 90 ÷ 6   **9.** 145 ÷ 5   **10.** 60 ÷ 4   **11.** 168 ÷ 4

12. Choose two of the exercises above. Explain why you chose the strategy you used.

Estimate each quotient using compatible numbers.

13. 249 ÷ 5   **14.** 639 ÷ 8   **15.** 498 ÷ 9   **16.** 798 ÷ 8

17. 288 ÷ 9   **18.** 179 ÷ 6   **19.** 204 ÷ 7   **20.** 155 ÷ 4

21. Choose two of the exercises above. Explain why you chose the compatible numbers you used.

Problem Solving

22. Find 123 ÷ 5 mentally by breaking apart 123 as 100 + 23. Explain your thinking.

23. Use Data Use the information about weekly dog food requirements on page 54. For how many weeks could you feed a Chihuahua with 28 pounds of dog food?

Be confident so you can do your best.

Midchapter ——— Checkup

Divide.
1. 89 ÷ 7   **2.** 265 ÷ 4

5. Estimate 538 ÷ 9 using compatible numbers.

Divide using mental math.
3. 155 ÷ 5   **4.** 287 ÷ 7

6. Use try and check to find two numbers that have a sum of 11 and a product of 24.

Problem-Solving Workshop

Explore as a Team

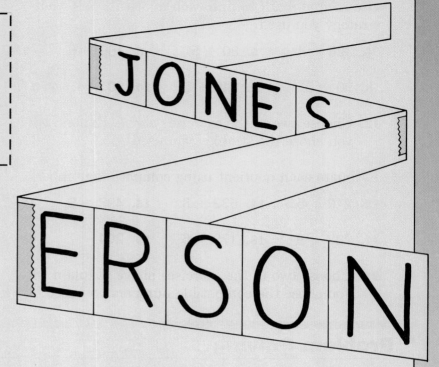

1. How many letters are in the longest last name of someone in your class? Shortest name?

2. Predict the average number of letters in the last names of your classmates.

3. Each member of your group writes his or her last name on a strip of squares, one letter to a square. Cut out the names and tape them together in one strip.

4. Count the number of last names in that strip. Fold the strip into that many equal parts. If there are four names, fold it into four equal parts. There should be the same number of letters in each part. Count the number of letters in each part. This is the average number of letters of the last names in your group.

5. What is the average number of letters of the last names in your group? (Do not count partial letters.)

6. Compare your group's results with those of other groups.

Explore with a Computer

Use the *Spreadsheet Workshop Project* for this activity.

1. At the computer, type two numbers whose sum is 15. What is their product? What other combinations of numbers add up to 15? What happens to the product each time you change these numbers? Keep a record of your results. What happens to the product as the first addend becomes larger and the second addend smaller?

2. What two numbers have a product of 144 and a sum of 25?

3. What two numbers have a product of 36 and a sum of 13?

4. What two numbers have the same product and sum?

Number-Sense Project

Look back at pages 120-121. Michelle did the paper clip drop. The table shows her result for 5 trials.

1. What was the total distance from the target for her 5 trials?

2. If she made 5 more trials, would you expect her total distance from the target to be about 20 cm or 50 cm? Why?

	Distance from Target
Trial	in Centimeters
1	8 cm
2	14 cm
3	9 cm
4	9 cm
5	1 cm

3. If you did the experiment, write a summary comparing your accuracy with Michelle's.

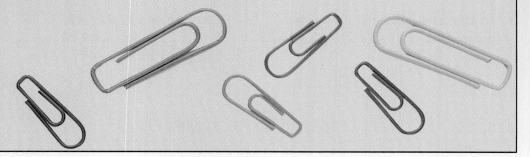

129

Dividing Larger Numbers

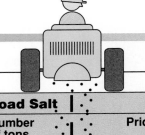

Build Understanding

Suppose you are the Commissioner of Public Works of the city of Frozen Tundra. How much would your city be paying per ton for road salt if you purchased 5 tons?

Since each ton costs the same, divide the 5-ton price by the number of tons. Find 3,695 ÷ 5.

Estimate: Use compatible numbers.
3,500 ÷ 5 = 700
Will the answer be more or less than $700?

Road Salt	
Number of tons	Price
1	$ 895
2	$1,695
3	$2,395
4	$2,995
5	$3,695

$$\begin{array}{r} 7 \\ 5\overline{)3,6\,9\,5} \\ 3\,5 \\ \hline 1 \end{array}$$ Divide.
Multiply.
Subtract and compare.

$$\begin{array}{r} 7\,3 \\ 5\overline{)3,6\,9\,5} \\ 3\,5\downarrow \\ \hline 1\,9 \\ 1\,5 \\ \hline 4 \end{array}$$ Bring down.
Divide.
Multiply.
Subtract and compare.

$$\begin{array}{r} 7\,3\,9 \\ 5\overline{)3,6\,9\,5} \\ 3\,5 \\ \hline 1\,9 \\ 1\,5\downarrow \\ \hline 4\,5 \\ 4\,5 \\ \hline 0 \end{array}$$ Bring down.
Divide.
Multiply.
Subtract and compare.

The cost per ton is $739.

■ **Talk About Math** When you estimated the answer above, how did you know that the answer would be more than the estimate?

Check Understanding

For another example, see Set C, pages 142-143.

Each exercise refers to steps in the example above.
Replace the blanks with *hundred(s)*, *ten(s)*, or *one(s)*.

1. In the first step, 36 __?__ are divided by 5 to give 7 __?__ with 1 __?__ left.

2. In the second step, 1 __?__ 9 __?__ becomes 19 __?__. There are 4 __?__ left.

Divide.

3. 3)129   4. 3)442   5. 5)359   6. 5)2,567

Practice

For More Practice, see Set C, pages 144-145.

Tell whether you would use paper and pencil or mental math. Then find each quotient.

7. $6\overline{)150}$ **8.** $5\overline{)240}$ **9.** $8\overline{)375}$ **10.** $3\overline{)693}$ **11.** $4\overline{)925}$

12. $3\overline{)881}$ **13.** $8\overline{)2,449}$ **14.** $2\overline{)1,599}$ **15.** $5\overline{)1,358}$ **16.** $7\overline{)3,577}$

17. $6\overline{)5,480}$ **18.** $8\overline{)1,768}$ **19.** $8\overline{)7,133}$ **20.** $6\overline{)1,889}$ **21.** $6\overline{)5,166}$

Problem Solving

22. There was $738 budgeted for new stop signs. Each sign costs $9. How many signs can be bought?

23. For Exercise 22, suppose that $745 was budgeted for the signs. What does the remainder represent?

24. How much more does it cost per ton to buy road salt one ton at a time than to buy it in a 5-ton load?

25. **Estimation** Which is closer to 68, 4×29 or $417 \div 6$?

Reading ——— Math

Using a Glossary Find each word in the glossary. Which statement best matches the glossary definition?

1. Divisor
  a. The number which is divided into equal groups
  b. The number that divides another number
  c. The smallest number in a division sentence

2. Quotient
  a. The answer when you divide
  b. The number of correct answers on a math quiz
  c. The largest number in a division sentence

Zeros in the Quotient

Build Understanding

A. The Lincoln Junior High Pep Club sold school T-shirts to raise money for new soccer uniforms. They collected $848 from the sales. If each T-shirt sold for $8, how many T-shirts did they sell?

Since each T-shirt cost the same, divide the total by the cost per T-shirt. Find 848 ÷ 8.

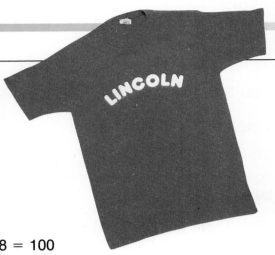

Estimate: Use compatible numbers. 800 ÷ 8 = 100

```
      1
  8)8 4 8     Divide.
    8         Multiply.
    ─         Subtract and
    0         compare.
```

```
     1 0
  8)8 4 8     Bring down.
    8 ↓       Divide. You cannot
    ───       divide 4 tens among
    0 4       8 groups.
              Write 0 in the quotient.
```

```
     1 0 6
  8)8 4 8     Bring down.
    8 ↓       Divide.
    ───       Multiply.
    0 4 8     Subtract and
      4 8     compare.
      ───
        0
```

The Pep Club sold 106 T-shirts.

B. Find $5.70 ÷ 3.

Think of $5.70 as 570 cents.
Write the answer in dollars and cents.

Has your school ever sold T-shirts to raise money for school activities?

```
      1 9 0
  3)5 7 0
    3
    ─
    2 7
    2 7
    ───
      0 0
```

```
    $1.9 0
  3)$5.7 0
    3
    ─
    2 7
    2 7
    ───
      0 0
```

■ **Talk About Math** For Example B, explain why it is necessary to write zero in the quotient.

Check Understanding

For another example, see Set D, pages 142–143.

Divide.

1. 8)165   **2.** 3)841   **3.** 4)$12.32   **4.** 6)3,604

5. Mental Math Explain how to find 3,612 ÷ 6 mentally.

Practice

For More Practice, see Set D, pages 144-145.

Tell whether you would use paper and pencil or mental math. Then find each quotient.

6. 6)365 **7.** 8)246 **8.** 7)770 **9.** 8)808 **10.** 4)435

11. 7)4,956 **12.** 6)4,321 **13.** 3)1,517 **14.** 6)4,863 **15.** 2)1,201

16. 8)$32.24 **17.** 5)$45.05 **18.** 9)$57.60 **19.** 3)$25.20 **20.** 7)$35.21

Mixed Practice **Remember** to watch the signs.

21. 208 ÷ 5 **22.** 824 + 926 **23.** 18 × 57

24. 1,280 − 571 **25.** 8 × 4,059 **26.** 7,473 ÷ 9

Problem Solving

27. The school provided $510 for 3 soccer trips. The same amount was used for each trip. How much was used for each trip?

Calculator Key in the numbers and operations in the order given. Tell the letter of the operation key that is the last one you can press so that the answer has fewer than five digits. Give that answer.

28. 49 $\overset{a}{\times}$ 87 $\overset{b}{+}$ 629 $\overset{c}{\div}$ 2 $\overset{d}{\times}$ 4 $\overset{e}{+}$ 357 $\overset{f}{-}$ 82 $\overset{g}{\div}$ 3 $\overset{h}{=}$

29. 381 $\overset{a}{+}$ 594 $\overset{b}{\div}$ 5 $\overset{c}{\times}$ 16 $\overset{d}{+}$ 5928 $\overset{e}{-}$ 827 $\overset{f}{\times}$ 2 $\overset{g}{+}$ 827 $\overset{h}{=}$

Number Sense Write the equation that is made when the operation sign shown in brackets is put in the correct place.

30. 1 0 5 5 = 21 [÷] **31.** 1 0 0 8 = 800 [×] **32.** 6 1 3 6 = 142 [+]

33. 6 0 6 6 = 101 [÷] **34.** 0 3 4 5 = 0 [×] **35.** 1 8 1 8 6 = 95 [−]

Finding Averages

Build Understanding

What is the average attendance for the four home games played so far by the Washington High football team?

Suppose that the same total number of people attended the four games but they were divided equally so that the same number attended each game. The number at each game is the average attendance.

To find the **average**, add to find the total. Then divide the sum by the number of addends.

Washington High School Home Football Games	
Opponent	Attendance
Jefferson High	3,262
Lincoln High	2,248
Madison High	2,000
Roosevelt High	1,810

Paper and Pencil

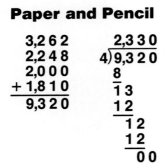

```
  3,2 6 2        2,3 3 0
  2,2 4 8     4)9,3 2 0
  2,0 0 0       8
+ 1,8 1 0      ‾13
  ‾‾‾‾‾         12
  9,3 2 0       ‾‾
                12
                12
                ‾‾
                 0 0
```

Calculator

3262 [+] 2248 [+]

2000 [+] 1810 [÷]

4 [=] *2330.*

The average attendance was 2,330.

Talk About Math Will the average attendance increase or decrease if the attendance at the fifth home game is 1,000? if the attendance at the fifth home game is 3,000? Explain your thinking.

Check Understanding

For another example, see Set E, pages 142-143.

1. Which game had the least attendance? Was the average more or less than this?

2. Which game had the greatest attendance? Was the average more or less than this?

Find the average of each group of numbers.

3. 13 4 2 9 7   **4.** 15 45 39 21   **5.** 7 12 9 19 8

6. Can the average of a group of numbers be greater than the largest number? Explain.

7. Can the average of a group of numbers be less than the smallest number? Explain.

Practice

For More Practice, see Set E, pages 144-145.

Use paper and pencil or a calculator to find the average of each group of numbers.

8. 2 7 4 5 7   **9.** 2 8 9 14 7   **10.** 18 12 10 12

11. 11 17 11 13   **12.** 14 15 26 21   **13.** 51 49 48 28

14. 156 129 144   **15.** 256 284 276   **16.** 5,254 1,226 3,351

Problem Solving

17. If only 630 people attended the fifth home game, what would be the average attendance?

18. If the team scored 168 points in 8 games, what was their average score per game?

Explore ———— Math

Calculator Use a calculator for the following exercises.

19. Press: 132 [−] 11. How many times do you have to press [=] to get a display of 0?

20. What is 132 ÷ 11?

21. Press: 177 [−] 15. How many times do you have to press [=] to get a display that is less than 15? What was the display when you stopped pressing [=]?

22. What is 177 ÷ 15?

Use the method shown in Exercises 19-22 to find each quotient.

23. 168 ÷ 12   **24.** 154 ÷ 14   **25.** 224 ÷ 18   **26.** 395 ÷ 50

Write an Equation

Build Understanding

There are many different kinds of transportation. In the deserts of Egypt, camel caravans are often used. If it took a caravan 8 days to travel 192 miles, how many miles did the caravan average each day?

Understand   The caravan covered 192 miles. It traveled for 8 days. You need to find how many miles it traveled each day if it traveled the same distance each day.

Plan and Solve   STRATEGY   *Write an equation* using n for the average distance traveled each day. Then solve the equation.

Distance traveled	Number of days	Average distance traveled each day
192 ÷	8 =	n

Estimate: $200 \div 8 = 25$

Paper and Pencil    **Calculator**

```
    2 4
  8)1 9 2
    1 6
    ---
      3 2
      3 2
      ---
        0   n = 24
```

192 ÷ 8 = 24.

$n = 24$

ANSWER   The caravan traveled an average of 24 miles each day.

Look Back   The answer is reasonable because the answer is close to the estimate. Check your division by using multiplication.

■ **Talk About Math**   Could you solve the problem using this equation: $8 \div 192 = n$? Explain why or why not.

Check Understanding

A train travels at 80 miles per hour. How far will it travel if it travels for 4 hours at this speed?

1. Which equation can you use to solve this problem?

   a. $80 \div 4 = n$ **b.** $4 \times 80 = n$

2. Solve the equation and give the answer in a sentence.

Practice

Write an equation. Then find the answer using paper and pencil or a calculator.

3. A dog sled team can travel 9 miles per hour at top speed. At this rate, how many hours will it take to travel 45 miles?

4. During a cruise, an ocean liner traveled 792 miles one day and 625 miles the next day. How far did it travel?

5. In quiet water, two people can paddle a canoe about 4 miles per hour. At this rate, if they paddled 96 miles, how many hours would it take?

6. In one hour, one of the fastest passenger trains can travel 228 miles and a jet can travel 552 miles. How much farther can the jet travel in one hour?

7. It might take you 324 hours to bicycle across the United States, coast to coast. If you walked this distance, it would probably take 3 times as long. How long would it take to walk?

Skills _____ **Review** pages 14-15, 22-23, 26-27, 30-31

Add or subtract. **Remember** to watch the signs.

1. 245 + 83	**2.** 943 − 72	**3.** 604 − 375
4. 654 + 928	**5.** 8,241 − 657	**6.** 5,926 + 3,829
7. 8,749 − 3,868	**8.** 35,284 + 8,391	**9.** 29,016 − 3,825
10. 98,347 − 29,492	**11.** 45,972 + 38,251	**12.** 34,258 + 95,114

Missing Factors

Build Understanding

A. Multiply or Divide?
Materials: 100 small objects
Groups: 4-6 students each

Number of groups	×	Number in each group	=	Total number
	×		=	
	×		=	

a. Each group splits into two teams, Team A and Team B. Each team should make a record sheet like the one at the right.

b. Team A organizes some of the objects into groups with the same number of objects in each group. Team A can use some or all of the objects. The objects should be grouped into 3 to 9 groups. Team B should not see what Team A is doing. Team A records the information on its record sheet.

c. Team A gives the objects it used to Team B with a clue that tells how many groups to use. Team B records the total number of objects and the number of groups on its record sheet. Team B groups the objects to find the correct number in each group, records the information, and compares its record with Team A's record.

d. What operation is Team B showing when it organizes the objects in this way?

e. The teams switch jobs and go through the steps again with a different number of objects. The teams should do this several times.

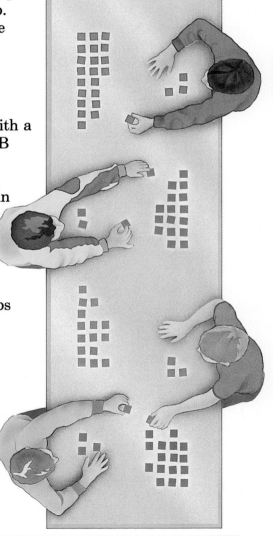

B. Find the missing factor in $3 \times n = 42$.

Divide to find the missing factor.

$$3 \times n = 42$$
$$n = 42 \div 3$$
$$n = 14$$

$$
\begin{array}{r}
14 \\
3\overline{)42} \\
3 \\
\hline
12 \\
12 \\
\hline
0
\end{array}
$$

■ **Write About Math** To find a missing factor, it is helpful to think of a family of facts such as the family shown at the right. Which fact would help you to find n in $4 \times n = 56$?

$$4 \times n = 56 \qquad 56 \div 4 = n$$
$$n \times 4 = 56 \qquad 56 \div n = 4$$

Write a family of facts for the equation in Example B.

Check Understanding

For another example, see Set F, pages 142-143.

Find the missing factor. Use families of facts to help.

1. $n \times 7 = 98$　　**2.** $864 = n \times 8$　　**3.** $7 \times n = 3,549$

Practice

For More Practice, see Set F, pages 144-145.

Find the missing factor. Use paper and pencil or a calculator.

4. $3 \times n = 57$　　**5.** $n \times 3 = 87$　　**6.** $252 = 9 \times n$

7. $n \times 8 = 544$　　**8.** $8 \times n = 688$　　**9.** $n \times 6 = 2,364$

10. $1,981 = 7 \times n$　　**11.** $4,445 = n \times 5$　　**12.** $4 \times n = 3,488$

13. $n \times 6 = 3,288$　　**14.** $9 \times n = 9,873$　　**15.** $3,928 = 4 \times n$

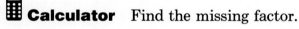 **Calculator** Find the missing factor.

16. $37 \times n = 185$　　**17.** $4,526 = 73 \times n$　　**18.** $4,234 = n \times 58$

Problem Solving

19. What is the missing factor if $8 \times n$ is as close as possible to 83?

20. What is the missing factor if $n \times 8$ is as close as possible to 162?

21. What is the missing factor if $n \times 8$ is as close as possible to 478?

22. What is the missing factor if $6 \times n$ is the least multiple of 6 that is greater than 65?

23. What is the missing factor if $n \times 6$ is a multiple of 6 that is closest to but less than 357?

24. What is the missing factor if $6 \times n$ is a multiple of 6 that is between 181 and 191?

Problem-Solving Review

Solve each problem.

1. Van has 97 flower bulbs. If he plants the same number of bulbs in each of 6 rows, how many bulbs will be in each row? How many will be left over?

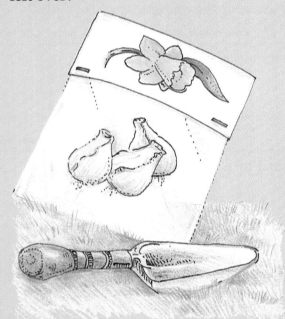

2. The product of two numbers is 91. Their sum is 20. What are the numbers?

3. There are 5,280 feet in 1 mile. If 4 people run a mile relay race, how far should each person run?

4. A baseball and a football cost a total of $27.88. The baseball costs $6.90. How much did the football cost?

5. If basketballs cost $14.75 each, how much will 6 basketballs cost?

6. In the past 4 days, Roger practiced the piano for 55 minutes, 65 minutes, 40 minutes, and 72 minutes. What was his average practice time?

7. You have 22 meters of fencing that comes in 1-meter sections. What is the greatest rectangular area you can enclose?

8. **Data File** Find the average cost of flying round-trip from Chicago to the cities shown on the chart on pages 244–245.

9. **Make a Data File** Find out how old the past 8 United States presidents were when they became president. What was the average age?

140

Explore with a Calculator

"Dividing the Treasure"

1. Play this game with a friend.

Exercises

Think about how you could key in the check facts on your calculator to find the remainder.

Press	Display
8 ÷ 5 =	1.6
10 ÷ 4 =	2.5
189 ÷ 6 =	31.5
7,162 ÷ 5 =	1,432.4
162 ÷ 7 =	23.142857
94 ÷ 7 =	13.428571
1,369 ÷ 3 =	456.33333
4,987 ÷ 8 =	623.375

Rules

• Each player chooses one of the division exercises below and finds the remainder using a calculator. During the game, an exercise may only be chosen once.
• The remainder tells each player how many squares the player may move.
• The first person to reach the buried treasure wins the game.

Check Facts
Think: 5 × 1 + ? = 8
Think: 4 × 2 + ? = 10

2. Make up some division exercises with remainders of 1, 2, or 3. Then play another game with your friend.

START

ADVANCE 2 SPACES

GO BACK 1 SPACE

LOSE 1 TURN

JAIL

GO TO JAIL

Reteaching

Set A pages 122–123

Find 327 ÷ 6.

```
      5              Quotient → 5 4 R3
  6)3 2 7      Divisor → 6)3 2 7 ← Dividend
    3 0                        3 0 ↓
      2                          2 7
                                 2 4
                                   3 ← Remainder
```

Remember to check the quotient by multiplying the quotient times the divisor and adding the remainder. This number and the dividend should be the same.

Divide.

1. 2)17   2. 8)33

3. 7)51   4. 4)31

5. 5)39   6. 4)254

7. 6)417   8. 8)628

9. 9)795   10. 5)439

Set B pages 126–127

Estimate 344 ÷ 9 using compatible numbers.

Choose numbers close to 344, 9, or both, that are easy to divide.

Think: 350 ÷ 10 = 35
         or 360 ÷ 9 = 40

Remember that there is more than one way to choose compatible numbers.

Estimate each quotient using compatible numbers.

1. 238 ÷ 6   2. 408 ÷ 7

3. 316 ÷ 4   4. 278 ÷ 5

5. 512 ÷ 9   6. 543 ÷ 8

7. 369 ÷ 7   8. 416 ÷ 6

9. 511 ÷ 5   10. 387 ÷ 9

Set C pages 130–131

Find 5,968 ÷ 8.

Estimate: Use compatible numbers.
          5,600 ÷ 8 = 700

```
          7 4 6
      8)5,9 6 8
        5 6 ↓ |
          3 6  |
          3 2 ↓
            4 8
            4 8
              0
```

Remember to estimate the quotient first to see if your answer is reasonable.

Tell whether you would use paper and pencil or mental math. Then find each quotient.

1. 5)450   2. 6)486

3. 7)440   4. 4)873

5. 8)648   6. 9)3,799

7. 6)1,478   8. 7)2,718

9. 9)4,797   10. 5)4,386

Set D pages 132–133

Find $832 \div 4$.

Estimate: Use compatible numbers.
$$800 \div 4 = 200$$

```
     2          2 0         2 0 8
4)8 3 2     4)8 3 2     4)8 3 2
  8           8↓           8  ↓
  0           0 3          0 3 2
                             3 2
                               0
```

Remember to write zeros in the quotient when needed. Tell whether you would use paper and pencil or mental math. Then find each quotient.

1. $4\overline{)323}$ **2.** $6\overline{)606}$

3. $7\overline{)4,221}$ **4.** $5\overline{)2,850}$

5. $3\overline{)1,229}$ **6.** $4\overline{)1,603}$

7. $8\overline{)4,165}$ **8.** $6\overline{)5,344}$

Set E pages 134–135

Find the average of this group of numbers.

41   52   48   43

To find the average:
  first, add to find the total,
  then divide the sum by the
  number of addends.

```
  4 1              4 6 ← Average
  5 2          4)1 8 4
  4 8            1 6
+ 4 3            ─────
─────            2 4
1 8 4            2 4
                 ─────
                   0
```

Remember that the average of a group of numbers cannot be greater than the largest number or smaller than the smallest number.

Use paper and pencil or a calculator to find the average of each group of numbers.

1. 7   5   4   8   6

2. 185   196   151   168

3. 2,341   1,846   2,860

Set F pages 138–139

Find the missing factor in

$4 \times n = 208.$

Divide by 4 to find the missing factor.

$n = 208 \div 4$

```
      5 2
4)2 0 8
  2 0
  ─────
    0 8
      8
    ─────
      0
n = 52
```

Remember that it is helpful to think of a family of facts. Find the missing factor.

1. $5 \times n = 185$

2. $n \times 3 = 93$

3. $288 = n \times 8$

4. $7 \times n = 3,073$

5. $2,892 = 6 \times n$

143

More Practice

Set A   pages 122–123

Divide. **Remember** to check your work.

1. $3\overline{)17}$ 2. $8\overline{)59}$ 3. $6\overline{)38}$ 4. $5\overline{)36}$ 5. $4\overline{)29}$

6. $9\overline{)84}$ 7. $6\overline{)84}$ 8. $7\overline{)91}$ 9. $4\overline{)86}$ 10. $5\overline{)89}$

11. $4\overline{)298}$ 12. $5\overline{)328}$ 13. $6\overline{)326}$ 14. $7\overline{)579}$ 15. $8\overline{)554}$

16. $6\overline{)567}$ 17. $4\overline{)390}$ 18. $5\overline{)423}$ 19. $8\overline{)634}$ 20. $9\overline{)569}$

21. $84 \div 9$ 22. $78 \div 7$ 23. $706 \div 8$ 24. $507 \div 6$

Set B   pages 126–127

Use mental math to find each quotient. Tell what strategy you used.

1. $366 \div 6$ 2. $90 \div 5$ 3. $140 \div 5$ 4. $248 \div 4$

5. $96 \div 8$ 6. $328 \div 8$ 7. $180 \div 9$ 8. $155 \div 5$

9. $219 \div 3$ 10. $287 \div 7$ 11. $168 \div 8$ 12. $240 \div 5$

13. Choose two of the exercises above. Explain why you chose the strategy you used.

Estimate each quotient using compatible numbers.

14. $196 \div 9$ 15. $430 \div 8$ 16. $558 \div 8$ 17. $619 \div 7$

18. $341 \div 7$ 19. $717 \div 9$ 20. $536 \div 6$ 21. $338 \div 5$

22. Choose two of the exercises above. Explain why you chose the compatible numbers you used.

Set C   pages 130–131

Tell whether you would use paper and pencil or mental math. Then find each quotient.

1. $8\overline{)176}$ 2. $6\overline{)283}$ 3. $5\overline{)320}$ 4. $9\overline{)738}$ 5. $7\overline{)226}$

6. $4\overline{)946}$ 7. $8\overline{)3,289}$ 8. $6\overline{)1,866}$ 9. $2\overline{)1,359}$ 10. $5\overline{)4,207}$

11. $6\overline{)2,597}$ 12. $8\overline{)5,752}$ 13. $7\overline{)1,575}$ 14. $3\overline{)1,783}$ 15. $5\overline{)4,643}$

16. $4\overline{)3,347}$ 17. $6\overline{)3,889}$ 18. $9\overline{)6,417}$ 19. $7\overline{)4,379}$ 20. $8\overline{)6,586}$

Set D pages 132–133

Tell whether you would use paper and pencil or mental
math. Then find each quotient.

1. $7\overline{)426}$　　2. $6\overline{)304}$　　3. $9\overline{)457}$　　4. $8\overline{)872}$　　5. $3\overline{)624}$

6. $6\overline{)5,430}$　　7. $2\overline{)1,618}$　　8. $9\overline{)1,807}$　　9. $4\overline{)1,840}$　　10. $8\overline{)3,247}$

11. $8\overline{)\$56.24}$　　12. $6\overline{)\$13.20}$　　13. $3\overline{)\$10.50}$　　14. $6\overline{)\$19.20}$　　15. $2\overline{)\$18.16}$

Mixed Practice　**Remember** to watch the signs.

16. $738 + 862$　　17. 17×48　　18. $1,470 - 482$

19. $7 \times 3,046$　　20. $309 \div 6$　　21. $6 \times 2,108$

22. $946 + 485$　　23. $2,376 - 1,469$　　24. $8,345 \div 9$

Set E pages 134–135

Use paper and pencil or a calculator to find the average of
each group of numbers.

1. 8　7　5　6　4　　2. 15　10　12　11　　3. 16　12　18　10

4. 18　13　14　15　　5. 19　14　21　18　　6. 52　45　44　47

7. 151　133　154　　8. 280　255　248　　9. 4,263　1,819　1,367

Set F pages 138–139

Find the missing factor.

1. $4 \times n = 96$　　2. $n \times 2 = 86$　　3. $432 = 8 \times n$

4. $n \times 6 = 318$　　5. $9 \times n = 711$　　6. $n \times 7 = 2,009$

7. $3,415 = n \times 5$　　8. $2,748 = n \times 4$　　9. $n \times 6 = 5,544$

10. $n \times 8 = 5,528$　　11. $7 \times n = 8,442$　　12. $3,174 = 3 \times n$

Calculator　Find the missing factor.

13. $43 \times n = 387$　　14. $3,886 = 67 \times n$　　15. $5,056 = 79 \times n$

16. $n \times 53 = 4,081$　　17. $5,762 = n \times 86$　　18. $7,644 = n \times 91$

Enrichment

Short Division

With one-digit divisors, you can save time and space by using the short form of division.

This shows the long form and the short form for 2,402 ÷ 7.

Long form

```
     3           34           343 R1
7)2,402      7)2,402      7)2,402
  21           21           21
   3           30           30
               28           28
                2           22
                            21
                             1
```

Short form

```
     3           3 4          3 4 3 R1
7)2,4³0 2    7)2,4³0²2     7)2,4³0²2
```

Divide. Use the short form.

1. 3)46   **2.** 8)395   **3.** 4)274   **4.** 6)745   **5.** 5)548

6. 7)751   **7.** 8)6,592   **8.** 3)1,362   **9.** 5)3,025   **10.** 8)4,163

11. 9)3,457   **12.** 7)5,106   **13.** 9)3,656   **14.** 8)4,237   **15.** 9)3,821

16. 7)2,656   **17.** 7)6,734   **18.** 4)2,987   **19.** 5)3,212   **20.** 8)9,673

Chapter 4 Review/Test

Divide.

1. $5\overline{)93}$ 2. $7\overline{)226}$

3. $6\overline{)5,321}$ 4. $9\overline{)4,188}$

5. $4\overline{)521}$ 6. $8\overline{)1,601}$

Estimate each quotient using compatible numbers.

7. $252 \div 5$ 8. $598 \div 6$

9. Suppose you break apart 318 in order to find $318 \div 3$ mentally. Should you use $300 + 18$ or $310 + 8$?

Find the average of each group of numbers.

10. 3 5 8 12

11. 54 80 91 95 100

12. 1,238 1,367 1,520

Find the missing factor.

13. $4 \times n = 84$

14. $n \times 6 = 228$

15. $9 \times n = 2,322$

16. If the average of 5 numbers is 9, could the largest number be 8? Explain.

Solve each problem.

17. Miss Watkins bought 4 new tires for $268. What was the cost of each tire?

18. Use try and check to find two numbers that have a sum of 17 and a product of 30.

19. Use the table below to find the average daily sales for the days shown.

Daily Sales

Monday	$786
Tuesday	$824
Wednesday	$767
Thursday	$825
Friday	$1,028

Read this problem. Then answer the questions below.

A machine produces 88 parts per hour. How many parts can the machine produce in 8 hours?

20. Which sentence could be completed to answer the question?

   a. The machine produces ▦ parts in 1 hour.
   b. The machine takes ▦ hours to produce 88 parts.
   c. In 8 hours the machine produces ▦ parts.

21. Write an equation and solve the problem.

22. **Write About Math** When you divide a number by 8, what is the greatest remainder you can get? Explain your answer.

Division with Two-Digit Divisors

Did You Know: Tolls are not only charged on roads, but they are also charged on some bridges, canals, and ferries.

Number-Sense Project

Estimate
Estimate how much money will be collected by 4 automatic toll gates during 1 hour of heavy traffic. Each car must pay a toll of 25¢.

Gather Data
Make your estimate and then gather estimates from 4 other people.

Analyze and Report
Compare your results with those of other students. Are there any patterns in the estimates? Do people in any age group tend to estimate higher than people in other groups?

Mental Math for Division

Build Understanding

A. Sgt. Wilson is a forest ranger. One of his duties is to collect information on bears in order to help decide which camps and trails should be closed due to danger from bears. During a 20-day span of time, there were 140 bear sightings reported by campers. What was the average number of sightings per day for this time?

Find 140 ÷ 20 using mental math.

Here is a mental math strategy that you can use when dividing mentally. Look for *special numbers* that are easy to divide.

140 ÷ 20 = 7   Think: 14 ÷ 2 = 7
So, 14 tens ÷ 2 tens = 7

The average number was 7 bear sightings per day.

B. Find 6,000 ÷ 30 mentally using special numbers.

You know 6 ÷ 3 = 2.
Think: 60 ÷ 30 = 2 since 30 × 2 = 60.
   600 ÷ 30 = 20 since 30 × 20 = 600.
   6,000 ÷ 30 = 200 since 30 × 200 = 6,000.

6,000 ÷ 30 = 200

C. Find 187 ÷ 30.

Another mental math strategy that you can use is to look for numbers that you can **break apart** into numbers that are easy to divide.

Think: 187 = 180 + 7

$$30\overline{)187}$$ Think:
$$30\overline{)180}^{6}$$ $$30\overline{)187}^{\,6\ R7}$$

■ **Write About Math**   Write a multiplication sentence that will help you find 2,400 ÷ 20 mentally.

150

Check Understanding

For another example, see Set A, pages 174–175.

Copy and complete.

1. $4,000 \div 10 = \blacksquare 00$

2. $800 \div 40 = 2\blacksquare$

3. $1,000 \div 50 = \blacksquare\blacksquare$

4. Find $180 \div 60$ using special numbers.

5. Find $368 \div 40$ by breaking apart one number.

Practice

For More Practice, see Set A, pages 176–177.

Use mental math to find each quotient. Tell which strategy you used.

6. $400 \div 40$

7. $80 \div 20$

8. $240 \div 80$

9. $254 \div 50$

10. $640 \div 80$

11. $491 \div 70$

12. $9,000 \div 30$

13. $326 \div 80$

14. $6,300 \div 90$

15. $180 \div 30$

16. $10,000 \div 20$

17. $452 \div 90$

18. Choose three of the exercises above. Explain why you chose the strategy you used.

Problem Solving

Use the information in the table. There are 30 days in April and June and 31 days in May. **Remember** to use mental math when it is helpful.

Ridge Park Bear Sightings			
Camp	April	May	June
North	0	0	0
South	60	50	20
East	51	160	35
West	26	40	5

19. What was the average number of bear sightings reported per day in April at the North Camp?

20. What was the average number of bear sightings reported per day in April at the South Camp?

21. How many bear sightings were reported in May in Ridge Park?

22. What is the average number of bear sightings reported per day in June in Ridge Park?

Estimating Quotients

Build Understanding

How many coins do you think the average person carries each day? One day, data was gathered from 31 people. Together they had a total of 157 coins. About how many coins did each person have?

Estimate 157 ÷ 31.

You can use **compatible numbers** as an estimation strategy when estimating quotients.

Substitute numbers that are close to the original numbers for the divisor, the dividend, or both. Choose numbers so you can divide easily.

157 ÷ 31   Think: 150 ÷ 30 = 5

Each person had about 5 coins.

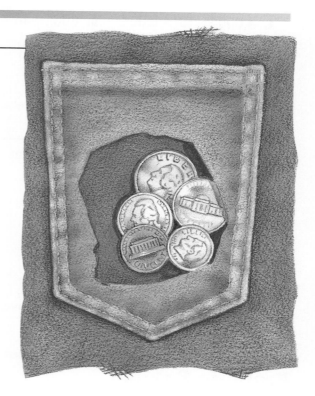

■ **Write About Math**   Often there can be more than one way to choose compatible numbers when estimating a quotient. List the compatible numbers that could be used for 358 ÷ 46 and for 4,581 ÷ 64.

Check Understanding

For another example, see Set B, pages 174–175.

Suppose you are to estimate the quotient of each of the given numbers divided by 60. What compatible number would you use for the given number?

1. 358   **2.** 661   **3.** 1,187   **4.** 6,258

5. Name some 2-digit numbers that would be compatible with 4,000 in 4,000 ÷ ▦▦.

Estimate each quotient. Tell what compatible numbers you used.

6. 345 ÷ 49   **7.** 421 ÷ 21   **8.** 4,611 ÷ 47   **9.** 8,109 ÷ 87

Practice

For More Practice, see Set B, pages 176–177.

Estimate each quotient. Tell what compatible numbers you used.

10. $554 \div 59$ **11.** $498 \div 49$ **12.** $349 \div 62$ **13.** $251 \div 39$

14. $816 \div 79$ **15.** $389 \div 41$ **16.** $634 \div 82$ **17.** $341 \div 73$

18. $7{,}209 \div 78$ **19.** $3{,}179 \div 83$ **20.** $2{,}438 \div 49$ **21.** $2{,}917 \div 63$

22. $8{,}221 \div 41$ **23.** $6{,}053 \div 59$ **24.** $8{,}905 \div 31$ **25.** $5{,}426 \div 62$

Problem Solving

26. If 21 people had 137 coins, give an estimate of about how many coins each person had.

27. If you have $5 in quarters, how many quarters do you have?

28. How much change will you get if you pay a $17.42 grocery bill with a twenty-dollar bill?

29. If you have 3 quarters, 2 dimes, 4 nickels, and 8 pennies, how much money do you have?

Reading ——— Math

Numbers and Symbols A bicycle club planned to ride a total of ___a___ miles on a trip Saturday. They plan to cover ___b___ miles in the morning. How many miles will they have left for the afternoon?

1. Describe what a represents.   **2.** Describe what b represents.

3. Which tells how to solve the problem? $a + b$ $a - b$ $a \div b$

The members of the club keep a record of the number of miles they ride each month. There are ___c___ members in the club. In June, the members rode a total of ___d___ miles. What is the average number of miles each member rode in June?

4. Describe what c represents.   **5.** Describe what d represents.

6. Which tells how to solve the problem? $c \div d$ $c \times d$ $d \div c$

One-Digit Quotients

Build Understanding

A. Division
Materials: Place-value materials
Groups: 3-4 students

a. You are to find the number in each group if 112 is divided equally into 18 groups. First show the number 112 with place-value materials.

c. Trade the tens for ones and divide. How many are in each group? Record your results.

b. Can you divide 1 hundred into 18 groups? Trade 1 hundred for 10 tens. Do you have enough tens to divide them into 18 groups?

d. Model the division for several other problems. Take turns deciding the number to divide and the number in each group. Use dividends of 120 or less and two-digit divisors. Record your results.

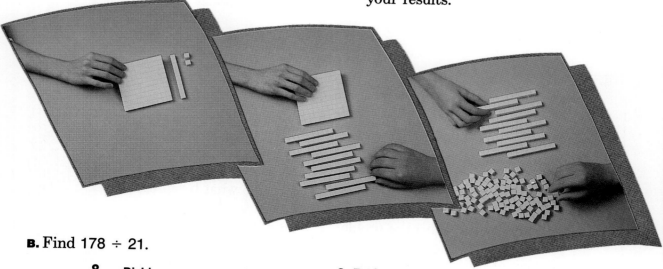

B. Find 178 ÷ 21.

$$\begin{array}{r} 8 \\ 21\overline{)178} \end{array}$$

Divide.
To find 178 ÷ 21, think: what is 17 ÷ 2? 8

$$\begin{array}{r} 8 \text{ R10} \\ 21\overline{)178} \\ \underline{168} \\ 10 \end{array}$$

Multiply.
Subtract and compare.

■ **Talk About Math** In Example B, explain why the 8 is placed above the digit in the ones place of the dividend.

154

Check Understanding

For another example, see Set C, pages 174–175.

Exercises 1-4 refer to Example B.

1. Why was 8 used as the quotient?

2. Where does the number 168 come from?

3. The last step is "Subtract and compare." What do you compare?

4. Explain how you would check this division.

Divide.

5. $31\overline{)96}$ **6.** $11\overline{)58}$ **7.** $23\overline{)138}$ **8.** $52\overline{)417}$ **9.** $71\overline{)570}$

Practice

For More Practice, see Set C, pages 176-177.

Tell whether you would use paper and pencil or mental math.
Then find each quotient.

10. $32\overline{)39}$ **11.** $23\overline{)98}$ **12.** $37\overline{)74}$ **13.** $20\overline{)87}$ **14.** $12\overline{)49}$

15. $40\overline{)98}$ **16.** $31\overline{)87}$ **17.** $50\overline{)350}$ **18.** $42\overline{)336}$ **19.** $54\overline{)165}$

20. $51\overline{)153}$ **21.** $30\overline{)601}$ **22.** $83\overline{)664}$ **23.** $43\overline{)175}$ **24.** $40\overline{)210}$

25. $58\overline{)182}$ **26.** $87\overline{)451}$ **27.** $60\overline{)305}$ **28.** $62\overline{)251}$ **29.** $74\overline{)166}$

Problem Solving

30. Liza watched a 90-minute television program. Write this time in hours and minutes.

31. Ed is 49 inches tall. Write this height in feet and inches.

32. Use Data Use the information in the table on page 151. What was the total number of bear sightings reported in April for Ridge Park?

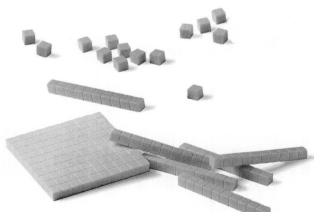

Estimation Louis used compatible numbers to estimate $2,485 \div 55$.

33. What compatible numbers did he use if his estimate was 50?

34. What compatible numbers did he use if his estimate was 40?

Adjusting the Quotient

Build Understanding

A. Mrs. Saito's science class was conducting experiments with eggs. There were 184 eggs to be shared equally among 23 students. How many eggs was this per student?

Find 184 ÷ 23.

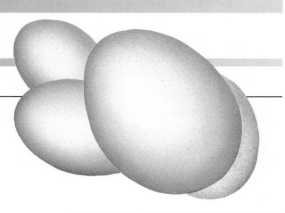

The shell of an egg contains pores so water and gases can pass through it.

Estimate: Use compatible numbers. 180 ÷ 20 = 9

Paper and Pencil

```
      9
2 3)1 8 4
  2 0 7
```
Divide.
Think:
What is 18 ÷ 2? 9
Multiply.
207 is greater than 184.

```
      8
2 3)1 8 4
  1 8 4
      0
```
Try 8.
Multiply.
Subtract and compare.

Calculator

184 ÷

23 = *8.*

Each student received 8 eggs.

B. Find 418 ÷ 42.

```
4 2)4 1 8
```
Divide.
Think:
What is 41 ÷ 4? 10
Since 10 × 42 is 420,
there are less than 10.

```
      9 R 40
4 2)4 1 8
  3 7 8
    4 0
```
Try 9.
Multiply.
Subtract and compare.

c.  **Calculator** Find 532 ÷ 56.

532 ÷ 56 = *9.5*

■ **Talk About Math** For Example A, explain where the number 207 came from and describe what it tells you about the quotient.

Check Understanding

For another example, see Set D, pages 174–175.

1. In the problem at the right, how was 6 selected for the quotient?

2. How do you know 6 will not work?

3. What number should you try next? Does it work?

4. What is the answer?

```
        6
1 4)6 8
    8 4
```

Divide.

5. $28\overline{)112}$ **6.** $12\overline{)90}$ **7.** $76\overline{)149}$ **8.** $12\overline{)57}$ **9.** $37\overline{)344}$

Practice

For More Practice, see Set D, pages 176–177.

Use paper and pencil or a calculator. Show each
answer as a quotient with a whole-number remainder
(if there is one) or as a decimal with one digit after
the decimal point.

10. $27\overline{)135}$ **11.** $29\overline{)116}$ **12.** $12\overline{)96}$ **13.** $68\overline{)375}$ **14.** $47\overline{)329}$

15. $38\overline{)228}$ **16.** $12\overline{)59}$ **17.** $14\overline{)55}$ **18.** $36\overline{)295}$ **19.** $26\overline{)159}$

20. $29\overline{)68}$ **21.** $58\overline{)103}$ **22.** $57\overline{)415}$ **23.** $96\overline{)642}$ **24.** $13\overline{)93}$

25. $15\overline{)53}$ **26.** $48\overline{)452}$ **27.** $19\overline{)49}$ **28.** $78\overline{)767}$ **29.** $86\overline{)832}$

Problem Solving

Eggs are sized by weight. The table at the right
gives information about egg classifications.

30. What is the minimum weight for
1 dozen medium eggs?

31. What is the minimum weight for
4 dozen large eggs?

32. If 5 dozen eggs weighed 150 ounces,
what kind of eggs were they?

33. What is the minimum weight for
48 extra large eggs?

34. The age of an egg can be tested using a float test.
A fresh egg will sink to the bottom of a container
of water and rest on its side. If 184 eggs were
tested and 135 of them sank and rested on their
sides, how many eggs were not fresh?

Egg Classifications

Weight class	Minimum weight per dozen
Small	18 ounces
Medium	21 ounces
Large	24 ounces
Extra Large	27 ounces
Jumbo	30 ounces

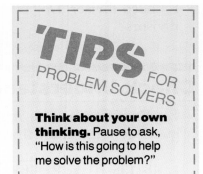

TIPS FOR PROBLEM SOLVERS

Think about your own thinking. Pause to ask, "How is this going to help me solve the problem?"

Using Rounded Divisors

Build Understanding

A. As you saw in the last lesson, sometimes you need to adjust your first try for the quotient because the quotient is too big. Sometimes it is helpful to round the divisor and use the rounded divisor to find the quotient.

Find 259 ÷ 38.

```
      6 R31
38)259    Divide.
   228    Think: 38 rounds to 40.
    31          What is 25 ÷ 4? 6
          Multiply.
          Subtract and compare.
```

When you use a rounded divisor to find the quotient, *be sure to use the actual divisor* when you multiply.

B. Sometimes when a rounded divisor is used, the first try for the quotient is too small, and the quotient must be adjusted.

Find 198 ÷ 28.

```
       6      Divide.                    7 R2
28)198        Think: 28 rounds to 30.  28)198      Try 7.
   168              What is 19 ÷ 3? 6      196      Multiply.
    30        Multiply.                      2      Subtract and compare.
              Subtract and compare.
              30 is greater than 28,
              so 6 is too small.
```

■ **Talk About Math** For both Examples A and B, tell what quotient you would have tried if you did not use a rounded divisor. Do you think it is helpful to use rounded divisors?

Check Understanding

For another example, see Set E, pages 174–175.

For Exercises 1-4, use rounded divisors. Tell what quotient you will try first. Then give the answer.

1. 48)139   **2.** 21)162   **3.** 39)196   **4.** 426 ÷ 58

158

Practice

For More Practice, see Set E, pages 176–177.

Use paper and pencil or a calculator. Show each answer
as a quotient with a whole-number remainder (if there is
one) or as a decimal with one digit after the decimal point.

5. 37)293 **6.** 77)691 **7.** 68)233 **8.** 19)146 **9.** 18)125

10. 89)573 **11.** 47)421 **12.** 56)501 **13.** 58)243 **14.** 48)153

15. 199 ÷ 39 **16.** 150 ÷ 17 **17.** 125 ÷ 16 **18.** 274 ÷ 67

Mixed Practice   Tell whether you would use paper and pencil,
a calculator, or mental math. Then find each answer.

19. 8,000 + 2,351 **20.** 3,421 − 2,985 **21.** 42 × 97 **22.** 364 ÷ 4

23. 5 × 804 **24.** 6,525 ÷ 8 **25.** 372 ÷ 81 **26.** 458 + 927

27. 342 × 9 **28.** 6,000 ÷ 30 **29.** 984 ÷ 27 **30.** 348 × 129

Problem Solving

31. Mental Math   Which of the following will help
you find 10,000 ÷ 200 mentally?

200 × 500   200 × 50

32. Number Sense   Find the missing digits
in the division problem at the right.
There is no remainder.

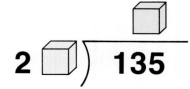

$2\,\square\,)\,\overline{135}$

Midchapter ✓ Checkup

Use mental math to find each
quotient.

1. 1,200 ÷ 40   **2.** 425 ÷ 60

Use compatible numbers to estimate
each quotient.

3. 3,498 ÷ 51   **4.** 2,543 ÷ 49

Divide.

5. 54)335   **6.** 13)118   **7.** 39)248   **8.** 26)135   **9.** 87)349

Problem Solving WORKSHOP

Number-Sense Project

Look back at pages 148-149.
A group of several students organized their data in three rows, one row for each age group.

1. How many adults did these students interview?

2. How many people in all did these students interview?

3. How many adults estimated that less than $100 was collected in an hour?

4. If $3,024.00 was collected in a day, what was the average amount per hour?

5. One type of automatic toll gate allows 1 car to pass every 4 seconds. If the toll is $0.25 per car, how much money would be collected in 1 hour by 4 of these gates during heavy traffic?

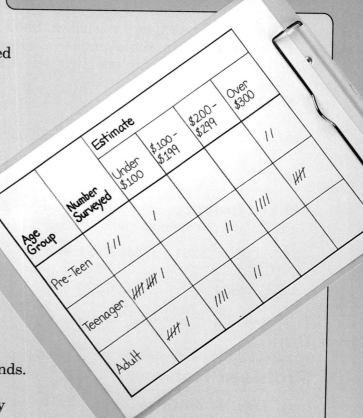

Age Group	Number Surveyed	Estimate			
		Under $100	$100 – $199	$200 – $299	Over $300
Pre-Teen	III	I		II	II
Teenager	HHH HHH I			IIII	IIII
Adult	HHH I			II	

Visual Thinking Activity

Here are four views of the same cube.

1. What color is opposite red?

2. What color is opposite orange?

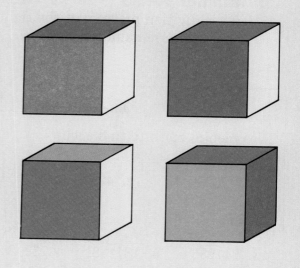

MATH laugh

Why is SMILES the longest word in the English language?

ANSWER:
Because there is a mile between the two Ss.

Real-Life Decision Making

On June 1, you have $70 to spend on your summer vacation. You get $5 a week allowance. You plan to ride horses at Gallager's Stables 10 to 15 times during the summer. You also need money for the movies and other summer activities.

1. If you pay separately for each horseback ride, what is the least amount of money you will spend?

2. If you buy a summer pass but ride only 10 times, how much money will be wasted?

3. If you buy a summer pass and ride 15 times, how much money will you save?

4. Decide how you will spend your money during summer vacation.

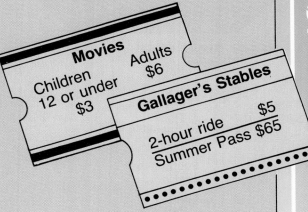

Movies
Children 12 or under $3
Adults $6

Gallager's Stables
2-hour ride $5
Summer Pass $65

Math-at-Home Activity

Take a survey of 9 people who live with or near you. Ask them if they think the same side of the moon always faces earth. Graph the results.

Does Same Side of Moon Always Face Earth?

Yes									
No									
	1	2	3	4	5	6	7	8	9

Number of answers

Two-Digit Quotients

Build Understanding

The drive from St. Louis to New Orleans is about 768 miles. If you used 24 gallons of gasoline on this trip, how many miles per gallon did you average?

Find 768 ÷ 24.

Estimate: Use compatible numbers. 800 ÷ 20 = 40   Will the answer be more or less than the estimate?

Each car in the U.S. uses an average of about 700 gallons of gasoline each year.

Calculator

768 ÷ 24 = *32.*

Paper and Pencil

$$\begin{array}{r} 3 \\ 24\overline{)768} \\ 72 \\ \hline 4 \end{array}$$

Divide.
Think:
24 rounds to 20.
What is 7 ÷ 2? 3
Multiply.
Subtract and compare.

$$\begin{array}{r} 32 \\ 24\overline{)768} \\ 72\downarrow \\ \hline 48 \\ 48 \\ \hline 0 \end{array}$$

Bring down.
Divide.
Think:
What is 4 ÷ 2? 2
Multiply.
Subtract and compare.

You averaged 32 miles per gallon.

■ **Talk About Math** When you estimated the answer above, how did you know that the answer would be less than the estimate?

Check Understanding

For another example, see Set F, pages 174–175.

1. **Estimation** Use compatible numbers to estimate the answers to Exercises 2-5.

Divide.

2. 32)544   **3.** 42)3,913   **4.** 27)605   **5.** 3,087 ÷ 58

Practice

For More Practice, see Set F, pages 176–177.

Use paper and pencil or a calculator. Show each answer as a
quotient with a whole-number remainder (if there is one) or as
a decimal with one digit after the decimal point. **Remember**
to estimate to tell if the answer is reasonable.

6. $20\overline{)920}$ **7.** $30\overline{)840}$ **8.** $43\overline{)995}$ **9.** $70\overline{)5,844}$ **10.** $80\overline{)3,511}$

11. $71\overline{)999}$ **12.** $38\overline{)871}$ **13.** $28\overline{)653}$ **14.** $73\overline{)4,535}$ **15.** $54\overline{)1,739}$

16. $611 \div 18$ **17.** $968 \div 39$ **18.** $2,325 \div 68$ **19.** $1,989 \div 58$

Problem Solving

Explore _____ Math

Calculator Sometimes the answer to a
word problem that is solved by division is the
remainder. But if you have used your calculator
to divide, the calculator will not show the
remainder.

Suppose you need to find the remainder for $6,591 \div 92$.

20. Enter the division problem and
press $\boxed{=}$. What is the display?

21. What is the whole-number part
of the display? This is the
quotient.

22. Multiply the quotient by the
divisor. What is the result?

23. Subtract from the dividend to
find the remainder. What is the
remainder?

Find each quotient and remainder using a calculator.
24. $842 \div 15$ **25.** $916 \div 18$ **26.** $789 \div 25$ **27.** $941 \div 42$

28. Describe how you could use the memory keys
to simplify this procedure.

Use your idea to find the quotient and remainder for the following.
29. $2,456 \div 37$ **30.** $3,613 \div 41$ **31.** $6,250 \div 98$ **32.** $4,978 \div 83$

Interpret the Remainder

PROBLEM SOLVING
GUIDE

Understand
QUESTION
FACTS
KEY IDEA

▌▙▶ **Plan and Solve**
STRATEGY
ANSWER

Look Back
SENSIBLE ANSWER
ALTERNATE APPROACH

Build Understanding

Connie has 250 telephone books to deliver. The books are packaged 18 books to a carton. How many cartons does Connie need to complete the order?

Understand   How many cartons does Connie need?
There are 18 books in a carton.
Connie needs a total of 250 books.
You need to find how many 18s there are in 250.

▌▙▶ **Plan and Solve**   STRATEGY   To find how many groups of 18 are in 250, use division.

$$\begin{array}{r} 13 \text{ R16} \\ 18\overline{)250} \end{array}$$

The quotient tells that 13 full cartons of books are needed. The remainder of 16 means you need 16 more books. So, you need one more carton to complete the order, even though you will not use all 18 books in the carton.

ANSWER   Connie needs 14 cartons of books.

Look Back   Since Connie needs 250 books, 13 cartons of 18 books is not enough because $13 \times 18 = 234$. Since $14 \times 18 = 252$, 14 cartons is enough.

■ **Talk About Math**   What question could you ask for the situation above that would use the quotient as the answer? the remainder as the answer?

Check Understanding

Use paper and pencil or a calculator to solve each problem.
Tell what you would do with the remainder.

1. If 250 names are printed in an office directory and each page holds 18 names, how many pages will be filled?

2. There were 250 directories to be packed. As many full cartons of 18 directories as possible were packed. How many directories were left over?

3. There are 250 guests invited to a phone company banquet. They will be seated at tables that can each seat 18. How many tables are needed to seat all the guests?

Practice

Use paper and pencil or a calculator to solve each problem.

4. Telephones are packaged 20 to a crate. The Kelso Building needs 150 telephones. How many crates have to be opened to fill the order?

5. If the installer uses as many full crates of 20 phones as he can, how many more phones will he need for the 150-phone order?

6. How many 12-foot sections of telephone wire can be cut from a 508-foot roll of wire?

7. How much will be left after as many 12-foot sections as possible have been cut from a 508-foot roll?

8. A telephone company truck can carry 55 telephone poles. How many truck loads will be needed to carry 692 poles?

9. Wall phones are packed 15 to a carton. The installer used as many full cartons as he could for an order of 76 wall phones. He took the rest from another full carton. How many phones were left in the partially used carton?

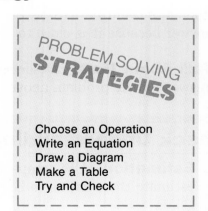

Choose a _____ Strategy

Phone Home If the operator told you to deposit 35 cents for a phone call, what coins could you use? Can you deposit exactly 35 cents using only
10. quarters?   11. dimes?   12. nickels?

13. Give an example of the coins you could use if you did not have any quarters.

14. How many different coin combinations can you use?

PROBLEM SOLVING
STRATEGIES

Choose an Operation
Write an Equation
Draw a Diagram
Make a Table
Try and Check

Three-Digit Quotients

Build Understanding

Every year, as a public health service, a local television station sponsors cholesterol testing. This year, the station set up 21 sites for testing. There were 8,673 people tested. What was the average number of people tested at each site?

Find 8,673 ÷ 21.

Estimate: Use compatible numbers.
8,000 ÷ 20 = 400

Paper and Pencil

```
      4
21)8,6 7 3
   8 4
   ───
     2
```

```
      4 1
21)8,6 7 3
   8 4↓
   ───
     2 7
     2 1
     ───
       6
```

```
      4 1 3
21)8,6 7 3
   8 4
   ───
     2 7
     2 1↓
     ───
       6 3
       6 3
       ───
         0
```

▦ Calculator

8673 ⎡÷⎤

21 ⎡=⎤ *413.*

Each site averaged 413 people tested. This is a reasonable answer because it is close to the estimate.

■ **Talk About Math**   Describe how you would check your answer for the problem above.

Check Understanding

For another example, see Set G, pages 174–175.

1. **Estimation**   Use compatible numbers to estimate the answers to Exercises 2-5.

2. 32)6,880   3. 18)2,359   4. 32)5,381   5. 4,603 ÷ 37

Practice

For More Practice, see Set G, pages 176–177.

Use paper and pencil or a calculator. Show each answer as a quotient with a whole-number remainder (if there is one) or as a decimal with one digit after the decimal point. **Remember** to estimate to tell if the answer is reasonable.

6. $40\overline{)8,745}$ **7.** $60\overline{)7,479}$ **8.** $27\overline{)6,641}$ **9.** $44\overline{)9,597}$ **10.** $62\overline{)7,936}$

11. $23\overline{)7,498}$ **12.** $52\overline{)8,049}$ **13.** $31\overline{)8,412}$ **14.** $22\overline{)9,331}$ **15.** $42\overline{)9,385}$

16. $5,885 \div 34$ **17.** $9,583 \div 43$ **18.** $3,977 \div 27$ **19.** $9,583 \div 57$

Problem Solving

20. Last year, 5,967 people had their cholesterol checked at 17 sites. What was the average number of people checked at each site?

21. The station donated $5 to a heart fund for every person checked. Since 8,673 people were checked, what was the total donation?

22. One site checked a total of 1,631 people in 3 days. An odd thing happened. On each of the 3 days, the number checked was double the number from the day before. How many people were checked on each of the 3 days?

Skills _____ Review   pages 46-71

Multiply.
1. 800×400 **2.** $320 \times 1,000$ **3.** 20×500 **4.** $2 \times 9 \times 5$

5. $(31 \times 25) \times 4$ **6.** 4×32 **7.** 8×725 **8.** $3,462 \times 9$

9. 5×421 **10.** 50×85 **11.** 629×300 **12.** 30×508

13. 29×53 **14.** 82×621 **15.** 307×921 **16.** 761×508

Zeros in the Quotient

Build Understanding

A. In a telephone book, there are 6,798 names that begin with the letter S. There are 22 pages in this section. On the average, how many names are on each page?

Find $6{,}798 \div 22$.

Estimate: Use compatible numbers.
$$6{,}000 \div 20 = 300$$

Paper and Pencil

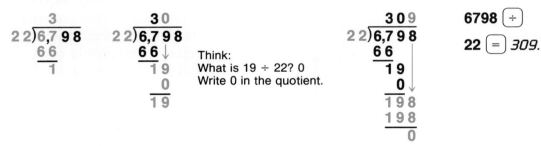

$$\begin{array}{r} 3 \\ 22\overline{)6{,}7\,9\,8} \\ \underline{6\,6} \\ 1 \end{array}$$

$$\begin{array}{r} 3\,0 \\ 22\overline{)6{,}7\,9\,8} \\ \underline{6\,6}\downarrow \\ 1\,9 \\ \underline{0} \\ 1\,9 \end{array}$$

Think:
What is $19 \div 22$? 0
Write 0 in the quotient.

$$\begin{array}{r} 3\,0\,9 \\ 22\overline{)6{,}7\,9\,8} \\ \underline{6\,6} \\ 1\,9 \\ \underline{0}\downarrow \\ 1\,9\,8 \\ \underline{1\,9\,8} \\ 0 \end{array}$$

▦ Calculator

6798 ⌷÷⌷

22 ⌷=⌷ *309.*

There are about 309 names on each page.

B. Find $7{,}624 \div 38$.

$$\begin{array}{r} 2\,0\,0 \text{ R24} \\ 38\overline{)7{,}6\,2\,4} \\ \underline{7\,6}\downarrow \\ 0\,2 \\ \underline{0}\downarrow \\ 2\,4 \\ \underline{0} \\ 2\,4 \end{array}$$

Think:
What is $2 \div 38$? 0
Write 0 in the quotient.

What is $24 \div 38$? 0
Write 0 in the quotient.

■ **Talk About Math** If you worked Example A and got 39 as the answer, how would you have known that it was not the correct answer? Would estimation have helped you?

168

Check Understanding

For another example, see Set H, pages 174–175.

1. **Estimation** Use compatible numbers to estimate the answers to Exercises 2-5.

2. $64\overline{)3,857}$ 3. $37\overline{)8,152}$ 4. $49\overline{)9,823}$ 5. $8,532 \div 21$

Practice

For More Practice, see Set H, pages 176–177.

Use paper and pencil or a calculator. Show each answer as a quotient with a whole-number remainder (if there is one) or as a decimal with one digit after the decimal point. **Remember** to estimate to tell if the answer is reasonable.

6. $73\overline{)2,953}$ 7. $57\overline{)1,155}$ 8. $42\overline{)9,664}$ 9. $28\overline{)9,815}$ 10. $34\overline{)7,041}$

11. $33\overline{)6,878}$ 12. $32\overline{)9,619}$ 13. $19\overline{)3,808}$ 14. $48\overline{)1,471}$ 15. $29\overline{)9,879}$

16. $9,104 \div 44$ 17. $5,402 \div 18$ 18. $9,217 \div 23$ 19. $6,530 \div 62$

Problem Solving

20. There are 3,440 names that begin with the letter K in a phone book. Each column contains 86 names. How many columns of names beginning with K are there?

21. There are about 309 names listed on each page of a telephone book. There are 182 pages of names. How many names are listed?

Number Sense Write the equation that is made when a division or multiplication sign is put in the correct position.

22. $3\ 5\ 6\ 4\ 1\ 8 = 198$ 23. $2\ 0\ 8\ 3\ 5 = 7,280$ 24. $9\ 9\ 1\ 8\ 2\ 9 = 342$

Critical Thinking In the last chapter, you used division to solve multiplication equations involving missing factors. In Chapter 1, you used subtraction to solve addition equations involving missing addends.

25. Do you think addition could be used to solve a subtraction equation such as $n - 15 = 9$? Explain your thinking.

26. What operation do you think could be used to solve a division equation such as $n \div 4 = 7$?

Choose an Operation

Build Understanding

When the McGee family travels by car, they record the different vanity license plates they see. When they get home, they add the license plates to an alphabetical master list that they keep with their computer. The list has 462 license plates on it. It is 14 pages long. On the average, how many plates are listed on each page?

PROBLEM SOLVING GUIDE

Understand
QUESTION
FACTS
KEY IDEA

→ **Plan and Solve**
STRATEGY
ANSWER

Look Back
SENSIBLE ANSWER
ALTERNATE APPROACH

Understand   You need to find how many plates are listed on each page. There are a total of 462 plates listed on 14 pages. You need to find how many plates there are in each of the 14 groups.

→ **Plan and Solve**   STRATEGY   Since you are finding the average number of plates, you divide.

Paper and Pencil

```
        3 3
1 4)4 6 2
      4 2
      ‾‾‾
        4 2
        4 2
        ‾‾‾
          0
```

Calculator

$462 \div 14 = 33.$

ANSWER   On the average, there are 33 plates listed on each page.

Look Back   Be sure to check your work.
$14 \times 33 = 462$. The answer is correct.

■ **Talk About Math**   Does the answer above mean that there are exactly 33 plates listed on each page?

Check Understanding

After their latest trip, the McGees' list grew from 462 plates to 491 plates. How many plates did they see on this trip?

1. Will you add, subtract, multiply, or divide?
2. Find the answer.
3. Explain why you chose the operation you used.

Practice

Tell whether to add, subtract, multiply, or divide. Then solve the problem using paper and pencil or a calculator.

4. Later, the McGees found a list of 38 plates in their car. When they added these to the 491 plates already listed, how many did they have in all?

5. If a state sets aside $15 of the profit from each vanity plate for the construction of rest stops, how many vanity plates need to be sold to total $6,450 for rest stops?

6. In one state, it costs $50 for a vanity plate. The cost for a regular plate is $24. How much more does a vanity plate cost?

7. If the McGees collect an average of 125 license plates each year, how many plates will they have after 10 years?

Choose a _____ Strategy

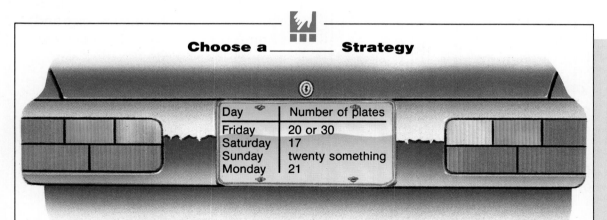

Day	Number of plates
Friday	20 or 30
Saturday	17
Sunday	twenty something
Monday	21

How Many Was That? Mitzi McGee was trying to remember the number of vanity plates they saw on each day of a 4-day trip. She knew that they averaged 24 plates each day. The table shows what she remembers about the number for each day.

8. What was the total number of plates seen on the 4-day trip?

What was the number of plates seen

9. on Sunday?
10. on Friday?

Problem-Solving Review

Solve each problem.

1. If you have 4 quarters, 3 dimes, and a nickel, how much money will you have left after paying $0.52 for an orange drink?

2. On a pictograph 1 wheel represents 70 cars sold. How many wheels would represent the 1,715 cars Mr. Ludwig sold?

3. How many 8-ounce hamburgers can you make with 216 ounces of hamburger?

4. On May 4, 1961, a manned balloon reached a height of 113,740 feet. On February 1, 1966, another balloon reached a height of 123,800 feet. How much higher did the second balloon go?

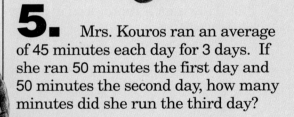

5. Mrs. Kouros ran an average of 45 minutes each day for 3 days. If she ran 50 minutes the first day and 50 minutes the second day, how many minutes did she run the third day?

6. **Data File** If you could watch meteor showers each night they are visible during one year, what is the average number of meteors per hour you would see? Use the chart on pages 244–245.

7. **Make A Data File** Find the price per case and the price per item for at least 4 different items that come in cases. Make a table to show the name of the item, the number of items per case, and the prices.

Explore with a Calculator

"A Question of Quotients"

You have been chosen by your classmates to be the school detective. Use your calculator to help you solve each case.

1. Students' seat assignments for the play will be decided by the quotient of the exercise they are assigned. To make sure these students have the correct seat number, find each quotient. If a quotient is wrong, give the correct answer.

a. Amy: 623 ÷ 89 = 7
b. Joe: 513 ÷ 57 = 9
c. Joy: 1,632 ÷ 48 = 34
d. Mel: 893 ÷ 47 = 18
e. Jan: 3,683 ÷ 127 = 27
f. Pam: 1,802 ÷ 106 = 17
g. Ben: 2,848 ÷ 89 = 30
h. Bob: 504 ÷ 36 = 14
i. Ian: 1,512 ÷ 72 = 21
j. Fay: 1,656 ÷ 92 = 16

2. Brandon had finished his homework when his puppy tracked mud all over it. Help him find the missing numbers.

a. ▦ ÷ 29 = 65
b. ▦ ÷ 71 = 21
c. ▦ ÷ 24 = 106
d. ▦ ÷ 53 = 41

3. Andy can remember only the first two numbers in the club's secret code. He knows he can divide the numbers at the right to get each number in the code.
Secret code: 23–17–▦

a. Help Andy find the quotient that is the missing number.

Club Code Clues	
56	2,108
124	3,393
117	1,288

173

Reteaching

Set A   pages 150–151

Find 362 ÷ 90.

Look for a way you can break apart the number so it is easy to divide.

Think: 362 = 360 + 2 and 4 × 90 = 360.

So $90\overline{)360}$ gives 4   and $90\overline{)362}$ gives 4 R2

Remember to look for numbers that you can break apart.

Use mental math to find each quotient.

1. 425 ÷ 60   2. 354 ÷ 70

3. 816 ÷ 90   4. 566 ÷ 80

5. 563 ÷ 80   6. 453 ÷ 50

Set B   pages 152–153

Estimate 334 ÷ 82 using compatible numbers.

Choose numbers that are close to 334, 82, or both. Think: 8 × 4 = 32. Replace 82 with 80 and 334 with 320.

$$320 ÷ 80 = 4$$

So 334 ÷ 82 is about 4.

Remember that there is more than one way to choose compatible numbers.

Estimate each quotient. Tell what compatible numbers you used.

1. 551 ÷ 79   2. 372 ÷ 92

3. 419 ÷ 64   4. 623 ÷ 71

Set C   pages 154–155

Find 257 ÷ 32.

```
        8 R1
3 2)2 5 7      To find 257 ÷ 32,
    2 5 6      think: what is 25 ÷ 3? 8
        1
```

Remember that the remainder must be less than the divisor.

Tell whether you would use paper and pencil or mental math. Then find each quotient.

1. $23\overline{)69}$ 2. $33\overline{)298}$

3. $52\overline{)423}$ 4. $40\overline{)370}$

Set D   pages 156–157

Find 339 ÷ 43.

```
        8
4 3)3 3 9      Think: What is 33 ÷ 4? 8
    3 4 4
```

Since 344 is greater than 339, try 7 in the quotient.

```
        7 R38
4 3)3 3 9
    3 0 1
       3 8
```

Remember to estimate the quotient first to see if your answer is reasonable.

Use paper and pencil or a calculator. Show each answer as a quotient with a whole-number remainder (if there is one).

1. $26\overline{)156}$ 2. $31\overline{)304}$

3. $13\overline{)67}$ 4. $32\overline{)254}$

5. $46\overline{)272}$ 6. $64\overline{)301}$

Set E   pages 158–159

Find 249 ÷ 47.

Round the divisor. Use the rounded divisor to find the quotient.

Think: 47 rounds to 50.
What is 24 ÷ 5? 4

```
         4                              5 R14
  47)2 4 9    Since 61 is greater   47)2 4 9
    1 8 8     than 47, try 5          2 3 5
    ─────     in the quotient.        ─────
      6 1                               1 4
```

Remember to use the actual divisor when you multiply and not a rounded divisor.

Use paper and pencil or a calculator. Show each answer as a quotient with a whole-number remainder (if there is one).

1. 68)364   **2.** 37)283

3. 27)168   **4.** 56)462

Set F   pages 162–163

Find 792 ÷ 44.

```
         1                      1 8
  44)7 9 2    What is    44)7 9 2
    4 4       7 ÷ 4? 1     4 4 ↓
    ───                    ─────
    3 5                    3 5 2    What is
                           3 5 2    35 ÷ 4? 8
                           ─────
                               0
```

Remember to use a rounded divisor to help you find the quotient.

Use paper and pencil or a calculator. Show each answer as a quotient with a whole-number remainder (if there is one).

1. 32)416   **2.** 40)960

3. 63)718   **4.** 54)1,415

Set G   pages 166–167

Find 6,275 ÷ 26.

```
       2              2 4               2 4 1 R9
26)6,2 7 5     26)6,2 7 5        26)6,2 7 5
   5 2            5 2 ↓             5 2
   ───            ─────            ─────
   1 0            1 0 7            1 0 7
                  1 0 4            1 0 4 ↓
                  ─────            ─────
                      3              3 5
                                     2 6
                                    ───
                                      9
```

Remember to estimate first to be sure the answer is reasonable.

Use paper and pencil or a calculator. Show each answer as a quotient with a whole-number remainder (if there is one).

1. 30)6,452   **2.** 34)7,177

3. 42)8,970   **4.** 53)5,892

Set H   pages 168–169

Find 7,368 ÷ 24.

```
       3              3 0               3 0 7
24)7,3 6 8     24)7,3 6 8        24)7,3 6 8
   7 2            7 2 ↓             7 2
   ───            ─────            ─────
     1            1 6              1 6
                    0             0 ↓
                  ─────            ─────
                  1 6              1 6 8
                                  1 6 8
                                  ─────
                                      0
```

Remember to write zeros in the quotient as needed.

Use paper and pencil or a calculator. Show each answer as a quotient with a whole-number remainder (if there is one).

1. 23)4,780   **2.** 42)8,728

3. 66)9,288   **4.** 16)9,637

More Practice

Set A   pages 150–151

Use mental math to find each quotient. Tell which
strategy you used.

1. $600 \div 60$	**2.** $280 \div 70$	**3.** $480 \div 80$	**4.** $242 \div 30$
5. $720 \div 90$	**6.** $362 \div 60$	**7.** $8,000 \div 40$	**8.** $356 \div 70$
9. $3,600 \div 40$	**10.** $210 \div 30$	**11.** $278 \div 90$	**12.** $486 \div 60$

13. Choose three of the exercises above. Explain why you
chose the strategy you used.

Set B   pages 152–153

Estimate each quotient. Tell what compatible numbers you used.

1. $476 \div 61$	**2.** $393 \div 48$	**3.** $652 \div 83$	**4.** $591 \div 57$
5. $272 \div 37$	**6.** $789 \div 82$	**7.** $356 \div 63$	**8.** $776 \div 38$
9. $4,314 \div 72$	**10.** $3,460 \div 47$	**11.** $5,719 \div 83$	**12.** $4,825 \div 51$
13. $8,186 \div 38$	**14.** $9,135 \div 31$	**15.** $4,901 \div 64$	**16.** $2,912 \div 42$

Set C   pages 154–155

Tell whether you would use paper and pencil or mental
math. Then find each quotient.

1. $41\overline{)85}$	**2.** $32\overline{)98}$	**3.** $20\overline{)68}$	**4.** $33\overline{)74}$	**5.** $21\overline{)88}$
6. $30\overline{)67}$	**7.** $21\overline{)84}$	**8.** $63\overline{)379}$	**9.** $60\overline{)420}$	**10.** $57\overline{)231}$
11. $80\overline{)642}$	**12.** $73\overline{)440}$	**13.** $52\overline{)315}$	**14.** $44\overline{)276}$	**15.** $82\overline{)578}$

Set D   pages 156–157

Use paper and pencil or a calculator. Show each answer
as a quotient with a whole number remainder (if there is
one) or as a decimal with one digit after the decimal point.

1. $24\overline{)94}$	**2.** $14\overline{)126}$	**3.** $16\overline{)128}$	**4.** $23\overline{)160}$	**5.** $37\overline{)259}$
6. $46\overline{)368}$	**7.** $24\overline{)174}$	**8.** $34\overline{)219}$	**9.** $54\overline{)369}$	**10.** $19\overline{)82}$
11. $48\overline{)348}$	**12.** $73\overline{)507}$	**13.** $59\overline{)413}$	**14.** $34\overline{)256}$	**15.** $86\overline{)579}$
16. $42\overline{)409}$	**17.** $87\overline{)325}$	**18.** $63\overline{)495}$	**19.** $76\overline{)511}$	**20.** $53\overline{)421}$

Set E pages 158–159

Use paper and pencil or a calculator. Show each answer
as a quotient with a whole number remainder (if there is
one) or as a decimal with one digit after the decimal point.

1. $47\overline{)256}$
2. $29\overline{)198}$
3. $18\overline{)161}$
4. $38\overline{)243}$
5. $19\overline{)125}$

6. $69\overline{)485}$
7. $57\overline{)470}$
8. $85\overline{)342}$
9. $38\overline{)316}$
10. $76\overline{)532}$

Mixed Practice Tell whether you would use paper and pencil,
a calculator, or mental math. Then find each answer.

11. $426 \div 6$
12. 37×58
13. $476 + 589$
14. $9,000 \div 30$

Set F pages 162–163

Use paper and pencil or a calculator. Show each answer
as a quotient with a whole number remainder (if there is
one) or as a decimal with one digit after the decimal point.

1. $40\overline{)920}$
2. $20\overline{)740}$
3. $34\overline{)821}$
4. $60\overline{)4,468}$
5. $30\overline{)2,572}$

6. $24\overline{)858}$
7. $67\overline{)802}$
8. $38\overline{)745}$
9. $34\overline{)1,479}$
10. $53\overline{)3,758}$

11. $763 \div 16$
12. $933 \div 46$
13. $3,444 \div 46$
14. $5,420 \div 62$

Set G pages 166–167

Use paper and pencil or a calculator. Show each answer
as a quotient with a whole number remainder (if there is
one) or as a decimal with one digit after the decimal point.

1. $80\overline{)8,963}$
2. $40\overline{)5,851}$
3. $38\overline{)8,092}$
4. $22\overline{)6,864}$
5. $46\overline{)6,079}$

6. $31\overline{)6,609}$
7. $26\overline{)6,275}$
8. $48\overline{)5,718}$
9. $54\overline{)9,637}$
10. $28\overline{)7,365}$

11. $7,348 \div 65$
12. $8,038 \div 34$
13. $8,833 \div 27$
14. $9,707 \div 77$

Set H pages 168–169

Use paper and pencil or a calculator. Show each answer
as a quotient with a whole number remainder (if there is
one) or as a decimal with one digit after the decimal point.

1. $46\overline{)3,689}$
2. $16\overline{)9,637}$
3. $23\overline{)4,780}$
4. $24\overline{)2,528}$
5. $43\overline{)8,908}$

6. $32\overline{)6,535}$
7. $28\overline{)8,665}$
8. $25\overline{)5,086}$
9. $19\overline{)3,239}$
10. $89\overline{)9,125}$

11. $5,632 \div 27$
12. $9,696 \div 94$
13. $8,515 \div 34$
14. $7,180 \div 66$

Enrichment

Divisibility Rules

Here are ways you can tell if a whole number is divisible by 2, 3, 5, 9, or 10.

2 A number is divisible by 2 if the ones digit is 0, 2, 4, 6, or 8.

86 is divisible by 2 because the ones digit is 6.

3 A number is divisible by 3 if the sum of the digits is divisible by 3.

876 is divisible by 3 because $8 + 7 + 6 = 21$, and 21 is divisible by 3.

5 A number is divisible by 5 if the ones digit is 5 or 0.

805 is divisible by 5 because the ones digit is 5.

9 A number is divisible by 9 if the sum of the digits is divisible by 9.

828 is divisible by 9 because $8 + 2 + 8 = 18$, and 18 is divisible by 9.

10 A number is divisible by 10 if the ones digit is 0.

940 is divisible by 10 because the ones digit is 0.

Copy and complete the table. The check marks show that 3,285 is divisible by 3, 5, and 9.

	Number	2	3	5	9	10
			Divisible by			
	3,285		✔	✔	✔	
1.	630					
2.	762					
3.	856					
4.	810					
5.	2,685					
6.	5,814					
7.	32,004					
8.	74,010					
9.	431,204					
10.	602,265					
11.	4,277,133					
12.	5,009,407					
13.	7,961,590					
14.	9,951,413					

15. If a number is divisible by 6, it is divisible by both 2 and 3. Describe how you can tell if a number is divisible by 6.

16. Tell which of the numbers in Exercises 1-14 are divisible by 6.

Chapter 5 Review/Test

Use mental math to find each quotient.

1. $500 \div 50$ **2.** $60 \div 20$

3. $630 \div 90$ **4.** $325 \div 8$

Use compatible numbers to estimate each quotient.

5. $562 \div 71$ **6.** $4{,}520 \div 49$

Divide. Show each answer as a quotient with a whole-number remainder (if there is one).

7. $35\overline{)40}$ **8.** $25\overline{)50}$

9. $71\overline{)230}$ **10.** $60\overline{)425}$

11. $39\overline{)137}$ **12.** $48\overline{)216}$

13. $42\overline{)505}$ **14.** $39\overline{)2{,}269}$

15. $17\overline{)5{,}457}$ **16.** $33\overline{)5{,}117}$

17. $42\overline{)841}$ **18.** $18\overline{)5{,}425}$

19. Suppose you want to find $216 \div 28$ by using a rounded divisor. Which is the correct method?

   a. Think: 28 rounds to 30.
       How many 3s in 21?

   b. Think: 216 rounds to 220.
       How many 2s in 22?

Solve each problem.

20. Sophie is 51 inches tall. Write this height in feet and inches.

21. A hotel offers its guests free trips to the airport by van. The van carries 14 passengers. If 62 people need rides, what is the least number of trips the van can make?

22. Eggs are packaged in cartons of 12 each. If a farmer has collected 520 eggs, how many cartons can be completely filled?

23. A computer printer will print 51 lines on each page. There are 1,530 lines to be printed. How many pages will be filled?

Read this problem. Then answer the questions below.

On a vacation trip, the Jimenez family traveled an average of 264 miles per day. They were gone for 12 days. How many miles did they travel?

24. One student got an answer of 22 miles for this problem. Is this answer reasonable? Why or why not?

25. Solve the problem.

26. **Write About Math** Explain how you chose the compatible numbers you used in Exercise 6.

Geometric Solids and Measurement

6

Did You Know:
In the United States, 41 people out of every 100 eat cereal for breakfast.

NUTRITION INFORMATION		
SERVING SIZE: 1 OZ (28.4 g, ABOUT 1 CUP)		
SERVINGS PER PACKAGE:		12
		WITH $\frac{1}{2}$ CUP VITAMINS A & D
	CEREAL	SKIM MILK
CALORIES	110	150
PROTEIN	6 g	10 g
CARBOHYDRATE	20 g	26 g
FAT	0 g	0 g
CHOLESTEROL	0 mg	0 mg
SODIUM	230 mg	290 mg
POTASSIUM	55 mg	260 mg

NUTRITION INFORMATION		
SERVING SIZE: 1 OZ (28.4 g, ABOUT 1 CUP)		
SERVINGS PER PACKAGE:		11
		WITH $\frac{1}{2}$ CUP VITAMINS A & D
	CEREAL	SKIM MILK
CALORIES	110	150
PROTEIN	2 g	6 g
CARBOHYDRATE	26 g	32 g
FAT	0 g	0 g
CHOLESTEROL	0 mg	0 mg
SODIUM	125 mg	190 mg
POTASSIUM	30 mg	230 mg

Number-Sense Project

Estimate
Predict how much of a difference there is in the number of calories in a 1-ounce serving of different breakfast cereals. Are there:
a. no differences?
b. small differences?
c. considerable differences?

Gather Data
Look at the boxes of 3 different types of cereal. Record the number of calories, grams of sucrose and other sugars, and milligrams of sodium in a 1-ounce serving of each cereal.

Analyze and Report
Make a table to show the data you collected. Write a summary statement telling how the cereals you checked differ in calories, sugars, and sodium per serving.

NUTRITION INFORMATION

SERVING SIZE: 1 OZ (28.4 g, ABOUT 1 CUP)
SERVINGS PER PACKAGE: 12

	CEREAL	WITH ½ CUP VITAMINS A & D SKIM MILK
CALORIES	100	140
PROTEIN	2 g	6 g
CARBOHYDRATE	24 g	30 g
FAT	0 g	0 g
CHOLESTEROL	0 mg	0 mg
SODIUM	290 mg	350 mg
POTASSIUM	35 mg	240 mg

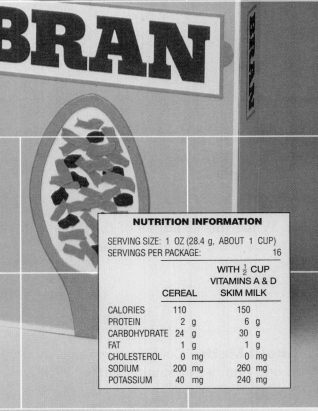

NUTRITION INFORMATION

SERVING SIZE: 1 OZ (28.4 g, ABOUT 1 CUP)
SERVINGS PER PACKAGE: 16

	CEREAL	WITH ½ CUP VITAMINS A & D SKIM MILK
CALORIES	110	150
PROTEIN	2 g	6 g
CARBOHYDRATE	24 g	30 g
FAT	1 g	1 g
CHOLESTEROL	0 mg	0 mg
SODIUM	200 mg	260 mg
POTASSIUM	40 mg	240 mg

Investigating Solid Shapes

Build Understanding

Mikoko likes to find different ways to display the photographs she has taken. Mikoko decided to put some of her photographs on cardboard cubes and to hang the cubes from the ceiling.

A. Cut It Out
Materials: 1-inch grid paper, ruler, scissors
Groups: Small groups of 2 or 3

a. A **cube** is a figure with six flat, square sides called **faces**. Draw a figure like this one, with the measures shown, on a piece of grid paper. If you cut the figure out and fold along the dotted lines, will you get a cube?

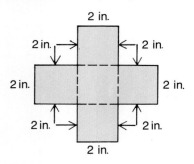

b. What could you add to this figure so that when you cut it out and fold it, you will get a cube?

c. Make the change you suggested in *Step b*. Cut out and fold the figure. Did you get a cube?

B. Mikoko tried several groupings of small cubes for a display of some of her larger photographs.

All of these shapes are **rectangular prisms**. When the 12 **edges** of the shape are the same length, the prism is a cube.

■ **Talk About Math** Could you make a solid cube with an odd number of smaller cubes? Explain.

Check Understanding

For another example, see Set A, pages 206–207.

Tell whether each of these shapes Mikoko made is a
cube, a *rectangular prism*, *both*, or *neither*.

1.

2.

3.

Practice

For More Practice, see Set A, pages 208–209.

Tell whether each object is like a *cube*, a *rectangular
prism*, *both*, or *neither*.

4.

5.

6.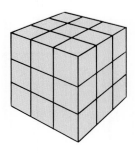

Problem Solving

Visual Thinking   Mikoko made this figure to
display her photographs. How many faces of the
small cubes can be seen if Mikoko places the
figure on the floor,

7. pushed into the corner of the room?

8. in the middle of the room?

Reading ——— Math

Diagrams and Pictures   Look at this
rectangular prism. How many cubes
1. can you see in the top layer?

2. can you see in the bottom layer?

3. are actually in the bottom layer?

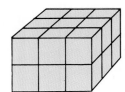

Finding Volume by Counting Cubes

Build Understanding

How is the word *volume* used in each sentence below?

Our encyclopedia has sixteen *volumes*.

Would you turn down the *volume* of the stereo?

One word can have several different meanings. In the top sentence, *volume* means *book in a set*. In the bottom sentence, *volume* means *loudness*.

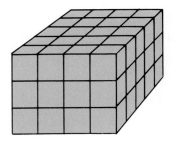

A. In mathematics, ***volume*** is the measure of the amount of space inside a solid figure.

One way to find the volume of a figure is to count the number of cubes that will "fill" the figure.

B. Each edge of this cube measures 1 inch. The volume of this cube is 1 ***cubic inch*** (1 cu in.).

C. What is the volume of this figure? Each cube represents 1 cubic inch.

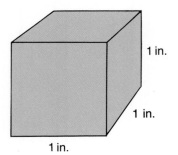

1 in.

1 in.

1 in.

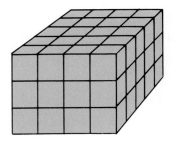

Count the number of cubes in the top layer. There are 20 cubes.

Each edge of this cube measures 1 centimeter. The volume of this cube is 1 ***cubic centimeter*** (1 cm³).

1 cm

1 cm

1 cm

Since there are 3 layers, there are 3 × 20, or 60, cubes.

The volume is 60 cubic inches (60 cu in.).

■ **Write About Math** Explain how you can find the number of cubes in the top layer without counting.

184

Check Understanding

For another example, see Set B, pages 206–207.

1. Each cube represents 1 cubic centimeter.
   Find the volume by counting cubes.

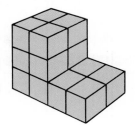

Practice

For More Practice, see Set B, pages 208–209.

Each cube represents 1 cubic centimeter. Find the
volume of each figure by counting cubes. **Remember** to
write the unit of measure.

2.

3.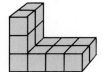

4.

Each cube represents 1 cubic inch. Find the volume of
each figure by counting cubes. **Remember** to write the
unit of measure.

5.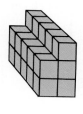

6.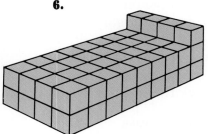

7.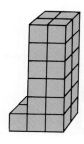

Problem Solving

8. Which is larger, a box with a volume of 64 cubic inches
   or a box with a volume of 64 cubic centimeters?

Volume

Build Understanding

A. Robert works at Sanchez Office Supply. He is stacking plastic storage crates on an area of the floor that is 6 feet long and 3 feet wide. Robert has enough storage crates to make 4 complete layers. What is the volume of the stack?

In the diagram, each small cube represents 1 cubic foot. The stack is 6 feet long, 3 feet wide, and 4 feet high. Find the number of cubes in the top layer.

Length		Width		Cubes in one layer
6	×	3	=	18

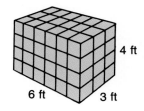

There are 4 layers of 18 cubes.

Cubes in one layer		Number of layers		Volume of stack
18	×	4	=	72

The volume of the stack is 72 cubic feet.

B. Find the volume of this rectangular prism.

You can find the volume by multiplying the length, the width, and the height.

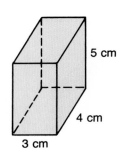

Length		Width		Height		Volume
4	×	3	×	5	=	60

The volume of the figure is 60 cubic centimeters.

■ **Talk About Math** Would the volume of the figure in Example B be different if the figure were turned over so a different face was on the bottom? Why or why not?

Check Understanding

For another example, see Set C, pages 206–207.

Find the volume of each rectangular prism.

1.

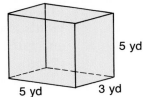

5 cm

12 cm   7 cm

2. Length: 9 inches
Width: 5 inches
Height: 3 inches

Practice

For More Practice, see Set C, pages 208–209.

Find the volume of each rectangular prism.

3.

5 yd

5 yd   3 yd

4.

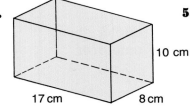

10 cm

17 cm   8 cm

5.

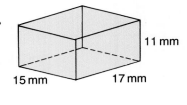

11 mm

15 mm   17 mm

Tell whether you would use paper and pencil, mental math,
or a calculator to find the volume of each rectangular
prism. Then find the volume.

6. Length: 13 ft
Width: 11 ft
Height: 12 ft

7. Length: 14 cm
Width: 4 cm
Height: 14 cm

8. Length: 15 in.
Width: 10 in.
Height: 10 in.

9. Length: 23 m
Width: 18 m
Height: 20 m

10. Length: 76 cm
Width: 50 cm
Height: 20 cm

11. Length: 84 m
Width: 26 m
Height: 30 m

Problem Solving

12. Will 4,000 cubic inches of packing material fit
into a box 20 inches long, 18 inches wide, and
9 inches high?

13. Critical Thinking Each box of computer
paper is 11 inches long and 10 inches wide. The
volume of each box is 1,320 cubic inches. How
tall is each box?

TIPS FOR PROBLEM SOLVERS

**Brainstorm to get
started**—one idea will
lead to another.

Customary Units of Capacity

Build Understanding

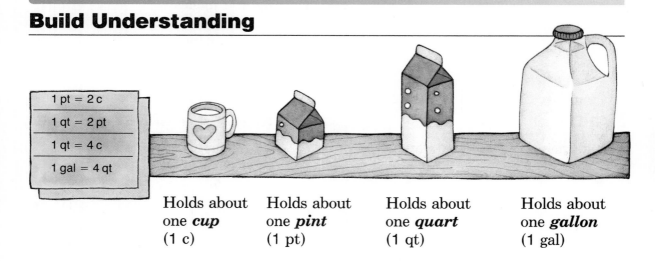

1 pt = 2 c
1 qt = 2 pt
1 qt = 4 c
1 gal = 4 qt

Holds about one *cup* (1 c)

Holds about one *pint* (1 pt)

Holds about one *quart* (1 qt)

Holds about one *gallon* (1 gal)

A. Shelley wanted to buy 2 gallons of milk. The store was out of gallon containers. How many quart containers would Shelley have to buy to get 2 gallons of milk?

The chart shows that 1 gallon equals 4 quarts. So 2 gallons is twice that amount, or 8 quarts. She would have to buy 8 quart containers.

B. Write 3 pints 1 cup in cups.

Use the chart. Multiply the number of pints by 2. Add the rest of the cups to find the total number of cups.

$$\begin{array}{r} 3 \\ \times\,2 \\ \hline 6 \\ +\,1 \\ \hline 7 \end{array}$$

3 pt 1 c = 7 c

C. Write 9 quarts in gallons and quarts.

Use the chart. Divide the number of quarts by 4. The remainder is the number of quarts left over.

$$\begin{array}{r} 2\ \text{R1} \\ 4\overline{)9} \\ 8 \\ \hline 1 \end{array}$$

9 qt = 2 gal 1 qt

Talk About Math In Example A, if the store were out of gallon and quart containers, how many pint containers would Shelley need?

Check Understanding

For another example, see Set D, pages 206–207.

1. **Estimation** Would you use cups or gallons to measure the amount of water needed to fill a kitchen sink?

2. **Estimation** Choose the most sensible measure for the amount of water needed to fill a flower vase.

    4 c   4 qt   4 gal

3. Write 2 qt 1 pt in pints.

4. Write 11 c in pints and cups.

Practice

For More Practice, see Set D, pages 208–209.

Estimation Would you use

5. cups or quarts to measure the amount of soup in a bowl?

6. pints or gallons to measure the amount of water a washing machine can hold?

Number Sense Tell which measure is larger.

7. 3 pt or 1 qt

8. 16 c or 2 qt

9. 1 gal or 5 qt

Estimation Choose the most sensible measure.

10. Glass of juice

    1 c   1 qt   1 gal

11. Pitcher of lemonade

    8 c   8 qt   8 gal

12. Baby bottle

    1 pt   1 qt   1 gal

Write each measure in pints.

13. 8 c

14. 12 qt

15. 8 qt 1 pt

16. 1 gal

Write each measure in quarts.

17. 16 pt

18. 7 gal

19. 8 c

20. 10 gal 3 qt

Write each measure in quarts and pints.

21. 9 pt

22. 25 pt

23. 34 c

24. 1 gal 2 c

Problem Solving

25. Shelley wanted to buy a quart of tomato juice. A 1-pint can of tomato juice costs $0.90. A 1-quart can costs $1.65. Which is the better buy for one quart of juice?

Metric Units of Capacity

Build Understanding

Jason Schwartz works at a zoo. Sometimes he has to feed baby animals whose mothers cannot take care of them.

A. The eyedropper Jason uses to feed very small animals holds about 1 *milliliter* (1 mL) of liquid.

The bottled water Jason drinks comes in a 1-*liter* (1 L) container.

One liter is 1,000 milliliters.

B. Estimation A plastic drinking cup holds about 250 milliliters. About how many cups of water could Jason pour from the 1-liter container?

One liter is 1,000 milliliters. Each time Jason pours a cup of water from the bottle, there are 250 milliliters less in the bottle.

1,000 − 250 − 250 − 250 − 250 = 0

Jason could pour about 4 cups from the 1-liter container.

c. How many milliliters is 16 liters?

Sixteen liters is
16 × 1,000 milliliters,
or 16,000 milliliters.

D. How many liters is 3,000 mL?

1,000 mL = 1 L

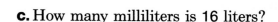
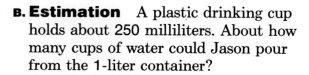

$$\begin{array}{r} 3 \\ 1{,}000\overline{)3{,}000} \\ 3{,}000 \\ \hline 0 \end{array}$$

Divide the number of milliliters by 1,000 to find the number of liters.

3,000 mL = 3 L

■ **Talk About Math** One cubic centimeter holds 1 milliliter of water. How many liters will 1,000 cubic centimeters hold?

Check Understanding

For another example, see Set E, pages 206–207.

Number Sense Tell which quantity is larger.

1. 951 L or 951 mL   **2.** 6 L or 5,699 mL   **3.** 2,500 mL or 3 L

Practice

For More Practice, see Set E, pages 208–209.

Estimation Would you use milliliters or liters to measure the amount of liquid each container can hold?

4. Hot water tank

5. Ice cube tray

6. Bird's water dish

Estimation Choose the more sensible measure.

7. Glass of milk
    25 mL 250 mL

8. Pitcher of water
    3 L 300 L

9. Sink
    1 L 10 L

Mental Math Write each measure in milliliters.

10. 3 L
    11. 9 L
    12. 15 L
    13. 20 L

Problem Solving

Calculator Solve each problem.

14. How many full cups of water can Jason pour from his 1-liter bottle if his cup holds about 190 mL?

15. How much water will be left in the bottle?

Midchapter _____ Checkup

1. Tell whether this figure is a cube, a rectangular prism, or neither.

2. Count the cubes to find the volume. Each cube represents 1 cubic inch.

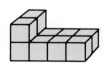

3. Find the volume of this rectangular prism.

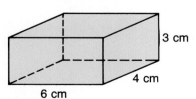

3 cm

4 cm

6 cm

Complete.

4. 8 qt = ▦ gal

5. 9 L = ▦ mL

Problem-Solving Workshop

Explore as a Team

1. Use cubes to make a new building shaped like the original Building A, but doubling its dimensions (length, width, and height).

Building A

Building A doubled

2. Discuss what happened to the total number of cubes and to the perimeter of the base when the dimensions of Building A were doubled.

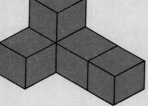

Building B (two views)

3. Double the dimensions of Building B.

4. Draw a picture of the base of the new Building B.

5. Write about the original and new Building B.

6. Predict what you think would happen if you tripled each dimension.

TIPS FOR **WORKING TOGETHER**

Involve your whole group. Help everyone to participate.

Math-at-Home Activity

Play this game with someone at home. Draw 16 dots, 4 in each row and column. Decide who will mark Xs and who will mark Os. Take turns marking any dot with your X or O.

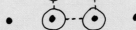
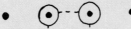

The winner is the first person to mark 4 dots that lie at the corners of a square.

Number-Sense Project

Look back at pages 180-181.

Two students collected the data shown in the tables below.

1. Which cereal has the greatest number of calories per serving?

2. If a person is trying to limit sugar intake, which cereals should be avoided?

3. In these samples is there a greater difference between cereals in calories, sugar, or sodium?

4. Is it important to pay attention to these differences? Why?

Student 1

Type/Brand of cereal	Amount of each ingredient per 1-ounce serving		
	Calories (without milk)	Sucrose and other sugars	Sodium
Brand A	100	5 g	160 mg
Brand B	90	0 g	0 mg
Brand C	110	9 g	280 mg

Student 2

Type/Brand of cereal	Amount of each ingredient per 1-ounce serving		
	Calories (without milk)	Sucrose and other sugars	Sodium
Brand D	120	12 g	250 mg
Brand E	90	5 g	200 mg
Brand F	130	15 g	150 mg

Customary Units of Weight

Build Understanding

A small head of lettuce weighs about 1 *pound*. A radish weighs about 1 *ounce*.

A. Tanika wants to get 35 ounces of green beans. Does she have 35 ounces if the food scale shows 2 pounds 3 ounces?

Look at this chart.

1 pound (lb) = 16 ounces (oz)
2,000 pounds = 1 ton (T)

Multiply the number of pounds and 16. Then add the remaining ounces to find the total number of ounces.

$$\begin{array}{r} 16 \\ \times\ 2 \\ \hline 32 \\ +\ 3 \\ \hline 35 \end{array}$$

Tanika has 35 ounces of beans.

B. Write 37 ounces in pounds and ounces.

Use the chart. Divide the number of ounces by 16. The remainder is the number of ounces left over.

$$\begin{array}{r} 2\ R5 \\ 16)\overline{37} \\ \underline{32} \\ 5 \end{array}$$

37 oz = 2 lb 5 oz

■ **Talk About Math** Why might someone say that a popular person has a "ton" of friends?

Check Understanding

For another example, see Set F, pages 206–207.

1. **Estimation** Would you use ounces, pounds, or tons to weigh a chair?

2. **Estimation** Choose the most sensible measure for the weight of a delivery truck.

   3 oz   3 lb   3 T

3. Write 3 lb 5 oz in ounces.

4. Write 19 oz in pounds and ounces.

Practice

For More Practice, see Set F, pages 208–209.

Estimation Would you use ounces, pounds, or tons to weigh a

5. pair of glasses?   6. bicycle?   7. bus?

Estimation Choose the most sensible measure.

8. Telephone
   4 oz   4 lb   4 T

9. Elephant
   5 oz   5 lb   5 T

10. Apple
    6 oz   6 lb   6 T

Write each measure in ounces.

11. 4 lb   12. 20 lb   13. 8 lb 9 oz   14. 25 lb 12 oz

Write each measure in pounds.

15. 6 T   16. 368 oz   17. 128 oz   18. 10 T

Write each measure in pounds and ounces.

19. 23 oz   20. 81 oz   21. 216 oz   22. 498 oz

Problem Solving

23. **Estimation** A piece of charcoal weighs about 2 ounces. About how many pieces of charcoal are in a 10-pound bag?

24. **Use Data** Use the chart on page 157. Write the minimum weight of one dozen jumbo eggs in pounds and ounces.

Metric Units of Mass

Build Understanding

A healthy diet includes plenty of fruits and vegetables.

A. A grape is about 1 *gram* (1 g). A bunch of bananas is about 1 *kilogram* (1 kg).

One kilogram is 1,000 grams.

B. How many grams is 3 kilograms?

Three kilograms is 3 × 1,000 grams, or 3,000 grams.

C. How many kilograms is 17,000 grams?

1,000 g = 1 kg

$$\begin{array}{r} 17 \\ 1,000\overline{)17,000} \\ \underline{17000} \\ 0 \end{array}$$

Divide the number of grams by 1,000 to find the number of kilograms.

A healthy diet includes 4 servings of fruits and vegetables daily.

■ **Talk About Math** A thousand meters is a kilometer. A thousand grams is a kilogram. What do you think *kilo-* means?

Check Understanding

For another example, see Set G, pages 206–207.

Number Sense Tell which quantity is larger.

1. 42 g or 42 kg   **2.** 6 kg or 5,232 g   **3.** 4 kg or 4,822 g

4. Estimation Would you use grams or kilograms to measure a large bag of potatoes?

5. Estimation Choose the more sensible measure for a melon.

5 g   5 kg

Practice

For More Practice, see Set G, pages 208–209.

Estimation   Would you use grams or kilograms to measure each of the following?

6. Tomato   **7.** Bag of apples   **8.** Bunch of parsley

Estimation   Choose the more sensible measure.

9. Strawberry   **10.** Banana   **11.** Bag of oranges

   15 g   15 kg   225 g   225 kg   3 g   3 kg

Write each measure in grams.

12. 2 kg   **13.** 28 kg   **14.** 75 kg   **15.** 57 kg

Write each measure in kilograms.

16. 3,000 g   **17.** 7,000 g   **18.** 12,000 g   **19.** 15,000 g

Problem Solving

20. If a whole watermelon is 6 kilograms and you cut out a 450-gram slice, how much remains?

21. Each bunch of grapes is 180 grams. Would 10 bunches be more than or less than 1 kilogram?

22. A bunch of bananas is about 1 kilogram. If the bunch contains 4 bananas, how many grams is each banana?

23. An apple is 138 grams, an orange is 131 grams, a stalk of celery is 40 grams, and a tomato is 135 grams. What is the total?

Skills _____ **Review**   pages 14–71

Add, subtract, or multiply.

1. 523 + 251   **2.** 938 − 33   **3.** 4,809 − 711

4. 519 + 3,265   **5.** 4 × 56   **6.** 19 × 91

7. 78 × 68   **8.** 571 × 3   **9.** 6 × 808

10. 774 × 91   **11.** 208 × 118   **12.** 1,011 × 10

Try and Check

Build Understanding

Megan has 60 pounds of camping gear to put in 4 packs. She wants 3 packs to be of equal weight and the fourth to weigh less than 10 pounds. Which items should she put in each of the 4 packs?

PROBLEM SOLVING
GUIDE

Understand
QUESTION
FACTS
KEY IDEA

▶ **Plan and Solve**
STRATEGY
ANSWER

Look Back
SENSIBLE ANSWER
ALTERNATE APPROACH

Understand   QUESTION   Which items should she put in each pack?

FACTS   The table gives the number of items and the weight of each item. Megan has 4 packs. One pack has to weigh less than 10 pounds. The other 3 packs have to be of equal weight.

KEY IDEA   Try to make 3 groups of equal weight and see if the fourth group weighs less than 10 pounds.

Camping Gear

Item	Number of items	Weight of each item
Mess kits	4	16 oz
Food sacks	2	12 lb
Craft kits	2	5 lb
Stove	1	3 lb
Tent	1	8 lb
First-aid kit	1	32 oz
Sports kit	1	9 lb

Plan and Solve   STRATEGY   Convert all the weight to pounds. Then list each item and its weight on a slip of paper. Try different groupings of the items. Since the 2 food sacks weigh 12 pounds each, put 1 food sack in Pack 1 and 1 food sack in Pack 2. Then try to find other items that total 12 pounds and put them in Pack 3. Repeat the process with the items of less weight.

ANSWER

Pack 1		Pack 2		Pack 3		Pack 4	
Food sack	12	Food sack	12	Sports kit	9	Tent	8
Craft kit	5	Craft kit	5	Stove	3	Mess kit	1
				First-aid kit	2		
				Mess kit	1		
				Mess kit	1		
				Mess kit	1		

Look Back SENSIBLE ANSWER The weight of each of the first three packs is 17 pounds. The fourth pack weighs 9 pounds, which is less than 10 pounds. The answer is sensible.

■ **Write About Math** Show how you could make each of the four packs have equal weight.

Check Understanding

Use the information on page 198 for Exercises 1–5.
Write the weight of each item in pounds.

1. First-aid kit

2. Mess kit

3. Could both food sacks be put in the same pack? Explain.

4. Could the 3 packs of equal weight contain only 12 pounds? Explain.

5. Show another way Megan could arrange the items in the packs.

Practice

For Problems 6–10, refer to the Example.

6. Put the stove, the first-aid kit, and a mess kit in Pack 4. Separate the remaining gear so that Packs 1, 2, and 3 are of equal weight.

7. If you put the first-aid kit and the sports kit together in a pack, is it possible to separate the remaining gear so that each of two packs weighs 20 pounds and each of two packs weighs 10 pounds? Explain.

On the trip home from camping, Megan's packs weighed 24 pounds less than when she started.

8. Why would the packs be 24 pounds lighter than before?

9. How much does the remaining gear weigh?

10. Show how Megan could arrange the remaining items to make each pack equal in weight.

Computing with Customary Measures

Build Understanding

A. Raoul works in a hardware and lumber store. A customer wants a wooden closet rod cut into 2 pieces. One piece must be 8 feet 3 inches long, and the other piece must be 2 feet 10 inches long. What is the smallest length that the original rod can be?

Find 8 feet 3 inches + 2 feet 10 inches.

Add the inches.
Add the feet.

$$
\begin{array}{r}
\textbf{8 ft} \quad \textbf{3 in.} \\
+\, \textbf{2 ft 10 in.} \\
\hline
\textbf{10 ft 13 in.} = \textbf{11 ft 1 in.}
\end{array}
$$

Rename the answer.
13 in. = 1 ft 1 in.

B. Find 12 lb 4 oz − 6 lb 9 oz.

Rename to
subtract ounces.
12 lb 4 oz = 11 lb 20 oz

Subtract ounces.
Subtract pounds.

$$
\begin{array}{rcr}
\textbf{12 lb 4 oz} & = & \textbf{11 lb 20 oz} \\
-\ \textbf{6 lb 9 oz} & = & \textbf{6 lb \ \ 9 oz} \\
\hline
& & \textbf{5 lb 11 oz}
\end{array}
$$

C. Find 3 × 7 gal 3 qt.

Multiply quarts.
Multiply gallons.

$$
\begin{array}{r}
\textbf{7 gal 3 qt} \\
\times \qquad \textbf{3} \\
\hline
\textbf{21 gal 9 qt} = \textbf{23 gal 1 qt}
\end{array}
$$

Rename the answer.
9 qt = 2 gal 1 qt

D. Find 8 ft 4 in. ÷ 5.

Write 8 feet 4 inches in inches. Then divide. Rename the answer.

8 ft 4 in. = 100 in.

100 in. ÷ 5 = 20 in.

20 in. = 1 ft 8 in.

■ **Write About Math** Explain how you could use mental math to find 3 hours 30 minutes ÷ 3.

Check Understanding

For another example, see Set H, pages 206–207.

Mental Math   Use mental math to find each missing number.

1. 7 yd 2 ft = 6 yd ▦ ft   **2.** 4 gal 1 qt = 3 gal ▦ qt   **3.** 5 lb 21 oz = 6 lb ▦ oz

4. 2 h 72 min = 3 h ▦ min   **5.** 5 h 19 min = 4 h ▦ min

Practice

For More Practice, see Set H, pages 208–209.

Mixed Practice   Find each answer.
Remember to watch the signs.

6.   3 gal 1 qt
  + 7 gal 3 qt

7.   8 ft 6 in.
  − 4 ft 8 in.

8.   6 ft 5 in.
  ×   4

9. 5 h 55 min ÷ 5

10.   6 h 40 min
  + 8 h 35 min

11.   14 min 20 sec
  −   7 min 32 sec

12. 2 yd 15 in. ÷ 3

13.   6 qt
  − 3 qt 3 c

14.   6 yd 2 ft 7 in.
  ×   5

Problem Solving

Explore _____ Math

One movie is exactly twice as long as another movie. The length of
the shorter movie is 1 hour 37 minutes 54 seconds. How long is the
other movie? Problems 15–17 show one way to find the answer.

15. How many seconds long is the
first movie?

16. How many seconds long is the
longer movie?

17. What is the length of the longer movie in hours,
minutes, and seconds?

18. Now find the length of the longer
movie by doubling the hours,
minutes, and seconds of the
shorter movie. Remember to
rename your answer.

19. Were your answers to Problems
17 and 18 the same? Which
method did you prefer for finding
the answer?

Use Data from a Table

Build Understanding

Do you feel colder on windy days? Your skin cools faster in a high wind than when it is exposed to the same temperature on a calm day.

The wind chill temperature is the temperature it seems to be because of the speed of the wind. What does the temperature seem to be when the air temperature is 20°F and the wind speed is 10 miles per hour?

PROBLEM SOLVING GUIDE

➡ **Understand**
QUESTION
FACTS
KEY IDEA

Plan and Solve
STRATEGY
ANSWER

Look Back
SENSIBLE ANSWER
ALTERNATE APPROACH

Wind Chill Table

Wind (mi per h)	Air Temperature (Fahrenheit)							
	25	20	15	10	5	0	−5	−10
5	21	19	12	7	0	−5	−10	−15
10	10	3	−3	−9	−15	−22	−27	−34
15	2	−5	−11	−18	−25	−31	−38	−45
20	−3	−10	−17	−24	−31	−39	−46	−53
25	−7	−15	−22	−29	−36	−44	−51	−59

Wind chill measurements were developed from experiments performed in Antarctica in 1939.

➡ **Understand**   QUESTION   What temperature does it seem to be when both the air temperature and wind speed are taken into account?

FACTS   The air temperature is 20°F. The wind speed is 10 miles per hour.

KEY IDEA   Use the data from the wind chill table.

Plan and Solve   Find the column for 20°F and the row for 10 miles per hour in the table. The point where the column and row meet gives the wind chill temperature. The wind chill is 3°F. It feels like it is 3°F outside.

Look Back   The wind blowing against your skin makes you colder, so the wind chill temperature should be lower than the thermometer reading. A wind chill of 3°F is lower than an air temperature of 20°F.

■ **Talk About Math** Which would feel colder: 20°F with a
25-mile-per-hour wind or 15°F with a 15-mile-per-hour wind?

Check Understanding

Find the wind chill temperature.

1. 10°F with a 25-mile-per-hour wind

2. −5°F with a 15-mile-per-hour wind

3. −10°F with a 20-mile-per-hour
wind

4. 0°F with a 25-mile-per-hour wind

Practice

If the wind is blowing at 20 miles per hour, what would the
actual temperature be if the wind chill temperature is

5. −17°F?   **6.** −53°F?   **7.** −10°F?   **8.** −39°F?

What would the wind speed be if the actual temperature is 0°F
and the wind chill temperature is

9. −22°F?   **10.** −44°F?   **11.** −5°F?   **12.** −39°F?

Choose a ———— Strategy

It's Cold Enough The air temperature was
25°F when a cold front moved in at noon. The
air temperature dropped 5 degrees each hour. The
wind speed was steady at 15 miles per hour.
What was the wind chill temperature at 4 P.M.?

13. How many hours are there
between noon and 4 P.M.?

14. How many degrees did the air
temperature drop by 4 P.M.?

15. What was the air temperature at 4 P.M.?

16. Use the table on page 202 to find the wind chill temperature at 4 P.M.

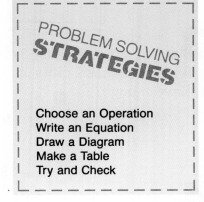

PROBLEM SOLVING
STRATEGIES

Choose an Operation
Write an Equation
Draw a Diagram
Make a Table
Try and Check

Solve each problem.

1. Josh has 750 centimeter cubes. Can he store all of them in a box 10 cm wide, 8 cm deep and 12 cm long?

2. Can Jenny ship two photo cubes in the box?

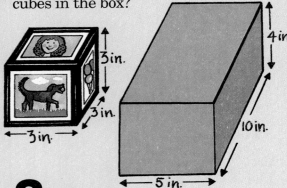

3. A recipe calls for 3 cups of milk. Alberto has 2 pints of milk. Does he have enough?

4. Iris has four 1-liter bottles of juice. Can she give each of the 12 people at her party 250 mL of juice?

5. Ms. Kenton plans to make 48 turkey sandwiches. If she needs 5 oz of turkey for each sandwich, how many pounds of turkey meat should she buy?

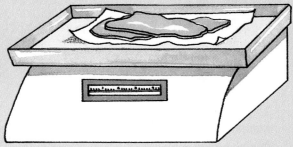

6. Brad has a box with a volume of 105 cubic cm. The length of each side is a whole number. What are the dimensions of the box?

7. **Data File** How many different size rectangular prisms can hold one million $1 bills? Use the information on pages 244–245 to help you decide. Draw and label each one.

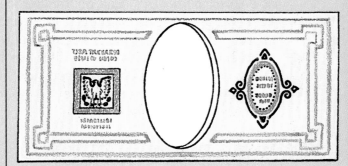

8. **Make a Data File** Which United States President's portrait is on each denomination of United States Savings Bonds?

Explore with a Calculator

"Turn up the volume."

At a State Mathematics Festival, student teams from each county receive the problem cards below. The team that finds all the missing sides first wins.

1. Use your calculator to solve the problems.

a. Facts: Rectangular prism
volume = 120 cm³
length = 5 cm
width = 3 cm
height = ?

b. Facts: Cube
volume = 343 cm³
length of a side = ?

c. Facts: Rectangular prism
volume = 336 cu in.
length = 7 in.
height = 8 in.
width = ?

d. Facts: Rectangular prism
volume = 1,210 cm³
height = 10 cm
width = 11 cm
length = ?

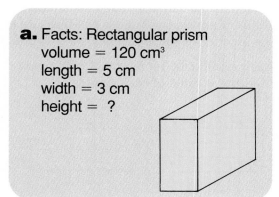
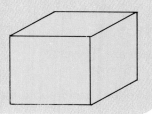

e. Facts: Rectangular prism
volume = 450 cm³
area of base = 75 m²
height = ?

f. Facts: Cube
volume = 1,728 cu in.
area of base = 144 sq in.
length of a side = ?

Reteaching

Set A pages 182–183

Each of the six faces of a cube is a square.

Each of the six faces of a rectangular prism is a rectangle.

Remember that a cube is a special rectangular prism.

Tell whether each object is like a cube, a rectangular prism, both a cube and a rectangular prism, or neither.

1.    2.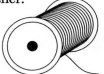

Set B pages 184–185

Each cube represents 1 cubic inch. What is the volume of this figure?

Each layer has 4 rows. Each row has 4 cubes.
4 × 4 = 16

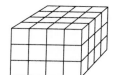

There are 3 layers.
3 × 16 = 48

The volume is 48 cubic inches.

Remember that volume is the measure of the amount of space inside a solid figure.

Each small cube represents 1 cubic inch. Find the volume of each figure.

1. 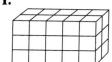   2.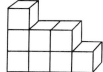

Set C pages 186–187

Find the volume of this figure.

Multiply the length, the width, and the height.

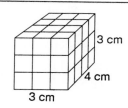
3 cm
4 cm
3 cm

Length   Width   Height   Volume
 4 cm × 3 cm × 3 cm = 36 cm³

Remember to write the unit of measure.

Find the volume of each figure.

1.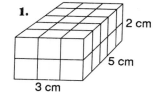
2 cm
5 cm
3 cm

2.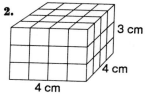
3 cm
4 cm
4 cm

Set D pages 188–189

Write 3 gallons in

a. quarts.   b. pints.

a. Since 1 gallon equals 4 quarts, 3 gallons equals 3 × 4 quarts, or 12 quarts.

b. Since 1 quart equals 2 pints, 12 quarts equals 12 × 2 pints, or 24 pints.

Remember that you multiply to change a larger unit of measure to a smaller unit of measure. Write each measure in quarts.

1. 4 gal   2. 5 gal

Write each measure in pints.

3. 6 qt   4. 6 gal

Independent Study RETEACHING

Set E   pages 190–191

Write 19 liters in milliliters.

Since 1 liter = 1,000 milliliters, 19 liters is 19 × 1,000 mL, or 19,000 mL.

Remember that 1 L = 1,000 mL.

Mental Math   Use mental math to write each measure in milliliters.

1. 4 L   **2.** 17 L

Set F   pages 194–195

Write 4 tons in

a. pounds.   **b.** ounces.

a. Since 1 ton is 2,000 pounds, 4 tons is 4 × 2,000 lb, or 8,000 lb.

b. Since 1 pound is 16 ounces, 8,000 lb is 8,000 × 16 oz, or 128,000 oz.

Remember that the abbreviation for pound is lb, ounce is oz, and ton is T.

Write each measure in ounces.

1. 36 lb   **2.** 2 T

Write each measure in pounds.
3. 12 T   **4.** 30 T

Set G   pages 196–197

How many kilograms is 21,000 grams? Since 1 kilogram is 1,000 grams, divide the number of grams by 1,000 to find the number of kilograms.

$$
\begin{array}{r}
2\,1 \\
1{,}0\,0\,0)\overline{2\,1{,}0\,0\,0} \\
\underline{2\,1{,}0\,0\,0} \\
0
\end{array}
$$
   21,000 g = 21 kg

Remember that you divide to change a smaller unit of measure to a larger unit of measure.

Write each measure in kilograms.

1. 6,000 g   **2.** 10,000 g

3. 18,000 g   **4.** 13,000 g

Set H   pages 200–201

Find 14 lb 6 oz − 7 lb 10 oz.

$$
\begin{array}{r}
14\ \text{lb}\ \ 6\ \text{oz} \\
-\ 7\ \text{lb}\ 10\ \text{oz}
\end{array}
$$

You cannot subtract 10 oz from 6 oz. Rename 14 lb 6 oz.

$$
\begin{array}{r}
13\ \text{lb}\ 22\ \text{oz} \\
-\ 7\ \text{lb}\ 10\ \text{oz} \\
\hline
6\ \text{lb}\ 12\ \text{oz}
\end{array}
$$
  14 lb = 13 lb 16 oz
  So, 14 lb 6 oz = 13 lb 22 oz

Remember that when you subtract measures, you may have to rename the minuend.

Subtract.

1.   11 lb 7 oz   **2.**   9 ft 3 in.
     − 9 lb 12 oz   − 5 ft 9 in.

3.   6 gal 1 qt   **4.**   14 yd 1 ft
     − 2 gal 3 qt   − 3 yd 2 ft

More Practice

Set A   pages 182–183

Tell whether each object is like a cube, like a rectangular prism, like both a cube and a rectangular prism, or like neither.

1.

2.

3.

Set B   pages 184–185

Each small cube in Exercises 1–4 represents 1 cubic centimeter. Find the volume of each figure. **Remember** to write the unit of measure.

1.    **2.**   **3.**   **4.**

Set C   pages 186–187

For Exercises 1–3, tell whether you would use paper and pencil, mental math, or a calculator to find the volume of each figure. Then find the volume.

1.  6 cm 8 cm 6 cm

2. 1 in. 10 in. 10 in.

3.

Set D   pages 188–189

Estimation   Choose the most sensible measure.

1. Gas tank of a car
   20 c   20 qt   20 gal

2. Teapot
   6 c   6 qt   6 gal

Write each measure in pints.
3. 3 gal   **4.** 4 qt   **5.** 7 gal   **6.** 5 qt

Write each measure in quarts.
7. 16 c   **8.** 4 gal   **9.** 8 pt   **10.** 32 c

Write each measure in quarts and pints.
11. 17 pt   **12.** 24 pt   **13.** 11 pt   **14.** 10 c

Set E pages 190–191

Estimation Choose the most sensible measure.

1. Tablespoon
   5 mL   15 mL   150 mL

2. Pail of water
   10 L   100 L   1,000 L

Mental Math Use mental math for Exercises 3–6.
Write each measure in milliters.

3. 5 L

4. 10 L

5. 13 L

6. 22 L

Set F pages 194–195

Write each measure in Exercises 1 and 2 in ounces and in
Exercises 3 and 4 in pounds.

1. 30 lb

2. 3 T

3. 5 T

4. 160 oz

Write each measure in pounds and ounces.

5. 20 oz

6. 42 oz

7. 88 oz

8. 164 oz

9. Write 4 qt 2 c in cups.

10. Write 4 lb 7 oz in ounces.

Set G pages 196–197

Choose the most sensible measure.

1. Couch
   100 g or 100 kg

2. Cat
   4 g or 4 kg

3. Shoelace
   1 g or 1 kg

Write each measure in Exercises 4 and 5 in grams and in
Exercises 6 and 7 in kilograms.

4. 3 kg

5. 10 kg

6. 8,000 g

7. 10,000 g

Set H pages 200–201

Mental Math Use mental math for Exercises 1 and 2.
Find the missing number.
1. 5 qt 1 pt = 4 qt ▦ pt

2. 9 ft 17 in. = 10 ft ▦ in.

Add, subtract, or multiply.

3.   3 ft 9 in.
   $+$ 4 ft 6 in.

4.   6 gal 1 qt
   $-$ 2 gal 3 qt

5.   7 h 25 min
   $+$ 4 h 45 min

6. 3×6 qt 1 pt

7. 5×3 yd 2 ft 9 in.

8. 6 ft 5 in. $-$ 2 ft 8 in.

Enrichment

Polyominoes

What do you notice about these figures?

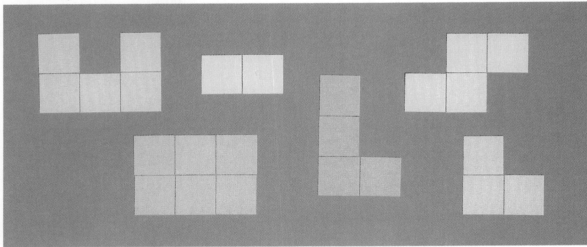

In each figure, all the squares are the same size. Each square shares at least one of its sides with another square.

All the figures shown above are **_polyominoes_**.

1. These figures are not polyominoes. Why not?

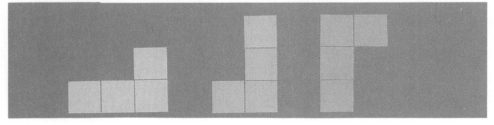

2. These figures are not considered different polyominoes. Why not?

3. How many different polyominoes are there for 4 squares? Draw each polyomino on grid paper.

4. How many different polyominoes are there for 5 squares? Draw each polyomino on grid paper.

210

Chapter 6 Review/Test

Tell whether each figure is a cube, a rectangular prism, both, or neither.

1.   **2.**

If each small cube represents 1 cm³, find the volume of the figure in

3. Item 1.   **4.** Item 2.

Find the volume of each figure.

5. 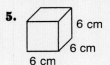 **6.**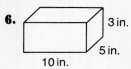

Choose the most sensible measure.

7. Capacity of a soup bowl

   2 c   2 qt   2 gal

8. Weight of a 10-year-old boy

   30 g   3 kg   30 kg

Complete.

9. 12 qt = ▦ gal

10. 6 L = ▦ mL

11. 16 lb = ▦ oz

12. 4,000 g = ▦ kg

Add or subtract.

13.   2 gal 2 qt   **14.**   6 ft 2 in.
     + 3 gal 3 qt   − 4 ft 5 in.

Use the table with the problem given below to answer Items 15 and 16.

Wind Chill Table

Wind (mi per h)	Temperature (Fahrenheit)							
	25	20	15	10	5	0	−5	−10
5	21	19	12	7	0	−5	−10	−15
10	10	3	−3	−9	−15	−22	−27	−34
15	2	−5	−11	−18	−25	−31	−38	−45
20	−3	−10	−17	−24	−31	−39	−46	−53
25	−7	−15	−22	−29	−36	−44	−51	−59

The wind is blowing at 25 miles per hour. If the wind-chill temperature is −15°F, what is the actual temperature?

15. To solve the problem, which would you look for in the table?

   a. −15 in the column for an actual temperature of −10°F
   b. −15 in the row for a wind of 25 mi per h
   c. −15 in the column for an actual temperature of 5°F
   d. −25 in the row for a wind of 15 mi per h

16. Solve the problem.

17. The table below shows how many cans of each kind of food Alice has. She wants to make three 10-pound packages. What should she put in each package?

Items	Number of Cans	Weight of Each Can
Peanuts	1	1 lb
Fruit	4	3 lb
Trail mix	4	2 lb
Ham	1	9 lb

18. Write About Math What makes a cube a special kind of rectangular prism?

Addition and Subtraction of Decimals 7

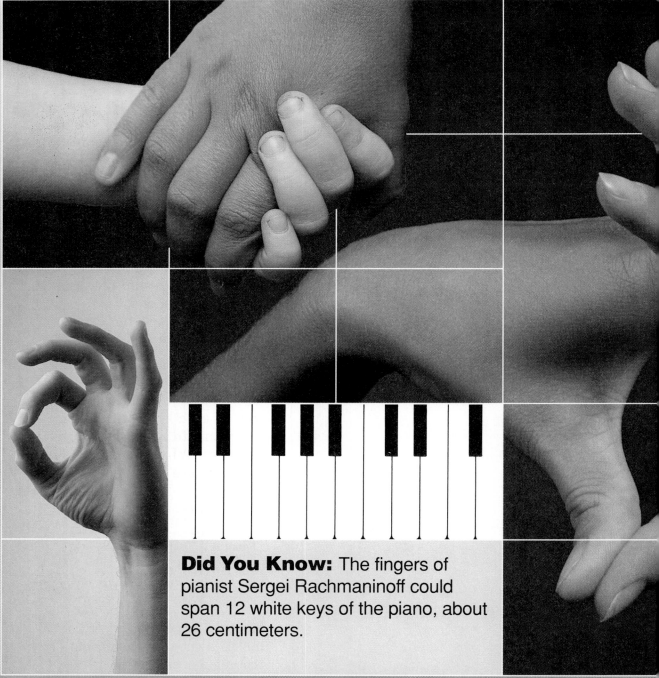

Did You Know: The fingers of pianist Sergei Rachmaninoff could span 12 white keys of the piano, about 26 centimeters.

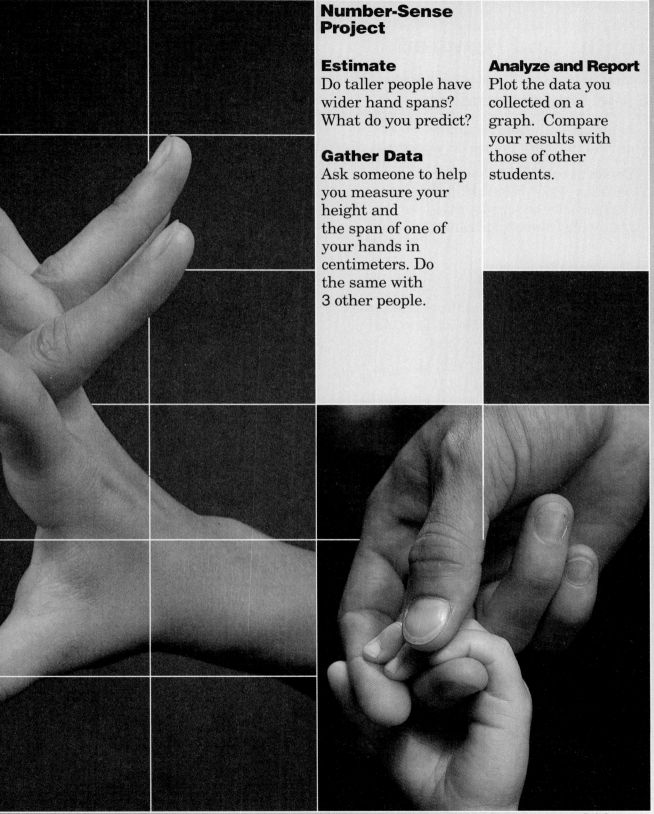

Number-Sense Project

Estimate
Do taller people have wider hand spans? What do you predict?

Gather Data
Ask someone to help you measure your height and the span of one of your hands in centimeters. Do the same with 3 other people.

Analyze and Report
Plot the data you collected on a graph. Compare your results with those of other students.

213

Tenths and Hundredths

Build Understanding

Numbers with decimal points are all around us. They are called *decimals*.

Decimals are used to name a fractional part. For 10 or 100 equal parts, the numbers can be written using our place-value system instead of fractions.

For sale 0.7 acre

A. Some decimals name numbers less than 1. The For Sale sign names 0.7 acre. An acre is a measure of land area.

Think of 1 acre divided into 10 equal parts. Each part is one *tenth* of an acre.

Read: seven tenths

$\frac{7}{10}$ or 0.7

B. Some decimals name numbers greater than 1. The package of meat weighs 2.93 pounds.

If each tenth is divided into 10 equal parts, then the whole square is divided into 100 equal parts. Each part is one *hundredth*.

Read: two and ninety-three hundredths

2 wholes $\frac{93}{100}$ or 0.93

$2\frac{93}{100}$ or 2.93

C. Our place-value system is based on 10. The chart shows the value of each digit in a decimal.

The decimal 0.7 means 7 of 10 equal parts. The decimal 2.93 means 2 wholes and 93 of 100 equal parts of another whole.

	Tens	Ones	Tenths	Hundredths
0.7		0	7	
2.93		2	9	3

■ **Write About Math** Use the hundredths model and the tenths model to show that 0.10 and 0.1 are equal.

Check Understanding

For another example, see Set A, pages 238-239.

Write a fraction and a decimal for each exercise.

1.   **2.**    **3.**   **4.**

5. Seventeen and one tenth

6. Four hundredths

7. Thirty and forty-five hundredths

8. What does the last word name when you read a decimal?

9. What word is used when you read the decimal point?

Practice

For More Practice, see Set A, pages 240–241.

Write a fraction and a decimal for each exercise.

10.   **11.**   **12.**   **13.**

14. Two tenths

15. Thirty-five hundredths

16. Three and four tenths

17. Forty and five hundredths

Write each decimal in words.

18. 0.7   **19.** 0.03   **20.** 6.8   **21.** 4.39   **22.** 5.02   **23.** 20.04

Problem Solving

Write each amount with a dollar sign and decimal point.

24. A package of notebook paper costs 60¢.

25. A pound of hamburger costs one dollar and forty-seven cents.

26. Two magazines cost five dollars and five cents.

27. Five pens were on sale for 98¢.

Thousandths

Build Understanding

Linda was designing letters using the squares on a grid.
She used a rectangle 50 squares long and 20 squares wide.
Can she fit the entire alphabet on the grid?

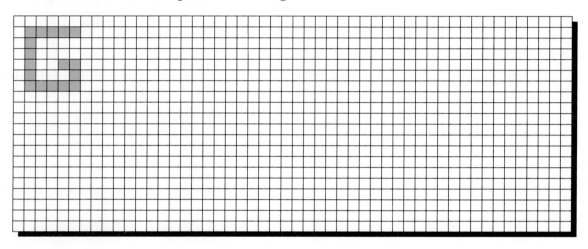

A. Designing Decimals
Materials: Grid paper, ruler, colored pencil

a. Make a rectangle 50 squares long and 20 squares wide.

b. Draw vowels on the grid. Remember to color only whole squares. Make the letters about the same size as the G.

B. What part of the rectangle is shaded to make the G?

The whole rectangle has 1,000 squares. Each square is *one thousandth* of the rectangle, or:

$$\frac{1}{1,000} \longleftarrow \text{1 of 1,000 equal parts}$$

Seventeen squares are shaded to make the G. The G uses *seventeen thousandths* of the rectangle, or:

$$\frac{17}{1,000} \longleftarrow \text{17 of 1,000 equal parts}$$

c. Remember that one decimal place shows tenths and two decimal places show hundredths. Three decimal places show thousandths.

Tens	Ones	Tenths	Hundredths	Thousandths		
	0	0	0	1	0.001	one thousandth
	0	0	1	7	0.017	seventeen thousandths

216

■ **Talk About Math**   If the rectangle in Example A represents one whole, how many squares are in one tenth of the rectangle? How many squares are in one hundredth of the rectangle?

Check Understanding

For another example, see Set B, pages 238–239.

Write a decimal to name the part of your rectangle you would shade to make

1. A.   **2.** E.   **3.** I.   **4.** O.   **5.** U.

6. How many squares in the grid would be shaded to show 1.0?

Complete. One whole equals

7. ▦ tenths.   **8.** ▦ hundredths.   **9.** ▦ thousandths.

Practice

For More Practice, see Set B, pages 240–241.

Write each number in words. **Remember** to use "and" for decimals greater than 1.

10. 0.008   **11.** 0.071   **12.** 0.378   **13.** 5.046   **14.** 93.607

Write a fraction and a decimal for each exercise.

15. Three thousandths

16. Thirty-two thousandths

17. Nine hundred fifty-seven thousandths

18. Seven hundred twenty thousandths

19. Ten and three hundred five thousandths

20. Forty-two and sixty-five thousandths

Problem Solving

21. One centimeter is what part of a meter?

22. One millimeter is what part of a meter?

23. A liter contains 1,000 milliliters. A quart is 946 milliliters. What part of a liter is a quart?

24. A kilometer is 1,000 meters. The length of a soccer field is 110 meters. What part of a kilometer is that?

25. Critical Thinking   How many thousandths are in one tenth? How many thousandths are in one hundredth?

Place Value

Build Understanding

A. The longest United States manned space mission was *Skylab 4*. It ended in 1974. The mission lasted 84 days, 1 hour, and 16 minutes. That time is the same as 2,017.267 hours.

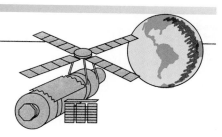

thousands	hundreds	tens	ones	tenths	hundredths	thousandths
2	0	1	7	2	6	7

2,017.267
two thousand, seventeen and
two hundred sixty-seven thousandths

The 2 at the left means 2 thousands and the 2 to the right means 2 tenths.

Skylab was the first space station launched by the U.S. space program.

B. What part of the rectangle is shaded?

Ones	Tenths	Hundredths	Thousandths
0	1	3	8

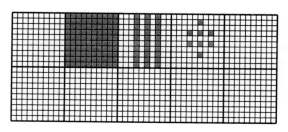

1 tenth, 3 hundredths, 8 thousandths
138 thousandths
0.138

C. The value of each place in a decimal is 10 times as large as the value of the place to its right.

1 ten = 10 ones
1 one = 10 tenths
1 tenth = 10 hundredths

■ **Talk About Math**   In the amount of money $34.53, the 3 in the tens place is how many times as large as the 3 in the hundredths place? Explain.

Check Understanding

For another example, see Set C, pages 238–239.

Use the number in Example A to answer the following questions.

1. What does the 6 mean?

2. What does the 0 mean?

3. How many times as large is the value of the 7 in the ones place than the value of the 7 in the thousandths place?

Practice

For More Practice, see Set C, pages 240–241.

Tell what 7 means in each number.

4. 71.3   **5.** 21.07   **6.** 9.703   **7.** 7,031.5   **8.** 3.027

Which decimals have

9. 4 in the tenths place?
   a. 40.12   **b.** 26.43   **c.** 13.146

10. 7 in the thousandths place?
   a. 413.57   **b.** 7,104.5   **c.** 2.357

11. 9 in the hundredths place?
   a. 123.49   **b.** 951.92   **c.** 23.509

12. 3 in the hundreds place?
   a. 5.035   **b.** 6,361.38   **c.** 37.36

Problem Solving

13. In the *Apollo* flight times, which 5 has a greater value? How much greater?

14. Which *Skylab* flight has a 0 in the thousandths place?

15. Critical Thinking Complete the pattern.

29.02, 29.04, 29.06, ▦, ▦

U.S. Space Missions

Mission	Flight Time (h)
Apollo 11	195.6
Apollo 17	301.85
Skylab 2	672.833
Skylab 3	1,427.15
Skylab 4	2,017.267

Explore ———— Math

Look for a pattern in the place-value chart in Example A.

16. How are the names of the places similar? How are they different?

17. Describe the pattern.

18. What name is used for the sixth decimal place?

Comparing and Ordering Decimals

Build Understanding

A. Two trails lead up Sugarloaf Mountain. Which distance is shorter?

Compare 0.5 and 0.75.

0.5 < 0.75

5 tenths is less than 75 hundredths. The shorter distance is 0.5 miles.

B. Compare 0.3 and 0.30.

0.3 = 0.30
0.3 and 0.30 are
equal decimals.

C. Compare 0.385 and 0.38.

0.385 ⬚ **0.38**
The ones are the same.
The tenths are the same.
The hundredths are the same.

0.385 ⬚ **0.380**
Think: 0.38 = 0.380
Compare the thousandths.
5 thousandths is greater than 0 thousandths.

0.385 > 0.38

D. Decimals can be shown on a number line in order from least to greatest.

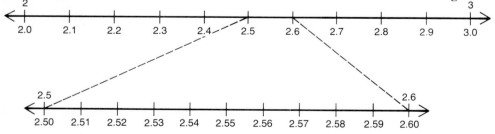

■ **Talk About Math** Explain how to write a decimal in thousandths equal to 3 tenths.

220

Check Understanding

For another example, see Set D, pages 238–239.

Compare the numbers. Use <, >, or =.

1. 0.8 ⬚ 0.3   **2.** 0.50 ⬚ 0.49   **3.** 0.316 ⬚ 0.314   **4.** 6.7 ⬚ 6.70

5. Write the missing numbers for A, B, C, and D.

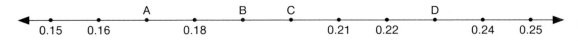

```
◄────●────●──────────A────────●────C──────●────●──────D──────●────●────►
    0.15  0.16         0.18      B           0.21  0.22        0.24  0.25
```

Practice

For More Practice, see Set D, pages 240–241.

Compare the numbers. Use <, >, or =. Draw a diagram if needed.

6. 0.4 ⬚ 0.6   **7.** 2.46 ⬚ 2.41   **8.** 0.5 ⬚ 0.416   **9.** 9.831 ⬚ 9.83

List the numbers in order from least to greatest. Use a number line if needed.

10. 0.4   0.7   0.3   **11.** 5.68   5.73   5.51   **12.** 0.483   0.481   0.486

13. 7.7   7.0   7.5   **14.** 27.3   27.31   27.03   **15.** 1.001   1.101   1.01

Problem Solving

16. Red trail is 1 mile long. There is a red flag at each end of the trail. A yellow flag is at each 0.1 mile. How many yellow flags are there?

17. Number Sense Write the greatest possible decimal having four different digits and a 3 in the hundredths place.

TIPS FOR PROBLEM SOLVERS

Visualize the problem in your mind to help you understand it better.

Midchapter ——— Checkup

Write a fraction and a decimal for each exercise.

1. Two and seven tenths   **2.** Forty-six hundredths   **3.** Eighteen thousandths

Tell what 6 means in each number.

4. 84.6   **5.** 26.1   **6.** 0.46   **7.** 5.016

Explore as a Team

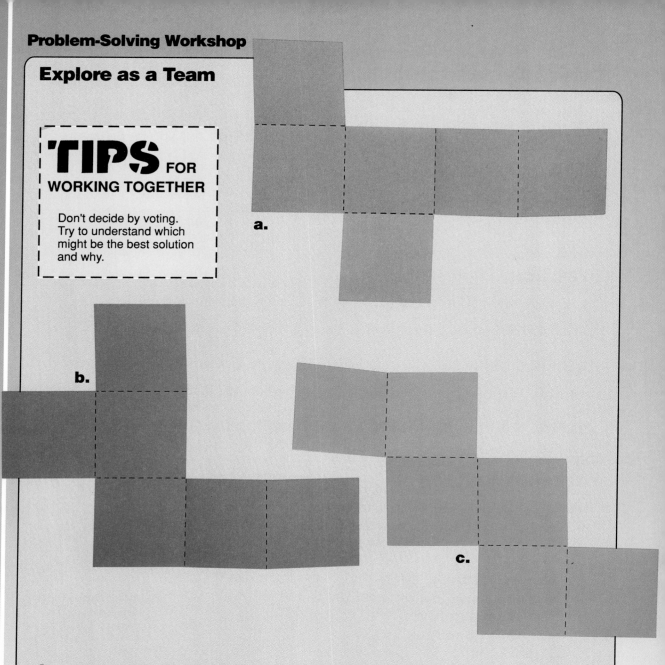

TIPS FOR **WORKING TOGETHER**

Don't decide by voting. Try to understand which might be the best solution and why.

a.

b.

c.

1. Which of the diagrams form cubes when folded along the dotted lines?

2. Use 1-inch or larger grid paper. Cut out different diagrams of 6 squares.

3. Fold the diagrams you made to see which ones can form cubes. Draw your diagrams on grid paper. Show which diagrams do and which do not form cubes.

Explore with a Computer

Use the *Spreadsheet Workshop Project* for this activity.
At the School Olympic Days, five students entered the softball throw event. Each student threw the ball three times. The distances were recorded in the spreadsheet.

1. At the computer, type the greatest distance each student threw the ball in the "Best" column. Use the **Sort** option to list the students in order by best throw. Find the student who is the overall winner.

Student	1st throw	2nd throw	3rd throw	Best
Carrie	25.73 m	26.35 m	26.4 m	
Roy	15.7 m	15.47 m	15.28 m	
Kyle	20.2 m	21.18 m	18.2 m	
Ingrid	15.07 m	13.07 m	14.9 m	
Edwardo	23.7 m	26.34 m	26.24 m	

2. The school record for the softball throw is 39.68 m. Estimate how much farther a student would have to throw the ball to break or tie the record.

Number-Sense Project

Look back at pages 212-213.
A number of centimeters can be written as a part of a meter.
Since there are 100 cm in 1 m, 1 cm is the same as 0.01 m.

Byron's hand span measured 9 cm or 0.09 m. His height measured 154 cm or 1.54 m.

Measure the width of each of the tracks. Write each measurement in centimeters and meters.

1.

2.

3.

Use Logical Reasoning

Build Understanding

West School has teams only in volleyball, swimming, soccer, and basketball. Erica, Justin, Molly, and Dave each play a different sport. Justin's sport does not use a ball. Molly is older than the volleyball player. Neither Molly nor Dave plays soccer. Who plays volleyball?

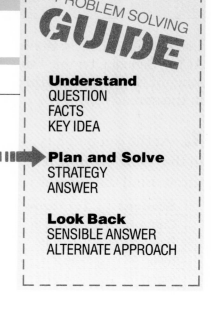

PROBLEM SOLVING
GUIDE

Understand
QUESTION
FACTS
KEY IDEA

IIII➤ **Plan and Solve**
STRATEGY
ANSWER

Look Back
SENSIBLE ANSWER
ALTERNATE APPROACH

Understand   Only one student plays volleyball. You know a ball is not used in swimming and people cannot be older than themselves.

IIII➤ **Plan and Solve**

STRATEGY   Logical reasoning is thinking in a sensible and orderly way to draw conclusions using known facts. Putting the facts in a chart can help.

Justin is the swimmer since his sport does not use a ball. Write yes for swimming and no for the other sports. Also, write no for swimming for the other students. Molly is not older than herself. Write no for her for volleyball. Since neither Molly nor Dave plays soccer, write no for them for soccer. The chart shows only Erica can play soccer. So she does not play volleyball.

	Volleyball	Basketball	Swimming	Soccer
Erica			no	
Justin	no	no	yes	no
Molly	no		no	no
Dave			no	no

ANSWER   Dave plays volleyball.

Look Back   Check that the answer fits all the facts.

■ **Talk About Math**   Who plays basketball? How does using facts together help you learn new facts?

Check Understanding

Organize the facts in a chart to answer each question.

Mr. Smythe, Mr. McCarthy, and Mrs. Roberts teach at West School. One of them teaches math, one teaches science, and one teaches reading. No one teaches a subject with the same first letter as his or her name. Mr. Smythe does not teach math.

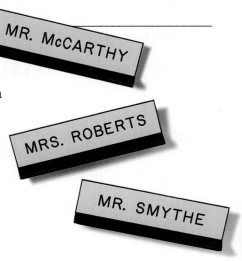

1. Who teaches reading?
2. Who teaches science?
3. Who teaches math?

Practice

Solve each problem. **Remember** to make a chart to help you.

4. Harold, Mary Ann, and Jorge each have a pet. One person has a dog, one a cat, and one a goldfish. One of the boys has a dog. The owner of the goldfish lives next to Mary Ann. Jorge does not have a dog. Which pet does each person own?

5. Jenni, Kevin, Susan, and Maria each bought different food for lunch. The menu choices were pizza, salad, hamburger, and fish sandwich. None of the girls ate salad. Susan and the girl who had pizza are in different grades. Maria had pickles on her hamburger. What did each person buy for lunch?

6. Tim, Jane, Alex, and Jessica get to school in different ways. One person walks, one rides a bicycle, one takes a bus, and one rides in a car. Neither girl walks to school. Neither Alex nor Jane rides to school in a bus or a car. The bus rider gets to school before Tim. How does each person get to school?

Rounding Decimals

Build Understanding

A. The average January temperatures for three cities are given in degrees Fahrenheit. Round each temperature to the nearest whole number.

City	Average January Temperature
Hartford	25.2°F
Cleveland	25.5°F
Spokane	25.7°F

Showing these temperatures on a number line will help.

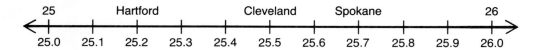

Hartford: 25.2 is closer to 25.

Cleveland: 25.5 is halfway between 25 and 26.
             Round a number halfway between two
             numbers to the larger number. Round
             25.5 to 26.

Spokane: 25.7 is closer to 26.

B. Round 15.064 to the nearest hundredth.

Steps

Find the place to be rounded.

Hundredths
↓
15.0̂64

Look at the digit to the right.

15.064   4 is less than 5.

If it is less than 5, the digit in the rounding place stays the same.

If it is 5 or more, add 1 to the digit in the rounding place.

Write the rounded decimal.

15.06   Drop digits to the right of the rounding place.

■ Talk About Math

Explain how to round these numbers to the nearest tenth using the number line.

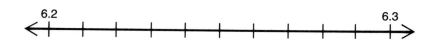

6.21   6.25   6.28

Check Understanding

For another example, see Set E, pages 238-239.

Round 6.28 to the nearest tenth.

1. What digit is in the rounding place?

2. What digit is to the right of the rounding place?

3. Does the rounding place change? If so, how?

4. What is 6.28 rounded to the nearest tenth?

Nick used the calculator to see if 1,107 was divisible by 439. The display showed *2.52164*. Round this to the nearest

5. one.   6. tenth.   7. hundredth.   8. thousandth.

Practice

For More Practice, see Set E, pages 240–241.

Round to the the nearest whole number.

9. 1.3   10. 58.7   11. 22.5   12. 0.6   13. 9.61

14. 5.05   15. 7.49   16. 29.5   17. 1.632   18. 0.980

Round to the nearest tenth.

19. 0.41   20. 1.75   21. 12.37   22. 8.03   23. 8.409

24. 14.07   25. 3.18   26. 17.56   27. 92.42   28. 18.99

Round to the nearest hundredth.

29. 0.675   30. 2.344   31. 74.009   32. 0.399   33. 0.595

34. 0.998   35. 5.972   36. 38.017   37. 17.003   38. 0.909

Problem Solving

39. Luis collected rainfall for a science project. He collected 0.325 inch one week and 0.335 the next week. In which week did it rain more?

40. Rosita hoped to collect 1.5 inches of rain for her project. She collected 1.46 inches. Did she have enough for her project?

41. The temperature in St. Louis is 78.9°F. Nashville is 79.4°F, and Charlotte is 78.5°F. List the cities in order from coolest to warmest.

Estimating Sums and Differences

Build Understanding

This table shows the average monthly rainfall in inches for Seattle, Washington.

A. About how many inches of rain will fall during the first three months of the year?

Use addition to find the total amount.

Estimate 6.04 + 4.22 + 3.59.

Month	Inches	Month	Inches
Jan.	6.04	July	0.74
Feb.	4.22	Aug.	1.27
Mar.	3.59	Sept.	2.02
Apr.	2.40	Oct.	3.43
May	1.58	Nov.	5.60
June	1.38	Dec.	6.33

You can estimate with decimals the same way you estimate with whole numbers.

Round to the nearest whole number.

```
6.04 →   6
4.22 →   4
+ 3.59 → + 4
        14
```

Add the front-end digits.

```
6.04 →   6
4.22 →   4
+ 3.59 → + 3
        13
```

About 13 or 14 inches of rain can be expected during January, February, and March.

B. Tropical rainstorms dropped 11.81 inches of rain in Louisiana during August and September. Florida received 7.39 inches. About how much more rain fell in Louisiana?

Use subtraction to compare two amounts.
Estimate 11.81 − 7.39.

Round to the nearest whole number.

```
 11.81 →   12
− 7.39 → −  7
           5
```

Subtract the front-end digits.

```
 11.81 →   11
− 7.39 → −  7
           4
```

About 4 or 5 inches more rain fell in Louisiana.

■ **Talk About Math** When both methods for estimating sums are used and the estimates are different, which method will always give the smaller sum? Explain.

Check Understanding

For another example, see Set F, pages 238–239.

For each exercise, estimate each sum or difference. Use both methods of estimating sums.

1. 3.9 + 6.7 + 9.2   **2.** 7.8 + 1.1 + 5.2   **3.** 12.19 − 6.82   **4.** 18.57 − 10.48

5. **Calculator** Find the exact sum or difference in Exercises 1-4. Which method of estimating is more accurate?

Practice

For More Practice, see Set F, pages 240–241.

Estimate each sum or difference. Round to the nearest whole number.

6.	**7.**	**8.**	**9.**	**10.**	**11.**
30.2	99.7	4.216	59.1	19.5	20.350
+ 15.5	+ 60.2	+ 8.190	− 19.8	− 4.6	− 14.627

Estimate each sum or difference. Use front-end digits.

12. 3.9 + 35.4   **13.** 48.3 − 6.1   **14.** 52.62 + 9.75   **15.** 78.03 − 10.48

16. 65.006 − 2.980   **17.** 88.4 + 5.2 + 6.7   **18.** 47.3 + 8.9 + 2.6

19. 71.94 − 3.28   **20.** 81.73 − 9.48   **21.** 27.953 + 1.276

Problem Solving

22. About how many inches of rain will fall in Seattle during April, May, and June?

23. About how many more inches of rain fell during the wettest month than during the driest month?

24. Use Data Use the table on page 219. About how many hours longer was the flight time of *Apollo 17* than the flight time of *Apollo 11*?

Skills_____ Review   pages 122-133

Divide.

1. 9)64   **2.** 9)604   **3.** 8)4,330   **4.** 7)5,816   **5.** 7)4,003

Too Much or Too Little Information

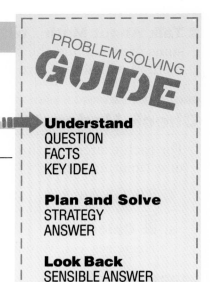

Understand
QUESTION
FACTS
KEY IDEA

Plan and Solve
STRATEGY
ANSWER

Look Back
SENSIBLE ANSWER
ALTERNATE APPROACH

Build Understanding

Cory bought a pair of blue cycling pants for $25.75, a pair of black ones for $28.88, and a touring helmet for $39.99. How much did he pay for the two pairs of cycling pants?

Understand   QUESTION   What was the cost of the two pairs of pants?

FACTS   Blue pants: $25.75; black pants: $28.88; helmet: $39.99

KEY IDEA   Find the total cost for pants only. The cost of the helmet is extra information.

Plan and Solve   To find the total cost of the pants, add the prices. First estimate. Then find the exact amount.

		Estimate	Exact Amount
$25.75	rounds to	$26	$25.75
+ 28.88	rounds to	+ 29	+ 28.88
		$55	$54.63

Cory paid $54.63 for the two pairs of pants.

Look Back   Since $54.63 is close to $55, the answer is sensible.

■**Talk About Math**   Why can't you tell how much change Cory received?

Check Understanding

Cory bought a pair of meshback gloves for $24.95. How much money does he have left?

1. What facts are given in the problem?

2. To find how much money is left, do you add, subtract, or multiply?

3. Can you solve this problem with the facts that are given? Why?

Practice

Solve each problem. If there is not enough information given to do so, write *too little information.*

4. Cory and his friends biked 3 hours in the morning. Then they stopped for 1 hour for lunch. They biked for 3 more hours after lunch. How many hours did they bike that day?

5. Cory had $15 with him, Al had $11, and Floyd had $9.60. How much money did they have in all?

6. Cory's 12-speed bike weighs 37 pounds. To it he added a seat pack of 215 cubic inches. What is the total weight of his bike, including the pack?

7. A 6-foot vinyl-covered steel cable with a combination barrel lock costs $14.99. A 2-pound steel U-lock with bracket and keys is $24.99. How much more is the U-lock than the barrel lock?

8. A seat pack cost $12.99. How much change did Cory get back?

9. Before lunch, the boys had spent only $7.00. How much money did they have after lunch?

10. Gumwall tires cost $12.99 and blackwall tires cost $12.49. Tire tubes cost $6.49 for standard tubes and $10.49 for puncture-resistant tubes. How much did Cory pay for new tires and tubes?

11. At the Rest Stop, hamburgers cost $1.59 each. A chicken sandwich costs $1.85. Cory and Hank each ordered a chicken sandwich. How much did they spend together for sandwiches?

Choose a _____ Strategy

Color Combos

12. Cory has 3 shirts: white, red, and yellow, and 2 pairs of biking pants: blue and black. How many different biking outfits could he have?

13. Cory also has 2 helmets: gold and silver. How many different biking outfits could he have?

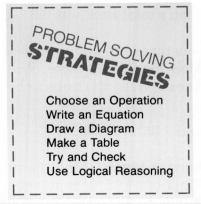

PROBLEM SOLVING
STRATEGIES

Choose an Operation
Write an Equation
Draw a Diagram
Make a Table
Try and Check
Use Logical Reasoning

Adding Decimals

Build Understanding

A. To make the swim team, Jason must swim 400 meters in less than 7 minutes. Jason swam the first 200 meters in 2.86 minutes. He swam the second 200 meters in 3.95 minutes. Did he make the team?

Use addition to find the *total* amount of time he took to swim 400 meters. Find 2.86 + 3.95.

Estimate using rounding. 3 + 4 = 7

Line up the decimal points.	Add the hundredths. 11 hundredths = 1 tenth 1 hundredth	Add the tenths. 18 tenths = 1 one 8 tenths	Add the whole numbers. Remember to place the decimal point in your answer.

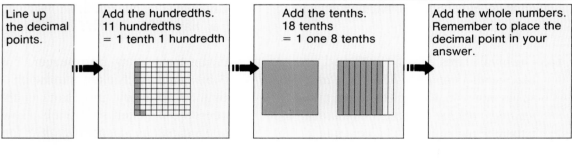

$$
\begin{array}{r} 2.86 \\ +\,3.95 \\ \hline \end{array}
$$

$$
\begin{array}{r} {\scriptstyle 1} \\ 2.8\,6 \\ +\,3.9\,5 \\ \hline 1 \end{array}
$$

$$
\begin{array}{r} {\scriptstyle 1\ 1} \\ 2.8\,6 \\ +\,3.9\,5 \\ \hline 8\,1 \end{array}
$$

$$
\begin{array}{r} {\scriptstyle 1\ 1} \\ 2.8\,6 \\ +\,3.9\,5 \\ \hline 6.8\,1 \end{array}
$$

Jason's total time was 6.81 minutes. He made the team.

B. Sometimes the numbers of decimal places are not the same. Writing zeros to make them the same is helpful.

Find 7.85 + 8.673.

$$
\begin{array}{r} 7.8\,5 \\ +\,8.6\,7\,3 \\ \hline \end{array}
\qquad
\begin{array}{r} {\scriptstyle 1\ 1} \\ 7.8\,5\,0 \\ +\,8.6\,7\,3 \\ \hline 1\,6.5\,2\,3 \end{array}
$$

c. Mental Math Find the sum of $1.98 and $2.95.
Think of $1.98 as 2¢ less than $2.00.
Think of $2.95 as 5¢ less than $3.00.
The sum is 7¢ less than $5.00, or $4.93.

■ **Talk About Math** The work at the right shows how one student found 16.05 + 21.834. What did the student do wrong?

$$\begin{array}{r} 16.005 \\ + 21.834 \\ \hline 37.839 \end{array}$$

Check Understanding

For another example, see Set G, pages 238–239.

Add.

1. $\begin{array}{r} 0.7 \\ + 0.8 \\ \hline \end{array}$ **2.** $\begin{array}{r} \$7.63 \\ + \$2.07 \\ \hline \end{array}$ **3.** $\begin{array}{r} \$86.75 \\ + \$26.58 \\ \hline \end{array}$ **4.** $\begin{array}{r} 3.20 \\ + 5.292 \\ \hline \end{array}$ **5.** $\begin{array}{r} 42.881 \\ + 8.95 \\ \hline \end{array}$

6. 6 + 8.2   **7.** 1.073 + 77.2   **8.** 14.62 + 917.1 + 0.629

Practice

For More Practice, see Set G, pages 240–241.

Add. **Remember** to estimate to be sure your answer makes sense.

9. $\begin{array}{r} 6.4 \\ + 9.8 \\ \hline \end{array}$ **10.** $\begin{array}{r} 82.7 \\ + 3.2 \\ \hline \end{array}$ **11.** $\begin{array}{r} \$6.37 \\ + \$10.45 \\ \hline \end{array}$ **12.** $\begin{array}{r} 42.9 \\ + 7.463 \\ \hline \end{array}$ **13.** $\begin{array}{r} 1.806 \\ + 4.29 \\ \hline \end{array}$

14. 10.8 + 12   **15.** $861.20 + $43.39   **16.** 8.91 + 11.4 + 0.006

17. 0.6 + 9.75 + 11   **18.** 13.9 + 236.7   **19.** $75.76 + $3.80

20. 0.4 + 90   **21.** $95.70 + $8.50   **22.** $20.10 + $12.80

23. 0.7 + 87.8   **24.** 50.5 + 8.176   **25.** 51.25 + 4.086

26. 13.8 + 8.62   **27.** 75.452 + 82.1   **28.** 15.84 + 9.216

29. 6.1 + 2.3 + 5.0   **30.** $91.75 + $2.39 + $16.56 **31.** 3.618 + 4.021 + 9.0

Problem Solving

Julio and Wally were one team, and Clyde and Tai were the other team in a two person 400-meter freestyle relay. Their times are shown in the table.

400-Meter Relay

Names	1st 200 m	2nd 200 m
Julio/Wally	2.92 min	4.01 min
Clyde/Tai	3.00 min	3.95 min

32. What was the total time for Julio and Wally?

33. What was the total time for Clyde and Tai?

34. Who won the relay?

233

Subtracting Decimals

Build Understanding

A. The school record for the 400-meter relay race was 65.5 seconds. This year's Whiz Kids would like to tie or break the record. It took them 53.96 seconds to run 300 meters. In how much time must they run the last 100 meters to tie the record?

Each person in a 400-meter relay runs 100 meters.

Use subtraction to find how much time is left. Find 65.5 − 53.96.

Estimate using front-end digits. 65 − 53 = 12

Line up the decimal points. Write 65.5 as 65.50. Rename to get 10 more hundredths. 1 tenth = 10 hundredths Subtract the hundredths.	Rename to get 10 more tenths. 5 ones 4 tenths = 4 ones 14 tenths Subtract the tenths.	Subtract the ones. Subtract the tens.

$$
\begin{array}{r}
{}^{4\,10} \\
6\,5.\cancel{5}\,\cancel{0} \\
-\,5\,3.9\,6 \\
\hline
4
\end{array}
\qquad
\begin{array}{r}
{}^{14}\!\!\!\!\!\!\!\!\!\!\!\!\! \\
{}^{4}\!\!\cancel{4}\,{}^{10} \\
6\,\cancel{5}.\cancel{5}\,\cancel{0} \\
-\,5\,3.9\,6 \\
\hline
.5\,4
\end{array}
\qquad
\begin{array}{r}
{}^{14}\!\!\!\!\!\!\!\!\!\!\!\!\! \\
{}^{4}\!\!\cancel{4}\,{}^{10} \\
6\,\cancel{5}.\cancel{5}\,\cancel{0} \\
-\,5\,3.9\,6 \\
\hline
1\,1.5\,4
\end{array}
$$

The Whiz Kids have to run the last 100 meters in 11.54 seconds to tie the record.

B. Find 36.8 − 32.476. Write 36.8 as 36.800.

$$
\begin{array}{r}
{}^{9} \\
{}^{7\,\cancel{10}\,10} \\
3\,6.\cancel{8}\,\cancel{0}\,\cancel{0} \\
-\,3\,2.4\,7\,6 \\
\hline
4.3\,2\,4
\end{array}
$$

■ **Talk About Math** Why is lining up the decimal points so important when adding and subtracting decimals?

Check Understanding

For another example, see Set H, pages 238–239.

Subtract.

.1. $5.65 − $4.34	2. 6.27 − 0.94	3. $18.63 − $12.69	4. 9.61 − 3.582	5. 85.089 − 54.12

6. 7 − 4.5   **7.** 5.17 − 3.5   **8.** 50.87 − 4.271

Practice

For More Practice, see Set H, pages 240–241.

Subtract. **Remember** to estimate to be sure your answer makes sense.

9.   7.8   10. $8.25   11. $16.35   12.   9.2   13.   15.406
    − 3.2   − $4.62   − $ 6.50   − 4.546   − 8.73

14. 21 − 3.183   15. 85.22 − 41.6   16. 37.49 − 33.392

17. $91.96 − $90.97   18. 17.78 − 4.7   19. 72.008 − 51.992

Mixed Practice   Tell whether you would use paper
and pencil or mental math. Then find each answer.

20. 5.03 + 4.387   21. 16 − 15.86   22. 18.932 + 6.6068   23. 403 + 27

24. 176 − 16   25. 49.071 + 20   26. 87.094 + 983   27. 874 − 15.473

28. 41.85 + ▦ = 45.35   29. ▦ − 0.409 = 3.421   30. ▦ − 37.74 = 377.76

Problem Solving

31. The Green Team ran the 400-meter relay race in 47.35 seconds.
    Their time for the first 300 meters was 35.58 seconds. What
    was their time for the last 100 meters?

32. At the age of 92, Duncan McLean ran a 100-meter race in
    21.7 seconds. This is 11.8 seconds slower than the 100-meter
    race he ran in 1904. What was his time for the race in
    1904?

33. **Estimation**   Sarah said that the sum of 8.946 and 7.692 is
    more than 16. Do you agree? Explain why or why not.

Reading ———— **Math**

Numbers and Symbols

▦ **Calculator**   Which key sequence matches Exercise 18?

a. 17 [.] 78 [+] 4 [.] 7 [=]   b. 4 [.] 7 [−] 17 [.] 78 [=]

c. 177 [.] 8 [−] 47 [.] [=]   d. 17 [.] 78 [−] 4 [.] 7 [=]

Problem Solving **REVIEW**

Solve each problem.

1. A kilogram is 1,000 grams. A quarter weighs 6 grams. What part of a kilogram is that?

2. A cubit is an ancient unit of measure based on the measure of the length of the forearm from the elbow to the end of the middle finger.

In ancient China, the cubit was 20.9 inches. In ancient Greece, the cubit was 18.2 inches. How much longer was the cubit in ancient China?

3. Janice ran 100 meters in 14.1 seconds. Beth's time was 14.01 seconds. Who won the race?

4. Monty, Ned, and Tony play different sports. The sports are basketball, golf, and swimming. Monty is not as tall as the basketball player. Ned does not use a ball in his sport. Which sport does each person play?

5. Wendy started to work at 9:00 A.M. She took a 1-hour lunch break and two 15-minute breaks. She left work at 4:30 P.M. How many hours did she work?

6. **Data File** Order the batting averages from highest to lowest given in the chart on pages 244-245. Who had the highest batting average?

7. **Make a Data File** Make a chart to show the average monthly rainfall in your state (or an area of your choice) for one year. What is the difference in the amount of rainfall between the wettest and the driest months?

Explore with a Calculator

"Scrambled Keys"

One afternoon Dave was trying to find as many different displays as he could using only the digits 2, 4, 5 and 6, one decimal point, and the operations of addition and subtraction. He kept a record of the displays but not the key sequences.

1. Use the digits 2, 4, 5, and 6 in each of the following sequences to get these displays.

a. ▦ ▦ ⬜.⬜ ▦ ⬜+⬜ ▦ ⬜=⬜ ⬜31.4⬜

b. ▦ ⬜.⬜ ▦ ⬜+⬜ ▦ ▦ ⬜=⬜ ⬜48.5⬜

c. ▦ ⬜.⬜▦ ⬜+⬜▦ ⬜+⬜ ▦ ⬜=⬜ ⬜13.4⬜

d. ⬜.⬜ ▦ ⬜+⬜ ▦ ▦ ⬜+⬜ ▦ ⬜=⬜ ⬜66.5⬜

e. ▦ ⬜+⬜ ▦ ▦ ⬜.⬜ ▦ ⬜=⬜ ⬜60.2⬜

f. ▦ ⬜+⬜ ▦ ⬜.⬜ ▦ ⬜−⬜ ▦ ⬜=⬜ ⬜1.6⬜

g. ▦ ⬜−⬜ ▦ ⬜.⬜ ▦ ⬜+⬜ ▦ ⬜=⬜ ⬜8.6⬜

h. ▦ ▦ ⬜+⬜ ⬜.⬜▦ ⬜−⬜ ▦ ⬜=⬜ ⬜22.5⬜

2. Use the operations addition or subtraction and one decimal point in each of the following sequences to get these displays.

a. 2 ▦ 6 ▦ 5 ▦ 4 ⬜=⬜ ⬜12.5⬜

b. 6 ▦ 2 ▦ 4 ▦ 5 ⬜=⬜ ⬜5.2⬜

c. 26 ▦ 4 ▦ 5 ⬜=⬜ ⬜30.5⬜

d. 5 ▦ 4 ▦ 2 ▦ 6 ⬜=⬜ ⬜6.8⬜

e. 2 ▦ 64 ▦ 5 ⬜=⬜ ⬜66.5⬜

f. 6 ▦ 4 ▦ 5 ▦ 2 ⬜=⬜ ⬜3.5⬜

Reteaching
Set A   pages 214–215

The decimal 0.5 means 5 of 10 equal parts. The decimal 4.86 means 4 wholes and 86 of 100 equal parts of another whole.

Tens	Ones	Tenths	Hundredths
	0	5	
	4	8	6

Remember that a fraction whose denominator is 10 or 100 can be written as a decimal.

Write a fraction and a decimal for each.

1.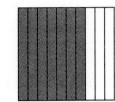

2. Three hundredths

3. Eight and five tenths

Set B   pages 216–217

The fraction $\frac{22}{1,000}$ means 22 of 1,000 equal parts. Three decimal places show thousandths.

Ones	Tenths	Hundredths	Thousandths
0	0	2	2

0.022 is read twenty-two thousandths.

Remember that one decimal place shows tenths and two decimal places show hundredths.

Write a fraction and a decimal for each.

1. Twenty-five thousandths

2. Four hundred thirty-seven thousandths

Set C   pages 218–219

This chart shows the value of each digit in 0.245.

Ones	Tenths	Hundredths	Thousandths
0	2	4	5

2 tenths, 4 hundredths, 5 thousandths
245 thousandths.

Remember that the value of each place in a decimal is 10 times as large as the value of the place to its right.

1. Tell what 4 means in 52.045.

2. Which decimals have 6 in the hundredths place?

   a. 32.006   **b.** 48.162   **c.** 51.069

Set D   pages 220–221

Compare 0.526 and 0.527.

Start at the left.   **0.526**
Compare digits in   **0.527**
the same place.

The ones, tenths, and
hundredths are the same.

6 thousandths is less than
7 thousandths.

0.526 < 0.527

Remember that writing zeros to the right of a decimal does not change its value.

Compare the numbers. Use <, >, or =.

1. 6.4 ▦ 6.40   **2.** 6.947 ▦ 6.946

List the numbers in order from least to greatest.

3. 3.28   3.82   3.58

Set E pages 226–227

Round 3.185 to the nearest hundredth.

The digit 8 is in the hundredths place.

The digit to the right of 8 is 5.

When the digit to the right is 5 or more, add 1 to the digit in the place to be rounded.

The answer is 3.19.

Remember that the digit in the place to be rounded stays the same if the digit to its right is less than 5.

Round to the nearest

1. whole number: 28.72

2. tenth: 16.04

3. hundredth: 42.015

Set F pages 228–229

Estimate 7.21 + 8.61 + 4.08.

Round to the nearest whole number.	Add the front-end digits.
7.21 ---> 7	7.21 ---> 7
8.61 ---> 9	8.61 ---> 8
+ 4.08 ---> 4	+ 4.08 ---> 4
20	19

The exact sum is about 19 or 20.

Remember that adding front-end digits will always give an estimate that is less than the actual sum.

Estimate each sum or difference. Round to the nearest whole number.

1. 6.84 + 9.32   **2.** 72.9 − 41.7

Estimate using front-end digits.

3. 49.81 − 3.75   **2.** 37.94 + 26.41

Set G pages 232–233

Find 8.97 + 9.339.

Estimate using rounding: 9 + 9 = 18.

Write 8.970 for 8.97 to make the number of decimal places the same.

```
         1        1 1       1 1
 8.970   8.970    8.970     8.970
+9.339  +9.339   +9.339    +9.339
    9       09      309    18.309
```

Remember to estimate the sum to be sure your answer makes sense.

Add.

1.	5.9	**2.**	43.8	**3.**	81.09
	+ 4.3		+ 16.1		+ 9.118

4. 12.9 + 8.3   **5.** 4.35 + 10.469

Set H pages 234–235

Find 36.07 − 29.481.

Estimate using front-end digits:
36 − 29 = 7

```
  15 9 16
  2 5 10 610
  36.070  ← Write 36.070 for 36.07.
 −29.481
   6.589
```

Remember to line up the decimal points, and write zeros so that each decimal will have the same number of decimal places. Subtract.

1.	6.5	**2.**	$7.46	**3.**	4.8
	− 2.4		− 4.52		− 2.902

4. 19 − 5.281   **5.** 13.89 − 8.8

More Practice

Set A pages 214–215

Write a fraction and a decimal for each exercise.

1. Six tenths

2. Forty-six hundredths

3. Two and eight hundredths

4. Twelve and three tenths

Write each decimal in words.

5. 0.8   **6.** 0.06   **7.** 7.3   **8.** 9.26   **9.** 3.04   **10.** 31.01

Set B pages 216–217

Write each number in words.

1. 0.005   **2.** 0.084   **3.** 0.647   **4.** 3.028   **5.** 93.109

Write a fraction and a decimal for each exercise.

6. Forty-one thousandths

7. Seven thousandths

8. Five hundred thirty-two thousandths

9. Fifty-four and forty-nine thousandths

Set C pages 218–219

Write what 3 means in each number.

1. 17.3   **2.** 62.023   **3.** 19.03   **4.** 9,305.6   **5.** 13.205

Which decimals have

6. 9 in the tenths place?
 a. 34.09   **b.** 19.02   **c.** 1.941

7. 5 in the thousandths place?
 a. 103.205   **b.** 82.254   **c.** 5,180.49

8. 2 in the hundredths place?
 a. 901.48   **b.** 851.021   **c.** 44.172

9. 6 in the hundredths place?
 a. 2.86   **b.** 684.13   **c.** 13.026

Set D pages 220–221

Compare the numbers. Use <, >, or =. Draw a diagram if needed.

1. 9.74 ▦ 9.72   **2.** 0.8 ▦ 0.7   **3.** 3.8 ▦ 3.80

4. 2.842 ▦ 2.843   **5.** 6.242 ▦ 6.42   **6.** 0.4 ▦ 0.395

List the numbers in order from least to greatest. Use a number line if needed.

7. 0.4   0.9   0.5   **8.** 3.48   7.06   3.19   **9.** 0.274   0.272   0.277

10. 5.1   1.5   1.7   **11.** 0.42   0.35   0.53   **12.** 2.896   8.629   6.928

Set E   pages 226–227

Round to the nearest whole number.

1. 4.6   **2.** 38.4   **3.** 0.738   **4.** 43.5   **5.** 8.04

Round to the nearest tenth.

6. 1.82   **7.** 0.86   **8.** 8.14   **9.** 6.305   **10.** 5.06

Round to the nearest hundredth.

11. 2.433   **12.** 8.049   **13.** 46.481   **14.** 11.006   **15.** 0.825

Set F   pages 228–229

Estimate each sum or difference. Round to the nearest whole number.

1. $\begin{array}{r} 41.4 \\ +\ 19.6 \end{array}$	**2.** $\begin{array}{r} 87.4 \\ +\ 62.2 \end{array}$	**3.** $\begin{array}{r} 6.256 \\ +\ 1.498 \end{array}$	**4.** $\begin{array}{r} 64.8 \\ -\ 32.4 \end{array}$	**5.** $\begin{array}{r} 49.6 \\ -\ 10.8 \end{array}$	**6.** $\begin{array}{r} 31.409 \\ -\ 13.811 \end{array}$

Estimate each sum or difference. Use front-end digits.

7. 4.82 + 20.06   **8.** 39.4 − 9.8   **9.** 87.33 − 20.48   **10.** 43.56 + 10.84

11. 83.106 − 4.612   **12.** 26.5 + 6.4 + 4.8   **13.** 66.6 + 7.8 + 9.3

Set G   pages 232–233

Add. **Remember** to line up the decimal points.

1. $\begin{array}{r} 7.6 \\ +\ 8.5 \end{array}$	**2.** $\begin{array}{r} 45.8 \\ +\ 6.1 \end{array}$	**3.** $\begin{array}{r} \$12.18 \\ +\ 5.61 \end{array}$	**4.** $\begin{array}{r} 91.4 \\ +\ 8.815 \end{array}$	**5.** $\begin{array}{r} 5.924 \\ +\ 3.47 \end{array}$

6. 12.1 + 20   **7.** 4.62 + 10.2 + 0.101   **8.** $731.40 + $42.59

9. 7.82 + 0.8 + 12   **10.** 15.8 + 147.7   **11.** 0.8 + 36.5

12. $26.84 + $4.60   **13.** 9.2 + 4.6 + 8.0   **14.** 4.183 + 1.204 + 6.0

Set H   pages 234–235

Subtract.

1. $\begin{array}{r} 9.7 \\ -\ 4.5 \end{array}$	**2.** $\begin{array}{r} \$6.48 \\ -\ 3.86 \end{array}$	**3.** $\begin{array}{r} \$25.66 \\ -\ 4.71 \end{array}$	**4.** $\begin{array}{r} 14.3 \\ -\ 3.429 \end{array}$	**5.** $\begin{array}{r} 18.204 \\ -\ 9.54 \end{array}$

6. 42 − 6.091   **7.** 63.48 − 53.7   **8.** 26.004 − 14.873

9. 29.46 − 8.4   **10.** $42.34 − $41.33   **11.** 48.26 − 36.168

12. 17.6 − 9.8   **13.** $9.00 − $5.49   **14.** 62.04 − 29.004

Enrichment

Prime and Composite Numbers

Mathematicians put numbers into two categories. They say a number is either prime or composite.

A whole number greater than 1 that has exactly two whole-number divisors is a **prime number**.

A whole number greater than 1 that is not a prime number, such as 12, is a **composite number**. A composite number has more than two whole-number divisors.

The number 2 has only two divisors: itself and 1. The number 2 is prime.

The number 12 has six divisors: 1, 2, 3, 4, 6, 12. When 12 is divided by each of these numbers, the remainder is 0. The number 12 is composite.

The number 1 has only one divisor: itself. The number 1 is neither prime nor composite.

The Sieve of Eratosthenes can be used to find prime numbers.

1. Copy the table of numbers from 1 to 50.
2. Cross out 1. 1 is not prime.
3. Circle 2. 2 is prime. Why?
4. Cross out all the numbers divisible by 2. Why are they not prime?
5. Circle 3. 3 is prime. Why?
6. Cross out all the numbers divisible by 3. Why are they not prime?
7. Circle 5. 5 is prime. Why?
8. Cross out all the numbers divisible by 5.
9. Circle 7. Why is 7 prime?
10. Cross out all the numbers divisible by 7.
11. The numbers left are prime. Circle them.
12. Extend the table of numbers to 100.
13. Repeat Steps 4, 6, 8, and 10.
14. List all the prime numbers to 100.

1	2	3	4	5	6	7	8	9	10
11	12	13	14	15	16	17	18	19	20
21	22	23	24	25	26	27	28	29	30
31	32	33	34	35	36	37	38	39	40
41	42	43	44	45	46	47	48	49	50

Chapter 7 Review/Test

Write a fraction and a decimal for each exercise.

1.

2. Sixteen and five hundredths

3. Six thousandths

Write each number in words.

4. 0.007   **5.** 6.021

Which decimal has

6. a 7 in the tenths place?

    a. 7.13   **b.** 1.73   **c.** 2.074

7. a 2 in the thousandths place?

    a. 0.203   **b.** 0.023   **c.** 0.302

8. Find a pattern. Write the missing decimals.

    17.02, 17.05, 17.08, ▦, ▦

Compare the numbers. Use <, >, or =.

9. 0.7 ▦ 0.53   **10.** 4.4 ▦ 4.40

11. Joel, Jill, and Janelle each are on a different team. One plays baseball, one plays volleyball, and one plays tennis. The sport that Jill plays does not use a net. Janelle does not play tennis. Who plays volleyball?

Round to the nearest tenth.

12. 0.73   **13.** 7.89

Round to the nearest hundredth.

14. 0.083   **15.** 19.729

Estimate each sum or difference. Round to the nearest whole number.

16. $\begin{array}{r} 40.1 \\ +\ 6.5 \end{array}$ **17.** $\begin{array}{r} 29.5 \\ -19.9 \end{array}$

Estimate each sum or difference. Use front-end digits.

18. 5.8 + 17.9   **19.** 58.7 − 10.9

Add.

20. $\begin{array}{r} 0.8 \\ +0.9 \end{array}$ **21.** $\begin{array}{r} 1.73 \\ +2.789 \end{array}$

22. 1.6 + 2.79   **23.** 17.8 + 0.9

Subtract.

24. 15.7 − 6.8   **25.** 32 − 1.63

26. The school record in relay race was 46.8 seconds. This year the record was broken by 1.9 seconds. What was the time this year?

Read the problem below. Then answer the questions.

Erin saved $12.75 toward the cost of a cassette player. How much more money does she need?

27. What additional data, if any, do you need to solve the problem?

28. **Write About Math** How would you write a decimal in the thousandths equal to 0.1?

243

DATA FILE

Data File

1. Round-Trip Fares From Chicago

1. Airfares
Round-trip means to go to a place and back again.

2. List
The list tells how many years would pass before the given population doubles.

3. Picture
One million $1 bills would fill two average size refrigerators.

4. Table
A meteor is a mass of rock that enters earth's atmosphere.

5. Chart
The chart shows the averages of leading hitters on August 18, 1989.

2. When Populations Will Double

U.S.A.	India	Japan
222.5 million	576.2 million	116.8 million
99 Years	36 Years	79 Years
Mexico	Poland	Australia
68.2 million	35.5 million	14.6 million
22 Years	71 Years	86 Years
Brazil	Iraq	Kenya
122 million	13.2 million	19.9 million
25 Years	20 Years	18 Years
France	U. S. S. R.	Sweden
53.6 million	266 million	8.3 million
198 Years	82 Years	1,386 Years
Egypt	China	
42.1 million	975 million	
26 Years	58 Years	

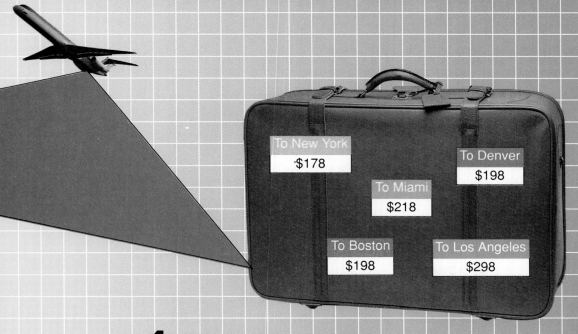

To New York
$178

To Denver
$198

To Miami
$218

To Boston
$198

To Los Angeles
$298

4. Meteor Showers

NAME	MONTH VISIBLE	METEORS PER HOUR	NIGHTS VISIBLE
Quadrantids	January	40	1
Lyrids	April	15	2
N. Aquarids	May	20	3
S. Aquarids	July	20	7
Perseids	August	50	4
Orionids	October	25	2
S. Taurids	November	15	1
Leonids	November	15	1
Geminids	December	50	2
Ursids	December	15	2

3. Weight and Volume of a Million Dollars

Volume — 42 cubic ft

Weight — more than 1 ton

5. Batting Average

Player	Batting Average
Baines, Harold	.315
Boggs, Wade	.338
Browne, Jerry	.309
Davis, Alvin	.332
Greenwell, Mike	.308
Lansford, Carney	.333
Puckett, Kirby	.339
Sax, Steve	.322
Sierra, Ruben	.312
Steinbach, Terry	.308
Yount, Robin	.326

Cumulative Review/Test Chapters 1–7

1. List these numbers in order from least to greatest.

   486   456   449

   a. 486 456 449
   b. 486 449 456
   c. 449 456 486
   d. 449 486 459

2. Multiply.

   412 × 80

   a. 32,096
   b. 32,860
   c. 32,960
   d. 3,286

3. Subtract.

   12,000
   − 3,278

   a. 9,278
   b. 8,278
   c. 8,722
   d. 9,722

4. Find the average of these numbers.

   18   18   22   30   37

   a. 18   **b.** 125   **c.** 25   **d.** 22

5. Divide.

   5)1,795

   a. 35
   b. 360
   c. 358
   d. 359

6. Find the missing factor.

   9 × n = 261

   a. 29   **c.** 2,349
   b. 252   **d.** 28

7. Find the quotient.

   7,200 ÷ 90

   a. 80   **c.** 800
   b. 8   **d.** 8,000

8. Use compatible numbers to estimate.

   6,310 ÷ 71

   a. 9   **b.** 90   **c.** 80   **d.** 900

9. Divide.

   16)3,201

   a. 2 R1
   b. 20 R1
   c. 200 R1
   d. 20

10. Find the volume.

    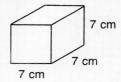

    a. 21 cm³   **c.** 343 cm³
    b. 49 cm³   **d.** 98 cm³

11. Complete.

    16 qt = ▦ gal

    a. 8
    b. 4
    c. 32
    d. 64

12. Complete.

    9 L = ▦ mL

    a. 90
    b. 900
    c. 9,000
    d. 90,000

Choose the most sensible measure.

13. Milk in a bowl of cereal

    a. 1 c   **b.** 1 pt   **c.** 1 qt   **d.** 1 gal

14. A grapefruit

    a. 7 lb   **b.** 70 lb   **c.** 7 T   **d.** 7 oz

15. When you convert from kg to g, you

    a. multiply by 1,000.
    b. divide by 1,000.
    c. multiply by 100.
    d. divide by 100.

Cumulative Review/Test Chapters 1–7 continued

16. Subtract.

7 ft 5 in.
− 4 ft 9 in.

a. 3 ft 4 in.   **c.** 2 ft 8 in.
b. 3 ft 8 in.   **d.** 2 ft 6 in.

17. Which digit in 0.715 is in the hundredths place?

a. 7   **c.** 5
b. 1   **d.** 0

18. Which decimal represents seven thousandths?

a. 0.700   **c.** 0.007
b. 0.070   **d.** 7000

19. Add.

2.9 + 3.78

a. 4.07   **c.** 5.68
b. 6.68   **d.** 5.87

20. Tell whether you would *add, subtract, multiply,* or *divide*. Then solve the problem.

An office supply store has 36 boxes of pencils. Each box holds 144 pencils. How many pencils are there in all?

a. Add; 180 boxes
b. Subtract; 108 boxes
c. Divide; 4 boxes
d. Multiply; 5,184 pencils

21. Plates are being packed 8 per box. There are 300 plates to be packed. How many boxes are needed?

a. 37 boxes   **c.** 4 boxes
b. 38 boxes   **d.** none of these

22. A relay team ran a race in 48.8 seconds. This was 1.9 seconds slower than the school record. What was the school record?

a. 50.7 sec   **c.** 47.1 sec
b. 46.9 sec   **d.** 36.9 sec

23. Jack is making a rectangular pen with 40 feet of fencing. What is the area of the largest pen he can make with the fencing?

a. 40 sq ft   **c.** 100 sq ft
b. 400 sq ft   **d.** 80 sq ft

Read the problem below. Then answer the question.

Alice has worked part-time as a cashier at Smith's Restaurant for 14 weeks. She earns $30 on Friday evenings and $45 working on Saturdays. How much does she earn each week?

24. Which information is not needed to solve the problem?

a. Alice's pay for Friday evening is $30.
b. Alice works only 2 days per week.
c. Alice has worked for 14 weeks.
d. She is paid $45 for working on Saturdays.

CUMULATIVE REVIEW/TEST

247

Multiplication of Decimals

Did You Know:
In 8 hours, a typical pack horse, or mule, can travel approximately 20 miles.
A horse-drawn carriage can travel approximately 40 miles in 8 hours.

Number-Sense Project

Estimate
What is the approximate distance around your school's playground?

Gather Data
Develop a method for estimating the distance. Then use the method to estimate the perimeter of the playground.

Analyze and Report
Describe how you estimated the distance around the playground. Compare estimates with other students.

THE OREGON TRAIL

WYOMING

NEBRASKA

Independence

KANSAS

MISSOURI

Extending Place Value

Build Understanding

A. Carla was trying out different keys on her calculator. She entered the number 37.150. The display looked like this:

$$\boxed{3\,7.15\,0}$$

There are three places to the right of the decimal point. Read: Thirty-seven and one hundred fifty thousandths

B. Next, Carla entered a 4. The display looked like this:

$$\boxed{3\,7.150\,4}$$

There are four decimal places to the right of the decimal point.
Read: Thirty-seven and one thousand five hundred four ten-thousandths

Electronic calculators perform calculations automatically by the use of miniature electronic circuits.

c. Carla then entered an 8. The display looked like this:

$$\boxed{3\,7.150\,48}$$

There are five decimal places to the right of the decimal point.
Read: Thirty-seven and fifteen thousand forty-eight hundred-thousandths

A place-value chart can be extended to show these decimal places.

hundred-thousands	ten-thousands	thousands	hundreds	tens	ones	tenths	hundredths	thousandths	ten-thousandths	hundred-thousandths
				3	7	1	5	0	4	8

37.15048

■ **Talk About Math** What two places are just to the right of the hundred-thousandths place?

Check Understanding

For another example, see Set A, pages 274-275.

Tell how many decimal places are in each number. Write each decimal in words.

1. 91.34   **2.** 3.7602   **3.** 192.64391   **4** 2.0003   **5.** 30.04017

6. How many zeros are between the decimal point and the one in the decimal for one hundred-thousandth?

7. If one ten-thousandth is written as a fraction, what number would be in the denominator?

Practice

For More Practice, see Set A, pages 276-277.

Look at each calculator display. Name the value of the last decimal place.

8. ⌐ 4812.67 ⌐   **9.** ⌐ 201.7802 ⌐   **10.** ⌐ 0.1823 ⌐

11. ⌐ 0.00491 ⌐   **12.** ⌐ 1900.1027 ⌐   **13.** ⌐ 81.20782 ⌐

For each number, name the place that contains an 8.

14. 5.008   **15.** 27.1811   **16.** 3.00087   **17.** 198.074

18. 817.473   **19.** 47.17468   **20.** 89.0631   **21.** 176.4832

Problem Solving

22. 🖩 **Calculator** Enter 12.34567 into a calculator. What number must you add so that the 6 in the display becomes a 9?

23. **Number Sense** Is a number with five decimal places always less than a number with one decimal place? Explain.

Reading ——— Math

Numbers and Symbols Use Exercises 14-21. Write the numbers that have

1. a 7 in the hundred-thousandths place.

2. a 2 in the ten-thousandths place.

3. a 9 in the tens place.

Multiplying a Decimal by a Whole Number

Build Understanding

A. Payday
Materials: Play money ($10 bills,
$1 bills, dimes, pennies)
Groups: Small groups

José works at the Great Movies Video Store
after school and on weekends. He earns $4.17
an hour.

On Thursday, he worked from 3:00 P.M. until
6:00 P.M. How much did José earn?

José worked for 3 hours. He earned $4.17
each hour.

Estimate: $4.17 is a little more than $4.00,
so José earned a little more than 3 × $4, or $12.

You can use play money to help solve problems
in which you need to multiply a decimal
by a whole number. Remember:

1 dollar	1 dime	1 penny
1 one	1 tenth	1 hundredth
1	0.1	0.01

a. Make 3 groups of $4.17.

b. Combine all of the similar coins and bills.
How many dollars do you have? How many
dimes? How many pennies?

c. How many pennies can you trade for dimes?
How many dimes can you trade for $1 bills?
How many dollars can you trade for $10 bills?

Add the value of all the bills and coins. How much
money do you have in all? How much did José earn?

B. Find 3 × 2.4.

You could use play money to model 3 groups of 2.4. Or you could use multiplication to find the total since you are combining groups of equal size.

| Multiply the tenths.
3 × 4 tenths = 12 tenths ‖‖‖
Rename as 1 one 2 tenths. | | Multiply the ones.
3 × 2 ones = 6 ones
6 ones + 1 one = 7 ones |

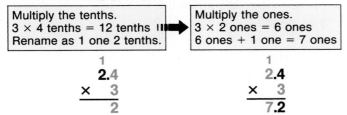

What do you do with play money that is the same as renaming?

C. Find 45 × 0.217.

```
    0.2 1 7    3 decimal places
  ×    4 5    0 decimal places
    1 0 8 5
    8 6 8 0
    9.7 6 5    3 decimal places
```

■ **Write About Math**   Find the products.

3 × 417   3 × 24   45 × 217

What can you say about these products and the products in Examples A, B, and C? Describe how to multiply a decimal by a whole number.

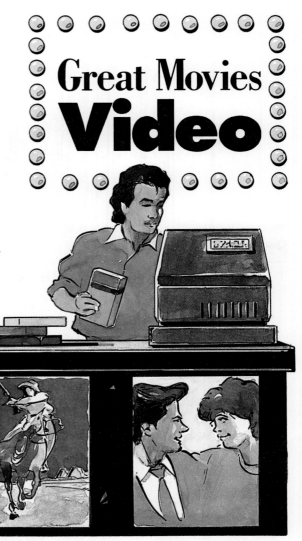

Check Understanding

For another example, see Set B, pages 274-275.

Suppose you are using play money to show 6 × 2.37.

1. How many pennies would you need?

2. How many dimes would you need?

3. How many dollars would you need?

4. How many decimal places will be in the product?

Copy each exercise. Place the decimal point in the product.

5. 2 × 1.74 = 348

6. 3 × 28.6 = 858

7. 8 × 5.27 = 4216

8. 9 × 6.43 = 5787

Practice

For More Practice, see Set B, pages 276-277.

Multiply. **Remember** to place the decimal point in the product.

9. 0.4 × 6

10. 0.09 × 3

11. 0.12 × 7

12. 8.3 × 6

13. 4.5 × 3

14. 2.81 × 4

15. 1.76 × 5

16. 3.03 × 6

17. 2.8 × 34

18. 6.2 × 13

19. 3.7 × 65

20. 0.17 × 14

21. 0.52 × 26

22. 0.208 × 21

23. 0.836 × 52

24. 7 × 2.3

25. 3 × 2.54

26. 4 × 0.205

27. 6 × 0.0513

28. 8 × 0.5149

29. 27 × 0.035

30. 38 × 0.22

31. 17 × 8.15

32. 54 × 6.02

Problem Solving

33. Mental Math On Friday José got paid $87.50 for the whole week. The week before, he earned $79.00. How much more did he earn this week than last?

34. On Saturday, José worked from 8:30 A.M. until 1:30 P.M. He did not get paid for the one hour he took off for lunch. At $4.17 an hour, how much did he earn?

35. Write a question for these data. A quarter is 1.8 millimeters thick. Tom has $12 in quarters.

36. It costs $2.00 plus 12¢ tax to rent a video for one night at Great Movies. The Gomezes kept a space adventure film for 5 nights. How much did they pay?

37. Tom's Videos rents videos for $1.00 the first night. Each additional night costs $2.50. Prices include tax. How many nights would you have to keep a video rented from Great Movies before the price would be cheaper than at Tom's Videos?

Organize your work to help you think clearly.

Skills _____ Review   pages 150-169

Divide.

1. $57\overline{)90}$ **2.** $50\overline{)212}$ **3.** $49\overline{)155}$ **4.** $89\overline{)356}$

5. $42\overline{)849}$ **6.** $50\overline{)4,745}$ **7.** $22\overline{)748}$ **8.** $46\overline{)2,391}$

9. $30\overline{)4,589}$ **10.** $48\overline{)6,796}$ **11.** $52\overline{)7,996}$ **12.** $74\overline{)9,546}$

13. $98\overline{)2,962}$ **14.** $51\overline{)6,656}$ **15.** $24\overline{)7,236}$ **16.** $61\overline{)199}$

17. $3,653 \div 41$ **18.** $8,001 \div 32$ **19.** $7,654 \div 76$

Choose an Operation

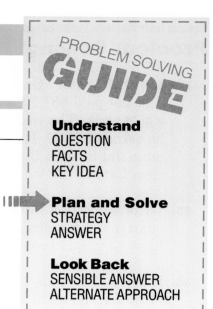

PROBLEM SOLVING GUIDE

Understand
QUESTION
FACTS
KEY IDEA

IIII➤ **Plan and Solve**
STRATEGY
ANSWER

Look Back
SENSIBLE ANSWER
ALTERNATE APPROACH

Build Understanding

The 5th-grade class at Elkins School was having a party to celebrate the upcoming wedding of its teacher, Miss Wolfe. Choy's mother bought four cheese and cracker trays for the party. Each tray cost $12.65. How much did Choy's mother pay for the four trays?

Understand   What was the total cost of the four cheese and cracker trays? Choy's mother bought 4 trays and each tray was the same price. Each tray cost $12.65.

IIII➤ **Plan and Solve**   STRATEGY   Since each tray was the same price, use multiplication to find the total cost.
Find $4 \times \$12.65$.
Estimate: $12.65 is about $13. $4 \times 13 = 52$

Paper and Pencil

$$\begin{array}{r} \$12.65 \\ \times 4 \\ \hline \$50.60 \end{array}$$

Calculator

Press: 12 [.] 65 [×] 4 [=]

Display: *50.6*

ANSWER   Choy's mother paid $50.60 for the four cheese and cracker trays.

Look Back   Check the answer using addition.

$12.65 + $12.65 + $12.65 + $12.65 = $50.60
The answer of $50.60 is close to the estimate of $52.
The answer is reasonable.

■ **Talk About Math**   Which computation method—paper and pencil, calculator, or mental math—would you prefer for working a problem in which you need to multiply an amount of money?

Check Understanding

To answer these questions, use the problem at the right.

1. What is the question?

2. What are the facts?

3. What operations would you use?

4. How will you know if your answer is reasonable?

> Brett's mother bought three rolls of crepe paper at $7.75 each and a box of balloons for $4.85. How much did she spend in all?

Practice

Tell which operation to use. Then solve the problem.

5. Three parents donated a meat tray. The tray cost $36. If they shared the cost equally, how much did each parent spend?

6. Mrs. Gallo, the principal, bought 5 cases of fruit drinks. Each case cost $8.79. How much did she spend?

7. If 28 students shared the cost of a gift for $112, how much did each contribute?

8. If 15 teachers gave a total of $178 for a gift that cost $169.75, how much money was left over?

Choose a _____ Strategy

Paper Routes Meg and Suzie deliver different newspapers on Monday through Saturday. Meg earns $0.06 for every paper she delivers. Suzie makes $13.00 a month plus $0.05 for every paper delivered. Use the calendar to help you answer the questions.

9. How much would each girl earn in September if each delivered 20 papers each day?

10. How much would each girl earn if she delivered 30 papers each day? 40 papers? 60 papers?

11. One September the girls earned the same salary and delivered the same number of papers. How much did each earn? How many newspapers were delivered each day?

S E P T E M B E R						
S	M	T	W	Th	F	S
	1	2	3	4	5	6
7	8	9	10	11	12	13
14	15	16	17	18	19	20
21	22	23	24	25	26	27
28	29	30				

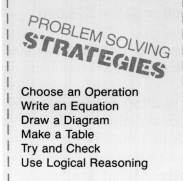

PROBLEM SOLVING STRATEGIES

Choose an Operation
Write an Equation
Draw a Diagram
Make a Table
Try and Check
Use Logical Reasoning

Mental Math for Multiplying by 10, 100, or 1,000

Build Understanding

Equipment used in different sports must meet standard measurements. A baseball must weigh between 5 ounces and 5.25 ounces.

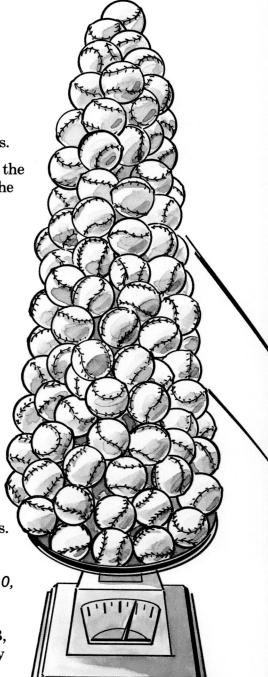

A. What is the most 10 baseballs could weigh?

If each of the 10 baseballs weighs 5.25 ounces, the total weight is 10 × 5.25 ounces. Estimate: Since 10 × 5 = 50, 10 × 5.25 must be more than 50 ounces.

You know 10 × 525 = 5,250. So 10 × 5.25 will have the same digits in the product but two digits will be to the right of the decimal point.

$$10 \times 5.25 = 52.50$$

The most 10 baseballs could weigh is 52.50 ounces.

B. What would be the most that 100 baseballs or 1,000 baseballs could weigh?

Use what you know about multiplying by 10, 100, or 1,000 and multiplying decimals by whole numbers.

Notice how the decimal point moves.

10 × 525 = 5,250	10 × 5.25 = 52.50
100 × 525 = 52,500	100 × 5.25 = 525.00
1,000 × 525 = 525,000	1,000 × 5.25 = 5,250.00

The most 100 baseballs could weigh is 525 ounces. The most 1,000 baseballs could weigh is 5,250 ounces.

To multiply a decimal by 10, 100, or 1,000, move the decimal point one place to the right for each zero in 10, 100, or 1,000.

■ **Write About Math** In the products in Example B, which zeros do not need to be written? Why can they be left off? Which zeros must be written? Why?

258

Check Understanding

For another example, see Set C, pages 274-275.

Match the product with the letter of the correct answer.

1. 1,000 × 2.7   **2.** 100 × 0.27   **3.** 10 × 0.027   **4.** 1,000 × 0.27

a. 27   **b.** 0.27   **c.** 270   **d.** 2,700

Practice

For More Practice, see Set C, pages 276-277.

Find each product. Use mental math.

5. 10 × 0.6   **6.** 100 × 0.06   **7.** 1,000 × 0.06   **8.** 10 × 4.3

9. 100 × 4.3   **10.** 1,000 × 4.3   **11.** 10 × 0.17   **12.** 0.4 × 100

13. 0.653 × 1,000   **14.** 1.09 × 10   **15.** 21.3 × 10   **16.** 10 × 0.007

17. 1,000 × 0.004   **18.** 0.46 × 1,000   **19.** 0.46 × 10,000   **20.** 0.46 × 100,000

Mixed Practice   Find the product.

21. 0.45 × 7   **22.** 4.7 × 8   **23.** 1.34 × 9   **24.** 8 × 2.6

25. 47 × 9   **26.** 18 × 19   **27.** 478 × 5   **28.** 282 × 11

Problem Solving

29. A tennis ball must weigh between 2 and 2.065 ounces. What is the maximum weight of 100 tennis balls?

30. A golf ball can weigh no more than 1.62 ounces. What is the maximum weight of 1,000 golf balls?

31. The smallest a football can be is 10.875 inches long. What is the smallest total length of 100 footballs laid end to end?

32. In the metric system, 1 kilogram equals 1,000 grams. How many grams are in 1.7 kilograms? How many grams are in 0.785 kilograms?

Estimating Products

Build Understanding

How tall will you be when you are an adult?

Growth Factor		
Age	Girls	Boys
8	1.29	1.39
9	1.24	1.33
10	1.18	1.28
11	1.13	1.23
12	1.08	1.19
13	1.04	1.15

A. In her science book, Lisa found a growth factor table for predicting adult height. To use the table, multiply the person's height in centimeters by the growth factor for the person's age.

Lisa is 10 years old and her height is 159 centimeters. The growth factor for a 10-year-old girl is 1.18. To estimate her adult height, she rounded each number.

1.18 × 159 → 1 × 200 = 200   1.18 rounds to 1.
159 rounds to 200.

Her adult height will be about 200 centimeters.

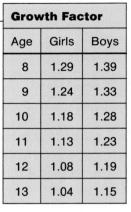

B. Estimate the product of 94.8 and 5.82. Substitute a compatible number to multiply mentally.

94.8 × 5.82 → 100 × 5.82 = 582

The product of 94.8 and 5.82 is about 582.

■ **Talk About Math**   Will the actual product in Example B be more than 582 or less? Why?

Check Understanding

For another example, see Set D, pages 274-275.

Match each with the most reasonable estimate.

1. 6.42 × 2.87   **2.** 9.75 × 2.2   **3.** 3.02 × 9.18   **4.** 42.3 × 7.04

   a. 280   **b.** 27   **c.** 18   **d.** 22

Estimate each product. Use your estimate to put the decimal point in each product.

5. 3.83 × 3.1 = 11873   **6.** 12.34 × 9.5 = 11723   **7.** 102.4 × 4.71 = 482304

Practice

For More Practice, see Set D, pages 276-277.

Estimate the products.

8. 3.22 × 5.7   **9.** 4.09 × 1.34   **10.** 23.7 × 8.5   **11.** 6.554 × 2.3

12. 63.5 × 4.9   **13.** 81.2 × 8.7   **14.** 92.5 × 1.07   **15.** 100.2 × 24.6

16. 0.34 × 0.99   **17.** 89.32 × 11.03   **18.** 123.4 × 10.8   **19.** 54.37 × 0.83

20. 1,034.25 × 7.17   **21.** 0.06 × $25   **22.** 1.25 × $150

Mixed Practice   Complete only those exercises with products less than 20.

23. 20 × 0.9   **24.** 20 × 0.09   **25.** 20 × 1.2   **26.** 20 × 2.4

27. 6 × 0.3   **28.** 6 × 3.9   **29.** 6 × 0.03   **30.** 6 × 3.1

Problem Solving

31. Number Sense   Adam told Lisa the product of 23.2 and 1.5 is 3.48. Was he correct? Explain.

32. Lisa said the product of 9.23 and 8.76 is less than 90. Explain her thinking.

Midchapter ———— Checkup

Write each decimal in words.

1. 82.47   **2.** 4.82604   **3.** 187.53282   **4.** 3.0006

Find the product.

5. 3 × $2.78   **6.** 6 × 36.7   **7.** 12 × 0.16   **8.** 23 × 0.107

9. 0.47 × 10   **10.** 0.407 × 100   **11.** 4.07 × 1,000   **12.** 1.01 × 100

13. Alfredo delivers pizzas after school. He earns $3.50 an hour. Last week he worked 11 hours. How much money did he earn?

Estimation   Estimate to place the decimal point in each product.

14. 3.96 × 2.72 = 107712   **15.** 21.2 × 1.03 = 21836

Problem-Solving Workshop

Real-Life Decision Making

You and 5 friends have $5 each to play miniature golf and buy pizza at the Pizza Shack. Two people want pepperoni, 2 people want sausage, and 2 people like all the toppings.

PIZZA TOPPINGS
pepperoni
sausage
mushrooms
onions
green pepper
broccoli

16-inch pizza

$9
serves 4–6 people
toppings: $1.50 each

12-inch pizza

$6.50
serves 2–3 people
toppings: $1 each

1. How much money does the group have in all?

2. What is the cost of 2 small pizzas with one topping each?

3. What is the cost of one large pizza with two toppings?

4. How much does it cost 6 people to play 2 games each? How much more would it cost them to play 3 games each?

5. Decide how you will spend the group money. What will you order? How many games of miniature golf will you play? Will any money be left?

Miniature Golf

Price per child
$1.00 for 1 game
$2.50 for 3 games

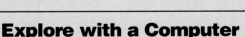

Explore with a Computer

Use the *Spreadsheet Workshop Project* for this activity.

1. Suppose you had $2.46 to spend on supplies for making friendship bracelets. At the computer, you will see the prices for the supplies. What could you buy? Type the number of each item you want to buy. Can you spend exactly $2.46?

2. What if you and two friends had $6.37 to spend for supplies together? If you each bought the same items, what could you buy?

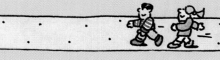

Number-Sense Project

Look back at pages 248-249.
Mr. Hill's class estimated the perimeter of the school's playground is about 1,300 feet, or 0.25 miles.

The class planned a route across the United States. For each lap a student walked around the playground, he or she moved a marker 0.25 miles along the route. If each of the 30 students in the class walked 1 lap, Mr. Hill moved the marker 30 × 0.25, or 7.5 miles.

1. In all, how many miles did the class walk on Tuesday, the 6th?

2. How many laps were logged on Wednesday, the 7th? What is a possible explanation for this number?

3. What was the greatest distance in miles covered by Mr. Hill's class in one day?

4. Write a statement comparing the perimeter of your playground to the one at Mr. Hill's school.

Log of the laps
Mr. Hill's class
walked in
12 days

Date	Day	Laps
1	Thursday	97
2	Friday	112
5	Monday	65
6	Tuesday	40
7	Wednesday	0
8	Thursday	101
9	Friday	135
12	Monday	150
13	Tuesday	90
14	Wednesday	148
15	Thursday	67
16	Friday	125

Problem Solving WORKSHOP

263

Multiplying by a Decimal

Build Understanding

A. On his last sales trip, Mr. McCall averaged 55 miles per hour driving on the interstate highway. How far did he travel in 3.5 hours?

He traveled the same distance each hour, so multiply to find the total distance.

Estimate: 4 × 55 = 220

```
    5 5
  × 3.5  ← 1 decimal place
    275
  1650
  192.5  ← 1 decimal place
```

Mr. McCall covered a distance of **192.5** miles.

East-west interstate highways have even numbers. Odd numbers are used for north-south highways.

B. Find 0.7 of 0.5. Use models to show how to place the decimal point.

Shade 0.5 of a square yellow.

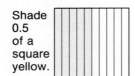

Separate each tenth into 10 equal parts. Shade 7 of the 10 equal parts red.

Name the number of parts of the square that are orange.

```
    0.5   1 decimal place
  × 0.7   1 decimal place
  0.3 5   2 decimal places
```

C. Find 4.12 × 6.89.

Estimate: 4 × 7 = 28

Step 1
Multiply as with whole numbers.

```
      689
    ×412
    1378
    6890
  275600
  283868
```

Step 2
Count the number of decimal places in both factors.

```
    6.8 9  ← 2 decimal places
  × 4.1 2  ← 2 decimal places
    1378
    6890
  275600
  283868
```

Step 3
The number of decimal places in the product is the total number of decimal places in the factors.

```
    6.8 9  ← 2 decimal places
  × 4.1 2  ← 2 decimal places
    1378
    6890
  275600
  28.3 8 6 8  ← 4 decimal places
```

■ **Write About Math**   What coin is one tenth of a dollar?
Write its value as a decimal. What coin is one tenth of a tenth
of a dollar? Write its value as a decimal.

Check Understanding

For another example, see Set E, pages 274-275.

Tell how many decimal places should be shown in each product.

1. 23×5.7 **2.** 2.3×5.7 **3.** 0.23×5.7 **4.** 0.23×0.57

5. 1.34×4.96 **6.** 0.46×1.56 **7.** 345×0.5 **8.** 1.25×1.25

Practice

For More Practice, see Set E, pages 276-277.

Multiply.

9. $\begin{array}{r} 0.7 \\ \times\, 0.4 \\ \hline \end{array}$
10. $\begin{array}{r} 0.3 \\ \times\, 0.5 \\ \hline \end{array}$
11. $\begin{array}{r} 7 \\ \times\, 0.6 \\ \hline \end{array}$
12. $\begin{array}{r} 0.54 \\ \times\, 0.7 \\ \hline \end{array}$
13. $\begin{array}{r} 2.9 \\ \times\, 5.4 \\ \hline \end{array}$

14. $\begin{array}{r} 8.4 \\ \times\, 0.6 \\ \hline \end{array}$
15. $\begin{array}{r} 23.7 \\ \times\, 0.12 \\ \hline \end{array}$
16. $\begin{array}{r} 23.9 \\ \times\, 0.2 \\ \hline \end{array}$
17. $\begin{array}{r} 9.12 \\ \times\, 0.22 \\ \hline \end{array}$
18. $\begin{array}{r} 2.126 \\ \times\, 8 \\ \hline \end{array}$

19. 721×0.3 **20.** 56.1×2.1 **21.** 3.16×0.9 **22.** 1.02×0.6

23. 0.9×5 **24.** 0.7×6 **25.** 0.4×0.87 **26.** 56×2.7

27. 0.04×5.7 **28.** 4.9×0.3 **29.** 0.2×78 **30.** 0.33×4.6

31. 34.1×0.3 **32.** 9.1×4.3 **33.** 0.25×65.1 **34.** 5.01×3.047

Problem Solving

Read for the facts to solve the problems.

35. On a previous trip, Mr. McCall averaged 54.5 miles per hour. If he traveled 7.5 hours, how many miles did he travel?

36. When Mr. McCall began his last trip, the odometer on his car read 34,512.9. The reading when he returned home was 35,389.2. How many miles did he travel?

37. If gas costs $1.18 a gallon and Mr. McCall bought 9 gallons, how much did he pay?

38. ▦ **Calculator**   The price of gas is $1.349 per gallon as shown on a pump. Mr. McCall bought 5.947 gallons. What total cost did the pump show?

Multiplying Decimals: Zeros in the Product

Build Understanding

A. At Val's Variety Store, Maria bought a notebook for $1.50. A state sales tax of 6 cents on each dollar is added to the cost of any purchase. How much tax did Maria pay?

To find the amount of the sales tax, multiply the cost by 0.06. Find 0.06 × 1.50.

| Multiply as with whole numbers. | Count the total number of decimal places in both factors. | You need to write another zero to place the decimal point. |

$$\begin{array}{r} 1.5\,0 \\ \times\, 0.0\,6 \\ \hline 9\,0\,0 \end{array}$$

$$\begin{array}{r} 1.5\,0 \leftarrow \text{2 decimal places} \\ \times\, 0.0\,6 \leftarrow \text{2 decimal places} \\ \hline 9\,0\,0 \leftarrow \text{4 decimal places} \\ \text{are needed.} \end{array}$$

$$\begin{array}{r} 1.5\,0 \\ \times\, 0.0\,6 \\ \hline 0.0\,9\,0\,0 \leftarrow \text{4 decimal places} \end{array}$$

Maria paid $0.09 in sales tax on her notebook.

B. Find 0.08 × 0.012.

$$\begin{array}{r} 0.0\,1\,2 \leftarrow \text{3 decimal places} \\ \times\quad 0.0\,8 \leftarrow \text{2 decimal places} \\ \hline 0.0\,0\,0\,9\,6 \leftarrow \text{5 decimal places} \end{array}$$

Need to write 3 extra zeros in product.

c. ▦ **Calculator**   Find 0.215 × 0.174.

Press: ⬚.⬚ 215 ⬚×⬚ ⬚.⬚ 174 ⬚=⬚

Display: *0.03741*

■ **Talk About Math**   In Example C, why are there only 5 decimal places in the product but 6 decimal places in the 2 factors?

Check Understanding

For another example, see Set F, pages 274-275.

Copy each exercise. Place the decimal point in the product. Write extra zeros when necessary.

1.	**2.**	**3.**	**4.**	**5.**
$\begin{array}{r} 0.07 \\ \times\ 0.3 \\ \hline 21 \end{array}$	$\begin{array}{r} 6.4 \\ \times 0.2 \\ \hline 128 \end{array}$	$\begin{array}{r} 0.18 \\ \times\ 0.4 \\ \hline 72 \end{array}$	$\begin{array}{r} 1.25 \\ \times 0.07 \\ \hline 875 \end{array}$	$\begin{array}{r} 0.09 \\ \times 0.06 \\ \hline 54 \end{array}$

Practice

For More Practice, see Set F, pages 276-277.

Multiply. **Remember** to write extra zeros when necessary.

6. 0.09 × 0.02   **7.** 0.004 × 9   **8.** 0.007 × 0.07   **9.** 0.025 × 0.04

10. 33 × 0.003   **11.** 1.4 × 0.004   **12.** 2.05 × 0.01   **13.** 45 × 0.002

14. 0.01 × 0.01   **15.** 0.125 × 0.08   **16.** 2.7 × 0.002   **17.** 0.025 × 2

Tell whether you would use paper and pencil, a calculator, or mental math. Then find each product.

18. 2.2 × 0.007   **19.** 0.22 × 0.007   **20.** 0.022 × 0.007

21. 0.2 × 0.2 × 0.2   **22.** 0.3 × 0.4 × 0.5   **23.** 1 × 0.03 × 0.05

Problem Solving

Use Data   Study the table of telephone rates on page 271. Find the cost of a call lasting 0.5 minute at the following times.

24. 11:00 A.M.   **25.** 6:00 P.M.   **26.** 6:00 A.M.

For each problem, multiply by 0.06 to find the sales tax.

27. Akato bought a felt-tipped pen at Val's for $1.00. How much was the sales tax?

28. What is the sales tax on a box of paper clips for 89 cents and a tablet for 46 cents?

Explore ———— Math

Easy Products   Complete, using paper and pencil or a calculator.

29. a. 0.1 × 7.52 = ▦
   b. 0.1 × 69.08 = ▦
   c. 0.1 × 547.6 = ▦
   d. 0.1 × 0.03 = ▦

30. a. 0.01 × 7.52 = ▦
   b. 0.01 × 69.08 = ▦
   c. 0.01 × 547.6 = ▦
   d. 0.01 × 0.03 = ▦

31. Describe an easy way to find the product of a decimal number and 0.1.

32. Describe an easy way to find the product of a decimal number and 0.01.

Exploring Division of Decimals

Build Understanding

Be Fair
Materials: Play money ($10 bills, $1 bills, dimes, and pennies)
Groups: Small groups

Daniel, RJ, and Scott have a lawn-raking business in the fall. One day they earned $17.25. How much was each boy's share of their earnings?

Find $17.25 ÷ 3.

a. Use play money to divide $17.25 into 3 equal shares.

b. First trade $10 for 10 $1 bills. How many dollars do you have in all?

c. Divide the dollars into 3 equal groups. How many dollars can each boy have? How many dollars are left over?

d. Trade the remaining dollars for dimes. How many dimes do you have in all? How many dimes can each boy have?

e. How many dimes are left over? Trade the extra dime for pennies. How many pennies do you have in all? How many can each boy have?

f. What is each boy's share?

■ **Talk About Math**   Find 1,725 ÷ 3. What can you say about this quotient and your answer to the problem above?

Check Understanding

For another example, see Set G, pages 274-275.

1. If you were dividing $18.40 among 4 girls, how many dollar bills would each girl get?

2. What would you do with the dollar bills that were left?

3. What coins would each girl get?

4. How much money would each girl get?

5. What is the quotient for 18.40 ÷ 4?

6. How could you show 7.2 ÷ 3 using money?

7. Find 41.5 ÷ 5.

Practice

For More Practice, see Set G, pages 276-277.

Divide. **Remember** to put the decimal point in the quotient.

8. 3.69 ÷ 3   9. 6.08 ÷ 4   10. 14.94 ÷ 6   11. 23.25 ÷ 5

12. 20.4 ÷ 3   13. 16.8 ÷ 7   14. 13.8 ÷ 6   15. 217.2 ÷ 4

16. 2.348 ÷ 4   17. 2.205 ÷ 9   18. 0.984 ÷ 8   19. 5.25 ÷ 5

Problem Solving

Use play money, if you need to, to solve these problems.

20. If you and two of your friends earned $8.43 together, what would your share be?

21. RJ worked for 2 hours, and Scott and Daniel each worked 1 hour. They were paid $21.60. How could the money be split fairly?

22. One day Scott worked for 2 hours raking a lawn, but Daniel worked for only 1 hour. The two boys earned $10.35. What would be a fair way to share the money? Why?

23. **Visual Thinking** You have quarters, nickels, pennies, and dimes in your pocket. There are 12 coins all together. There are 2 large silver coins, 3 small silver coins, and 3 medium silver coins. The rest are copper coins. What is the total?

Multiple-Step Problems

PROBLEM SOLVING GUIDE

Build Understanding

Floyd's father bought a fishing vest for his son's birthday. It was gray with 17 pockets and cost $26.60. A state sales tax of 5 cents on each dollar is added to the cost of every purchase. What was the total cost of the fishing vest, including tax?

Understand   QUESTION   What was the total cost including tax?

FACTS   The vest cost $26.60. The sales tax is 5 cents on every dollar.

KEY IDEA   You need to find the amount of sales tax on $26.60. The sales tax then must be added to the cost of the vest to find the total cost.

Plan and Solve   First, compute the sales tax. The tax is 5 cents on each dollar, so multiply $26.60 by 0.05. To find the total cost, add sales tax to the cost of the vest.

Find 0.05 × $26.60.	2 6.6 0
Estimate:	× 0.0 5
0.05 × 30 = 1.50	1.3 3 0 0

The sales tax is $1.33.

Find $26.60 + $1.33.	2 6.6 0
Estimate:	+ 1.3 3
27.00 + 1.00 = 28.00	2 7.9 3

The total cost, including tax, was $27.93.

Look Back   The computed sales tax and total cost are close to the estimates. The answer is reasonable.

■ Talk About Math   If an item is on sale, do you pay tax on the original price or on the sale price?

Understand
QUESTION
FACTS
KEY IDEA

Plan and Solve
STRATEGY
ANSWER

Look Back
SENSIBLE ANSWER
ALTERNATE APPROACH

Check Understanding

Use the problem at the right to answer these questions.

1. What is the question?

2. What are the facts?

3. How would you solve the problem?

> Floyd's father bought a canvas creel that cost $20.25. What is the total cost of this purchase if the sales tax is the same as in the example?

Practice

Solve each problem. Use a sales tax of 5 cents on the dollar.

4. A customer bought a landing net for $16. What is the total cost of the net, including sales tax?

5. Mr. Cardona bought 2 fly fishing videotapes at $45 each. What was his total cost, including tax?

6. Mrs. Torres bought a graphite rod for $57.55 and a reel for $49.05. What is the total cost, including sales tax?

7. Tom's Tackle Shop donates 1 cent of every dollar in sales to a conservation fund. How much would be donated for $110 in sales?

8. **Calculator** Explain how to do this problem with your calculator: $26.60 × 1.05.

9. **Critical Thinking** Why is the answer in Problem 8 the same as the answer in the example?

Choose a _____ Strategy

Timed Talk The cost of a long distance call depends on the distance and the time of day the call is made. Here is a table of rates for telephone calls.

Time of day	Cost of first minute	Cost for each additional minute
11:00 P.M. to 8:00 A.M.	$0.25	$0.18
8:00 A.M. to 5:00 P.M.	$0.62	$0.43
5:00 P.M. to 11:00 P.M.	$0.38	$0.26

10. How much would it cost to make a 3-minute call at noon? at 8:00 P.M.? at 6:00 A.M.?

11. How much would it cost to make a 20-minute call at noon? at 8:00 P.M.? at 6:00 A.M.?

12. The cost of a 7:30 A.M. call was $2.05. How long was the call?

Solve each problem.

1. Find the cost of 3 rolls of film if each roll costs $2.49.

2. Parking at Ace Garage costs $2.25 for the first hour and $0.75 for each additional hour. How much would it cost to park for 4 hours?

3. Mr. Wilkinson wants to plant 5 rows of raspberries. Each row is 20 feet long. If he places a plant every 2 feet, how many raspberry plants does he need?

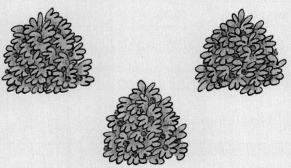

4. If sales tax is 6%, find the total cost of an $18 basketball.

5. Each of the 15 members of a baseball team gave $3 for a gift for the coach. The gift cost $42.80. How much money was left?

6. A dime weighs 2 grams. How much does $10 worth of dimes weigh?

7. **Data File** Ron and his two brothers want to buy season tickets to the orchestra concerts. The most they can spend as a family for tickets is $300. Use the price chart on pages 380–381. Which tickets can they buy? Which ones would you buy? Why?

8. **Make a Data File** Find the current rates for mailing envelopes by first-class that range in weight from 1 ounce to 1 pound. Make a chart to show the data.

Explore with a Calculator

"Order, please!"

Estelle works at The Paper Pound. She fills out the forms for telephone orders. All of the paper products are sold by the pound.

PRICE LIST			
Price per pound		Price per pound	
Typing paper	$1.29	Note pads	$0.98
Stationery		Notebook Paper	
white	$1.56	white	$1.18
assorted colors	$1.68	assorted colors	$1.36
Letter envelopes	$0.42	Mailing envelopes	$6.84

For each item, estimate to find which choice is the cost.
Then find the actual cost.

1. 4 lb of typing paper

a. $516　**b.** $51.60　**c.** $5.16

2. 8 lb of note pads

a. $7.84　**b.** $784　**c.** $78.40

3. 15 lb of letter envelopes

a. $630　**b.** $6.30　**c.** $6.75

4. 2.5 lb of white notebook paper

a. $29.50　**b.** $2.95　**c.** $3.20

5. 4.25 lb of white stationery

a. $66.30　**b.** $7.02　**c.** $6.63

6. 0.75 lb of mailing envelopes

a. $11.97　**b.** $5.13　**c.** $51.30

7. Mary would like to buy 3 pounds of typing paper and 4.75 pounds of colored notebook paper. Will $10 be enough money to pay for the order?

8. Ann ordered 4.5 pounds of letter envelopes, 7.25 pounds of mailing envelopes, and 6 pounds of note pads. What is the total cost of the order?

Reteaching

Set A   pages 250–251

This chart shows the value of each digit in 3.04263, which is read as: three and four thousand two hundred sixty-three hundred-thousandths.

hundred-thousands	ten-thousands	thousands	hundreds	tens	ones	tenths	hundredths	thousandths	ten-thousandths	hundred-thousandths
					3	0	4	2	6	3

Remember that the decimal point separates the ones place from the tenths place.

Name the value of the last decimal place.

1. 364.825   **2.** 247.6837

For each number, name the place that contains a 6.

3. 5.206   **4.** 14.39763

Set B   pages 252–255

Find 32 × 0.366.

Multiply as with whole numbers

```
      0.3 6 6      3 decimal places
    ×     3 2      0 decimal places
      ─────────
        7 3 2
      1 0 9 8
      ─────────
    1 1.7 1 2      3 decimal places
```

Remember to place the decimal point in the product.

Multiply.

1.   0.7   **2.**   0.04   **3.**   0.16
       × 7   ×   9   ×   4

4. 5 × 3.47   **5.** 8 × 0.314

Set C   pages 258–259

To multiply a decimal by 10, 100, or 1,000, move the decimal point one place to the right for each zero in 10, 100, or 1,000.

Find 100 × 0.3.

Since there are two zeros in 100, move the decimal point two places to the right.

100 × 0.3 = 30

Remember that you may have to write zeros in the product when multiplying a number by 10, 100, or 1,000.

Find each product. Use mental math.

1. 10 × 0.8   **2.** 100 × 0.08

3. 1,000 × 0.49   **4.** 32.5 × 100

Set D   pages 260–261

Estimate the product 48.3 × 102.6. Use a compatible number, a number that is easy to multiply, for 102.6.

100 × 48.3 = 4830

Notice that a zero was written after 3 in the product.

Remember that an estimated product will be larger than the actual product if you substitute a larger number for one of the factors.

Estimate the product.

1. 4.45 × 3.7   **2.** 8.04 × 2.52

3. 94.1 × 1.12   **4.** 48.6 × 9.47

Set E   pages 264–265

Find 7.43 × 3.79.
Estimate: 7 × 4 = 28

Multiply as with whole numbers.

$$
\begin{array}{r}
7.4\,3 \\
\times\,3.7\,9 \\
\hline
6\,6\,8\,7 \\
5\,2\,0\,1 \\
2\,2\,2\,9 \\
\hline
2\,8\,1\,5\,9\,7 \\
\end{array}
$$

Count the number of decimal places in both factors.
7.43: 2 places; 3.79; 2 places; total 4

Write the product with 4 decimal places:
28.1597

Remember that the number of decimal places in the product is the total number of decimal places in the factors.

Multiply.

1.	0.6 × 0.3	**2.**	0.9 × 0.4
3.	8 × 0.7	**4.**	0.49 × 0.5
5.	24.2 × 0.06	**6.**	8.32 × 0.33

Set F   pages 266–267

Find 3.72 × 0.007.
Multiply as with whole numbers.

$$
\begin{array}{rl}
3.7\,2 & \text{2 decimal places} \\
\times\,0.0\,0\,7 & \text{3 decimal places} \\
\hline
2\,6\,0\,4 & \\
\end{array}
$$

The total number of decimal places needed is 5. Write an extra zero to show the fifth place.

3.72 × 0.007 = 0.02604

Remember that you may have to have to write zeros when you place the decimal point in the product.

Multiply.

1. 0.08 × 0.03   **2.** 0.006 × 8

3. 3.09 × 0.01   **4.** 55 × 0.005

5.	0.007 × 3.8	**6.** 0.075 × 4

Set G   pages 268–269

Find $17.45 ÷ 5.

Think: Divide $17 among 5 people. Each would receive $3 from the $17.

Trade the remaining dollars for dimes.
$2 = 20 dimes   Divide 20 dimes among the 5 people. Each would get 4 dimes.

Now divide the 45¢ among the 5 people. Each will get 9¢.
So each person receives:
three $1 bills + 4 dimes + 9 cents

$3.00 + 0.40 + 0.09 = $3.49

So $17.45 ÷ 5 = $3.49.

Remember to place the decimal point in the quotient directly above the decimal point in the dividend. Then divide as with whole numbers.

Divide.

1. 16.8 ÷ 4   **2.** 42.6 ÷ 3

3. 20.55 ÷ 5   **4.** 54.6 ÷ 6

5. 3.28 ÷ 8   **6.** 38.5 ÷ 7

7. 6.03 ÷ 9   **8.** 2.52 ÷ 6

More Practice
Set A   pages 250–251

Look at each calculator display. Name the value of the
last decimal place.

1. *3678.582*   2. *456.89*   3. *80.43052*   4. *527.0745*

For each number, name the place that contains a 7.

5. 16.071   6. 36.287   7. 5.03087   8. 701.342

9. 827.133   10. 472.0912   11. 320.744   12. 58.18307

Set B   pages 252–255

Multiply. **Remember** to place the decimal point in the
product.

1. 0.8	2. 0.34	3. 0.05	4. 7.4	5. 6.5
× 9	× 6	× 7	× 4	× 5

6. 4.32	7. 3.87	8. 3.2	9. 7.07	10. 0.504
× 3	× 6	× 44	× 9	× 32

11. 6 × 4.7   12. 4 × 5.63   13. 9 × 0.802   14. 48 × 0.66   15. 68 × 4.07

Set C   pages 258–259

Find each product. Use mental math.

1. 10 × 0.9   2. 100 × 0.09   3. 1,000 × 0.09   4. 10 × 6.7

5. 100 × 6.7   6. 1,000 × 6.7   7. 10 × 0.28   8. 0.6 × 100

Mixed Practice   Find the product.

9. 0.83 × 6   10. 7.9 × 5   11. 1.62 × 8   12. 474 × 12

Set D   pages 260–261

Estimate the product.

1. 6.43 × 8.7   2. 34.5 × 6.6   3. 3.07 × 1.85   4. 24.5 × 3.91

5. 73.9 × 2.4   6. 490 × 5.33   7. 106.9 × 11.1   8. 0.48 × 1.09

Mixed Practice   Complete only those exercises with
products less than 30.

9. 30 × 1.1   10. 30 × 0.99   11. 8.4 × 3.7   12. 7.03 × 4.8

13. 0.8 × 32   14. 5.4 × 5.9   15. 30 × 1.4   16. 7 × 4.9

276

Set E   pages 264–265

Multiply.

1. $\begin{array}{r} 0.8 \\ \times\,0.4 \\ \hline \end{array}$	**2.** $\begin{array}{r} 0.6 \\ \times\,0.7 \\ \hline \end{array}$	**3.** $\begin{array}{r} 9 \\ \times\,0.5 \\ \hline \end{array}$	**4.** $\begin{array}{r} 0.83 \\ \times\,\,0.6 \\ \hline \end{array}$	**5.** $\begin{array}{r} 3.7 \\ \times\,8.2 \\ \hline \end{array}$
6. $\begin{array}{r} 6.8 \\ \times\,0.4 \\ \hline \end{array}$	**7.** $\begin{array}{r} 41.5 \\ \times\,0.17 \\ \hline \end{array}$	**8.** $\begin{array}{r} 35.9 \\ \times\,\,0.3 \\ \hline \end{array}$	**9.** $\begin{array}{r} 8.13 \\ \times\,0.33 \\ \hline \end{array}$	**10.** $\begin{array}{r} 2.385 \\ \times\,\,\,\,\,6 \\ \hline \end{array}$
11. $\begin{array}{r} 682 \\ \times\,\,0.9 \\ \hline \end{array}$	**12.** $\begin{array}{r} 65.4 \\ \times\,7.1 \\ \hline \end{array}$	**13.** $\begin{array}{r} 4.18 \\ \times\,0.6 \\ \hline \end{array}$	**14.** $\begin{array}{r} 1.08 \\ \times\,0.4 \\ \hline \end{array}$	**15.** $\begin{array}{r} 68.5 \\ \times\,\,\,\,4 \\ \hline \end{array}$

16. 0.7×9 **17.** 0.4×5 **18.** 5.6×0.5 **19.** 0.2×46

20. 44.2×0.6 **21.** 8.2×6.7 **22.** 0.35×85.2 **23.** 0.44×6.7

Set F   pages 266–267

Multiply. **Remember** to write extra zeros if necessary.

1. $\begin{array}{r} 0.07 \\ \times\,0.06 \\ \hline \end{array}$	**2.** $\begin{array}{r} 0.008 \\ \times\,\,\,\,\,\,7 \\ \hline \end{array}$	**3.** $\begin{array}{r} 0.009 \\ \times\,\,0.09 \\ \hline \end{array}$	**4.** $\begin{array}{r} 0.048 \\ \times\,\,0.05 \\ \hline \end{array}$

5. 1.6×0.006 **6.** 55×0.005 **7.** 35×0.003 **8.** 4.06×0.01

9. 0.145×0.06 **10.** 0.001×0.01 **11.** 0.075×4 **12.** 3.8×0.004

For Exercises 13–19, tell whether you would use paper and pencil, a calculator, or mental math. Then find each product.

13. 4.4×0.006 **14.** 0.44×0.006 **15.** 0.044×0.006

16. $\begin{array}{r} 832.4 \\ \times\,\,0.01 \\ \hline \end{array}$	**17.** $\begin{array}{r} 940.11 \\ \times\,\,\,\,\,100 \\ \hline \end{array}$	**18.** $\begin{array}{r} 76.2 \\ \times\,\,\,\,5 \\ \hline \end{array}$	**19.** $\begin{array}{r} 16.94 \\ \times\,\,0.02 \\ \hline \end{array}$

Set G   pages 268–269

Divide.

1. $24.3 \div 3$ **2.** $81.9 \div 9$ **3.** $16.35 \div 5$ **4.** $34.32 \div 8$

5. $192.6 \div 6$ **6.** $30.8 \div 4$ **7.** $26.6 \div 7$ **8.** $410.4 \div 8$

9. $3.304 \div 4$ **10.** $0.714 \div 6$ **11.** $4.401 \div 9$ **12.** $3.864 \div 7$

13. $59.6 \div 2$ **14.** $19.16 \div 4$ **15.** $31.8 \div 3$ **16.** $25.25 \div 5$

Enrichment

Equal Metric Measures

When you know the measure of an object, you can find its
measure in a smaller unit by *multiplying*.

The Statue of Liberty is 0.04605 kilometer tall.
How many meters tall is it?

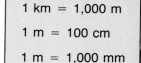

Since 1 kilometer equals 1,000 meters, you need
to multiply. Find 0.04605 × 1,000.

$$0.04605 \times 1{,}000 = 46.05$$

The Statue of Liberty is 46.05 meters tall.

1 km = 1,000 m
1 m = 100 cm
1 m = 1,000 mm
1 cm = 10 mm
1 kg = 1,000 g
1 L = 1,000 mL

Multiply to find the missing measure.

1. Height of a giraffe
   0.00599 km = ⫶⫶⫶ m

2. Anaconda snake
   11.2 m = ⫶⫶⫶ cm

3. Fork length
   14.3 cm = ⫶⫶⫶ mm

4. Length of ribbon
   2.56 m = ⫶⫶⫶ mm

5. Length of a trail
   3.4 km = ⫶⫶⫶ m

6. Bottle of juice
   0.496 L = ⫶⫶⫶ mL

When you know the measure of an object, you can
find its measure in a larger unit by *dividing*.

The Statue of Liberty has a mass of
204,000,000 grams. How many kilograms is it?

Since 1,000 grams equals 1 kilogram, you need to
divide. Find 204,000,000 ÷ 1,000.

$$204{,}000{,}000 \div 1{,}000 = 204{,}000$$

The mass of the Statue of Liberty is
204,000 kilograms.

Divide to find the missing measure.

7. Fishing rod
   165 cm = ⫶⫶⫶ m

8. Mass of a melon
   2,482 g = ⫶⫶⫶ kg

9. Watch
   20.5 g = ⫶⫶⫶ kg

10. Capacity of a glass
    265 mL = ⫶⫶⫶ L

11. Length of a field
    827 m = ⫶⫶⫶ km

12. Capacity of a jar
    869 mL = ⫶⫶⫶ L

Which measure is greater?

13. 4,775 g or 5.2 kg

14. 0.235 m or 25 cm

15. 6.1 cm or 64.2 mm

Chapter 8 Review/Test

For each number, name the place that contains a 5.

1. 3.075   **2.** 52.138

Tell how many decimal places should be shown in each product.

3. 8.2 × 3.6   **4.** 1.75 × 1.75

Multiply.

5.   0.07
       × 18

6.   0.729
       ×   64

7.   0.8
       × 0.4

8.   3.14
       × 1.86

9. 0.07 × 0.9   **10.** 0.075 × 0.3

Estimate each product.

11. 2.87 × 5.43   **12.** 92.6 × 9.92

Find each product. Use mental math.

13. 10 × 0.9   **14.** 0.46 × 100

15. 1,000 × 68.5   **16.** 0.82 × 10,000

Divide.

17. 1.95 ÷ 5   **18.** 18.9 ÷ 9

Tell what operation you would use to solve Items 19 and 20. Then solve.

19. Four friends shared the cost of a $56 gift equally. How much did each friend pay?

20. A machine part weighs 1.34 ounces. How much do 100 parts weigh?

Read this problem. Then answer the questions below.

The Langer family bought a new chair for $195 and a table for $152. The sales tax is 6 cents on each dollar. What is the total cost?

21. Which could you use as the *first steps* in solving this problem?

   a. 195 − 152 = 43
      0.06 × 43 = 2.58
   b. 195 + 152 = 347
      0.06 × 347 = 20.82
   c. 195 × 0.06 = 11.70
      195 − 11.70 = 183.30
   d. 195 + 152 = 347
      347 + 6 = 353

22. Solve the problem.

23. **Write About Math** Explain how to multiply a decimal by 100 mentally.

Patterns and Coordinate Graphing

Did You Know: The most common street name in the United States is Park. Washington is the second most common. Maple is third in popularity.

Number-Sense Project

Estimate
What different plans do you think people would suggest for naming streets on a city map?

Gather Data
Interview three older people. Have each person look at a layout of streets around a central square. Ask them what plan they would use to name the streets.

Analyze and Report
Make a list of the different plans that were suggested. Compare your results with those of other students.

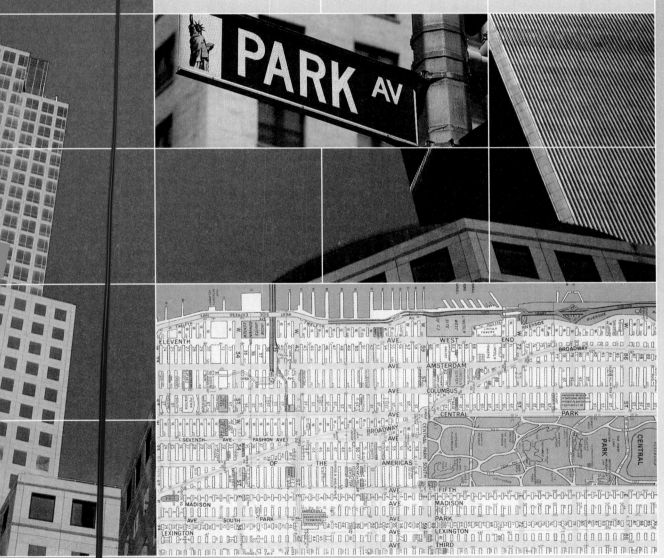

Patterns

Build Understanding

Kathryn, a display designer, is arranging cups in a store window. She has red, blue, and yellow cups. She began arranging the cups as shown below. If she continues in the same way, what would be the color of the next five cups?

The colors form a *pattern*. A pattern is a general idea by which things can be arranged or events can happen in an organized way.

The cups are arranged in a certain order by color. The colors are 1 red, 1 blue, 1 yellow, 2 red, 1 blue, 1 yellow, 3 red, 1 blue. The pattern is: the number of red cups increases by 1 and each group of red cups is separated by 1 blue and 1 yellow cup.

The next five cups would be yellow, red, red, red, red.

■ **Write About Math** Make a list of five places where you see patterns each day. Describe each pattern.

Check Understanding

For another example, see Set A, pages 300–301.

Tell what would be the next color in each pattern.

1.  2.

Draw the next figure in each pattern.

3. 4.

Practice

For More Practice, see Set A, pages 302–303.

Draw the next three figures in each pattern.

5.

6.

7.

8.

9.

10.

11.

12.

Problem Solving

13. Kathryn used 20 place mats in the display. The mats were green, brown, and orange. Arrange them in a pattern.

14. She used 7 white mugs, 9 glass mugs, and 8 tan mugs in the display. How many mugs did she use in all?

15. Create your own pattern. Ask a classmate to try to find the pattern.

16. Number Sense Look for a pattern on the cards. What number does the third card show?

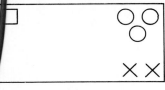

132

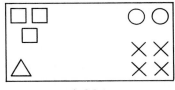

1,324

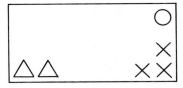

Skills ——— Review

pages 232-236

Use a calculator, paper and pencil, or mental math to find each answer. Tell which method you used and why.

1.
```
  91.75
   2.39
+ 16.56
```
2.
```
  $6.27
-  5.00
```
3.
```
  13.875
   2.98
+  8.096
```
4. $12.45 + $3.69

5. 54.87 − 26.453

Number Patterns

Build Understanding

Into how many sections can you fold a piece of paper?

Forever Folding
Materials: A sheet of paper

a. Fold a sheet of paper in half by putting opposite sides together. Then unfold the paper. How many sections are there?

b. Refold the paper. Then fold it in half again. Undo both folds. How many sections are there?

c. Make a table like the one shown to record the results of each fold.

Number of folds	0	1	2	3		
Number of sections	1	2				

d. Redo the first and second folds. Then fold the paper again. Undo the folds to find the number of sections. Record the number in the table.

e. The pattern in the table tells you what number of sections the paper can be folded into.

■ **Talk About Math** Describe the pattern in the table. Show the pattern is correct by folding the paper five times. Did you get the right number of sections?

Check Understanding

For another example, see Set B, pages 300–301.

1. How many sections would you have after six folds?

2. To get 128 sections, how many folds would you make?

3. Continue the toothpick pattern to make 3 more squares.

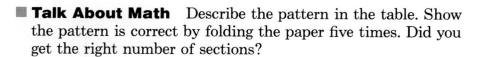

4. Complete the table.

Number of

Squares	1	2	3	4	5	6
Toothpicks	4	7	10			

284

Practice

For More Practice, see Set B, pages 302–303.

Draw the next three figures in each pattern.
Copy and complete each table.

5.

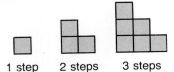

1 step 2 steps 3 steps

6. Number of

Steps	1	2	3	4	5	6
Squares	1	3	6			

7. How many squares are in 10 steps?

8.

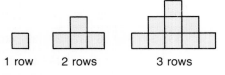

1 row 2 rows 3 rows

9. Number of

Rows	1	2	3	4	5	6
Squares	1	4	9			

10. How many squares are in 10 rows?

11.

3 sides 4 sides 5 sides

12. Number of

Sides	3	4	5	6	7	8
Triangles	1	2	3			

13. How many triangles are in a figure with 10 sides?

Problem Solving

In the school cafeteria, 4 people can sit
together at 1 table. If 2 tables are
placed together, 6 people can sit
together.

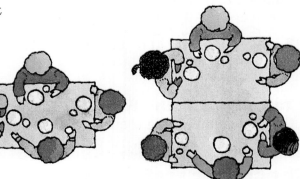

How many tables must be placed
together in a row to seat

14. 10 people? **15.** 20 people? **16.** 30 people?

If the tables are placed together in a row, how many
people can be seated using

17. 10 tables? **18.** 15 tables? **19.** 20 tables?

Number Relationships

Build Understanding

When the counting numbers are written in an array, many patterns are formed. Look at the 8-by-8 array. Do you see any patterns?

1	2	3	4	5	6	7	8
9	10	11	12	13	14	15	16
17	18	19	20	21	22	23	24
25	26	27	28	29	30	31	32
33	34	35	36	37	38	39	40
41	42	43	44	45	46	47	48
49	50	51	52	53	54	55	56
57	58	59	60	61	62	63	64

A. A *diagonal* has one pattern. The numbers are: 1, 10, 19, 28, 37, 46, 55, 64.

The pattern is add 9 to get the next number.

+9 +9 +9 +9 +9 +9 +9
1, 10, 19, 28, 37, 46, 55, 64

B. A sequence is a set of numbers formed by a pattern.

Describe the pattern in this sequence. Then write the next four numbers.

3, 7, 5, 9, 7, 11, . . .   The three dots tell you the pattern continues in the same way.

To find a pattern, compare each number with the number before it. The second number is 4 more than the first. The third number is 2 less than the second number, and so on.

+4 −2 +4 −2 +4 −2 +4 −2 +4
3, 7, 5, 9, 7, 11, 9, 13, 11, 15, . . .

■ Talk About Math What operation can be used to get the next number in a sequence?

Check Understanding

For another example, see Set C, pages 300–301.

1. Write the sequence of numbers in the other diagonal for the array above. Describe the pattern.

2. Where are the even numbers in the array above? the odd numbers?

Describe the pattern in each sequence. Then write the next four numbers.

3. 6, 13, 20, 27, 34

4. 2, 7, 4, 9, 6, 11

286

Practice

For More Practice, see Set C, pages 302–303.

Describe the pattern in each sequence.
Then write the next four numbers.

5. 5, 9, 13, 17, . . .

6. 36, 31, 26, 21, . . .

7. 7, 9, 5, 7, . . .

8. 1, 2, 4, 8, 16, . . .

9. 2, 8, 7, 28, . . .

10. 5, 10, 7, 14, . . .

11. 9, 11, 8, 10, 7, . . .

12. 0.05, 0.1, 0.15, . . .

13. 1.2, 2.7, 4.2, . . .

14. 3, 7, 5, 10, 14, . . .

Problem Solving

15. **Calculator** Find this product: your
age × 37 × 21 × 13. Find the product for other
ages. Describe the pattern.

16. **Critical Thinking** During a gas shortage,
owners of license plates ending in even digits can
buy gas on even-numbered dates. Owners of
plates ending in odd digits can buy gas on
odd-numbered dates. Which kind of plate will
allow more days to buy gas? Why?

Explore ———— Math

Make a 10-by-10 array, a 6-by-6 array, and a 4-by-4 array of
the counting numbers. For each array start with the number 1.

17. Describe the patterns in both diagonals for each array.

18. List the patterns for those arrays and the array on page 286
in a table.

19. Predict the patterns in the diagonals for other arrays of
counting numbers.

20. Check your predictions by making the arrays.

Find a Pattern

Build Understanding

Six teams are playing in the first round of a volleyball tournament. Each team will play one match against each of the other teams. How many matches will there be?

Understand What is the total number of matches among the six teams? Each team is to play each other team only once.

IIII➡ **Plan and Solve**

Plan and Solve STRATEGY Find the number of matches with 2 teams, 3 teams, and 4 teams. Try to find a pattern in the number of matches as the number of teams increases.

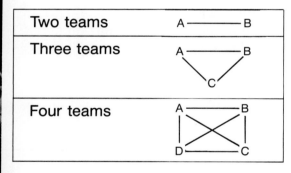

Two teams	A————B
Three teams	A————B C
Four teams	A————B D————C

Number of teams	Number of matches
2	1
3	3
4	6
5	
6	

+2
+3

According to this pattern, add 4 to find the number of matches among 5 teams. Then add 5 to find the number of matches among 6 teams.

ANSWER There will be 15 matches.

Look Back List the matches or draw diagrams to check that the pattern works.

■ **Talk About Math** In the diagrams in the example, what does each line segment show?

Check Understanding

1. How many matches would be played among eight teams?

2. How many tennis matches would be needed for nine players to play each other once?

Practice

3. Each team has 12 players. If each Tiger shakes hands with each Eagle, how many handshakes are there in all?

4. There are 32 teams in an elimination tournament. In the first round, every team plays one game. Only the winners play another game in the second round. How many games would be played until one team won the tournament?

5. If 16 teams played in an elimination tournament, how many rounds would be played until one team won?

TIPS FOR PROBLEM SOLVERS

Share your thinking with others. Explaining your ideas helps you think better.

Volleyball became an official sport of the Olympic Games in 1964.

Midchapter _____ Checkup

1. Draw the next figure.

2. Use this pattern to complete the table.

Number of

Squares	1	2	3	4	5	6
Dots	4	6	8			

3. Write the next three numbers.
3, 5, 7, 9, . . .

4. Each of the 5 players on the Lions says hello to each of the 5 Bears, and each Bear answers. How many hellos are spoken?

Number-Sense Project

Look back at pages 280-281.
Tell if you think these statements
are *seldom true*, *sometimes true*, or
always true. Consult an atlas or
maps to help you decide.

1. Interstate highways which run
north and south have odd numbers,
and interstate highways which run
east and west have even numbers.

2. An organized plan was used to
name the streets in your school's
neighborhood.

3. Streets in the center of large
cities are named according to a
plan of some type.

Math-at-Home Activity

Play *Find the
Spaceship* with
someone at home.

Each player labels
a five-by-five grid.

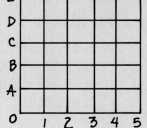

Each player secretly marks 3 points
in a row, column, or diagonal to
show where the other player's lost
spaceship is. Do not let the other
player see your grid.

Players take turns trying to find each
point of their spaceship. To guess,
name the number and letter of a
point. The other player marks the
point named with an **X** and tells if
the point is in the spaceship. The
first player to get an **X** on each
spaceship point wins.

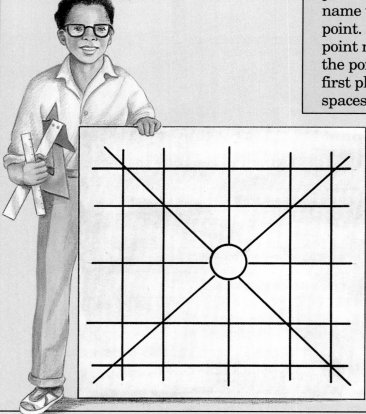

What plan would you
use if you were the
city planner and could
name the streets in
this town?

Problem Solving WORKSHOP

Explore as a Team

1. Draw the next figure in each pattern.

2. Find the perimeter for each figure. What pattern does your team see in the perimeters?

3. Predict the perimeter of the fifth figure in each pattern.

4. Draw the fifth figures. Were your predictions correct?

5. Draw other figures that have a perimeter of 12 cm.

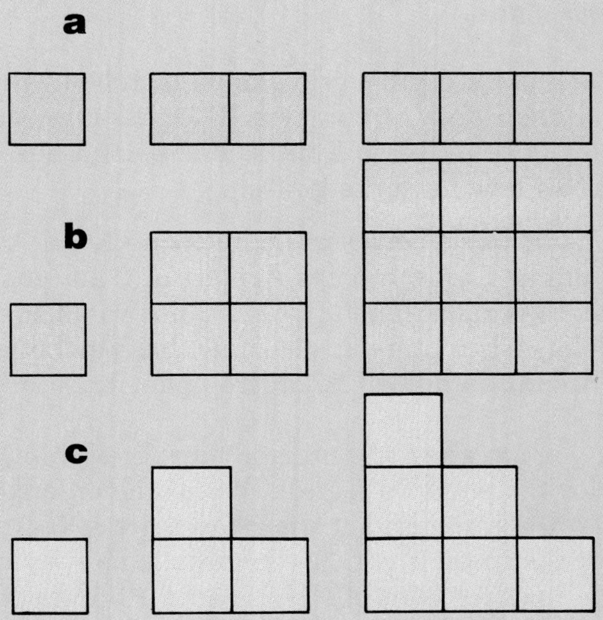

a

b

c

Explore with a Computer

Use the *Graphing and Probability Workshop Project* for this activity.

1. You can plan your own city on a grid of ordered pairs. On the screen you will see a grid with one location marked A at the center. Suppose this spot marks a statue in the center of the city.

2. Plan other points on the map. You may add houses, apartment buildings, stores, parks, or other important features of a city.

3. Plot the points on the map by entering an ordered pair in the table. Label the points with letters.

4. When you are finished marking your map, use the **Print** option to make a printout of the graph. On the printout write what each letter on the map represents.

Locating Points with Ordered Pairs

Build Understanding

A forest ranger maps where lightning has struck. To show the exact spot of a lightning strike, the ranger uses a grid.

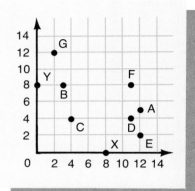

A. Each point on this grid can be matched with an *ordered pair* of numbers. The first number shows how far right to go from 0. The second number shows how far up to go from 0.

The distance between the lines on the grid represents 2 units. To reach point A, start at 0 and move 12 units right. Then move 5 units up on that line. Point A is 5 units up that line, halfway between the lines for 4 and 6. The ordered pair for A is (12, 5).

B. If you are given the ordered pair for a point, you can *plot* the point on a grid. To plot the ordered pair (7, 10) on the grid at the right, start at 0. Move 7 units to the right. Seven units is halfway between the lines for 6 and 8. Then move 10 units up. Draw a dot and label the point (7, 10).

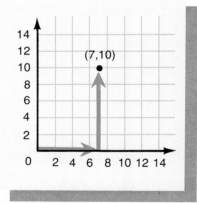

■ **Talk About Math** Find Point G and Point E. How are the ordered pairs for these points alike? How are they different?

Check Understanding

For another example, see Set D, pages 300–301.

Use the grid in Example A.

1. Point B is _____ units to the right of 0 and _____ units up.

2. Write the ordered pairs for Point B and for Point C.

3. Name two points on the grid that are 4 units up from 0.

4. What point is at (11, 8)?

5. Write the ordered pair for Point X.

Practice

Use the grid at the right. Write the
letter that names the point located by
each ordered pair.

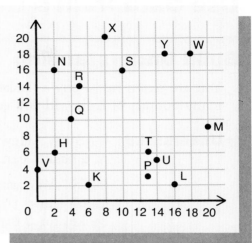

6. (2, 6)   **7.** (16, 2)   **8.** (18, 18)

9. (8, 20)   **10.** (0, 4)   **11.** (6, 2)

Write the ordered pair for each point.
Remember to use parentheses and a comma.

12. N   **13.** Q   **14.** Y   **15.** T

16. U   **17.** M   **18.** S   **19.** P

Make a grid in which each unit on the grid
represents 2 units. Label your grid from
0 to 20 in both directions. Then plot and
label each point.

20. A (8, 2)   **21.** B (6, 12)   **22.** C (20, 4)   **23.** D (10, 10)

24. E (7, 6)   **25.** F (2, 9)   **26.** G (14, 11)   **27.** J (11, 13)

28. Mixed Practice Make a grid. Plot and connect the points
in order. Continue the pattern.

(0, 2) (0, 1) (1, 1) (1, 2) (2, 2) (2, ▦) (▦, 1) (▦, ▦)

Problem Solving

An archaeologist uses a grid to map the location of artifacts.
The corners of each room are given by the ordered pairs below.
Plot the points for each room on the same grid, and connect
them to show the floor plan.

29. Main Hall: (1, 6); (1, 1); (9, 1); (9, 6)

30. Kitchen: (1, 6); (4, 6); (4, 9); (1, 9)

31. Bedroom: (4, 6); (9, 6); (9, 9); (4, 9)

32. Treasury: (1, 9); (4, 9); (4, 11); (1, 11)

33. List the ordered pairs for some artifacts found in
each room. Ask a classmate to find the location of
the items.

293

Use Data from a Graph

PROBLEM SOLVING
GUIDE

▶ **Understand**
QUESTION
FACTS
KEY IDEA

Plan and Solve
STRATEGY
ANSWER

Look Back
SENSIBLE ANSWER
ALTERNATE APPROACH

Build Understanding

You are planning to buy a basket of fruit. How many pounds of fruit will you get for $10?

▶ **Understand**   QUESTION   How many pounds of fruit in a basket can you buy for $10?

FACTS   You want to spend $10. The graph shows the cost of fruit in a basket for 0 through 5 pounds of fruit.

KEY IDEA   You need to find how many pounds of fruit you can buy for $10 by reading the graph.

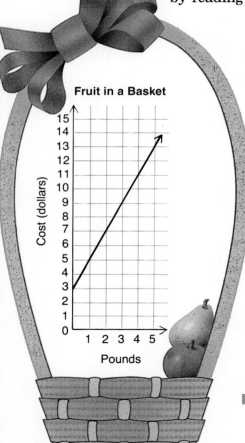

Fruit in a Basket

Plan and Solve

Find $10 on the left side of the graph. Move across to the graph line. Then move straight down to find the number of pounds.

The number of pounds is halfway between 3 and 4. You can buy about $3\frac{1}{2}$ pounds for $10.

Look Back

The answer is reasonable because a $3\frac{1}{2}$-pound basket costs more than a 3-pound basket and less than a 4-pound basket.

How much of the $10 is the cost for the fruit? Each cost includes $3 for the basket. If you did not have the graph, what other information would you need to find the number of pounds of fruit?

■ **Talk About Math**   Explain how you could use data from the graph to find amounts or costs that are not on the graph. For example, how could you find how many pounds you can buy for $20?

Check Understanding

1. How much would 2 pounds of fruit in a basket cost?

2. How much would $4\frac{1}{2}$ pounds of fruit in a basket cost?

3. What size basket of fruit could you buy for $12?

4. What does the point (0, 3) tell you?

Practice

Use the graph at the right.

5. How many pounds of dried fruit could you buy for $8? for $12?

6. How much would 4 pounds cost?

7. How much does the basket cost?

8. How much does 1 pound of dried fruit without a basket cost?

9. **Mental Math** How many pounds with a basket could you buy for $14? $20?

10. How much does $2\frac{1}{2}$ pounds without a basket cost?

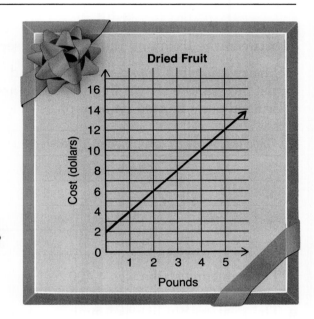

Dried Fruit

Cost (dollars) / Pounds

Choose a Strategy

Basket Bonanza On Sports Day, Bob, Rhoda, and Sue played on the winning basketball team.

11. Bob made 3 more baskets than Sue. Sue made 2 fewer baskets than Rhoda. Altogether they scored 26 baskets. How many baskets did each of them make?

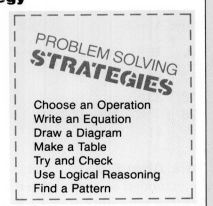

PROBLEM SOLVING STRATEGIES

Choose an Operation
Write an Equation
Draw a Diagram
Make a Table
Try and Check
Use Logical Reasoning
Find a Pattern

Number Relationships and Ordered Pairs

Build Understanding

A. The distance in feet between you and a lightning strike can be computed if you count the seconds between the flash and the thunder. Then multiply the number of seconds by 1,100.

How far away was a lightning strike if the time between the flash and thunder was 4 seconds?

The relationship between the time and distance can be shown in a table and as ordered pairs plotted on a graph.

Time (seconds)	Distance (feet)	Ordered Pair
1	1,100	(1, 1,100)
2	2,200	(2, 2,200)
3	3,300	(3, 3,300)
4	4,400	(4, 4,400)

The lightning strike was 4,400 feet away.

B. The relationship between numbers can be stated using a rule. In the table below, the relationship between A and B is given by the rule $A + 5$. The rule can be used to find more numbers or missing numbers.

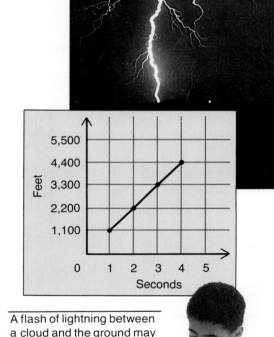

A flash of lightning between a cloud and the ground may be up to 9 miles long.

Rule: $A + 5$

A	B	$A + 5$
7	12	
18	23	
26	▓▓	$26 + 5$
▓▓	41	$n + 5$

■ **Talk About Math** Can the graph in Example A be extended to show longer amounts of time? Why or why not?

Check Understanding

For another example, see Set E, pages 300–301.

1. What rule would state the relationship between the time and distance in Example A?

2. Write a rule for the relationship between A and B in Example B using subtraction.

Practice

For More Practice, see Set E, pages 302-303.

Find the missing numbers. Write the rule.

3.

A	B
16	42
15	
9	
4	30

4.

A	B
3	9
6	18
10	
	27

5.

A	B
15	8
21	
14	
13	6

6.

A	B
	16
	8
16	21
69	74

Find the rule.

7.

A	B
8	64
3	24
5	40
9	72

8.

A	B
19	13
22	16
9	3
11	5

9.

A	B
2	14
12	84
6	42
4	28

10.

A	B
48	12
60	15
36	9
0	0

Problem Solving

Make a table to show the relationship between time and distance for a car traveling at

11. 35 miles per hour.
12. 55 miles per hour.
13. 65 miles per hour.

14. On one grid, graph the ordered pairs in Problems 11-13.

15. **Use Data** Use the graph on page 293. Write the ordered pair for Point R.

Reading ——— Math

Vocabulary Use the words to complete the sentences.

The numbers 2, 4, 6, 8, . . . is a __1.__ of numbers. When written (2, 4) (6, 8), the numbers are __2.__. If you __3.__ them on a grid, you will get two __4.__. The __5.__ of 2, 4, 6, 8, . . . is add 2 to get the next __6.__.

number
pattern
ordered pairs
sequence
points
plot

Problem Solving REVIEW

Solve each problem.

1. Mary Ellen arranged coins in the pattern shown.

If she has 12 coins, what is their total value?

2. A train made 12 stops before arriving at Ridersville. One passenger got on at the first stop, three at the second stop, five at the third stop, seven at the fourth stop, and so on. If no one got off the train, how many passengers arrived at Ridersville?

3. How much fence will Mr. Lee need to enclose a vegetable garden 12 feet wide and 24 feet long?

4. How many fence posts will Mr. Lee need if he puts one every 4 feet?

5. Brad made this "bow tie" pattern with toothpicks.

If he used 36 toothpicks in all, how many " bow ties" did he make?

6. Data File Use the data on pages 380–381. Estimate the number of nights vacationers spent away from home per trip in 1986. From this data, would you predict the number of nights spent away from home in 1989 was more or less than in 1988?

7. Make a Data File Find the latitude and longitude of 5 places you would like to visit. For each place, write the data in an ordered pair with latitude first.

Explore with a Calculator

"Pattern Search"

1. Ted and Carol were playing *Find the Pattern* on their calculators. They used different patterns to make sequences of numbers. The other person would try to find the pattern from seeing only the display.

This sequence was made by using the pattern add 2 to get the next number.

    1, 3, 5, 7, 9

The key sequence Ted used was:

Press: 1   +   2   +   2   +   2   +   2

Carol used an easier way that works on most calculators. She used this key sequence:

Press: 1   +   2   =   =   =   =

Use your calculator to make the following pattern.

    a. Start with 1. Add 8. Give the first five numbers in the pattern.

    b. Start with 5. Add 13. Give the first five numbers in the pattern.

2. Other patterns involve more than one operation. Look at this pattern.
1, 3, 7, 15, 31, . . .
Each number is 2 times the number before it plus 1.

Describe the pattern for each sequence. Then write the next three numbers in the sequence.

    a. 1, 11, 111, 1111, 11111, . . .

    b. 5, 9, 21, 57, 165, . . .

    c. 2, 12, 62, 312, 1562, . . .

Reteaching

Set A pages 282–283

A pattern is a general idea by which things can be arranged or events can happen in an organized way. Draw the next three figures in this pattern.

To do this, describe the pattern: triangle, square, circle, triangle, square.
The pattern repeats after three figures. So the next three figures are:

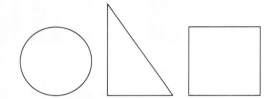

Remember that the description of a pattern of geometric figures can involve different types of changes, such as color, size, position, and shape.

Draw the next three figures in each pattern.

1.

2.

3.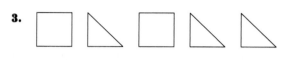

4.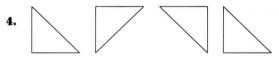

Set B pages 284–285

Draw the next two figures in this pattern.

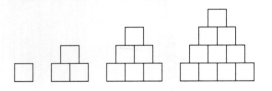

First, describe the pattern: To get the next figure, add a row to the previous figure. The new row has 1 more square than the bottom row of the previous figure.

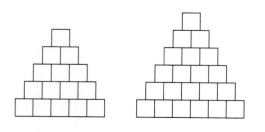

Remember that a pattern is a general idea by which things, such as geometric figures or numbers, can be arranged in an organized manner.

Draw the next three figures in the pattern.

1.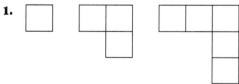

2.

Set C   pages 286–287

A sequence is a set of numbers formed by a pattern.

Describe the pattern in this sequence. Then write the next three numbers.

3, 6, 9, 12, 15, . . .

The pattern is to add 3 to get the next number.

$$+3 \ +3 \ +3 \ \ +3 \ \ +3 \ \ +3 \ \ +3$$
3, 6, 9, 12, 15, 18, 21, 24

Remember that to find a pattern, compare each number with the number before it.

Describe the pattern in each sequence. Then write the next four numbers.

1. 5, 10, 15, 20, . . .

2. 49, 43, 37, 31, . . .

3. 1, 10, 19, 28, . . .

Set D   pages 292–293

Each point on this grid can be matched with an ordered pair of numbers.

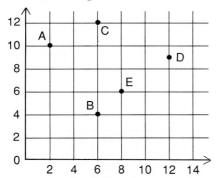

To reach point E, start at 0. Move 8 units to the right. Then move 6 units up that line. The ordered pair for E is (8, 6).

Remember that the first number in an ordered pair tells how many units to move to the right. The second number tells how many units to move up.

Use the grid at the left. Write the ordered pair for each point.

1. A   **2.** B   **3.** C   **4.** D

Make a grid in which units on the grid represent 2 units. Label your grid 0 to 12 in both directions. Then plot and label each point.

5. E (6, 4)   **6.** F (4, 6)
7. G (8, 12)   **8.** H (12, 9)

Set E   pages 296–297

Write a rule for the numbers on the table at the right.

Each number in the B column is 2 times the number in the A column. The missing number in B is 2 × 5, or 10.

A	B
1	2
2	4
4	8
5	▒

Remember that if the rule for finding the numbers in column B uses addition, then you find the numbers in column A by using subtraction.

Find the missing numbers. Write the rule.

1.

A	B
4	16
8	20
12	▒
16	▒

2.

A	B
3	8
4	9
▒	10
▒	11

More Practice

Set A   pages 282–283

Draw the next three figures in each pattern.

1. △ □ △ □

2. ○ △ ▽ ○

3. ▽ ▽ □ ▽ ▽ □

4. □ □ ○ ○ △ □ □

5. △ ▷ ▽ ◁ △

6. □ ◺ □ □ ◺ ◺ □ □ □

7. □ ○□ □○□ ○□○□

8. □ ◹ ⊠ ⊠ ⊠

Set B   pages 284–285

Draw the next three figures in each problem. Copy and
complete each table.

1.

2. Number of

Rows	1	2	3	4	5	6
Squares	1	4	9	▦	▦	▦

3. How many squares in 10 rows?

4.

5. Number of

Rows	1	2	3	4	5	6
Squares	1	4	7	▦	▦	▦

6. How many squares in 10 rows?

Set C   pages 286–287

Describe the pattern in each sequence. Then write the
next four numbers.

1. 3, 9, 15, 21, . . .

2. 44, 41, 38, 35, . . .

3. 10, 20, 30, 40, . . .

4. 1, 3, 9, 27, . . .

5. 2, 6, 4, 12, . . .

6. 4, 9, 8, 13, . . .

7. 3, 9, 8, 24, . . .

8. 1, 3, 2, 4, . . .

Set D pages 292–293

Use the grid at the right. Write the letter that names the point located by each ordered pair.

1. (4, 6) **2.** (18, 8) **3.** (14, 14)

4. (10, 6) **5.** (6, 0) **6.** (12, 18)

Write the ordered pair for each point.

7. F **8.** A **9.** H

10. J **11.** N **12.** B

Make a grid in which each unit on the grid represents 2 units. Label your grid from 0 to 20 in both directions. Then plot and label each point.

13. A (10, 6) **14.** B (4, 14) **15.** C (8, 16) **16.** D (20, 0)

17. E (9, 12) **18.** F (12, 11) **19.** G (13, 18) **20.** H (16, 9)

21. Mixed Practice Make a grid. Plot and connect the points in order. Continue the pattern.
(0, 0) (1, 2) (2, 1) (3, 4) (4, 3) (5, ▦) (▦, 5) (▦, ▦)

Set E pages 296–297

Find the missing numbers. Write the rule.

1.

A	B
13	28
12	▦
8	▦
3	18

2.

A	B
2	10
4	20
8	▦
▦	60

3.

A	B
20	14
30	▦
25	▦
8	2

4.

A	B
▦	20
▦	15
20	28
34	42

Find the rule.

5.

A	B
3	15
9	45
4	20
8	40

6.

A	B
12	8
26	22
8	4
16	12

7.

A	B
3	27
10	90
6	54
1	9

8.

A	B
5	14
17	26
39	48
21	30

Enrichment

Prime Factorization

Mattie has 6 new mugs. How can she arrange them in even rows?

1 row of 6 mugs  $1 \times 6 = 6$

2 rows of 3 mugs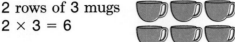
$2 \times 3 = 6$

3 rows of 2 mugs $3 \times 2 = 6$

Mattie sees that the possible arrangements for the mugs give her the factors of 6. She knows that 2 and 3 are prime numbers. Therefore, 2 and 3 are *prime factors* of 6.

To write the prime factors of a composite number, divide by prime numbers until all the factors are prime. You can use a factor tree.

$18 = 2 \times 9$
      prime composite

$9 = 3 \times 3$
    prime   prime

The prime factorization of 18 is $2 \times 3 \times 3$.

Find the missing numbers.

1. 12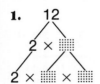

2. 15

3. 30

4. 27

5. 24

6. 25

7. 24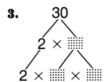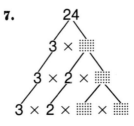

8. 32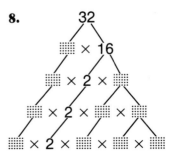

Make a factor tree for each number.

9. 54   **10.** 48   **11.** 16   **12.** 22   **13.** 30   **14.** 49

Independent Study ENRICHMENT

Chapter 9 Review/Test

1. Draw the next three figures in the pattern.

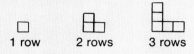

2. Draw the next three figures in the pattern. Then copy and complete the table below.

1 row   2 rows   3 rows

Number of

Rows	1	2	3	4	5	6
Squares	1	3	5			

Describe the pattern in each sequence. Then write the next four numbers.

3. 7, 12, 17, 22, . . .

4. 8, 12, 10, 14, 12, . . .

Use the grid at the right for Items 5–8.

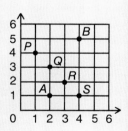

Write the letter that names the point located by the ordered pair.

5. (3, 2)   **6.** (1, 4)

Write the ordered pair for each point.

7. A   **8.** B

Use the graph below to answer Items 9 and 10.

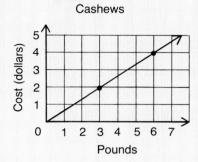

9. Which information from the graph could you use to find how many pounds you can buy for $3?

   a. 3 pounds of cashews cost $2.
   b. $3 is halfway between the cost of 3 pounds and the cost of 6 pounds.
   c. 6 pounds cost $4.

10. How many pounds of cashews can you buy for $3?

11. Five brothers will each play 1 game of chess with every other brother. How many games will they play?

Find the rule.

12.

A	B
5	30
3	18
7	42
10	60

13.

A	B
20	15
10	5
6	1
12	7

14. **Write About Math** Explain in your own words how you found the rule in Item 13.

Fraction Concepts

10

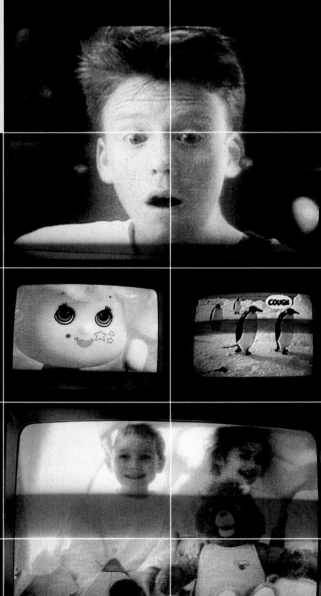

Number-Sense Project

Estimate

Estimate how many minutes of each $\frac{1}{2}$ hour of your favorite TV program is commercial time.

Gather Data

Record the starting and stopping time of each commercial break during $\frac{1}{2}$ hour of your favorite TV program.

Analyze and Report

Make a graph to show the number of minutes used for commercials and for the program during your $\frac{1}{2}$ hour program. Compare your results with other students.

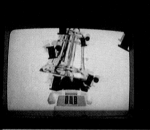

Fractions

Build Understanding

A. Paula Calhoun is a chef. She baked a loaf of banana bread. She divided the loaf into 12 equal pieces.

A fraction can name part of a whole. The picture shows 11 out of the 12 pieces of banana bread.

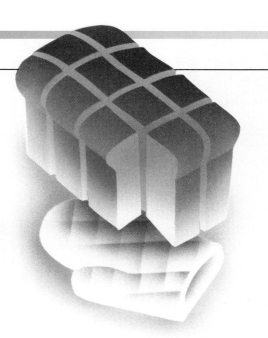

Number of pieces shown → 11 ← **Numerator**
Number of equal pieces → 12 ← **Denominator**
in whole loaf

eleven twelfths

$\frac{11}{12}$ of the whole loaf is shown.

B. For a fruit salad, Paula uses 2 pears, 1 pineapple, and 2 apples.

A fraction can also name part of a set.

Two out of 5 pieces of fruit are pears.

Number of pears → 2
Number of pieces of fruit → 5

$\frac{2}{5}$ of the pieces of fruit are pears.

C. Fractions can be used to name points on a number line.

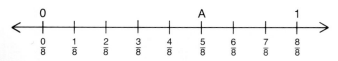

The fraction $\frac{5}{8}$ is a name for point A.

■ **Talk About Math**   What different ways can fractions be used?

308

Check Understanding

For another example, see Set A, pages 334–335.

Complete each sentence.

1. The ___?___ of a fraction names the number of parts you are talking about.

2. The ___?___ of a fraction names the number of equal parts in the whole amount.

Use the figure at the right. What fraction

3. names the part that is not shaded?

4. names the part that is shaded?

Use the number line. What fraction

5. names the point labeled 0?

6. names the point labeled 1?

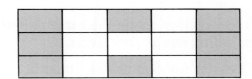

7. names the point labeled A?

Practice

For More Practice, see Set A, pages 336–337.

Write the fraction to name the part that is shaded.

What fraction of the

8.

9.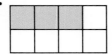

10. apples are red?

11. eggs are brown?

12. Write a fraction to name the point labeled A.

Write the fraction.

13. Three fourths

14. Five eighths

15. One half

16. Two thirds

17. Eight eighths

18. Seven sixteenths

Problem Solving

19. A package of cheese has 16 slices. Paula used 4 slices on sandwiches. What part of the cheese did she use?

20. Paula works at the restaurant Healthy Haven. What fraction of the letters in that name are Hs?

Equal Fractions

Build Understanding

Each pitcher has the same amount of cranberry juice.

Fractions that name the same amount are called *equal fractions.*

To find a fraction that is equal to a fraction, you can multiply the numerator and the denominator by the same number (not zero).

$$\frac{1}{2} \begin{array}{c} \nearrow 1 \times 6 \searrow \\ = \\ \searrow 2 \times 6 \nearrow \end{array} \frac{6}{12}$$

To find a fraction that is equal to a fraction, you can divide the numerator and the denominator by the same number (not zero).

$$\frac{4}{16} \begin{array}{c} \nearrow 4 \div 2 \searrow \\ = \\ \searrow 16 \div 2 \nearrow \end{array} \frac{2}{8}$$

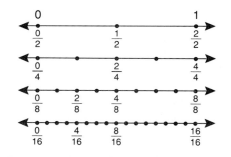

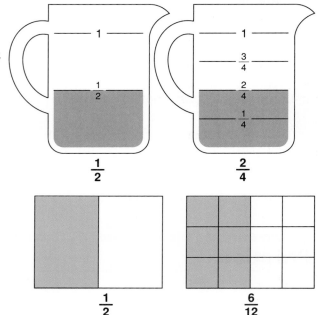

■ **Write About Math** If a fraction is equal to $\frac{1}{2}$, can its denominator be an odd number? Can its numerator be an odd number? Why?

Check Understanding

For another example, see Set B, pages 334–335.

Use the pictures. Write equal fractions for the shaded part.

1.

2.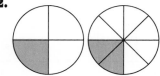

3.

4. Multiply to find equal fractions.

$\frac{3}{4} = \frac{6}{}$

5. Divide to find equal fractions.

$\frac{4}{6} = \frac{}{3}$

6. Tell whether the fractions are equal. Explain why or why not.

$\frac{1}{2}$ $\frac{5}{11}$

Practice

For More Practice, see Set B, pages 336–337.

Multiply to find equal fractions.

7. $\frac{1}{3} = \frac{3}{}$

8. $\frac{3}{8} = \frac{6}{}$

9. $\frac{2}{3} = \frac{}{15}$

10. $\frac{5}{5} = \frac{}{10}$

11. $\frac{3}{4} = \frac{}{20}$

12. $\frac{9}{12} = \frac{36}{}$

13. $\frac{3}{10} = \frac{21}{}$

14. $\frac{8}{11} = \frac{}{187}$

Divide to find equal fractions.

15. $\frac{8}{12} = \frac{2}{}$

16. $\frac{6}{9} = \frac{}{3}$

17. $\frac{10}{25} = \frac{2}{}$

18. $\frac{16}{32} = \frac{}{8}$

19. $\frac{20}{40} = \frac{}{2}$

20. $\frac{16}{48} = \frac{1}{}$

21. $\frac{20}{36} = \frac{}{9}$

22. $\frac{217}{420} = \frac{31}{}$

Mixed Practice Multiply or divide to find equal fractions.

23. $\frac{5}{8} = \frac{}{16}$

24. $\frac{9}{12} = \frac{3}{}$

25. $\frac{3}{14} = \frac{6}{}$

26. $\frac{4}{6} = \frac{}{24}$

Tell whether the fractions are equal. Explain why or why not.

27. $\frac{3}{5}$ $\frac{12}{20}$

28. $\frac{20}{28}$ $\frac{3}{4}$

29. $\frac{7}{8}$ $\frac{28}{36}$

30. $\frac{14}{20}$ $\frac{7}{10}$

Problem Solving

Solve each problem.

31. Judy used 8 of 12 boxes of raisins for school lunches. Write this as a fraction. Write two equal fractions.

32. Critical Thinking How is the denominator related to the numerator in all fractions equal to $\frac{1}{4}$?

Fractions in Lowest Terms

Build Understanding

In the United States, 10 out of the 50 states, or $\frac{10}{50}$ of the states, have names consisting of two words. South Dakota is one example.

To show this number more simply, you can write the fraction $\frac{10}{50}$ in *lowest terms*.

A fraction is in lowest terms when the only number that both the numerator and denominator can be divided by is 1. The numerator and denominator are the *terms* of a fraction.

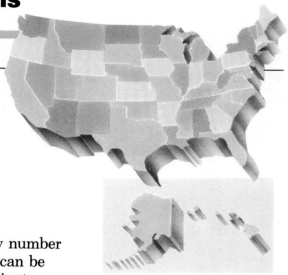

Five of the 50 states border the Gulf of Mexico.

A. One way to write $\frac{10}{50}$ in lowest terms is to do the work like this.

You can divide both 10 and 50 by 2 to find a fraction equal to $\frac{10}{50}$.

$$\frac{10}{50} \overset{10 \div 2}{\underset{50 \div 2}{=}} \frac{5}{25}$$

Since you can divide 5 and 25 by 5, $\frac{5}{25}$ is not in lowest terms.

$$\frac{5}{25} \overset{5 \div 5}{\underset{25 \div 5}{=}} \frac{1}{5}$$

The fraction $\frac{1}{5}$ is in lowest terms because both 1 and 5 can be divided only by 1.

B. Another way is to divide both the numerator and denominator by the *greatest common factor*. The greatest common factor is the greatest number that is a factor of each number.

List all the factors of 10 and 50.
10: 1, 2, 5, 10
50: 1, 2, 5, 10, 25, 50
The greatest common factor is 10.

$$\frac{10}{50} \overset{10 \div 10}{\underset{50 \div 10}{=}} \frac{1}{5}$$

A fraction is in lowest terms when the greatest common factor of both terms is 1.

■ **Talk About Math** What number is a common factor of every number?

312

Check Understanding

For another example, see Set C, pages 334–335.

Tell whether each fraction is in lowest terms. Why or why not?

1. $\frac{6}{15}$ **2.** $\frac{3}{4}$ **3.** $\frac{8}{10}$ **4.** $\frac{3}{7}$ **5.** $\frac{15}{30}$

Write the greatest common factor of the numerator and denominator.

6. $\frac{12}{15}$ **7.** $\frac{5}{10}$ **8.** $\frac{5}{20}$ **9.** $\frac{6}{9}$ **10.** $\frac{2}{3}$

Practice

For More Practice, see Set C, pages 336–337.

Write the greatest common factor of the numerator and denominator.

11. $\frac{8}{12}$ **12.** $\frac{9}{12}$ **13.** $\frac{13}{20}$ **14.** $\frac{5}{25}$ **15.** $\frac{16}{20}$

Write each fraction in lowest terms.

16. $\frac{3}{6}$ **17.** $\frac{4}{12}$ **18.** $\frac{10}{15}$ **19.** $\frac{8}{18}$ **20.** $\frac{6}{9}$

21. $\frac{18}{20}$ **22.** $\frac{20}{50}$ **23.** $\frac{15}{30}$ **24.** $\frac{16}{24}$ **25.** $\frac{133}{203}$

Problem Solving

Write each answer in lowest terms.

26. Five out of 50 states have land borders on the Pacific Ocean. What fraction of the states border the Pacific Ocean?

27. Fourteen out of 50 states border the Atlantic Ocean. What fraction of the states border the Atlantic Ocean?

Explore ———— Math

28. Start with the fraction $\frac{1}{2}$. Add 1 to each term of the fraction. Is the resulting fraction equal to $\frac{1}{2}$?

29. Pick another fraction. Add the same number to both terms of the fraction. Is the resulting fraction equal to the original fraction?

30. Does adding the same number to both the numerator and the denominator of a fraction give an equal fraction?

Mixed Numbers

Build Understanding

Carpenters often make measurements longer than one inch. The nail in the picture is $2\frac{1}{4}$ inches long.

The number $2\frac{1}{4}$ is a **mixed number**. Every mixed number is made up of a whole number and a fraction.

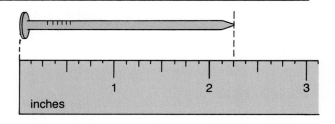

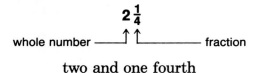

$$2\frac{1}{4}$$
whole number ⎯⎯⎯↑ ↑⎯⎯⎯ fraction

two and one fourth

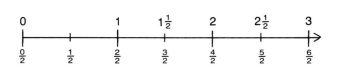

Think of a ruler as a combination of number lines. These number lines show that mixed numbers and improper fractions can name the same point. A fraction equal to or greater than 1 is an **improper** fraction. A fraction less than 1 is a **proper** fraction.

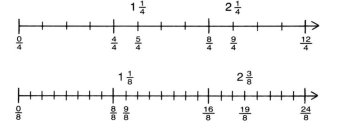

■ **Talk About Math** Is $\frac{4}{4}$ proper or improper?

Check Understanding

For another example, see Set D, page 334–335.

Write a mixed number for each picture.

1. How many melons?

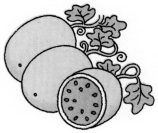

2. How many cups of punch?

3. How many pans of muffins?

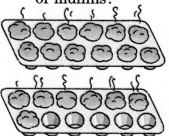

4. How much is shaded?

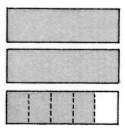

Practice

For More Practice, see Set D, pages 336–337.

Write a mixed number.

5. One and two fifths

6. Four and three tenths

7. Two and five eighths

Use these number lines for Exercises 8–13. **Remember** that one point on a number line can have more than one name.

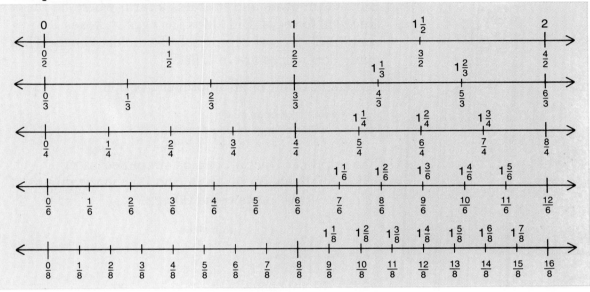

8. Name three fractions equal to $\frac{1}{2}$.

9. What fraction is equal to $\frac{6}{8}$?

10. What mixed number is equal to $\frac{4}{3}$?

11. What whole number is equal to $\frac{12}{6}$?

12. What fraction in sixths is closest to $\frac{1}{8}$?

13. Which fraction is less, $\frac{3}{4}$ or $\frac{4}{6}$?

Problem Solving

14. Lucas cut 6 pieces of wood from one board. Each piece is $\frac{1}{4}$ foot long. If Lucas used all of the board, how long was it?

 Skills _____ Review   pages 220–221

Use >, <, or = to compare.

1. 7.2 ⬚ 0.72   **2.** 4.5 ⬚ 4.50   **3.** 9.07 ⬚ 9.7   **4.** 7.463 ⬚ 7.467

Improper Fractions, Quotients, and Mixed Numbers

Build Understanding

Bill Stahm owns and operates a farm where he raises chickens for eggs. Bill ships the eggs in boxes containing flats of eggs. Each flat holds 30 eggs. How many dozen eggs are in a flat?

You could think of an improper fraction.

$\dfrac{30}{12}$ ← Number of eggs in all
     ← Number of eggs in one dozen

The improper fraction can be simplified using division. Divide 30 by 12 to find how many groups of 12 eggs can be made using 30 eggs.

$$30 \div 12 \qquad 12\overline{)30} \quad 2\tfrac{6}{12} \begin{array}{l} \leftarrow \text{Remainder} \\ \leftarrow \text{Divisor} \end{array}$$

There are 2 dozen eggs with 6 eggs left over. Show those eggs as part of a dozen by writing the fraction $\frac{6}{12}$. The fraction $\frac{6}{12}$ can be written in lowest terms.

$$\frac{30}{12} = 2\frac{6}{12} = 2\frac{1}{2}$$

A flat is $2\frac{1}{2}$ dozen eggs.

■ **Write About Math**   Is any improper fraction equal to $\frac{2}{3}$? Why or why not?

Check Understanding

For another example, see Set E, pages 334–335.

1. Write $16 \div 5$ as an improper fraction.

2. Write $3\overline{)5}$ as an improper fraction.

3. Write $7 \div 8$ as a fraction.

Refer to the example at the right.

4. What is the divisor?

5. What is the remainder?

$$73 \div 5 \qquad \frac{73}{5} \qquad 5\overline{)73}$$

6. Express the quotient as a mixed number.

316

Practice

For More Practice, see Set E, pages 336–337.

Write a whole number or a mixed number for each improper fraction. **Remember** to write each fraction in lowest terms.

7. $\frac{34}{10}$ **8.** $\frac{27}{6}$ **9.** $\frac{48}{9}$ **10.** $\frac{54}{4}$ **11.** $\frac{51}{18}$

12. $\frac{75}{20}$ **13.** $\frac{16}{12}$ **14.** $\frac{24}{14}$ **15.** $\frac{288}{9}$ **16.** $\frac{264}{18}$

Tell whether you would use paper and pencil or mental math. Write each quotient as a whole number, mixed number, or proper fraction.

17. $3\overline{)17}$ **18.** $6\overline{)25}$ **19.** $9\overline{)147}$ **20.** $5\overline{)65}$ **21.** $24\overline{)60}$

22. $12\overline{)147}$ **23.** $30\overline{)303}$ **24.** $26\overline{)260}$ **25.** $15\overline{)5}$ **26.** $76\overline{)1,349}$

Problem Solving

Write the answer as a mixed number with the fraction in lowest terms.

27. If Bill ships 3,976 eggs, how many dozen eggs is this?

28. Bill worked 57 hours in 6 days. What was the average number of hours he worked per day?

Midchapter _____ Checkup

1. Write a fraction to name the shaded part.

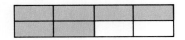

2. Write a fraction to name the fraction of glasses that are full.

3. Multiply to find an equal fraction. $\frac{5}{12} = \frac{}{24}$

4. Divide to find an equal fraction. $\frac{30}{50} = \frac{3}{}$

5. Write $\frac{12}{18}$ as a fraction in lowest terms.

6. Write a mixed number for *two and nine tenths.*

7. Write a mixed number for $\frac{37}{9}$.

8. Write $50 \div 12$ as a mixed number.

Explore as a Team

1. How many different ways can you cut a 3-inch by 5-inch card into 8 equal pieces? All pieces have to be the same size and shape.

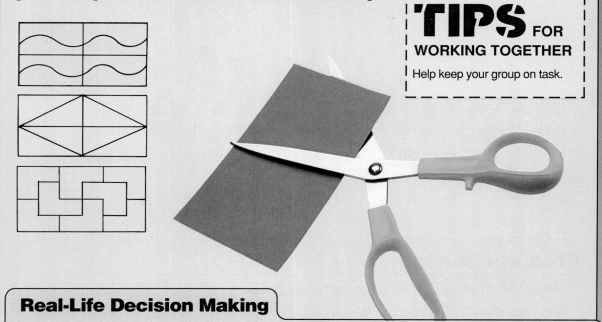

TIPS FOR **WORKING TOGETHER**

Help keep your group on task.

Real-Life Decision Making

Your neighbor hired you and your friend to shovel the snow off her sidewalks. Her front sidewalk and back sidewalk are the same size.

Your friend forgot to show up, so you did the front sidewalk alone. When your friend came, you were ready to start shoveling the back sidewalk. The two of you shoveled the back sidewalk together.

How should you split the money?

Explore with a Computer

Use the *Fractions Workshop Project* for this activity.

1. Divide the first unit into 3 equal parts. Shade $\frac{1}{3}$ of the unit.

2. Divide the second unit into six equal parts. Divide the third unit into twelve equal parts. Shade parts of these units to equal $\frac{1}{3}$. How many parts did you shade?

3. Shade parts of all the units to show $\frac{2}{3}$. How many parts did you shade?

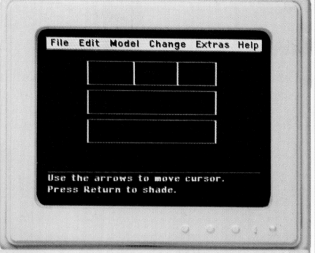

File Edit Model Change Extras Help

Use the arrows to move cursor.
Press Return to shade.

Number-Sense Project

Look back at pages 306-307.

A student made the chart below showing how time was used during $\frac{1}{2}$ hour of her favorite program.

| Time | | Type of Program/Elapsed Time | | |
Start	Stop	Commercial	Program	Other
7:30	7:33	3 min		
7:33	7:40		7 min	
7:40	7:42	2 min		
7:42	7:48		6 min	
7:48	7:51	3 min		
7:51	7:52			1 min
7:52	7:58		6 min	
7:58	8:00	2 min		

a. How many minutes of the program were used for commercials?

b. What fraction of the program was used for commercials?

c. One minute was classified as other. What could this minute have been used for?

d. What patterns do you notice in the amount of time used for commercials in the TV programs you watch?

319

Fractions and Estimation

Build Understanding

A. Sometimes you can solve problems involving fractions by estimating. What fraction of each box of crayons is red?

None are red.

$\frac{0}{12}$

One half are red.

$\frac{1}{2}$

All are red.

$\frac{12}{12}$

Almost none are red.

$\frac{1}{12}$

About $\frac{1}{2}$ are red.

$\frac{5}{12}$

Almost all are red.

$\frac{11}{12}$

B. To estimate with mixed numbers, round to the nearest whole number. Round $2\frac{3}{4}$ to the nearest whole number.

$2\frac{3}{4}$ is between the whole numbers 2 and 3.

When a fraction is $\frac{1}{2}$ or greater, round to the nearest whole number.

To the nearest whole number, $2\frac{3}{4}$ is about 3.

■ **Talk About Math** When the fraction part of a mixed number is less than $\frac{1}{2}$, would you round up or down? Explain.

Check Understanding

For another example, see Set F, pages 334–335.

Number Sense   Answer the following questions.

1. When the numerator and denominator of a proper fraction are almost the same size, is the fraction closest to 0, $\frac{1}{2}$, or 1?

2. When twice the numerator is close to the denominator, is the fraction closest to 0, $\frac{1}{2}$, or 1?

3. When the denominator is much larger than the numerator, is the fraction closest to 0, $\frac{1}{2}$, or 1?

Practice

For More Practice, see Set F, pages 336–337.

For each fraction, estimate if the fraction is closest to 0, to $\frac{1}{2}$, or to 1.

4. $\frac{1}{20}$ 5. $\frac{24}{25}$ 6. $\frac{11}{10}$ 7. $\frac{9}{20}$ 8. $\frac{99}{100}$ 9. $\frac{3}{100}$

10. $\frac{50}{100}$ 11. $\frac{2}{25}$ 12. $\frac{27}{50}$ 13. $\frac{9}{16}$ 14. $\frac{29}{32}$ 15. $\frac{16}{32}$

Round each mixed number to the nearest whole number.

16. $4\frac{2}{3}$ 17. $9\frac{3}{8}$ 18. $12\frac{2}{5}$ 19. $3\frac{7}{9}$ 20. $9\frac{5}{11}$ 21. $48\frac{6}{12}$

Problem Solving

22. The lengths of three crayons were $5\frac{3}{8}$ inches, $4\frac{1}{4}$ inches, and $3\frac{3}{4}$ inches. About how long was each crayon?

23. **Critical Thinking**   Can a proper fraction be greater than 1? Explain.

Reading ——— Math

Numbers and Symbols   Tell if you read each expression from top to bottom, from left to right, or from right to left. Write each expression in words.

1. $\frac{16}{3}$ 2. $3\overline{)16}$ 3. $16 \div 3$ 4. 14×12 5. $19 - 14$

Work Backward

Build Understanding

Brian is raising gerbils that other students will use in a science project. Some gerbils will be fed vitamins to see if they grow faster than gerbils that are not fed vitamins.

Brian gives $\frac{1}{2}$ of the gerbils he has to Susan. Then Susan gives $\frac{1}{2}$ of these gerbils to Yolanda. Yolanda then gives $\frac{1}{2}$ of her gerbils to Chen. Chen has 4 gerbils.

How many gerbils did Brian have before he gave any away?

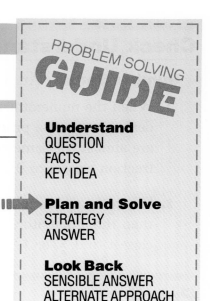

PROBLEM SOLVING GUIDE

Understand
QUESTION
FACTS
KEY IDEA

➤ **Plan and Solve**
STRATEGY
ANSWER

Look Back
SENSIBLE ANSWER
ALTERNATE APPROACH

Understand How many gerbils did Brian have when he started the project? Brian gives $\frac{1}{2}$ of the gerbils to Susan. She gives $\frac{1}{2}$ of those gerbils to Yolanda. Yolanda gives $\frac{1}{2}$ of those gerbils to Chen. Chen has 4 gerbils. Chen has the fewest gerbils.

➤ **Plan and Solve** STRATEGY   Start with the number of gerbils Chen has and work backward to find the original number.

Chen has 4 gerbils. This is half the gerbils that Yolanda had. So Yolanda had 8 gerbils.

Since 8 gerbils is half the number that Susan had, Susan had 16 gerbils.

Since 16 is half the number of gerbils that Brian had, then Brian had 32 gerbils.

ANSWER   Brian started with 32 gerbils.

Look Back Check your work by starting with 32 gerbils. Go through the steps in the problem and see if the result is 4.

■ **Talk About Math** How do you "undo" the result of adding 10? subtracting 5? multiplying by 2? dividing by 3?

Check Understanding

One gerbil gained 2 ounces in week 1, 1 ounce in week 2, and 3 ounces in week 3. The gerbil weighed 15 ounces at the end of week 3. How much did the gerbil weigh

1. at the end of week 2?   **2.** at the end of week 1?

3. What was the original weight of the gerbil at the beginning of the project?

Practice

4. One gerbil lost 1 ounce in week 1, gained 2 ounces in week 2, and then gained 3 ounces in week 3. What was the original weight of the gerbil if it weighed 14 ounces at the end of week 3?

5. Brian also raises guinea pigs. One time he gave $\frac{1}{3}$ of his guinea pigs to Lila. Lila gave 5 away and had 2 left. How many guinea pigs did Brian originally have?

6. For a science project, the teacher divided the class into 3 groups. There were 7 students in each group. The two students who were not in any group kept records of the class's project. How many students were there in the class?

7. Brian, Susan, Yolanda, and Chen helped raise money for the Science Fair. Brian raised $\frac{1}{3}$ as much as Susan. Yolanda raised $\frac{1}{2}$ as much as Susan but $3 less than Chen. Chen raised $15. How much money did each student raise?

Choose a _____ Strategy

Zoo-onomics On a science field trip, each student paid $3 for admission to the zoo. Half of the students also spent $4 each in the gift shop for books on animal care.

8. If 10 students had gone on the trip, how much would they have spent in all?

9. If the students spent $80 in all at the zoo, how many students went on the trip?

Finding the Least Common Denominator

Build Understanding

Sometimes estimation is not exact enough to compare fractions. Comparing, adding, and subtracting fractions are easier when they have the same denominator.

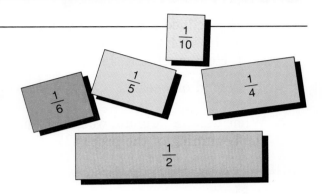

 A. Denominator Detectives
Materials: Fraction models
Groups: Work with a partner

a. Use your fraction models to find fractions equal to $\frac{1}{2}$. Try to cover exactly the piece for $\frac{1}{2}$ using the piece for thirds, then fourths, and so on. Make a list of the fractions equal to $\frac{1}{2}$.

b. Your partner should find fractions equal to $\frac{2}{3}$ in the same way. Remember that the model for $\frac{2}{3}$ must be covered exactly. Make a list of fractions equal to $\frac{2}{3}$.

c. Compare the lists. What fractions on both lists have denominators in common? Which common denominator is the least?

d. Write fractions equal to $\frac{1}{2}$ and $\frac{2}{3}$ using the ***least common denominator***.

B. Write $\frac{3}{4}$ and $\frac{5}{6}$ with the least common denominator. Since you do not always have fraction models with you, here is another way to find least common denominators.

List the multiples of both 4 and 6.

Multiples of **4: 4, 8, 12, 16, 20, 24, 28**
Multiples of **6: 6, 12, 18, 24, 30, 36, 42**

Common multiples are 12 and 24.
The least common multiple is 12.
Use 12 for the least common denominator.

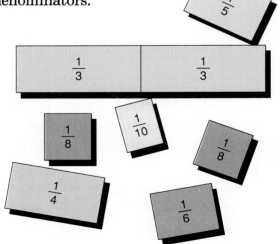

$$\frac{3}{4} \overset{\times 3}{\underset{\times 3}{=}} \frac{9}{12} \qquad\qquad \frac{5}{6} \overset{\times 2}{\underset{\times 2}{=}} \frac{10}{12}$$

■ **Write About Math**   Write the fractions in Example B with two more common denominators. What is an advantage to using the least common denominator?

Check Understanding

For another example, see Set G, pages 334–335.

1. Use fraction models to find the least common denominator for $\frac{1}{3}$ and $\frac{1}{4}$. Draw the pieces to show your answer.

2. List multiples to find the least common denominator for $\frac{1}{3}$ and $\frac{1}{4}$.

3. Write fractions with the least common denominator for $\frac{1}{3}$ and $\frac{1}{4}$.

4. What is the least common denominator for $\frac{4}{5}$ and $\frac{3}{5}$?

Practice

For More Practice, see Set G, pages 336–337.

Write the fractions with the least common denominator.

5. $\frac{3}{8}, \frac{3}{4}$

6. $\frac{2}{5}, \frac{3}{10}$

7. $\frac{1}{3}, \frac{1}{12}$

8. $\frac{1}{2}, \frac{3}{4}$

9. $\frac{1}{6}, \frac{1}{2}$

10. $\frac{7}{10}, \frac{1}{4}$

11. $\frac{5}{6}, \frac{2}{3}$

12. $\frac{1}{2}, \frac{3}{5}$

13. $\frac{3}{4}, \frac{2}{5}$

14. $\frac{1}{6}, \frac{2}{9}$

15. $\frac{1}{3}, \frac{3}{4}$

16. $\frac{1}{3}, \frac{1}{2}$

17. $\frac{3}{5}, \frac{3}{7}$

18. $\frac{2}{3}, \frac{2}{5}$

19. $\frac{1}{2}, \frac{4}{9}$

20. $\frac{1}{10}, \frac{5}{6}$

21. $\frac{1}{2}, \frac{3}{4}, \frac{5}{6}$

22. $\frac{2}{3}, \frac{1}{6}, \frac{3}{8}$

23. $\frac{3}{10}, \frac{7}{12}, \frac{11}{15}$

Problem Solving

Critical Thinking   Work with your partner. Explain your thinking to another pair of students.

24. For each of Exercises 5–9, compare the denominators of the fractions and the least common denominator. What do you notice? Does this always happen?

25. For each of Exercises 15–19, compare the denominators of the fractions and the least common denominator. What do you notice? Does this always happen?

26. What number is always a common denominator of two fractions? Is it always the least common denominator? Use examples to explain your answer.

27. Select any two fractions with different denominators. How many common denominators can you find? How many least common denominators are there?

Comparing and Ordering Fractions

Build Understanding

A. Martha is using a recipe for pumpkin bread that calls for $\frac{2}{3}$ cup of milk. She has $\frac{3}{4}$ of a cup. Does she have enough milk?

Compare $\frac{2}{3}$ and $\frac{3}{4}$.

$\frac{2}{3}$	⠿	$\frac{3}{4}$	The denominators are not the same.
↓		↓	
$\frac{8}{12}$	⠿	$\frac{9}{12}$	Write the fractions with the least common denominator.
$\frac{8}{12}$	<	$\frac{9}{12}$	Compare the numerators. $8 < 9$, so $\frac{8}{12} < \frac{9}{12}$.
↓		↓	
$\frac{2}{3}$	<	$\frac{3}{4}$	$\frac{2}{3}$ is less than $\frac{3}{4}$.

Martha has enough milk.

B. Compare $2\frac{1}{5}$ and $2\frac{2}{3}$.

$2\frac{1}{5}$	⠿	$2\frac{2}{3}$	The whole numbers are the same.
↓		↓	
$2\frac{3}{15}$	⠿	$2\frac{10}{15}$	Compare the fractions. First write the fractions with the least common denominator.
$2\frac{3}{15}$	<	$2\frac{10}{15}$	$\frac{3}{15}$ is less than $\frac{10}{15}$.
↓		↓	
$2\frac{1}{5}$	<	$2\frac{2}{3}$	$2\frac{1}{5}$ is less than $2\frac{2}{3}$.

C. Write $\frac{1}{3}$, $\frac{5}{18}$, and $\frac{4}{9}$ in order from least to greatest.

$\frac{1}{3}$	$\frac{5}{18}$	$\frac{4}{9}$	
$\frac{6}{18}$	$\frac{5}{18}$	$\frac{8}{18}$	Write the fractions with the least common denominator.
$\frac{5}{18}$	$\frac{6}{18}$	$\frac{8}{18}$	Compare the numerators.
↓	↓	↓	
$\frac{5}{18}$	$\frac{1}{3}$	$\frac{4}{9}$	Write the fractions in order.

■ **Talk About Math** If two fractions have the same numerator but different denominators, how can you tell which fraction is larger without finding a common denominator?

326

Check Understanding

For another example, see Set H, pages 334–335.

Tell which fraction or mixed number is greater.

1. $\frac{3}{4}$ $\frac{9}{16}$

2. $\frac{1}{3}$ $\frac{5}{9}$

3. $2\frac{1}{2}$ $1\frac{5}{16}$

4. $3\frac{4}{5}$ $3\frac{1}{5}$

Order the fractions or mixed numbers from least to greatest.

5. $\frac{3}{4}$ $1\frac{1}{4}$ $\frac{5}{8}$

6. $\frac{2}{5}$ $\frac{7}{10}$ $\frac{3}{10}$

Practice

For More Practice, see Set H, pages 336–337.

Compare the fractions, whole numbers, and mixed numbers.
Use <, >, or =. **Remember** to find the least common denominator.

7. $\frac{1}{2}$ ⬚ $\frac{2}{3}$

8. $\frac{1}{3}$ ⬚ $\frac{4}{9}$

9. $\frac{2}{5}$ ⬚ $\frac{1}{2}$

10. $\frac{3}{4}$ ⬚ $\frac{2}{5}$

11. $\frac{2}{3}$ ⬚ $\frac{4}{6}$

12. $\frac{5}{6}$ ⬚ $\frac{3}{4}$

13. 1 ⬚ $\frac{3}{8}$

14. $\frac{3}{4}$ ⬚ $\frac{6}{8}$

15. $1\frac{3}{5}$ ⬚ $2\frac{1}{5}$

16. $5\frac{1}{2}$ ⬚ $3\frac{3}{4}$

17. 3 ⬚ $5\frac{5}{16}$

18. $7\frac{5}{12}$ ⬚ $6\frac{2}{3}$

19. $5\frac{1}{3}$ ⬚ $5\frac{1}{5}$

20. $6\frac{7}{10}$ ⬚ $6\frac{1}{15}$

21. $4\frac{7}{16}$ ⬚ $4\frac{1}{2}$

22. $\frac{311}{200}$ ⬚ $1\frac{1}{2}$

Write the fractions, whole numbers, and mixed numbers in order from least to greatest.

23. $\frac{2}{3}$ $\frac{1}{2}$ $\frac{1}{3}$

24. $1\frac{3}{4}$ $1\frac{1}{8}$ $1\frac{3}{8}$

25. $1\frac{1}{2}$ 2 $\frac{3}{8}$

26. $\frac{3}{8}$ $\frac{1}{4}$ $\frac{9}{16}$

27. $2\frac{7}{8}$ $2\frac{1}{2}$ $2\frac{1}{3}$

28. $4\frac{1}{6}$ $4\frac{2}{5}$ $4\frac{1}{3}$

Problem Solving

Read for the facts to solve the problems.

29. The pumpkin bread recipe calls for $\frac{3}{4}$ cup of shortening. Martha has $\frac{5}{8}$ of a cup. Does she have enough shortening?

30. Martha made two loaves of pumpkin bread the same size. She cut one into 12 equal slices and the other into 16 equal slices. Which slices were larger?

31. Use Data Refer to the fractions in Example A and Example B on page 308. Which fraction is larger?

327

Fractions and Decimals

Build Understanding

A. Scientists have estimated that less than three tenths of the earth's surface is land. The number *three tenths* can be written either as a decimal or as a fraction.

$$0.3 = \frac{3}{10}$$

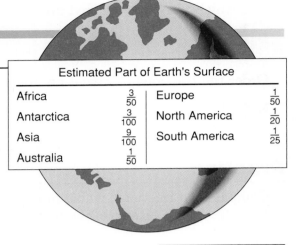

Estimated Part of Earth's Surface			
Africa	$\frac{3}{50}$	Europe	$\frac{1}{50}$
Antarctica	$\frac{3}{100}$	North America	$\frac{1}{20}$
Asia	$\frac{9}{100}$	South America	$\frac{1}{25}$
Australia	$\frac{1}{50}$		

About $\frac{7}{10}$ of the earth's surface is water or ice.

B. South America covers about $\frac{1}{25}$ of the earth's surface. Rename $\frac{1}{25}$ as a fraction with a denominator of 100. Then write it as a decimal.

$$\frac{1}{25} \xrightarrow[\;25 \times 4\;]{\;1 \times 4\;} \frac{4}{100} = 0.04$$

C. **Calculator** Write $\frac{7}{50}$ as a decimal. Use your calculator to divide the numerator by the denominator.

Press: 7 ÷ 50 =

Display: *0.14*

■ **Talk About Math** What is $6\frac{2}{5}$ as a decimal? If you used a calculator, what keys would you press to get the correct display of 6.4? Remember that $6\frac{2}{5}$ means $6 + \frac{2}{5}$.

Check Understanding

For another example, see Set I, pages 334–335.

1. Write 0.8 as a fraction. Then write it in lowest terms.

2. Write 0.25 as a fraction in lowest terms.

3. Write 0.325 as a fraction in lowest terms.

4. Write 2.35 in lowest terms.

5. Write $\frac{7}{5}$ as a fraction with denominator 10. Then write it as a decimal.

6. Write $\frac{9}{20}$ as a fraction with denominator 100. Then write it as a decimal.

Practice

For More Practice, see Set I, pages 336–337.

Write each decimal as a fraction or a mixed number. **Remember** to write all fractions in lowest terms.

7. 0.7   **8.** 0.4   **9.** 0.6   **10.** 0.9

11. 0.24   **12.** 0.36   **13.** 1.24   **14.** 3.48

15. 0.025   **16.** 0.175   **17.** 2.144   **18.** 12.056

Mental Math   Write each fraction with a denominator of 10, 100, or 1,000. Then write it as a decimal.

19. $\frac{1}{4}$ **20.** $\frac{3}{20}$ **21.** $\frac{1}{2}$ **22.** $\frac{9}{50}$

23. $\frac{7}{25}$ **24.** $\frac{9}{250}$ **25.** $\frac{9}{125}$ **26.** $\frac{7}{500}$

Calculator   Write each fraction as a decimal.

27. $\frac{3}{4}$ **28.** $\frac{1}{8}$ **29.** $\frac{1}{5}$ **30.** $\frac{3}{8}$

31. $\frac{3}{16}$ **32.** $\frac{27}{50}$ **33.** $\frac{1}{50}$ **34.** $\frac{3}{40}$

Estimation   Is each fraction closest to 0, to $\frac{1}{2}$, or to 1?

35. $\frac{49}{100}$ **36.** $\frac{3}{100}$ **37.** $\frac{887}{1,000}$ **38.** $\frac{250}{500}$

For Exercises 39–42, tell whether you would use paper and pencil, mental math, or a calculator. Then change each fraction to a decimal.

39. $\frac{9}{25}$ **40.** $\frac{19}{95}$ **41.** $\frac{7}{20}$ **42.** $\frac{12}{25}$

Problem Solving

43. Compare the fractional parts of the earth's surface taken up by Africa and South America. Which is greater?

44. Order the fractional parts of the earth's surface taken up by the continents from least to greatest.

TIPS FOR PROBLEM SOLVERS

Share your thinking with others. Explaining your ideas helps you think better.

329

Interpret the Remainder

Build Understanding

Rita sells office equipment. Each day, she reports the orders she takes.

DAILY REPORT

Sales Agent: _Rita Landry_   DATE: _July 17_

CUSTOMER	ORDER NO.	AMOUNT	SHIPPING DATE
1. *Star Co.*	4123	$1342.20	Oct. 24
2. *Star Co.*	4124	238.17	Sept. 11
3. *Compco*	4125	2841.32	Sept. 18
4. *Action Co.*	4126	137.50	Oct. 15

Understand
QUESTION
FACTS
KEY IDEA

Plan and Solve
STRATEGY
ANSWER

Look Back
SENSIBLE ANSWER
ALTERNATE APPROACH

Each daily report sheet has **9** lines. How many sheets did Rita need to report **67** orders?

Understand   How many daily report sheets did Rita use for 67 orders? Each sheet is a list for 9 orders. She must use enough sheets to list all the orders.

Plan and Solve   STRATEGY   Find how many groups of 9 are in 67, and how many are left over. Divide 67 by 9.

$$9)\overline{67} \quad 7\frac{4}{9}$$

$$\frac{63}{4}$$

The quotient is 7, and the remainder is 4. There are 7 groups of 9, and 4 are left over.

ANSWER   Rita had to use 8 sheets of report paper: 7 full sheets and 1 sheet with 4 orders. Even though she would only use a fraction of the page, Rita would still need 8 sheets.

Look Back   Check the answer. Since 7 × 9 = 63, 7 full sheets can list 63 names. The eighth sheet lists 4 names. All the names are listed.

■ **Talk About Math**   When division is used to solve a problem, in what three ways might the answer be used?

Check Understanding

Nova Computers are shipped in crates. Each crate holds 12 computers.

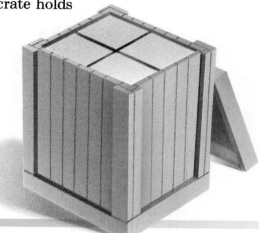

1. If 150 computers are shipped, how many crates can be completely filled?

2. How many computers will be left over?

3. How many crates are needed in all?

4. Each full crate weighs 260 pounds. What is the average weight of each computer?

Practice

5. Each page of Rita's checkbook has 4 checks. She wrote 58 checks. How many full pages did she use? How many checks on the next page did she use?

6. Calculators are packed 8 to a box. Rita can order only full boxes. A customer wants to buy 100 calculators. How many boxes are needed to complete the order?

7. Packages of computer paper are shipped in cartons of 24 packages. If a full carton weighs 36 pounds, what is the weight of each package of computer paper?

Choose a _____ Strategy

Yoshi has 9 coins. He spends a quarter in the bakery and 5 cents in the grocery store. Now he has only 23 cents left. What coins did he have before shopping?

8. If he has 23 cents left, how much money did he have before spending the quarter and 5 cents?

9. How many coins could he use to spend 5 cents?

10. What coins did Yoshi have before shopping?

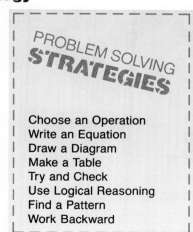

PROBLEM SOLVING
STRATEGIES

Choose an Operation
Write an Equation
Draw a Diagram
Make a Table
Try and Check
Use Logical Reasoning
Find a Pattern
Work Backward

Problem Solving REVIEW

Solve each problem.

1. What fraction of the stripes on the American flag are red?

2. Of the 50 United States, 8 have names that begin with the letter M. What fraction, in lowest terms, of the United States have names that do not begin with the letter M?

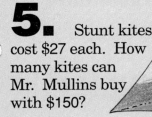

3. Lonna has 3 cats. One weighs $6\frac{3}{4}$ lb, one weighs $7\frac{1}{8}$ lb, and the third weights $6\frac{7}{8}$ lb. About how much does each cat weigh?

4. Of Vince's shirts, $\frac{1}{3}$ are blue. Of the remaining shirts, $\frac{1}{2}$ are striped. The other 3 shirts are yellow. How many shirts does Vince have?

5. Stunt kites cost $27 each. How many kites can Mr. Mullins buy with $150?

6. Use the bar graph below. What fraction of the people surveyed chose a cruise as a favorite vacation?

Favorite Vacation

7. **Data File** Using the weather map on pages 380–381, find the number of cities with a high temperature of exactly 83°. What fraction of the Michigan cities shown had that temperature?

8. **Make a Data File** Find pictures of flags of different countries. List 10 countries whose flags are divided into thirds. Draw the flags.

Explore with a Calculator

"Is that a fact?"

1. Mrs. Brown's class is sponsoring Decimal Days. Students who can find the most mixed numbers in their daily reading and correctly convert them to decimals will receive a trophy.

Mrs. Brown started them off with this fact: The length of the longest snake at the nature center is about $37 \frac{1}{4}$ inches.

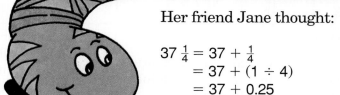

Sally thought:

$37 \frac{1}{4} = \frac{149}{4}$

$149 \div 4 = 37.25$

Her friend Jane thought:

$37 \frac{1}{4} = 37 + \frac{1}{4}$
$= 37 + (1 \div 4)$
$= 37 + 0.25$
$= 37.25$

Sally presses: 4 ⊠ 37 ⊞ 1 ⊡ 4 ⊟
Her display shows: | 37.25 |

Jane presses: 1 ⊡ 4 ⊞ 37 ⊟
Her display shows: | 37.25 |

2. Help Sally win the trophy. She found these facts. Use a calculator method to change each of these mixed numbers to a decimal.

a. The tongue of a blue whale weighs about $2 \frac{1}{2}$ tons.

b. A baby whale's head is about $2 \frac{4}{5}$ yards long.

c. An Alaskan sled dog can pull $2 \frac{1}{4}$ times as much as its body weight.

d. A box turtle lives $1 \frac{3}{5}$ times as long as a human being.

e. A baby rhinoceros weighs about $72 \frac{3}{4}$ pounds at birth.

f. A baby gorilla weighs about $3 \frac{3}{8}$ pounds at birth.

g. Find at least 5 more examples of mixed numbers in your newspaper or encyclopedia. Then change them to decimals.

Reteaching

A fraction can be used to name part of a set.

Three of 7 coins are dimes. Write this as a fraction.

$\dfrac{3}{7}$ ← Number of dimes
   ← Total number of coins

Remember that the denominator is the number of objects in the set.

What fraction of the

1. glasses have straws?   **2.** candles are lit?

Find equal fractions: $\dfrac{3}{8} = \dfrac{9}{\square}$

To find equal fractions, you can multiply both the numerator and the denominator by the same number (not zero).

So $\dfrac{3}{8}$ $\dfrac{9}{24}$ 3×3 8×3

Remember that you can divide the numerator and denominator by the same number (not zero) to find equal fractions. Multiply or divide to find equal fractions.

1. $\dfrac{3}{5} = \dfrac{12}{\square}$ **2.** $\dfrac{6}{12} = \dfrac{1}{\square}$ **3.** $\dfrac{5}{8} = \dfrac{10}{\square}$

4. $\dfrac{14}{16} = \dfrac{\square}{8}$ **5.** $\dfrac{16}{18} = \dfrac{\square}{9}$ **6.** $\dfrac{3}{4} = \dfrac{\square}{12}$

Write $\dfrac{8}{12}$ in lowest terms.

You can divide both 8 and 12 by 2.

$\dfrac{8}{12} = \dfrac{4}{6}$ $8 \div 2$ $12 \div 2$

You can divide both 4 and 6 by 2.

$\dfrac{4}{6} = \dfrac{2}{3}$ Lowest terms $4 \div 2$ $6 \div 2$

Remember that the greatest common factor can be used to write a fraction in lowest terms.

Write each fraction in lowest terms.

1. $\dfrac{5}{15}$ **2.** $\dfrac{16}{28}$ **3.** $\dfrac{4}{16}$

4. $\dfrac{3}{9}$ **5.** $\dfrac{12}{16}$ **6.** $\dfrac{14}{35}$

You can use the number lines on page 315 to find equal fractions, mixed numbers, and improper fractions. What mixed number is equal to $\dfrac{5}{3}$?

Look at the number line for thirds.

$\dfrac{5}{3} = 1\dfrac{2}{3}$

Remember that a point on a number line can have more than one name. Use the number lines on page 315 to answer these questions.

1. What mixed number is equal to $\dfrac{11}{8}$?

2. What fraction is equal to $\dfrac{2}{3}$?

Set E   pages 316–317

Write a whole number or a mixed number for $\frac{26}{4}$.

Divide.

$$4\overline{)2\,6}$$

$6\frac{2}{4}$ ← Remainder
← Divisor

The fraction $\frac{2}{4}$ can be written in lowest terms. So $\frac{26}{4} = 6\frac{2}{4} = 6\frac{1}{2}$.

Remember that an improper fraction names a number greater than or equal to 1.

Write a whole number or a mixed number for each improper fraction. Write each fraction in lowest terms.

1. $\frac{20}{6}$ **2.** $\frac{36}{12}$ **3.** $\frac{36}{8}$

Set F   pages 320–321

Round $1\frac{3}{8}$ to the nearest whole number.

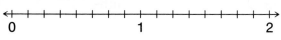

0   1   2

$1\frac{3}{8}$ is closer to 1. So, $1\frac{3}{8}$ rounds to 1.

Remember to round to the next whole number if the fraction is $\frac{1}{2}$ or greater. Round each mixed number to the nearest whole number.

1. $3\frac{2}{3}$ **2.** $4\frac{3}{10}$ **3.** $6\frac{5}{12}$

Set G   pages 324–325

Write $\frac{7}{8}$ and $\frac{1}{12}$ with the least common denominator.

List multiples of each denominator.
Multiples of 8: 8, 16, 24, 32, 40
Multiples of 12: 12, 24, 36, 48
The least common multiple of 8 and 12 is 24.

$\frac{7}{8} = \frac{21}{24}$ ← 7×3
← 8×3

$\frac{1}{12} = \frac{2}{24}$ ← 1×2
← 12×2

Remember that multiplying the numerator and denominator by the same number does not change the value of the fraction.

Write the fractions with the least common denominator.

1. $\frac{2}{5}, \frac{1}{6}$ **2.** $\frac{1}{3}, \frac{2}{9}$ **3.** $\frac{5}{6}, \frac{4}{9}$

Set H   pages 326–327

Compare $2\frac{5}{6}$ and $2\frac{7}{8}$.

Write the fractions with the least common denominator, 24.

$2\frac{5}{6} = 2\frac{20}{24}$ $2\frac{7}{8} = 2\frac{21}{24}$

Since $2\frac{20}{24} < 2\frac{21}{24}$, then $2\frac{5}{6} < 2\frac{7}{8}$

Remember that the inequality symbol always points to the smaller number.

Compare the fractions, whole numbers, and mixed numbers. Use $<$, $>$, or $=$.

1. $\frac{3}{4}$ ⬚ $\frac{1}{2}$ **2.** $\frac{3}{8}$ ⬚ $\frac{5}{12}$ **3.** $1\frac{3}{4}$ ⬚ $1\frac{9}{12}$

Set I   pages 328–329

The number nine tenths can be written as a decimal or as a fraction.

$0.9 = \frac{9}{10}$

Remember that the first place to the right of the decimal point is the tenths place.

Write each decimal as a fraction. Write all fractions in lowest terms.

1. 0.8   **2.** 0.32   **3.** 0.202

More Practice

Set A pages 308–309

What fraction of the

1. letters are Es? **2.** symbols are dollar signs? **3.** punctuation marks are commas?

E E G T E % $ # ? , , ? ! !

4. Write a fraction to name the point labeled B.

$$0 \qquad\qquad B \qquad 1$$

Write the fraction.

5. Three fifths **6.** Five sixths **7.** One fourth **8.** Seven sixteenths

Set B pages 310–311

Multiply to find each fraction.

1. $\frac{1}{4} = \frac{4}{}$ **2.** $\frac{5}{8} = \frac{15}{}$ **3.** $\frac{5}{6} = \frac{}{24}$ **4.** $\frac{7}{7} = \frac{}{14}$

Divide to find each fraction.

5. $\frac{24}{32} = \frac{}{4}$ **6.** $\frac{9}{24} = \frac{}{8}$ **7.** $\frac{30}{36} = \frac{5}{}$ **8.** $\frac{10}{12} = \frac{5}{}$

Set C pages 312–313

Write the greatest common factor of the numerator and denominator.

1. $\frac{6}{15}$ **2.** $\frac{11}{19}$ **3.** $\frac{18}{24}$ **4.** $\frac{16}{36}$ **5.** $\frac{15}{35}$

Write each fraction in lowest terms.

6. $\frac{4}{8}$ **7.** $\frac{6}{18}$ **8.** $\frac{10}{45}$ **9.** $\frac{15}{60}$ **10.** $\frac{9}{24}$

Set D pages 314–315

Write a mixed number.

1. One and three fourths **2.** Two and five sixths **3.** Five and two fifths

Use the number lines on page 315 to answer the questions.

4. What fraction is equal to $\frac{4}{6}$? **5.** What whole number is equal to $\frac{8}{4}$?

6. What mixed number is equal to $\frac{5}{4}$? **7.** What improper fraction is equal to $1\frac{5}{6}$?

8. Which fraction is less, $\frac{2}{3}$ or $\frac{4}{8}$? **9.** Which number is greater, $1\frac{3}{8}$ or $\frac{7}{4}$?

Set E pages 316–317

Write a whole number or a mixed number for each improper fraction. **Remember** to write each fraction in lowest terms.

1. $\frac{21}{4}$ **2.** $\frac{26}{6}$ **3.** $\frac{48}{15}$ **4.** $\frac{68}{17}$ **5.** $\frac{34}{16}$

Tell whether you would use paper and pencil or mental math. Write each quotient as a whole number, a mixed number, or a proper fraction.

6. $4\overline{)19}$ **7.** $8\overline{)33}$ **8.** $9\overline{)263}$ **9.** $12\overline{)136}$ **10.** $20\overline{)4}$

Set F pages 320–321

For each fraction, estimate if the fraction is closest to 0, to $\frac{1}{2}$, or to 1.

1. $\frac{1}{15}$ **2.** $\frac{9}{17}$ **3.** $\frac{9}{15}$ **4.** $\frac{2}{13}$ **5.** $\frac{13}{25}$ **6.** $\frac{39}{41}$

Round each mixed number to the nearest whole number.

7. $5\frac{1}{4}$ **8.** $3\frac{5}{8}$ **9.** $10\frac{5}{9}$ **10.** $14\frac{7}{11}$ **11.** $8\frac{7}{14}$ **12.** $6\frac{2}{5}$

Set G pages 324–325

Write the fractions with the least common denominator.

1. $\frac{1}{6}, \frac{3}{4}$ **2.** $\frac{1}{3}, \frac{1}{15}$ **3.** $\frac{3}{10}, \frac{1}{5}$ **4.** $\frac{5}{6}, \frac{3}{8}$ **5.** $\frac{1}{4}, \frac{2}{5}$

Set H pages 326–327

Compare the fractions, whole numbers, and mixed numbers. Use $<$, $>$, or $=$. **Remember** to find the least common denominator.

1. $\frac{5}{8} \ \square \ \frac{3}{4}$ **2.** $\frac{2}{3} \ \square \ \frac{3}{5}$ **3.** $1 \ \square \ \frac{7}{8}$ **4.** $4\frac{1}{4} \ \square \ 4\frac{1}{5}$

Write the fractions, whole numbers, and mixed numbers in order from least to greatest.

5. $\frac{7}{8}, \frac{3}{4}, \frac{5}{6}$ **6.** $1\frac{2}{3}, 1\frac{3}{8}, 1\frac{1}{4}$ **7.** $\frac{1}{3}, \frac{2}{5}, \frac{1}{6}$

Set I pages 328–329

Write each decimal as a fraction or a mixed number. **Remember** to write all fractions in lowest terms.

1. 0.3   **2.** 0.46   **3.** 2.38   **4.** 0.275

Mental Math Write each fraction with a denominator of 10, 100, or 1,000. Then write it as a decimal.

5. $\frac{1}{5}$ **6.** $\frac{4}{25}$ **7.** $\frac{9}{500}$ **8.** $\frac{3}{4}$

Enrichment

Terminating and Repeating Decimals

Byron was using his calculator to change the fractions on page 329 to decimals. After he finished with those fractions, he thought he would try some others. Here are the fractions he tried, along with the results:

$\frac{5}{12}$ **Press:** 5 ÷ 12 =   **Display:** 0.4166666

$\frac{6}{11}$ **Press:** 6 ÷ 11 =   **Display:** 0.5454545

$\frac{7}{32}$ **Press:** 7 ÷ 32 =   **Display:** 0.21875

The decimals for $\frac{5}{12}$ and $\frac{6}{11}$ are **repeating decimals**. A repeating decimal has a digit or pattern of digits that repeats endlessly. To write a repeating decimal, put a bar over the digit or digits that repeat.

$$0.4166666\ldots = 0.41\overline{6} \qquad 0.5454545\ldots = 0.\overline{54}$$

The decimal for $\frac{7}{32}$ is a **terminating decimal**. Terminating decimals have digits in an exact number of decimal places.

 **Calculator**   Use your calculator to change these fractions to decimals.

1. $\frac{3}{4}$ 2. $\frac{5}{8}$ 3. $\frac{4}{9}$ 4. $\frac{5}{6}$ 5. $\frac{17}{20}$ 6. $\frac{5}{24}$

7. $\frac{11}{32}$ 8. $\frac{8}{15}$ 9. $\frac{13}{16}$ 10. $\frac{29}{40}$ 11. $\frac{9}{11}$ 12. $\frac{7}{18}$

13. For each fraction, write the prime factorization of the denominator.

14. What are the prime factors of denominators in fractions that become terminating decimals?

15. What are the prime factors of denominators in fractions that become repeating decimals?

16. How can you tell if a fraction will be a terminating or a repeating decimal by looking at the denominator?

Chapter 10 Review/Test

Write a fraction to name the shaded part.

1.

2.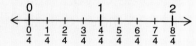

Multiply or divide to find equal fractions.

3. $\frac{7}{8} = \frac{14}{\boxed{}}$

4. $\frac{10}{20} = \frac{\boxed{}}{2}$

Write each fraction in lowest terms.

5. $\frac{10}{16}$

6. $\frac{12}{20}$

7. What mixed number equals $\frac{5}{4}$?

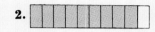

Write a whole number or a fraction for each improper fraction.

8. $\frac{19}{8}$

9. $\frac{30}{10}$

For each fraction, estimate if the fraction is closer to 0, to $\frac{1}{2}$, or to 1.

10. $\frac{1}{12}$

11. $\frac{29}{32}$

Write the fractions with the least common denominator.

12. $\frac{7}{16}$ $\frac{3}{8}$

13. $\frac{2}{3}$ $\frac{1}{4}$

Compare the fractions, whole numbers, and mixed numbers.

14. $\frac{5}{8}$ ▦ $\frac{1}{2}$

15. 7 ▦ $6\frac{2}{3}$

Write each decimal as a fraction or a mixed number.

16. 0.8

17. 2.19

18. Hal picked some tomatoes and gave $\frac{1}{2}$ of them to Melissa. She gave 4 away and had 3 left. How many tomatoes did Hal pick?

Read this problem. Then answer the questions below.

Arturo is packing glasses in boxes that hold 8 glasses each. If he has 50 glasses to pack, how many boxes will he need?

19. Which statement describes a method for getting a reasonable answer?

   a. Divide. Use the whole-number part of the quotient.
   b. Divide. Use the remainder.
   c. Divide. Write the quotient as a mixed number.
   d. Divide. Add 1 to the whole number part of the quotient, if the remainder is not zero.

20. Solve the problem.

21. **Write About Math** Write a sentence in which a fraction is used to name part of a set.

Exploring Addition and Subtraction of Fractions

11

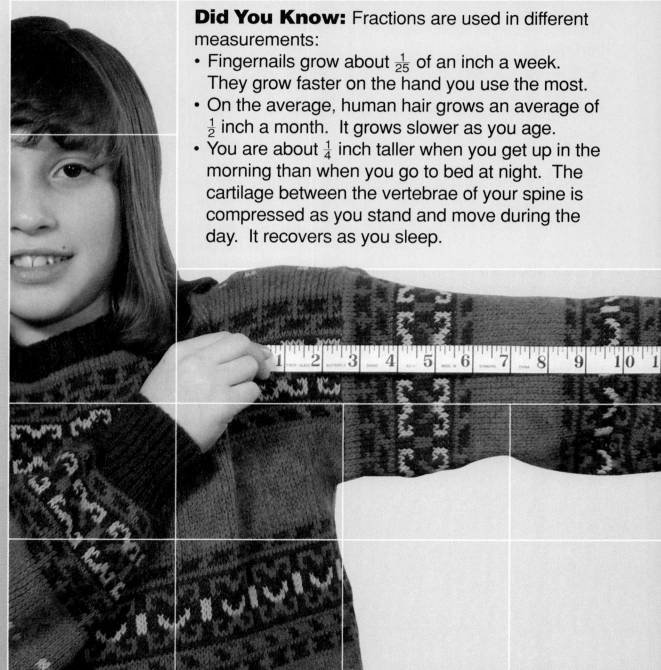

Did You Know: Fractions are used in different measurements:

- Fingernails grow about $\frac{1}{25}$ of an inch a week. They grow faster on the hand you use the most.
- On the average, human hair grows an average of $\frac{1}{2}$ inch a month. It grows slower as you age.
- You are about $\frac{1}{4}$ inch taller when you get up in the morning than when you go to bed at night. The cartilage between the vertebrae of your spine is compressed as you stand and move during the day. It recovers as you sleep.

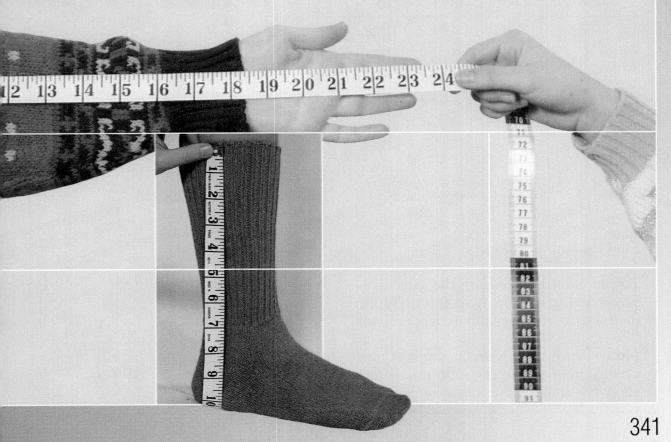

Number-Sense Project

Estimate
Who can estimate the length of short lines more accurately: adults or students your age?

Gather Data
Draw 5 lines on a sheet of paper from 1 to 8 inches long. Have 2 adults and 2 classmates estimate the length of your lines to the nearest $\frac{1}{4}$ inch.

Analyze and Report
Compute the accuracy of the different estimates. Share your results with other students. Who was more accurate in estimating?

Adding Fractions: Same Denominator

Build Understanding

A. Harry fed his baby sister, Mary, a bottle of warm milk. First, he fed her 4 ounces of milk. Later, he fed her 4 ounces more. What fraction of a pint did Mary drink?

There are 16 ounces in a pint. Each ounce is $\frac{1}{16}$ of a pint. So, 4 ounces equals $\frac{4}{16}$ of a pint.

Use addition to find the total.

4 ounces	4 sixteenths
+ 4 ounces	+ 4 sixteenths
8 ounces	8 sixteenths

A number line can be used to show the addition.

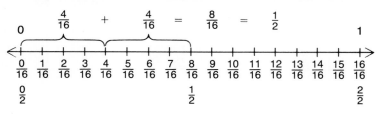

$$\frac{4}{16} \quad + \quad \frac{4}{16} \quad = \quad \frac{8}{16} \quad = \quad \frac{1}{2}$$

$$\begin{array}{c} \frac{4}{16} \\ + \frac{4}{16} \\ \hline \frac{8}{16} = \frac{1}{2} \end{array}$$

The fractions have the same denominator, 16. Add the numerators. $\frac{4}{16} + \frac{4}{16} = \frac{4+4}{16} = \frac{8}{16}$

Write the fraction in lowest terms to name the sum more simply.

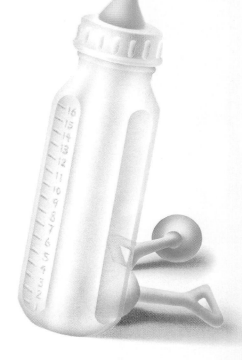

Mary drank $\frac{1}{2}$ pint of milk.

B. Find the sum of $\frac{3}{4}$ and $\frac{3}{4}$.

To add two fractions with the same denominator, add the numerators. Write their sum over the common denominator.

Always write the answer in simplest form. Change improper fractions to mixed numbers and write fractions in lowest terms.

$$\begin{array}{c} \frac{3}{4} \\ + \frac{3}{4} \\ \hline \frac{6}{4} = 1\frac{2}{4} = 1\frac{1}{2} \end{array}$$

■ **Talk About Math** How are units such as ounces like the denominator sixteenths?

Check Understanding

For another example, see Set A, pages 374–375.

Add these fractions. **Remember** to simplify the answer if necessary.

1.

$\frac{1}{5} + \frac{2}{5}$

2.

$\frac{4}{8} + \frac{1}{8}$

3.

$\frac{2}{9} + \frac{4}{9}$

4. 3 sixths + 2 sixths

5.
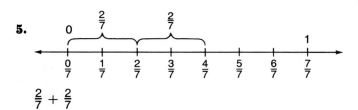

$\frac{2}{7} + \frac{2}{7}$

Practice

For More Practice, see Set A, pages 376–377.

Add the fractions. **Remember** to simplify the answer if necessary.

6. $\frac{1}{5}$
$+\frac{1}{5}$

7. $\frac{4}{10}$
$+\frac{5}{10}$

8. $\frac{2}{8}$
$+\frac{3}{8}$

9. $\frac{2}{8}$
$+\frac{4}{8}$

10. $\frac{6}{12}$
$+\frac{3}{12}$

11. $\frac{7}{11} + \frac{4}{11}$

12. $\frac{3}{9} + \frac{7}{9}$

13. $\frac{4}{5} + \frac{3}{5} + \frac{1}{5}$

14. $\frac{5}{12} + \frac{7}{12} + \frac{6}{12}$

Problem Solving

Solve the problem.

15. Mary drank the first part of her bottle in 3 minutes. She drank the second part in 5 minutes. She drank the last part in 2 minutes. What fraction of an hour did Mary take to drink her bottle?

Visualize the problem in your mind to help you understand it better.

343

Subtracting Fractions: Same Denominator

Build Understanding

A. Greta's house is $\frac{1}{5}$ of a mile from the Twin Oaks shopping mall. Flora's house is $\frac{4}{5}$ of a mile from the mall. How much farther is Flora's house from the mall than Greta's house?

Use subtraction to compare the distances. Find $\frac{1}{5}$ from $\frac{4}{5}$.

You can use a number line to show the subtraction.

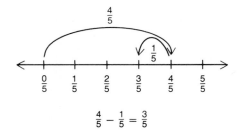

$$\frac{4}{5} - \frac{1}{5} = \frac{3}{5}$$

4	**fifths**
− 1	**fifth**
3	**fifths**

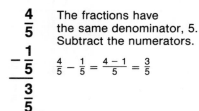

$\frac{4}{5}$ The fractions have the same denominator, 5. Subtract the numerators.

$-\frac{1}{5}$ $\frac{4}{5} - \frac{1}{5} = \frac{4-1}{5} = \frac{3}{5}$

$\frac{3}{5}$

Flora's house is $\frac{3}{5}$ mile farther from the mall than Greta's house.

B. Find the difference between $\frac{4}{6}$ and $\frac{1}{6}$.

To subtract two fractions with the same denominator, subtract the numerators.

Write their difference over the common denominator.

$$\frac{4}{6}$$
$$-\frac{1}{6}$$

$$\frac{3}{6} = \frac{1}{2}$$

Write the fraction in lowest terms to name the difference more simply.

■ **Talk About Math**   Explain how to check subtraction using the exercises in Examples A and B.

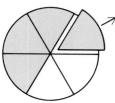

344

Check Understanding

For another example, see Set B, pages 374–375.

Subtract these fractions. Write the difference in simplest form.

1.

$\frac{5}{6} - \frac{1}{6}$

2.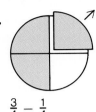

$\frac{3}{4} - \frac{1}{4}$

3.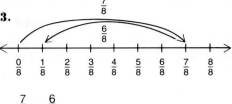

$\frac{7}{8} - \frac{6}{8}$

4. 5 sevenths − 2 sevenths

5. Explain in your own words how to subtract fractions with the same denominator.

Practice

For More Practice, see Set B, pages 376–377.

Subtract the fractions. **Remember** to simplify the answers if necessary.

6. $\frac{2}{4} - \frac{1}{4}$

7. $\frac{5}{6} - \frac{2}{6}$

8. $\frac{7}{9} - \frac{5}{9}$

9. $\frac{12}{13} - \frac{10}{13}$

10. $\frac{5}{5} - \frac{1}{5}$

11. $\frac{9}{10} - \frac{7}{10}$

12. $\frac{20}{24} - \frac{12}{24}$

13. $\frac{13}{17} - \frac{3}{17}$

14. $\frac{8}{9} - \frac{3}{9}$

15. $\frac{12}{10} - \frac{2}{10}$

16. $\frac{3}{8} - \frac{3}{8}$

17. $\frac{9}{6} - \frac{3}{6}$

Mixed Practice   Add or subtract these fractions. Write your answer in simplest form. Check your work.

18. $\frac{3}{4} + \frac{5}{4}$

19. $\frac{11}{28} + \frac{13}{28}$

20. $\frac{7}{21} + \frac{7}{21}$

21. $\frac{5}{9} + \frac{4}{9}$

22. $\frac{17}{10} - \frac{7}{10}$

23. $\frac{15}{22} - \frac{4}{22}$

24. $\frac{6}{14} - \frac{4}{14}$

25. $\frac{21}{13} - \frac{17}{13}$

Problem Solving

Read for the facts to solve the problems.

26. Franco takes 18 minutes to walk to the mall. William can walk there in only 8 minutes. By what fraction of an hour longer does it take Franco to walk to the mall?

27. Franco spent 23 minutes shopping for school supplies. He spent another 18 minutes shopping for gym equipment. How many minutes did he spend in all?

Adding and Subtracting Mixed Numbers: Same Denominator

Build Understanding

A. Lou and Gina were helping their father make a carrot salad for a party. They used $8\frac{1}{3}$ cups of shredded carrots and $4\frac{1}{3}$ cups of raisins. How many cups would a mixing bowl need to hold for just these two ingredients?

Use addition to find a total.
Find $8\frac{1}{3} + 4\frac{1}{3}$.

$$8\frac{1}{3}$$
$$+\ 4\frac{1}{3}$$
$$\overline{12\frac{2}{3}}$$

Add the fractions.
Add the whole numbers.

The bowl must hold at least $12\frac{2}{3}$ cups.

B. Estimation   Is the sum of $10\frac{3}{4}$ and $12\frac{3}{4}$ greater than or less than 23?

First look at the sum of the whole numbers.

$$10 + 12 = 22$$

Then estimate whether the sum of the fractions is more than or less than 1.

$$\frac{3}{4} + \frac{3}{4} = \text{▦}$$

Both fractions are greater than $\frac{1}{2}$. The sum of the fractions will be greater than 1.

The sum $10\frac{3}{4} + 12\frac{3}{4}$ is greater than 23.

C. Find $19\frac{3}{4} - 17\frac{1}{4}$.

$$19\frac{3}{4}$$
$$-\ 17\frac{1}{4}$$
$$\overline{2\frac{2}{4}} = 2\frac{1}{2}$$

First, subtract the fractions. Then subtract the whole numbers.

Write the answer in simplest form.

■ **Talk About Math**   When estimating the sum or difference of mixed numbers, how can comparing each fraction with $\frac{1}{2}$ be helpful?

346

Check Understanding

For another example, see Set C, pages 374–375.

Choose the correct answer.

1. $1\frac{1}{6}$ **a.** $5\frac{5}{12}$ **b.** $5\frac{5}{6}$ **c.** $6\frac{5}{6}$
     $+4\frac{4}{6}$

2. $5\frac{4}{5}$ **a.** $2\frac{1}{5}$ **b.** $1\frac{5}{5}$ **c.** $2\frac{3}{5}$
     $-3\frac{1}{5}$

3. Estimation Is the sum $3\frac{5}{8} + 4\frac{2}{8}$ more than or less than $7\frac{1}{2}$? Explain your answer.

Practice

For More Practice, see Set C, pages 376–377.

Add. **Remember** to write your answers in simplest form.

4. $1\frac{5}{9}$ **5.** $8\frac{1}{12}$ **6.** $3\frac{2}{8}$ **7.** $14\frac{3}{15}$ **8.** $21\frac{4}{17}$
   $+4\frac{4}{9}$ $+\frac{10}{12}$ $+7\frac{3}{8}$ $+12\frac{3}{15}$ $+9\frac{3}{17}$

9. $8\frac{1}{4} + 10\frac{1}{4} + 6\frac{1}{4}$ **10.** $7\frac{1}{16} + \frac{3}{16} + 4\frac{1}{16}$ **11.** $5\frac{1}{5} + 10\frac{2}{5} + \frac{1}{5}$

Subtract. **Remember** to write your answers in simplest form.

12. $2\frac{8}{14}$ **13.** $6\frac{8}{9}$ **14.** $18\frac{8}{12}$ **15.** $11\frac{13}{15}$ **16.** $21\frac{19}{24}$
   $-1\frac{5}{14}$ $-3\frac{3}{9}$ $-7\frac{1}{12}$ $-5\frac{9}{15}$ $-8\frac{16}{24}$

Estimation Estimate to answer each question.

17. Is the sum more than or less than 16?

$7\frac{1}{5} + 8\frac{3}{5}$

18. Is the sum more than or less than $5\frac{1}{2}$?

$3\frac{2}{4} + 2\frac{1}{4}$

19. Is the answer more than or less than $10\frac{1}{2}$?

$15\frac{3}{8} - 5\frac{2}{8}$

Problem Solving

20. Write a problem using this information: Mrs. Russo made $11\frac{1}{3}$ quarts of lemonade. Then she made $14\frac{2}{3}$ quarts of orangeade.

21. Amy has a pint container of yogurt. A recipe for onion dip calls for $\frac{3}{4}$ cup of yogurt. Does Amy have enough yogurt to make the recipe three times?

Adding Mixed Numbers: Renaming Sums

Build Understanding

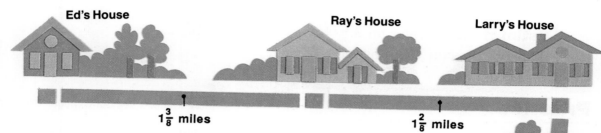

Ed's House   Ray's House   Larry's House

$1\frac{3}{8}$ miles $1\frac{2}{8}$ miles

A. Ed walked to Ray's house. Ed and Ray walked to Larry's house. Larry's mom drove the 3 boys to Frank's house. How far did Ed travel to go to Frank's house?

Use addition to find the total distance.

Find $1\frac{3}{8} + 1\frac{2}{8} + 4\frac{5}{8}$.

Estimate using the whole numbers.
$1 + 1 + 4 = 6$

Add the fractions.
Add the whole numbers.

$$1\frac{3}{8}$$
$$1\frac{2}{8}$$
$$+ 4\frac{5}{8}$$
$$\overline{6\frac{10}{8}} = 7\frac{1}{4}$$

Rename the sum.

$6\frac{10}{8} = 6 + \frac{10}{8}$

$= 6 + 1\frac{2}{8}$

$= 7\frac{2}{8} = 7\frac{1}{4}$

Ed traveled $7\frac{1}{4}$ miles.

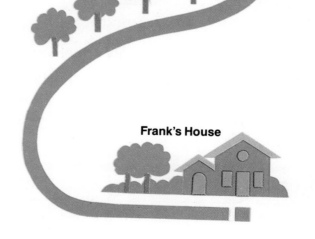

$4\frac{5}{8}$ miles ⟶

Frank's House

B. Mental Math Sometimes you can add mixed numbers mentally. Look for fractions whose sum will equal 1.

Find $1\frac{4}{5} + 1\frac{3}{5} + 2\frac{1}{5}$.

$1\frac{4}{5} + 1\frac{3}{5} + 2\frac{1}{5}$ $\frac{4}{5} + \frac{1}{5} = \frac{5}{5} = 1$

$1 + 1 + 1\frac{3}{5} + 2 = 5\frac{3}{5}$

■ **Talk About Math** How would you use the fraction part of the mixed numbers in Example A to find an estimate closer to the actual sum?

348

Check Understanding

For another example, see Set D, pages 374–375.

For Exercises 1 and 2, tell which is the correct answer.

1. $2\frac{3}{8} + \frac{3}{8} + 5\frac{4}{8}$

   a. $8\frac{1}{2}$ **b.** $8\frac{1}{4}$ **c.** 8

2. $17\frac{5}{6} + 7\frac{2}{6}$

   a. $24\frac{5}{6}$ **b.** $25\frac{1}{6}$ **c.** $25\frac{7}{6}$

Mental Math   Use mental math to add these fractions.

3. $1\frac{2}{3} + 2\frac{1}{3} + \frac{1}{3}$ 4. $2\frac{1}{5} + 3\frac{4}{5} + 4\frac{2}{5}$ 5. $2\frac{3}{8} + 1\frac{3}{8} + 5\frac{5}{8}$

Practice

For More Practice, see Set D, pages 376–377.

Add. **Remember** to write your answers in simplest form.

6. $\frac{3}{6}$
   $+ 1\frac{5}{6}$

7. $\frac{1}{2}$
   $+ 1\frac{1}{2}$

8. $1\frac{3}{4}$
   $+ 5\frac{1}{4}$

9. $7\frac{14}{15}$
   $+ 8\frac{8}{15}$

10. $16\frac{1}{13}$
    $+ 16\frac{12}{13}$

11. $21\frac{5}{10}$
    $+ 13\frac{9}{10}$

12. $7 + 21\frac{2}{3} + 6\frac{2}{3}$

13. $10\frac{1}{4} + 10\frac{3}{4} + 6\frac{1}{4}$

14. $4\frac{2}{3} + 14\frac{2}{3} + 2\frac{1}{3}$

Mental Math   Use mental math to add these fractions.

15. $1\frac{5}{8} + 1\frac{3}{8} + 2\frac{1}{8}$ 16. $6\frac{1}{3} + 2\frac{1}{3} + 1\frac{2}{3}$ 17. $5\frac{3}{5} + 5\frac{3}{5} + \frac{2}{5}$

Problem Solving

Use the map to help you solve the problems.

18. How far is it from Anna's house to Fred's house?

19. How much farther is it from school to Fred's house than from Lou's house to Fred's house?

20. How much farther is it from the school to Lou's house than from Lou's house to Anna's house?

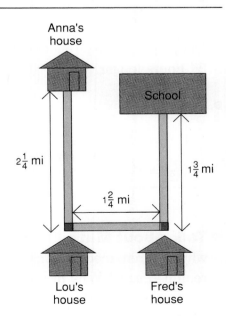

Anna's house

School

$2\frac{1}{4}$ mi

$1\frac{3}{4}$ mi

$1\frac{2}{4}$ mi

Lou's house

Fred's house

Subtracting from a Whole Number

Build Understanding

A. Manuel is a pianist. He is preparing for a concert. He has practiced $3\frac{1}{4}$ hours so far today. He practices 7 hours every day. How much longer must he practice?

Since you want to know how much time is left, subtract.
Find $7 - 3\frac{1}{4}$.

To subtract fourths from 7, rename 7 as a mixed number with the fraction part in fourths.

$$\begin{array}{l} 7 \\ -3\frac{1}{4} \\ \hline \end{array} \qquad \begin{array}{l} 7 = 6 + 1 \\ = 6 + \frac{4}{4} \end{array}$$

$$\begin{array}{rcl} 7 & = & 6\frac{4}{4} \\ -3\frac{1}{4} & = & 3\frac{1}{4} \\ \hline & & 3\frac{3}{4} \end{array}$$

Manuel must practice for $3\frac{3}{4}$ hours longer.

B. Find $1 - \frac{7}{12}$.

$$\begin{array}{rcl} 1 & = & \frac{12}{12} \\ -\frac{7}{12} & = & \frac{7}{12} \\ \hline & & \frac{5}{12} \end{array}$$

Rename 1 as $\frac{12}{12}$.
Subtract the fractions.

■ **Talk About Math** In Example B, why is 1 renamed as $\frac{12}{12}$? Could 1 be renamed as $\frac{4}{4}$? Why or why not?

The standard piano keyboard has 88 keys that are arranged according to pitch.

Check Understanding

For another example, see Set E, pages 374–375.

Use the pictures to rename each whole number.

1.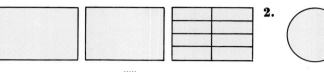

$$3 = 2\frac{}{8}$$

2.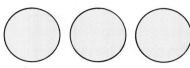

$$4 = 3\frac{}{}$$

Rename each whole number.

3. $1 = \frac{}{8}$ **4.** $3 = 2\frac{}{6}$ **5.** $6 = 5\frac{}{12}$ **6.** $15 = 14\frac{}{10}$

Copy and complete each subtraction exercise.

7.
$$5 = 4\frac{}{8}$$
$$-2\frac{3}{8} = 2\frac{3}{8}$$

8.
$$9 = 8\frac{}{}$$
$$-3\frac{7}{12} = 3\frac{}{12}$$

9.
$$1 = \frac{}{}$$
$$-\frac{2}{5} = \frac{2}{}$$

Practice

For More Practice, see Set E, pages 376–377.

Subtract. **Remember** to write your answers in simplest form.

10.
$$1$$
$$-\frac{7}{10}$$

11.
$$2$$
$$-1\frac{6}{11}$$

12.
$$4$$
$$-2\frac{1}{2}$$

13.
$$7$$
$$-3\frac{14}{15}$$

14.
$$5$$
$$-2\frac{9}{10}$$

15.
$$6$$
$$-1\frac{1}{6}$$

16.
$$12$$
$$-8\frac{7}{9}$$

17.
$$20$$
$$-3\frac{1}{4}$$

18.
$$25$$
$$-13\frac{5}{7}$$

19.
$$32$$
$$-30\frac{4}{5}$$

20. $1 - \frac{7}{16}$ **21.** $3 - 1\frac{17}{20}$ **22.** $32 - 17\frac{9}{11}$ **23.** $46 - 1\frac{14}{17}$ **24.** $42 - 41\frac{12}{13}$

Problem Solving

25. Manuel spends $2\frac{1}{2}$ hours practicing exercises during his 7 hours of daily practice. How much of his practice time is left to practice the pieces he will play?

26. Manuel's last concert was $2\frac{3}{4}$ hours long. Before the concert, he practiced for $3\frac{3}{4}$ hours. How many hours did Manuel play the piano that day?

Subtracting Mixed Numbers with Renaming

Build Understanding

The first time Shaun tried an experiment in science class, he used $7\frac{3}{8}$ inches of wire. The second time he did the experiment, he needed only $5\frac{7}{8}$ inches. How many inches more did he use in the first experiment than in the second experiment?

You want to find how many more inches. You can subtract. Find $7\frac{3}{8} - 5\frac{7}{8}$.

You cannot subtract the fractions because $\frac{7}{8}$ is greater than $\frac{3}{8}$. Rename $7\frac{3}{8}$.

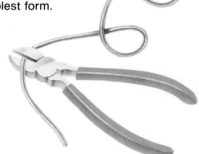

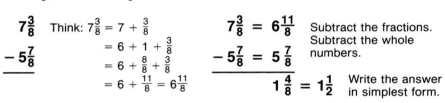

$$\begin{array}{l} 7\frac{3}{8} \\ -5\frac{7}{8} \end{array}$$

Think: $7\frac{3}{8} = 7 + \frac{3}{8}$
$= 6 + 1 + \frac{3}{8}$
$= 6 + \frac{8}{8} + \frac{3}{8}$
$= 6 + \frac{11}{8} = 6\frac{11}{8}$

$$\begin{array}{rl} 7\frac{3}{8} &= 6\frac{11}{8} \\ -5\frac{7}{8} &= 5\ \frac{7}{8} \\ \hline &1\frac{4}{8} = 1\frac{1}{2} \end{array}$$

Subtract the fractions. Subtract the whole numbers.

Write the answer in simplest form.

Shaun used $1\frac{1}{2}$ inches more wire in the first experiment.

■ **Talk About Math** In the example, why is 1 renamed as $\frac{8}{8}$ and not $\frac{7}{7}$ or $\frac{6}{6}$?

Check Understanding

For another example, see Set F, pages 374–375.

Use the pictures to help you rename the mixed numbers.

1.

$2\frac{5}{6} = 1\frac{}{6}$

2.

$3\frac{1}{4} = 2\frac{}{4}$

3.

$1\frac{2}{3} = \frac{}{3}$

Copy and complete the renaming of each mixed number.

4. $7\frac{3}{4} = 6\frac{}{4}$ **5.** $2\frac{2}{9} = 1\frac{}{9}$ **6.** $12\frac{3}{10} = 11\frac{}{10}$ **7.** $25\frac{7}{12} = 24\frac{}{12}$

Copy and complete each subtraction exercise.

8. $6\frac{1}{3} = 5\frac{▦}{3}$

 $-3\frac{2}{3} = 3\frac{2}{3}$
_____

9. $4\frac{1}{6} = 3\frac{▦}{▦}$

 $-2\frac{5}{6} = 2\frac{5}{6}$
_____

10. $11\frac{3}{5} = ▦\frac{▦}{▦}$

 $-9\frac{4}{5} = 9\frac{4}{▦}$
_____

For More Practice, see Set F, pages 376–377.

Practice

Subtract. **Remember** to write the answer in simplest form.

11. $4\frac{1}{4}$
$-1\frac{3}{4}$
_____

12. $9\frac{3}{8}$
$-5\frac{5}{8}$
_____

13. $7\frac{2}{5}$
$-2\frac{4}{5}$
_____

14. $6\frac{1}{6}$
$-2\frac{5}{6}$
_____

15. $4\frac{5}{8}$
$-1\frac{7}{8}$
_____

16. $3\frac{1}{5}$
$-1\frac{3}{5}$
_____

17. $13\frac{3}{5} - 4\frac{4}{5}$

18. $12\frac{7}{16} - 10\frac{11}{16}$

19. $8\frac{5}{9} - \frac{8}{9}$

20. $14\frac{1}{12} - 1\frac{7}{12}$

21. $24 - 8\frac{1}{2}$

22. $36 - 28\frac{2}{3}$

23. $16 - 2\frac{3}{4}$

24. $12 - 4\frac{5}{12}$

Problem Solving

Read for the facts to solve the problems.

25. For an experiment on the eating habits of gerbils, Ruth put $3\frac{1}{5}$ cups of feed in the gerbils' cage. After 3 days, only $1\frac{4}{5}$ cups were left. How much feed did the gerbils eat?

26. Connie's corn plant was $9\frac{3}{8}$ inches tall on Monday. The plant grew $2\frac{5}{8}$ inches during the week. How tall was the corn plant on Friday?

✓
Midchapter _____ Checkup

Add or subtract. Write your answers in simplest form.

1. $\frac{5}{8} + \frac{3}{8}$

2. $7\frac{12}{14} + 2\frac{3}{14}$

3. $\frac{3}{5} - \frac{2}{5}$

4. $3\frac{7}{12} - 1\frac{5}{12}$

5. $12 + 1\frac{2}{3} + 5\frac{2}{3}$

6. $9\frac{3}{4} + 9\frac{1}{4} + 5\frac{3}{4}$

7. $24 + 3\frac{5}{12} + 7\frac{9}{12}$

8. $16\frac{7}{18} - 3\frac{11}{18}$

9. $8\frac{3}{18} - 4\frac{12}{18}$

10. $36 - 17\frac{12}{22}$

11. $20 - 4\frac{1}{5}$

Explore as a Team

1. Play *Multiples and Factors* with another player. You will need a new game mat for each game you play. To make a game mat, write the numbers from 1 to 30 on a piece of paper.

• Players take turns. Player A marks an **X** on a *multiple*. Player B marks an **O** on each of the *factors* of Player A's multiple.

• Then Player B marks an **O** on a new multiple. Player A marks **X**s on all of the unmarked factors of Player B's multiple. (Never mark numbers already marked.)

• You may only mark a multiple that still has some factors left for the other player to mark.

• When no more moves are left on the mat, count your points (numbers you marked).

• The player with the greatest number of points is the winner.

2. Discuss with your team.

a. 9 has 3 factors: 1, 9, and 3. Find other numbers with exactly 3 factors.

b. What is the largest factor the other player can get when you mark 30? 29? 28?

c. Which first moves give the other player exactly 1 point?

d. What are the best moves? What are the worst moves?

Multiples and Factors

① ② ③ ④ 5

⑥ 7 8 9 10

11 1̷2̷ 13 14 15

16 17 18 19 20

21 22 23 24 25

26 27 28 29 30

TIPS FOR
WORKING TOGETHER

Tell someone when they do or say something that helps you.

Explore with a Computer

Use the *Fractions Workshop Project* for this activity.

Maria is planning a dinner. A recipe calls for $4\frac{3}{8}$ cups of rice. Maria has $1\frac{1}{2}$ cups of rice. Find how much more rice she needs to buy.

1. At the computer, use the **Mark** option to divide the circles to have equal parts.

2. Use the **Shade** option to fill $4\frac{3}{8}$.

3. Using the **Erase** option, take away $1\frac{1}{2}$ of the shaded parts. How much is left?

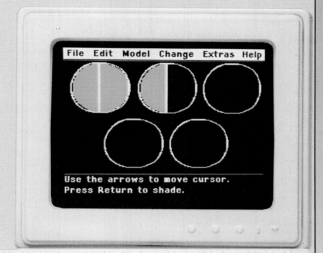

File Edit Model Change Extras Help

Use the arrows to move cursor.
Press Return to shade.

Number-Sense Project

Look back at pages 340-341.
A student collected these estimates.

Line	Estimates in inches				Actual length
	Adult 1	Adult 2	Classmate 1	Classmate 2	
1	3	$3\frac{3}{4}$	4	$3\frac{1}{4}$	$3\frac{1}{4}$
2	6	6	6	6	$6\frac{1}{4}$
3	7	$6\frac{1}{2}$	$6\frac{1}{2}$	7	$7\frac{1}{2}$
4	1	$1\frac{1}{4}$	1	$1\frac{3}{4}$	$1\frac{1}{4}$
5	$5\frac{1}{4}$	6	$5\frac{3}{4}$	$5\frac{3}{4}$	$5\frac{3}{4}$

a. How far off was Adult 1 in estimating Line 3?

b. Find the total amount Classmate 1 was off in estimating all 5 lines.

c. Who was the most accurate in their estimates?

d. Write a statement comparing the accuracy of the two adults to the accuracy of the two classmates.

Adding and Subtracting Fractions: Related Denominators

Build Understanding

A. Mr. Nochim is building a fence. He wants to bolt two boards together. One board is $\frac{3}{4}$ inch thick and the other is $\frac{1}{2}$ inch thick. To decide on a length of bolt to use he must find the total thickness of the two boards.

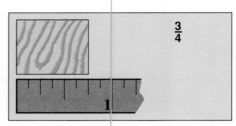

You can see from the rulers that

$$
\begin{array}{rl}
\textbf{3 fourths} & = \textbf{3 fourths} \\
+\ \textbf{1 half} & = \textbf{2 fourths} \\
\hline
& \textbf{5 fourths} = 1\tfrac{1}{4}
\end{array}
$$

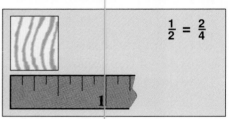

Mr. Nochim needs a bolt longer than $1\frac{1}{4}$ inches.

When you add or subtract fractions, think of the denominators as units. To name the sum or difference, you must use the same size units.

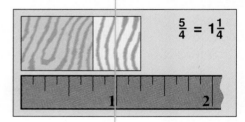

B. Find $\frac{1}{4} + \frac{7}{12}$.

$\dfrac{1}{4}$ The denominators are different. Find a common denominator.

$+\dfrac{7}{12}$ Remember that sometimes one of the denominators is the least common denominator.

$\dfrac{1}{4} = \dfrac{3}{12}$

$+\dfrac{7}{12} = \dfrac{7}{12}$

$\rule{1.5cm}{0.4pt}$

$\dfrac{10}{12} = \dfrac{5}{6}$

12 is the least common denominator. Write equal fractions with the least common denominator. Add the fractions.

Write the answer in simplest form.

$$\overset{\times\,3}{\underset{\times\,3}{\frac{1}{4} \quad \frac{3}{12}}}$$

C. Find $\frac{2}{3} - \frac{1}{6}$.

$\dfrac{2}{3} = \dfrac{4}{6}$

$-\dfrac{1}{6} = \dfrac{1}{6}$

$\rule{1.5cm}{0.4pt}$

$\dfrac{3}{6} = \dfrac{1}{2}$

■ **Talk About Math** In Example A, why is 4 better than 8 or 16 for a common denominator? Could you use 2 as a common denominator?

356

Check Understanding

Copy and complete to find equal fractions.

1. $\frac{1}{6} = \frac{\blacksquare}{12}$ **2.** $\frac{1}{4} = \frac{\blacksquare}{16}$ **3.** $\frac{2}{3} = \frac{\blacksquare}{9}$ **4.** $\frac{3}{5} = \frac{\blacksquare}{15}$ **5.** $\frac{4}{7} = \frac{\blacksquare}{14}$

Copy and complete each exercise.

6. $\frac{1}{4} = \frac{\blacksquare}{8}$
$+\frac{3}{8} = \frac{\blacksquare}{8}$
_____

7. $\frac{5}{6} = \frac{\blacksquare}{6}$
$-\frac{2}{3} = \frac{\blacksquare}{6}$
_____

8. $\frac{1}{3} = \frac{\blacksquare}{\blacksquare}$
$+\frac{8}{9} = \frac{8}{\blacksquare}$
_____

9. $\frac{7}{16} = \frac{\blacksquare}{\blacksquare}$
$-\frac{1}{8} = \frac{\blacksquare}{\blacksquare}$
_____

Practice

Add or subtract by finding a common denominator.
Remember to write your answers in simplest form.

10. $\frac{1}{8} + \frac{3}{4}$ **11.** $\frac{5}{8} - \frac{1}{2}$ **12.** $\frac{1}{6} + \frac{1}{2}$ **13.** $\frac{1}{4} + \frac{5}{8}$ **14.** $\frac{2}{5} - \frac{1}{10}$ **15.** $\frac{2}{9} + \frac{1}{3}$

16. $\frac{1}{5}$
$+\frac{7}{10}$
_____

17. $\frac{1}{6}$
$+\frac{7}{12}$
_____

18. $\frac{1}{4}$
$-\frac{1}{8}$
_____

19. $\frac{4}{5}$
$-\frac{3}{10}$
_____

20. $\frac{1}{2}$
$+\frac{3}{8}$
_____

21. $\frac{5}{6}$
$-\frac{2}{3}$
_____

22. $\frac{3}{4} + \frac{11}{12}$ **23.** $\frac{3}{5} - \frac{4}{15}$ **24.** $\frac{5}{8} + \frac{3}{4}$ **25.** $\frac{7}{15} + \frac{1}{5}$ **26.** $\frac{5}{6} - \frac{1}{12}$ **27.** $\frac{4}{5} - \frac{2}{15}$

Mixed Practice Add or subtract. **Remember** to write your answers in simplest form.

28. $2\frac{1}{5} + 3\frac{2}{5}$ **29.** $1\frac{5}{8} + 2\frac{3}{8}$ **30.** $3\frac{5}{6} - 2\frac{1}{6}$ **31.** $5\frac{3}{4} - 1\frac{1}{4}$

32. $4 - 1\frac{2}{3}$ **33.** $8 - 3\frac{1}{5}$ **34.** $1\frac{3}{4} + 2\frac{1}{2} + 2\frac{1}{4}$ **35.** $3\frac{3}{5} + 2\frac{9}{10} + 1\frac{4}{5}$

Problem Solving

Solve each problem.

36. Mr. Nochim attached the gate to the fence in $\frac{3}{4}$ hour. He took $\frac{2}{12}$ hour to put the handle on the gate. How much time in all did he work on the gate?

37. Jackie is nailing two boards together. Both boards are $\frac{1}{4}$ inch thick. Will a nail $\frac{3}{8}$ of an inch long go through both boards?

Use Alternate Strategies

Build Understanding

Mr. Alfano plans to put a chef's work table in the middle of his restaurant kitchen. The kitchen is $12\frac{1}{2}$ feet wide and 18 feet long. The table is 6 feet long and $3\frac{1}{2}$ feet wide. He plans 3 feet of walking space on each side of the table. How much space will be left for cabinets along each end of the room?

Understand Find how much space will not be used for the table or for walking. The kitchen is $12\frac{1}{2}$ feet by 18 feet. The table is 6 feet by $3\frac{1}{2}$ feet. Allow 3 feet on each side of the table.

Plan and Solve Make a drawing on grid paper. Let the side of each square represent one foot. Draw the table and show the walking space. Count the squares to find the space left.

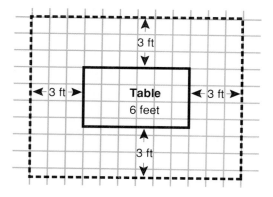

By counting squares, you can see that 12 feet of the 18-foot length are used. Since 6 feet are left, this leaves 3 feet along each end of the room for cabinets.

 **Look Back** ALTERNATE APPROACH You can find the amount of space along each end by first subtracting the used space from the length.

Room	18
Table	− 6
	12
Walking space (2 × 3)	− 6
	6

Then divide by 2 to allow equal space at each end. 6 ÷ 2 = 3

PROBLEM SOLVING GUIDE

Understand
QUESTION
FACTS
KEY IDEA

Plan and Solve
STRATEGY
ANSWER

Look Back
SENSIBLE ANSWER
ALTERNATE APPROACH

■ **Talk About Math** Could you choose a different operation to solve this problem? Explain.

Check Understanding

Use information in the Example to answer these questions.

1. How much space will be left for cabinets along the other two sides of the room?

2. In the Look Back step, why must you subtract twice the measure of the walking space?

Practice

3. Mr. Alfano wants to install a window in the front wall. The wall is 12 feet tall and 30 feet wide. The window will be 5 feet by 20 feet. If the window is centered in the wall, how much wall space will be left on each side?

4. Mr. Alfano's kitchen is 9 feet high. He plans to install floor cabinets with countertops that are $3\frac{3}{4}$ feet high and wall cabinets that are $2\frac{1}{4}$ feet high. How much wall space will be left above the countertops?

5. In the back of Mr. Alfano's restaurant is a patio that is 26 feet by $22\frac{1}{2}$ feet. He wants to plant a rectangular garden in the center. If he wants to leave $8\frac{1}{2}$ feet on each side for seating, how big can the garden be?

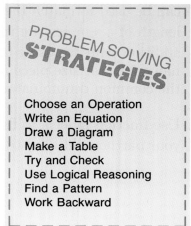

Choose a _____ Strategy

A Fraction of the Value Mr. Gary Johnson's fifth-grade class gave a fraction value to each letter of the alphabet. Students found the value of their first names by adding the letter values together.

$A = \frac{1}{24}$, $B = \frac{2}{24}$, $C = \frac{3}{24}$, $D = \frac{4}{24}$, and so on.

6. What is the value of the teacher's first name?

7. Which day of the week has a whole-number value?

PROBLEM SOLVING
STRATEGIES

Choose an Operation
Write an Equation
Draw a Diagram
Make a Table
Try and Check
Use Logical Reasoning
Find a Pattern
Work Backward

Adding Fractions: Different Denominators

Build Understanding

You know how to find the sum of fractions with the same denominator. How do you think you can find the sum of fractions with different denominators?

A. Fraction Match
Materials: Fraction models
Groups: With a partner

a. Find $\frac{1}{2} + \frac{1}{3}$ using fraction models.

b. Place the piece that shows one whole on your desk as a reference. Below it, place the pieces that show $\frac{1}{2} + \frac{1}{3}$ end to end.

c. To find the fraction that names the sum, place fraction pieces below them. Try halves. Is the sum equal to a number of halves?

d. Try thirds. Is the sum equal to a number of thirds? Continue using different size pieces for other fractions until you find a size that matches the length of $\frac{1}{2} + \frac{1}{3}$.

e. After you find a piece that can be used to match the length of $\frac{1}{2} + \frac{1}{3}$, rewrite the addition sentence using the name for that size piece as the common denominator.

$$\frac{1}{2} = \frac{}{}$$
$$+\frac{1}{3} = \frac{}{}$$

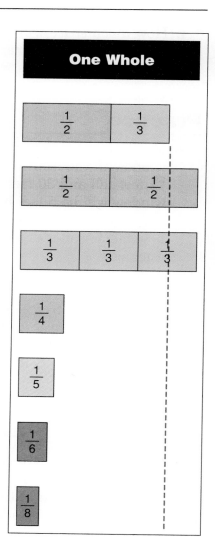

f. Use fraction models to find $\frac{2}{3} + \frac{3}{4}$. You and your partner will need to use both sets of pieces.

When you add fractions, think of the denominators as units, as the sizes of the pieces of your fraction models. To name a sum, you must use the same size units. So, before adding fractions, find equal fractions with a common denominator.

B. Find $\frac{1}{6} + \frac{3}{10}$.

The denominators are different. Find a common denominator.

$$\frac{1}{6}$$
$$+\frac{3}{10}$$

Think:
Multiples of 6: 6, 12, 18, 24, 30 , 36, . . .
Multiples of 10: 10, 20, 30 , . . .

Write equal fractions. Add the fractions.

$$\frac{1}{6} = \frac{5}{30}$$
$$+\frac{3}{10} = \frac{9}{30}$$
$$\frac{14}{30} = \frac{7}{15}$$

C. Find $\frac{3}{8} + \frac{1}{6} + \frac{1}{4}$.

The denominators are different. Find a common denominator.

$$\frac{3}{8}$$
$$\frac{1}{6}$$
$$+\frac{1}{4}$$

Think:
Multiples of 8: 8, 16, 24, 32, . . .
8 is a multiple of 4 but not a multiple of 6.
16 is a multiple of 4 but not a multiple of 6.
24 is a multiple of 4 and 6.

Write equal fractions. Add the fractions.

$$\frac{3}{8} = \frac{9}{24}$$
$$\frac{1}{6} = \frac{4}{24}$$
$$+\frac{1}{4} = \frac{6}{24}$$
$$\frac{19}{24}$$

D. Mental Math When adding three or more fractions, look for sums of 1 to help you add mentally.

Find $\frac{2}{3} + \frac{1}{8} + \frac{1}{3}$.

$$\frac{2}{3} + \frac{1}{8} + \frac{1}{3} \qquad \frac{2}{3} + \frac{1}{3} = \frac{3}{3} = 1$$

$$1 + \frac{1}{8} = 1\frac{1}{8}$$

■ **Talk About Math** Can you use a common denominator greater than the least common denominator? Explain why or why not.

Check Understanding

For another example, see Set G, pages 374–375.

1. If you were adding $\frac{1}{3}$ and $\frac{1}{4}$, name two of the common denominators that could be used.

2. What is the least common denominator of $\frac{1}{3}$ and $\frac{1}{4}$?

Copy and complete each exercise.

3. $\frac{1}{6} = \frac{}{12}$

$+\frac{1}{4} = \frac{}{12}$

4. $\frac{3}{8} = \frac{}{}$

$+\frac{5}{12} = \frac{}{24}$

5. $\frac{7}{10} = \frac{}{}$

$+\frac{1}{4} = \frac{}{}$

6. $\frac{5}{9} = \frac{}{}$

$+\frac{5}{6} = \frac{}{}$

Practice

For More Practice, see Set G, pages 376–377.

Find each sum. **Remember** to write your answer in simplest form.

7. $\frac{4}{9}$
$+\frac{5}{6}$

8. $\frac{5}{8}$
$+\frac{7}{12}$

9. $\frac{11}{15}$
$+\frac{7}{10}$

10. $\frac{9}{10}$
$+\frac{1}{6}$

11. $\frac{5}{12}$
$+\frac{7}{8}$

12. $\frac{4}{9}$
$+\frac{7}{15}$

13. $\frac{3}{8} + \frac{1}{6}$

14. $\frac{5}{12} + \frac{2}{3}$

15. $\frac{1}{3} + \frac{5}{6}$

16. $\frac{3}{4} + \frac{1}{5}$

17. $\frac{1}{2} + \frac{9}{11}$

18. $\frac{3}{5} + \frac{3}{4}$

19. $\frac{4}{5} + \frac{1}{2}$

20. $\frac{5}{6} + \frac{4}{7}$

21. $\frac{1}{6}$
$\frac{3}{4}$
$+\frac{1}{2}$

22. $\frac{3}{8}$
$\frac{5}{6}$
$+\frac{1}{3}$

23. $\frac{5}{9}$
$\frac{1}{6}$
$+\frac{2}{3}$

24. $\frac{3}{4}$
$\frac{5}{6}$
$+\frac{2}{3}$

25. $\frac{5}{12}$
$\frac{2}{3}$
$+\frac{1}{8}$

26. $\frac{1}{6}$
$\frac{3}{8}$
$+\frac{7}{12}$

Mental Math   Use mental math to find each sum.

27. $\frac{1}{4} + \frac{3}{5} + \frac{3}{4}$

28. $\frac{2}{5} + \frac{1}{2} + \frac{3}{5}$

29. $\frac{5}{8} + \frac{3}{8} + \frac{4}{5}$

30. $\frac{4}{7} + \frac{1}{6} + \frac{5}{6}$

31. $\frac{1}{8} + \frac{2}{3} + \frac{7}{8}$

32. $\frac{3}{4} + \frac{2}{7} + \frac{5}{7}$

33. $\frac{4}{5} + \frac{1}{3} + \frac{1}{5}$

34. $\frac{7}{9} + \frac{2}{9} + \frac{4}{5}$

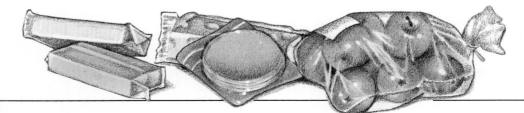

Problem Solving

Use the information on Mrs. Briggman's shopping list at the right.

35. How many pounds of cheese did Mrs. Briggman buy?

36. How many pounds of meat did Mrs. Briggman buy?

37. Did she buy more cheese or more meat?

Critical Thinking Use the digits in the box below to solve these problems. Use each digit only once in a solution.

Shopping List

$\frac{2}{3}$ pound – Colby cheese

$\frac{3}{4}$ pound – bologna

$\frac{1}{2}$ pound – turkey

$\frac{1}{3}$ pound – corned beef

$\frac{7}{8}$ pound – American cheese

$\frac{1}{4}$ pound – Swiss cheese

3 pounds – apples

1	2	3	4	6	8

38. Write two fractions that have a sum of 1.

39. Write two fractions that have a sum less than 1.

40. Write two fractions that have a sum between 1 and 2.

Explore ———— Math

An ancient Egyptian papyrus shows only unit fractions. A *unit fraction* has 1 as the numerator. Some examples of unit fractions are:

$\frac{1}{2}, \frac{1}{3}, \frac{1}{4}, \frac{1}{5}, \frac{1}{8}, \frac{1}{12}$

The Egyptians wrote other fractions as the sum of unit fractions. For example:

$\frac{3}{4} = \frac{1}{4} + \frac{2}{4}$

Reduce $\frac{2}{4}$ to lowest terms.

$\frac{3}{4} = \frac{1}{4} + \frac{1}{2}$

Write each fraction as the sum of two unit fractions.

41. $\frac{2}{7}$ **42.** $\frac{3}{10}$ **43.** $\frac{5}{12}$ **44.** $\frac{8}{15}$ **45.** $\frac{5}{8}$

Subtracting Fractions: Different Denominators

Build Understanding

Brett and Donna were making oatmeal cookies for their school fun fair. Their recipe calls for $\frac{3}{4}$ cup of oatmeal and $\frac{2}{3}$ cup of flour. How much more oatmeal than flour is called for in this recipe?

You want to compare the amount of flour with the amount of oatmeal. You can subtract. Find $\frac{3}{4} - \frac{2}{3}$.

If you try to use fraction models for this subtraction, you see that a common denominator is needed to tell how much larger $\frac{3}{4}$ is than $\frac{2}{3}$.

The denominators are different. Find a common denominator.

$$\frac{3}{4}$$
$$-\frac{2}{3}$$

Think:
Multiples of 4: 4, 8, $\boxed{12}$, 16, . . .
Multiples of 3: 3, 6, 9, $\boxed{12}$, . . .

Write equal fractions. Subtract the fractions.

$$\frac{3}{4} = \frac{9}{12}$$
$$-\frac{2}{3} = \frac{8}{12}$$
$$\frac{1}{12}$$

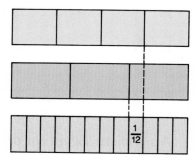

The recipe calls for $\frac{1}{12}$ cup more oatmeal than flour.

■ **Talk About Math** What can you do to always find a common denominator for two fractions with different denominators?

Check Understanding

For another example, see Set H, pages 374–375.

Copy and complete each exercise.

1. $\frac{5}{6} = \frac{}{12}$
   $-\frac{1}{4} = \frac{}{12}$

2. $\frac{4}{5} = \frac{}{}$
   $-\frac{1}{2} = \frac{}{10}$

3. $\frac{3}{4} = \frac{}{}$
   $-\frac{3}{8} = \frac{}{}$

4. $\frac{5}{8} = \frac{}{}$
   $-\frac{1}{6} = \frac{}{}$

364

Practice

For More Practice, see Set H, pages 376–377.

Find each difference. **Remember** to write your answer in simplest form.

5. $\dfrac{3}{4}$
$-\dfrac{1}{10}$

6. $\dfrac{5}{8}$
$-\dfrac{1}{12}$

7. $\dfrac{17}{20}$
$-\dfrac{3}{8}$

8. $\dfrac{9}{10}$
$-\dfrac{5}{6}$

9. $\dfrac{4}{15}$
$-\dfrac{1}{10}$

10. $\dfrac{1}{2}$
$-\dfrac{1}{9}$

11. $\dfrac{4}{5} - \dfrac{2}{3}$

12. $\dfrac{3}{4} - \dfrac{1}{3}$

13. $\dfrac{2}{5} - \dfrac{1}{6}$

14. $\dfrac{7}{8} - \dfrac{2}{5}$

15. $\dfrac{3}{4} - \dfrac{1}{5}$

16. $\dfrac{7}{9} - \dfrac{7}{12}$

17. $\dfrac{3}{4} - \dfrac{3}{20}$

18. $\dfrac{5}{9} - \dfrac{1}{4}$

Problem Solving

Solve each problem.

19. A fruit salad recipe calls for $\dfrac{5}{8}$ cup of raisins. Brett has only $\dfrac{1}{6}$ cup of raisins. How many more cups of raisins does he need?

20. The recipe calls for $\dfrac{7}{8}$ cup of chopped watermelon and $\dfrac{2}{3}$ cup of chopped honeydew melon. How many cups of melon is this?

Skills ———— Review pages 312–329

Write each fraction in lowest terms.

1. $\dfrac{9}{12}$ **2.** $\dfrac{15}{30}$ **3.** $\dfrac{6}{18}$ **4.** $\dfrac{3}{9}$ **5.** $\dfrac{18}{30}$ **6.** $\dfrac{36}{84}$

For Exercises 7–10, tell whether you would use pencil and paper, mental math, or a calculator. Then change each fraction to a decimal.

7. $\dfrac{3}{4}$ **8.** $\dfrac{13}{20}$ **9.** $\dfrac{48}{25}$ **10.** $\dfrac{188}{50}$

Write each improper fraction as a whole number or mixed number.

11. $\dfrac{24}{10}$ **12.** $\dfrac{46}{7}$ **13.** $\dfrac{58}{9}$ **14.** $\dfrac{65}{13}$ **15.** $\dfrac{146}{8}$ **16.** $\dfrac{180}{11}$

Adding Mixed Numbers: Different Denominators

Build Understanding

A. Mr. Bosnak is a butcher at the Harvest Faire supermarket. A customer ordered meat for chop suey. To fill the order, Mr. Bosnak chopped $3\frac{5}{8}$ pounds of beef and $2\frac{3}{4}$ pounds of pork. What is the total weight of the meat?

Since you need to find a total, use addition.

Estimate: Both $\frac{5}{8}$ and $\frac{3}{4}$ are greater than $\frac{1}{2}$. $4 + 3 = 7$

The denominators are different. Find a common denominator.

Write equal fractions. Add the mixed numbers.

$$3\frac{5}{8}$$
$$+2\frac{3}{4}$$

$$3\frac{5}{8} = 3\frac{5}{8}$$
$$+2\frac{3}{4} = 2\frac{6}{8}$$

Write the answer in simplest form.

$$5\frac{11}{8} = 5 + 1\frac{3}{8} = 6\frac{3}{8}$$

Mr. Bosnak chopped $6\frac{3}{8}$ pounds of meat to fill the order.

B. Mental Math When adding mixed numbers, look for fractions whose sum will equal 1 to help you add mentally.

Find $4\frac{1}{4} + 2\frac{2}{3} + 1\frac{3}{4}$.

$$4\frac{1}{4} + 2\frac{2}{3} + 1\frac{3}{4} \qquad \frac{1}{4} + \frac{3}{4} = \frac{4}{4} = 1$$

$$1 + 4 + 2\frac{2}{3} + 1 = 8\frac{2}{3}$$

■ **Talk About Math** Explain how you could find a range to estimate the total weight in Example A.

Check Understanding

For another example, see Set I, pages 374–375.

Find each sum.

1. $3\frac{5}{8}$
   $+2\frac{1}{6}$

2. $4\frac{5}{6}$
   $+1\frac{1}{9}$

3. $6\frac{7}{10}$
   $+3\frac{3}{4}$

4. $5\frac{5}{6}$
   $+5\frac{9}{10}$

5. $3\frac{8}{9}$
   $+12\frac{5}{6}$

Practice

For More Practice, see Set I, pages 376–377.

Add. **Remember** to write your answers in simplest form.

6. $12\frac{1}{2}$
   $+\ 3\frac{2}{3}$

7. $13\frac{5}{8}$
   $+12\frac{7}{12}$

8. $6\frac{9}{10}$
   $+3\frac{5}{8}$

9. $4\frac{3}{4}$
   $+2\frac{2}{3}$

10. $42\frac{3}{10}$
    $+15\frac{1}{3}$

11. $13\frac{1}{4}$
    $2\frac{5}{6}$
    $+\ 1\frac{2}{3}$

12. $2\frac{3}{8}$
    $5\frac{1}{2}$
    $+14\frac{1}{6}$

13. $12\frac{7}{12}$
    $3\frac{3}{4}$
    $+\ 2\frac{5}{8}$

14. $4\frac{7}{15}$
    $10\frac{4}{9}$
    $+\ 2\frac{1}{5}$

15. $17\frac{13}{18}$
    $15\frac{5}{12}$
    $+\ 3\frac{4}{9}$

16. $10\frac{3}{4} + 13\frac{2}{5}$

17. $4\frac{7}{9} + 20\frac{7}{18}$

18. $19\frac{3}{4} + 5\frac{5}{6}$

19. $35\frac{1}{4} + 12\frac{7}{12}$

Mental Math   Find each sum mentally.

20. $3\frac{1}{3} + 1\frac{4}{5} + 2\frac{2}{3}$

21. $4\frac{5}{8} + 1\frac{1}{2} + 2\frac{3}{8}$

22. $2\frac{3}{7} + 1\frac{4}{7} + 4\frac{3}{4}$

23. $13\frac{11}{12} + 4\frac{1}{12} + 1\frac{2}{3}$

24. $2\frac{3}{4} + 12\frac{5}{6} + 1\frac{1}{4}$

25. $13\frac{5}{8} + 2\frac{4}{5} + 1\frac{6}{5}$

Problem Solving

Read for the facts to solve each problem.

26. A shipment of fruit included two crates of apples, each weighing $45\frac{5}{8}$ pounds, and a crate of pears weighing $17\frac{7}{10}$ pounds. How many pounds did the three crates weigh?

27. A customer ordered 8 pounds of chicken. Mr. Bosnak filled the order with three chickens. One chicken weighed $2\frac{3}{4}$ pounds and another weighed $3\frac{1}{2}$ pounds. How much did the third chicken weigh?

Subtracting Mixed Numbers: Different Denominators

Build Understanding

How much longer was the triple jump that won the gold medal in 1980 than the triple jump that won in 1984?

Use subtraction to compare the distances. Since the number of feet are the same, find $11\frac{1}{8} - 7\frac{1}{2}$.

Estimate: Use the whole number parts.
$11 - 7 = 4$

Olympic Gold Medals Triple Jump			
1976	Viktor Saneyev USSR	56 ft	$8\frac{3}{4}$ in.
1980	Jaak Uudmare USSR	56 ft	$11\frac{1}{8}$ in.
1984	Al Joyner USA	56 ft	$7\frac{1}{2}$ in.
1988	Histo Markov Bulgaria	57 ft	$9\frac{1}{4}$ in.

A first-place Olympic medal is made of silver with a gold coating.

Find a common denominator.	Write equal fractions. Try to subtract.	Rename, if necessary. Subtract.
$11\frac{1}{8}$	$11\frac{1}{8} = 11\frac{1}{8} =$	$10\frac{9}{8}$
$- 7\frac{1}{2}$	$- 7\frac{1}{2} = 7\frac{4}{8} =$	$7\frac{4}{8}$
		$3\frac{5}{8}$

The triple jump that won in the 1980 Olympics was $3\frac{5}{8}$ inches longer.

■ **Talk About Math**   What other numbers could have been used as a common denominator?

Check Understanding

For another example, see Set J, pages 374–375.

Find each difference.

1. $7\frac{1}{4}$
   $-4\frac{1}{6}$

2. $5\frac{1}{4}$
   $-1\frac{1}{3}$

3. $4\frac{5}{8}$
   $-3\frac{1}{6}$

4. $9\frac{8}{9}$
   $-2\frac{5}{6}$

5. $12\frac{1}{4} - 3\frac{3}{10}$

Number Sense   Answer each question.

6. Can a common denominator of a pair of fractions ever be smaller than either of the denominators?

7. Do the subtraction in the Example two more times, each time with a different common denominator. Do you get the same answer? Why or why not?

Practice

For More Practice, see Set J, pages 376–377.

Subtract. **Remember** to write your answers in simplest form.

8. $11\frac{7}{8}$
$-\ 4\frac{5}{6}$

9. $17\frac{8}{9}$
$-\ 9\frac{1}{2}$

10. $24\frac{7}{12}$
$-19\frac{7}{8}$

11. $34\frac{5}{6}$
$-17\frac{5}{8}$

12. $40\frac{1}{3}$
$-13\frac{7}{10}$

13. $26\frac{3}{8}$
$-\ 8\frac{7}{12}$

14. $14\frac{8}{9}$
$-\ 1\frac{3}{4}$

15. $32\frac{1}{3}$
$-23\frac{5}{8}$

16. $56\frac{5}{12}$
$-\ 8\frac{2}{9}$

17. $33\frac{4}{5}$
$-\ 6\frac{5}{6}$

18. $6\frac{3}{10} - 2\frac{1}{4}$

19. $7\frac{2}{5} - 3\frac{1}{2}$

20. $5\frac{7}{10} - 5\frac{5}{16}$

21. $12\frac{1}{9} - 11\frac{2}{7}$

Problem Solving

22. The world record for the pole vault was set by the Russian Sergey Bubka in 1988 at 19 feet $10\frac{1}{2}$ inches. The American record was set in 1987 by Joe Dial at 19 feet $10\frac{1}{4}$ inches. How much higher is the world record?

23. American Jackie Joyner-Kersee won the 1988 gold medal for the long jump with a jump of 24 feet $3\frac{1}{2}$ inches. She set an American record in 1987 at 24 feet $5\frac{1}{4}$ inches. How much longer was her record jump?

Reading ———— Math

Numbers and Symbols Match each term in the left column with its example. Use each letter only once.

1. Common denominator
2. Fraction
3. Simplest form
4. Least common denominator
5. Mixed number
6. Rename

a. $3\frac{1}{2}$

b. $\frac{1}{2} + \frac{1}{3} = \frac{3}{6} + \frac{2}{6}$

c. $\frac{1}{2} + \frac{1}{3} = \frac{6}{12} + \frac{4}{12}$

d. $\frac{11}{8} = 1\frac{3}{8}$

e. $5\frac{2}{3} = 4\frac{5}{3}$

f. $\frac{4}{7}$

Solve a Simpler Problem

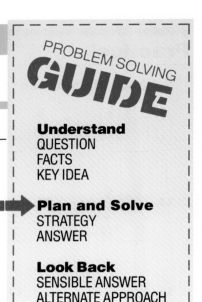

PROBLEM SOLVING

GUIDE

Understand
QUESTION
FACTS
KEY IDEA

▶ **Plan and Solve**
STRATEGY
ANSWER

Look Back
SENSIBLE ANSWER
ALTERNATE APPROACH

Build Understanding

The Cloth Company sells material and other sewing needs. As material is cut from a bolt, the clerk marks how much material is left. Mrs. Trygar bought material to make 2 skirts for each of her daughters. She needed $1\frac{7}{8}$ yards for one size skirt and $2\frac{1}{4}$ yards for the other. The material was cut from a bolt with $31\frac{1}{3}$ yards. How much material was left on the bolt?

Understand   How many yards of material are left? The bolt had $31\frac{1}{3}$ yards. The clerk cut 2 pieces $1\frac{7}{8}$ yards long and 2 pieces $2\frac{1}{4}$ yards long.

**Plan and Solve**   STRATEGY   Sometimes the numbers make a problem look difficult. Replace them with simpler numbers to help you decide how to solve the problem. Then use the actual numbers.

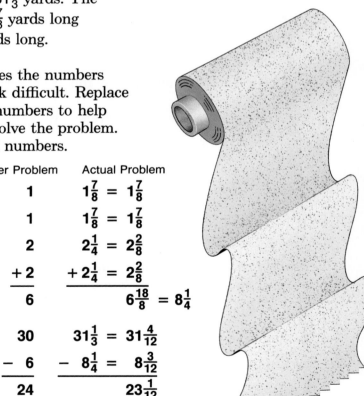

	Simpler Problem	Actual Problem
Find the total amount cut from the bolt.	1	$1\frac{7}{8} = 1\frac{7}{8}$
	1	$1\frac{7}{8} = 1\frac{7}{8}$
	2	$2\frac{1}{4} = 2\frac{2}{8}$
	$+2$	$+2\frac{1}{4} = 2\frac{2}{8}$
	6	$6\frac{18}{8} = 8\frac{1}{4}$
Find the amount left on the bolt.	30	$31\frac{1}{3} = 31\frac{4}{12}$
	-6	$-8\frac{1}{4} = 8\frac{3}{12}$
	24	$23\frac{1}{12}$

ANSWER   The bolt has $23\frac{1}{12}$ yards of material left.

Look Back   Be sure you subtracted the lengths of all the pieces of material that were cut from the bolt. Check your computation.

■ **Talk About Math** Explain how you could solve the problem using another method.

Check Understanding

1. What numbers would you use to make the problem simpler?

2. Solve the problem.

> The first three sales from a new $45\frac{1}{2}$-yard bolt were $2\frac{5}{8}$ yards, $5\frac{2}{3}$ yards, and $4\frac{1}{4}$ yards. How many yards were left on the bolt?

Practice

3. A pattern for the front of a penguin puppet is a square measuring $4\frac{1}{2}$ inches on each side. Judy has a piece of white material that is 15 inches wide and 20 inches long. How many patterns can she cut out?

4. **Use Data** Use the information in the table on page 368. In 1985, Willie Banks set a world record with a triple jump of 58 feet $11\frac{1}{2}$ inches. How much longer was this jump than the gold medal jump in 1976?

5. **Calculator** Linda worked $7\frac{3}{4}$ hours each of 6 days last week at The Cloth Company. If she is paid $7.20 per hour, how much did she earn last week?

6. Jane wants to sew a ruffle around the 4 sides of a bedspread that is $2\frac{1}{3}$ yards long and $1\frac{5}{6}$ yards wide. To make the ruffle, she needs twice the length and twice the width. How much material does she need?

─────── **Choose a ⎯⎯⎯ Strategy** ───────

Follow the Leader
7. On a long hike, Joseph, Rhonda, Bob, and Steve took turns leading. Joseph led for $4\frac{1}{2}$ miles. This was $1\frac{1}{2}$ miles less than Rhonda led. Rhonda led twice as far as Bob. Steve led 2 miles less than Bob. How long was the hike?

Solve each problem.

1. Jake had 15 minutes to finish a test. He spent 7 minutes on the true-false questions and 5 minutes on the essay question. What fraction of the time was left to check his work?

2. Brenda worked $2\frac{1}{2}$ hours on a book report and then played a computer game for $1\frac{5}{6}$ hours. How much longer did she spend on her book report than on the computer game?

3. Leroy is $55\frac{1}{2}$ inches tall. LuAnne is $1\frac{3}{4}$ inches taller than Linda. Linda is $3\frac{1}{8}$ inches shorter than Leroy. How tall are Linda and LuAnne?

4. Ms. McRae wants to fence in an area $24\frac{1}{2}$ feet wide and $29\frac{1}{4}$ feet long for her chickens. How much wire does she need for the fence?

5. A zookeeper asked a group of people if they took the elephant ride or the camel ride. The circle graph shows the results.

a. What fraction of the people surveyed took only the elephant ride?

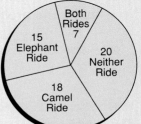

Both Rides 7

15 Elephant Ride

20 Neither Ride

18 Camel Ride

b. What fraction of the people surveyed took the elephant ride?

6. **Data File** Using the chart of heights on page 380–381, find the difference in height between Manute Bol and the top of a telephone booth.

7. **Make a Data File** Organize data about types of programs on TV during the evening hours for 1 week. Include the number of hours used for news, information, comedy, and drama. Show the data in a chart.

Problem Solving REVIEW

Explore with a Calculator

"Did you get the point?"

1. Karen and Nancy each chose a game card to play *Five-in-A-Row*. The first player to cover 5 squares in a row, in a column, or in a diagonal wins the game.

Five-In-A-Row *Karen*

3.125	9.4375	7.75	2.3125	5.8
4.6	10.75	8.1	7.8	6.5
9.375	3.8	10.75	6.2	7.425
3.4	4.875	3.125	9.375	13.8
4.75	1.2	6.325	3.5	8.1

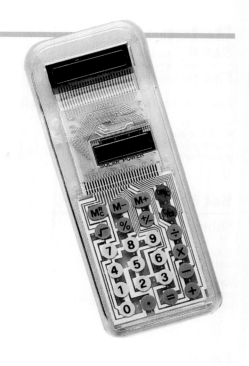

Five-In-A-Row *Nancy*

13.8	8.475	7.6	14.8	2.75
4.5	17.1875	21.4	7.25	8.375
1.25	3.5	5.8	10.75	4.3
7.425	12.6	19.8	1.25	2.25
1.2	8.9	7.5	3.125	3.4

2. Change each improper fraction or mixed number to a decimal. Use your calculator.

a. $\frac{5}{4}$ **b.** $1\frac{1}{5}$ **c.** $2\frac{3}{4}$

d. $\frac{7}{2}$ **e.** $\frac{17}{5}$ **f.** $\frac{11}{8}$ **g.** $6\frac{1}{2}$

h. $\frac{19}{5}$ **i.** $3\frac{1}{8}$ **j.** $7\frac{3}{4}$ **k.** $5\frac{4}{5}$ **l.** $\frac{9}{6}$

m. $\frac{39}{8}$ **n.** $\frac{43}{4}$ **o.** $\frac{39}{5}$ **p.** $7\frac{7}{16}$ **q.** $9\frac{3}{8}$

r. $13\frac{4}{5}$ **s.** $\frac{59}{8}$ **t.** $17\frac{3}{16}$

3. Cover the numbers of each exercise on both cards. Which girl won the game?

Reteaching

Set A   pages 342–343

Find the sum of $\frac{3}{8}$ and $\frac{7}{8}$.

Add the numerators.

$$\frac{3}{8}$$

Write the sum over the common denominator.

$$+\frac{7}{8}$$
$$\frac{10}{8} = 1\frac{2}{8} = 1\frac{1}{4}$$

Remember to change improper fractions to mixed numbers and write fractions in lowest terms. Add the fractions.

1. $\frac{5}{6}$ **2.** $\frac{3}{5}$ **3.** $\frac{1}{4}$
  $+\frac{3}{6}$ $+\frac{1}{5}$ $+\frac{2}{4}$

Set B   pages 344–345

Subtract: $\frac{5}{8} - \frac{1}{8}$.

Subtract the numerators.

$$\frac{5}{8}$$

Write the difference over the common denominator.

$$-\frac{1}{8}$$
$$\frac{4}{8} = \frac{1}{2}$$

Remember to simplify the answers if necessary. Subtract the fractions.

1. $\frac{4}{6} - \frac{1}{6}$ **2.** $\frac{11}{12} - \frac{5}{12}$

3. $\frac{7}{10} - \frac{3}{10}$ **4.** $\frac{19}{20} - \frac{7}{20}$

Set C   pages 346–347

Find the sum of $6\frac{1}{5}$ and $8\frac{3}{5}$.

Add the fractions.

$$6\frac{1}{5}$$
$$+8\frac{3}{5}$$
$$\frac{4}{5}$$

Add the whole numbers.

$$6\frac{1}{5}$$
$$+8\frac{3}{5}$$
$$14\frac{4}{5}$$

Remember to write fractions in lowest terms. Add or subtract.

1. $2\frac{1}{3}$ **2.** $15\frac{7}{8}$ **3.** $25\frac{1}{6}$
  $+7\frac{1}{3}$ $-8\frac{3}{8}$ $+4\frac{1}{6}$

Set D   pages 348–349

Find $2\frac{1}{4} + 3\frac{3}{4} + 3\frac{2}{4}$.

$2\frac{1}{4} + 3\frac{3}{4} + 3\frac{2}{4} = 8\frac{6}{4}$

Rename: $8\frac{6}{4} = 8 + \frac{6}{4}$

$= 8 + \frac{4}{4} + \frac{2}{4}$

$= 8 + 1 + \frac{2}{4} = 9\frac{2}{4} = 9\frac{1}{2}$

Remember to rename a sum if it contains an improper fraction. Add.

1. $4\frac{1}{4} + 6\frac{3}{4}$ **2.** $3\frac{5}{6} + 9\frac{5}{6}$

3. $3\frac{3}{8} + 2\frac{5}{8} + 5\frac{3}{8}$ **4.** $4\frac{2}{5} + 5\frac{4}{5} + 4\frac{3}{5}$

Set E   pages 350–351

Find $4 - 2\frac{3}{8}$.

Rename 4: $4 = 3\frac{8}{8}$
$$-2\frac{3}{8} = 2\frac{3}{8}$$
$$1\frac{5}{8}$$

Think:
$4 = 3 + 1$
$= 3 + \frac{8}{8}$

Remember that a whole number can be renamed as a mixed number. Subtract.

1. $5 - 2\frac{4}{5}$ **2.** $9 - 4\frac{1}{6}$

3. $2 - 1\frac{3}{4}$ **4.** $6 - 3\frac{3}{7}$

Set F pages 352–353

Find $8\frac{1}{6} - 4\frac{5}{6}$.

Rename $8\frac{1}{6}$:

$$8\frac{1}{6} = 7\frac{7}{6}$$
$$-\,4\frac{5}{6} = 4\frac{5}{6}$$
$$\overline{\qquad\quad 3\frac{2}{6} = 3\frac{1}{3}}$$

Think:
$$8\frac{1}{6} = 7 + 1 + \frac{1}{6}$$
$$= 7 + \frac{6}{6} + \frac{1}{6}$$
$$= 7\frac{7}{6}$$

Remember that renaming a mixed number is sometimes necessary when subtracting mixed numbers. Subtract.

1. $6\frac{1}{5} - 3\frac{2}{5}$ **2.** $3\frac{1}{8} - 1\frac{3}{8}$

Set G pages 360–363

Find $\frac{4}{5} + \frac{2}{3}$.

Write equal fractions with a common denominator of 15.

$$\frac{4}{5} = \frac{12}{15}$$
$$+\frac{2}{3} = \frac{10}{15}$$
$$\overline{\qquad \frac{22}{15} = 1\frac{7}{15}}$$

Remember to make a list of multiples for each denominator to find a common denominator. Find each sum.

1. $\frac{3}{4}$ **2.** $\frac{5}{6}$ **3.** $\frac{3}{8}$
$+\frac{1}{8}$ $+\frac{1}{10}$ $+\frac{5}{6}$

Set H pages 364–365

Find $\frac{5}{6} - \frac{3}{8}$.

A common denominator is 24.

$$\frac{5}{6} = \frac{20}{24}$$
$$-\frac{3}{8} = \frac{9}{24}$$
$$\overline{\qquad \frac{11}{24}}$$

Remember that you can always find a common denominator by multiplying the denominators. Find each difference.

1. $\frac{4}{5}$ **2.** $\frac{2}{3}$ **3.** $\frac{7}{8}$
$-\frac{1}{4}$ $-\frac{3}{5}$ $-\frac{1}{12}$

Set I pages 366–367

Find $4\frac{7}{10} + 2\frac{5}{6}$.

$$4\frac{7}{10} = 4\frac{21}{30}$$
$$+\,2\frac{5}{6} = 2\frac{25}{30}$$
$$\overline{\qquad 6\frac{46}{30} = 6 + 1\frac{16}{30} = 7\frac{16}{30} = 7\frac{8}{15}}$$

Remember that fractions must have the same denominator before you can add them.

Add.

1. $5\frac{2}{3}$ **2.** $2\frac{3}{10}$ **3.** $9\frac{4}{7}$
$+6\frac{1}{4}$ $+2\frac{1}{5}$ $+3\frac{1}{2}$

Set J pages 368–369

Find $8\frac{3}{4} - 3\frac{4}{5}$.

$$8\frac{3}{4} = 8\frac{15}{20} = 7\frac{35}{20}$$
$$-\,3\frac{4}{5} = 3\frac{16}{20} = 3\frac{16}{20}$$
$$\overline{\qquad\qquad\qquad 4\frac{19}{20}}$$

Remember that there is more than one number that you can use as a common denominator.

Subtract.

1. $10\frac{2}{3}$ **2.** $7\frac{1}{2}$ **3.** $12\frac{1}{10}$
$-8\frac{5}{6}$ $-3\frac{3}{5}$ $-6\frac{1}{4}$

More Practice

Set A   pages 342–343

Add the fractions. **Remember** to simplify the answer if necessary.

1. $\frac{5}{8} + \frac{2}{8}$
2. $\frac{2}{6} + \frac{1}{6}$
3. $\frac{4}{7} + \frac{2}{7}$
4. $\frac{1}{5} + \frac{3}{5}$

5. $\frac{3}{13} + \frac{7}{13}$
6. $\frac{3}{8} + \frac{7}{8}$
7. $\frac{2}{7} + \frac{4}{7} + \frac{3}{7}$
8. $\frac{4}{9} + \frac{5}{9} + \frac{7}{9}$

Set B   pages 344–345

Subtract the fractions. **Remember** to simplify the answer if necessary.

1. $\frac{7}{8} - \frac{3}{8}$
2. $\frac{7}{10} - \frac{3}{10}$
3. $\frac{5}{6} - \frac{1}{6}$
4. $\frac{4}{5} - \frac{2}{5}$

5. $\frac{5}{9} - \frac{2}{9}$
6. $\frac{5}{8} - \frac{1}{8}$
7. $\frac{9}{13} - \frac{6}{13}$
8. $\frac{9}{10} - \frac{3}{10}$

Set C   pages 346–347

Add. **Remember** to write your answers in simplest form.

1. $3\frac{1}{5} + 6\frac{2}{5}$
2. $6\frac{7}{10} + 1\frac{1}{10}$
3. $8\frac{3}{10} + 2\frac{3}{10}$
4. $7\frac{5}{12} + 3\frac{1}{12}$

Subtract. **Remember** to write your answers in simplest form.

5. $11\frac{9}{10} - 6\frac{3}{10}$
6. $9\frac{7}{12} - 1\frac{5}{12}$
7. $6\frac{11}{16} - 2\frac{3}{16}$
8. $15\frac{17}{20} - 8\frac{11}{20}$

Set D   pages 348–349

Add. **Remember** to write your answers in simplest form.

1. $2\frac{4}{5} + 3\frac{3}{5}$
2. $5\frac{5}{12} + 6\frac{11}{12}$
3. $8\frac{7}{10} + 9\frac{9}{10}$
4. $9\frac{3}{4} + 6\frac{1}{4}$

5. $13 + 9\frac{3}{4} + 5\frac{3}{4}$
6. $4\frac{7}{13} + 2\frac{9}{13} + 6\frac{1}{13}$
7. $8\frac{3}{7} + 1\frac{4}{7} + 6\frac{5}{7}$

Set E   pages 350–351

Subtract. **Remember** to write your answers in simplest form.

1. $3 - \frac{3}{10}$
2. $7 - 2\frac{2}{5}$
3. $6 - 3\frac{4}{7}$
4. $11 - 4\frac{5}{9}$
5. $13 - 8\frac{5}{8}$

6. $2 - \frac{9}{14}$
7. $36 - 21\frac{7}{12}$
8. $29 - 18\frac{5}{6}$
9. $18 - 12\frac{7}{10}$

Set F   pages 352–353

Subtract. **Remember** to write the answer in simplest form.

1. $8\frac{2}{5}$ $-3\frac{3}{5}$
2. $8\frac{3}{8}$ $-6\frac{7}{8}$
3. $10\frac{5}{9}$ $-4\frac{7}{9}$
4. $12\frac{2}{5}$ $-3\frac{4}{5}$
5. $16\frac{5}{12}$ $-9\frac{11}{12}$
6. $14\frac{1}{6}$ $-10\frac{5}{6}$

Set G   pages 360–363

Find each sum. **Remember** to write your answer in simplest form.

1. $\frac{3}{8}$ $+\frac{5}{6}$
2. $\frac{7}{10}$ $+\frac{3}{4}$
3. $\frac{3}{4}$ $+\frac{6}{7}$
4. $\frac{5}{9}$ $+\frac{1}{6}$
5. $\frac{2}{3}$ $+\frac{5}{9}$
6. $\frac{11}{12}$ $+\frac{1}{8}$

7. $\frac{1}{5} + \frac{3}{4} + \frac{1}{2}$
8. $\frac{5}{6} + \frac{4}{9} + \frac{1}{3}$
9. $\frac{3}{4} + \frac{7}{12} + \frac{5}{8}$

Set H   pages 364–365

Find each difference. **Remember** to write your answer in simplest form.

1. $\frac{3}{4}$ $-\frac{2}{5}$
2. $\frac{11}{12}$ $-\frac{3}{8}$
3. $\frac{7}{10}$ $-\frac{1}{4}$
4. $\frac{5}{9}$ $-\frac{1}{2}$
5. $\frac{3}{5}$ $-\frac{1}{6}$
6. $\frac{5}{9}$ $-\frac{5}{12}$

7. $\frac{3}{10} - \frac{1}{5}$
8. $\frac{2}{3} - \frac{1}{6}$
9. $\frac{5}{6} - \frac{1}{4}$
10. $\frac{5}{6} - \frac{7}{9}$

Set I   pages 366–367

Add. **Remember** to write your answer in simplest form.

1. $6\frac{3}{4} + 8\frac{1}{3}$
2. $5\frac{4}{5} + 9\frac{1}{6}$
3. $3\frac{1}{9} + 7\frac{5}{6}$
4. $4\frac{11}{12} + 8\frac{5}{6}$

5. $16\frac{2}{5} + 17\frac{1}{3}$
6. $19\frac{5}{6} + 17\frac{1}{2}$
7. $8\frac{2}{5} + 10\frac{3}{4}$
8. $25\frac{3}{10} + 21\frac{1}{6}$

Set J   pages 368–369

Subtract. **Remember** to write your answer in simplest form.

1. $5\frac{3}{10}$ $-2\frac{4}{5}$
2. $8\frac{1}{5}$ $-6\frac{3}{8}$
3. $10\frac{1}{9}$ $-8\frac{3}{4}$
4. $16\frac{5}{12}$ $-9\frac{7}{8}$
5. $21\frac{2}{7}$ $-18\frac{3}{5}$

6. $8\frac{3}{10} - 5\frac{5}{8}$
7. $4\frac{1}{2} - 2\frac{3}{5}$
8. $9\frac{1}{4} - 6\frac{7}{10}$
9. $14\frac{2}{9} - 11\frac{7}{12}$

Enrichment

Betweenness for Fractions

A. You know there is no whole number between 3 and 4. Between any two fractions, however, there is another fraction. To find a fraction between $\frac{3}{8}$ and $\frac{4}{8}$, think of dividing the number line from 0 to 1 into 16 equal parts instead of 8 equal parts. What fraction appears between $\frac{3}{8}$ and $\frac{4}{8}$ on the number line?

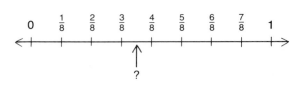

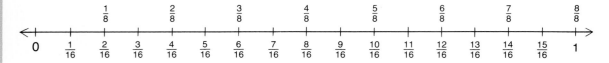

A fraction between $\frac{3}{8}$ and $\frac{4}{8}$ is $\frac{7}{16}$.

B. You can also use a common denominator to find a fraction between two fractions. Find a fraction between $\frac{5}{6}$ and $\frac{7}{8}$.

First, rename the fractions using a common denominator.

$$\frac{5}{6} = \frac{20}{24} \qquad \frac{7}{8} = \frac{21}{24}$$

Then find a fraction between $\frac{20}{24}$ and $\frac{21}{24}$. Use 2×24 to find a common denominator.

$$\frac{20}{24} = \frac{40}{48} \qquad \frac{21}{24} = \frac{42}{48}$$

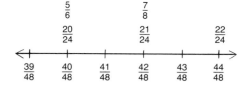

A fraction between $\frac{5}{6}$ and $\frac{7}{8}$ is $\frac{41}{48}$.

Find a fraction between each pair of fractions.

1. $\frac{2}{5}$ and $\frac{3}{5}$ **2.** $\frac{21}{24}$ and $\frac{22}{24}$ **3.** $\frac{1}{3}$ and $\frac{2}{3}$ **4.** $\frac{3}{7}$ and $\frac{4}{7}$

5. $\frac{1}{9}$ and $\frac{1}{6}$ **6.** $\frac{2}{5}$ and $\frac{1}{2}$ **7.** $\frac{7}{8}$ and $\frac{9}{10}$ **8.** $\frac{6}{6}$ and $\frac{7}{6}$

Chapter 11 Review/Test

Add or subtract. Write the answers in simplest form.

1. $\frac{1}{8} + \frac{3}{8}$

2. $\frac{3}{10} + \frac{3}{10}$

3. $\frac{11}{12} - \frac{1}{12}$

4. $\frac{5}{6} - \frac{1}{6}$

5. $\begin{array}{r} 4\frac{9}{16} \\ + 2\frac{1}{16} \\ \hline \end{array}$

6. $\begin{array}{r} 6\frac{11}{15} \\ - 1\frac{10}{15} \\ \hline \end{array}$

7. $2\frac{7}{8} + 3\frac{3}{8}$

8. $5\frac{4}{5} + 3\frac{3}{5}$

9. $\begin{array}{r} 9 \\ - 2\frac{1}{8} \\ \hline \end{array}$

10. $\begin{array}{r} 10 \\ - 2\frac{2}{3} \\ \hline \end{array}$

11. $\begin{array}{r} 6\frac{1}{3} \\ - 2\frac{2}{3} \\ \hline \end{array}$

12. $\begin{array}{r} 10\frac{1}{12} \\ - 5\frac{5}{12} \\ \hline \end{array}$

13. $\begin{array}{r} \frac{3}{4} \\ + \frac{1}{8} \\ \hline \end{array}$

14. $\begin{array}{r} \frac{9}{10} \\ - \frac{1}{5} \\ \hline \end{array}$

15. $\frac{1}{6} + \frac{1}{4}$

16. $\frac{1}{2} + \frac{1}{5} + \frac{3}{10}$

17. $\frac{9}{10} - \frac{1}{15}$

18. $\frac{3}{8} - \frac{1}{3}$

19. $7\frac{1}{3} + 3\frac{3}{4}$

20. $6\frac{1}{12} - 3\frac{3}{8}$

21. Is the sum $7\frac{7}{8} + 5\frac{3}{4}$ more than or less than $12\frac{1}{2}$?

Copy and complete.

22. $\begin{array}{r} 7 = 6\frac{\boxed{}}{5} \\ - 2\frac{2}{5} = 2\frac{2}{5} \\ \hline 4\frac{3}{5} \end{array}$

23. $\begin{array}{r} \frac{1}{9} = \frac{\boxed{}}{18} \\ + \frac{5}{6} = \frac{\boxed{}}{18} \\ \hline \frac{\boxed{}}{18} \end{array}$

Solve each problem.

24. A carpenter cut $\frac{1}{2}$ foot from a board that was $3\frac{1}{4}$ feet long. How long was the board after the cut?

25. A room is 20 feet long by 12 feet wide. A rug that is 15 feet long by 9 feet wide is placed in the center of the room so that equal space is left at each end. How much space will be left at each end?

Read the problem below. Then answer the question.

Julie spent $2\frac{1}{2}$ hours one day baby-sitting and $3\frac{1}{4}$ hours the next. She was paid $2 per hour. How many hours did she work in all?

26. Which is the correct answer for the problem?

   a. $5\frac{3}{4}$ dollars

   b. $5\frac{3}{4}$ days

   c. $5\frac{3}{4}$ hours

27. **Write About Math** What must be true for a number to be a common denominator of two fractions with different denominators?

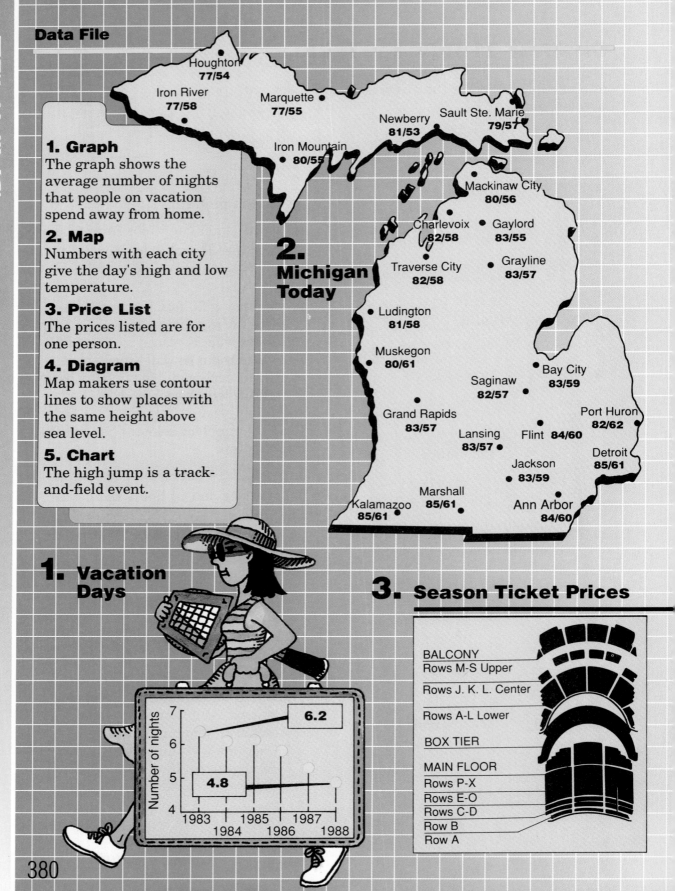

Data File

1. Graph
The graph shows the average number of nights that people on vacation spend away from home.

2. Map
Numbers with each city give the day's high and low temperature.

3. Price List
The prices listed are for one person.

4. Diagram
Map makers use contour lines to show places with the same height above sea level.

5. Chart
The high jump is a track-and-field event.

2. Michigan Today

Houghton 77/54
Iron River 77/58
Marquette 77/55
Newberry 81/53
Sault Ste. Marie 79/57
Iron Mountain 80/55
Mackinaw City 80/56
Charlevoix 82/58
Gaylord 83/55
Traverse City 82/58
Grayline 83/57
Ludington 81/58
Muskegon 80/61
Bay City 83/59
Saginaw 82/57
Grand Rapids 83/57
Port Huron 82/62
Lansing 83/57
Flint 84/60
Detroit 85/61
Jackson 83/59
Marshall 85/61
Kalamazoo 85/61
Ann Arbor 84/60

1. Vacation Days

Number of nights

6.2

4.8

1983 1984 1985 1986 1987 1988

3. Season Ticket Prices

BALCONY
Rows M-S Upper

Rows J. K. L. Center

Rows A-L Lower

BOX TIER

MAIN FLOOR
Rows P-X
Rows E-O
Rows C-D
Row B
Row A

DATA FILE

380

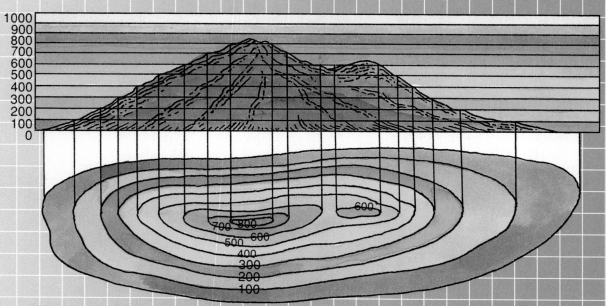

4. Topographic Maps

5. Chart of Heights

Highest jump by a horse: 8 $\frac{1}{12}$ ft.

Cuba's Javier Sotomayor's high jump: 8 ft (July 1989)

Normal ceiling in a house: 8 ft

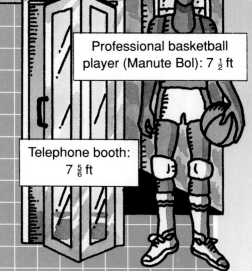

Professional basketball player (Manute Bol): 7 $\frac{1}{2}$ ft

Telephone booth: 7 $\frac{5}{6}$ ft

	Thursday A-B-C Series 10 Concerts	Friday A-B Series 7 Concerts	Saturday A-B Series 10 Concerts
MAIN FLOOR			
Rows A	$ 50	$ 35	$ 50
B	125	87.50	135
C-D	200	140	220
E-O	390	273	440
P-X	315	220.50	350
BALCONY			
Rows A-L	390	273	440
J-K-L (Center)	315	220.50	350
M-S	250	175	280

1. Multiply.

$$\begin{array}{r} 23 \\ \times 41 \\ \hline \end{array}$$

a. 843
b. 64
c. 943
d. 115

2. Multiply.

30 × 800

a. 240
b. 2,400
c. 24,000
d. 240,000

3. Divide.

21)1,315

a. 63 R2
b. 62 R12
c. 62 R13
d. 67 R8

4. Subtract.

$$\begin{array}{r} 4,826 \\ -3,459 \\ \hline \end{array}$$

a. 1,367
b. 1,477
c. 1,467
d. 1,377

Choose the most sensible measure.

5. Length of a needle

a. 40 m
b. 40 mm
c. 40 dm
d. 40 cm

6. Find the perimeter.

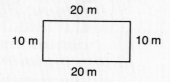

a. 200 m
b. 30 m
c. 50 m
d. 60 m

7. Subtract.

$$\begin{array}{r} 7 \text{ ft } 2 \text{ in.} \\ -3 \text{ ft } 7 \text{ in.} \\ \hline \end{array}$$

a. 4 ft 5 in.
b. 3 ft 5 in.
c. 3 ft 7 in.
d. 4 ft 7 in.

8. What decimal represents three thousandths?

a. 0.300
b. 0.030
c. 0.003
d. 0.3

9. Multiply.

$$\begin{array}{r} 2.6 \\ \times 0.3 \\ \hline \end{array}$$

a. 6.18
b. 0.78
c. 7.8
d. 0.618

10. Multiply.

0.93 × 100

a. 9.3
b. 93
c. 930
d. 9,300

11. Look for the pattern. Then give the next number in the sequence.

3   13   12   22   21   31

a. 30
b. 41
c. 32
d. 33

12. Which ordered pair names the point labeled by *A*?

a. (1, 4)
b. (4, 1)
c. (0, 4)
d. (4, 0)

13. Find the rule.

A	B
2	8
3	12
4	16
5	20

a. 4 × A = B
b. 4 × B = A
c. A + B = 10
d. A ÷ 4 = B

14. What is $\frac{20}{30}$ in lowest terms?

   a. $\frac{10}{15}$ **b.** $\frac{4}{6}$ **c.** $\frac{2}{3}$ **d.** $\frac{3}{5}$

15. What is the least common denominator for $\frac{2}{3}$ and $\frac{1}{4}$?

   a. 6   **b.** 12   **c.** 8   **d.** 7

16. Which number sentence is true?

   a. $\frac{3}{8} > \frac{1}{2}$ **c.** $\frac{8}{16} = \frac{7}{15}$

   b. $7\frac{1}{5} < 8\frac{1}{3}$ **d.** $\frac{3}{4} < \frac{5}{8}$

17. Add.

   $\frac{1}{10} + \frac{1}{10}$

   a. $\frac{1}{10}$

   b. $\frac{1}{5}$

   c. $\frac{1}{100}$

   d. $\frac{1}{20}$

18. Subtract.

   $\frac{11}{12}$
   $-\frac{1}{3}$

   a. $\frac{7}{12}$

   b. $\frac{7}{24}$

   c. $\frac{10}{9}$

   d. $\frac{10}{12}$

19. Subtract.

   12
   $-7\frac{5}{8}$

   a. $4\frac{3}{8}$

   b. $5\frac{5}{8}$

   c. $4\frac{5}{8}$

   d. $5\frac{5}{8}$

20. Mrs. Hayes trimmed $\frac{1}{2}$ foot from the length of a curtain that was $4\frac{1}{4}$ feet long. How long was the curtain after she trimmed it?

   a. $3\frac{3}{4}$ feet   **c.** $4\frac{1}{4}$ feet

   b. $3\frac{1}{5}$ feet   **d.** $4\frac{1}{2}$ feet

Make a chart to solve the following problem.

21. Vic, Tess, Frank, and Sue each had a different snack. The choices were fruit cup, muffin, oatmeal cookies, or carrot sticks. None of the boys ate cookies. Vic and the boy who had carrot sticks have different teachers. Tess had jam on her muffin. Who had fruit cup?

   a. Frank   **c.** Tess
   b. Sue   **d.** Vic

22. Oranges are packed 8 to a sack. How many sacks are needed for 70 oranges?

   a. 7 sacks   **c.** 6 sacks
   b. 8 sacks   **d.** 9 sacks

Read the problem below. Then answer the question.

Mr. Jones bought a jacket for $95 and a sweater for $39. The sales tax was 6 cents on the dollar. What was the total cost?

23. Which method can be used to solve the problem?

   a. $95 + 39 = 134$

   b. $95 + 39 = 134$ 134
   $134 \times 0.06 = 8.04$ $+\quad 8.04$
   $\overline{142.04}$

   c. $95 \times 0.06 = 5.70$ 5.70
   $39 \times 0.06 = 2.34$ $+2.34$
   $\overline{8.04}$

   d. $95 + 39 + 6 = 140$

Exploring Multiplication of Fractions

Did You Know: A good way for two people to share something that needs to be cut into two parts: one person cuts the thing in two, and the other person gets the half of his or her choice.

Number-Sense Project

Estimate
What ways do people use to estimate or divide something into "equal shares"?

Gather Data
Present a series of problems to 3 people and see what methods they use to divide things into "equal shares."

Analyze and Report
Compare your findings with those of other students. How many different ways of sharing were used?

Using Pictures to Multiply Fractions

Build Understanding

Forests once covered about $\frac{3}{5}$ of the earth's land surface. Today, only about $\frac{1}{2}$ of those forest areas remain. What fraction of the earth's land surface is now covered by forests?

You can draw a picture to help you find $\frac{1}{2}$ of $\frac{3}{5}$.

First shade $\frac{3}{5}$.   Next shade $\frac{1}{2}$ of that.

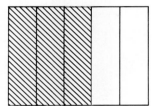 

In the second picture, how many equal parts are in the whole? What is the value of each of these parts? How many parts are shaded twice?

The diagrams show that $\frac{1}{2}$ of $\frac{3}{5}$ is $\frac{3}{10}$. Multiplication can be used to find a fraction of a number.

$$\frac{1}{2} \times \frac{3}{5} = \frac{3}{10}$$

About $\frac{3}{10}$ of the earth's land surface is covered by forests.

■ **Talk About Math**   Do you think you would get the same product for $\frac{1}{2} \times \frac{3}{5}$ if you shaded $\frac{1}{2}$ first? Why or why not? Draw a picture to see if your reasoning is correct.

Forests cover about one third of the land area in the United States.

Check Understanding

For another example, see Set A, pages 408–409.

Use the picture to find each product.

1. $\frac{1}{4}$ of $\frac{1}{2}$
$\frac{1}{4} \times \frac{1}{2}$

2. $\frac{3}{4}$ of $\frac{2}{5}$
$\frac{3}{4} \times \frac{2}{5}$
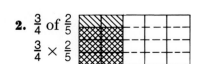

3. Write a number sentence for this picture. Try to find another number sentence.

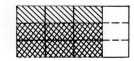

4. Draw a picture to find each product.

a. $\frac{1}{3}$ of $\frac{1}{2}$ **b.** $\frac{2}{3}$ of $\frac{1}{4}$

$\frac{1}{3} \times \frac{1}{2}$ $\frac{2}{3} \times \frac{1}{4}$

Practice

For More Practice, see Set A, pages 410–411.

Use the picture to find the product.

5. $\frac{1}{4}$ of $\frac{1}{3}$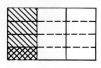

$\frac{1}{4} \times \frac{1}{3}$

6. $\frac{1}{2}$ of $\frac{3}{4}$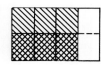

$\frac{1}{2} \times \frac{3}{4}$

7. $\frac{2}{3}$ of $\frac{1}{6}$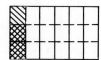

$\frac{2}{3} \times \frac{1}{6}$

8. $\frac{2}{3}$ of $\frac{2}{5}$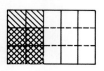

$\frac{2}{3} \times \frac{2}{5}$

9. $\frac{5}{6}$ of $\frac{1}{4}$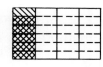

$\frac{5}{6} \times \frac{1}{4}$

10. $\frac{3}{4}$ of $\frac{3}{4}$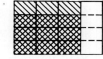

$\frac{3}{4} \times \frac{3}{4}$

Write a number sentence that states what each picture shows.

11. 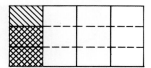   **12.**    **13.**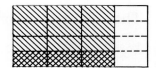

Draw a picture to find each product.

14. $\frac{1}{2}$ of $\frac{1}{2}$ **15.** $\frac{1}{3}$ of $\frac{1}{4}$ **16.** $\frac{1}{3}$ of $\frac{1}{3}$ **17.** $\frac{2}{3}$ of $\frac{1}{2}$

$\frac{1}{2} \times \frac{1}{2}$ $\frac{1}{3} \times \frac{1}{4}$ $\frac{1}{3} \times \frac{1}{3}$ $\frac{2}{3} \times \frac{1}{2}$

18. $\frac{1}{6}$ of $\frac{1}{3}$ **19.** $\frac{5}{6}$ of $\frac{1}{2}$ **20.** $\frac{2}{3}$ of $\frac{4}{5}$ **21.** $\frac{4}{5}$ of $\frac{3}{5}$

$\frac{1}{6} \times \frac{1}{3}$ $\frac{5}{6} \times \frac{1}{2}$ $\frac{2}{3} \times \frac{4}{5}$ $\frac{4}{5} \times \frac{3}{5}$

Problem Solving

Solve each problem by drawing a picture.

22. Land covers $\frac{2}{7}$ of the earth's surface. If $\frac{1}{3}$ of the land is in Asia, what fraction of the earth's surface is land in Asia?

23. About $\frac{1}{6}$ of the world's land is in North America. About $\frac{2}{5}$ of the land in North America is in Canada. What fraction of the world's land is in Canada? Draw a picture to help you.

Multiplying Fractions

Build Understanding

George makes furniture with tiles laid into the top. For one table, $\frac{3}{4}$ of the tiles are blue. Birds are painted on $\frac{1}{3}$ of the blue tiles. What part of the table top is blue tiles with birds painted on them?

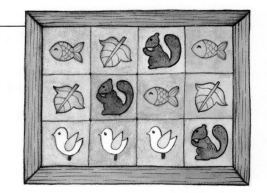

$\frac{1}{3}$ of $\frac{3}{4}$ is $\frac{1}{3} \times \frac{3}{4}$

The picture shows that $\frac{1}{3} \times \frac{3}{4} = \frac{3}{12}$. Do you see another way to find the answer?

You could multiply numerators.

$\frac{1}{3} \times \frac{3}{4} = \frac{3}{}$

Then multiply denominators.

$\frac{1}{3} \times \frac{3}{4} = \frac{3}{12}$

On the table top, $\frac{3}{12}$ or $\frac{1}{4}$ of the tiles are blue and have birds painted on them.

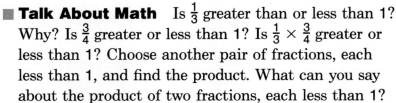

■ **Talk About Math**   Is $\frac{1}{3}$ greater than or less than 1? Why? Is $\frac{3}{4}$ greater or less than 1? Is $\frac{1}{3} \times \frac{3}{4}$ greater or less than 1? Choose another pair of fractions, each less than 1, and find the product. What can you say about the product of two fractions, each less than 1?

Check Understanding

For another example, see Set B, pages 408–409.

1. How can you write $\frac{2}{3}$ of $\frac{5}{6}$ as a product?

2. How can you multiply fractions without drawing a picture?

3. Find $\frac{2}{3} \times \frac{5}{6}$ without drawing a picture.

4. Find $\frac{5}{6}$ of $\frac{2}{3}$. How does the answer compare to $\frac{2}{3}$ of $\frac{5}{6}$?

Practice

For More Practice, see Set B, pages 410–411.

Multiply. **Remember** to multiply the numerators and multiply the denominators.

5. $\frac{3}{4} \times \frac{5}{6}$ **6.** $\frac{1}{10} \times \frac{1}{10}$ **7.** $\frac{3}{4} \times \frac{1}{4}$ **8.** $\frac{3}{8} \times \frac{2}{3}$

9. $\frac{1}{6} \times \frac{5}{6}$ **10.** $\frac{1}{8} \times \frac{1}{4}$ **11.** $\frac{3}{5} \times \frac{7}{8}$ **12.** $\frac{1}{4} \times \frac{5}{6}$

13. $\frac{1}{2} \times \frac{3}{4}$ **14.** $\frac{11}{12} \times \frac{3}{4}$ **15.** $\frac{1}{3} \times \frac{1}{2}$ **16.** $\frac{1}{6} \times \frac{3}{4}$

17. Number Sense   You know that $\frac{1}{2} \times \frac{1}{3} = \frac{1}{6}$ and $\frac{1}{6} \times \frac{5}{6} = \frac{5}{36}$. What does $\frac{1}{2} \times \frac{1}{3} \times \frac{5}{6}$ equal?

Multiply. **Remember** to write each product in simplest form.

18. $\frac{1}{4} \times \frac{2}{5} \times \frac{3}{4}$ **19.** $\frac{2}{3} \times \frac{1}{5} \times \frac{5}{6}$ **20.** $\frac{1}{2} \times \frac{2}{3} \times \frac{3}{8}$

21. Number Sense   Is the product of three fractions, each being less than 1, greater than or less than 1?

22. **Calculator**   Use your calculator to find a decimal for each fraction in Exercise 18. Multiply the decimals.

Problem Solving

23. For a kitchen counter, George uses white tiles for $\frac{2}{3}$ of the tiles. Of the white tiles, $\frac{2}{5}$ have a leaf design. What part of the total tiles are white with a leaf design?

24. The top of a dining table is covered with tiles. Of these tiles, $\frac{5}{6}$ are black, and $\frac{1}{3}$ of the black tiles form the border. What part of the total tiles are used for the border?

Skills ———— Review   pages 22–163

Find each answer.
1. $189 + 334$ **2.** $1{,}994 - 881$ **3.** $700 - 132$ **4.** 349×765

5. $1{,}250 \div 25$ **6.** $3{,}001 - 728$ **7.** $226 + 987$ **8.** 657×200

Multiplying Fractions and Whole Numbers

Build Understanding

A. Egg Carton Fractions
Materials: Counters
Groups: With a partner

a. Draw a diagram like the picture to act as an egg carton. How many parts are in the whole egg carton?

b. Think of separating the carton into 3 equal parts. What fraction of the whole carton is each part?

c. Put counters into $\frac{1}{3}$ of the spaces. How many spaces have counters?

d. Use your answer from Step c to find $\frac{1}{3}$ of 12. Remember that $\frac{1}{3}$ of 12 means $\frac{1}{3} \times 12$.

e. Next put counters into $\frac{2}{3}$ of the spaces. What is $\frac{2}{3}$ of 12? What is $\frac{2}{3} \times 12$?

B. You can use multiplication of fractions to check your work in the activity.

Any whole number can be written as a fraction with the whole number as the numerator and 1 as the denominator.

$\frac{1}{3} \times 12 = \frac{1}{3} \times \frac{12}{1}$ Multiply the numerators.
Multiply the denominators.

$= \frac{12}{3}$

$= 4$ Write the product in simplest form.

$\frac{2}{3} \times 12 = \frac{2}{3} \times \frac{12}{1}$

$= \frac{24}{3}$

$= 8$

c. Find $\frac{3}{4}$ of 14.

$$\frac{3}{4} \times 14 \qquad \text{Write 14 as a fraction.}$$

$$\frac{3}{4} \times \frac{14}{1} = \frac{42}{4} \qquad \text{Multiply the fractions.}$$

$$= 10\frac{2}{4}$$

$$= 10\frac{1}{2} \qquad \begin{array}{l}\text{Write the product}\\ \text{in simplest form.}\end{array}$$

D. Mental Math You can use mental math to multiply a fraction and a whole number.

Find $\frac{4}{5}$ of 25.

Think: $\frac{1}{5}$ of 25 is 5.

$\qquad \frac{4}{5}$ of 25 is 4×5.

So, $\frac{4}{5}$ of 25 is 20.

E. Estimation You can estimate the product of a fraction and a whole number.

Find $\frac{1}{3}$ of 25.

$\frac{1}{3}$ of 25 is about $\frac{1}{3}$ of 24.   Think: What multiple of 3 is close to 25?

$$\frac{1}{3} \times 24 = \frac{1}{3} \times \frac{24}{1} = \frac{24}{3} = 8$$

So, $\frac{1}{3}$ of 25 is about 8.

■ **Talk About Math** When you multiply $\frac{1}{3} \times 5 \times 12$, is it easier to multiply $\frac{1}{3}$ and 5 first or to multiply $\frac{1}{3}$ and 12 first? Why?

Check Understanding

For another example, see Set C, pages 408–409.

Choose the best answer for Exercises 1 and 2.

1. To multiply a whole number and a fraction, you should first

  a. write the whole number as a fraction.

  b. write the fraction as a whole number.

  c. round the fraction to the nearest whole number.

2. To write a whole number as a fraction, you should write

  a. 1 in the numerator and the whole number in the denominator.

  b. the product of the whole number and 1.

  c. the whole number in the numerator and 1 in the denominator.

Write each whole number as a fraction.

3. 7   **4.** 17   **5.** 737   **6.** 1

Mental Math   Complete the following.

7. Since $\frac{1}{5}$ of 30 is 6, $\frac{3}{5}$ of 30 is ▦.

8. Since $\frac{1}{8}$ of 16 is 2, $\frac{7}{8}$ of 16 is ▦.

Estimation   Choose the best estimation method.

9. $\frac{1}{3}$ of 31   **a.** 31 + 3   **b.** $\frac{1}{3}$ of 30   **c.** 30 × 3

10. $\frac{1}{4}$ of 25   **a.** $\frac{1}{4}$ of 24   **b.** 4 + 25   **c.** 4 × 25

Practice

For More Practice, see Set C, pages 410–411.

Multiply. **Remember** to write the product in simplest form.

11. $\frac{3}{4} \times 12$ **12.** $\frac{7}{8} \times 24$ **13.** $15 \times \frac{3}{5}$ **14.** $\frac{1}{5} \times 2$

15. $\frac{7}{8} \times 40$ **16.** $6 \times \frac{5}{9}$ **17.** $\frac{2}{3} \times 7$ **18.** $\frac{5}{6} \times 15$

19. $\frac{4}{7} \times 14$ **20.** $\frac{3}{4} \times 3$ **21.** $9 \times \frac{4}{18}$ **22.** $\frac{1}{8} \times 32$

Mental Math   Use mental math to find each product.

23. $\frac{1}{5} \times 100$ **24.** $\frac{2}{3} \times 30$ **25.** $\frac{4}{5} \times 50$ **26.** $\frac{5}{6} \times 60$

27. $\frac{1}{3} \times 15 \times 6$ **28.** $\frac{1}{4} \times 5 \times 20$ **29.** $7 \times \frac{1}{5} \times 25$ **30.** $\frac{1}{10} \times 30 \times 4$

Estimation   Estimate each product.

31. $\frac{1}{4} \times 39$ **32.** $\frac{2}{3} \times 29$ **33.** $\frac{2}{5} \times 24$ **34.** $17 \times \frac{1}{9}$

35. $32 \times \frac{2}{3}$ **36.** $\frac{1}{5} \times 34$ **37.** $\frac{3}{4} \times 98$ **38.** $\frac{1}{6} \times 50$

39. Number Sense   Look at the products you
found in Exercises 11–22. Are any products
greater than the whole number in the exercise?
Write a statement about the product of a proper
fraction and a whole number.

Problem Solving

Kristen saw signs advertising sales at almost every store in the mall. For each regular price in Problems 40–45, find how many dollars would be saved on each item during the sale.

40. Sweater $30

41. Coat $64

42. Gloves $12

43. Watch $100

44. Boots $48

45. Jeans $25

Midchapter Checkup

Use the picture to find each product.

1. $\frac{1}{3}$ of $\frac{2}{5}$
$\frac{1}{3} \times \frac{2}{5}$

2. $\frac{1}{2}$ of $\frac{1}{3}$
$\frac{1}{2} \times \frac{1}{3}$

3. $\frac{2}{3}$ of $\frac{1}{4}$
$\frac{2}{3} \times \frac{1}{4}$

Find each product.

4. $\frac{1}{3} \times \frac{5}{6}$

5. $\frac{1}{5} \times \frac{1}{4}$

6. $\frac{2}{3} \times \frac{3}{8}$

7. $7 \times \frac{3}{5}$

8. $6 \times \frac{2}{3}$

9. $\frac{5}{8} \times 16$

Mental Math   Find each product mentally.

10. $\frac{2}{3}$ of 12

11. $\frac{4}{5}$ of 20

12. $\frac{7}{8}$ of 24

393

Problem-Solving Workshop

Real-Life Decision Making

You and your friends are planning a bicycle trip in Spotted Deer Park. You will begin the ride at Winding Road Lodge at 9:00 A.M. You must be back at the lodge by 3:30 P.M. Make a schedule for your bicycle trip in the park.

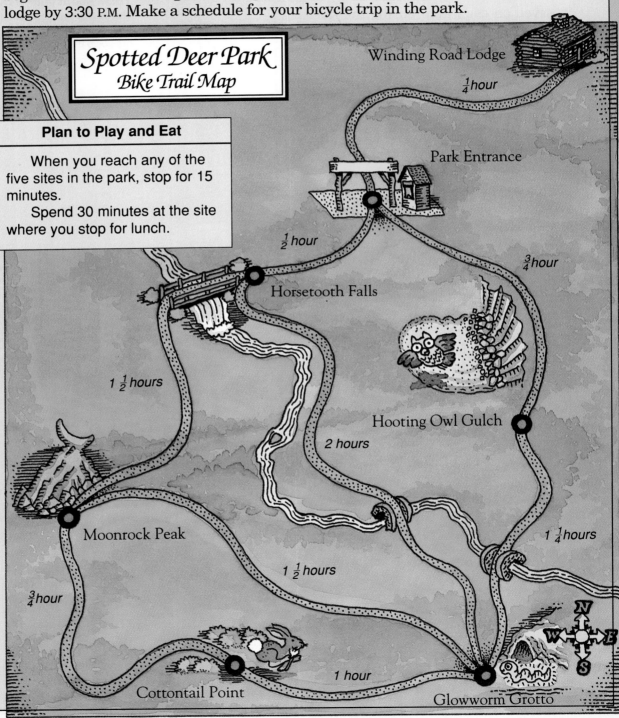

Spotted Deer Park
Bike Trail Map

Plan to Play and Eat

When you reach any of the five sites in the park, stop for 15 minutes.

Spend 30 minutes at the site where you stop for lunch.

Winding Road Lodge

$\frac{1}{4}$ hour

Park Entrance

$\frac{1}{2}$ hour

$\frac{3}{4}$ hour

Horsetooth Falls

$1\frac{1}{2}$ hours

2 hours

Hooting Owl Gulch

Moonrock Peak

$\frac{3}{4}$ hour

$1\frac{1}{2}$ hours

$1\frac{1}{4}$ hours

Cottontail Point

1 hour

Glowworm Grotto

394

Number-Sense Project

Look back at pages 384-385. Giving everyone an equal share is not always easy to do. Erwin and his two sisters received a package of things to be divided equally among them. What is his "equal share" in each case below?

a. 24 baseball cards

b. 5 dozen postcards

c. Two identical 12-inch strips of garden seeds

d. One $2 coupon to be used for a $5 pizza

Math-at-Home Activity

Take a survey of 12 people who live with or near you. Ask them which is the capital of Florida: Miami, Jacksonville, or Tallahassee.

Copy this circle. Make a circle graph of their answers. Use:
M or red for Miami,
J or blue for Jacksonville,
T or yellow for Tallahassee.

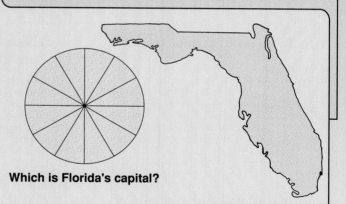

Which is Florida's capital?

Critical Thinking Activity

a. Who owns $\frac{1}{2}$ as much land as Michelle?

b. Who owns $\frac{1}{3}$ as much land as Christine?

c. Who owns $\frac{1}{3}$ as much land as Patrick?

b. Which two people together own $\frac{3}{8}$ of the land?

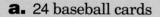

Michelle $\frac{1}{2}$		
Patrick $\frac{1}{4}$	Christine $\frac{1}{8}$	
	Paul $\frac{1}{24}$	Dorothy $\frac{2}{24}$

Mixed Numbers as Improper Fractions

Build Understanding

A. Sophia is having carpeting installed in her hallway. The hallway is $3\frac{1}{2}$ feet wide. How many $\frac{1}{2}$-foot-wide carpet tiles will fit across the hallway?

Think of a picture of the hallway.

Think: 1 is the same as 2 halves.

3 is the same as 6 halves.

So, $3\frac{1}{2}$ is the same as 7 halves.

The width of the hallway can be carpeted with 7 tiles that are $\frac{1}{2}$ foot wide.

B. Write $3\frac{1}{2}$ as an improper fraction.

$3\frac{1}{2} = 3 + \frac{1}{2}$

$\phantom{3\frac{1}{2}} = \frac{3}{1} + \frac{1}{2}$

$\phantom{3\frac{1}{2}} = \frac{6}{2} + \frac{1}{2}$

$\phantom{3\frac{1}{2}} = \frac{7}{2}$

C. Mental Math A shortcut can be used to change a mixed number to an improper fraction.

$5\frac{3}{4} = \frac{23}{4}$

■ **Write About Math** Explain why the shortcut in Example C works. Draw a picture to help you.

Check Understanding

For another example, see Set D, pages 408–409.

1. Write both a mixed number and an improper fraction for each lettered point.

Write each mixed number as an improper fraction.

2. $2\frac{3}{4}$ **3.** $1\frac{7}{8}$ **4.** $5\frac{2}{3}$ **5.** $4\frac{3}{5}$

Practice

For More Practice, see Set D, pages 410–411.

Write each mixed number as an improper fraction.

6. $4\frac{1}{6}$ **7.** $3\frac{1}{4}$ **8.** $5\frac{3}{8}$ **9.** $16\frac{2}{3}$ **10.** $8\frac{2}{9}$

11. $5\frac{3}{10}$ **12.** $3\frac{3}{7}$ **13.** $11\frac{2}{9}$ **14.** $21\frac{2}{5}$ **15.** $14\frac{1}{3}$

16. $12\frac{1}{2}$ **17.** $8\frac{3}{10}$ **18.** $12\frac{2}{6}$ **19.** $13\frac{1}{9}$ **20.** $9\frac{7}{7}$

Mixed Practice   Write a mixed number or a whole number for each fraction.

21. $\frac{17}{3}$ **22.** $\frac{13}{10}$ **23.** $\frac{25}{5}$ **24.** $\frac{28}{7}$ **25.** $\frac{21}{3}$

26. $\frac{33}{8}$ **27.** $\frac{16}{2}$ **28.** $\frac{25}{3}$ **29.** $\frac{29}{1}$ **30.** $\frac{21}{5}$

Problem Solving

Solve each problem.

31. When measuring a window for blinds, Sophia found that the window was $31\frac{3}{4}$ inches wide. Write $31\frac{3}{4}$ as an improper fraction.

32. When measuring a room for carpeting, Sophia found the room was 18 feet 5 inches long. Write 18 feet 5 inches as a mixed number. Write the mixed number as an improper fraction.

Critical Thinking   Answer each question.

33. Choose the answer that makes a true statement. Improper fractions are always

   a. greater than 0 and less than 1.
   b. greater than 1 and less than 10.
   c. greater than or equal to 1.
   d. greater than 10.

34. Which two statements are true about the product of a whole number that is not zero and an improper fraction?

   a. The product is between 0 and 1.
   b. The product is less than the whole number.
   c. The product is greater than or equal to the whole number.
   d. The product equals the improper fraction when the whole number is 1.

Multiplying Mixed Numbers

Build Understanding

A. To make a fishing pole, Mike uses $5\frac{2}{3}$ feet of line. How much line does he need for 6 fishing poles?

Since the same amount of line is used for each pole, multiply.

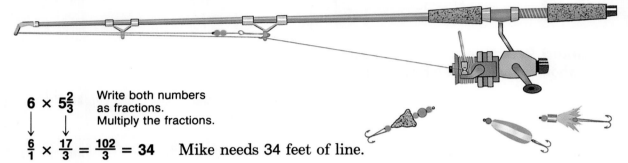

$6 \times 5\frac{2}{3}$ Write both numbers as fractions.
Multiply the fractions.

$\frac{6}{1} \times \frac{17}{3} = \frac{102}{3} = 34$ Mike needs 34 feet of line.

B. Find $5\frac{1}{2} \times 4\frac{2}{3}$.

$5\frac{1}{2} \times 4\frac{2}{3}$ Write both mixed numbers as fractions.

$\frac{11}{2} \times \frac{14}{3} = \frac{154}{6}$ Multiply.

$= 25\frac{4}{6}$

$= 25\frac{2}{3}$ Write the fraction in simplest form.

C. Estimation You can use estimation to check if your answer is reasonable. Estimate $5\frac{1}{2} \times 4\frac{2}{3}$.

$5\frac{1}{2}$ is between 5 and 6.

$4\frac{2}{3}$ is between 4 and 5.

Since $4 \times 5 = 20$ and $5 \times 6 = 30$, the product is between 20 and 30.

■ **Talk About Math** In Example A, how do you know, before you multiply, that the answer is greater than 30?

Check Understanding

For another example, see Set E, pages 408–409.

Complete. **Remember** to write the product in simplest form.

1. $\frac{3}{4} \times 1\frac{1}{2} = \frac{3}{4} \times \frac{⬚}{2} = \frac{⬚}{8} = ⬚$

2. $2\frac{1}{3} \times 3 = \frac{⬚}{3} \times \frac{⬚}{1} = \frac{⬚}{3} = ⬚$

3. $2\frac{3}{4} \times 1\frac{2}{3} = \frac{⬚}{4} \times \frac{⬚}{3} = \frac{⬚}{12} = ⬚$

4. $4 \times 3\frac{2}{5} = \frac{⬚}{1} \times \frac{⬚}{5} = \frac{⬚}{⬚} = ⬚$

5. $\frac{2}{3} \times 6\frac{1}{2} = \frac{⬚}{⬚} \times \frac{⬚}{2} = \frac{⬚}{⬚} = ⬚$

6. $1\frac{2}{5} \times 3\frac{3}{4} = \frac{⬚}{⬚} \times \frac{⬚}{⬚} = \frac{⬚}{⬚} = ⬚$

398

Practice

For More Practice, see Set E, pages 410–411.

Multiply. **Remember** to estimate to be sure your answer is reasonable.

7. $3\frac{3}{5} \times 6\frac{1}{2}$ **8.** $2\frac{4}{5} \times 7$ **9.** $\frac{3}{4} \times 5\frac{1}{6}$ **10.** $2 \times 4\frac{5}{6}$ **11.** $3 \times 2\frac{5}{7}$

12. $4\frac{1}{3} \times 1\frac{2}{3}$ **13.** $6\frac{1}{8} \times 2\frac{2}{5}$ **14.** $5 \times 5\frac{4}{5}$ **15.** $10 \times 3\frac{2}{7}$ **16.** $\frac{1}{3} \times 6\frac{2}{3}$

17. $4\frac{3}{4} \times 2\frac{3}{8}$ **18.** $2 \times 4\frac{1}{5}$ **19.** $3 \times 2\frac{2}{3}$ **20.** $1\frac{1}{2} \times 4$ **21.** $5\frac{1}{2} \times 5\frac{1}{8} \times \frac{3}{4}$

Mixed Practice   Multiply. **Remember** to write the product in simplest form.

22. $\frac{3}{8} \times \frac{1}{4}$ **23.** $12 \times \frac{5}{6}$ **24.** $9 \times 2\frac{4}{9}$ **25.** $2\frac{1}{3} \times 1\frac{4}{5}$ **26.** $14 \times 4\frac{5}{7}$

Problem Solving

Solve each problem.

27. Mike has $4\frac{1}{2}$ bags of bread crumbs. Each full bag weighs $2\frac{3}{4}$ pounds. How many pounds of bread crumbs does Mike have?

28. Mike gave $\frac{1}{2}$ of a $20\frac{5}{8}$-ounce fish to his uncle. How much did his uncle's portion weigh?

29. Number Sense   Is the product $2\frac{1}{8} \times 4\frac{1}{6}$ greater than or less than 8?

30. Number Sense   Is the product $3\frac{7}{8} \times 6\frac{4}{5}$ closer to 18 or to 28?

Explore _____ Math

Find each product.

31. $\frac{3}{8} \times \frac{8}{3}$ **32.** $7 \times \frac{1}{7}$ **33.** $1\frac{2}{3} \times \frac{3}{5}$ **34.** $\frac{4}{25} \times 6\frac{1}{4}$

35. What pattern do you notice for each product?

Numbers whose product is 1 are called ***reciprocals***.
Find the reciprocal of each number.

36. $\frac{3}{5}$ **37.** $\frac{7}{3}$ **38.** $6\frac{2}{3}$ **39.** $5\frac{3}{4}$

Use Data from a Table

Build Understanding

PROBLEM SOLVING GUIDE

Length	Weight	Time
1 foot = 12 inches 1 yard = 3 feet 1 mile = 5,280 feet	1 pound = 16 ounces 1 ton = 2,000 pounds	1 minute = 60 seconds 1 hour = 60 minutes 1 day = 24 hours

Understand
QUESTION
FACTS
KEY IDEA

Plan and Solve
STRATEGY
ANSWER

Look Back
SENSIBLE ANSWER
ALTERNATE APPROACH

An Asian elephant weighs about $3\frac{1}{2}$ tons. It normally walks at 4 miles per hour. It can run at 25 miles per hour. What is the weight of the elephant in pounds?

Understand QUESTION How many pounds does an Asian elephant weigh?

FACTS An elephant weighs $3\frac{1}{2}$ tons.

KEY IDEA Use data from the table of weights to find the number of pounds in one ton. For $3\frac{1}{2}$ tons, there will be $3\frac{1}{2}$ times the number of pounds in one ton.

Plan and Solve Since 1 ton is 2,000 pounds, $3\frac{1}{2}$ tons will be $3\frac{1}{2} \times 2,000$ pounds.

Elephants are classified as an endangered species.

Paper and Pencil

$$3\frac{1}{2} \times 2,000 = \frac{7}{2} \times \frac{2,000}{1}$$
$$= 7,000$$

Calculator

3.5 ⊠ 2000 ⊟ *7000.*

An Asian elephant weighs about 7,000 pounds.

Look Back Estimate $3\frac{1}{2} \times 2,000$. $3\frac{1}{2}$ is between 3 and 4. $3 \times 2,000 = 6,000$ and $4 \times 2,000 = 8,000$. The answer is reasonable.

■ **Write About Math** What information from the tables would you use to find the weight of the elephant in ounces? Write a number sentence.

400

Check Understanding

1. An Asian elephant carried a load of logs for $1\frac{3}{4}$ miles. Find the distance in feet.

   $1\frac{3}{4}$ miles $= 1\frac{3}{4} \times$ ▦ feet

   $\qquad\qquad = $ ▦ feet

2. The elephant took $\frac{3}{4}$ hour to walk this distance. Find the time in minutes.

   $\frac{3}{4}$ hour $= \frac{3}{4} \times$ ▦ minutes

   $\qquad\qquad = $ ▦ minutes

Practice

3. If an elephant walks 4 miles per hour, how far can it walk in $3\frac{5}{6}$ hours?

4. Bennie the elephant is $8\frac{2}{3}$ feet tall. What is his height in inches?

5. An elephant worked for $2\frac{2}{5}$ hours lifting logs. How many minutes was this? How many seconds was this?

6. If each elephant can carry up to 600 pounds of cargo, how many elephants are needed to carry 3,400 pounds of cargo?

7. A mother elephant weighed 6,200 pounds. This was 3,700 pounds more than her baby's weight. Find the baby's weight.

8. **Calculator** At 25 miles per hour, how many feet would an elephant run in 1 hour? How many feet would it run in 1 minute?

Choose a ——— Strategy

Roses for Everyone Jill cut some roses from her garden. James cut a dozen roses and gave $\frac{1}{2}$ of them to Jill. Then Jill gave Janelle $\frac{1}{2}$ of all the roses she had. When Jill gave Pedro 5 roses, she only had 1 left. How many roses did Jill have originally?

9. How many roses would Jill have if Pedro returned the roses?

10. If Janelle then returned her roses how many roses would Jill have?

11. If James took his roses back, how many roses would Jill have?

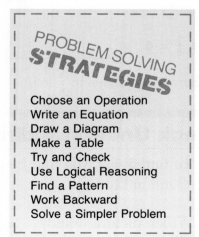

PROBLEM SOLVING STRATEGIES

Choose an Operation
Write an Equation
Draw a Diagram
Make a Table
Try and Check
Use Logical Reasoning
Find a Pattern
Work Backward
Solve a Simpler Problem

Exploring Division by Fractions

Build Understanding

A. Ben is packing lunches for his friends. He has 5 oranges. He wants to put $\frac{1}{2}$ orange into each lunch. How many lunches can have $\frac{1}{2}$ orange?

To find how many halves are in 5, divide 5 by $\frac{1}{2}$.

Use a picture to help.

$5 \div \frac{1}{2} = 10$

Ben can put $\frac{1}{2}$ orange in 10 lunches.

B. Each slice of a loaf of bread is $\frac{1}{8}$ of the loaf. How many slices are in $\frac{1}{2}$ loaf? Find how many eighths are in $\frac{1}{2}$.

Use a picture to help.

$\frac{1}{2} \div \frac{1}{8} = 4$

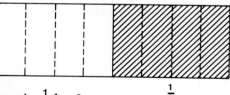

There are 4 slices in $\frac{1}{2}$ loaf.

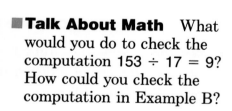

■ **Talk About Math** What would you do to check the computation $153 \div 17 = 9$? How could you check the computation in Example B?

Check Understanding

For another example, see Set F, pages 408–409.

1. To find $3 \div \frac{1}{2}$, you find how many ▦ are in ▦.

2. To find $\frac{1}{2} \div \frac{1}{4}$, you find how many ▦ are in ▦.

3. Which picture would help you to find how many eighths are in $\frac{1}{4}$, or $\frac{1}{4} \div \frac{1}{8}$?

a. 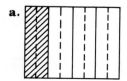   **b.**    **c.**

402

Practice

For More Practice, see Set F, pages 410–411.

Use the pictures to complete the divisions.

4.

How many thirds are in 3?

$3 \div \frac{1}{3} = $ ▦

5.

How many fourths are in 2?

$2 \div \frac{1}{4} = $ ▦

6.

How many halves are in 5?

$5 \div \frac{1}{2} = $ ▦

7.

How many thirds are in 4?

$4 \div \frac{1}{3} = $ ▦

8.

How many sixths are in $\frac{1}{2}$?

$\frac{1}{2} \div \frac{1}{6} = $ ▦

9.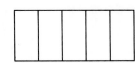

How many fifths are in $\frac{3}{5}$?

$\frac{3}{5} \div \frac{1}{5} = $ ▦

Write a division sentence for each picture.

10.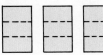

11.

12.

Problem Solving

Use a picture to solve each problem.

13. Alice has 3 melons. She wants to serve $\frac{1}{4}$ melon to each guest. How many guests will get $\frac{1}{4}$ melon?

14. There is $\frac{1}{3}$ of a meat loaf left. Bill has cut it so that each piece is $\frac{1}{12}$ of the original meat loaf. How many pieces does Bill have?

Reading ———— Math

Following Examples

1. In Example A, how many oranges were being divided?

2. By what number was the number of oranges being divided?

3. What was the answer?

Choose an Operation

Build Understanding

Stores often have sales to attract customers. They offer a discount that reduces the price of items they sell. What is the sale price of a shirt that regularly costs $18?

Understand How much will the shirt cost on sale? The regular price is $18 and $\frac{1}{3}$ of that price will be taken off $18. The amount taken off is called the discount.

Understand
QUESTION
FACTS
KEY IDEA

Plan and Solve
STRATEGY
ANSWER

Look Back
SENSIBLE ANSWER
ALTERNATE APPROACH

**Plan and Solve** STRATEGY First find the amount of the discount. Find $\frac{1}{3}$ of 18.

$$\frac{1}{3} \times 18 = \frac{1}{3} \times \frac{18}{1} = \frac{18}{3} = 6$$

The amount of the discount is $6.

To find the sale price, subtract the discount from the regular price.

```
$ 1 8    regular price
-   6    discount
$ 1 2    sale price
```

ANSWER The sale price of the shirt is $12.

Look Back The answer is reasonable since the sale price should be less than the regular price, and $12 is less than $18.

■ **Talk About Math** If the discount is $\frac{1}{3}$, the sale price is $\frac{2}{3}$ of the regular price. Find $\frac{2}{3}$ of $18. Is the answer the same as above?

Check Understanding

The regular price of a pair of running shoes is $24.

1. What is $\frac{1}{4}$ of $24?

2. What is the amount of the discount?

3. What is the sale price?

Practice

4. Appliances are selling for $\frac{1}{4}$ off. The original price of a stove was $456. What is the amount of discount and the sale price?

5. Jeff bought a parka for $\frac{1}{3}$ off the original price, which was $36. How much was the discount? What was the sale price?

6. Originally, a pearl necklace cost $65 and a pair of earrings cost $15. Both items were on sale for $\frac{1}{4}$ off. How much would it cost for the necklace and earrings on sale?

7. Mr. Clark bought an oil filter that originally cost $14.25 for his car. The filter was marked $\frac{1}{3}$ off. How much change did he get from $10.00?

8. Fred bought a jacket on sale for $\frac{1}{3}$ off. The original price was $75. The sales tax was $0.06 on each dollar. What was the total amount Fred paid for the jacket?

9. The sale price of a sofa is $180. The original price was $240. How much is the discount? What fraction of the original price is saved?

Use Data   Refer to Problems 40–45 on page 393. Find the sale price.

10. Sweater   11. Coat   12. Gloves   13. Watch   14. Boots   15. Jeans

Choose a ———— Strategy

16. *Teamwork*   Ruth, Linda, Karen, and Marlene are each on a different team—volleyball, soccer, swimming, and tennis. Ruth is older than the volleyball player. The volleyball player, the tennis player, and Marlene all live on the same street. Linda is the only one who knows how to swim.

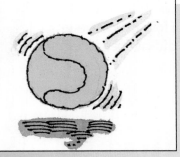

Problem-Solving Review

Solve each problem.

1. Three melons cost $2. Paul bought 2 melons. How much did he pay?

2. Of the 30 students in a play, $\frac{5}{6}$ had speaking parts. How many students had speaking parts?

3. Together Joy and James picked $13\frac{5}{8}$ pounds of blueberries. If they divided the amount of berries equally, how many pounds did each person get?

4. Larry lost $2\frac{1}{2}$ pounds per week for 6 weeks. How much weight did he lose in all?

5. Mira rode her horse for 2 hours and 20 minutes. If she rode $4\frac{1}{2}$ miles per hour, how far did she ride?

6. A protoceratops was 6 feet long. Its eggs were about 8 inches long. How many times as long as its egg was the protoceratops?

7. **Data File** Jolene wants to sew 3 pairs of shorts for her brother. Using the information on pages 528-529, find the amount of fabric and the amount of braid trim she must buy.

8. **Make a Data File**
For one day, estimate the quantity of food you eat and drink. Use a chart that shows the number of calories in various foods. Find the number of calories you consumed in one day.

Explore with a Calculator

"Fraction Tags"

1. The clerks at Merchandise Plus marked each item with a red sale tag. Joan used her calculator to find the discount and the sale price.

Joan wants to buy a coat selling at $\frac{1}{4}$ off the regular price of $32. Find the sale price.

Press:	*Display:*	
MRC MRC		Clears calculator
32 M+	M 32.	Stores regular price in memory
÷ 4 =	M 8.	Finds $\frac{1}{4}$ of 32 (amount of discount)
M−	M 8.	Subtracts discount from regular price
MRC	M 24.	Recalls sale price from memory

2. Use your calculator to find the discount and sale price for a

a. suit.

b. skirt.

c. jacket.

d. pair of shoes.

Reteaching

Set A pages 386–387

Draw a picture to find
$\frac{1}{3}$ of $\frac{3}{4}$.

First shade $\frac{3}{4}$.   Next shade $\frac{1}{3}$ of that.

Of the 12 parts in the second picture,
3 parts are shaded twice.

$\frac{1}{3}$ of $\frac{3}{4}$ is $\frac{3}{12}$, or $\frac{1}{4}$.

Remember to write the product in simplest form.

Use the picture to find the product.

1. $\frac{1}{2}$ of $\frac{2}{3}$

2. $\frac{3}{4}$ of $\frac{3}{5}$

Set B pages 388–389

Find $\frac{7}{8}$ of $\frac{4}{5}$.

To multiply fractions, multiply the numerators and multiply the denominators. Write the answer in simplest form.

$$\frac{7}{8} \times \frac{4}{5} = \frac{7 \times 4}{8 \times 5}$$
$$= \frac{28}{40} \text{ or } \frac{7}{10}$$

Remember that the product of two fractions is less than 1 if both fractions are less than 1.

Multiply.

1. $\frac{3}{5} \times \frac{3}{4}$ 2. $\frac{1}{8} \times \frac{5}{6}$

3. $\frac{7}{8} \times \frac{2}{5}$ 4. $\frac{3}{4} \times \frac{3}{4}$

Set C pages 390–393

Find $\frac{3}{8}$ of 18.

$\frac{3}{8}$ of 18 means $\frac{3}{8} \times 18$.

Multiply the fractions.

$$\frac{3}{8} \times \frac{18}{1} = \frac{54}{8} \qquad \text{Think: } 8\overline{)54}$$
$$= 6\frac{6}{8}$$
$$= 6\frac{3}{4}$$

Remember that any whole number can be written as a fraction with the whole number as the numerator and 1 as the denominator.

Multiply. Remember to write the product in simplest form.

1. $\frac{5}{6} \times 18$ 2. $\frac{3}{7} \times 21$

3. $9 \times \frac{3}{4}$ 4. $12 \times \frac{2}{5}$

5. $16 \times \frac{3}{8}$ 6. $\frac{3}{10} \times 22$

Set D   pages 396–397

Write $4\frac{3}{5}$ as an improper fraction.

$4\frac{3}{5} = 4 + \frac{3}{5}$

$\quad = \frac{4}{1} + \frac{3}{5}$

Rename $\frac{4}{1}$ with a denominator of 5 so it can be added to $\frac{3}{5}$.

$\quad = \frac{20}{5} + \frac{3}{5}$

$\quad = \frac{23}{5}$

Remember that when you write a mixed number as an improper fraction, you can check by writing the improper fraction as a mixed number.

Write each mixed number as an improper fraction.

1. $5\frac{1}{8}$ **2.** $9\frac{3}{5}$

3. $12\frac{3}{4}$ **4.** $16\frac{2}{3}$

Set E   pages 398–399

Find $3\frac{2}{3} \times 4\frac{1}{2}$.

To multiply with mixed numbers, write the mixed numbers as improper fractions.

$3\frac{2}{3} \times 4\frac{1}{2} = \frac{11}{3} \times \frac{9}{2}$

$\quad = \frac{99}{6}$

$\quad = 16\frac{3}{6}$

$\quad = 16\frac{1}{2}$

Remember that you should estimate to check if your answer is reasonable.

Multiply.

1. $2\frac{1}{2} \times 4\frac{1}{5}$ **2.** $4\frac{2}{5} \times 6$

3. $8\frac{1}{3} \times 4\frac{1}{6}$ **4.** $\frac{1}{3} \times 6\frac{1}{2}$

5. $6\frac{3}{5} \times 1\frac{2}{3}$ **6.** $\frac{1}{4} \times 8\frac{1}{2}$

7. $10 \times 4\frac{3}{5}$ **8.** $2 \times 6\frac{7}{8}$

Set F   pages 402–403

How many eighths are in 3?

Find $3 \div \frac{1}{8}$.

Draw squares to show 3 and divide each into 8 equal parts.

Count the total number of parts. So $3 \div \frac{1}{8} = 24$.

Remember that you can check the answer when dividing by multiplying the quotient by the divisor. This number should be equal to the dividend.

Use the pictures to complete the divisions.

1.   **2.**

How many fourths are in 3?   How many fifths are in 4?

$3 \div \frac{1}{4} = $ ▦ $4 \div \frac{1}{5} = $ ▦

409

More Practice

Set A   pages 386–387

Use the pictures to find the product.

1. $\frac{2}{3}$ of $\frac{3}{5}$

   $\frac{2}{3} \times \frac{3}{5}$

2. $\frac{3}{4}$ of $\frac{4}{5}$

   $\frac{3}{4} \times \frac{4}{5}$

3. $\frac{2}{3}$ of $\frac{4}{5}$

   $\frac{2}{3} \times \frac{4}{5}$

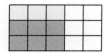 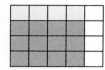 

Write a number sentence that states what each picture shows.

4.

5.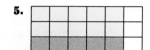

6.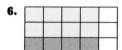

Draw a picture to find each product.

7. $\frac{1}{2}$ of $\frac{1}{3}$

   $\frac{1}{2} \times \frac{1}{3}$

8. $\frac{1}{3}$ of $\frac{1}{6}$

   $\frac{1}{3} \times \frac{1}{6}$

9. $\frac{3}{4}$ of $\frac{3}{5}$

   $\frac{3}{4} \times \frac{3}{5}$

10. $\frac{1}{4}$ of $\frac{2}{5}$

    $\frac{1}{4} \times \frac{2}{5}$

Set B   pages 388–389

Multiply.

1. $\frac{1}{4} \times \frac{1}{6}$

2. $\frac{3}{4} \times \frac{3}{8}$

3. $\frac{2}{3} \times \frac{7}{8}$

4. $\frac{2}{5} \times \frac{2}{3}$

5. $\frac{5}{6} \times \frac{3}{4}$

6. $\frac{7}{8} \times \frac{3}{4}$

7. $\frac{5}{12} \times \frac{1}{3}$

8. $\frac{1}{8} \times \frac{5}{6}$

Set C   pages 390–393

Multiply. **Remember** to write the product in simplest form.

1. $\frac{1}{3} \times 21$

2. $\frac{3}{4} \times 16$

3. $24 \times \frac{7}{8}$

4. $\frac{1}{6} \times 42$

5. $\frac{2}{5} \times 20$

6. $\frac{2}{3} \times 8$

7. $\frac{5}{6} \times 10$

8. $\frac{3}{8} \times 48$

Mental Math   Use mental math to find each product.

9. $\frac{1}{5} \times 25$

10. $\frac{7}{8} \times 80$

11. $6 \times \frac{1}{3} \times 8$

12. $\frac{1}{5} \times 12 \times 10$

Estimation   Estimate each product.

13. $\frac{1}{5} \times 97$

14. $\frac{2}{3} \times 58$

15. $\frac{1}{4} \times 76$

16. $\frac{1}{6} \times 29$

Set D pages 396–397

Write each mixed number as an improper fraction.

1. $8\frac{1}{3}$ **2.** $5\frac{1}{4}$ **3.** $7\frac{2}{5}$ **4.** $9\frac{1}{6}$ **5.** $12\frac{2}{3}$ **6.** $14\frac{3}{5}$

Mixed Practice Write a mixed number or a whole number for each fraction.

7. $\frac{18}{7}$ **8.** $\frac{21}{4}$ **9.** $\frac{32}{8}$ **10.** $\frac{63}{7}$ **11.** $\frac{37}{5}$ **12.** $\frac{18}{1}$

Set E pages 398–399

Multiply. **Remember** to estimate to be sure your answer is reasonable.

1. $2\frac{1}{2} \times 1\frac{2}{3}$ **2.** $4\frac{1}{2} \times 1\frac{7}{8}$ **3.** $1\frac{2}{3} \times 3\frac{3}{4}$ **4.** $\frac{3}{4} \times 4\frac{1}{4}$

5. $9\frac{1}{6} \times 8\frac{3}{5}$ **6.** $4\frac{2}{3} \times 3\frac{5}{8}$ **7.** $3\frac{1}{10} \times 5$ **8.** $6\frac{3}{8} \times 5\frac{1}{5}$

Mixed Practice Multiply. **Remember** to write the product in simplest form.

9. $\frac{1}{6} \times \frac{5}{8}$ **10.** $20 \times \frac{4}{5}$ **11.** $\frac{3}{10} \times \frac{5}{6}$ **12.** $16 \times 2\frac{1}{8}$

13. $\frac{1}{3} \times 2\frac{1}{6}$ **14.** $\frac{5}{6} \times 15$ **15.** $\frac{4}{5} \times \frac{7}{8}$ **16.** $1\frac{1}{8} \times 2\frac{4}{7}$

Set F pages 402–403

Use the pictures to complete the divisions.

1.  **2.**   **3.**

How many fourths are in 5?

$5 \div \frac{1}{4} = $ ▦

How many eighths are in 2?

$2 \div \frac{1}{8} = $ ▦

How many sixths are in $\frac{1}{2}$?

$\frac{1}{2} \div \frac{1}{6} = $ ▦

Write a division sentence for each picture.

4.   **5.**   **6.**

Enrichment

Shortcut in Multiplying Fractions

You can use a shortcut to find $\frac{3}{4} \times \frac{6}{7}$.

Carl multiplied like this.

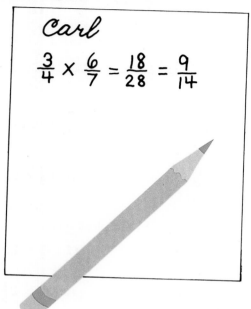

Clyde used a shortcut to multiply.

He divided one numerator and one denominator by the same number, 2.

Here is another example of how to use the shortcut.

$$5 \div 5$$

$$\overset{1}{\cancel{5}} \times \frac{6}{\underset{5}{\cancel{25}}} = \frac{6}{35}$$

$$25 \div 5$$

Multiply. Use the shortcut.

1. $\frac{2}{3} \times \frac{1}{4}$
2. $\frac{4}{7} \times \frac{3}{4}$
3. $\frac{3}{4} \times \frac{1}{3}$
4. $\frac{4}{7} \times \frac{5}{12}$
5. $\frac{3}{10} \times \frac{5}{8}$

6. $\frac{1}{2} \times \frac{2}{3}$
7. $\frac{1}{6} \times \frac{4}{5}$
8. $\frac{5}{12} \times \frac{8}{9}$
9. $\frac{9}{10} \times \frac{7}{15}$
10. $\frac{7}{25} \times \frac{10}{11}$

11. $\frac{6}{7} \times \frac{5}{9}$
12. $\frac{5}{6} \times \frac{4}{7}$
13. $\frac{5}{6} \times 12$
14. $24 \times \frac{3}{8}$
15. $16 \times \frac{3}{4}$

Chapter 12 Review/Test

1. Write a number sentence that states what the picture shows.

Multiply.

2. $\frac{1}{2} \times \frac{5}{6}$ **3.** $\frac{1}{8} \times \frac{1}{8}$

4. $\frac{2}{3} \times 24$ **5.** $\frac{1}{3} \times 7$

6. $7\frac{1}{2} \times \frac{1}{5}$ **7.** $3\frac{1}{3} \times 1\frac{3}{4}$

Write each mixed number as an improper fraction.

8. $3\frac{1}{6}$ **9.** $2\frac{3}{8}$

10. Use the picture to answer the question.

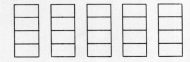

How many fourths are in 5?

11. If you find the product of two fractions, each less than 1, will the product be less than or greater than 1?

Solve each problem.

12. George has 5 quarts of juice. He will serve each guest $\frac{1}{4}$ quart of juice. How many guests will get $\frac{1}{4}$ quart of juice?

13. In one class, $\frac{1}{3}$ of the students are in the band. Of these students, $\frac{1}{2}$ are also in the chorus. What fraction of the students are in both the band and the chorus?

14. Use the table below to solve the problem.

1 minute = 60 seconds
1 hour = 60 minutes
1 day = 24 hours

A sailboat makes a trip that lasts $2\frac{1}{2}$ days. How many hours is this?

Read the problem below. Then answer the question.

Jeffry bought a sweater on sale for $\frac{1}{3}$ off. The original price was $27. How much change did he receive from $30?

15. Which of the following statements is true?

a. The discount is $27.

b. The discount is $\frac{1}{3}$ of $27.

c. The discounted price is $27.

16. **Write About Math**   How do you find the product of two fractions?

413

Statistics, Graphing, and Probability

13

Number-Sense Project

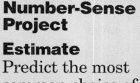

Estimate
Predict the most common choice of a pet by people who live in in a city.

Gather Data
Show 5 people a list of pets and ask them what their first choice would be if they lived in a city.

Analyze and Report
Write several sentences to compare your prediction with the data you collected. Compare your results with those of other students.

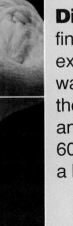

Did You Know: A poll was taken to find the most popular choice for an exotic pet. The most common choice was a monkey, second was a lion, and there was a tie between an elephant and a tiger for third place. More than 60 animals were named, even a skunk, a hyena, and an alligator.

415

Collecting Data

Build Understanding

What subjects do you think students like best?

In a national survey, students named their favorite subject. The results, in order, were math, science, gym, and art. Carmen wondered whether students in her school would choose the same subjects in the same order.

 **Understand**

QUESTION   How can Carmen collect data that she can compare with the results of the national survey?

FACTS   She knows the national survey results and which subjects are taught in her school.

KEY IDEA   Carmen could survey all the students in her school. Or she could ask a *sample*, a small number of students. In a random sample, all students have an equal chance of being chosen.

Plan and Solve   Carmen chose four students from each room by drawing their names from a hat. She asked them, "What is your favorite subject?" She recorded the results in a frequency table.

Favorite subject	Tally	Number of students
Math	### ### ### ///	18
Science	### ### ////	14
Gym	### ### ### ### ////	24
Art	### /	6
Reading	### ### ###	15
Social Studies	### ///	8

She ordered her data. In order, the favorites were gym, math, reading, and science. Her results differed from those in the national survey.

Look Back   Are the frequencies and ordering correct?

PROBLEM SOLVING
GUIDE

Understand
QUESTION
FACTS
KEY IDEA

Plan and Solve
STRATEGY
ANSWER

Look Back
SENSIBLE ANSWER
ALTERNATE APPROACH

■ **Talk About Math** Suppose Carmen had counted smiles during a lesson in each subject. Would that have been a good way to collect data? Why or why not? When could observation be used to collect data?

Check Understanding

1. Why do you think Carmen decided to survey only some students?

2. Why should a sample be chosen randomly?

3. How might the results have differed if Carmen had surveyed only fifth graders?

4. How might the results have differed if Carmen had surveyed all students?

5. How might the results have differed if students had chosen from a list of subjects?

Practice

For each item, tell whom you would survey and the question you would ask.

6. Favorite sport of students in your state

7. Favorite pet of people in your community

8. Favorite color of students in your class

9. Favorite food of students in your school

Choose a ———— Strategy

The Mummies Have It!

10. The class voted on what to see at the museum. Each student had one vote. Jewelry got 5 votes. Costumes got 9 votes. The mummies won by getting 6 votes more than the runner-up. These 6 votes were $\frac{1}{5}$ of all the votes cast. Sculpture got the rest of the votes. How large is the class? How many votes did each kind of exhibit get?

Organizing Data

Build Understanding

What kind of job would you like after you finish school?

A. Aki collected data for a social studies report on new jobs expected to be available in the year 2000. With her data, she prepared a table to display the information.

After looking at the table, Aki saw that she could display her information better if she put it into a *bar graph.* A bar graph is one way to display information using numbers. The display helps you to compare quantities easily. How would you find the number of new jobs in food services from the graph?

Find the bar for food services. Move down from the end of the bar to the number on the horizontal scale.

What Kind of Job...

Type of Job	Number of New Jobs
Health Offices	1,400,000
Personnel	832,000
Food Services	2,500,000
Construction	890,000
Nursing	852,000

Where the New Jobs Will Be

Health Offices

Personnel

Food Services

Construction

Nursing

| 0 | 0.5 | 1 | 1.5 | 2 | 2.5 |

Number of Jobs (in millions)

Preferred Jobs

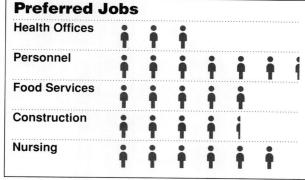

Health Offices

Personnel

Food Services

Construction

Nursing

Each 🚶 stands for two students.

B. Stella asked 50 students which of these jobs they preferred. The *pictograph* shows the results. A pictograph is another way to display quantities. It uses pictures or symbols.

How many students prefer personnel work?

Since 🚶 stands for two students, ╻ stands for one student.

There were 13 students who preferred personnel work.

c. Earl wants to find a restaurant job in Rocky City. Rocky City is a ski resort that also has a famous summer music festival. The ***broken-line graph*** shows the number of restaurant jobs available throughout the year in Rocky City.

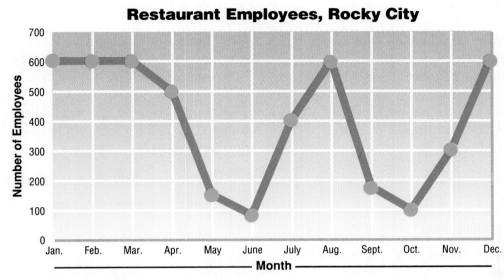

Restaurant Employees, Rocky City

About how many people are employed in Rocky City restaurants in August?

Find August on the horizontal scale. Move straight up to the point on the grid. From that point, move along the grid line straight across to the vertical scale.

About 600 people work in Rocky City restaurants in August.

A broken-line graph can show how quantities change over time. Only the graph points, and not the line segments in between, show data.

■ **Talk About Math** Would you use a broken-line graph to compare the salaries for different jobs? Explain.

Check Understanding

For another example, see Set A, pages 444-445.

Use the graphs in Examples A, B, and C.

1. How many more of the students surveyed preferred nursing over construction work?

2. Could you use a pictograph instead of a bar graph for the data in Example A? Explain.

3. Could you use a broken-line graph instead of the pictograph in Example B? Explain.

4. Does the graph in Example C show how many people worked in Rocky City restaurants May 1-8? Explain.

5. How many more people worked in Rocky City restaurants in April than in May?

6. How many fewer people worked in Rocky City restaurants in October than in August?

Practice

For More Practice, see Set A, pages 446-447.

Answer the questions.

7. This graph shows how many years of school are needed for some jobs. Which kind of work takes the longest time in school?

8. Which jobs need the least time in school?

9. How many more years of school does a veterinarian need than a dental hygienist?

10. What kind of graph would best show how the number of students who work part time has increased over the years?

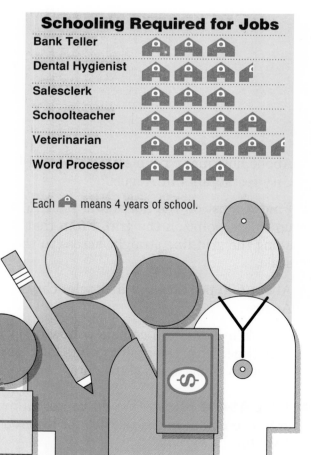

Schooling Required for Jobs

Bank Teller

Dental Hygienist

Salesclerk

Schoolteacher

Veterinarian

Word Processor

Each 🏠 means 4 years of school.

11. The weekly incomes for five types of work are as follows: Construction, $450; Mining, $531; Factory, $406; Transportation, $472; Trade, $365. Organize these data into a table. What kind of graph would you use to show these data? Why?

12. Five after-school jobs were listed in the school paper. Seven students applied for baby-sitting, 3 for dog walking, 15 for lawn mowing, 8 for newspaper delivery, and 2 for weeding. Put these data into a table. What kind of graph would you use to show the data? Why?

13. Make a graph to show the data given in Problem 11.

14. Make a graph to show the data given in Problem 12.

15. This table shows the weekly incomes for the jobs listed in Problem 12. What kind of graph would you use to show the data? Why?

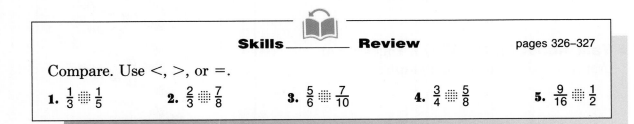

Type of Work	Baby-Sitting	Dog Walking	Lawn Mowing	Newspaper Delivery	Weeding
Weekly Salary	$12	$10	$24	$18	$16

16. Make a graph to show the data given in Problem 15.

Problem Solving

Solve these problems.

17. Number Sense In Example C, during which month were there twice as many restaurant workers as the month before?

18. Critical Thinking In Example B, about half the students Stella surveyed were female. Does this fact mean that 6 of the 12 students who chose nursing were females? Explain.

Skills ——— **Review**   pages 326–327

Compare. Use <, >, or =.

1. $\frac{1}{3} \ \vdots\vdots \ \frac{1}{5}$ **2.** $\frac{2}{3} \ \vdots\vdots \ \frac{7}{8}$ **3.** $\frac{5}{6} \ \vdots\vdots \ \frac{7}{10}$ **4.** $\frac{3}{4} \ \vdots\vdots \ \frac{5}{8}$ **5.** $\frac{9}{16} \ \vdots\vdots \ \frac{1}{2}$

Making a Broken-Line Graph

Build Understanding

ACTIVITY

Check the Census Counts
Materials: Ruler, grid paper

How can you tell if the number of people in your community is growing?

Every ten years the people of the United States are counted by the Bureau of the Census. This population census tells the size and other characteristics of the population. How has the size of the population of your community changed over the last 40 years?

a. *Gather data* Obtain the results of the population censuses for your community from 1950 to 1990. Ask for the data at a public library or a government office.

b. Write a title for the graph.

c. Put the years on the horizontal scale. Label the scale.

d. Decide how to round the numbers.

e. Choose numbers for the vertical scale. Be sure the smallest and largest numbers of the data fit on the graph. Write the numbers for the scale and label it.

f. Plot the points and connect them.

g. What trend does the graph show?

■ **Talk About Math** Why is this kind of graph called a broken-line graph?

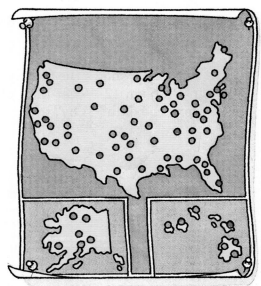
The year 1990 was the 200th anniversary of the population census in the U.S.

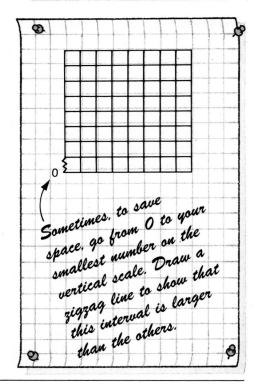
0

Sometimes, to save space, go from 0 to your smallest number on the vertical scale. Draw a zigzag line to show that this interval is larger than the others.

Check Understanding

For another example, see Set B, pages 444–445.

Use your data and graph.

1. What is the size of the first interval on the vertical scale?

2. What is the size of the other intervals on the vertical scale?

3. Does the graph show the size of the population in 1965? Explain your answer.

4. Would a broken-line graph best show the difference in the sizes of the 1970 and 1990 populations?

Practice

For More Practice, see Set B, pages 446–447.

Use the table below to make two broken-line graphs showing the following. **Remember** to draw a zigzag line on the population scale to save space.

5. Size of the U.S. population, aged 5-17 years, 1960-2010, rounded to the nearest million

6. Size of the total U.S. population, 1960-2010, rounded to the nearest ten million

U S Population (in millions), 1960-2010*						
Age Range	1960	1970	1980	1990*	2000*	2010*
5-17 years	44.2	52.6	47.2	45.6	48.8	45.7
All Ages	180.7	205.1	227.8	250.4	268.3	282.6

* projected data for 1990-2010

7. How has the population changed in the 5-17 year age range since 1960?

8. Has the size of the total population changed in the same way?

Problem Solving

Read for the facts to solve the problems.

9. The Census Bureau estimated that 1,041,400 U.S. residents were touring foreign countries on May 1, 1988. Of these, 209,900 were in Canada and 203,100 were in Mexico. How many tourists were visiting other countries on that day?

10. Use the table above. How many people does the Census Bureau expect will be living in the United States in 2010? What is the projected increase in U.S. population from 1990 to 2010?

Reading and Interpreting a Line Graph

Build Understanding

Have you ever tried to estimate how long it would take you to finish reading a book?

A **line graph** shows the rate at which something happens. This line graph shows how many book pages Ron reads in 1 hour, 2 hours, and so on, when he is reading for his own enjoyment. At this rate, how long will it take Ron to read 30 pages?

On the graph, follow the dotted line from 30 pages to the right until it meets the blue line. Follow the dotted line down from that point to the hours at the bottom.

At this rate, Ron will spend $1\frac{1}{2}$ hours reading 30 pages of his book.

Ron's Reading for Enjoyment Rate

■ **Talk About Math** How is a line graph different from a broken-line graph? How are the two kinds of graphs alike?

How many books have you read for enjoyment this year?

Check Understanding

1. How long does it take Ron to read 40 pages?

2. How would you find the number of pages Ron can read in 1 hour?

3. How long do you think it takes Ron to read 50 pages?

4. How many pages does Ron read in $3\frac{1}{2}$ hours?

Practice

This graph shows how many book pages Ron can carefully review when he is studying for a test. Use this graph and the one on page 424.

5. Ron is going to study for his social studies test from 7:00 to 8:00 tonight. How many pages will he review?

6. The chapter Ron is studying is 30 pages long. How much time should he put aside for studying the chapter?

7. How many pages of his favorite storybook could Ron read in the same amount of time he put aside for studying?

8. If Ron has 50 pages to study next week, how much time should he leave for studying on each of the five school nights?

Ron's Reading for Studying Rate

Problem Solving

Estimation   Use estimation to solve each problem.

9. Ron is reading a book that has 719 pages. Use the graph on page 424. About how long will it take Ron to read the entire book?

10. Read a story for 15 minutes, and note how many pages you read. About how many pages could you read in an hour?

11. About how many hours will it take you to read 719 pages?

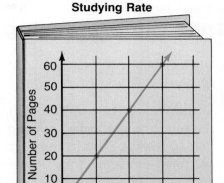

TIPS FOR PROBLEM SOLVERS

Compare problems to help you relate new problems to ones you've solved before.

Making a Line Graph

Treadmill at 4 Miles Per Hour		
Number of Miles	Number of Minutes	Ordered Pairs
0	0	(0,0)
1	15	(1,15)
3	▒	(3,▒)
5	▒	(▒,▒)
8	▒	(▒,▒)

Build Understanding

ACTIVITY

Walk a Mile on a Graph
Materials: Ruler, grid paper

Walking on a treadmill is good exercise. You can make a line graph to show how long it would take you to walk a certain number of miles on a treadmill set for 4 miles an hour. At this rate, you can walk 1 mile in 15 minutes.

a. Copy and complete the table.

b. Draw a grid like the one shown at the right. What labels will you use for the scales? Label them, and write a title for the graph.

c. What intervals will you use to show the minutes and the miles? Write the intervals along the scales.

d. Where will you draw the line on the graph? On your graph, plot the ordered pairs shown in your table. Draw a line to connect them.

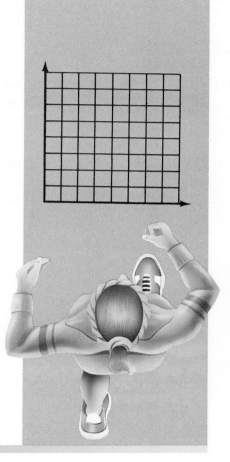

■ **Talk About Math** Explain how you could use the graph to find how long it would take to walk a number of miles that are not shown in the table or on the graph.

Check Understanding

For another example, see Set C, pages 444–445.

Use your table and graph to answer the questions.

1. How far can you walk in 30 minutes?

2. How far can you walk in 1 hour?

3. How long will it take to walk 6 miles?

4. How long will it take to walk 9 miles?

Practice

For More Practice, see Set C, pages 446–447.

Suppose you set the speed of the treadmill at 2 miles an hour. At this rate, how many minutes would it take to walk

5. 1 mile?   **6.** 3 miles?   **7.** 6 miles?

Use the information in Exercises 5-7 to make a table showing ordered pairs for the following.

8. Time taken to walk 3 miles

9. Distance covered in 180 minutes

10. Use the data from your table to make a line graph. **Remember** to plan the intervals so the least and greatest numbers will fit on the graph.

Use your graph to answer the questions.

11. How long does it take to walk 4 miles?

12. How far can you walk in 150 minutes?

Problem Solving

Answer each question.

13. If you walked for 15 minutes at 2 miles an hour, 30 minutes at 4 miles an hour, and another 15 minutes at 2 miles an hour, how far would you walk?

14. **Critical Thinking** Suppose you walked for 45 minutes at 4 miles an hour. How long would your friend have to walk at 2 miles an hour to cover the same distance?

Midchapter ✓ Checkup

1. Whom would you survey and what question would you ask to find the favorite Major League baseball team of students in your school?

2. When is a broken-line graph best used?

3. What does the zigzag line on a scale of a broken-line graph mean?

4. What does a line graph show?

5. How can each point on a line graph be named?

Problem Solving WORKSHOP

Real-Life Decision Making

Suppose you found these two unusual types of graphs in a newspaper. They show the weekly allowance of 19 students in your town. The graphs show the same information but in different ways.

Box Plot

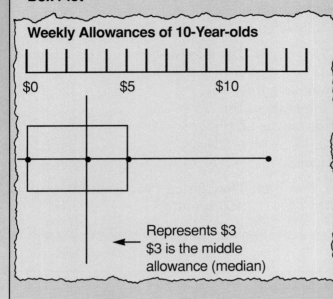

Weekly Allowances of 10-Year-olds

$0 $5 $10

Represents $3
$3 is the middle
allowance (median)

Stem-and Leaf Plot

**Weekly Allowances
for 10-Year-olds**

0	000000	6 people receive
1	5	$0 allowance
2		
3	00055	Stem Leaf
4	0	4 | 0 means 1 person
5	00	receives $4.00
6	5	6 | 5 means 1 person
7		receives $6.50
8	0	
9		
10	0	
11		
12	0	
13		
14		

The **box plot** shows that most of the 10-year-old students surveyed receive from $0 to $5 weekly allowance.

The **stem-and-leaf plot** shows that the most common allowance for the 10-year-olds surveyed is $0. Three of those surveyed receive $3 and two receive $3.50.

1. You want a raise in your allowance. Decide which graph you would use to persuade your family that you should get a raise.

2. You want to ask the newspaper some questions about the people surveyed. What questions will help you decide whether the graphs are representative of most 10-year-olds?

Explore with a Computer

Use the *Graphing and Probability Workshop Project* for this activity.

At the computer, run a probability experiment. Choose to roll cubes. The computer adds the numbers that come up on each cube.

1. Have the computer roll the cubes 20 times. View the data as a **Bar graph.** Which number was rolled the most? Which number was rolled the least?

2. Predict which number would be rolled the most if you have the computer roll the cubes 200 times. Try this experiment. View the data as a **Bar graph.** Compare your prediction with the results on the computer.

3. Why do you think certain numbers are rolled more often than other numbers?

Number-Sense Project

Look back at pages 414-415.

A class collected this data. They asked a number of people what would be their first choice of a pet if they lived in a city.

Pet	Age Group		
	Child	Teen	Adult
Bird	12	14	5
Cat	36	19	42
Dog	16	12	14
Fish	12	18	6
Gerbil	5	0	0

a. Write a statement about the popularity of the gerbil as a pet according to this data.

b. Write a summary explaining the differences in the adults' choices for a pet as compared to the teenagers' choices.

c. How might the results have differed if the people surveyed did not have a list from which to choose?

Math-at-Home Activity

Try this experiment at home. Predict how many times a paper cup will land *top down* if you flip it 50 times.

Flip the cup 10 times. Record the results on a graph.

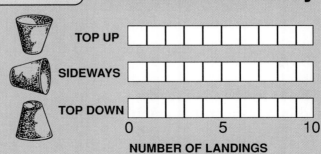

TOP UP

SIDEWAYS

TOP DOWN

0   5   10

NUMBER OF LANDINGS

Do you want to change your prediction? Continue the activity, until you have flipped the cup 50 times.

Make a Graph

Build Understanding

Len Barsky became manager of a music store, Jazz, Rock, and More, in April. He wants to show the increase in sales since he became manager.

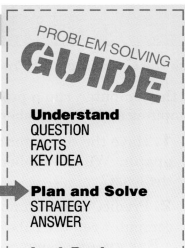

PROBLEM SOLVING
GUIDE

Understand
QUESTION
FACTS
KEY IDEA

▐▐▐▶ **Plan and Solve**
STRATEGY
ANSWER

Look Back
SENSIBLE ANSWER
ALTERNATE APPROACH

Understand How can Len best show how sales have increased since he became manager? He knows the monthly sales from January through June. A graph is a good way to display data.

▐▐▐▶ **Plan and Solve** STRATEGY Len needs to decide what kind of graph to make. A bar graph and a pictograph show quantities and are used to make comparisons. A broken-line graph shows changes in quantities over time.

ANSWER Len decided to make a broken-line graph. He titled the graph and labeled the scales. He rounded the monthly sales to the nearest $500 and then plotted the points to show the sales for each month.

Look Back The graph shows the increase in sales beginning in April. Are exact amounts shown? Are exact amounts necessary?

■ **Talk About Math** Is it easier to interpret data displayed in a table or in a graph? Explain.

Total Sales, Jan.-June	
Month	Dollars
January	$3,689
February	3,402
March	3,150
April	5,287
May	8,102
June	9,608

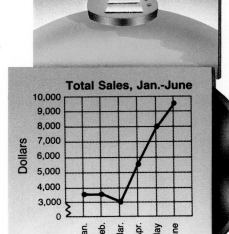

Total Sales, Jan.-June

Check Understanding

Use the table at the right to answer Problems 1–3.

1. What kind of graph would you make from the data?

2. Make a graph of the data in the table.

3. What numbers did you use as labels to show sales in dollars?

4. When would you use a pictograph instead of a bar graph?

April Sales by Salesperson

Rivera	$1,280
Jones	1,230
Dennis	1,000
Okada	1,717

Practice

Which kind of graph would you use for each situation? Why?

5. Number of compact discs sold by each salesperson in July

6. Total sales in one month of each of the three best-selling records

7. Number of tapes sold monthly from July through December

8. Decrease in the number of albums sold over 6 months

Answer each question.

9. During an August sale, albums were 2 for $4.00. Make a graph to show the prices of 4, 6, 8, and 10 albums.

10. What kind of graph did you make to show the data in Problem 9? Why?

Choose a _____ Strategy

Hidden Faces

11. Each face of a cube is numbered 1 to 6 using triangles. Here are 3 views of the *same* cube. Tell what number is opposite:
   a. 5 **b.** 1 **c.** 3

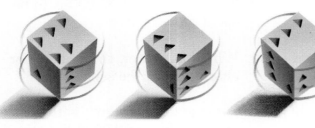

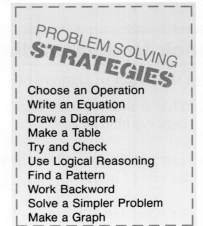

PROBLEM SOLVING
STRATEGIES

Choose an Operation
Write an Equation
Draw a Diagram
Make a Table
Try and Check
Use Logical Reasoning
Find a Pattern
Work Backward
Solve a Simpler Problem
Make a Graph

Circle Graphs

Build Understanding

A budget is a plan for spending money. Do you have a budget for your money?

A *circle graph* compares parts of a whole. This circle graph shows the budget made by the Sunnyhill School's student council. The whole circle stands for the whole amount in the budget. Each section of the circle shows how a fraction of the whole is to be spent. Since each section shows a fraction of the whole, the sum of the fractions must be 1.

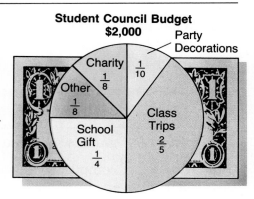

Student Council Budget
$2,000

A. On which item is the most money to be spent?

Find the largest section of the graph.

The most money is to be spent on class trips.

B. How much money is planned for party decorations?

Find $\frac{1}{10}$ of $2,000. $2,000 \div 10 = 200$

The budget shows $200 can be spent on party decorations.

■ **Talk About Math**   If the money to be spent on the school gift were $\frac{1}{5}$ of the whole $2,000, would any other sections of the graph have to change? Explain.

Check Understanding

For another example, see Set D, pages 444-445.

Use the graph to answer the questions.

1. What fraction of the $2,000 is to be spent on charity?

2. Two fifths of the $2,000 is to be spent on what item?

3. How much money is to be spent on the school gift?

4. Which is greater, the amount for charity or for the school gift?

5. For every circle graph, is the sum of the fractions that name the parts always 1? Explain.

6. For every circle graph, is the whole amount always $2,000? Explain.

Practice

For More Practice, see Set D, pages 446–447.

Juana earns $40 each week by doing chores in her neighborhood. The circle graph shows her budget for the week.

What fraction of the $40 does she budget for

7. entertainment?   **8.** snacks?

9. For which item does Juana set aside the most money?

10. What is the main idea of this circle graph?

a. How much Juana earns in a week

b. How much she spends in a week

c. How all parts of her weekly earnings are to be used

Juana's Weekly Budget

Transportation $\frac{1}{8}$

Other $\frac{1}{8}$

Savings $\frac{3}{10}$

Snacks $\frac{1}{4}$

Entertainment $\frac{1}{5}$

Mental Math   How much money did Juana budget each week for

11. entertainment?   **12.** savings?   **13.** transportation?   **14.** snacks?

Problem Solving

Read for the facts to solve the problems.

15. How much more money does Juana put into savings than she spends on transportation?

16. Use the circle graph on page 432. How much more did the student council plan to spend on charity than on party decorations?

 Calculator   Use the circle graph above to answer Problems 17-19. If Juana earns $32 a week, in 52 weeks how much does she

17. earn?   **18.** save?   **19.** spend?

Skills_____ Review   pages 396–397

Write each mixed number as an improper fraction.

1. $2\frac{3}{8}$ **2.** $1\frac{7}{10}$ **3.** $4\frac{1}{2}$ **4.** $5\frac{3}{4}$ **5.** $7\frac{2}{3}$ **6.** $11\frac{3}{5}$

Line Plots in Statistics

Build Understanding

Statistics is a branch of mathematics in which data are collected, organized, and analyzed.

A. Here are quiz scores for 19 students:

90, 75, 95, 75, 95, 90, 90, 85, 80, 95,
70, 95, 95, 80, 75, 100, 65, 100, 100

These scores can be organized in a frequency table or in a *line plot*.

Score	Tally	Frequency
100	///	
95	////	3
90	///	5
85	/	3
80	//	1
75	///	2
70	/	3
65	/	1
		1

B. The *median* is the middle number in a set of data. You can put the test scores in order to find the median.

65, 70, 75, 75, 75, 80, 80,
85, 90, 90, 90, 95, 95, 95,
95, 95, 100, 100, 100

The median is the tenth score, 90.

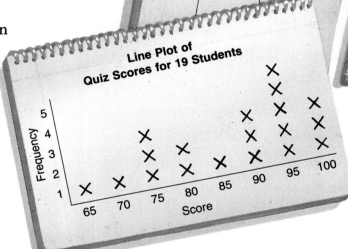

Line Plot of Quiz Scores for 19 Students

C. To find the *average*, or *mean*, for a set of scores, add to find the total. Then divide by the number of scores.

Hyung's quiz scores were 70, 70, 60, 80, 90, 50. What was the mean?

Hyung's mean score was 70.

D. When there is an even number of scores, the median is the mean of the two middle scores. Find the median:

75, 80, 80, 90, 95, 100

The median is 85.

E. The *mode* is the number that occurs most often in a set of data. In Example A, the mode is 95.

■ **Talk About Math** Could there ever be more than one mode? Explain.

434

Check Understanding

For another example, see Set E, pages 444–445.

Use the line plot for Reba's test scores to answer the questions.

1. How many scores are greater than 80?

2. How many scores are there in all?

3. What is the mode?

4. What is the median?

5. What is the mean?

Reba's Test Scores

Frequency				
4		X		
3	X	X		
2	X	X	X	
1	X	X	X	X
	70	80	90	100

Scores

Practice

For More Practice, see Set E, pages 446–447.

Use these data for Exercises 6-10:
90, 70, 60, 70, 90, 100, 80, 70, 65, 55.

6. Make a frequency table.

7. Draw a line plot.

8. Find the mean.

9. Find the median.

10. Find the mode.

Use these data for Exercises 11-15:
100, 92, 92, 96, 88, 88, 88, 96, 92, 94, 90, 88.

11. Make a frequency table.

12. Draw a line plot.

13. **Calculator**   Find the mean.

14. Find the median.

15. Find the mode.

Problem Solving

16. **Critical Thinking**   What do you think would happen to the mean in Example A if the lowest score was 75?

Reading ———— Math

Vocabulary   The middle number in a set of data is called the __1.__ .

If you add a set of scores and then divide by the number of addends, you find the __2.__ .

The number that occurs most frequently in a set of data is the __3.__ .

Outcomes

Build Understanding

In some games you make words with letter tiles. What words could you make with the tiles shown?

Margo put these ten letter tiles into a bag. Then she drew a letter without looking.

When Margo draws a tile, she is *certain* to draw some letter. Could she draw a K? a T? Drawing a K is one possible **outcome.** There are no tiles with T, so drawing a T is *impossible.*

Margo can think of many words with M. She does not like to make words with K. Since there is one M and one K, drawing an M and drawing a K are *equally likely.*

Margo knows that most words have vowels. Only two of the tiles have vowels (I,O). The rest have consonants. When Margo draws a tile without looking, the letter on it is *more likely* to be a consonant than a vowel.

■ **Write About Math**   If you were making words by drawing tiles from the bag, is it more likely that you could use an L or a Q? Give a reason for your answer.

Check Understanding

For another example, see Set F, pages 444–445.

Norm draws a letter from the bag described above without looking. For each exercise, are the two outcomes equally likely? If not, which outcome is more likely?

1. Draw a Q or draw a J.

2. Draw an L or a letter not an L.

3. Draw a letter in Norm's name or draw a letter not in his name.

4. Draw a letter in Norm's name or draw a letter in Kip's name.

Practice

For More Practice, see Set F, pages 446–447.

Thom placed these cards face down and mixed them up. Then he drew a card and recorded the number on it.

5. List all the possible outcomes.

6. Is Thom more likely to draw a 6 or to draw a 3?

7. Order all the possible outcomes from least likely to most likely.

8. Is Thom more likely to draw an odd number or an even number?

9. Gabe spins each spinner once. What are the possible outcomes for the colors the two spinners will land on?

Problem Solving

10. **Critical Thinking**   In a game, Kimi spins the spinner shown. She needs to get a vowel to win. She thinks, "All the outcomes on this spinner are equally likely, so I have as good a chance to get a vowel as a consonant." Is Kimi correct about her chances? Why or why not?

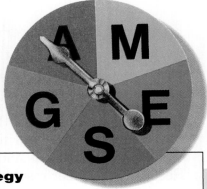

Choose a ▬▬ **Strategy**

In a certain game, you spin the spinner shown with Problem 10. Then you flip a coin and get heads or tails.

11. What are all the possible outcomes? How many possible outcomes are there?

12. Jan wins if she gets M and tails on her next turn. She loses if she gets any other outcome. Is Jan more likely to win or to lose?

437

Experiments

Build Understanding

The Road Home
Materials: Spinner as shown; 3-6 markers
Groups: 3-6 students

a. Each time it is your turn, choose a color and spin. If the spinner lands on the color you chose, move your marker this number of squares: red, 1; blue, 3; yellow, 5.

b. Make a table for 6 turns.

Player	Turn 1	Turn 2
	Spinner Landed on	Spinner Landed on
1		
2		

Keep track of each player's first 3 turns.

c. After each player has had 3 turns, study the table. How many times did the spinner land on red? on blue? on yellow?

d. Predict how many times the spinner will land on red, blue, and yellow during the next 3 turns. Write your predictions and continue playing. Record the spinner results in the table.

e. Compare your predictions and finished table. If everyone took 24 turns, do you think the results would be closer to your predictions? Why?

f. Think about the spinner results and play the game again. This time use what you know to try to reach Home before anyone else.

■ **Talk About Math** Explain your strategy for playing this game. How did you develop your strategy?

Check Understanding

For another example, see Set G, pages 444–445.

Use the spinner and your table to answer the questions.

1. When you spin, what color are you most likely to land on?

2. What color are you least likely to land on?

3. Why do you think you are more likely to land on one color than another?

Practice

For More Practice, see Set G, pages 446–447.

For Exercises 4-6, make a spinner like the one shown.

4. Write how many times you think the spinner will land on each color in 28 spins.

5. Work alone or with your group. Record the results of 28 spins.

6. Were your predictions close to the results? Why might they be very different?

Problem Solving

Explore ——— Math

The most common letters in English, listed in order, are **E, T, A, O, N, R, I,** and **S.** Choose two paragraphs from any book to answer the following questions.

7. Tally how many times each letter of the alphabet appears in your two paragraphs.

8. For the two paragraphs that you chose, list the eight most common letters in order.

9. Compare and contrast your results to the list of the most common letters above. Try to explain any differences.

10. If you tallied the letters on the last page of a dictionary, how would you expect the results to be different?

Fractions and Probability

Build Understanding

A. Karl puts these tiles into a bag and draws one without looking. He records the letter in a tally chart, returns the tile to the bag, and draws again. If he repeats this activity many times, what fraction of the time would you expect him to get an R?

One of the 8 tiles has an R. In many draws, you would expect about $\frac{1}{8}$ of the letters drawn to be R.

Probability tells how likely it is that an outcome will happen. The probability of an outcome is written as a fraction. The probability of drawing an R is

$$\frac{\textbf{Number of favorable outcomes}}{\textbf{Number of possible outcomes}} = \frac{\textbf{Number of tiles with R}}{\textbf{Total number of tiles}} = \frac{1}{8}$$

B. If you drew 80 times from the bag, about how many times would you expect to get a G?

The probability of drawing a G is

$$\frac{\textbf{Number of favorable outcomes}}{\textbf{Number of possible outcomes}} = \frac{\textbf{Number of tiles with G}}{\textbf{Total number of tiles}} = \frac{2}{8} = \frac{1}{4}$$

You would expect to get a G on about $\frac{1}{4}$ of 80 draws, or about 20 times.

$\frac{1}{4}$ of 80 = 20

■ **Talk About Math** Which is more likely, drawing an N or drawing an R? Would you expect the probability of drawing N to be a fraction greater or less than $\frac{1}{8}$?

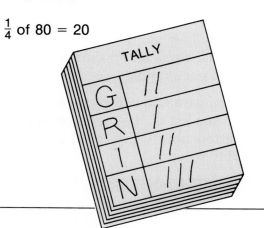

TALLY	
G	//
R	/
I	//
N	///

Check Understanding

For another example, see Set H, pages 444–445.

1. Karl's bag has 3 Ns, so the probability of getting an N is $\frac{3}{\blacksquare}$.

2. The bag has 8 tiles, so the probability of getting an I is $\frac{\blacksquare}{8}$.

3. About how many times would you expect to get an I in 80 draws?

4. Name two outcomes that are equally likely when Karl draws a tile.

Practice

For More Practice, see Set H, pages 446–447.

Take each of the following words one at a time. Suppose you put the tiles that spell the word in a bag and draw a letter without looking. What is the probability of getting an L?

5. GLADLY   6. LOLLIPOP   7. ELEVATOR   8. EXPERIMENT

The numbers 1 through 6 appear on the 6 faces of this number cube. When the cube is rolled, all the faces have the same chance to come up. Find the probability of getting each result on one roll.

9. a 5   10. a 2   11. a 6   12. an odd number

13. a number less than 5   14. a number less than 7

Problem Solving

Critical Thinking   The spinner has the names of all the members of the bicycle club. The member whose name is spun will be leader for a month. Give a reason why you think each statement below is correct or incorrect.

15. "There are more boys than girls in the club, so Jim is more likely to win than Gina."

16. "Hal won the spin last month, so this month he is less likely to win than the other members."

Solve each problem.

1. A pen and an eraser together cost about $1.10. The pen costs a dollar more than the eraser. How much does the eraser cost?

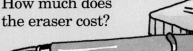

2. A company makes 3,500 softballs each day. The softballs are packed in boxes of 16. How many boxes can be filled with the softballs made in 1 day?

3. Mrs. Kraus needs $6\frac{1}{2}$ gallons of juice for the picnic. If Uncle Joe brings $2\frac{1}{2}$ gallons, Aunt Celia brings $2\frac{1}{3}$ gallons, and cousin Lenny brings $1\frac{3}{4}$ gallons, will there be enough juice?

4. Matt practiced piano for 65 minutes on Monday and for 32 minutes on Tuesday. How many hours and minutes did he practice the two days?

5. Raoul has 7 pairs of crew socks. Three pairs have red rings on them. The other 4 pairs have blue rings on them. What is the probability of pulling one sock with a red ring from the drawer without looking?

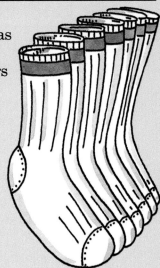

6. **Data File** Using the line graph on pages 528–529, estimate the difference in population between the United States and Canada in 1850, and in 1982.

7. **Make a Data File** Each day for one week, count the number of people in your class wearing blue or another color of your choice. Display the data using two different kinds of graphs.

Explore with a Calculator

"About Average"

1. Play the *Average Game* with a friend.

Rules

• Each player writes the following before each round:

	Estimated average	Number line	Actual average
Round 1			

• Estimate the average of the numbers in that box.

• Use the estimate to choose the number line that will contain the average.

After both players choose a number line, find the actual average.

Scoring

• Each player receives 1 point for choosing the correct number line.

• Each player receives 1 point for finding the correct answer on the calculator.

• Each player loses 1 point for finding an incorrect answer on the calculator.

• The player with the most points at the end of 12 rounds wins.

Round 1	**Number Lines**	**Round 9**
43, 61, 52	A 40 49 D 50 59	94, 81, 82, 95
Round 2	B 90 99 E 80 89	**Round 10**
83, 76, 87	C 70 79 F 60 69	98, 82, 87, 97

Round 3	**Round 5**	**Round 7**	**Round 11**
58, 61, 61	85, 72, 71	90, 87, 90, 97	58, 72, 43, 71
Round 4	**Round 6**	**Round 8**	**Round 12**
60, 62, 72, 74	65, 68, 71	100, 77, 80, 79	62, 81, 77, 71, 64

Reteaching

Set A   pages 418–421

Bar graphs and pictographs can make it easy to compare quantities. A broken-line graph shows change over time.

Remember that one type of graph may be better to use than another type of graph depending, on the type of data.

What kind of graph would you use to show these data? Why?

1. The average annual rainfall in each of 5 major cities

2. The average annual rainfall in one city over the last 8 years

Set B   pages 422–423

Follow these steps to make a broken-line graph:

1. Write the title for the graph.
2. Label the horizontal scale and write the months, or years, or other time interval.
3. Label the vertical scale and write the number for the scale.
4. Plot the points and connect them.

Remember that a zigzag line can be used on the vertical scale to save space from 0 to the smallest number.

Make a broken-line graph of these data.

White House Visitors (in thousands)

Month	Jan.	Feb.	Mar.	Apr.	May	June
Number	48	60	100	180	172	168

Set C   pages 426–427

Follow these steps to make a line graph:

1. Complete a table of ordered pairs.
2. Write the title for the graph.
3. Number and label the scales.
4. Plot the ordered pairs from the table.
5. Draw a line to connect the points.

Remember to plan the intervals so the least and the greatest numbers will fit on the graph. Copy and complete this table. Then make a line graph.

Car Traveling 20 Miles Per Hour

Number of Minutes	Number of Miles	Ordered Pairs
15	5	(15, 5)
30	10	(▦, 10)
▦	20	(▦, ▦)
▦	30	(▦, ▦)

Set D   pages 432–433

This circle graph shows how a student spent each part of a weekday. The largest section is "sleeping." How many hours does $\frac{1}{3}$ represent?

$\frac{1}{3} \times 24 = 8$ hours

Remember that each section shows a fraction of the whole. So the sum of the fractions must be 1.

What fraction of a day does the student spend

1. at school?   2. playing?

How many hours are spent

3. studying?   4. playing?

Set E   pages 434–435

A line plot can be drawn for these pulse rates.

70, 75, 75, 90, 80, 70, 80, 80, 75, 85, 80, 70, 85, 85, 80, 85, 80, 75, 75

Pulse Rate	Frequency
70	3
75	5
80	6
85	4
90	1

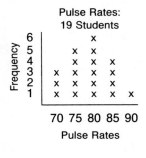

Pulse Rates: 19 Students

70 75 80 85 90
Pulse Rates

Remember that a frequency table helps you organize the data.

Make a frequency table and draw a line plot for the test scores below.

80, 90, 70, 80, 80, 90, 70, 70, 80, 100, 70, 60, 80, 80, 90, 60

Set F   pages 436–437

If you spin this spinner, the three possible outcomes are A, B, and C. Remember that outcomes are not always equally likely.

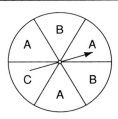

1. Are you more likely to spin an A or a B?

2. Order all the possible outcomes from least likely to most likely.

3. If there were 3 As and 3 Bs on the spinner, what could you conclude?

Set G   pages 438–439

If you spin the spinner in Set F, you are most likely to land on A, because there are more As than Bs or Cs.

Remember that each section of a spinner is the same size.
Make a spinner like the one shown in Set F.

1. Write how many times you think the spinner will land on each letter in 12 spins.

2. Record the results of 12 spins.

3. Were your predictions close to the results? Why might they be very different?

Set H   pages 440–441

If you spin the spinner in Set F, the probability of landing on C is $\frac{1}{6}$.
If you spin it 24 times, you would expect it to stop on C 4 times because

$\frac{1}{6} \times 24 = 4$

Remember that there are 6 possible places for the spinner to stop.

What is the probability of stopping on

1. A?   **2.** B?

More Practice

Set A   pages 418–421

This table shows the top speed of some animals in miles per hour.

Animal	Speed
Rabbit	35
Lion	50
Elephant	25
Zebra	40
Cat	30

1. What kind of graph would you use to show the data? Why?

2. Jamie collected the following data about the top speed in miles per hour of 5 sea creatures. Sea turtle: 20; bluefish: 40; sailfish: 60; dolphin: 25; baleen whale: 20. Organize the data in a table.

3. What kind of graph would you use to show these data?

4. Make a graph to show these data.

Set B   pages 422–423

Use the table to make a broken-line graph for

1. black and white receivers.

2. color receivers.

U.S. Production of Television Receivers (in millions)

Year	1977	1978	1979	1980	1981	1982
Black/White	2.4	2.7	2.5	2.7	2.4	2.7
Color	4.7	5.3	5.2	6.2	6.7	6.9

3. How has the number of black and white receivers changed since 1977?

4. Has the number of color televisions changed in the same way?

Set C   pages 426–427

This table shows how long it would take to drive a certain number of miles.

Car Traveling 60 Miles Per Hour

Number of Minutes	Number of Miles	Ordered Pairs
0	0	(0, 0)
10	10	(10, ▦)
20	▦	(▦, ▦)
40	▦	(▦, ▦)
60	▦	(▦, ▦)

1. Copy and complete the table.

Suppose the speed is reduced to 30 miles per hour. At this rate, how many minutes would it take to drive

2. 10 miles?   3. 20 miles?   4. 60 miles?

5. Make a table like the one at the left for a car traveling 30 miles per hour. Use 0, 10, 20, 40 and 60 for the number of minutes.

6. Use the data from your table to make a line graph.

Set D pages 432–433

Nick received $80 for his birthday. The circle graph shows how he plans to spend this money. What fraction of the $80 did he budget for

1. clothes?   **2.** savings?

Mental Math How much money did Nick budget for
3. clothes?   **4.** entertainment?

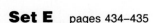

Set E pages 434–435

Use these test scores: 75, 80, 85, 80, 70, 100, 65, 80, 90, 65.

1. Make a frequency table.   **2.** Draw a line plot.   **3.** Find the mean.

4. Find the median.   **5.** Find the mode.

Set F pages 436–437

Amy placed these cards face down and mixed them. Then she drew a card and recorded the number on it.

| 5 | 5 | 5 | 5 | 6 |

1. Is Amy more likely to draw a 5 or to draw a 7?

| 6 | 7 | 7 | 7 | 8 |

2. Order all the possible outcomes from least likely to most likely.

3. Is Amy more likely to draw an odd number or an even number?

Set G pages 438–439

For Exercises 1–3, make a spinner like the one shown.

1. Write how many times you think the spinner will land on each letter in 24 spins.

2. Record the results of 24 spins.

3. Were your predictions close to the results? Why might they be very different?

Set H pages 440–441

Use each of the following words one at a time. Suppose you put the tiles that spell the word in a bag and draw a letter without looking. What is the probability of drawing an A?

1. FLORIDA   **2.** KANSAS   **3.** ALABAMA   **4.** MONTANA

Independent Study MORE PRACTICE

447

Enrichment

Order of Operations

What is the value of $9 + 4 \times 3$?

Ralph said the value was 39. Juana said it was 21.

Ralph did the addition, then the multiplication. Juana did the multiplication, then the addition. Who was right?

To avoid such confusion, mathematicians follow a standard *order of operations*.

1. First do all operations within parentheses.

$(3 + 4) \times 6 - (52 - 4) \div 6$

2. Then multiply and divide in order from left to right.

$7 \times 6 - 48 \div 6$

3. Then add and subtract in order from left to right.

$42 - 8$

34

Which operation should be done first: addition, subtraction, multiplication, or division?

1. $3 \times 4 + 12$ **2.** $27 \div (7 - 4)$ **3.** $14 - 8 \div 4 + 6$

Choose the correct value.

4. $(6 + 12) \div 3$
    a. 20   **b.** 6   **c.** 14

5. $(24 \div 6) \times 6 - (36 \div 18)$
    a. 16   **b.** 22   **c.** 12

6. $10 - 3 \times 3 + 5$
    a. 26   **b.** 56   **c.** 6

7. $24 - (16 \div 2) \times 2$
    a. 20   **b.** 32   **c.** 8

Find the value of each expression.

8. $10 - 4 \times 2$ **9.** $(6 \times 5) + (3 \times 5)$ **10.** $27 \div 3 + 9$

11. $6 + 3 \times 9 - 3$ **12.** $(15 + 5) \times 4 - 16$ **13.** $18 - 3 - 2 + 9 \times 2$

14. $(10 \times 8) \div 4 + 5$ **15.** $9 + (8 \div 2) \times (18 \div 3)$

Chapter 13 Review/Test

1. If you conducted a survey to find the favorite movie of students in your school, tell whom you would survey and the question you would ask.

2. Steve asked 20 students what their favorite pet was. The pictograph shows the results. How many students prefer a dog for a pet?

Favorite Pets

Dog	⚲ ⚲ ⚲ ⚲ ⚲	
Cat	⚲ ⚲ ⚲	Each ⚲
Bird	⚲ ⚲	stands for
Hamster	⚲	2 students

Use the table to answer the question.

Year	1986	1987	1988	1989	1990
Sales (in thousands)	$185	$200	$220	$248	$300

3. The table shows the annual sales for a company. If you were making a broken-line graph to show this data, what numbers would you use when labeling the scale for sales?

4. This graph shows the distance traveled by a train in 5 hours.

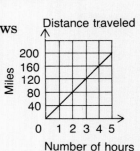

How long does it take the train to travel 160 miles?

5. Use the line graph in Item 4. What ordered pair would you use to show how long it takes the train to travel 120 miles?

6. What kind of graph would you use to show the total sales in one month for each of five salespersons? Why?

7. If a fruit market sells $1,200 worth of fruit, how much more money did the market take in for apples than for bananas?

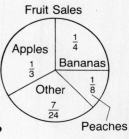

On 10 tests, Sarah got these scores: 80, 90, 95, 75, 90, 95, 100, 85, 95, 95.

8. Draw a line plot of her scores.

9. Find the mean of Sarah's scores.

Suppose these cards are face down.

9	6	6	9	5	9

10. Pick one card. List the possible outcomes from least to most likely.

11. If you pick one card from the cards above and then replace it, how many times would you expect to get a 9 in 24 picks?

12. What is the probability of getting a 6 in one draw?

13. Use the graph in Item 4. Alan said that the train travels 800 miles in 10 hours. Is this a reasonable answer? Why or why not?

14. **Write About Math** Can you know in advance how an experiment will turn out?

449

Geometry

14

Did You Know:
A group of students flew a train of kites to an altitude of 35,530 feet. About how many miles is that altitude? About how many miles of line do you think were needed to lift the kites to that altitude?

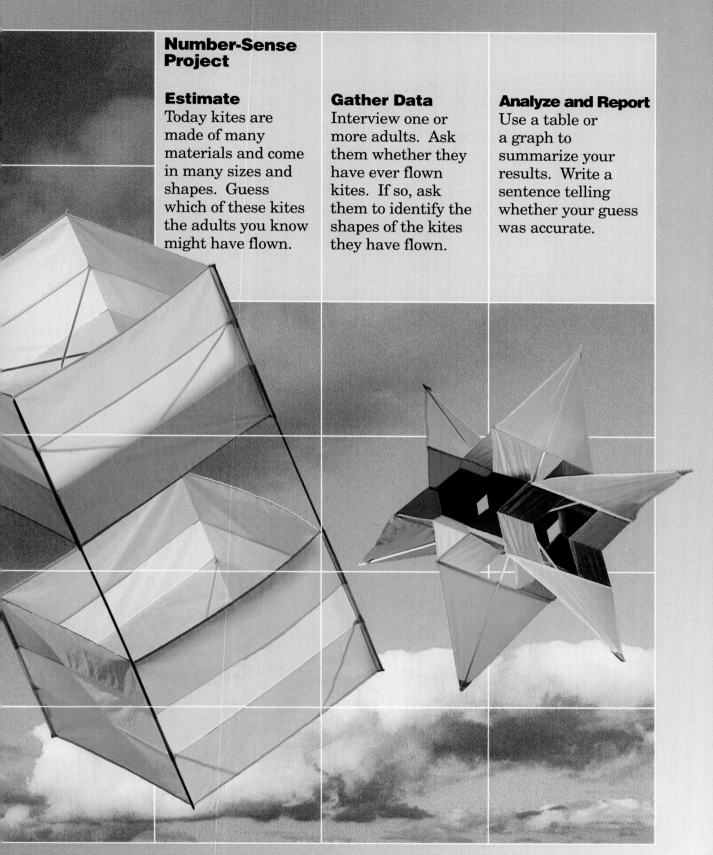

Number-Sense Project

Estimate
Today kites are made of many materials and come in many sizes and shapes. Guess which of these kites the adults you know might have flown.

Gather Data
Interview one or more adults. Ask them whether they have ever flown kites. If so, ask them to identify the shapes of the kites they have flown.

Analyze and Report
Use a table or a graph to summarize your results. Write a sentence telling whether your guess was accurate.

Solid Shapes

Paul and Melissa used these pieces of plywood to build a ramp for their brother, Brad.

A. What do you notice about the surfaces of these objects?

All of the surfaces of these objects are flat.

What do you notice about the surfaces of these objects?

Some of the surfaces of these objects are not flat.

452

B. A geometric solid that has all flat surfaces is a ***polyhedron***. Which of these solid shapes are polyhedrons?

| Sphere | Cylinder | Cone | Triangular Prism | Rectangular Prism | Pyramid | Cube |

The first three shapes are not polyhedrons because they have some curved surfaces. The other shapes have all flat surfaces, so they are polyhedrons.

C. Some polyhedrons are ***prisms***.

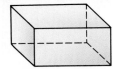 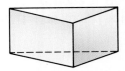

Rectangular prism   Cube   Triangular prism

Some polyhedrons are ***pyramids***.

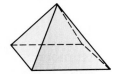 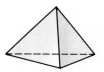

Rectangular pyramid   Square pyramid   Triangular pyramid

D. Each surface of a polyhedron is a ***face***. Two faces of a polyhedron meet to form an ***edge***. The edges meet to form a ***vertex***.

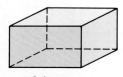 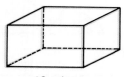 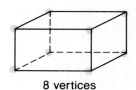

6 faces   12 edges   8 vertices

Talk About Math   Name some everyday items that are polyhedrons. Name some everyday items that are not polyhedrons.

Check Understanding

For another example, see Set A, pages 488–489.

Tell which solid at the right Paul and Melissa could build with the pieces of plywood.

1. 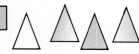   **a.**   **b.**   **c.**

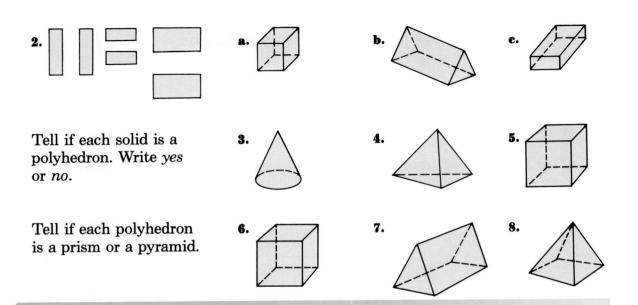

2. a.   b.   c.

Tell if each solid is a polyhedron. Write *yes* or *no*.

3.   **4.**   **5.**

Tell if each polyhedron is a prism or a pyramid.

6.   **7.**   **8.**

Practice

For More Practice, see Set A, pages 490–491.

Tell if each object shown in the picture below is a polyhedron. Write *yes* or *no*. If it is a polyhedron, tell whether it is a prism or a pyramid.

9. Tent   **10.** Paper towels   **11.** Soap bubbles   **12.** Aquarium   **13.** Number cube

Complete the table.

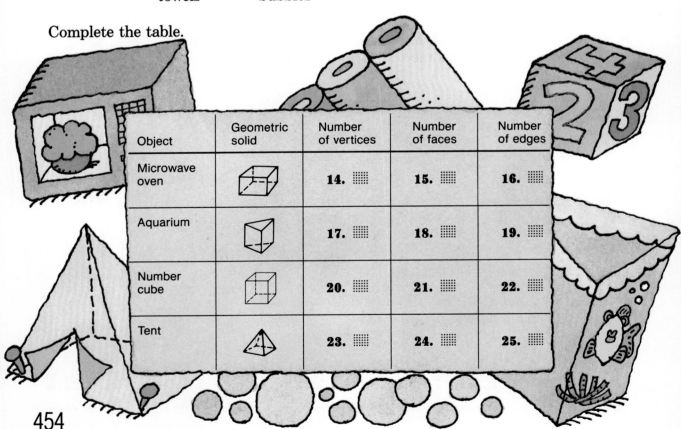

Object	Geometric solid	Number of vertices	Number of faces	Number of edges
Microwave oven		**14.**	**15.**	**16.**
Aquarium		**17.**	**18.**	**19.**
Number cube		**20.**	**21.**	**22.**
Tent		**23.**	**24.**	**25.**

454

Problem Solving

Tell how many pieces of plywood are needed to make each object.

26.

27.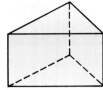

Visual Thinking Suppose you traced each face of each solid. Sketch all the different figures you would draw.

28.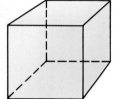

29.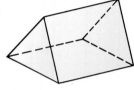

30.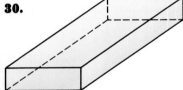

31.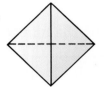

Skills _____ **Review**   pages 328–329

Write each fraction as a decimal.

1. $\frac{1}{2}$ **2.** $\frac{1}{4}$ **3.** $\frac{3}{5}$ **4.** $2\frac{7}{10}$

5. $\frac{3}{4}$ **6.** $6\frac{9}{25}$ **7.** $1\frac{7}{50}$ **8.** $3\frac{4}{5}$

Write each decimal as a fraction in lowest terms.

9. 0.6   **10.** 0.15   **11.** 0.1   **12.** 0.75

13. 6.25   **14.** 3.7   **15.** 9.03   **16.** 0.99

Polygons

Build Understanding

A. The figures you get when you trace the faces of a polyhedron are *polygons*.

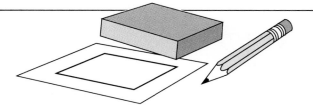

Each of these polygons could be the face of a polyhedron.

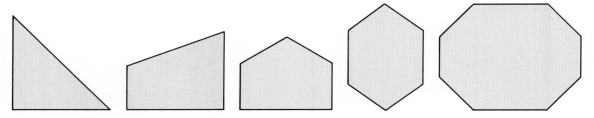

B. Polygons are named by the number of *sides* they have.

| Triangle | Quadrilateral | Pentagon | Hexagon | Octagon |

C. What makes the polygons in Example B and the polygons in Example A different?

Some of the sides of each polygon in Example A have different lengths. The sides of each polygon in Example B have the same length. The polygons in Example B are *regular polygons*.

D. Two sides of a polygon meet to form a *vertex*. How many vertices does this figure have?

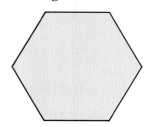

This hexagon has 6 vertices.

■ **Talk About Math** What is another name for a quadrilateral that is a regular polygon?

456

Check Understanding

For another example, see Set B, pages 488–489.

Match each polygon with its name from the list below.

1.
2.
3.
4.
5.

a. Triangle   **b.** Quadrilateral   **c.** Pentagon   **d.** Hexagon   **e.** Octagon

Use the figures in Exercises 1–5 to answer Exercises 6–8.

6. Which of the figures are regular?

7. How many sides does the figure in Exercise 3 have?

8. How many vertices does the figure in Exercise 4 have?

Practice

For More Practice, see Set B, pages 490–491.

Name the polygon you see. Then tell how many sides and vertices the polygon has.

9.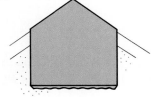

10.

11.

12.

13.

14.

Problem Solving

Name the polygons you would get if you traced each face of these polyhedrons.

15.

16.

17. Critical Thinking   What is the relationship between the edge of a polyhedron and the side of a polygon traced from one of the faces of the polyhedron?

457

Basic Geometric Ideas

Build Understanding

A. All the edges of a polyhedron and all the sides of a polygon are *segments*. A segment is part of a *line*.

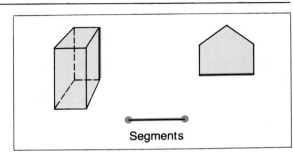
Segments

In polyhedrons and in polygons, all the segments meet at *points* called vertices. Sometimes a point is represented by a dot.

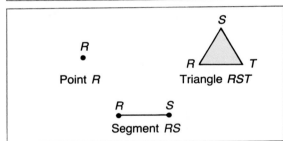
Points

Points are often labeled to help you tell them apart. Polygons and other geometric figures are often named by their points.

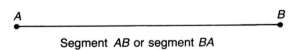

Point *R*   Triangle *RST*

Segment *RS*

B. You know that a segment is part of a line. How many *endpoints* does this segment have?

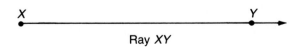
Segment *AB* or segment *BA*

A segment has two endpoints. Points *A* and *B* are endpoints.

A *ray* is also part of a line. A ray goes on and on in one direction. How many endpoints does this ray have?

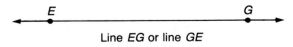
Ray *XY*

A ray has one endpoint.
Point *X* is the endpoint of ray *XY*.

In geometry, a line goes on and on in two directions. Does a line have any endpoints?

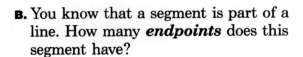
Line *EG* or line *GE*

A line has no endpoints.

458

c. *Parallel lines* are lines that never meet.

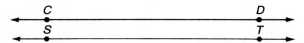

Lines *CD* and *ST* are parallel lines.

D. *Intersecting lines* are lines that meet in a point.

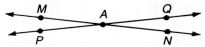

Lines *MN* and *PQ* are intersecting lines. They meet at point *A*.

■ **Talk About Math** In Example B, is "ray *YX*" another name for ray *XY*?

Check Understanding

For another example, see Set C, pages 488–489.

Use the figures at the right to complete these sentences.

1. Another name for line *AB* is line ▦.

2. Point C is the ▦ of ray *CD*.

3. Lines *EF* and *GH* are ▦ lines.

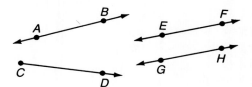

Practice

For More Practice, see Set C, pages 490–491.

Name each figure.

4. R ——— S **5.** B **6.** K ——————— L

7. C ——— D **8.** N ——— M **9.** W ——— V

Use the figure at the right for Exercises 10–12. Name

10. four points. **11.** a pair of parallel lines.

12. a pair of intersecting lines.

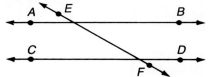

Problem Solving

Critical Thinking Use the figure at the right.

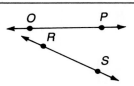

13. Are these lines parallel lines or intersecting lines?

14. How many different lines can you draw through point *R*?

15. How many different lines can you draw through points *R* and *P*?

Triangles

Build Understanding

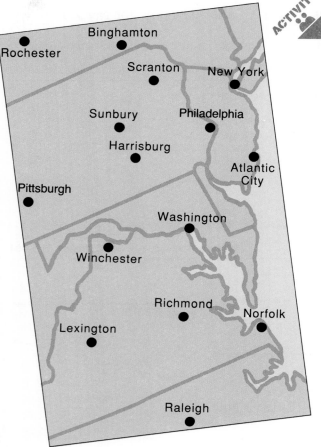

ACTIVITY

A. Go to Any Length
Materials: Ruler, paper
Groups: With a partner

a. Locate any three cities on this map.

b. Trace the dots that represent the locations of the three cities.

c. Draw 3 line segments connecting the dots you made. Unless the cities you selected are in a straight line, the figure you draw will be a ***triangle***.

d. Label the dots, *R*, *E*, and *J*.

e. In your triangle *REJ*, which is greater: the distance from *R* to *J* to *E* or the distance from *R* straight to *E*? Measure to check.

f. Practice constructing triangles using different cities on the map. Is the result you got in *Step e* true for all the triangles? Summarize your results.

B. Triangles can be named according to the lengths of their sides.

Triangle GHJ is an ***equilateral triangle.***	Triangle DEF is an ***isosceles triangle.***	Triangle ABC is a ***scalene triangle.***
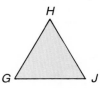	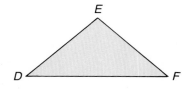	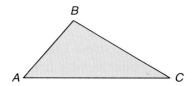
All three sides of an equilateral triangle are equal in length.	At least two sides of an isosceles triangle are equal in length.	None of the sides of a scalene triangle are equal in length.

■ **Talk About Math** Could an isosceles triangle also be an equilateral triangle? Explain your answer.

Check Understanding

For another example, see Set D, pages 488–489.

Name each triangle. Then tell whether the triangle is equilateral, isosceles, or scalene.

1.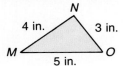

2.

3.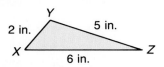

4.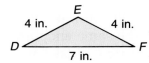

Practice

For More Practice, see Set D, pages 490–491.

Measure each side of each triangle. Then tell whether the triangle is equilateral, isosceles, or scalene.

5.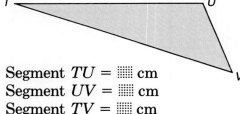

Segment TU = ▦ cm
Segment UV = ▦ cm
Segment TV = ▦ cm

6.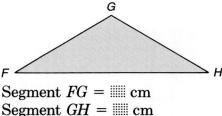

Segment FG = ▦ cm
Segment GH = ▦ cm
Segment FH = ▦ cm

7.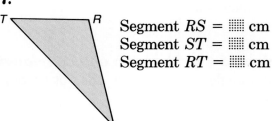

Segment RS = ▦ cm
Segment ST = ▦ cm
Segment RT = ▦ cm

8.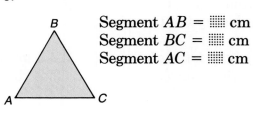

Segment AB = ▦ cm
Segment BC = ▦ cm
Segment AC = ▦ cm

Problem Solving

9. **Visual Thinking** On a map, a line drawn from Hilltop to Milltown measures 6 cm. A line drawn from Milltown to River City measures 7 cm. How long could a line drawn from Hilltop to River City be?

461

Angles

Build Understanding

What do you think will happen when the laser beam is pointed at a mirror?

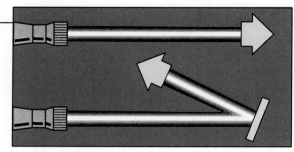

When the laser beam hits the mirror, it bounces off and goes in another direction. The path of the laser beam suggests an **angle**.

A. Ray *ED* and ray *EF* form an angle. Both rays have the same endpoint. Point *E* is the **vertex** of the angle. The two rays are the **sides** of the angle.

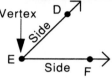

Angle *DEF* or angle *FED*
$\angle DEF$ or $\angle FED$ or $\angle E$

B. A **right angle** looks like a square corner.

An **acute angle** is smaller than a right angle.

An **obtuse angle** is larger than a right angle.

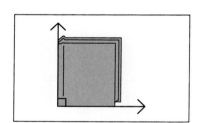

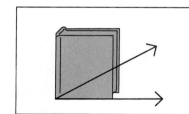

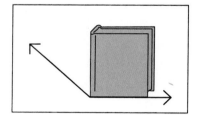

C. You have seen how the sides of a triangle can be used to classify the triangle. The angles of a triangle also can be used to classify the triangle.

A **right triangle** has one right angle.

An **acute triangle** has three acute angles.

An **obtuse triangle** has one obtuse angle.

The right angle is $\angle A$.

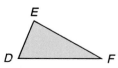

The acute angles are $\angle D$, $\angle E$, and $\angle F$.

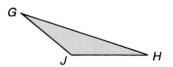

The obtuse angle is $\angle J$.

■ **Talk About Math** Does an obtuse triangle have any acute angles? Does an acute triangle have any obtuse angles?

Check Understanding

[For another example, see Set E, pages 488–489.]
For another example, see Set E, pages 488–489.

Tell which geometric idea is suggested.

1.  **2.**  **3.**

Tell whether each statement is *true* or *false*.

4. Another name for angle *JKL* is angle *LKJ*.

5. The vertex of ∠*RST* is *R*.

6. A right angle is larger than an acute angle.

7. An obtuse triangle has 3 obtuse angles.

Practice

For More Practice, see Set E, pages 490–491.

Name each angle. Then tell whether the angle is right, acute, or obtuse.

8.
X
Y   Z

9.
K
L   M

10.
P
Q   R

Use the figure at the right for Exercises 11–13.

11. Name two obtuse angles.

12. Name one right angle.

13. Name one acute angle.

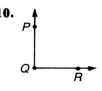

Tell whether each triangle is right, acute, or obtuse.

14. 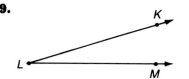 **15.** **16.**

Problem Solving

Tell whether each angle formed by the laser beams looks like it is right, acute, or obtuse.

17. 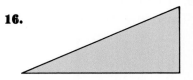 **18.**

Using a Protractor

Build Understanding

Bob is a carpenter. When he needs to cut pieces of wood, he can use a ***protractor*** to find the measures of the angles.

A. The unit used to measure an angle is the ***degree***. A protractor is marked with 180 degrees. What is the measure of ∠XYZ?

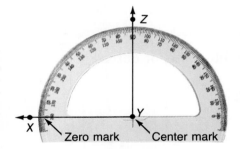

Zero mark   Center mark

The measure of ∠XYZ is 90°.

To find the measure of an angle with a protractor, put the center mark of the protractor on the vertex of the angle. Place the zero mark on one of the rays. Then use the scale with that zero mark to find the measure of the angle.

B. How would you draw an angle with a measure of 110°?

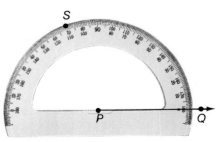

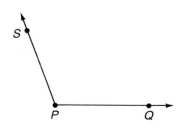

First, draw a ray. Point *P* will be the vertex of the angle.	Put the center mark of a protractor on point *P*. Put a zero mark on the ray. Using the scale with that zero mark, mark point *S* at 110°.	Draw ray *PS*. The measure of ∠SPQ is 110°.

c. The angle in Example A is a **_right angle._** Its measure is 90°. The angle in Example B is an **_obtuse angle_**. Its measure is greater than 90° and less than 180°. An **_acute angle_** has a measure of less than 90°.

What kind of angle is ∠BCD?

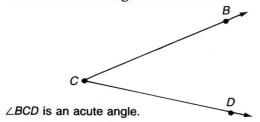

∠BCD is an acute angle.

D. What do you notice about the angles formed by these intersecting lines?

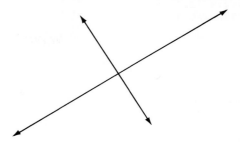

The intersecting lines form right angles. Intersecting lines that form right angles are **_perpendicular lines_**.

■ **Talk About Math**   Explain why you think a protractor has two scales.

Check Understanding

Find the measure of each angle. Then tell whether the angle is right, acute, or obtuse.

1. ∠ABC

2. ∠EBC

3. ∠DBC

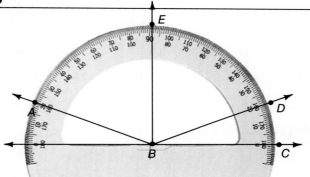

Use a protractor to tell whether each pair of intersecting lines is perpendicular. Answer *yes* or *no*.

4.

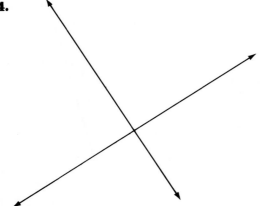

5.

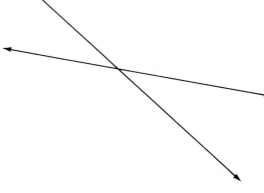

Practice

Estimation Estimate the measure of each angle.
Then use a protractor to find the measure.

6.

7.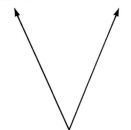

8.

9.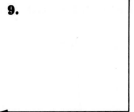

10.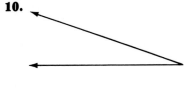

11.

Use a protractor to draw an angle for each measure given.

12. 25°   **13.** 135°   **14.** 60°   **15.** 150°   **16.** 90°   **17.** 75°

Problem Solving

Explore _____ Math

18. Use a protractor to measure the angles in triangle *ABC*. Find the sum of the angle measures.

19. Draw several other triangles, and measure their angles. For each triangle, find the sum of the angle measures.

20. Use your answers to Problems 18–19 to tell if this statement is true or false.

The sum of the measures of the angles of a triangle is 180°.

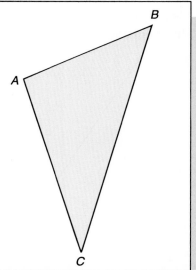

1. Tell which of the figures below are polyhedrons.

a.

b.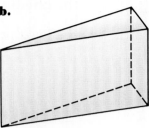

c.

Name each figure.

2.

3.
B •

4.

5.

Use the figure at the right for Exercises 6–8.

6. Name a pair of intersecting lines.

7. Name a pair of parallel lines.

8. Use a protractor to measure ∠FGX. Tell whether it is right, acute, or obtuse.

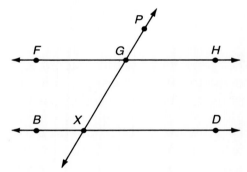

Name each polygon.

9.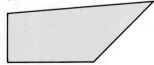

10.

11.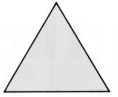

Complete each sentence.

12. A scalene triangle has ▦ sides of the same length.

13. All three sides of a(n) ▦ triangle are equal in length.

Explore as a Team

1. Which triangle do you think has the greatest perimeter?

2. Which triangle do you think has the least perimeter?

3. Work with other students to find ways to measure the perimeter of each triangle. Record the perimeter of each triangle. Were your predictions correct?

4. How many different triangles with a perimeter of 15 cm can your team find? Use only whole number measures for the lengths of the sides.

TIPS FOR
WORKING TOGETHER

To make sure your group understands the task or solution have each group member say it in his/her own words, summarize the steps, or give an example.

MATH
Laugh

A. What kind of triangle never makes a mistake?

B. What geometric figure represents a lost parrot?

ANSWERS:
A. Right triangle
B. Polygon

468

Explore with a Computer

Use the *Geometry Workshop Project* for this activity.

Brett plans to be an architect. He likes to draw unusual designs of homes and floor plans like the one shown here.

1. At the computer, use the **Draw** option to create an original floor plan for a home.

2. Print a copy of your floor plan and label the rooms that make up your home.

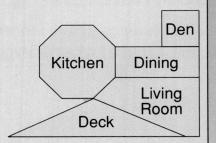

Number-Sense Project

Look back at pages 450-451.
Use the kite designs sketched at the right. Identify which kites match the descriptions below.

a. Contains at least three different triangles.

b. Contains two congruent triangles.

c. Contains a hexagon.

Math-at-Home Activity

Play *Adjacent Squares* with someone at home. Make a grid like this one.

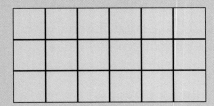

Each player needs 12 markers. Players take turns placing markers on one or two squares at a time.

If a player covers two squares, the squares must be adjacent (share one side).

Adjacent   Not Adjacent

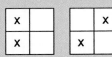

The player who covers the last square wins.

469

Quadrilaterals

Build Understanding

Alaska and Hawaii became
states in 1959.

This map shows the states in the
continental United States. The shapes
of several of the states suggest
quadrilaterals. A quadrilateral is a
figure with four sides and four angles.

A.

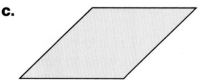

A **trapezoid** is a quadrilateral with
exactly one pair of parallel sides.

B.

A **parallelogram** is a quadrilateral
with opposite sides parallel. The
opposite sides have the same measure.

C.

A **rhombus** is a parallelogram with
all sides the same length.

D.

A *rectangle* is a parallelogram with four right angles.

E.

A *square* is a rectangle with all sides the same length.

■ **Talk About Math** Is a square always a rhombus? Is a rhombus always a square? Explain.

Check Understanding

For another example, see Set F, pages 488–489.

Use the map on page 470. Tell which quadrilateral each state suggests.

1. TN   **2.** WY   **3.** NV   **4.** CO   **5.** VT

Practice

For More Practice, see Set F, pages 490–491.

Name each quadrilateral.

6.

7.

8.

9.

10.

11.

12. Is this figure a quadrilateral?

Problem Solving

Visual Thinking Tell which segments at the right could be put together to form each figure. Sketch the figure.

13. Parallelogram   **14.** Rhombus

15. Square   **16.** Trapezoid

a —————————   b ———————
a —————————   b ———————
a —————————   c ——————
a —————————

Circles

Build Understanding

A. Going in Circles
Materials: Paper clips of various sizes, two pencils
Groups: With a partner

a. Use a paper clip and two pencils as shown at the right.

b. Hold one pencil in place and move the other pencil around until you return to the beginning point.

c. The shape you drew should be a *circle*. All the points of a circle are the same distance away from the *center* of the circle. The point made by the pencil you held in place is the center of the circle.

d. Repeat these steps using a paper clip of a different length. What do you notice about the size of the circle and the length of the paper clip?

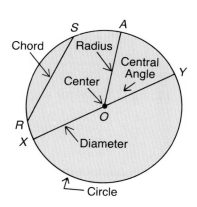

B. The circle at the right is circle *O*. The center is point *O*. A *radius* is a segment from the center to any point on the circle. Segment *OA* is a radius of this circle.

A segment through the center that connects two points on the circle is a *diameter* of the circle. Segment *XY* is a diameter of this circle.

A segment that has both endpoints on the circle is a *chord*. Segment *RS* is a chord.

An angle whose vertex is the center of the circle is a *central angle*. Angle *YOA* is a central angle.

■ Talk About Math Name two more radii of this circle. What can you say about the relationship between a radius and a diameter of a circle?

Check Understanding

For another example, see Set G, pages 488–489.

Tell whether each statement is *true* or *false*.

1. A circle can have more than one center.

2. A circle can have more than one diameter.

3. A circle can have more than one radius.

4. A circle can have more than one chord.

5. A circle can have more than one central angle.

Practice

For More Practice, see Set G, pages 490–491.

Use circle *C* at the right for Exercises 6–10.

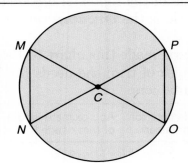

6. Name each segment that is a radius.

7. Name each segment that is a diameter.

8. Name each segment that is a chord.

9. Name each central angle.

10. Name four angles in the figure that are not central angles.

Problem Solving

Use circle *O* at the right for Problems 11–13.

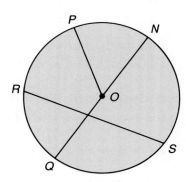

11. Can a radius be a diameter? a chord? Explain.

12. Are the angles formed by segments *RS* and *NQ* central angles? Explain.

13. Are points *N, P, S, Q*, and *R* the same distance from the vertex of the central angle? Explain.

14. **Use Data** Use the circle graph on page 432. If the total number of degrees in the central angles shown is 360°, how many degrees are there in the central angle for School Gift?

473

Circumference

Build Understanding

Marti makes fabric-covered containers to sell in her gift shop. Each container top has fancy piping trim along the outside edge.

A. The length of the trim Marti needs for each container is the distance around the edge of the top. The distance around a circle is the ***circumference***.

B. Marti made this chart to help her find the length of trim she needs for certain containers.

Diameter of container	Approximate length of trim needed
3 in.	$9\frac{1}{2}$ in.
5 in.	$15\frac{3}{4}$ in.
8 in.	$25\frac{1}{4}$ in.
12 in.	$37\frac{3}{4}$ in.

What do you notice about the relationship between the length of the trim and the diameter of the container?

The trim is always a little more than 3 times the length of the diameter.

c. Estimation   Estimate the length of trim Marti needs for a container with a diameter of 24 inches.

24 × 3 = 72   The circumference is about 3 times the length of the diameter.

Marti needs about 72 inches of trim.

■ **Talk About Math**   How could you use what you know about the relationship between the lengths of a radius and a diameter of a circle to estimate the circumference of a circle with a radius of 15 centimeters?

Check Understanding

Complete the chart below.

Radius	Diameter	Approximate circumference
5 cm	10 cm	**1.** ▦ cm
8 cm	**2.** ▦ cm	**3.** ▦ cm
4. ▦ cm	20 cm	**5.** ▦ cm
6. ▦ cm	**7.** ▦ cm	48 cm

Practice

Estimation Estimate the circumference of each object in Exercises 8–13. **Remember** to label each unit of measure.

8. Clock with a diameter of 14 cm

9. Paint can with a diameter of 5 in.

10. Volleyball with a radius of 5 in.

11. Penny with a diameter of 19 mm

12. Table with a diameter of 45 in.

13. Popcorn tin with a radius of 17 cm

Complete each sentence. For any circle,

14. an estimate for the circumference is about ▦ times the length of the diameter.

15. the circumference divided by the length of the diameter is about ▦.

Estimation For each circumference given, estimate the diameter.

16. 54 in.   **17.** 72 cm   **18.** 108 cm   **19.** 24 in.   **20.** 42 in.   **21.** 132 cm

Problem Solving

22. Will a container top with a diameter of 9 centimeters fit on a container with a radius of 5 centimeters?

23. A button has a diameter of 2 centimeters. Will it fit through a buttonhole that is 1.5 centimeters long?

24. Marti has 8 feet of red trim. About how many containers with diameters of 5 inches can Marti trim using the red trim?

Congruent Figures

Build Understanding

Paula makes paperweights. The piece of felt she glues on the bottom of each paperweight is exactly the same size and shape as the bottom of the paperweight.

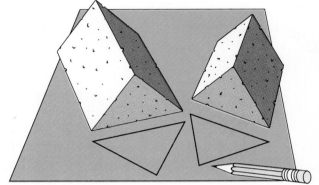

A. Figures that have the same size and shape are ***congruent***.

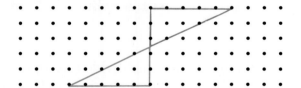

You can ***slide*** one triangle on top of the other triangle to see that both triangles are the same size and shape.

B. These figures are congruent.

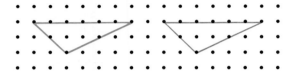

You can ***turn*** one of these figures to see that both figures are the same size and shape.

C. These figures are congruent.

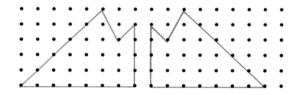

You can ***flip*** one of these figures on top of the other to see that the figures are the same size and shape.

D. The triangles are congruent because they have the same size and the same shape. The rectangles are not congruent.

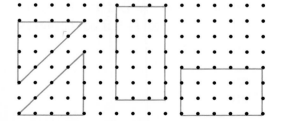

E. The diagonal segments are congruent because they have the same length. The vertical segments are not congruent.

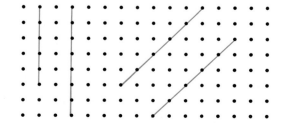

■ **Talk About Math**   How could you be sure two figures in different positions are congruent?

Check Understanding

For another example, see Set H, pages 488–489.

Tell whether the segments or figures are congruent. Write *yes* or *no*.

1. 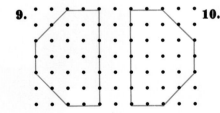 2.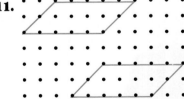

Practice

For More Practice, see Set H, pages 490–491.

Tell whether the segments or figures are congruent. Write *yes* or *no*.

3.  4.  5.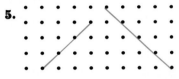

6. 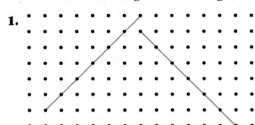 7.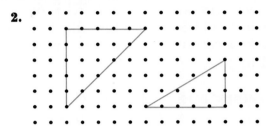

8.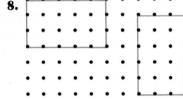

9. 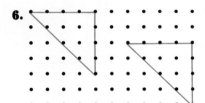 10. 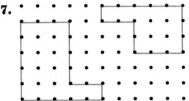 11.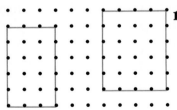

Problem Solving

12. For each pair of congruent figures in Exercises 6–11, tell whether you would flip, slide, or turn one figure to put it exactly on top of the other figure. In some cases, you may have to do a combination of these.

Draw a Diagram

Build Understanding

Steve Park is an architect. He is designing a tile floor. Could Steve use tiles like the one shown to make a rectangular floor with no spaces between the tiles?

Understand
QUESTION   Could tiles like the one shown be put together to form a solid rectangle?

FACTS   Only one size and shape will be used. The tiles must form a rectangle. There must be no space between tiles.

KEY IDEA   You can draw a diagram to help you answer the question.

Understand
QUESTION
FACTS
KEY IDEA

➤ **Plan and Solve**
STRATEGY
ANSWER

Look Back
SENSIBLE ANSWER
ALTERNATE APPROACH

➤ **Plan and Solve**
STRATEGY   Trace the figure at the right. Then cut it out. Use the cut-out figure to draw more congruent figures. Determine if there is any way to draw the figures so that they form a solid rectangle.

ANSWER   Steve could not use the octagonal tiles for his design because they cannot be put together to form a solid rectangle.

The smooth surface on ceramic tiles is called *glazing*.

Look Back   SENSIBLE ANSWER   You drew congruent figures. You tried to position the figures to make a solid rectangle. Your answer is sensible.

■ **Talk About Math**   What do you notice about the angles of an octagon? How could you have used the measures of the angles of an octagon to solve this problem?

Check Understanding

Draw a diagram to help you decide whether Steve could use tiles of each shape for a solid rectangular floor. Answer *yes* or *no*.

1.   2.   3.

Practice

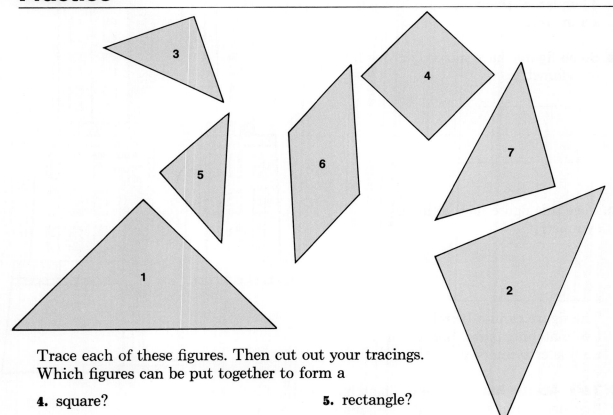

Trace each of these figures. Then cut out your tracings. Which figures can be put together to form a

4. square?   **5.** rectangle?

6. parallelogram?   **7.** trapezoid?

479

Symmetry

Build Understanding

Where could you fold this plan for a building so that the two parts match exactly?

A fold line drawn vertically down the middle of the plan shows two matching parts.

A. If a figure can be folded so that one part fits exactly over the other part, then the figure has *symmetry*. The fold line is a *line of symmetry*.

There is only one way the plan at the right could be folded so that one half fits exactly over the other half.

The plan of the building has one line of symmetry.

B. Some figures have more than one line of symmetry.

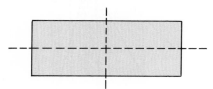

C. Does this figure have a line of symmetry?

The figure cannot be folded to make two matching parts. Some figures have no line of symmetry.

■ **Talk About Math** Are the matching parts of a figure that has symmetry congruent? Explain your answer.

Check Understanding

For another example, see Set I, pages 488–489.

Trace each figure. Then draw the lines of symmetry. How
many lines of symmetry does each figure have?

1.

2.

3.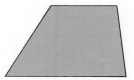

Practice

For More Practice, see Set I, pages 490–491.

Copy each figure. Draw each line of symmetry. How
many lines of symmetry does each figure have?

4.

5.

6.

7.

8.

9.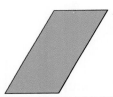

Problem Solving

The dashed line is the line of symmetry. Trace each
figure and the dashed line. Then draw the other part
of the figure.

10.

11.

12.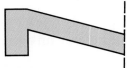

TIPS FOR
PROBLEM SOLVERS

Compare problems
to help you relate new
problems to ones you've
solved before.

Similar Figures

Build Understanding

Ismael is an artist. His friend Alice wanted him to paint a mural for her new restaurant. The small image Ismael placed in his slide projector and the large image that appears on the wall suggest *similar figures*.

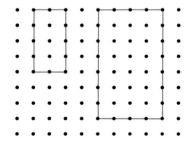

A. Similar figures have the same shape but not necessarily the same size. Are these triangles similar?

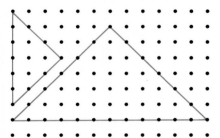

Both figures have the same shape. Each side of the large triangle is twice as long as the corresponding side of the small triangle. The triangles are similar.

B. Are these rectangles similar?

The second rectangle is twice as wide as the first rectangle, but it is not twice as long. They are not similar figures.

■ **Talk About Math**   Are congruent figures similar? Explain your answer.

482

Check Understanding

Tell whether the figures are similar. Write *yes* or *no*.

1. 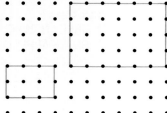   **2.** 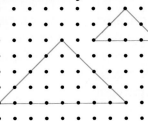   **3.**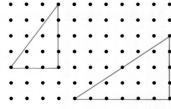

Practice

Tell whether the figures are similar. Write *yes* or *no*.

4. 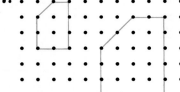   **5.** 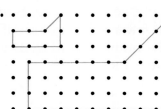   **6.**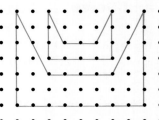

7.    **8.**   **9.**

Problem Solving

Use these figures for Problems 10–11.

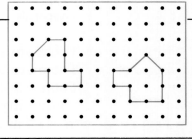

10. Copy these figures onto grid paper.

11. Number Sense Draw similar figures with sides that are three times as long.

Reading ———— Math

Vocabulary Complete each sentence.

1. Congruent segments have equal ▦.

2. A quadrilateral has ▦ sides.

3. An ▦ triangle has one obtuse angle.

4. A unit used to measure angles is the ▦.

Find a Pattern

Build Understanding

In Ms. Sanford's geometry class, the students learned that a *diagonal* is a segment that connects one vertex of a polygon to another vertex but is not a side of the polygon. One question on a quiz was: How many diagonals does a heptagon have?

Understand How many different segments can be drawn that connect the vertices of a heptagon but are not sides of the heptagon? A heptagon is a seven-sided polygon.

Plan and Solve STRATEGY Drawing the heptagon and all the diagonals might get confusing. Start with a polygon with fewer sides and see if there is a pattern in the number of diagonals as the number of sides increases.

Triangle	Quadrilateral	Pentagon	Hexagon	Heptagon
3 sides	4 sides	5 sides	6 sides	7 sides
0 diagonals	2 diagonals	5 diagonals	9 diagonals	

There are 2 more diagonals in a quadrilateral than a triangle. There are 3 more diagonals in a pentagon than a quadrilateral. There are 4 more diagonals in a hexagon than a pentagon. Continuing the pattern, a heptagon will have 5 more diagonals than a hexagon.

ANSWER A heptagon has 14 diagonals.

Look Back You could draw a picture of a heptagon with its diagonals. Be sure you draw all the diagonals and have counted all of them.

■ **Talk About Math** Explain how you would find how many diagonals a decagon has. A decagon is a 10-sided polygon.

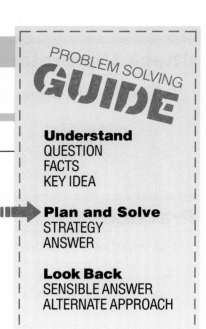

PROBLEM SOLVING
GUIDE

Understand
QUESTION
FACTS
KEY IDEA

Plan and Solve
STRATEGY
ANSWER

Look Back
SENSIBLE ANSWER
ALTERNATE APPROACH

Check Understanding

How many triangles can you make by drawing diagonals
from one vertex of a decagon? Start by drawing polygons
with fewer sides. How many triangles can you make in a

1. quadrilateral?   **2.** pentagon?   **3.** hexagon?

Use the pattern you found in Problems 1–3 to complete this table.

Number of sides	4	5	6	7	8	9	10
Number of triangles	**4.**	**5.**	**6.**	**7.**	**8.**	**9.**	**10.**

Practice

If you measure the three angles in any triangle and find the sum of
the measures, the total is 180°. What is the sum of the angle
measures of a decagon? Start with a polygon with fewer sides. Use
the pattern you found in Problems 1–10 for the number of triangles
in each polygon. What is the sum of the angle measures

11. of a quadrilateral?   **12.** of a pentagon?   **13.** of a decagon?

14. How many triangles can you make
by drawing diagonals from one
vertex of a 100-sided polygon?

15. 🖩 **Calculator**   What is the sum
of the angle measures of a
100-sided polygon?

Choose a ▨ Strategy

Green or Not?   There are 27 small white cubes
in the large cube. The top, bottom, and four sides
of the large cube are painted green. How many of
the small cubes have

16. no faces that are painted green?

17. 1 green face?

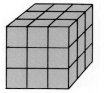

18. 2 green faces?

19. 3 green faces?

PROBLEM SOLVING STRATEGIES

Choose an Operation
Write an Equation
Draw a Diagram
Make a Table
Try and Check
Use Logical Reasoning
Find a Pattern
Work Backward
Solve a Simpler Problem
Make a Graph

Problem Solving REVIEW

Solve each problem.

1. Students in Mrs. Grant's class are making masks from 8-inch diameter paper plates. Marco has 28 inches of yarn. Does he have enough yarn to put around the circumference of the mask?

2. Glenn went to lunch after he went to the library and before he went to the bookstore. Right after lunch, he went to the bank. The post office was his first stop that morning. List Glenn's stops from first to last.

3. Photo reprints cost $0.65 each. Can Darryl have 15 reprints made for less than $10?

4. The Williamson's circular swimming pool has a diameter of 30 feet. If Mike swims along the edge of the pool, about how many times should he swim around the pool to swim $\frac{1}{4}$ mile (1,320 feet)?

5. Two numbers have a sum of 34 and a product of 285. What are the numbers?

6. **Data File** George wants to make a Chinese lantern kite as shown in the diagram on pages 528-529. If he makes the diameter of each circle 12 inches long, about how many inches will each circle be in circumference?

7. **Make a Data File** Find the regulation size of balls used in at least five different sports. List them in order from smallest to largest in circumference.

Explore with a Calculator

"Riddle-Ometry"

What does a snail leave behind when he leaves home?

1. Complete the exercises to find the answer to the riddle. They review vocabulary taught in the chapter. For Exercises a–f, you will need to replace the figure with its word name before you can solve the problem. Use your calculator to help you find each answer.

a. Count the number of letters in an ⬡ and in a ☐. Multiply the two numbers. Then multiply by 8.

b. Count the number of letters in a ◺. Add 7. Then count the number of letters in SYMMETRY and multiply your sum by that number.

c. Find the area. Multiply that number by 9.

d. Find the perimeter. Add that number to 769.

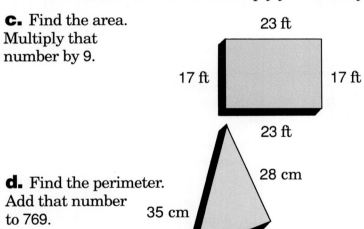

e. Count the number of letters in a RHOMBUS and in a ▱. Multiply those two numbers. Then divide that product by 7.

f. Count the number of E's in CIRCUMFERENCE, VERTICES, SYMMETRY, and ☐. Multiply that number by itself.

g. Find the sum of your answers to Exercises a-f. Then multiply by 14 and add 8,115.

h. Turn your calculator display upside down. If you have completed the exercises correctly, the answer in your display is the answer to the riddle.

Explore with a CALCULATOR

487

Reteaching

Set A pages 452–455

A geometric solid that has all flat surfaces is a polyhedron. This pyramid has 5 flat surfaces, or faces. It has 8 edges and 5 vertices.

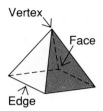

Remember that two faces meet to form an edge and three or more edges meet to form a vertex. This pyramid has

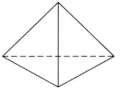

1. ▦ vertices.

2. ▦ edges.

3. ▦ faces.

Set B pages 456–457

The left-hand pyramid in Set A shows two types of polygons. Three of the faces are triangles. The bottom face is a quadrilateral.

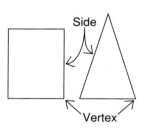

Remember that two sides of a polygon meet to form a vertex. This polygon has

1. ▦ sides

2. ▦ vertices.

3. Name the polygon.

Set C pages 458–459

A segment is named by its two endpoints.

A · —————— · B
Segment *AB* or segment *BA*

A line is named by two points on it. A line has no endpoints.

← · —————— · →
       C   *D*
Line *CD* or line *DC*

A ray is named by its endpoint and one other point on it.

· —————→
E   *F*
Ray *EF*

Remember that the endpoint of a ray is the point named first.

Use this figure for the exercises.

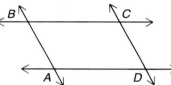

1. Name two rays with endpoint *A*.

2. Name two lines passing through *C*.

Set D pages 460–461

Here are three types of triangles.

Equilateral

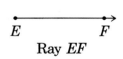
6 cm 6 cm
6 cm

Isosceles

8 cm 8 cm
6 cm

Scalene

7 cm   12 cm
10 cm

All sides equal

Two sides equal

No sides equal

Remember that an equilateral triangle is also an isosceles triangle.

1. Segment *AB* = ▦ cm

2. Segment *BC* = ▦ cm

3. Segment *AC* = ▦ cm

4. What type is the triangle?

Set E pages 462–463

A right angle looks like a square corner. A corner of a book page forms a right angle.

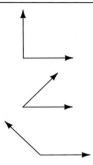

An acute angle is smaller than a right angle.

An obtuse angle is larger than a right angle.

Remember that when using 3 points to name an angle, the vertex is always the middle point. Which angle is

1. obtuse?

2. right?

3. acute?

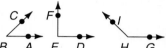

Set F pages 470–471

A trapezoid has one pair of parallel sides.

A parallelogram has two pairs of parallel sides.

Remember that a parallelogram is a rhombus if all its sides have the same length. Name each quadrilateral.

1. 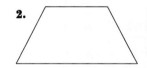   2.

Set G pages 472–473

Both endpoints of segment *AB* are on the circle.
Segment *AB* is a chord.

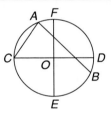

Remember that a chord through the center of a circle is a diameter.

1. Name four chords of circle *O*.

2. Name two diameters of circle *O*.

Set H pages 476–477

Some ways of moving a polygon are: *Slide:* Move it in any direction, as if on a sled. *Flip:* Flip it over a line, as if turning a page in a book. *Turn:* Turn it on a vertex, as if the vertex was nailed down.

Remember that congruent figures have the same size and shape. Would you slide, flip, or turn one figure to show it is congruent to the other?

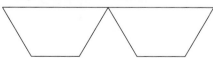

Set I pages 480–481

A square has 4 lines of symmetry because there are 4 ways to fold it so that one half of the figure fits the other half exactly.

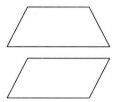

Remember that a figure may have 0, 1, or more lines of symmetry. How many lines of symmetry does each figure have?

1.    2.

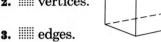

More Practice

Set A pages 452–455

This rectangular prism has

1. ▦ faces.

2. ▦ vertices.

3. ▦ edges.

This triangular prism has

4. ▦ faces.

5. ▦ vertices.

6. ▦ edges.

Set B pages 456–457

Tell which polygon you see. Then tell how many sides and vertices each polygon has.

1.

2.

3. ROAD CONSTRUCTION AHEAD

Set C pages 458–459

Use the figure at the right for Exercises 1–4.

1. Name a ray.

2. Name a line.

3. Name a pair of intersecting lines.

4. Name a pair of parallel lines.

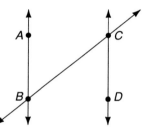

Set D pages 460–461

Measure each side of each triangle. Then tell whether the triangle is equilateral, isosceles, or scalene.

1. Segment AB = ▦ cm

Segment AC = ▦ cm

Segment BC = ▦ cm

2. Segment DE = ▦ cm

Segment DF = ▦ cm

Segment EF = ▦ cm

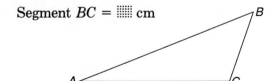

Set E pages 462–463

Use the figure at the right for Exercises 1–3.

1. Name two right angles.

2. Name one acute angle.

3. Name two obtuse angles.

Set F   pages 470–471

Name each quadrilateral.

1.    **2.**    **3.**

Set G   pages 472–473

Use circle O for Exercises 1–4. Name each segment that is

1. a radius.   **2.** a chord.   **3.** a diameter.

4. Name each central angle of circle O.

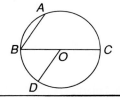

Set H   pages 476–477

Tell whether the figures are congruent. Write *yes* or *no*.

1. 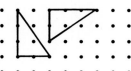   **2.** 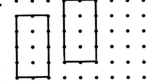   **3.**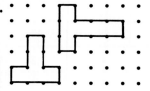

4. For each pair of congruent figures in Exercises 1–3, tell whether you would flip, slide, or turn one figure to show it is congruent to the other figure.

Set I   pages 480–481

Copy each figure. Draw each line of symmetry. How many lines of symmetry does each figure have?

1.   **2.**    **3.**

Enrichment

Surface Area

To find the *surface area* of a solid shape, add the areas of all the faces.

Find the surface area of this prism. Think of the figure as being taken apart.

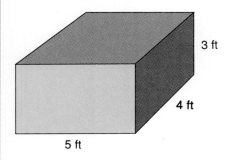

3 ft

4 ft

5 ft

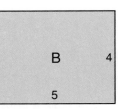

A 4

3

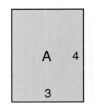

B 4

5

C 4

3

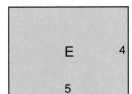

D 3

5

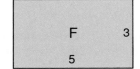

E 4

5

F 3

5

Make a table showing the area of each face.
Remember to multiply the length and width to find the area of each rectangle.

	Face	Length (ft)	Width (ft)	Area (sq ft)
1.	A	4	3	
2.	B	5	4	
3.	C	4	3	
4.	D	5	3	
5.	E	5	4	
6.	F	5	3	

7. What is the surface area of the figure?

Find the surface area to answer each question.

8. How much wrapping paper is needed to cover this box?

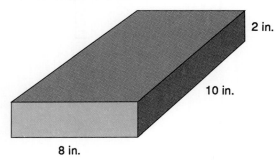

2 in.

10 in.

8 in.

9. How much paint is needed to cover this container?

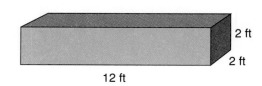

2 ft

2 ft

12 ft

Chapter 14 Review/Test

Is each polyhedron a prism or a pyramid?

1.

2.

How many sides does each have?

3. Pentagon   **4.** Octagon

Name each figure.

5.
R   S

6.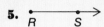
X   Y

Tell whether each triangle is *equilateral, isosceles,* or *scalene.*

7.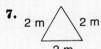
2 m   2 m
2 m

8.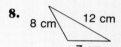
8 cm   12 cm
7 cm

Use a protractor to measure each angle. Then tell whether the angle is *right, acute,* or *obtuse.*

9.

10.

11. Use a protractor to draw an angle with a measure of 30°.

Name each quadrilateral.

12.

13.

14. Estimate the circumference of a circle with a diameter of 12 inches.

15. A diameter is a segment from the center of a circle to any point on the circle. Write *yes* or *no.*

16. Are the figures congruent? Write *yes* or *no.*

17. Could tiles like the ones shown cover a floor with no spaces between the tiles?

18. How many lines of symmetry does the figure at the right have?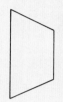

19. Are the figures similar? Write *yes* or *no.*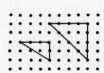

Read the problem below. Then answer Items 20–21.

How many cuts would be made on a pizza shaped like a pentagon if cuts are made on all the diagonals?

20. Which is another way of asking the question in the problem?

   a. How many pieces of pizza can be cut from a pizza shaped like a pentagon?

   b. How many sides in a pentagon?

   c. How many diagonals does a pentagon have?

21. Solve the problem.

22. Write About Math Can parallel lines ever be perpendicular to each other? Why or why not?

493

Ratio, Proportion, and Percent

Did You Know: Early bikes were called high wheelers. Those "wheels" moved on a direct drive system. There were no chains to make a gear system. Each turn of the pedal made the wheel go around one time.

Number-Sense Project

Estimate
Using the fastest gear, estimate how many times the back wheel of a bike will go around (without coasting) when you move the pedal so it makes one revolution.

Gather Data
Ask a student to hold up the back wheel of a bike while you turn the pedal around one time. Hold a finger against the tire to keep the wheel from coasting. Count the number of revolutions.

Analyze and Report
Count the number of back tire revolutions for one turn of the pedal using the highest and lowest gears. Make a table or graph to show your results. Share your results with other students.

Meaning of Ratio

Build Understanding

The students at Washington School held a talent show. The first act of the show featured 5 singers and 2 dancers.

A. A *ratio* is one way to compare two quantities. The ratio of singers to dancers is 5 to 2. This ratio can be written as 5 to 2 or 5 : 2.

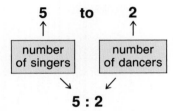

The order of comparison is important.

The ratio of dancers to singers is 2 to 5. This ratio is written 2 to 5 or 2 : 5.

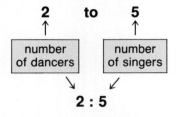

B. A ratio can compare a part to a total. The first act of the talent show featured a total of 7 performers. The ratio of singers to performers is 5 to 7. The ratio is written as 5 to 7 or 5 : 7.

The ratio of dancers to performers is 2 to 7. The ratio is written as 2 to 7 or 2 : 7.

■ **Talk About Math** If you know the ratio of boys to girls is 3 to 4, how do you find the ratio of girls to boys? of boys to the total number of performers? How do you decide which number to write first in a ratio?

Check Understanding

For another example, see Set A, pages 522–523.

The performers in the second act of the talent show were jugglers and musicians. Write each ratio.

1. Jugglers to musicians

2. Musicians to jugglers

3. Musicians to performers

4. Jugglers to performers

Practice

For More Practice, see Set A, pages 524–525.

The musicians for the third act needed drums, guitars, and trumpets. Write each ratio.

5. Guitars to trumpets

6. Drums to instruments

7. Guitars to instruments

8. Instruments to trumpets

Suppose students used 5 red, 4 blue, and 2 white rolls of streamers to decorate the stage. Explain each ratio.

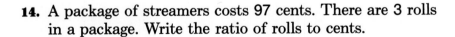

9. 5 : 2   10. 4 : 5   11. 2 : 4   12. 5 : 11   13. 4 : 11

14. A package of streamers costs 97 cents. There are 3 rolls in a package. Write the ratio of rolls to cents.

Problem Solving

15. Kevin needs 7 rolls of red and 8 rolls of white streamers. Packages are sold containing 3 rolls of a single color. How many packages of each color does he need to buy?

16. The only coins Kevin has are quarters and dimes. The ratio of his dimes to his coins is 7 : 23. How much money does he have? Does he have enough to buy the streamers he needs? Use the information in Exercises 14 and 15.

Equal Ratios

Build Understanding

One of the water rides at Colossal Park has boats that look like logs. Each log can hold 5 people.

A. Ratio Rides
Materials: Pencils, small objects
Groups: With a partner

a. Use small objects to represent riders. Use pencils to represent logs. Show the ratio of riders to logs, 5 : 1.

b. Show the ratio of riders to logs when there are 2 logs and 10 riders.

The ratio is 5 riders to 1 log, or 5 : 1, and 10 riders to 2 logs, or 10 : 2.

The ratio 10 : 2 is equal to the ratio 5 : 1.

c. Use your materials to find another ratio equal to 5 : 1 when there are 4 full logs.

d. How many ratios can you find equal to 5 : 1?

B. You can use pictures to write a list of equal ratios. There are 3 triangular flags and 2 square flags on each post.

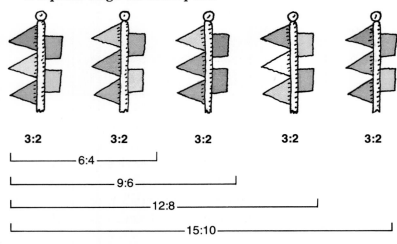

| 3:2 | 3:2 | 3:2 | 3:2 | 3:2 |

|———— 6:4 ————|

|———————— 9:6 ————————|

|———————————— 12:8 ————————————|

|———————————————— 15:10 ————————————————|

■ Talk About Math

Suppose the first number in a ratio is greater than the second. In an equal ratio, will the first number also be greater than the second? Explain.

Check Understanding

For another example, see Set B, pages 522–523.

1. In another ride, there are 4 riders to a car. Use objects to complete the list of equal ratios.

2. If each car holds 3 riders, use the picture to complete the list of equal ratios.

Riders : Cars
4 : 1   8 : ▦   ▦ : ▦   ▦ : ▦   ▦ : ▦

Car : Riders

1 : 3   2 : ▦   ▦ : 9   4 : ▦   ▦ : ▦

Practice

For More Practice, see Set B, pages 524–525.

3. In a game, you are allowed 5 tries to make a basket. Use objects to complete the list of equal ratios.

Tries : Baskets
5 : 1   10 : ▦   ▦ : ▦   ▦ : ▦   ▦ : ▦

Use the picture to write a list of equal ratios.

4. 4 red stripes and 3 blue stripes are on each T-shirt.

Red stripes : Blue stripes   4 : 3   ▦ : 6   12 : ▦   16 : ▦   ▦ : ▦

5. Each ride lasts 10 seconds and goes 90 meters.

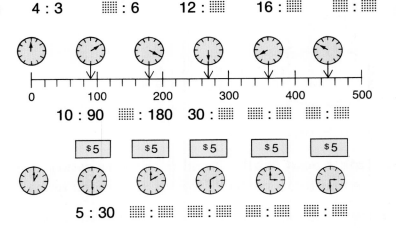

Seconds : Meters   10 : 90   ▦ : 180   30 : ▦   ▦ : ▦   ▦ : ▦

6. It costs $5 to rent a paddle boat for 30 minutes.

Dollars : Minutes   5 : 30   ▦ : ▦   ▦ : ▦   ▦ : ▦   ▦ : ▦

Problem Solving

7. **Visual Thinking** Two fences each measure 40 feet. Each has a post every 10 feet. The first fence is in a straight line. The other forms a square. Are the ratios for the number of feet of fence to the number of posts the same for both fences? Why or why not? Use graph paper to show how you solved the problem.

Finding Equal Ratios

Build Understanding

A. Leland owns the Bicycle Fix-it Shop. He can repair 4 bicycles in 2 hours. The ratio of bicycles to hours can be written in three different ways.

4 to 2   **4 : 2** $\dfrac{4}{2}$

B. This ratio can be used to find the number of bicycles Leland can repair during different amounts of time.

$$\underset{2 \div 2}{\overset{4 \div 2}{\dfrac{4}{2}}} = \dfrac{2}{1} \qquad \underset{2 \times 2}{\overset{4 \times 2}{\dfrac{4}{2}}} = \dfrac{8}{4}$$

C. Find n in $\dfrac{2}{3} = \dfrac{12}{n}$.

$$\dfrac{2}{3} = \dfrac{12}{n}$$

$$\underset{3 \times 6}{\overset{2 \times 6}{\dfrac{2}{3}}} = \dfrac{12}{18} \qquad \begin{array}{l}\text{Since } 2 \times 6 = 12, \\ \text{multiply } 3 \times 6 \text{ to find } n.\end{array}$$

$$n = 18$$

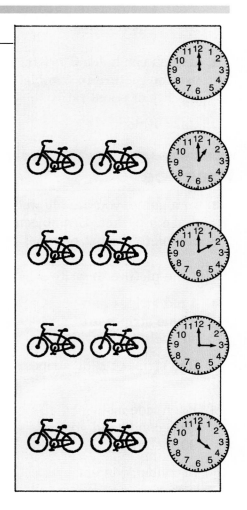

■ **Talk About Math** $\dfrac{3}{5}$ and $\dfrac{6}{10}$ are equal ratios. How are the first terms related? How are the second terms related?

Check Understanding

For another example, see Set C, pages 522–523.

Tell how to find the equal ratios.

1. $\dfrac{4}{5} = \dfrac{16}{20}$ Multiply 4 and 5 by ⸛.

2. $\dfrac{24}{21} = \dfrac{8}{7}$ Divide 24 and 21 by ⸛.

3. $\dfrac{9}{4} = \dfrac{18}{8}$ Multiply 9 and 4 by ⸛.

Complete each list of equal ratios.

4. $\dfrac{3}{4} = \dfrac{⬚}{8} = \dfrac{9}{⬚} = \dfrac{⬚}{16} = \dfrac{15}{⬚}$

5. $\dfrac{4}{5} = \dfrac{⬚}{10} = \dfrac{12}{⬚} = \dfrac{⬚}{20} = \dfrac{20}{⬚}$

Practice

For More Practice, see Set C, pages 524–525.

Complete each list of equal ratios.

6. $\frac{2}{7} = \frac{}{14} = \frac{6}{} = \frac{}{28} = \frac{}{35}$

7. $\frac{5}{8} = \frac{10}{} = \frac{}{24} = \frac{}{32} = \frac{25}{}$

8. $\frac{4}{5} = \frac{}{10} = \frac{12}{} = \frac{}{20} = \frac{20}{}$

9. $\frac{11}{12} = \frac{22}{} = \frac{}{36} = \frac{}{48} = \frac{55}{}$

Find n.

10. $\frac{5}{2} = \frac{10}{n}$

11. $\frac{3}{4} = \frac{n}{12}$

12. $\frac{9}{5} = \frac{27}{n}$

13. $\frac{4}{3} = \frac{n}{15}$

14. $\frac{3}{2} = \frac{n}{18}$

15. $\frac{5}{6} = \frac{40}{n}$

16. $\frac{7}{11} = \frac{n}{33}$

17. $\frac{4}{7} = \frac{28}{n}$

18. $\frac{3}{10} = \frac{9}{n}$

19. $\frac{3}{13} = \frac{15}{n}$

20. $\frac{2}{15} = \frac{14}{n}$

21. $\frac{5}{8} = \frac{100}{n}$

22. $\frac{17}{3} = \frac{n}{15}$

23. $\frac{12}{15} = \frac{36}{n}$

24. $\frac{14}{30} = \frac{n}{90}$

Multiply or divide to find the equal ratio.

25. Buy 2 brake pads for $7. $\frac{2}{7} = \frac{6}{}$

26. Spend 132 minutes to assemble 4 bicycles. $\frac{132}{4} = \frac{}{1}$

27. Write 4 equal ratios. Replace 3 mirrors in 10 minutes.

28. Write 3 equal ratios. Spend $6 for 48 wheel spokes.

Problem Solving

29. Leland can stack 9 bicycle tires on each rack at the shop. How many racks does he need to stack 36 bicycle tires?

30. Leland orders 8 new 18-inch bicycle tires for every 5 new 26-inch bicycle tires. If 25 of the 26-inch tires were ordered, how many 18-inch tires were ordered?

Skills ———— Review   pages 214–267

Add, subtract, or multiply.

1. $\begin{array}{r} 0.72 \\ + 0.49 \end{array}$ **2.** $\begin{array}{r} 0.72 \\ \times 0.49 \end{array}$ **3.** $\begin{array}{r} 0.72 \\ - 0.49 \end{array}$ **4.** $\begin{array}{r} 5.68 \\ - 0.204 \end{array}$ **5.** $\begin{array}{r} 0.205 \\ \times \quad 92 \end{array}$ **6.** $\begin{array}{r} 0.809 \\ + 15.2 \end{array}$

7. $82.4 + 3.65$ **8.** $19.5 - 14.7$ **9.** 3.2×7.91

Proportions

Build Understanding

Color	Number of Teams
Blue	18
White	17
Red	15
Orange	6
Yellow	6

A. The most common colors worn by Major League baseball teams are listed in the chart. The Rockford Little League has 4 teams that wear orange and 12 teams that wear blue on their uniforms. Is the ratio of teams that wear orange to the teams that wear blue the same for both leagues?

Major League   Orange → $\dfrac{6}{18} = \dfrac{12}{36}$
Blue ⟶

Little League   Orange → $\dfrac{4}{12} = \dfrac{8}{24} = \dfrac{12}{36}$
Blue ⟶

Since each list of equal ratios shows 12 orange and 36 blue, the ratios 6:18 and 4:12 are equal.

$\dfrac{6}{18} = \dfrac{4}{12}$ 6×12 and 4×18 are **cross-products** of these two ratios.
$6 \times 12 = 72$ and $4 \times 18 = 72$

If two ratios are equal, their cross-products are equal.
Two ratios that are equal form a **proportion**.

B. If the Rockford Little League wanted to have the same ratio of red to blue on their uniforms as the Major Leagues do, how many teams would wear red? Cross-products can be used to find a missing number in a proportion.

Major League   Little League

Red → $\dfrac{15}{18} = \dfrac{n}{12}$ Write a proportion.
Blue →   Use n for the missing number.

$18 \times n = 15 \times 12$ Find the cross-products. Since the ratios are equal, the cross-products are equal.
$18 \times n = 180$ Multiply.

$n = 180 \div 18$ Divide to find n.

$n = 10$

The Rockford Little League would have 10 teams wearing red.

502

■ **Talk About Math**   Why is the proportion $\frac{15}{18} = \frac{12}{n}$ not correct for Example B?

Check Understanding

For another example, see Set D, pages 522–523.

Find the cross-products. Then tell if the ratios are equal.

1. $\frac{3}{9}$ $\frac{4}{12}$

2. $\frac{4}{3}$ $\frac{9}{6}$

3. $\frac{3}{6}$ $\frac{5}{10}$

4. $\frac{15}{6}$ $\frac{10}{4}$

5. $\frac{12}{7}$ $\frac{9}{6}$

6. $\frac{20}{9}$ $\frac{25}{10}$

7. Number Sense   Would the missing number in the proportion $\frac{15}{20} = \frac{12}{n}$ be greater than or less than 12? How do you know?

Practice

For More Practice, see Set D, pages 524–525.

Solve each proportion using cross-products.

8. $\frac{2}{n} = \frac{3}{15}$

9. $\frac{n}{6} = \frac{3}{9}$

10. $\frac{4}{6} = \frac{14}{n}$

11. $\frac{n}{8} = \frac{9}{12}$

12. $\frac{20}{6} = \frac{10}{n}$

13. $\frac{4}{16} = \frac{3}{n}$

14. $\frac{2}{n} = \frac{5}{20}$

15. $\frac{9}{15} = \frac{12}{n}$

16. $\frac{n}{18} = \frac{16}{36}$

17. $\frac{12}{40} = \frac{18}{n}$

For Exercises 18–22, tell whether you would use paper and pencil or mental math. Then solve the proportion.

18. $\frac{5}{n} = \frac{10}{12}$

19. $\frac{n}{8} = \frac{8}{64}$

20. $\frac{10}{6} = \frac{15}{n}$

21. $\frac{6}{n} = \frac{7}{14}$

22. $\frac{n}{12} = \frac{3}{2}$

Problem Solving

23. Sam bought 6 baseballs for $14. How many baseballs can he buy for $21?

24. Gerry bought a baseball cap for $4.70 and a bat for $8.65. How much change will he get from $20?

25. The Rockford Twins practice 4 times in 7 days. How many times will they practice in 2 weeks?

26. The league can buy 15 pairs of baseball socks for $20. How much would 24 pairs of socks cost?

Write an Equation

Build Understanding

An encyclopedia showed a *scale drawing* of a Northwest Coast Indian totem pole that was carved in the early 1800s. In the drawing, 2 inches represents 15 feet. What is the actual height of the totem pole?

Understand How tall is the actual totem pole? In the picture, it is 5 inches tall. The scale in the drawing is the ratio of 2 to 15. It compares drawing height to actual height.

**Plan and Solve**

STRATEGY   Write a ratio for the totem pole to compare drawing height to actual height. Write a proportion using the two ratios.

Scale   Totem pole
$$\frac{2}{15} = \frac{5}{n}$$
← Drawing (inches)
← Actual (feet)

Solve the proportion.

	Paper and Pencil	**Calculator**
Find the cross-products.	$2 \times n = 15 \times 5$	$15 \boxed{\times} 5$
Multiply.	$2 \times n = 75$	$\boxed{\div} 2 \boxed{=} \; 37.5$
Divide.	$n = 37\frac{1}{2}$	

ANSWER   The actual height of the totem pole is $37\frac{1}{2}$ feet.

Look Back The drawing height of 5 inches is a little more than twice the 2 inches in the scale. The actual height is more than twice the 15 feet in the scale. The answer is reasonable.

■ **Talk About Math**   Could you also solve the problem with the proportion $\frac{15}{2} = \frac{n}{5}$? with the proportion $\frac{2}{15} = \frac{n}{5}$? Explain why or why not.

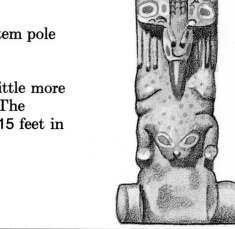

Northwest Coast Indians lived along the Pacific Ocean from northern California to southern Alaska.

Check Understanding

1. Measure the canoe. Use the scale 2 inches → 14 feet. Which of these proportions will not help you find the actual length? Why?

   a. $\frac{2}{14} = \frac{n}{3}$ **b.** $\frac{2}{14} = \frac{3}{n}$ **c.** $\frac{2}{3} = \frac{14}{n}$

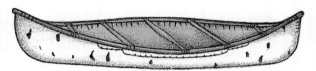

2. Find the actual length of the canoe.

Practice

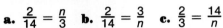

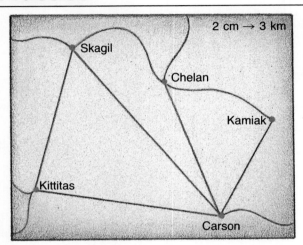

2 cm → 3 km

Measure the map distance to find the actual distance between Carson and the other Indian villages. **Remember** to use a proportion to find the actual distance.

3. Skagil   4. Chelan

5. Kittitas   6. Kamiak

Midchapter ———— Checkup

1. Use the items at the right. Write a ratio that compares the number of necklaces to the number of baskets.

2. Complete the list of equal ratios.

   $\frac{7}{3} = \frac{}{6} = \frac{21}{} = \frac{}{}$

3. Multiply or divide to find equal ratios.

   $\frac{21}{42} = \frac{7}{}$

4. Find the cross-products. Tell if the ratios are equal.

   $\frac{7}{12} \quad \frac{6}{9}$

5. Use cross-products to solve the proportion.

   $\frac{6}{n} = \frac{7}{14}$

6. In the map above, measure the distance between Kittitas and Skagil. Then use a proportion to find the actual distance.

Problem Solving WORKSHOP

Explore as a Team

1. Work with another student to cut a piece of string the same length as your height.

2. How many times will that length of string wrap around your head, wrist, elbow, knee, and ankle?

3. Record your results. Write a ratio to compare the number of times the string wraps safely around your head, wrist, and so on, to 1 (the number of times the string reaches your height).

	Number of times string wraps around	Number of times string reaches your height	Ratio
Head		1	
Wrist		1	

 FOR
WORKING TOGETHER
Remember, you can disagree without being disagreeable.

Explore with a Computer

Use the *Spreadsheet Workshop Project* for this activity.

Mary and Helen volunteer to read articles to senior citizens. Each week Mary visits 2 people for 1 hour each. Helen visits 3 people for 45 minutes each.

	People Visited	Minutes Each	Minutes/ Week	Hours/ Month
Mary				
Helen				

1. At the computer, enter this data in the spreadsheet. Who volunteers more time each month? How much more?

2. Find the ratio of the minutes Mary visits each person to the minutes Helen visits each person.

Real-Life Decision Making

You want to buy Puffy Crunch Popcorn. Your mother says you can buy it if you can prove that it is a better buy than Movie Time Popcorn. Is Puffy Crunch a better buy? Why?

$1.44

96¢

Visual Thinking Activity

How many cubes were used to build this staircase? Remember to count the cubes you cannot see.

Number-Sense Project

Look back at pages 494-495.

Most bicycles use gears consisting of a chain and different size sprockets. The size of the sprocket is determined by the number of teeth.

a. The high gear formed by this sprocket setup has a ratio of 54:14. Would the back wheel make more than one revolution or less than one revolution each time you turn the pedals?

Gear Ratio:

Number of teeth in front sprocket
―――――――――――
Number of teeth in rear sprocket

b. Based on the 54:14 ratio, describe what the back wheel does every time there is a complete revolution of the pedals.

507

Ratios and Percents

Build Understanding

A newspaper poll asked 100 children, ages 5 to 12, what they wanted to be when they grew up. They were asked to pick one of the choices in the chart. The chart shows how many children selected each choice.

A. Grown-up Percents
Materials: Grid paper, 5 different color crayons or markers
Groups: With a partner

a. Outline a 10-by-10 grid. How many squares are enclosed in the outline?

b. Using a different color for each choice, show the number of children who made each choice by coloring squares in the grid. Color one square for each child.

c. Copy the chart. For each choice write a ratio comparing the number of children who selected that choice to the total number of children polled.

What do you want to be when you grow up?

Happily married	38
Rich	24
Healthy	19
Surrounded by friends	14
Other	5
Total children polled	100

B. When a number is compared to 100, the comparison can be written as a ratio, or as a ***percent***. Percent means *per one hundred*. The symbol for percent is %.

The selection of the choice *Happily married* by 38 of the 100 children can be shown in different ways.

The grid shows 38 out of 100 squares colored.

The ratio of children who made this choice to the total is written 38 to 100, or 38:100, or $\frac{38}{100}$.

The percent of children who made this choice is written 38%.

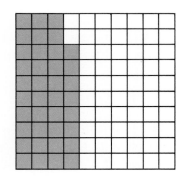

■ **Talk About Math** On a 10-by-10 grid, how many squares would be colored to show 100%? How many squares would be colored to show 0%?

508

Check Understanding

For another example, see Set E, pages 522–523.

Use the 10-by-10 grid at the right. Write a ratio and a percent to name the part shaded

1. red.　　**2.** blue.

3. green.　　**4.** yellow.

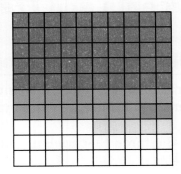

Practice

For More Practice, see Set E, pages 524–525.

Write each ratio as a percent.

5. $\frac{18}{100}$　　**6.** $\frac{50}{100}$　　**7.** $\frac{5}{100}$　　**8.** $\frac{100}{100}$　　**9.** $\frac{27}{100}$　　**10.** $\frac{20}{100}$

11. 2 to 100　　**12.** 75 to 100　　**13.** 1 to 100　　**14.** 43 to 100

15. 25:100　　**16.** 43:100　　**17.** 99:100　　**18.** 32:100

Write each percent as a ratio in fraction form.

19. 26%　　**20.** 7%　　**21.** 67%　　**22.** 90%　　**23.** 9%　　**24.** 1%

25. 39%　　**26.** 19%　　**27.** 82%　　**28.** 29%　　**29.** 16%　　**30.** 12%

Estimation Use the data from the chart in Example A to tell if each statement is true or false.

31. Almost 40% of the children chose *Happily married*.

32. Almost 50% of the children chose *Other*.

33. About 1 out of 5 chose *Healthy*.

34. About $\frac{1}{4}$ chose *Rich*.

Problem Solving

Out of 100 cars, 13 are sports cars.

35. What percent are sports cars?

36. What percent are not sports cars?

37. Of the 13 sports cars, 9 are red. What percent of the 100 cars are red sports cars?

Percents and Fractions

Build Understanding

For a science project, Melanie counted and identified birds that came near her home.

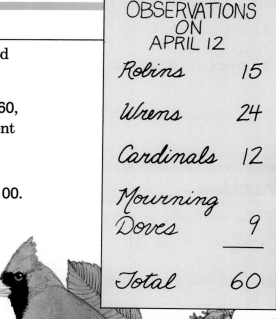

OBSERVATIONS ON APRIL 12

Robins	15
Wrens	24
Cardinals	12
Mourning Doves	9
Total	60

A. Of the birds that Melanie saw, 15 out of 60, or $\frac{1}{4}$ of the birds, were robins. What percent of the birds were robins?

Since percent means *per hundred*, find an equal fraction with a denominator of 100.

Fraction ⟶ Percent

$$\frac{1}{4} \overset{\times\ 25}{=} \frac{25}{100} = 25\%$$
$$\times\ 25$$

25% of the birds were robins.

B. Melanie found that 40% of the birds she saw were wrens. What fraction of the birds were wrens?

Write the percent as a fraction with a denominator of 100. Write a fraction in lowest terms.

Percent ⟶ Fraction

$$40\% = \frac{40}{100} \overset{\div\ 20}{=} \frac{2}{5}$$
$$\div\ 20$$

$\frac{2}{5}$ of the birds were wrens.

■ **Talk About Math** Melanie saw no woodpeckers. What fraction is that? What percent is it? What fraction and percent would describe the situation if all the birds she saw were the same type of bird?

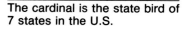

The cardinal is the state bird of 7 states in the U.S.

Check Understanding

For another example, see Set F, pages 522–523.

Complete.

1. $\frac{7}{10} = \frac{\text{▦}}{100}$
$= \text{▦}\%$

2. $\frac{3}{4} = \frac{\text{▦}}{100}$
$= \text{▦}\%$

3. $\frac{3}{5} = \frac{\text{▦}}{100}$
$= \text{▦}\%$

4. Write a percent for $\frac{4}{5}$.

5. Write a fraction in lowest terms for 25%.

Practice

For More Practice, see Set F, pages 524–525.

Write each percent as a fraction in lowest terms.

6. 27% **7.** 13% **8.** 1% **9.** 30% **10.** 50% **11.** 45% **12.** 4% **13.** 100%

Write each fraction as a percent.

14. $\frac{23}{100}$ **15.** $\frac{9}{100}$ **16.** $\frac{81}{100}$ **17.** $\frac{3}{10}$ **18.** $\frac{4}{25}$ **19.** $\frac{1}{5}$ **20.** $\frac{19}{20}$ **21.** $\frac{1}{4}$

Problem Solving

Melanie put her second day's observation in a circle graph. Use it to find these percents.

22. Woodpeckers   **23.** Blue jays

24. Wrens   **25.** Cardinals

26. Robins   **27.** Doves

28. Only 5% of the children did science projects on birds. What fraction did not do projects on birds?

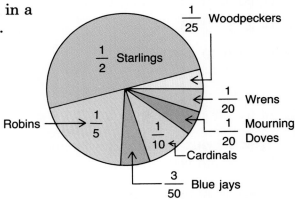

Explore ———— Math

Write a fraction in lowest terms for each percent.
Describe the pattern.
29. 50% **30.** 100% **31.** 150% **32.** 200% **33.** 250% **34.** 300% **35.** 350%

36. When a percent is greater than 100%, a fraction equal to it is greater than what number?

Percents and Decimals

Build Understanding

Many states charge a sales tax on items you buy. A tax of $0.06 on each dollar spent is a ratio of 6 cents to 100 cents. A sales tax is often named as a percent.

A. Decimals that name hundredths can easily be written as percents. Remember that percent means *per hundred*.

$$0.06 = \frac{6}{100} = 6\%$$

A tax of $0.06 on a dollar is a 6% tax.

B. Write 0.4 as a percent. First find the equal decimal in hundredths.

Think: $\frac{4}{10} = \frac{40}{100}$

$$0.4 = 0.40 = 40\%$$

C. Percents can be written as decimals.

30% means 30 per hundred or 30 hundredths.
$$30\% = 0.30 = 0.3$$

9% means 9 per hundred or 9 hundredths.
$$9\% = 0.09$$

■ **Talk About Math** How would you write 140% as a decimal? How would you show it using 10-by-10 grids?

Check Understanding

For another example, see Set G, pages 522–523.

Write a decimal and a percent for each picture.

1.

2.

3.

4.

5. Complete the table.

Percent	50%	7%			
Decimal			0.29	0.3	0.03

Practice

For More Practice, see Set G, pages 524–525.

Write each percent as a decimal.

6. 23%   **7.** 94%   **8.** 45%   **9.** 6%   **10.** 1%   **11.** 9%

12. 90%   **13.** 25%   **14.** 99%   **15.** 80%   **16.** 100%   **17.** 10%

Write each decimal as a percent.

18. 0.43   **19.** 0.65   **20.** 0.91   **21.** 0.19   **22.** 0.07   **23.** 0.04

24. 0.5   **25.** 0.3   **26.** 0.02   **27.** 0.1   **28.** 0.10   **29.** 1.00

Mixed Practice   Complete the table.

Percent	**30.**	30%	**33.**	**35.**	**36.**	5%
Decimal	0.2	**31.**	0.25	0.75	0.44	**38.**
Lowest Terms Fraction	$\frac{1}{5}$	**32.**	**34.**	$\frac{3}{4}$	**37.**	**39.**

Problem Solving

40. Judy's state charges a 3% sales tax on food items. Toni's state charges a 5% sales tax on food items. How much more on every dollar does Judy save than Toni on food purchases?

41. Critical Thinking   During weekend sales, Big Bob sells items at 60% of the regular price. During the Giant Sale at the end of the year, items are sold at 60% *off* the regular price. How much more on every dollar will you save if you buy an item at the Giant Sale instead of buying it at a weekend sale?

TIPS FOR PROBLEM SOLVERS

Compare problems to help you relate new problems to ones you've solved before.

60%

Finding a Percent of a Number

Build Understanding

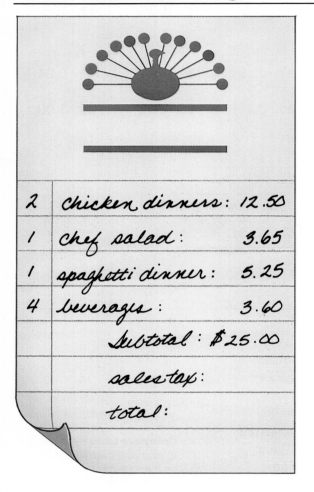

2 chicken dinners: 12.50
1 chef salad: 3.65
1 spaghetti dinner: 5.25
4 beverages: 3.60
Subtotal: $25.00
sales tax:
total:

Mr. and Mrs. Rivera and their children had lunch at the Blue Peacock Restaurant. Their total bill was $25.

In restaurants, people leave a tip for the person who serves them. The usual tip is 15% of the cost of the food. What is the tip on $25?

Since 15% means 15¢ for each dollar, find 15% of 25.

Write the percent as a decimal.

15% = 0.15

Then multiply.

$$\begin{array}{r} 25 \\ \times\,0.15 \\ \hline 125 \\ 250 \\ \hline 3.75 \end{array}$$

The tip is $3.75. The Riveras left $3.75 for the tip.

■ **Talk About Math** How could you do the computation in the example using a calculator? Try to use the %ﾠkey.

Check Understanding

For another example, see Set H, pages 522–523.

Find the percent of each number.

1. 8% of 90　　**2.** 12% of 70　　**3.** 7% of 45　　**4.** 50% of 83

5. 40% of 19　　**6.** 75% of 86　　**7.** 30% of 210　　**8.** 60% of 185

Practice

For More Practice, see Set H, pages 524–525.

Find the percent of each number.

9. 10% of 50　　　**10.** 80% of 35　　　**11.** 75% of 12　　　**12.** 6% of 300

13. 60% of 300　　**14.** 40% of 18　　　**15.** 4% of 150　　　**16.** 7% of 70

17. 35% of 70　　　**18.** 5% of 36　　　**19.** 90% of 150　　**20.** 1% of 18

Number Sense　Write >, <, or =.

21. 100% of 65 ▦ 65　　**22.** 85% of 65 ▦ 65　　**23.** 125% of 65 ▦ 65

24. 50% of 45 ▦ 45　　**25.** 99% of 87 ▦ 87　　**26.** 25% of 40 ▦ 40

Problem Solving

Solve each problem.

27. Mr. Rivera's state charges a 6% sales tax. What is the amount of tax he paid on his bill of $25?

28. What was the cost of the food and tax for the Riveras' meal? What was the total cost including the tip as well?

Use Data　Use the data in the table on page 84.

29. 75% of 1 foot = ▦ inches

30. 50% of 1 mile = ▦ yards

31. 20% of 1 mile = ▦ feet

32. 25% of 1 yard = ▦ inches

Reading ——— Math

Vocabulary and Percents　Use the clues given to form the word described.

1. In the word "lesson," 50% of the letters spell the name of a family member.

2. In the word "must," 75% of the letters spell the word for the answer to an addition problem.

3. In the word "sport," 60% of the letters spell the word for the opposite of "bottom."

4. In the word "cheap," 100% of the letters spell the name of a fruit.

Estimating a Percent of a Number

Build Understanding

The United States Census Bureau estimates that 18% of the population will be between 5 and 17 years old in 1990. If the city of Oak Hill, West Virginia, has a population of 7,800 in 1990, about how many people will be in the 5-to-17 age group?

To find an estimate of the population, use numbers compatible with the percent and the population. Compatible numbers are close to the original numbers and are easy to use in computation.

18% is about 20%.
7,800 is about 8,000.

A. Find 20% of 8,000 to estimate the population.

$$\begin{array}{r} 8,000 \\ \times\ \ 0.20 \\ \hline 1,600.00 \end{array}$$
Write 20% as a decimal.
Then multiply.

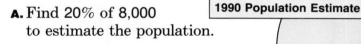

1990 Population Estimate

18%
5 to 17
years old

B. You can also use a fraction to estimate the population. Find 20% of 8,000.

$\frac{1}{5}$ **of 8,000**   Write 20% as a fraction.
$20\% = \frac{20}{100} = \frac{1}{5}$

$\frac{1}{5} \times \frac{8,000}{1} = \frac{8,000}{5} = 1,600$

Oak Hill will have about 1,600 people in the 5-to-17 age group.

■ **Talk About Math**   Here is a chart of useful percent–fraction equivalents.

$10\% = \frac{1}{10}$ $20\% = \frac{1}{5}$ $25\% = \frac{1}{4}$ $50\% = \frac{1}{2}$

What fraction would you use to estimate 50% of a number? 20% of a number? How could you find a fraction equal to 60%? equal to 75%?

Check Understanding

For another example, see Set I, pages 522–523.

For each percent, name a compatible number and its equal fraction.

1. $48\% \to 50\% = \frac{1}{\square}$

2. $26\% \to \square\% = \frac{\square}{\square}$

3. $9\% \to \square\% = \frac{\square}{\square}$

4. $19\% \to \square\% = \frac{\square}{\square}$

Choose the best estimate. **Remember** to use compatible numbers.

5. 49% of 81   **a.** 50   **b.** 40   **c.** 75   **d.** 38

6. 18% of $59.45   **a.** $12   **b.** $1.20   **c.** $20   **d.** $18

Practice

For More Practice, see Set I, pages 524–525.

Estimate each answer.

7. 9% of 21   **8.** 26% of 97   **9.** 73% of 101   **10.** 53% of 997

11. 19% of 79   **12.** 96% of 220   **13.** 9% of $29   **14.** 98% of $52.30

Problem Solving

Use the table for Problems 15–19.
Estimate these populations in 1980.

15. Under 5 years old in Stamford

16. Between 45 and 62 years old in Orlando

17. Between 20 and 44 years old in Memphis

18. About how many more children under 5 were in Louisville than in Grand Rapids?

19. About how many fewer people, ages 5 to 19, were in Ocala than in Wichita?

1980 Census

7% of the population: under 5 years old
24%: between 5 and 19 years old
37%: between 20 and 44 years old
19%: between 45 and 62 years old

Metropolitan Area	Population
Stamford, Connecticut	198,854
Grand Rapids, Michigan	601,680
Orlando, Florida	699,906
Wichita, Kansas	411,870
Ocala, Florida	122,088
Louisville, Kentucky	956,480
Memphis, Tennessee	913,472

Explore ———— Math

Find the percent of each number. What do you notice about each pair of answers? Describe a method you could use to find the percent of the numbers mentally.

20. What is 50% of 80?   80% of 50?   **21.** What is 25% of 40?   40% of 25?

Mental Math   Exchange the percent and the number to compute mentally.

22. 22% of 50   **23.** 88% of 25   **24.** 12% of 75

Too Much or Too Little Information

PROBLEM SOLVING GUIDE

||► **Understand**
QUESTION
FACTS
KEY IDEA

Plan and Solve
STRATEGY
ANSWER

Look Back
SENSIBLE ANSWER
ALTERNATE APPROACH

Build Understanding

Rosa earns $2 per hour babysitting. The regular price of a hat she wants to buy is $16. How much will the hat cost with a 30% discount?

Understand   QUESTION   What is the sale price of the hat?

FACTS   The regular price is $16. The discount is 30%. The fact that Rosa earns $2 per hour babysitting is extra information.

KEY IDEA   A discount is an amount taken off the regular price. To find the sale price, subtract the discount from the regular price.

Plan and Solve   Find 30% of $16 to find the amount of discount.

Paper and Pencil

$$\begin{array}{r} 1\,6 \\ \times\, 0.3\,0 \\ \hline 4.8\,0 \end{array}$$

📟 Calculator

Press: **16** ⊗ **30** %

Display: *4.8*

The discount is $4.80. Subtract to find the sale price.

$$\begin{array}{r} 1\,6.0\,0 \\ -\;\;4.8\,0 \\ \hline 1\,1.2\,0 \end{array}$$

Press: **16** ⊖ **4.8** =

Display: *11.2*

The hat will cost $11.20 on sale.

Look Back   The answer is reasonable. A discount of 50% would be the same as half price. 30% is less than 50%. The discount of $4.80 is less than half of $16.

■ **Talk About Math**   If the question had asked whether Rosa had enough money to buy the hat, could you have answered it? What additional information would you need?

Check Understanding

Use the information in the Example. Solve each problem. If there is not enough information given, write *too little information*.

1. Joanna worked 10 hours delivering newspapers last week. How much money will she have left if she buys the same hat on sale?

2. After another week, the same hat will sell for a price of 40% off the regular price. What will be the new sale price?

Practice

Solve each problem. If there is not enough information given, write *too little information*.

3. Mary bought a blouse on sale for $14. The discount was 30%. How much change did she get from $20?

4. Blair wanted to buy jeans at 20% off the original $40 price. How much did the jeans cost on sale?

5. Sue's Sneaker Den has 18 different brands of sneakers in stock. 65% of the sneakers were low-cuts. What percent of the sneakers were high-tops?

6. The Clothes Closet was having a year-end sale. Julie bought 2 pairs of slacks. The regular price was $16.95 for each pair. What was the sale price?

Choose a ———— Strategy

Speedy Discount

7. What is the price of a $150 10-speed bicycle with a 20% discount?

8. If you pay cash, there is a 5% discount off the sale price. What is the price of the bike with a 20% discount followed by a 5% discount for cash?

9. Is a 20% discount followed by a 5% discount the same as a 25% discount?

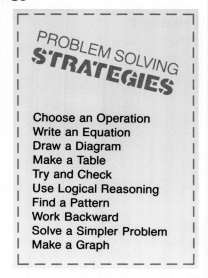

PROBLEM SOLVING
STRATEGIES

Choose an Operation
Write an Equation
Draw a Diagram
Make a Table
Try and Check
Use Logical Reasoning
Find a Pattern
Work Backward
Solve a Simpler Problem
Make a Graph

Problem-Solving Review

Solve each problem.

1. Two pencils cost $0.25. How much do 12 pencils cost?

2. Joe's garden is 30 feet long and 10 feet wide. He wants the rows to be $2\frac{1}{2}$ feet apart. In each row he will leave 2 feet between plants. To plant the most plants, should he plant the rows to run the length or the width of his garden?

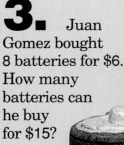

3. Juan Gomez bought 8 batteries for $6. How many batteries can he buy for $15?

4. A recipe calls for 3 cups of water for every 2 cups of fruit juice. How many cups of water are needed for 6 cups of juice?

5. The distance from Quiet Village to Scenic Bluff is $1\frac{1}{2}$ inches on a map. If the map scale is 1 inch equals 6 miles, how far is it from Quiet Village to Scenic Bluff?

6. A newspaper story reported that 60% of the 40 people surveyed knew how to play a musical instrument. How many of the people surveyed did not know how to play a musical instrument?

7. Data File A survey asked 1,000 consumers what is their favorite color of sneaker. Using the chart on pages 528–529, find how many people would have bought black sneakers.

8. Make a Data File Find at least six examples of "2 for" or "3 for" coupons or advertisements. For each one, make a table to show the cost of up to 12 items.

Explore with a Calculator

"Key Percents"

1. Juan and Ricky were shopping at the mall.

a. Juan purchased a shirt at a 20% discount. The regular price was $18. What was the sale price?

Juan, Ricky, and the sales clerk all used calculators to find the sale price.

Juan

[MRC] [MRC]
18 [M+]
[×] [.] 2 [=] [M−]
[MRC]
[14.4]

Ricky

18 [×] [.] 8 [=]
[14.4]

Sales clerk

18 [−] 20 [%]
[14.4]

Choose one of these calculator methods to find the discount price for each item Juan and Ricky bought.

b. Sweater
Regular price: $35
Discount: 10%

c. Pair of jeans
Regular price: $32
Discount: 20%

d. Shirt
Regular price: $26
Discount: 25%

Try to find at least two ways to solve each of these problems using the calculator. Hint: These are not all discount problems.

e. Juan's mother bought a new car for $12,500. She paid a 6% sales tax. What was the total cost, including tax?

f. Ricky's mother wanted to buy a small television that was priced at $250. Before she could buy it, the price increased by 15%. What will the set cost her now?

g. Ricky bought a new stereo. The regular price was $458, but it was on sale at a 30% discount. How much did he pay?

h. Juan bought a shirt. The regular price was $19, but it was on sale at a 20% discount. He must pay a 5% sales tax on this purchase. What was his total cost, including tax?

521

Reteaching

Set A pages 496–497

The U.S. flag has 7 red stripes and 6 white stripes. You can write four ratios to compare the stripes.
Red stripes to white stripes   7 : 6
White stripes to red stripes   6 : 7
Red stripes to total stripes   7 : 13
White stripes to total stripes   6 : 13

Remember that the order in which you compare two quantities is important. The pet shop has 4 canaries and 6 parakeets. Write the following ratios.

1. Canaries to parakeets

2. Parakeets to canaries

3. Canaries to the total number of birds

Set B pages 498–499

At Ace Sports, there are 3 tennis balls in a can. No matter how many cans you buy, the ratio of cans to tennis balls stays the same.

Number of cans to number of balls

Number of cans $\nearrow$ 1 : 3 $\nwarrow$ Number of balls
$\searrow$ 2 : 6 $\swarrow$

The ratio 1 : 3 equals the ratio 2 : 6.

Remember that there is no end to the number of ratios that you can find that equal a given ratio.

Use the picture to write a list of equal ratios.

The car goes 20 miles on 1 gallon of gas.

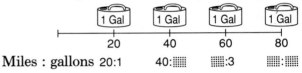

Miles : gallons 20:1   40:▒   ▒:3   ▒:▒

Set C pages 500–501

Find n in $\frac{7}{3} = \frac{28}{n}$.

Since $7 \times 4 = 28$, multiply 3 by 4 to find n.

$$\frac{7}{3} \quad \frac{28}{12}$$
$$7 \times 4$$
$$3 \times 4$$
$$n = 12$$

Remember that both multiplication and division can be used to find equal ratios.

Find n.

1. $\frac{5}{2} = \frac{15}{n}$ **2.** $\frac{12}{20} = \frac{n}{5}$

3. $\frac{5}{6} = \frac{n}{30}$ **4.** $\frac{3}{8} = \frac{18}{n}$

Set D pages 502–503

Solve this proportion.

$\frac{6}{14} = \frac{9}{n}$

Use cross-products.

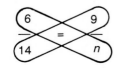

$6 \times n = 14 \times 9$
$6 \times n = 126$
$n = 126 \div 6$
$n = 21$

Remember to check the answer by replacing n in the proportion. Then see if the cross-products are equal.

Solve each proportion using cross-products.

1. $\frac{n}{6} = \frac{6}{9}$ **2.** $\frac{8}{10} = \frac{12}{n}$

3. $\frac{6}{n} = \frac{9}{12}$ **4.** $\frac{12}{9} = \frac{n}{12}$

Set E   pages 508–509

In a poll of 100 people, 55 chose red as their favorite color. What percent of these people liked red the best?

When a number is compared to 100, the comparison can be written as a ratio or as a percent.

$$\frac{\text{Number who chose red} \rightarrow}{\text{Number polled} \rightarrow} \frac{55}{100}, \text{ or } 55\%$$

Remember that percent means per hundred.

Write each ratio as a percent.

1. $\frac{20}{100}$ 2. $\frac{37}{100}$

3. $\frac{4}{100}$ 4. $\frac{10}{100}$

5. 3 to 100   6. 49 : 100

Set F   pages 510–511

Write 38% as a fraction in lowest terms. Write the percent as a fraction with a denominator of 100. Then reduce the fraction to lowest terms.

$$38\% = \frac{38}{100} \xrightarrow[\div 2]{\div 2} \frac{19}{50}$$

Remember that you reduce a fraction to lowest terms by dividing the numerator and denominator by common factors.

Write each percent as a fraction in lowest terms.

1. 22%   2. 60%   3. 47%   4. 75%

Set G   pages 512–513

Write 56% as a decimal.

56% means 56 per hundred or 56 hundredths. So

$$56\% = 0.56$$

Remember that per hundred means hundredths.

Write each percent as a decimal.

1. 32%   2. 68%   3. 4%

Set H   pages 514–515

Find 6% of 80.
Write 6% as a decimal. $6\% = 0.06$
Then multiply:

$$\begin{array}{r} 8\,0 \\ \times\,0.0\,6 \\ \hline 4.8\,0 \end{array}$$

Remember to place the decimal point in the product.

Find the percent of each number.

1. 20% of 60   2. 8% of 40

Set I   pages 516–517

Estimate 73% of 310.
Use compatible numbers.
73% is about 75%.   310 is about 300.

Find 75% of 300.
Using decimals: $300 \times 0.75 = 225$
Using fractions: $300 \times \frac{3}{4} = 225$

Remember that the actual answer will be greater than the estimate if both compatible numbers are smaller than the given numbers.

Estimate each answer.

1. 12% of 47   2. 23% of 95

3. 48% of 63   4. 98% of 77

More Practice

Set A   pages 496–497

Write each ratio.

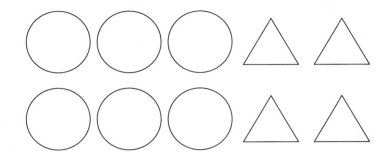

1. Circles to triangles

2. Triangles to circles

3. Circles to all the figures

4. Triangles to all the figures

Set B   pages 498–499

Use the pictures to write a list of equal ratios.

1. You can rent 3 movie videos for $5.

   Dollars : videos

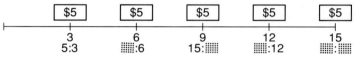

2. A pump pumps 4 gallons every 10 minutes.

   Gallons : minutes

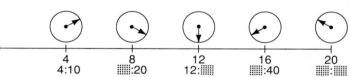

Set C   pages 500–501

Complete each list of equal ratios.

1. $\frac{3}{8} = \frac{▦}{16} = \frac{9}{▦} = \frac{▦}{32} = \frac{▦}{40}$

2. $\frac{5}{6} = \frac{10}{▦} = \frac{▦}{18} = \frac{▦}{24} = \frac{25}{▦}$

Find n.

3. $\frac{3}{2} = \frac{18}{n}$

4. $\frac{5}{8} = \frac{n}{48}$

5. $\frac{3}{7} = \frac{27}{n}$

6. $\frac{2}{3} = \frac{n}{39}$

7. $\frac{5}{4} \times \frac{45}{n}$

Multiply or divide to find the equal ratio.

8. Use 2 cups of flour to make 16 muffins $\frac{2}{16} = \frac{▦}{48}$

9. Spend 96 minutes to balance 16 tires $\frac{96}{16} = \frac{▦}{1}$

Set D   pages 502–503

Solve each proportion using cross-products.

1. $\frac{4}{n} = \frac{18}{27}$

2. $\frac{6}{8} = \frac{9}{n}$

3. $\frac{n}{12} = \frac{10}{5}$

4. $\frac{n}{12} = \frac{15}{20}$

5. $\frac{n}{30} = \frac{16}{20}$

6. $\frac{14}{24} = \frac{21}{n}$

7. $\frac{5}{4} = \frac{n}{20}$

8. $\frac{16}{6} = \frac{n}{9}$

9. $\frac{10}{3} = \frac{n}{12}$

10. $\frac{16}{n} = \frac{40}{35}$

Set E   pages 508–509

Write each ratio as a percent.

1. $\frac{22}{100}$ **2.** $\frac{60}{100}$ **3.** $\frac{3}{100}$ **4.** $\frac{39}{100}$ **5.** $\frac{9}{100}$ **6.** $\frac{99}{100}$

7. 4 to 100   **8.** 35 to 100   **9.** 66 : 100   **10.** 82 : 100

Write a ratio for each percent.

11. 29%   **12.** 6%   **13.** 51%   **14.** 80%   **15.** 2%   **16.** 18%

Set F   pages 510–511

Write each percent as a fraction in lowest terms.

1. 25%   **2.** 27%   **3.** 3%   **4.** 40%   **5.** 90%   **6.** 64%

Write each fraction as a percent.

7. $\frac{8}{100}$ **8.** $\frac{32}{100}$ **9.** $\frac{72}{100}$ **10.** $\frac{4}{10}$ **11.** $\frac{3}{20}$ **12.** $\frac{3}{5}$

Set G   pages 512–513

Write each percent as a decimal.

1. 28%   **2.** 39%   **3.** 53%   **4.** 2%   **5.** 50%   **6.** 7%

Write each decimal as a percent.

7. 0.38   **8.** 0.84   **9.** 0.52   **10.** 0.05   **11.** 0.2   **12.** 0.20

Set H   pages 514–515

Find the percent of each number.

1. 90% of 60   **2.** 10% of 80   **3.** 50% of 120   **4.** 4% of 400

5. 30% of 200   **6.** 8% of 110   **7.** 6% of 200   **8.** 45% of 90

9. 75% of 40   **10.** 1% of 26   **11.** 80% of 160   **12.** 2% of 52

Number Sense Write >, <, or =.

13. 25% of 8 ▒ 25   **14.** 90% of 82 ▒ 82   **15.** 10% of 40 ▒ 3

Set I   pages 516–517

Estimate each answer.

1. 19% of 43   **2.** 8% of 54   **3.** 23% of 82   **4.** 97% of 340

5. 54% of 92   **6.** 11% of 78   **7.** 78% of 202   **8.** 27% of 155

Enrichment

Making a Circle Graph

A *circle graph* shows how parts make up a whole or 100%. The sections of the circle are parts representing percents.

The graph at the right shows the percent of pages in a home catalog that advertises different kinds of products.

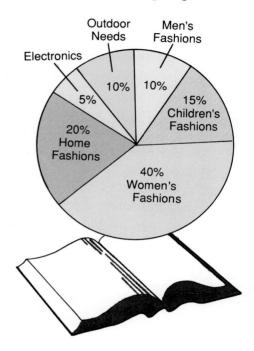

Advertising Pages

1. The most pages of advertising were for women's fashions. What percent of the pages advertised women's fashions?

2. Which products had the fewest pages of advertising? What percent of the total pages was it?

3. Which two kinds of products have the same number of pages of advertising? What is the percent of these two together?

4. What percent of the catalog was used to advertise children's clothing?

You can make a circle graph. Each mark on the circle below shows one tenth or 10% of the circle. To draw the circle graph that shows the percent of Help Wanted ads in the daily newspaper for different types of jobs, do this:

5. Trace the circle.

6. Using the marks as your guide, draw lines from the center of the circle to the outside to show the following percents. Label each section. The first one is done for you.

  a. 25% Office Help

  b. 20% Food Services

  c. 30% Health Services

  d. 10% Maintenance

  e. 10% Construction

  f. 5% Other

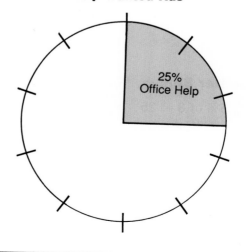

Help Wanted Ads

Chapter 15 Review/Test

1. The price of paper towels is $2 for 3 rolls. Write the ratio of rolls to dollars.

2. Each basket holds 4 pears. Use the pictures to write two more equal ratios.

1:4   :8   :12

3. Complete the list of equal ratios.

$$\frac{3}{8} = \frac{6}{} = \frac{}{24} = \frac{}{32}$$

Solve each proportion using cross-products.

4. $\frac{9}{10} = \frac{n}{20}$ **5.** $\frac{12}{16} = \frac{9}{n}$

Write each ratio as a percent.

6. $\frac{87}{100}$ **7.** 98:100

Write each percent as a fraction in lowest terms.

8. 31%   **9.** 60%

Write each fraction as a percent.

10. $\frac{3}{10}$ **11.** $\frac{3}{4}$

Write each percent as a decimal.

12. 79%   **13.** 46%

Write each decimal as a percent.

14. 0.33   **15.** 0.07

Find the percent of each number.

16. 10% of 60   **17.** 5% of 16

Estimate each percent.

18. 21% of 41   **19.** 49% of 98

20. A survey showed that 58 people out of 100 watch a certain television program. What percent is this?

Read the problem below. Choose the equation you can use to solve the problem. Then solve the problem.

21. A book showed a scale drawing of a room in which 2 inches represented 15 feet. In the drawing the room was 3 inches long. What was the actual length of the room?

a. $\frac{2}{15} = \frac{3}{n}$ **b.** $\frac{2}{15} = \frac{n}{3}$

Read the problem below. Then answer the question.

Jason bought 3 cassettes that were on sale. The original price for each cassette was $9.98. How much did he pay?

22. Is there *too much* or *too little* information given to solve the problem?

23. **Write About Math** If the cross-products of two ratios are equal, what do you know about the ratios?

1. **Favorite Sneaker Color**

Red 2%

Blue 5%

Gray 5%

Black 9%

Other 10%

White 69%

2. **Population Growth**

1. Chart
The chart shows the results of a survey of 1,000 consumers.

2. Graph
The dotted parts show the projected growth in population.

3. List
The pattern lists the amount of fabric, braid, and elastic needed for different sizes.

4. Diagram
The kite is made with 3 circles of bamboo supported by strips crossing in the center.

5. Drawing
This is the floor plan of a split-level house. The measurement 10' 4" means 10 feet 4 inches.

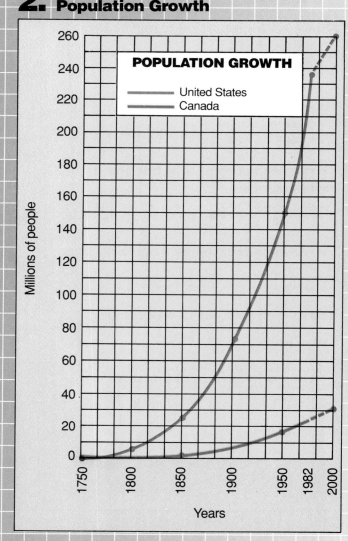

POPULATION GROWTH

United States
Canada

Millions of people

260
240
220
200
180
160
140
120
100
80
60
40
20
0

1750 1800 1850 1900 1950 1982 2000

Years

3. Sewing Pattern

Shorts are encased in fold over braid and have elastic waistline casing.

Top has neck and armholes encased in fold over braid.

BODY MEASUREMENTS

Chest	22	23	24	25	Inches
Waist	$20\frac{1}{2}$	21	$21\frac{1}{2}$	22	Inches
Hip	—	24	25	26	Inches
Back-neck to waist	9	$9\frac{1}{2}$	10	$10\frac{1}{2}$	Inches
Sizes	3	4	5	6	
Shorts 60 in. wide	$\frac{3}{8}$	$\frac{3}{8}$	$\frac{3}{8}$	$\frac{3}{8}$	Yards
Knitted fold over braid $\frac{3}{8}$ in. wide	$1\frac{3}{8}$	$1\frac{3}{8}$	$1\frac{3}{8}$	$1\frac{3}{8}$	Yards
Pajama Elastic-$\frac{5}{8}$ yd of $\frac{3}{4}$in. wide					
Top 60 in. wide	$\frac{1}{2}$	$\frac{1}{2}$	$\frac{1}{2}$	$\frac{1}{2}$	Yard
Knitted fold over braid $\frac{5}{8}$ in. wide	$1\frac{5}{8}$	$1\frac{5}{8}$	$1\frac{5}{8}$	$1\frac{5}{8}$	Yards

Master Bedroom
17' 0" x 12' 1"

WALK IN CLOSET

BATH

Bedroom 2
12' 0" x 10' 1"

Bedroom 3
10' 1" x 10' 0"

5. Floor Plan

OPTIONAL FIREPLACE

Family Room
17' 0" x 12' 1"

Breakfast
11' 8" x 10' 8"

Kitchen
9' 11" x 9' 10"

Dining
10' 4" x 10' 0"

POWDER ROOM

Living Room
18' 0" x 13' 1"

Foyer

Garage
22' 4" x 20' 1"

4. Lantern Kite

15 in.

30 in.

15 in.

Cumulative Review/Test Chapters 1–15

1. Multiply.

$$\begin{array}{r} 32 \\ \times\,58 \end{array}$$

a. 1,336   **c.** 1,856
b. 1,646   **d.** 1,214

2. Find the missing addend.

$518 + n = 736$

a. 118   **c.** 1,254
b. 218   **d.** 1,244

3. What does the 4 in 1.347 mean?

a. 4 tenths   **c.** 4 thousandths
b. 4 hundredths   **d.** 4 hundreds

4. What is the least common denominator for $\frac{2}{3}$ and $\frac{2}{5}$?

a. 15   **c.** 30
b. 8   **d.** 5

5. Add.

$\frac{5}{6} + \frac{7}{9}$

a. $\frac{1}{18}$
b. $1\frac{11}{18}$
c. $\frac{14}{15}$
d. $1\frac{1}{2}$

6. What is $\frac{12}{18}$ written in lowest terms?

a. $\frac{2}{3}$ **c.** $\frac{6}{9}$
b. $\frac{1}{3}$ **d.** $\frac{1}{12}$

7. Divide.

$3,661 \div 9$

a. 46 R7   **c.** 406 R7
b. 406 R3   **d.** 47 R7

8. Multiply.

$\frac{1}{3} \times \frac{2}{5}$

a. $\frac{2}{8}$
b. $\frac{3}{8}$
c. $\frac{2}{15}$
d. $\frac{5}{6}$

9. Subtract.

$$\begin{array}{r} \$87.46 \\ -\,85.57 \end{array}$$

a. $1.89   **c.** $2.99
b. $0.89   **d.** $2.89

10. Multiply.

$1\frac{2}{3} \times \frac{3}{5}$

a. $\frac{8}{15}$
b. $1\frac{6}{15}$
c. $2\frac{7}{9}$
d. 1

11. Name the figure.

a. Segment   **c.** Line
b. Ray   **d.** Vertex

12. Multiply.

$$\begin{array}{r} 0.046 \\ \times\,0.004 \end{array}$$

a. 0.0184   **c.** 0.00184
b. 0.000184   **d.** 0.184

13. Ms. Martino's state charges a sales tax of 8%. How much tax will she pay on a purchase of $100?

a. $8.00   **c.** $0.80
b. $80   **d.** $0.08

14. Which triangle is equilateral?

a. 8 ft 8 ft 10 ft

c. 2 in. 4 in. 3 in.

b. 7 m 7 m 7 m

d. 3 cm 5 cm 4 cm

15. Mark, Juan, Nora, and Miko helped collect money to sponsor a school fair. Mark raised $\frac{1}{2}$ as much as Juan. Nora raised $\frac{1}{3}$ as much as Juan but $4 more than Miko. Miko raised $12. How much did Mark collect?

a. $16 **c.** $24
b. $48 **d.** $40

16. Solve the proportion.

$$\frac{8}{10} = \frac{4}{n}$$

a. 10 **c.** 3.2
b. 8 **d.** 5

17. Which division sentence is shown by the picture?

a. $3 \div \frac{1}{4} = 12$ **c.** $12 \div \frac{1}{2} = 6$
b. $\frac{1}{4} \div 3 = 12$ **d.** $3 \div 12 = 4$

18. What is 62% written as a fraction in lowest terms?

a. $\frac{62}{100}$ **c.** $\frac{31}{50}$
b. $\frac{31}{100}$ **d.** $\frac{62}{25}$

19. Sheila bought a dress for $\frac{1}{3}$ off the original price. The original price was $39. How much change did she receive from $50?

a. $13 **c.** $26
b. $24 **d.** $37

20. The graph shows the number of miles traveled by a car in 5 hours.

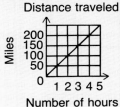

Distance traveled

Miles: 200, 150, 100, 50, 0

Number of hours: 1 2 3 4 5

How far did the car go in 4 hours?

a. 50 miles **c.** 150 miles
b. 100 miles **d.** 200 miles

Read the problem below. Then answer the question.

The All-City Swatters play 74 baseball games each year. They won 47 games in 1987, 68 games in 1988, 54 games in 1989, and 67 games in 1990. What was the mean number of games won by the Swatters for these 4 years?

21. What is the correct answer?

a. 59 teams **c.** 59 losses
b. 59 games **d.** 59 players

22. Suppose you place the five cards shown below face down and pick one without looking. What is the probability of picking a 2?

| 1 | 2 | 2 | 3 | 4 |

a. 2 **b.** $\frac{2}{5}$ **c.** $\frac{2}{4}$ **d.** $\frac{1}{4}$

Whole Numbers Through Hundred-Thousands

Review

The standard form of the number three hundred twenty-four thousand, seven hundred sixteen is 324,716. The comma separates the number into the thousands period and the ones period.

thousands period			ones period		
hundred-thousands	ten-thousands	thousands	hundreds	tens	ones
3	2	4	7	1	6

Practice

Tell which digits are in the thousands period in each number.

1. 403,248　　　　**2.** 36,975　　　　**3.** 916,720　　　　**4.** 3,062

Tell what the 6 in each number means.

5. 276,503　　　　**6.** 567,224　　　　**7.** 42,765　　　　**8.** 602,431

Write each number in words.

9. 226,700　　　**10.** 79,462　　　**11.** 913,810　　　**12.** 4,136

13. 168,204　　　**14.** 380,566　　　**15.** 48,013　　　**16.** 506,742

What number is 10,000 more? 1,000 less?

17. 3,002　　　**18.** 79,401　　　**19.** 123,421　　　**20.** 90,742

21. 68,450　　　**22.** 495,700　　　**23.** 428,000　　　**24.** 300,050

Write each number in standard form.

25. Fifty thousand, fifty

26. Forty-five thousand, one

27. Four hundred fifty-three thousand, two hundred ninety-eight

28. Three hundred thirty-seven thousand, twenty-seven

Comparing and Ordering Numbers

Review

A. Compare 2,301 and 2,320. Use > or <.

2,301 ▦ 2,320
The thousands digits are the same.
The hundreds digits are the same.
Compare the tens.
0 tens is less than 2 tens.

2,301 < 2,320   2,301 is less than 2,320.

B. List the numbers 6,587, 5,742, and 5,683 in order from least to greatest.

5,683 < 5,742   Compare the numbers
5,742 < 6,587   two at a time.

5,683   5,742   6,587

Practice

Compare these numbers. Use >, <.

1. 641 ▦ 582   **2.** 198 ▦ 219   **3.** 753 ▦ 735

4. 345 ▦ 362   **5.** 823 ▦ 328   **6.** 472 ▦ 412

7. 749 ▦ 794   **8.** 2,753 ▦ 2,548   **9.** 7,346 ▦ 7,463

10. 5,483 ▦ 5,427   **11.** 3,862 ▦ 3,892   **12.** 4,375 ▦ 4,372

13. 5,831 ▦ 6,854   **14.** 3,148 ▦ 3,143   **15.** 8,344 ▦ 8,234

List the numbers in order from least to greatest.

16. 73   85   67   **17.** 43   34   39   **18.** 857   875   837

19. 685   653   638   **20.** 721   689   719   **21.** 206   260   200

22. 1,764   3,851   2,735   **23.** 2,753   3,465   2,956   **24.** 8,357   8,372   7,328

25. 3,042   3,205   4,320   **26.** 4,981   4,672   4,913   **27.** 5,701   5,077   5,071

28. 356   653   365   366   553   563   **29.** 1,674   768   678   756   1,763

533

Addition and Subtraction Basic Facts

Review

John has 3 apples and 7 oranges.

A. How many pieces of fruit does he have?

Find 3 + 7.

$$
\begin{array}{rl}
3 & \text{Addend} \\
+7 & \text{Addend} \\
\hline
10 & \text{Sum}
\end{array}
\qquad
\begin{array}{r}
7 \\
+3 \\
\hline
10
\end{array}
$$

He has 10 pieces of fruit.

B. How many more oranges does he have than apples?

Find 7 − 3.

$$
\begin{array}{rl}
7 & \text{Minuend} \\
-3 & \text{Subtrahend} \\
\hline
4 & \text{Difference}
\end{array}
$$

He has 4 more oranges than apples.

Practice

Find each sum or difference.

1. $\begin{array}{r}4\\+5\\\hline\end{array}$	**2.** $\begin{array}{r}9\\+8\\\hline\end{array}$	**3.** $\begin{array}{r}6\\+2\\\hline\end{array}$	**4.** $\begin{array}{r}9\\-3\\\hline\end{array}$	**5.** $\begin{array}{r}8\\-0\\\hline\end{array}$	**6.** $\begin{array}{r}11\\-6\\\hline\end{array}$
7. $\begin{array}{r}12\\-9\\\hline\end{array}$	**8.** $\begin{array}{r}1\\+2\\\hline\end{array}$	**9.** $\begin{array}{r}8\\+5\\\hline\end{array}$	**10.** $\begin{array}{r}5\\-4\\\hline\end{array}$	**11.** $\begin{array}{r}17\\-8\\\hline\end{array}$	**12.** $\begin{array}{r}6\\+9\\\hline\end{array}$

13. 0 + 3   **14.** 4 + 6   **15.** 6 + 7   **16.** 9 + 2   **17.** 7 + 8   **18.** 3 + 4

19. 7 − 1   **20.** 16 − 7   **21.** 10 − 5   **22.** 12 − 8   **23.** 13 − 7   **24.** 16 − 9

25. 4 − 0   **26.** 14 − 9   **27.** 4 + 8   **28.** 7 + 3   **29.** 13 − 5   **30.** 7 − 2

31. 4 + 4   **32.** 9 + 5   **33.** 16 − 8   **34.** 15 − 8   **35.** 3 + 8   **36.** 2 + 3

37. 6 + 0   **38.** 4 + 2   **39.** 14 − 7   **40.** 18 − 9   **41.** 6 + 5   **42.** 7 + 2

43. 8 + 9   **44.** 9 + 1   **45.** 11 − 3   **46.** 8 + 2   **47.** 10 − 3   **48.** 11 − 7

49. 5 − 5   **50.** 9 − 5   **51.** 8 − 6   **52.** 6 + 7   **53.** 8 + 4   **54.** 9 + 9

Adding and Subtracting Money

Review

Add or subtract money the same way you add or
subtract whole numbers.

A. Find $13.55 + $1.25.

$$\begin{array}{r} \$13.55 \\ +\quad 1.25 \\ \hline \$14.80 \end{array}$$

Use the decimal point
to line up dollars and cents.
Write the decimal point and
dollar sign in the answer.

B. Find $23.50 − $12.98.

$$\begin{array}{r} \$23.50 \\ -\ 12.98 \\ \hline \$10.52 \end{array}$$

Practice

Find each sum or difference.

1. $13.34 + 1.87

2. $27.45 + 6.98

3. $3.52 + 9.64

4. $34.86 + 19.92

5. $46.95 + 81.63

6. $10.00 − 7.63

7. $14.61 − 1.87

8. $32.65 − 17.98

9. $22.50 − 11.16

10. $57.75 − 32.07

11. $26.89 + 30.68

12. $68.97 + 7.23

13. $89.53 − 34.62

14. $20.02 − 12.47

15. $50.75 − 21.75

16. $0.97 11.54 + 23.02

17. $63.62 7.47 + 3.89

18. $6.99 0.27 + 13.15

19. $79.18 32.82 + 8.47

20. $14.19 23.20 + 10.98

21. $0.37 + $7.73

22. $23.99 − $4.99

23. $34.86 − $19.92

24. $50.75 − $1.99

25. $12.71 + $6.92

26. $33.50 − $18.98

27. $16.15 + $40.21

28. $3.99 + $45.90

29. $55.32 − $14.90

30. $32.09 + $41.32

31. $56.66 − $42.19

32. $0.98 + $90.56

33. $4.82 + $12.65 + $8.99 + $72.36

34. $4.50 + $2.75 + $8.25 + $10.50

35. $10.19 + $0.97 + $1.25 + $4.55

36. $3.12 + $14.15 + $5.67 + $2.39

535

Addition and Subtraction Families of Facts

Review

Number sentences that are related make up a family of facts.

A. Write a family of facts using 6, 8, and 14.

$6 + 8 = 14$ $\qquad$ $14 - 8 = 6$
$8 + 6 = 14$ $\qquad$ $14 - 6 = 8$

B. Find the missing number.

$6 + \text{▦} = 14$

$\text{▦} + 6 = 14$, $14 - 6 = \text{▦}$, and $14 - \text{▦} = 6$
are from the same fact family as $6 + \text{▦} = 14$.
Since $14 - 6 = 8$, the missing addend is 8.

Practice

Write a family of facts using the given numbers.

1. 3, 5, 8 $\qquad$ **2.** 4, 7, 11 $\qquad$ **3.** 6, 6, 12 $\qquad$ **4.** 7, 0, 7 $\qquad$ **5.** 9, 1, 10

6. 8, 1, 9 $\qquad$ **7.** 2, 8, 10 $\qquad$ **8.** 3, 3, 6 $\qquad$ **9.** 9, 4, 13 $\qquad$ **10.** 0, 9, 9

11. 7, 5, 12 $\qquad$ **12.** 6, 9, 15 $\qquad$ **13.** 7, 7, 14 $\qquad$ **14.** 1, 3, 4 $\qquad$ **15.** 9, 9, 18

16. 4, 5, 9 $\qquad$ **17.** 3, 7, 10 $\qquad$ **18.** 6, 7, 13 $\qquad$ **19.** 3, 8, 11 $\qquad$ **20.** 9, 7, 16

Use a family of facts to help you find the missing number.

21. $\text{▦} + 3 = 7$ $\qquad$ **22.** $4 + \text{▦} = 10$ $\qquad$ **23.** $\text{▦} - 5 = 5$ $\qquad$ **24.** $16 - \text{▦} = 9$

25. $\text{▦} + 8 = 11$ $\qquad$ **26.** $16 - \text{▦} = 8$ $\qquad$ **27.** $\text{▦} - 9 = 5$ $\qquad$ **28.** $4 + \text{▦} = 8$

29. $13 - \text{▦} = 8$ $\qquad$ **30.** $\text{▦} + 8 = 12$ $\qquad$ **31.** $\text{▦} + 2 = 11$ $\qquad$ **32.** $\text{▦} - 4 = 1$

33. $\text{▦} + 2 = 8$ $\qquad$ **34.** $\text{▦} - 0 = 8$ $\qquad$ **35.** $11 - \text{▦} = 5$ $\qquad$ **36.** $\text{▦} + 8 = 17$

37. $12 - \text{▦} = 5$ $\qquad$ **38.** $3 + \text{▦} = 10$ $\qquad$ **39.** $\text{▦} + 9 = 18$ $\qquad$ **40.** $\text{▦} - 3 = 6$

41. $\text{▦} + 4 = 9$ $\qquad$ **42.** $7 - \text{▦} = 4$ $\qquad$ **43.** $9 + \text{▦} = 12$ $\qquad$ **44.** $7 + \text{▦} = 13$

Multiplication Basic Facts

Review

How many balloons are in the picture?
There are 4 groups with 5 balloons in each group.

$4 \times 5 = 20$
       └─ Product
There are 20 balloons.

Practice

Find each product.

1. $\begin{array}{r} 7 \\ \times 1 \\ \hline \end{array}$	**2.** $\begin{array}{r} 7 \\ \times 6 \\ \hline \end{array}$	**3.** $\begin{array}{r} 4 \\ \times 0 \\ \hline \end{array}$	**4.** $\begin{array}{r} 6 \\ \times 2 \\ \hline \end{array}$	**5.** $\begin{array}{r} 8 \\ \times 7 \\ \hline \end{array}$	**6.** $\begin{array}{r} 1 \\ \times 3 \\ \hline \end{array}$
7. $\begin{array}{r} 8 \\ \times 5 \\ \hline \end{array}$	**8.** $\begin{array}{r} 5 \\ \times 9 \\ \hline \end{array}$	**9.** $\begin{array}{r} 9 \\ \times 6 \\ \hline \end{array}$	**10.** $\begin{array}{r} 8 \\ \times 3 \\ \hline \end{array}$	**11.** $\begin{array}{r} 9 \\ \times 3 \\ \hline \end{array}$	**12.** $\begin{array}{r} 5 \\ \times 7 \\ \hline \end{array}$
13. $\begin{array}{r} 7 \\ \times 8 \\ \hline \end{array}$	**14.** $\begin{array}{r} 9 \\ \times 9 \\ \hline \end{array}$	**15.** $\begin{array}{r} 6 \\ \times 6 \\ \hline \end{array}$	**16.** $\begin{array}{r} 4 \\ \times 7 \\ \hline \end{array}$	**17.** $\begin{array}{r} 8 \\ \times 2 \\ \hline \end{array}$	**18.** $\begin{array}{r} 7 \\ \times 9 \\ \hline \end{array}$

19. 8×5 **20.** 2×8 **21.** 9×5 **22.** 4×8 **23.** 6×5

24. 9×8 **25.** 4×3 **26.** 2×9 **27.** 3×7 **28.** 4×6

29. 3×8 **30.** 9×7 **31.** 6×5 **32.** 4×5 **33.** 6×4

34. 6×8 **35.** 8×8 **36.** 7×7 **37.** 3×9 **38.** 5×5

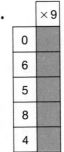

Complete each table.

39.

	$\times 6$
7	
5	
2	
3	
8	

40.

	$\times 4$
4	
2	
8	
7	
9	

41.

	$\times 9$
0	
6	
5	
8	
4	

42.

	$\times 7$
7	
1	
5	
6	
2	

Measuring in Inches

Review

Measured to the nearest inch, this key is about 2 inches long.

Most rulers do not show fraction names. But you need to know the fractions on a ruler when reading measurements to the nearest half inch and quarter inch. Remember that $\frac{1}{2}$ inch is the same as $\frac{2}{4}$ inch.

To the nearest half inch, the key is about $1\frac{1}{2}$ inches long.

To the nearest quarter inch, the key is about $1\frac{3}{4}$ inches long.

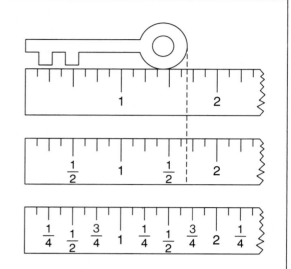

Practice

Measure each line segment below to the nearest

1. inch.   **2.** half inch.   **3.** quarter inch.

a. ———————

b. ————————————

c. ——————————————

d. —————

e. ———

f. ——————————

g. ———————————————————

h. ———————————————————

Use a ruler to draw a segment

4. 4 inches long.   **5.** $5\frac{3}{4}$ inches long.   **6.** $3\frac{1}{2}$ inches long.

7. $1\frac{1}{4}$ inches long.   **8.** $\frac{3}{4}$ inch long.   **9.** $2\frac{1}{4}$ inches long.

Measuring in Centimeters

Review

Measure the length of the lace to the
nearest centimeter.

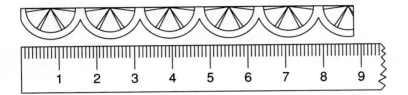

The end of the lace is closer to **9** centimeters than
8 centimeters. To the nearest centimeter, the lace
is about **9** centimeters long.

Practice

Measure each line segment to the nearest centimeter.

1. ────────────

2. ──────────

3. ──────

4. ───────────────

5. ────────────────

6. ──────────────────

7. ───────────────────────

8. ────────────────────────

9. ───────────────────────────

Use a metric ruler to draw line segments of the following lengths.

10. 6 centimeters

11. 5 centimeters

12. 8 centimeters

13. 10 centimeters

14. 2 centimeters

15. 4 centimeters

16. 1 centimeter

17. 9 centimeters

18. 15 centimeters

Division Basic Facts

Review

Jane needs 15 buttons. The buttons are packaged in groups of 3. How many packages does she need?

Use division to find how many groups of 3.

15 ÷ 3 = 5 ← Quotient

She needs to buy 5 packages of buttons.

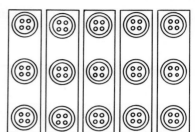

Practice

Find each quotient.

1. 2)4   **2.** 6)12   **3.** 4)16   **4.** 3)18   **5.** 6)24

6. 4)8   **7.** 3)27   **8.** 2)14   **9.** 5)15   **10.** 6)6

11. 12 ÷ 3   **12.** 9 ÷ 3   **13.** 6 ÷ 2   **14.** 18 ÷ 9   **15.** 0 ÷ 7

16. 56 ÷ 7   **17.** 30 ÷ 6   **18.** 7 ÷ 1   **19.** 24 ÷ 8   **20.** 72 ÷ 9

21. 72 ÷ 8   **22.** 48 ÷ 8   **23.** 64 ÷ 8   **24.** 40 ÷ 5   **25.** 36 ÷ 9

26. 63 ÷ 9   **27.** 35 ÷ 5   **28.** 5 ÷ 1   **29.** 45 ÷ 5   **30.** 21 ÷ 7

31. 42 ÷ 6   **32.** 20 ÷ 4   **33.** 36 ÷ 4   **34.** 27 ÷ 9   **35.** 81 ÷ 9

36. 8 ÷ 8   **37.** 30 ÷ 5   **38.** 45 ÷ 9   **39.** 63 ÷ 7   **40.** 54 ÷ 9

Complete each table.

41.

÷ 6	
36	
48	
54	
18	
0	

42.

÷ 4	
28	
32	
12	
24	
4	

43.

÷ 7	
28	
14	
42	
7	
49	

44.

÷ 8	
56	
40	
0	
32	
16	

Multiplication and Division Families of Facts

Review

Four number sentences can be written for this array.

$6 \times 4 = 24$ 6 rows of 4 is 24.

$4 \times 6 = 24$ 4 columns of 6 is 24.

$24 \div 4 = 6$ 24 divided into rows of 4 is 6 rows.

$24 \div 6 = 4$ 24 divided into columns of 6 is 4 columns.

These four number sentences form a family of facts.

Practice

Write the family of facts for each picture.

1.
2.

Write the other facts from each family.

3. $4 \times 5 = 20$ **4.** $8 \times 3 = 24$ **5.** $18 \div 3 = 6$ **6.** $12 \div 4 = 3$

7. $28 \div 4 = 7$ **8.** $5 \times 6 = 30$ **9.** $16 \div 4 = 4$ **10.** $9 \times 5 = 45$

Write the multiplication and division family of facts
for each set of numbers.

11. 4, 36, 9   **12.** 56, 8, 7   **13.** 5, 8, 40   **14.** 12, 6, 2

15. 7, 49, 7   **16.** 48, 6, 8   **17.** 1, 8, 8   **18.** 3, 7, 21

19. 72, 8, 9   **20.** 9, 54, 6   **21.** 4, 8, 32   **22.** 63, 7, 9

23. 27, 3, 9   **24.** 9, 81, 9   **25.** 7, 5, 35   **26.** 7, 42, 6

Meaning of Equal Fractions

Review

Find 4 equal fractions for $\frac{1}{2}$.

Compare the fraction bar that shows 2 halves with each of the other fraction bars.

$\frac{1}{2} = \frac{2}{4}$ $\frac{1}{2} = \frac{3}{6}$

$\frac{1}{2} = \frac{4}{8}$ $\frac{1}{2} = \frac{5}{10}$

$\frac{1}{2}$		$\frac{1}{2}$	

| $\frac{1}{4}$ | $\frac{1}{4}$ | $\frac{1}{4}$ | $\frac{1}{4}$ |

| $\frac{1}{6}$ | $\frac{1}{6}$ | $\frac{1}{6}$ | $\frac{1}{6}$ | $\frac{1}{6}$ | $\frac{1}{6}$ |

| $\frac{1}{8}$ | $\frac{1}{8}$ | $\frac{1}{8}$ | $\frac{1}{8}$ | $\frac{1}{8}$ | $\frac{1}{8}$ | $\frac{1}{8}$ | $\frac{1}{8}$ |

| $\frac{1}{10}$ | $\frac{1}{10}$ | $\frac{1}{10}$ | $\frac{1}{10}$ | $\frac{1}{10}$ | $\frac{1}{10}$ | $\frac{1}{10}$ | $\frac{1}{10}$ | $\frac{1}{10}$ | $\frac{1}{10}$ |

Practice

Use the fraction bars above to find equal fractions. Write the fraction.

1. 4 equal fractions for $\frac{2}{4}$

2. 1 equal fraction for $\frac{6}{8}$

Use the fraction bars to write equal fractions for the amount shaded.

3.

$\frac{3}{4} = \frac{}{8}$

4.

$\frac{2}{3} = \frac{}{9}$

5.

$\frac{1}{4} = \frac{}{8}$

6.

$\frac{}{2} = \frac{}{6}$

7.

$\frac{}{} = \frac{}{8}$

8.

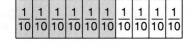

$\frac{}{} = \frac{}{}$

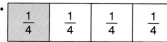

Pictographs

Review

The pictograph shows the number of students in each grade at Hilldale School who are members of the bicycle club. How many of the members are in fifth grade?

Each ☺ stands for 2 students. So, 6 ☺ stand for 6 × 2 students, or 12 students.

The bicycle club has 12 members in the fifth grade.

Number of Bicycle Club Members

Second Grade	☺
Third Grade	☺ ☺
Fourth Grade	☺ ☺ ☺ ☺ ☺
Fifth Grade	☺ ☺ ☺ ☺ ☺ ☺
Sixth Grade	☺ ☺ ☺

Each ☺ stands for 2 students.

Practice

Use the pictograph above to answer questions 1–8.

How many members are in

1. second grade?
2. third grade?
3. fourth grade?
4. sixth grade?

5. Which grade has the most students who belong to the bicycle club?

6. Which grade has the fewest students who belong to the bicycle club?

7. Does second grade or fourth grade have more students who belong to the bicycle club?

8. How many students at Hilldale School belong to the bicycle club?

9. Make a pictograph to show the data in the table.
   Remember to
   a. title the graph.
   b. list the items that the data are about.
   c. decide on a picture.
   d. decide how many each picture will stand for.

Favorite Dog Survey	
Type of dog	Number of votes
Beagle	9
Poodle	6
Collie	15
Golden Retriever	12

Bar Graphs

Review

The bar graph shows the favorite colors of students in Ernie's fifth grade class.

How many students like purple best?

The bar for purple stops at 5.
So, **5** students like purple best.

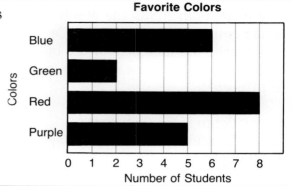

Favorite Colors

Practice

Use the bar graph above to answer questions 1–6.

1. How many students like green best?

2. How many students like red best?

3. How many students like blue best?

4. Which color is liked best?

5. Which color is liked the least?

6. Do more students like purple or blue best?

7. Make a bar graph to show the data in the table. Remember to
  a. title the graph.
  b. list the items the data are about.
  c. decide how to label the number scale.
    To label the scale, you can count
    by 1s or 2s or 3s and so on.

Number of Tickets Sold	
Alan	16
Alice	10
Aaron	4
Beth	8
Bart	2
Chad	14

Broken-Line Graphs

Review

The broken-line graph shows the number of aluminum cans saved by Jim's family for recycling during the first week of April. How many cans did Jim's family save on April 2?

Find April 2 along the bottom of the grid. Follow the grid line for April 2 straight up to the graph point.

Follow the grid line across to the number of cans.

They saved 6 cans on April 2.

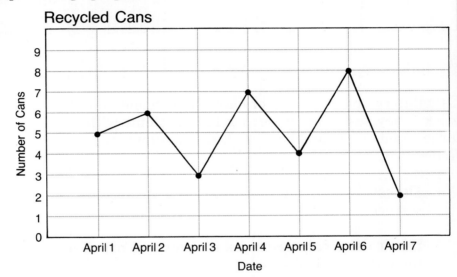

Practice

Use the broken-line graph above to answer each question.
How many cans were saved on

1. April 1?   **2.** April 5?   **3.** April 3?   **4.** April 7?

5. On what date were 7 cans saved?   **6.** On what date were 8 cans saved?

7. On what date were the most cans saved?   **8.** On what date were the fewest cans saved?

9. How many more cans were saved on April 4 than on April 5?   **10.** Were more cans saved on April 6 than on April 1?

11. What was the total number of cans saved on April 1 and April 2?   **12.** What was the total number of cans saved?

Independent Study Handbook

Contents

How to Use a Calculator

Calculators are used in everyday life at home and at work. They save time when solving problems with large numbers or problems with many numbers. *Remember*:

▶ **Do** estimate to check whether you pushed the correct buttons.

▶ **Don't** use a calculator when paper and pencil or mental math is faster.

Calculator displays

▶ **Number of digits** How many digits will your calculator display? If you press 99,999 × 99,999 to generate a number with more digits than the display can show, most calculators will show some kind of "error" message.

▶ **Unnecessary zeros** If you add 2.10 and 3.20, does your display show 5.3 or 5.30? Calculators usually drop unnecessary zeros.

▶ **Rounding** If you divide 2 by 3, do you see 0.6666666 or 0.6666667? Many calculators drop any digits after 8 digits, rather than round.

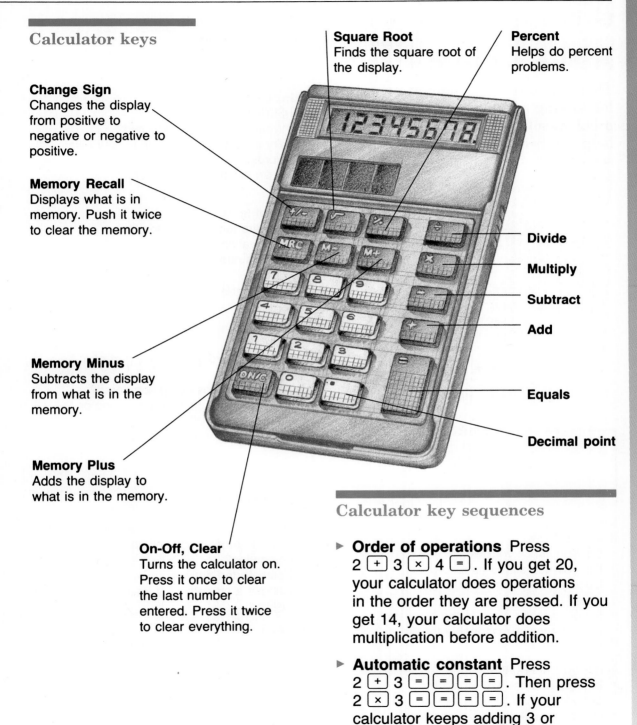

Calculator keys

Change Sign
Changes the display from positive to negative or negative to positive.

Memory Recall
Displays what is in memory. Push it twice to clear the memory.

Memory Minus
Subtracts the display from what is in the memory.

Memory Plus
Adds the display to what is in the memory.

On-Off, Clear
Turns the calculator on. Press it once to clear the last number entered. Press it twice to clear everything.

Square Root
Finds the square root of the display.

Percent
Helps do percent problems.

Divide

Multiply

Subtract

Add

Equals

Decimal point

Calculator key sequences

▶ **Order of operations** Press 2 ⊞ 3 ⊠ 4 ⊜. If you get 20, your calculator does operations in the order they are pressed. If you get 14, your calculator does multiplication before addition.

▶ **Automatic constant** Press 2 ⊞ 3 ⊜ ⊜ ⊜ ⊜. Then press 2 ⊠ 3 ⊜ ⊜ ⊜ ⊜. If your calculator keeps adding 3 or multiplying by 2, your calculator has an automatic constant.

547

Problem-Solving Help File

Use these pages when you need help with problem solving.

Problem-Solving Guide

There is no recipe or magic formula for solving problems. But keeping a problem-solving guide in mind can help you become a better problem solver.

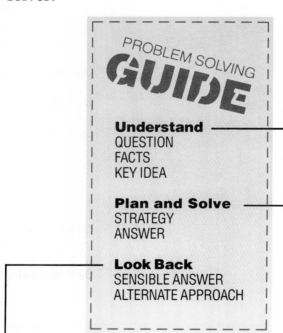

PROBLEM SOLVING GUIDE

Understand
QUESTION
FACTS
KEY IDEA

Plan and Solve
STRATEGY
ANSWER

Look Back
SENSIBLE ANSWER
ALTERNATE APPROACH

Understand
QUESTION
▶ What are you asked to find?
▶ Try to state the question in your own words.
▶ Is an exact answer needed?

FACTS
▶ What facts are given?
▶ Is there too much or too little information?
▶ Is data needed from a picture, table, graph?
▶ Do you need to collect some data?

KEY IDEA
▶ How are the facts and the question related?
▶ Are there groups that are part of a whole?
▶ Are two groups being compared?
▶ Are there groups that are joining or separating?
▶ Are there groups of the same size?

Plan and Solve
STRATEGY
▶ What can you do to solve the problem?
▶ Can the problem be solved by computing?
▶ Estimate the answer.
▶ Choose a strategy. Try another, if needed.

ANSWER
▶ Give the answer in a sentence.
▶ Do you need to interpret a remainder?
▶ Is rounding needed?

Look Back
SENSIBLE ANSWER
▶ Did you check your work?
▶ Did you use all the needed data?
▶ Does your answer have the correct units?
▶ Is your answer close to the estimate?
▶ Is your answer reasonable for the situation?

ALTERNATE APPROACH
▶ Is there another way to get the same answer?
▶ Could you use the same strategy differently?
▶ Would another strategy be faster or simpler?

Problem-Solving Strategies

You might think of problem-solving strategies as problem-solving tools that you own and use when needed. One or more strategies might be used for a problem. And if one strategy doesn't work, try another one.

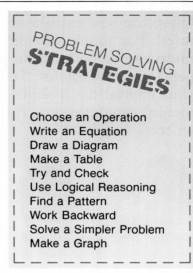

PROBLEM SOLVING STRATEGIES

Choose an Operation
Write an Equation
Draw a Diagram
Make a Table
Try and Check
Use Logical Reasoning
Find a Pattern
Work Backward
Solve a Simpler Problem
Make a Graph

TIPS FOR PROBLEM SOLVERS

Don't give up. Some problems take longer than others.

Problem-Solving Behaviors and Attitudes

When you solve problems, do you give up quickly or lack confidence? Behaviors and attitudes can affect your work. So, remember these tips. They can help you become a better problem solver.

Tips for Problem Solvers

- ▶ **Don't give up.** Some problems take longer than others.

- ▶ **Be flexible.** If you get stuck, try another idea.

- ▶ **Be confident** so you can do your best.

- ▶ **Take risks.** Try your hunches. They often work.

- ▶ **Brainstorm to get started**—one idea will lead to another.

- ▶ **Visualize the problem** in your mind to help you understand it better.

- ▶ **Compare problems** to help you relate new problems to ones you've solved before.

- ▶ **Think about your thinking.** Pause to ask, "How is this going to help me solve the problem?"

- ▶ **Share your thinking with others.** Explaining your ideas helps you think better.

- ▶ **Organize your work** to help you think clearly.

Mental Math Strategies

Often the best calculator is your own mind. For simple calculations, mental math can be better than paper and pencil or a calculator. To sharpen your mental math skills, use the mental computation strategies shown on these pages.

Breaking Apart Numbers

Break apart one or more numbers to get numbers that are easier to use.

54 + 23

54 + 20 + 3   Break apart 23.
74 + 3
77

87 × 2

(80 + 7) × 2   Break apart 87.
(80 × 2) + (7 × 2)   Use the distributive
160 + 14   property.
174

35 + 48

(30 + 5) + (40 + 8)   Break apart 35 and 48.
(30 + 40) + (5 + 8)   Regroup the numbers.
70 + 13
83

Compatible Numbers

Compatible numbers are pairs of numbers that are easy to use. Look for numbers like 1, 10, 100 or 3, 30, 300 that are easy to use.

40 + 30   **28 × 10**
70   280

180 ÷ 60
3

When there are 3 or more numbers, look for pairs of numbers that are compatible.

3 + 48 + 7

3 + 7 + 48
10 + 48
58

$\frac{1}{3}$ **× 7 × 12**

$\frac{1}{3}$ × 12 × 7

4 × 7
28

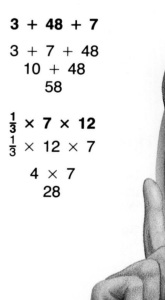

Using Equivalent Forms

Divide to find "fraction of."

$$\frac{1}{3} \times 180$$
$$180 \div 3$$
$$60$$

Change decimals or percents to fractions to get a number that is easier to use.

25% of 32

$$\frac{1}{4} \text{ of } 32$$
$$32 \div 4$$
$$8$$

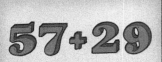

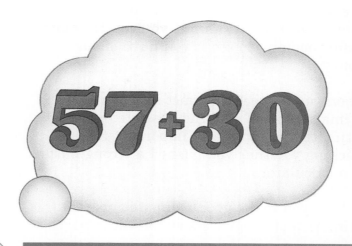

Compensation

Change one number to make it easy to use. Then change the answer to compensate.

57 + 29

$57 + 30 = 87$	Add 1 to 29 to get 30.
$87 - 1 = 86$	Subtract 1 from the answer.

165 − 97

$165 - 100 = 65$	Add 3 to 97 to get 100.
$65 + 3 = 68$	Add 3 to the answer.

Change one number to make it easy to use. Then change the other number to compensate.

66 + 19

$65 + 20$	Add 1 to 19 and subtract
85	1 from 66.

157 − 98

$159 - 100$	Add 2 to 98 and to 157.
59	

Estimation Strategies

In everyday life, an exact answer is often unnecessary. For example, you can estimate while shopping to see if you have enough money.

When you do need an exact answer, estimation helps you find possible errors. Estimation is especially important for checking whether you pushed a wrong button on a calculator.

To help you make good estimates, use the estimation strategies shown on these pages.

Front-End Digits

Use just the first digit in each number to help you make an estimate.

$$
\begin{array}{rr}
173 & 100 \\
421 & 400 \\
+348 & +300 \\
\hline
& 800 \\
\end{array}
$$

Since $73 + 21 + 48$ is about 100, you can also adjust the estimate by adding 100 to get 900.

$$4\tfrac{1}{2} + 6\tfrac{5}{8} + 2\tfrac{1}{3}$$
$$4 \ + \ 6 \ + 2$$
$$12$$

Rounding

Round to one nonzero digit.

$$
\begin{array}{rr}
425 & 400 \\
\times 28 & \times \ \ 30 \\
\hline
& 12{,}000 \\
\end{array}
$$

Round to the same place.

$$
\begin{array}{rr}
28.45 & 28 \\
- \ 3.79 & - \ 4 \\
\hline
& 24 \\
\end{array}
$$

$$13\tfrac{1}{4} + 8\tfrac{7}{8}$$
$$13 + 9$$
$$22$$

Round to the nearest half.

$$\tfrac{3}{8} + 2\tfrac{5}{8} + \tfrac{1}{4}$$
$$\tfrac{1}{2} + 2\tfrac{1}{2} + \tfrac{1}{2}$$
$$3\tfrac{1}{2}$$

Round both numbers up and both numbers down to get a range.

57×84 $\quad 60 \times 90 = 5{,}400$
$\quad\quad\quad\quad 50 \times 80 = 4{,}000$

57×84 is between 4,000 and 5,400.

Substituting Compatible Numbers

Use numbers that are close to the original numbers.

$23\overline{)476}$

$24\overline{)480}$ or $23\overline{)460}$ or $25\overline{)500}$

$23\overline{)476}$ is about 20.

$24 \times 78 \times 4$

$25 \times 78 \times 4$

100×78

$24 \times 78 \times 4$ is about 7,800.

$\frac{1}{3} \times 187$

$\frac{1}{3} \times 180$

$\frac{1}{3} \times 187$ is about 60.

26% of 32

25% of 32

$\frac{1}{4} \times 32$

26% of 32 is about 8.

Clustering

Look for groups of numbers that are close to the same number.

6,278	Each number
6,589	is about 6,000,
5,893	so the sum is
+6,134	about
	4 × 6,000 or
	24,000.

$4\frac{7}{8} + 5\frac{1}{5} + 4\frac{2}{3}$

Each number is about 5, so the sum is about 3×5 or 15.

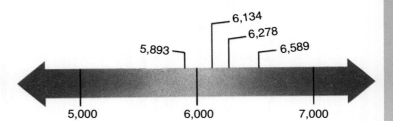

Comparing to a Reference Point

Compare the numbers to numbers you can work with easily.

| 346 | Both numbers are less than 500, so the |
| +438 | sum is less than 1,000. |

$\frac{5}{8} + \frac{3}{5}$ Both numbers are greater than $\frac{1}{2}$, so the sum is greater than 1.

Math Study Skills

Try these math study skills to help you do your best.

Before a Lesson

▶ **Preview the lesson.** Look over the lesson to see what it's about.

▶ **Set a purpose.** Are you about to learn a new topic or revisit a familiar one?

▶ **Recall what you know.** What have you learned about this topic previously?

Build Understanding

Reading the lesson

▶ **Read slowly.** Don't try to read a math book as fast as a story book.

▶ **Learn vocabulary and symbols.** Note new math terms and symbols. Use the glossary and index. Watch for words like "product" that have other meanings outside of math.

▶ **Read diagrams, tables, graphs.** Use a ruler to help you read rows and columns.

▶ **Do the examples.** Work the examples yourself as you go through them.

Doing Activities

▶ **Use materials.** Keep the materials organized. Use them to explore new ideas.

▶ **Work with others.** When you work with others, use the tips for working together given on page 556.

Build Understandin

A. A market gets boxes of 24 heads in each box. heads of lettuce are in

Since each box contai same number of he

Check Understanding

Trying on your own

▶ **Note what you don't understand.** When you try some exercises, be aware of what you don't understand.

▶ **Reread the lesson.** When you don't understand, reread the "Build Understanding" section.

Preventing errors

▶ **Find another example.** When you need another example, turn to the "Reteaching" set at the back of the chapter.

▶ **Try again.** Keep trying until you feel you understand.

Practice and Problem Solving

Reading the exercises

▶ **Read directions.** Read carefully.

▶ **Read word problems.** Read slowly and reread, if needed.

Doing written work

▶ **Show your work.** Record what you did. Make your paper easy to follow and the answer easy to find.

▶ **Check your work.** Read what you write.

▶ **Find more practice.** Use the "More Practice" at the back of the chapter when needed.

After a Lesson

▶ **Look back.** Summarize the lesson. Would you be able to teach it to another student?

▶ **Connect to other lessons.** Think about how this lesson is related to other lessons.

Working in Groups

When you do math working with others, you'll learn more math, you'll learn how to work as a team, and you'll enjoy math more.

Roles for Group Members

When you work in a group, it can be helpful for each person to have a role. Some roles are:

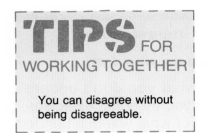

TIPS FOR WORKING TOGETHER

You can disagree without being disagreeable.

- **Reporter**—This person summarizes the group's thinking.

- **Encourager**—This person encourages group members to take part and to work together well.

- **Recorder**—This person records the group's work.

- **Checker**—This person asks group members to explain their thinking or may ask others if they agree.

- **Materials Manager**—This person gets any materials that are needed and returns them at the end of class.

Tips for Working Together

Here are some tips for working well with others in a group.

- Involve your whole group. Help everyone to participate.

- Help keep your group on task.

- To make sure your group understands the task or solution, have each group member say it in his or her own words, summarize the steps, or give an example.

- Work as a group. If you understand, help another group member. Don't work ahead of the others.

- Be a good tutor. Make up similar problems or easier ones to help someone understand.

- When you are unsure, ask someone in your group for help or say you don't understand.

- Tell someone when he or she does or says something that helps you.

- Don't decide by voting. Try to understand which might be the best solution and why.

- Remember, you can disagree without being disagreeable.

Tables

Metric System

Length

10 millimeters (mm)	= 1 centimeter (cm)
10 centimeters 100 millimeters	= 1 decimeter (dm)
10 decimeters 100 centimeters	= 1 meter (m)
1,000 meters	= 1 kilometer (km)

Area

100 square millimeters (mm²)	= 1 square centimeter (cm²)
10,000 square centimeters	= 1 square meter (m²)
100 square meters	= 1 are (a)
10,000 square meters	= 1 hectare (ha)

Volume

1,000 cubic millimeters (mm³)	= 1 cubic centimeter (cm³)
1,000 cubic centimeters	= 1 cubic decimeter (dm³)
1,000,000 cubic centimeters	= 1 cubic meter (m³)

Mass (weight)

1,000 milligrams (mg)	= 1 gram (g)
1,000 grams	= 1 kilogram (kg)
1,000 kilograms	= 1 metric ton (t)

Capacity

1,000 milliliters (mL)	= 1 liter (L)

Time

60 seconds	= 1 minute
60 minutes	= 1 hour
24 hours	= 1 day
7 days	= 1 week
365 days 52 weeks 12 months	= 1 year
366 days	= 1 leap year

Addition-Subtraction Table

+	0	1	2	3	4	5	6	7	8	9
0	0	1	2	3	4	5	6	7	8	9
1	1	2	3	4	5	6	7	8	9	10
2	2	3	4	5	6	7	8	9	10	11
3	3	4	5	6	7	8	9	10	11	12
4	4	5	6	7	8	9	10	11	12	13
5	5	6	7	8	9	10	11	12	13	14
6	6	7	8	9	10	11	12	13	14	15
7	7	8	9	10	11	12	13	14	15	16
8	8	9	10	11	12	13	14	15	16	17
9	9	10	11	12	13	14	15	16	17	18

Multiplication-Division Table

×	1	2	3	4	5	6	7	8	9
1	1	2	3	4	5	6	7	8	9
2	2	4	6	8	10	12	14	16	18
3	3	6	9	12	15	18	21	24	27
4	4	8	12	16	20	24	28	32	36
5	5	10	15	20	25	30	35	40	45
6	6	12	18	24	30	36	42	48	54
7	7	14	21	28	35	42	49	56	63
8	8	16	24	32	40	48	56	64	72
9	9	18	27	36	45	54	63	72	81

Customary System

Length

12 inches (in.)	= 1 foot (ft)
3 feet 36 inches	= 1 yard (yd)
1,760 yards 5,280 feet	= 1 mile (mi)
6,076 feet	= 1 nautical mile

Area

144 square inches (sq in.)	= 1 square foot (sq ft)
9 square feet	= 1 square yard (sq yd)
4,840 square yards	= 1 acre (A)

Volume

1,728 cubic inches (cu in.)	= 1 cubic foot (cu ft)
27 cubic feet	= 1 cubic yard (cu yd)

Weight

16 ounces (oz)	= 1 pound (lb)
2,000 pounds	= 1 ton (T)

Capacity

8 fluid ounces (fl oz)	= 1 cup (c)
2 cups	= 1 pint (pt)
2 pints	= 1 quart (qt)
4 quarts	= 1 gallon (gal)

Glossary

Acute angle An angle with a measure less than 90°.

Acute triangle Triangle with three acute angles.

Add To find the total by putting together two or more quantities.

Angle ($\angle$) Two rays with the same endpoint.

Area A number given in square units that indicates the size of the inside of a plane figure.

Associative property (Grouping property) The way in which addends (or factors) are grouped does not affect the sum (or product).
$(7 + 2) + 5 = 7 + (2 + 5)$
$(7 \times 2) \times 5 = 7 \times (2 \times 5)$

Average A number obtained by dividing the sum of two or more addends by the number of addends.

Base (Geometry) A name used for a side of a polygon or surface of a solid figure.

Betweenness property For any two numbers, there is another number between them.

Box plot A way of displaying data to show the median values.

Breaking apart numbers Changing the form of a number so it is easier to use when computing. 23 can be changed to 20 + 3.

Broken-line graph A drawing that shows how quantities change over time.

Central angle An angle with its vertex at the center of a circle.

Chord A segment with both endpoints on a circle. A diameter is a special chord.

Circle A plane figure with all points the same distance from a given point called the *center*.

Circle graph A drawing that compares the parts of a quantity with the whole quantity.

Circumference The distance around a circle.

Clustering An estimation method used when all the numbers are close to the same number.

Combinations of numbers Computing by using numbers in an order that makes the computation easier.

Common denominator A common multiple of two or more denominators. A common denominator for $\frac{1}{6}$ and $\frac{3}{8}$ is 48.

Common factor A number that is a factor of two or more numbers. A common factor of 6 and 12 is 3.

Common multiple A number that is a multiple of two or more numbers.

Commutative property (Order property) The order in which numbers are added (or multiplied) does not affect the sum (or product).
$4 + 6 = 6 + 4$
$4 \times 6 = 6 \times 4$

Compass An instrument used for drawing circles and for doing geometric constructions.

Compatible number A number close to the number in a problem being solved that is easy to use in mental computation.

Compensation Changing a number by adding to it, or subtracting from it, so it is easier to use when computing. Then changing the answer to make up for the change.

Complements Two numbers with a sum that has only the digit 9.

Composite number A whole number, greater than 0, that has more than two factors.

Cone A solid figure formed by connecting a circle to a point not in the plane of the circle.

Congruent figures Figures with the same size and shape.

Coordinates *See* ordered pair.

Cross-products The cross-products of the ratios $\frac{3}{4}$ and $\frac{9}{12}$ are 3×12 and 4×9.

Cube A prism with all square faces.

Customary units of measure A system for measuring length in *inches, feet, yards,* and *miles;* capacity in *cups, pints, quarts,* and *gallons;* weight in *ounces, pounds,* and *tons;* temperature in *degrees Fahrenheit.*

Cylinder A solid figure with two circular bases that are parallel and congruent.

Data A collection of gathered information that has not been organized.

Daylight-saving time Time that is one hour ahead of standard time.

Decimal A number that names a whole and/or fractional parts with denominators of 10 (*tenths*), 100 (*hundredths*), or 1,000 (*thousandths*). In standard form, a point separates the whole number and fraction parts.

Degree (of an angle) A unit for measuring angles.

Denominator The number below the line in a fraction. It names the number of equal parts or objects.

Diagonal A segment with two nonadjacent vertices of a polygon as its endpoints.

Diameter In a circle, a segment that passes through the center and that has both endpoints on the circle.

Difference The number found by subtracting one number from another.

Digit One of the symbols used for writing numbers: 0, 1, 2, 3, 4, 5, 6, 7, 8, and 9.

Distributive property When a factor is a sum, multiplying each addend before adding does not change the product.

Divide To separate a total amount into an equal number of groups, or into groups of equal size.

Dividend A number that is divided by another number.

Divisible One number is divisible by another if the remainder is zero after dividing.

Divisor The number by which another number is divided.

Edge Segment where two faces of a polyhedron meet.

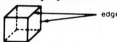

Endpoint The point at the end of a segment or a ray.

Equal decimals Decimals that name the same number. 1.8 and 1.80 are equal decimals.

Equal fractions Fractions that name the same number. $\frac{2}{3}$ and $\frac{8}{12}$ are equal fractions.

Equation A number sentence used to show how the parts of a problem are related.

Equilateral triangle Triangle with three congruent sides.

Estimate A number about the same as another number. A name used for a calculation not requiring an exact answer.

Even number A whole number with 0, 2, 4, 6, or 8 in the ones place.

Expanded form A way to write a number to show the value of each digit.

Face Flat surface that is part of a polyhedron.

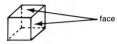

Factor (1) A number to be multiplied. (2) A number that divides evenly into a given second number is a factor of that number.

Favorable outcome A result in a probability experiment that meets a specific condition.

Flip A change in location of a figure by flipping it over a line, creating a mirror image (reflection) of the figure.

Fraction A number that names a part of a whole or of a set. It is written in the form $\frac{a}{b}$.

Frequency The number of times a certain item occurs in a set of data.

Front-end digit The digit in a number that has the greatest place value.

Graph A drawing used to show information in an organized way. Some types of graphs are *bar graphs* and *pictographs.*

Greatest common factor (1) The greatest number that is a factor of two or more numbers. (2) The greatest number that divides two or more numbers with no remainder.

Hexagon A six-sided polygon.

Improper fraction A fraction whose numerator is greater than or equal to its denominator.

Inequality A number sentence using the greater than (>) or less than (<) symbol.

Integers The whole numbers and their opposites. Some integers are $+3$, -3, 0, $+16$, -16.

Intersecting lines Lines that meet at a point.

Isosceles triangle Triangle with two congruent sides.

Least common denominator (LCD) The least common multiple of the denominators of two or more fractions. The least common denominator of $\frac{1}{2}$ and $\frac{2}{3}$ is 6.

Least common multiple (LCM) The smallest number that is a common multiple of two given numbers. The least common multiple for 6 and 8 is 24.

Line A set of points continuing without end in opposite directions.

Line graph A drawing that shows the rate at which something happens.

Line plot A graph that uses Xs to show information and compare quantities.

Line of symmetry A line on which a figure can be folded into two congruent parts.

Lowest terms A fraction for which 1 is the greatest common factor of both the numerator and the denominator.

Mean Average of a group of numbers. The mean of 2, 4, 5, 6, 6 is $23 \div 5$, or 4.6.

Median The middle number in a group of numbers when the numbers are listed in order. The median of 2, 4, 5, 6, 6 is 5.

Metric units of measure A system for measuring length in *millimeters, centimeters, decimeters, meters,* and *kilometers;* capacity in *milliliters* and *liters;* mass in *grams* and *kilograms;* temperature in *degrees Celsius.*

GLOSSARY

Mixed number A number that has a whole number part and a fraction part.

Mode Number that occurs most often in a set of data.

Multiple The number that is the product of a number and a whole number.

Multiply To find the total by putting together groups of equal size, or to find the number that is "times as many" as another number.

Negative number A number less than 0, such as -5 or -10.

Numerator The number above the line in a fraction. It names the number of objects or parts under consideration.

Obtuse angle An angle with a measure greater than 90° and less than 180°.

Obtuse triangle Triangle with one obtuse angle.

Octagon An eight-sided polygon.

Odd number A whole number with 1, 3, 5, 7, or 9 in the ones place.

Ordered pair Two numbers arranged so there is a first number and a second number, used to locate a point on a grid.

Order of operations Rules for finding the value of an expression.

Outcome A possible result in a probability experiment.

Palindrome A set of letters that read the same forward and backward.

Parallel lines Lines in a plane that never meet.

Parallelogram A quadrilateral with opposite sides parallel and congruent.

Pattern A general idea by which things can be arranged or events can happen in an organized way.

Pentagon A five-sided polygon.

Percent (%) A ratio that compares a number to 100. 45% means 45 hundredths.

Perimeter The sum of the lengths of the sides of a polygon.

Period A group of three digits in a number separated by a comma.

Perpendicular lines Lines that intersect to form right angles.

Place value The number each digit represents is determined by the position the digit occupies.

Plane A flat surface that extends without end in all directions.

Plot To find the location of a point on a grid using an ordered pair.

Point An exact location in space.

Polygon A closed plane figure made by line segments.

Polyhedron A solid figure made of flat surfaces called *faces*. Each face is a polygon.

Polyomino A figure made of squares that are the same size. Each square shares at least one of its sides with another square.

Positive number A number greater than 0, such as $+35$.

Prime factorization A number written as the product of prime numbers. $30 = 2 \times 3 \times 5$

Prime number A whole number, greater than 1, that has exactly two factors: itself and 1.

Prism A polyhedron with two parallel, congruent faces, called *bases*. All other faces are parallelograms.

triangular prism

bases rectangular prism

Probability A number from 0 to 1 that tells how likely it is that a given event will occur. The closer to 1, the *more likely* the event is to occur. The closer to 0, the *less likely* it is to occur.

Product The number found by multiplying numbers.

Proper fraction A fraction that is less than 1.

Property of one The product of one and a number is that number.

Property of zero The sum of zero and a number is that number. The product of zero and a number is zero.

Proportion A statement that two ratios are equal. $\frac{2}{5} = \frac{12}{30}$

Protractor An instrument used to measure angles.

Pyramid The solid figure formed by connecting points of a polygon to a point not in the plane of the polygon. The polygon and its interior is the *base*.

triangular pyramid

rectangular pyramid

Quadrilateral A four-sided polygon.

Quotient The answer after dividing one number by another.

Radius (1) In a circle, a segment that connects the center of the circle with a point on the circle. (2) The distance from the center to a point on the circle.

radius

560

Range (1) The difference between the greatest and the least numbers in a set of data. (2) An estimate consisting of a greater and lesser possible answer.

Rate A ratio that compares one quantity to a different kind of quantity.

Ratio A pair of numbers that expresses a rate or a comparison.

Ray A set of points that has one endpoint and that extends without end in one direction.

Reciprocals Two numbers whose product is 1. $\frac{3}{4}$ and $\frac{4}{3}$ are reciprocals because $\frac{3}{4} \times \frac{4}{3} = 1$.

Rectangle A parallelogram with four right angles.

Reference point When estimating, a number used for comparison with other numbers.

Regular polygon A polygon with all sides congruent and all angles congruent.

Repeating decimal A decimal in which one or more digits keep repeating, such as 0.518181818...

Remainder The number that is left over after dividing.

Rhombus A parallelogram with four congruent sides.

Right angle An angle with a measure of 90°.

Right triangle Triangle with one right angle.

Rounded number A number expressed to the nearest 10, 100, 1,000, and so on. 368 rounded to the nearest 10 is 370; rounded to the nearest 100 is 400.

Sample Part of a group upon which an experiment or survey is conducted.

Scale drawing A drawing made so that distances in the drawing are proportional to actual distances.

Scalene triangle Triangle with no congruent sides.

Segment Two points and the straight path between them.

Sequence A set of numbers formed by a pattern.

Side (1) A segment used to form a polygon. (2) A ray used to form an angle.

Similar figures Figures with the same shape but not necessarily the same size.

Slide A change in location of a figure by moving it without turning it.

Solid figure A figure with three dimensions: length, width, and height.

Special numbers Numbers like 1, 10, 100, or 3, 30, 300 that are easy to use when computing mentally.

Sphere A solid figure with all points the same distance from a given point called the *center*.

Square (Geometry) A rectangle with four congruent sides. (Numeration) To multiply a number by itself.

Square numbers A sequence of numbers that can be shown by dots arranged in the shape of a square.

Standard form The notation for writing numbers using the digits 0-9 and each place represents a power of ten.

Statistics Numerical facts that are collected, organized, and analyzed.

Stem-and-leaf plot A way to display numerical data in which tens digits (stems) appear in a vertical line and ones digits (leaves) appear in horizontal lines.

Subtract To find how many are left when some are taken away, or to compare two quantities.

Sum The number found by adding numbers.

Surface area The sum of the areas of all the surfaces of a solid figure.

Symmetric figure A plane figure that can be folded in half so the two halves match.

Terminating decimal A decimal with an exact number of nonzero digits, such as 0.375.

Terms The numerator and denominator of a fraction.

Trapezoid A quadrilateral with one pair of parallel sides.

Tree diagram An organized way to list all possible outcomes of an experiment.

Triangle A three-sided polygon.

Turn A change in location of a figure by moving it around a given point.

Unit fraction A fraction with a numerator of one.

Vertex (1) The common endpoint of two rays that form an angle. (2) The point of intersection of two sides of a polygon. (3) The point of intersection of the edges of a polyhedron.

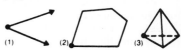

Volume A number given in cubic units that indicates the size of the inside of a space figure.

Whole number One of the numbers 0, 1, 2, 3, and so on.

Index